THE AUTHOR

A native New Yorker and son of an Irish immigrant, John A. Barnes has worked as a reporter and editorial writer for the *Washington Times,* the *Boston Herald,* and *The Detroit News* as well as for political columnists Rowland Evans and Robert Novak. A graduate of New York University, he has written for *Reader's Digest,* the *Wall Street Journal, American Spectator, The New Republic, Washington Monthly,* and many other publications. He is now a national issues reporter in New York for *Investor's Business Daily.* This is his first book.

IRISH-AMERICAN
L A N D M A R K S

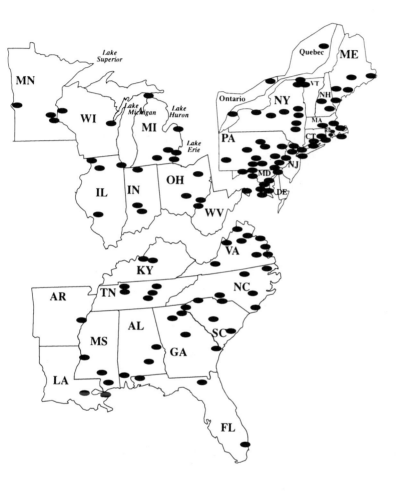

Irish-American Landmarks is a reference source that brings to life the sites in the U.S. and Canada that help comprise the rich history of the Irish in America since the 1700s. The guide contains:

- sketches on 300 sites related to Irish-American history, including

museums	memorials
battlefields	historic homes
neighborhoods	parks
historic buildings	monuments

- sites in 46 states, as well as Ontario and Quebec, listed alphabetically within 5 regions: Northeast, Southeast, Great Lakes/Ohio Valley, Great Plains, and West and Pacific

- practical information for planning visits to sites, including:

exhibits	telephone
location	admission
hours	

- map of the United States showing site locations

- five regional maps with locators identifying the sites

- more than 100 illustrations of landmarks and people

- foreword by Eoin McKiernan, columnist for *Irish America* magazine and founder of the Irish American Cultural Institute

- timeline noting important dates in Irish-American history

- bibliography of selected further reading

- site index listing landmarks by type

- subject index of people, places, and events mentioned in the text

IRISH-AMERICAN
LANDMARKS
A TRAVELER'S GUIDE

John A. Barnes

foreword by
Eoin McKiernan
Founder of the
Irish American Cultural Institute
St. Paul, Minnesota

 **Gale Research**

An International Thomson Publishing Company

I(T)P
NEW YORK • LONDON • BONN • BOSTON • DETROIT • MADRID
MELBOURNE • MEXICO CITY • PARIS • SINGAPORE • TOKYO
TORONTO • WASHINGTON • ALBANY NY • BELMONT CA • CINCINNATI OH

Allison McNeill, Rebecca Nelson, *Developmental Editors;* Lawrence W. Baker, *Managing Editor;* Christine Nasso, *Acquisitions Editor; with thanks to:* Kelle Sisung and Jolen Gedridge; Pamela A. E. Galbreath, *Cover and Page Designer;* Cynthia Baldwin, *Product Design Manager;* Sherrell Hobbs, *Desktop Publisher/Map Designer;* Barbara J. Yarrow, *Graphic Services Supervisor;* Pamela Hayes, *Photography Coordinator;* Willie Mathis, *Camera Operator;* Mary Kelley, *Production Associate;* Evi Seoud, *Assistant Production Manager;* Mary Beth Trimper, *Production Director;* Kweli Jomo, *Data Entry Associate;* Gwendolyn S. Tucker, *Data Entry Coordinator;* Benita L. Spight, *Data Entry Services Manager*

FRONT COVER PHOTOS: St. Patrick's Day Parade, New York City, *AP/Wide World Photos;* John F. Kennedy, *courtesy of Gale International Portrait Gallery;* John F. Kennedy National Historic Site; Irish Brigade Memorial. BACK COVER PHOTO: St. Patrick's Cathedral.

While every effort has been made to ensure the reliability of the information presented in this publication, Gale Research Inc. does not guarantee the accuracy of the data contained herein. Gale accepts no payment for listing; and inclusion in the publication of any organization, agency, institution, publication, service, or individual does not imply endorsement of the editors or publisher. Errors brought to the attention of the publisher and verified to the satisfaction of the publisher will be corrected in future editions.

∞™This book is printed on acid-free paper that meets the minimum requirements of American National Standard for Information Sciences—Permanence Paper for Printed Library Materials. ANSI Z39.48-1984.

Library of Congress Cataloging-in-Publication Data

Barnes, John 1960–
    Irish-American Landmarks: A Traveler's Guide/by John Barnes.
    p. cm.
    Includes bibliographical references and index.
    ISBN 0-8103-9603-3 (alk. paper)
    1. Irish Americans—History. 2. Historic sites—United States—Guidebooks.
    3. United States—Guidebooks. I. Title.
E184.I6.B27 1995
973'.049162–dc20
                                                95-17204
                                                CIP

Printed in the United States of America

10 9 8 7 6 5 4 3 2 1

For my mother,
Mary Bridget McAuliffe Barnes
And to the memory of my father,
Thomas Desmond Barnes
(1925–86)
Native of Ireland,
Citizen of the United States,
Korean War Veteran,
New York City Police Officer,
Gentleman

CONTENTS

GREAT PLAINS

WEST AND PACIFIC

THE IRISH CONNECTION

By Eoin McKiernan, Ph.D., Litt.D.

Founder of the Irish American Cultural Institute
Editor emeritus *Eire-Ireland*
Irish America magazine columnist

Having been among the earliest to arrive in what is now the United States and, at one time, constituting close to one-half of the foreign-born population here, the Irish have remained a very visible people in this country. Though they are no longer present in that proportion, almost 44 million people claimed an Irish heritage in the 1990 U.S. census.

Curiously, the Irish are the only ethnic group so far to have had their celebratory day, St. Patrick's Day, adopted as an unofficial national holiday. No doubt this has as much to do with the rites of Spring as an occasion to honor St. Patrick. Nonetheless, it is meaningful that in every single state, parades and festivities mark March 17 with an underlying consciousness that binds together all who think of themselves as Irish. Even those who may have a vast ignorance of Irish history or culture are, for that one day, Irish in spirit.

For Irish-Americans and non-Irish alike, this book is a rich quarry. The author, John Barnes, aims to instruct and to delight and does so very well. He offers all readers colorful snapshots of America's social and political history, which is so intertwined with the story of the Irish in America.

The Irish came to the United States mainly as rebels fleeing the noose; as Presbyterians, Quakers, and Catholics escaping the discriminations imposed by the Anglican state at home; or, later, by the failure of the one crop—the potato—so many were forced to subsist on.

Before the larger waves of immigration during the mid-1800s, the Irish were already in the New World. Many had fished the North Atlantic from Britain and Ireland to Newfoundland. Consequently, they called Newfoundland *Talamh an Eisc* (Bridge of Fish). In later years, the movement of Irish settlers from Newfoundland to Maine and Massachusetts introduced a new phrase to the language: "Down East."

There is even a 16th-century record of an Irishman, Edward Nugent, who made his way into history by shooting an Indian chief in 1586 in what is now North Carolina. In the next century Oliver Cromwell transported numbers of unwilling—"disaffected"—Irish to the West Indies, some of whom, in time, made their way to the North American mainland. So, the Irish connection with North America is, at least, four centuries old.

The Irish made a special impact in America throughout the 18th century: pioneering the westward and southern frontiers; as signers of the Declaration of Independence; in the person of John Mitchel, the risk-taking printer of that "seditious" document *United Irishman;* in the ranks of the Continental Army; and in Irish-born Charles Thomson, a key person in the Continental Congress and the one to whom the Congress turned to notify George Washington of his election to the presidency.

To use historian Lord Macaulay's phrase, "Every schoolboy knows" that, during the American War of Independence, the British House of Lords was reassured that there was no real disaffection in the Colonies— except on the part of His Majesty's Irish subjects there. This view of the staunchness of the Irish was confirmed when the British Commander-in-Chief in America, Sir Henry Clinton, recommended that his divisions be strengthened by drawing troops from Ireland "whence the rebels them-selves drew most of their best soldiers."

It is remarkable, too, how Irish-American history entwines with that of other nations. Both Spain and France had Irish Brigades in their service: Spain's Regimento de Hibernia, under the command of Colonel Arturo O'Neill, defeated the English at the battle of Pensacola; while both the Regiments du Dillon and du Walsh fought as part of the French forces at Yorktown where England met its final defeat in Colonial America.

The largest exodus from Ireland to the United States and Canada arrived between 1841 and 1860, owing to blight on the potato, the main food of millions of people. During that period, one and three quarter million immigrants arrived, filling mostly eastern seaboard ghettos. By 1860, the Irish-born accounted for one-quarter of the population in New York City, Jersey City, and Boston. For most, the conditions of their existence were appalling, their lives brutish and shortened. Yet Orestes Brownson, the social critic of the era, perceiving a fundamental dignity in the newcomers, burst forth in prophecy: "Out of these narrow lanes, dirty streets, damp cellars, and suffocating garrets, will come forth some of the noblest sons of our country whom she will delight to own and honor."

The Irish made—and continue to make—considerable contributions to the fabric of America: to the military (earning more Congressional Medals of Honor than any other foreign-born group); to labor organiza-tions (Mother Jones, Mike Quill, George Meany); to government (thirteen presidents); to literature (Eugene O'Neill, Flannery O'Connor); to music (Thomas Moore, Victor Herbert); to sculpture (Augustus St. Gaudens); to architecture (James Hoban, Louis Sullivan); and to business (W. R. Grace, James Concannon) just to name a few.

Possibly the single greatest—and most basic—contribution the Irish made was the continuing impetus they have given to the development of the democratic spirit. The Irish entered into a relatively stable society but from their early days tested the limitations placed upon political, personal, and social freedom.

Irish-American Landmarks is an excellent, readable, and valuable compendium which should have pride of place in every Irish-American home.

Who is Irish-American? President Woodrow Wilson, who sometimes boasted about his Irish grandparents in political speeches, nevertheless denounced what he called "hyphenated-Americans." Legendary New York Governor Al Smith could claim but one Irish grandparent, yet he enthusiastically and wholeheartedly described himself as Irish-American, and was accepted by the public as such.

Does Irish ancestry, however diluted and remote, qualify one as an Irish-American? In a country where over 40 percent of the population lays claim to at least one Irish ancestor, such a definition would be both absurdly vague and include a great many people who would not only fail to be recognized by most disinterested observers as Irish-Americans, but probably would not think of themselves as such either.

In compiling this book, I have tried to stay as close to Irish roots as possible. Obviously, landmarks associated with people born in Ireland who made a name for themselves on this side of the Atlantic were at the top of my list. Next were those sites having to do with someone whose parents—one or both of them—were born in Ireland. In the case of places tied to Irish-Americans whose ancestry was more distant, I tried to find out if the person was aware of his or her Irish roots or if they were touched by what might broadly be described as "the Irish-American experience." Some sites have been excluded because I could not find reliable research material on the backgrounds of the people associated with them. Of course these pages do not tell the story of every Irish-American: For many, including the accomplished and the noteworthy, there is no landmark—no place that a traveler can visit to learn that person's story.

Sharp-eyed readers will no doubt locate instances where I have departed from this criteria in including some sites and that I have left out others that are worthy of inclusion. For instance, I have included landmarks related only to those U.S. presidents who are of Irish ancestry through the direct paternal line. I have also included some sites for people who were not Irish, but who had interesting Irish connections, such as Pennsylvania founder William Penn (Penn's Landing in Philadelphia) and Indiana poet James Whitcomb Riley (Riley Birthplace Museum in Greenfield and Riley Home in Indianapolis).

I have also chosen sites and people regardless of religious affiliation. Some historians will argue with this approach, saying that including Roman Catholic and Protestant Irish in the same volume creates an affinity that does not exist. Perhaps this is true, but many of Ireland's greatest patriots, such as Wolfe Tone and Robert Emmet, were Protestants. It is also the position of many Irish and Irish-Americans that the experiences of Presbyterian and Episcopal Irish are a part of the national tradition.

In researching and writing this book, I made every effort to discover the real story behind many well-known anecdotes and to present the facts as fairly as possible.

I beg the reader to understand that it would be impossible to include everything and everyone. For instance, a whole volume could be written on the Irish sites of New York City alone. I do, of course, invite readers to provide suggestions for any future editions of this book. And while I have made every effort to ensure accuracy, errors and omissions no doubt will occur. All responsibility for them, of course, lies with me.

The photographs in the book come from a wide array of sources. Those photos without attribution are images I captured in my travels.

ACKNOWLEDGEMENTS

So many are involved in the production of a book that it is impossible to adequately thank everyone. Still, I am indebted to the following individuals:

George Cantor, my former colleague at *The Detroit News* and the author of *Historic Landmarks of Black America, North American Indian Landmarks,* and *Pop Culture Landmarks.* George's efforts gave me the inspiration to tackle this project.

Early in the research for *Irish-American Landmarks,* I chanced across a copy of *The Irish Volunteer* and decided to contact the editor, Charles Laverty. He and I soon became fast friends. A bloodhound in tracking down Irish-American military history, Charles generously provided me with a list of sites he had compiled over the years, which proved invaluable in getting me started.

In that treasure trove of Irish-America that is Boston, Bill O'Donnell of the Boston Redevelopment Authority pointed me to James Ford's invaluable *Irish Walking Tour of Boston,* which made me aware of many sites. James Ford himself sent me additional material, which was very useful. David Wadsworth, curator of the Cohasset Historical Society, took time to show me the St. John's Cross in Cohasset Cemetery. Also, I wish to thank the marvelously helpful staff at the John F. Kennedy Library.

Throughout this project, I never ceased to be amazed by the role played by coincidence (or was it fate?). I dropped by *The San Francisco Chronicle* offices to see my friends Dan Rosenheim and Jonathan Marshall, only to discover that another friend, Ben Wildavsky, was also working at the paper. It was Ben who called my attention to the book, *California: The Irish Dream* by Patrick Dowling. Pat, still hale in his eighties, generously invited me to his home and inscribed a copy of his book, without which the California chapter of this work would not be so rich.

Patricia Harty, the editor-in-chief of *Irish America* magazine, kindly put up with my questions and allowed me to look through back issues of the magazine and photocopy articles that were invaluable to my research.

I would also like to thank those who so graciously agreed to serve as advisers to this project: James S. Rogers, executive director of the Irish American Cultural Institute in St. Paul, Minnesota; Peter Quinn, chief speechwriter at Time-Warner Inc. and editor of *The Recorder,* the journal of the American-Irish Historical Society; Timothy Sarbaugh, associate professor of history at Gonzaga University, Spokane, Washington; and Jack Weaver, professor of English at Winthrop University, Rock Hill, South Carolina.

I would also like to pay tribute to the late Dennis Clark, scholar of Irish history and a moving force within the Balch Institute of Ethnic Studies, who had agreed to become an adviser to this project only weeks before his untimely death.

I also extend my thanks to William J. Durkin, a fellow Bronx boy and the man who taught me to play the bagpipes. Bill, and his brother Johnny, were unfailingly supportive and the source of much inspiration.

I would like to thank my former colleagues at *The Detroit News* editorial page, especially Thomas J. Bray, truly the finest individual anyone could ever work for. Thanks also to the staffs at the public libraries in Troy, Michigan, and Chesapeake, Virginia.

Thanks to Christine Nasso, Rebecca Nelson, and Allison McNeill, my editors at Gale Research/Visible Ink Press, for their unfailing courtesy and helpfulness at many difficult moments.

I would especially like to thank my family. My brother Thomas, his wife Liz, and my sister Joan were all sources of inspiration, as was my uncle, Jerry McAuliffe. I also recall fondly the memory of my grandfather, John McAuliffe of New Market, county Cork. One of the greatest pleasures of this project was discovering that the tales about the Irish and Irish-Americans with which he captivated me as a boy were (mostly) true.

And most of all I would like to thank my mother, Mary Bridget McAuliffe Barnes, whose love and belief in me and this project sustained me through hard times. The only regret she, I, and all of us share at the completion of this book is that my father, Thomas Desmond Barnes, who left Dublin in 1948 for a new and uncertain life in a strange country, did not live to see it.

J.A.B.
Brooklyn, New York
April 1995

CONNECTICUT

DELAWARE

MAINE

MARYLAND

MASSACHUSETTS

NEW HAMPSHIRE

NEW JERSEY

NEW YORK

ONTARIO

PENNSYLVANIA

QUEBEC

RHODE ISLAND

VERMONT

WASHINGTON
D.C.

*Glorious
St. Patrick's
Cathedral in
New York City.*
See page 106.

CONNECTICUT

1 Memorial to Irish Soldiers in French Service, Middlebury
2 Knights of Columbus Grand Council Museum, New Haven
3 Monte Cristo Cottage, New London

DELAWARE

4 Hagley Museum and Eleutherian Mills, Wilmington

MAINE

5 St John's Church, Bangor
6 *Margaretta* Incident, Machias Bay
7 St. Patrick's Church, Newcastle
8 Gorham's Corner, St. Dominic's Church, Portland
9 Montpelier, Thomaston

MARYLAND

10 Carroll-Barrister House, Annapolis
11 Antietam Natl Battlefield, Antietam
12 Basilica of the Assumption, Baltimore
13 B & O Railroad Museum, Baltimore
14 Carroll Mansion, Baltimore
15 Ft. McHenry, Baltimore
16 Homewood, Baltimore
17 B & O Railroad Station Museum, Ellicott City
18 John Hughes Cabin/Mt. St. Mary's College, Emmitsburg
19 Cemetery of St. Mary's Catholic Church, Rockville
20 George Meany Labor Archives, Silver Spring
21 Antrim, Taneytown
22 St. Francis Xavier and Old Bohemia Mission, Warwick

MASSACHUSETTS

23 Bellevue Apts, Boston
24 Boston Common, Boston
25 Boston Massacre Memorial, Boston
26 Cardinal Cushing Memorial Pk, Boston
27 Copley Square, Trinity Church, Boston
28 Deer Island, Boston
29 Doyle's Cafe, Boston
30 Edwin O'Connor Apt House, Boston
31 Great Hunger Memorial, Boston
32 James Michael Curley House, Boston
33 James Family Home, Boston
34 JFK Library and Museum, Boston
35 John Singleton Copley Studio, Boston
36 John Boyle O'Reilly Memorial, Boston
37 Louis Sullivan Birthplace, Boston
38 Maurice Tobin Statue, Boston
39 Old City Hall, Boston

40 Patrick Collins Memorial, Boston
41 Rose Fitzgerald Kennedy Birthplace, Boston
42 Shelton Hall, Boston
43 South Boston, Boston
44 St. Stephen's Church, Boston
45 JFK Natl Historic Site, Brookline
46 St. John's Memorial, Cohasset
47 Connie Mack Birthplace, East Brookfield
48 Whaling Museum, Catalpa Memorial, New Bedford

NEW HAMPSHIRE

49 Augustus Saint Gaudens Natl Historic Site, Plainfield
50 Fort Constitution, Portsmouth

NEW JERSEY

51 American Labor Museum/Botto House, Haledon
52 City Hall, Jersey City
53 Dean William McNulty Memorial/St. John the Baptist, Paterson
54 Paterson Museum, Paterson

NEW YORK

55 Charter Day Commemoration, Albany
56 Irish-American Heritage Museum, East Durham
57 Johnson Hall State Historic Site, Johnstown
58 Al Smith House, New York
59 American Irish Historical Society, New York
60 Ellis Island, Castle Clinton, Statute of Liberty, South St. Seaport, New York
61 5th Ave./St. Pat's Day Parade, New York
62 Fire Dept. Museum, New York
63 Five Points Site, New York
64 Fr. Francis J. Duffy Memorial, New York
65 George M. Cohan Memorial, New York
66 Jimmy Walker Home, New York
67 Police Academy Museum, New York
68 St. James Church, New York
69 St. Patrick's Cathedral, New York
70 St. Paul's Chapel, New York
71 69th Regiment Armory, New York
72 Tammany Hall, New York
73 Thomas Moore Memorial, New York
74 Victor Herbert Memorial, New York
75 Woodside, New York
76 Macdonough Memorial, Plattsburgh
77 Grave of Catherine de Valera, Rochester
78 Patrick O'Rorke Memorial, Rochester
79 Saratoga Natl Historical Pk, Saratoga
80 Erie Canal Museum, Syracuse
81 James Connolly Memorial, Troy

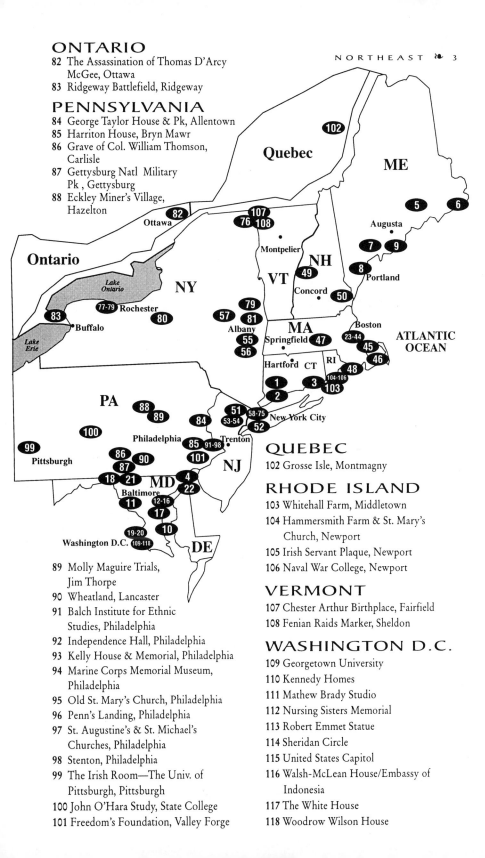

ONTARIO
82 The Assassination of Thomas D'Arcy McGee, Ottawa
83 Ridgeway Battlefield, Ridgeway

PENNSYLVANIA
84 George Taylor House & Pk, Allentown
85 Harriton House, Bryn Mawr
86 Grave of Col. William Thomson, Carlisle
87 Gettysburg Natl Military Pk , Gettysburg
88 Eckley Miner's Village, Hazelton

89 Molly Maguire Trials, Jim Thorpe
90 Wheatland, Lancaster
91 Balch Institute for Ethnic Studies, Philadelphia
92 Independence Hall, Philadelphia
93 Kelly House & Memorial, Philadelphia
94 Marine Corps Memorial Museum, Philadelphia
95 Old St. Mary's Church, Philadelphia
96 Penn's Landing, Philadelphia
97 St. Augustine's & St. Michael's Churches, Philadelphia
98 Stenton, Philadelphia
99 The Irish Room—The Univ. of Pittsburgh, Pittsburgh
100 John O'Hara Study, State College
101 Freedom's Foundation, Valley Forge

QUEBEC
102 Grosse Isle, Montmagny

RHODE ISLAND
103 Whitehall Farm, Middletown
104 Hammersmith Farm & St. Mary's Church, Newport
105 Irish Servant Plaque, Newport
106 Naval War College, Newport

VERMONT
107 Chester Arthur Birthplace, Fairfield
108 Fenian Raids Marker, Sheldon

WASHINGTON D.C.
109 Georgetown University
110 Kennedy Homes
111 Mathew Brady Studio
112 Nursing Sisters Memorial
113 Robert Emmet Statue
114 Sheridan Circle
115 United States Capitol
116 Walsh-McLean House/Embassy of Indonesia
117 The White House
118 Woodrow Wilson House

CONNECTICUT

MEMORIAL TO IRISH SOLDIERS IN FRENCH SERVICE

On the afternoon of May 11, 1745, the Battle of Fontenoy was going badly for King Louis XV of France. The English duke of Cumberland, who would achieve notoriety a year later as "Bloody Cumberland" after the defeat of Bonnie Prince Charlie (Prince Charles Edward Stuart) at Culloden, had mown down the French center, threatening the entire French position. After a hasty conference with Marshal Maurice Saxe, the king authorized that the six regiments of the Irish Brigade be thrown into the fray in a do-or-die effort to save the day.

For the first time since the early 17th century, Irish troops got to meet their English oppressors head-on in a pitched battle, and the Irish did not disappoint. With their pipers playing "St. Patrick's Day" and "The White Cockade," the Regiments du Clare, Dillon, Berwick, Bulkley, Rothe, and Lally moved forward. The Irish cannon raked holes in the English line like scythes through wheat. In bitter hand-to-hand fighting with the elite Brigade of Guards, the Irish turned the tide of battle and broke the English offensive that year. The cost: 400 Irish killed out of 4,000 engaged.

Irish troops had been in French service at least since 1607, when the rebellion against English rule led by the Earls of Tyrone and of Tyrconnell was crushed and the "Flight of the Earls" commenced. By 1688, France had about 6,000 Irish troops in service. After the flight of James II in that year, the trickle became a flood. No one knows the numbers of Irish who went into mercenary service on the Continent in the late seventeenth and early eighteenth centuries, but estimates as high as 250,000 have been made.

These regiments had Irish officers as well, and many of them went on to achieve the highest ranks in the French army, up to and including marshal of France. Marshal Patrice MacMahon, a descendant of the "Wild

Geese" who served Napoleon III in the 1870 war with Prussia, went on to become president of France.

These troops served France loyally until the French Revolution destroyed the old Royalist army. Two of the Irish Brigade regiments, the Regiment du Walsh and the Regiment du Dillon, served in the Americas after Benjamin Franklin concluded the alliance with France in 1778. These troops marched through Connecticut on their way to what would be the final major battle of the Revolution at Yorktown.

❧ **EXHIBITS:** The inscription reads, "Camp of the French Army en route to Yorktown, June 27, 1981." It was erected in 1904 by Dennis H. Tierney of the American-Irish Historical Society. Another memorial to these troops is in Southington at a place called French Hill. It was erected by Capt. Lawrence O'Brien of the American-Irish Historical Society in 1912. ❧ **LOCATION:** The monument to the Irish troops in French service is located in a park in Middlebury called Rochambeau Heights. Follow Artillery to where it curves into Break Neck Hill Rd. The monument is about 600 feet into the woods. ❧ **HOURS:** Dawn to dusk. ❧ **ADMISSION:** Free

NEW HAVEN

KNIGHTS OF COLUMBUS GRAND COUNCIL MUSEUM

Irish Catholics were forbidden by papal edict to join "secret societies" such as the Masons, which were said to have atheistic overtones. That stricture, however, meant that Catholics excluded themselves from organizations to which movers and shakers, both locally and nationally, belonged. They also lacked a real organization to provide mutual protection and support within a community that was frequently indifferent or even hostile to their needs.

Father Michael McGivney, a son of famine immigrants, thought that had to change. Roman Catholics, too, should have their own fraternal organization, through which they could help society as well as one another. In January 1882, he began a series of meetings at his parish parochial house at St. Mary's Church in New Haven. He and nine associates eventually formed the Knights of Columbus, an organization consciously modeled on the Masonic orders, with secret initiation rituals and oaths. The Knights received their first official recognition on March 29, 1882, when they were chartered by the state of Connecticut.

Official church recognition took a bit longer, because the hierarchy were suspicious of anything that smacked of Masonry, and the order was initially slow to spread outside of Connecticut. The papal nuncio soon pronounced his blessing, however, and the Knights were well on their way to becoming one of the country's great social service organizations, embracing an estimated one million-plus members.

Today, the Knights are known mostly for selling insurance to their members, getting Columbus Day declared a national holiday, and offering correspondence courses in everything from Catholicism to foreign languages. All cardinals, archbishops, and bishops are technically members, whether they attend meetings or not.

Needless to say, the Masons cast a jaundiced eye on the new organization, and lurid stories regularly appeared in the press about how the Knights' oath required the killing of Protestants and Masons. In 1912, the Knights offered a $25,000 reward to anyone who could prove the false oath was legitimate. To prove their point further, the Knights' leadership took the unprecedented step of showing the true oath, which doesn't mention Protestants or Masons, to a group of Masons, and the controversy blew over.

&. **EXHIBITS:** The museum contains displays on the life of Father McGivney and his two brothers, who succeeded him as national chaplain of the order, as well as displays on the Knights' many other activities. &. **LOCATION:** One Columbus Plaza in downtown New Haven. &. **HOURS:** Monday–Friday, 8–4:30. Weekends by appointment. &. **ADMISSION:** Free &. **TELEPHONE:** (203) 772-2130.

NEW LONDON

MONTE CRISTO COTTAGE

The stormy marriage of James and Ella O'Neill played itself out inside the walls of this modest cottage. Had they but known what the future would hold, the two might have been moved to be more pleasant to each other. For their youngest child, Eugene, was quietly taking it all in. Today, almost anywhere where Eugene O'Neill's plays are performed, you can see his family twist themselves in knots on the stage before your very eyes.

In recent years, critics and biographers have begun paying more attention to O'Neill's heritage and the influence it had on his life and career as America's greatest playwright. Certainly the playwright himself acknowledged the debt: "The critics have missed the important thing about me and my work," he wrote in a 1945 letter to his son. "The fact that I am Irish." His third wife, the half-mad Carlotta, described her husband as "a rough, tough black Irishman. . . . a tough Mick . . . who loved only his work."

O'Neill's father, James, emigrated to America from Kilkenny as a 10–year-old during the famine. Unlike most other immigrants, who set to work in factories, James decided on a career as an actor and made himself a great success. He loved to tell his sons that the O'Neills were the greatest and most powerful clan in Ulster. He fancied himself a descendant of the great Hugh O'Neill, earl of Tyrone, who, between 1598 and 1601, led the insurrection against English rule that had come closest to success before the 20th century.

James named his youngest son Eugene in the mistaken belief that it was the English transliteration of the Gaelic name Eoghan, after Eoghan O'Neill, another Celtic warrior. The playwright, in turn, named one of his own sons Shane, after yet another Celtic chieftain. Eugene O'Neill's middle name, Gladstone, was taken from William Ewart Gladstone, four times England's prime minister and a hero to the Irish for his vain support of home rule. The playwright's daughter, who was disowned by her father after she married film director and actor Charlie Chaplin under semi-scandalous circumstances, was given the Gaelic name of Oona.

Eugene O'Neill did his growing up backstage. As he grew older, his father was prosperous enough to send young Gene away to Catholic boarding schools and Princeton University for one year. (He is said to have thrown a beer bottle through then-university Pres. Woodrow Wilson's window.) O'Neill became unhinged for a time, however, after he became sickened by his father's endless portrayals of Edmond Dantes in *The Count of Monte Cristo* and his realization that his mother's morphine addiction was caused by her difficulties in giving birth to him. In 1909, he ran off to sea, getting drunk and wandering from port to port for the next few years. He became so depressed at one point he made a half-hearted attempt at suicide.

A bout with tuberculosis in 1912 was the event that changed his life. Forced to dry out and look hard at himself, he realized his true calling and began writing plays. In 1916, the Provincetown Players, a group of ama-teur actors on Cape Cod, successfully staged his short play about the sea, *Bound East for Cardiff,* and his career was launched.

O'Neill rebelled against the existing Irish-American theatrical tradi-tion. His father was only one of many Irish-born actors treading the American stage in the nineteenth century, and the "stage Irishman" was a staple of the vaudeville theater. Performing families like "The Three Keatons" (Buster Keaton and his parents) and "The Four Cohans" (George M. and family) were among the most popular acts of their day. Edward Harrigan and Tony Hart enjoyed a long and successful run with their "Mulligan Guard" series of musical comedies in the 1880s.

Eugene O'Neill was a far more serious sort. No O'Neill character would wish anyone "top o' the mornin' to ya." As O'Neill's father commented after watching his son's first big success, the Pulitzer Prize-winning *Beyond the Horizon,* "What are you trying to do, son? Make the audience go home and commit suicide?"

O'Neill never let up, mining his own family's history for material, though the dramatic version was usually far more incredible than anything that (probably) happened in real life. *Desire Under the Elms* concerned a lustful father, a weak son, and an adulterous wife who murders her own infant daughter. These shocking themes, drawn from classical Greek drama, vastly elevated the quality of American playwriting (and didn't hurt ticket sales either).

It wasn't all glumness in the O'Neill world, however. In 1933, he wrote his only comedy, *Ah Wilderness!,* which clearly has autobiographical themes. He meant the play as something of a joke, simply to prove that he could laugh as well as frown. It probably had a more serious meaning, however, as a nostalgic wish for what O'Neill had wanted his childhood to be: a happy home where parents spent time with their children and enjoyed their company.

But it is the great tragedy *Long Day's Journey Into Night* that figures most prominently with Monte Cristo Cottage. The play features the disintegration of an Irish-American theatrical family named "The Tyrones." The father is an actor who once had great promise, but has reduced himself to pathetic but popular roles in order to pay the mortgage on his estate. The mother is a withdrawn, neurotic morphine addict, floating down the long staircase in a perpetual trance. It won O'Neill a posthumous Pulitzer Prize (his fourth) and secured this Irish-American's reputation for all time as one of America's greatest playwrights. (*See* Danville, California for more on O'Neill.)

❧ EXHIBITS: Thanks to O'Neill's intricate stage directions for his plays, it has been possible to re-create the Victorian sitting room precisely as it is described in *Long Day's Journey Into Night.* The other rooms contain O'Neill memorabilia, as well as displays on many other aspects of the American theater. There is a short multimedia presentation on the playwright's life. Nearby is the Eugene O'Neill Memorial Theater Center (305 Great Neck Rd., Waterford), which frequently presents productions of O'Neill's work, as well as that of other playwrights. ❧ LOCATION: 1½ miles south of U.S. 1 at 325 Pequot Ave. ❧ HOURS: Monday–Friday 1–4 from early April to mid-December. ❧ ADMISSION: Adult $3; $1 for 13 and under. ❧ TELEPHONE: (203) 443-0051; Eugene O'Neill Memorial Theater Center: (203) 443-5378.

DELAWARE

HAGLEY MUSEUM AND ELEUTHERIAN MILLS

When E. I. du Pont built his famed gunpowder mills here in 1802, few were eager for the dangerous work. So he imported Irish workers at company expense and shiploads of immigrants soon began docking at Newcastle. Naturally, du Pont was anxious to maintain the loyalty of a workforce that was (literally) atop a powder keg. So he built housing for them, and his sons constructed a church, St. Joseph's-on-the-Brandywine, as a religious and social center for the workers and their families.

The first Irish in Delaware thus did not live in crowded slums, but in purpose-built housing probably considerably better than they had seen before. Irish labor later helped build the nearby Chesapeake and Delaware Canal and the New Castle— Frenchtown Railroad, where they again spent most of their time in work camps, isolated from the general population.

After the potato blight, however, immigration increased and the Irish experience in Delaware became similar to that elsewhere on the eastern seaboard, with the poor neighborhoods of Wilmington filling up with immigrants. The Irish constituted the largest foreign-born population in the city throughout the 19th century. Their numbers peaked around 1900, when 4,870 Wilmingtonians listed Ireland as their place of birth, 6 percent of the total population and 38 percent of the foreign-born.

The Hagley powder works remained in operation until 1921. In World War I, 40 percent of all the gunpowder used by U.S. forces was manufactured here.

* **EXHIBITS:** The 230-acre site along the Brandywine River features restored examples of worker housing and a school. A restored mill from 1814 contains exhibits on the many products manufactured here besides

9

gunpowder, such as flour, paper, and iron. Also on the grounds is
Eleutherian Mills, the du Pont family home for five generations. &
LOCATION: Route 141, just outside Wilmington. & HOURS: April
through December, 9:30–4:30 daily. January through March, guided tour
1:30 Monday–Friday, 9:30–4:30 Saturday–Sunday. & ADMISSION:
$9.75 adults; $7.50 seniors (62 and older) and students; $3.50 children
(ages 6–14); free for children 6 years and younger; $26.50 family. &
TELEPHONE: (302) 658-2400.

MAINE

ST. JOHN'S CHURCH

Cholera had broken out in Ireland in 1832, and many Irish who did not die of the disease took ship for America. Because the British government subsidized passage to Canada, in order to encourage the peopling of British North America, fares were lower than aboard ships headed directly to the United States. Consequently, many Irish immigrants landed at Quebec, or in the Maritime Provinces. Few, however, wished to linger under the detested Union Jack, and at the first opportunity they boarded ships or took to the roads headed south. Since these immigrants were counted as coming from Canada rather than Ireland, the official U.S. census figures of the period tend to understate the true level of Irish immigration to the United States.

There were Irish in Maine before the 1830s (*see* Newcastle, Maine). In addition to the Maine O'Briens mentioned elsewhere, there were the Kavanaghs of Newcastle, who were wealthy and established by the time the cholera immigrants arrived and who eventually produced the state's first Irish-Catholic governor in 1843.

These earlier immigrants, however, did nothing to prepare the mostly Yankee residents of Maine for the horde of Catholic peasantry bearing down upon them from the north in the early 1830s. Maine was "fatally situated," wrote the town fathers of Bangor to Gov. Samuel Smith in 1832, to receive "a whole host of paupers."

And come they did. Almost overnight, it seemed, Bangor's population was 20 percent Irish-born. Their labor fueled the hungry sawmills in the woods above Bangor. The seemingly endless stands of white pine were stripped to satisfy the craving of the growing eastern cities for ever more timber. So numerous were the immigrants and so packed were the slums that a Yankee observer noted that "Bangor has become a young New York." He didn't mean the comparison as a compliment.

Not surprisingly, clashes soon took place. In one of the first such incidents in the United States, an anti-Irish riot by mostly Yankee sailors gripped Bangor for several nights in July 1833. Appalled by the incident, the Yankee elite sought to cover it up, and it will never be known just how many Irish were killed. There was so much looting, burning, and general roughing up of Irish residents that many families fled to the safety of the nearby woods. It would be the first of several such encounters over the next few decades, both in Bangor and nationally.

As in many places, the most visible evidence of the Irish presence is in the churches they built. In Bangor the church is St. John's. Completed in 1855, it is largely the legacy of two Irish Bangorites, Timothy Field and James O'Donahue. Both men struck out from Bangor for California when word of the gold rush filtered back east. They returned as rich men to their adopted city a few years later.

One of the most famous priests associated with St. John's was Father John Bapst. Unlike virtually all his parishioners, Bapst was not Irish but Swiss, and he spoke scarcely a word of English. More devout than prudent, he went on a crusade in the early 1850s to have the Roman Catholic Bible replace the King James Version in Maine's public schools.

When Yankee Protestants in the United States expressed suspicion of the Catholic church's intentions toward the American experiment, the existence of priests such as Bapst proved they were not wholly hallucinating. Many, perhaps a majority, of Irish Catholics believed the civil power *ought* to be subordinate to the religious. It took several decades for this attitude to change.

Needless to say, Father Bapst's action was the equivalent of waving a red flag in front of the bull of anti-immigrant Know-Nothingism and the prelate was very nearly martyred for his trouble. On the night of October 14, 1854, he was cornered by a Know-Nothing mob in the town of Ellsworth, tarred and feathered, and run out of town on a rail.

&. **EXHIBITS:** The church is located in the middle of what was once a thriving Irish neighborhood. The baptismal font in the church was donated by mining magnate James Donahue and bears his name. &. **LOCATION:** St. John's is at 207 York St. in downtown Bangor, between Boyd and Newbury streets. &. **HOURS:** Church office: 8–12 and 1–5 daily. Church hours are variable, but the key to view the interior is available at the rectory. &. **ADMISSION:** None, but donations appreciated. &. **TELEPHONE:** (207) 942-6941.

MACHIAS BAY

MARGARETTA INCIDENT

By June 1775, word of the battles at Lexington and Concord had reached this isolated settlement on the far northeastern shore of Maine. Most of the townspeople were sympathetic to the Patriot cause, but had little opportunity to demonstrate it until June 2, when the sloops *Polly* and *Unity*, accompanied by the British gunboat *Margaretta*, arrived from Boston.

The two sloops were carrying badly needed supplies for the settlement after the harsh winter. The gunboat was present to ensure that the lumber the sloops would be carrying back in return—which was to be used to build barracks for the British troops then occupying Boston—would not be interfered with.

Sympathizing with the revolutionaries in far-off Massachusetts was one thing, openly joining in the insurrection by taking hostile action against a British man-o'-war was quite another, and a town council was called. Chairing it was Col. Benjamin Foster, leader of the local militia, and Capt. Jeremiah O'Brien, a 41-year-old sea captain. The latter was the eldest son of Morris O'Brien, a Dublin native and original settler of the Machias Bay area.

The men of the town, gathered in a field, debated their course of action throughout the morning of Sunday, June 11. Finally, Foster, weary of the long discussion, leapt over a local stream appropriately named the Rubicon. He challenged all the men who were in favor of taking action against the British ships to follow him. Almost all did.

Armed with a swords, pitchforks, axes, and a few primitive guns, the men endeavored to capture the British officers while they were attending church. Alerted to the approaching rebel band, however, the British made good their escape through the church windows and immediately cast off in the *Margaretta*. The British commander, Lieutenant Moore, warned the inhabitants that if any effort was made to seize the sloops, he would fire on the town.

Undeterred, 40 of the motley armed band boarded the *Unity* and, with O'Brien in command by unanimous consent, commenced their pursuit of the British gunboat.

The *Unity* caught up with the *Margaretta* the next day, June 12. O'Brien called across to Moore to surrender, which the latter refused to do. Wishing to avoid an armed confrontation, however, the British commander decided instead to try to reach Boston. But the *Unity* proved the faster vessel and soon caught up. Moore even cast his lifeboats adrift in an effort to lighten his vessel, but in vain. Finally, with few alternatives remaining, he opened fire on the fast-closing *Unity*.

O'Brien and his crew fired back, "with good effect" according to one witness. Soon, the two vessels came alongside and a short, sharp fight ensued. Moore made a gallant effort, personally throwing hand grenades at the rebels, but O'Brien was soon the first American aboard the British ship and a hand-to-hand melee on her deck commenced. A few moments later, Lt. Moore fell mortally wounded and his second-in-command had no stomach for continuing the fight. With seven dead on either side, the *Margaretta* became the first British warship to be captured by American arms.

O'Brien received the thanks of the Massachusetts legislature in a resolution dated June 26, 1775. He then proceeded to arm the *Unity* with the guns of the *Margaretta* and began patrolling the Maine coast. A month after the *Margaretta* incident, O'Brien captured two more British vessels, this time without firing a shot, and he once again received the thanks of the Massachusetts legislature. O'Brien turned his habit of capturing British warships into a full-time occupation as a privateer, capturing British vessels throughout the Western Hemisphere until he himself was captured in 1780. A year later, however, he successfully escaped and took command of another raider, named the *Hibernia* after the land of his ancestors.

Following the revolution, O'Brien lived quietly in Maine. Pres. James Madison appointed him customs collector for the Machias district in 1811, a position he held until his death in 1818. In honor of the action that author James Fenimore Cooper dubbed "the Lexington of the Seas," Secretary of the Navy John D. Long named a torpedo boat the *Jeremiah O'Brien*. (*See* San Francisco, California.)

❧ **EXHIBITS:** There are several sites in Machias related to Jeremiah O'Brien and the capture of the *Margaretta*. A marker along Main Street indicates where O'Brien's house stood. Another marker, along Route 92, just outside town, indicates the site of the town meeting where it was decided that action would be taken. Burnham Tavern, which was used as a hospital for the wounded after the *Margaretta* incident, is at Main and Free streets. and is now a museum with exhibits relating to the battle. Jeremiah O'Brien and his five brothers, who also took part in the action, are buried in the O'Brien churchyard.   ❧ **LOCATION:** Machias is on state Route 1, which runs parallel with the Atlantic Ocean, about 250 miles from Portland.   ❧ **HOURS:** Burnham Tavern Museum, Main Street: June–August, 10–5, Monday–Friday; Saturday 10–3. Other times by appointment.   ❧ **ADMISSION:** Free   ❧ **TELEPHONE:** (207) 255-4432.

NEWCASTLE

ST. PATRICK'S CHURCH

Roman Catholics were still a despised, distrusted sect in Puritan Massachusetts (of which Maine was still a part) when a small group of Irish immigrants founded St. Patrick's in 1796. St. Patrick's claims to be the oldest continuously functioning Catholic church in New England. The steeple contains a bell by Paul Revere, cast in 1818, the year of his death.

❧ **LOCATION:** 2½ miles north of U.S. 1 on ME 215 (Academy Rd.). ❧ **HOURS:** 9 A.M. to dusk. ❧ **ADMISSION:** None, but donations appreciated. ❧ **TELEPHONE:** (207) 563-3240.

PORTLAND

GORHAM'S CORNER, ST. DOMINIC'S CHURCH

Gorham's Corner was the center of Irish settlement in Maine's largest city, and in Maine, the five-throated intersection became as notorious for rowdiness as "Five Points" did in New York City.

Indeed, as James Mundy notes in *Hard Time, Hard Men: The Irish in Maine*, it was news when *nothing* happened at Gorham's Corner. On June 6, 1859, the *Portland Advertiser* reported incredulously that peace had reigned at Gorham's Corner on the previous Saturday night.

The Portland Irish came to Maine later than the Bangor Irish, for the former were mostly famine Irish, poorer and less well educated than the "cholera Irish" of 1832–33. Things were little better in the Portland slums than in Bangor, however. Conditions in the city were so horrific that in 1849, the Yankee-dominated city council passed a special appropriation for the "overseers of the poor," especially "destitute Irishmen." Three years later, the mayor grumbled that while the Irish constituted one-eighth of the city's population, they were nearly half the population of the Alms House.

But the Portland Irish survived and went on to exert their influence in their adopted country. And few exerted greater influence than John Martin Feeney aka, film director John Ford. (*See* Monument Valley, Utah). Ford was actually born in nearby Cape Elizabeth, but was baptized at St. Dominic's Church, four blocks west of Gorham's Corner.

❧ **EXHIBITS:** A plaque marks the corner. ❧ **LOCATION:** Gorham's Corner is located along the Portland waterfront, at the intersection of Pleasant, Fore, Yorke, Danforth and Center streets. St. Dominic's Church is on State Street at Danforth. ❧ HOURS: St. Dominic's is open daily. Inquire at church office to see the interior. ❧ TELEPHONE: St. Dominic's: (207) 773-8146.

THOMASTON

MONTPELIER

General Henry Knox was one of the most distinguished of Revolutionary War leaders and the first secretary of war under the Constitution.

Knox's parents came from the north of Ireland and he was an active participant in Irish activities, belonging to the Friendly Sons of St. Patrick in Philadelphia and the Charitable Irish Society in Boston.

This is not Knox's original 1795 house, but a reproduction.

❧ EXHIBITS: The house contains original furnishings. ❧ LOCATION: On High Street, near the intersection of U.S. 1 and ME 131. ❧ HOURS: Wednesday–Sunday 9–5:30, Memorial Day–Labor Day. ❧ ADMISSION: $2; seniors free. ❧ TELEPHONE: (207) 354-8062.

MARYLAND

CARROLL-BARRISTER HOUSE

The only Roman Catholic to sign the Declaration of Independence was born here on September 19, 1737. According to his biographers, the family was descended from the "old Irish princely family of the Carrolls of Ely O'Carroll, Kings County, Ireland."

Princely or not, the Carrolls certainly did well in the New World, for Charles was undoubtedly the richest man to put his name to the instrument of independence. He thus had by far the most to lose if the revolution failed. Some joked that there were so many Carrolls in Maryland that Charles was the only man who felt compelled to give his address on the Declaration. (*See* Baltimore, Maryland.)

This massive three-and-one-half story gabled house was built two years before young Charles's birth by his father, Charles Carroll. A chapel on the upper floor, 40 feet long, was the first Roman Catholic place of worship in Annapolis. In 1852, the property was presented to the Redemptorist order by Carroll's grandchildren.

🞜 **EXHIBITS:** The house was moved here from its original location on Duke of Gloucester Street near St. Mary's Church. It now houses administrative offices of the college. 🞜 **LOCATION:** On King George Street, on the campus of St. John's College. 🞜 **HOURS:** Tours of the campus are available by appointment. 🞜 **TELEPHONE:** (410) 263-2371.

ANTIETAM

ANTIETAM NATIONAL BATTLEFIELD

An Irish Brigade existed for a century in the service of the king of France, between Sarsfield's defeat at Limerick in 1690 and the abolition of the old Royalist army by the French Revolution in 1791. It was the memory of that unit, and its victory over the elite British Brigade of Guards at the Battle of Fontenoy in 1745, that partly inspired the organization of the Irish Brigade in the American Civil War. (*See* Middlebury, Connecticut for more on the French army's Irish Brigade; *see* Pensacola, Florida for information on the Irish Brigade of the Spanish army.)

As with so much Irish-American history, the story of the brigade began in Ireland during the potato famine of the 1840s. Under the devastating impact of that disaster, many politically active Irishmen became dissatisfied with the nonviolent nationalism of Daniel O'Connell. Calling their movement "Young Ireland," they began advocating the violent overthrow of British rule in Ireland.

One of the most vociferous members of Young Ireland was Thomas Francis Meagher (pronounced MAH-r), a 25-year-old lawyer from a well-off Catholic family from county Waterford. A fiery orator, his strident calls for action earned him the nickname "Meagher of the Sword." He unsuccessfully stood for Parliament in 1848 and, after a trip to the Continent to solicit support for an uprising in Ireland, he returned bearing with him the first Irish tricolor, modeled on the French one. He used the occasion of the presentation of this flag on July 11, 1848, to make a fiery speech, for which he was promptly arrested. This was nearly a month before the abortive rising in Tipperary on August 5, 1848.

Tried for treason and found guilty, Meagher was sentenced to death, a sentence that was commuted to life imprisonment in the notorious Van Diemen's Land (Tasmania). In 1852, however, he escaped and made his way to New York City. There, he married the daughter of a wealthy merchant and resumed his career as a lawyer, newspaper editor, and agitator for Irish independence.

With the coming of the Civil War, Meagher suspected that British sympathies lay with the Confederacy, and he promptly raised a company for Michael Corcoran's 69th New York State Militia. When Corcoran was captured at Bull Run (*see* Richmond, Virginia), Meagher took command of one of the future brigade's regiments with the understanding that Maj. General James Shields (*see* St. Paul, Minnesota, Carrollton, Missouri, and Washington, D.C.) would command the newly forming Irish Brigade.

Shields, however, refused to take a step down in rank to brigadier general, and the mantle of leadership fell to Meagher. He spent the winter of 1861 and 1862 forming the Irish Brigade, which initially consisted of the

63rd, 69th, and 88th New York regiments. The very un-Irish Massachusetts 29th, consisting of Bay State blue bloods whose names would have been unsurprising on the *Mayflower,* was added to bring the formation up to brigade strength. Meagher, however, goodnaturedly referred to the men of the 29th as "Irishmen in disguise," and the units fought well together.

Meagher's commission as a brigadier general came through in February 1862 and he assumed command of the brigade in Virginia a month later. Although a "political" general, Meagher proved himself a brave and capable battlefield commander and he would lead the brigade in its most famous actions.

Although there were other "ethnic" units in the Union army in the Civil War, the Irish Brigade was special. Its Irish-Catholic character was intended as a statement to an overwhelmingly Protestant and skeptical America that the Irish were worthy of being treated as full-fledged Americans. Its presence in the Army of the Potomac was meant as a rebuke to those who believed the "popish" Catholics could never truly give their loyalty to their adopted land.

Indeed, the Irish immigrants were by no means natural recruits for the Union cause. The Irish who settled in the South, after all, had little difficulty rallying to Confederate service. The immigrants who arrived in New York, Boston, and Philadelphia had been received with little enthusiasm by their new countrymen and had been relegated to the lowest-paid jobs under the worst working conditions: canal diggers, railroad workers, stevedores, millwrights, and so on.

Indeed, the Irish came so cheap they actually pushed free blacks out of many low-paying occupations (a situation deplored by no less than Frederick Douglass). The Irish, therefore, had little enthusiasm for any cause that threatened to bring thousands more even poorer blacks northward to compete for jobs at the lower rung of the social ladder.

Nevertheless, volunteer they did. As outlined by Lawrence Frederick Kohl in his introduction to the new edition of D. F. Conyngham's 1866 classic *The Irish Brigade and its Campaigns,* there were four main reasons. The first was Irish-American nationalism. In his recruiting speeches, Meagher emphasized the debt of the Irish to the nation that offered them "asylum and an honorable career." John Boyle O'Reilly's *Boston Pilot* urged its readers to "Stand by the Union; fight for the Union; die by the Union."

A second reason was the hope that high-profile Irish participation in the war would erase nativist prejudices. Blacks, when they were permitted to enlist later in the war, hoped for the same. Neither group really had its hopes fulfilled, at least not until many years after the war.

The third reason for volunteering was, as noted earlier, perceived British sympathy for the Confederacy. The Irish saw that John Bull was already warily eyeing the United States as a future rival for world power. Obviously, the break-up of the United States would destroy that possibility. And a greatly weakened United States would mean little hope of using American power to one day secure Irish independence.

Finally, many Irish just plain needed the work. The country was in an economic slump around the beginning of the war and jobs were scarce. In the absence of any kind of social welfare system, the choice sometimes came down to joining the army or starvation.

Once in the field, the Irish Brigade carved out a tremendous record for itself in almost every major engagement in the eastern theater of the Civil War. "(W)hen anything absurd, forlorn, or desperate was to be attempted, the Irish Brigade was called upon," wrote George Alfred Townsend, an English war correspondent who ordinarily had little use for the Irish.

One of the advantages enjoyed by the Irish Brigade over other Union units was the presence in its ranks of a substantial number of officers and men with previous military experience. Capt. P. F. Clooney of the 88th New York had served with the papal army in the Italian wars of unification. W. L. D. O'Grady had served with the British Royal Marines before emigrating to the United States. "He volunteered for the 88th only two hours after landing in New York," writes Kohl, "giving his address on the enlistment papers as 'my regiment.'"

The presence of these men helped the raw recruits adjust better to military life and not make the mistakes that led to so many noncombatant deaths in other regiments. On average, two Civil War soldiers died of disease for every one that was killed in battle. In the Irish Brigade, those numbers were reversed. "These men knew how to remain healthy in camp and on the march," writes Kohl, "so that they could make their sacrifices where they counted."

And sacrifice they did, for the brigade's casualties were always among the highest. Though the brigade never put more than 3,000 men into the field at any one time, it suffered over 4,000 casualties in the course of the war. Out of more than 2,000 Union army regiments and units, two from the brigade, the 69th New York and the 28th Massachusetts, ranked in the top ten for the highest casualties. All of the brigade's regiments ranked in the top 300 for casualties.

The brigade's baptism of fire took place during Gen. George McClellan's ill-starred Peninsular Campaign of 1862. The brigade did yeoman service in the battles of the Seven Days: Fair Oaks, Savage's Station, Malvern Hill, and so on. (See Richmond, Virginia.)

The confused and bloody clash that took place at Antietam on September 17, 1862, was the Irish Brigade's next major engagement. Lee had invaded Maryland in hopes of achieving foreign recognition of the Confederacy and relieving battered Virginia during the fall harvest season. The

Shouting "Raise the colors and follow me!" is Thomas Meagher, as his troops charge into the Battle of Antietam. (Copyright 1991 Mort Künstler, Inc. Original painting by Mort Künstler.)

Union army, once again under the ultracautious command of George McClellan, moved north to intercept. The two forces clashed near the small town of Sharpsburg on Antietam Creek. The result was the bloodiest day in American history.

The Irish Brigade was part of the division commanded by Brig. Gen. Israel Bush Richardson, a well-respected commander who had earned the nickname "Fighting Dick" in the Mexican War. With the Irish Brigade in the lead, Richardson's division came up around 10:30 A.M. to the place that would become known in history as "the Bloody Lane."

Meagher's plan was for the brigade to pause at the top of the ridgeline above the lane and fire two volleys, then charge with the bayonet at Confederate Brig. Gen. George Anderson's North Carolina Brigade, which was holding the far side of the lane. As soon as the Irish crested the ridge, however, Anderson's brigade blasted them with musketry, causing the color-bearers of the 69th New York to go down.

Drawing his sword and spurring his horse, Meagher turned to his men and shouted, "Raise the colors and follow me!" Capt. James McGee of the 69th seized the fallen emerald banner and held it high in response. A Confederate bullet promptly clipped the staff in two. As McGee bent to retrieve the flag a second time, a bullet went through his cap, but miraculously, did not hit him. Irish luck must have been with him, for he held up the flag and waved it defiantly. The hailstorm of Confederate lead, how-ever, was too much for any unit, no matter how courageous, to bear. The brigade fell back, with some of its regiments suffering 60 percent casualties.

In his official report, Meagher noted that his horse had been shot from under him and that he had to be carried unconscious from the field. Unkinder critics claimed he was drunk, a report that reached northern newspapers and which Meagher heatedly denied. True or not, it would have been understandable. Rare was the officer in either army who did not fortify himself with some "whiskey courage" before battle.

After the battle, the Irish Brigade retired to Harpers Ferry to recuper-ate. The blueblood 29th Massachusetts transferred out and was replaced by the Irish 28th Massachusetts and 116th Pennsylvania.

🍂 EXHIBITS:There are plans to erect a memorial plaza to the Irish Brigade at Antietam, though this has not come to fruition yet. A 26-minute film is shown on the hour and an 18-minute slide show is shown on the half-hour. There are oil murals depicting various scenes of the battle by James Hope, a veteran, and various exhibits related to the Battle of Antietam and the Civil War. 🍂 LOCATION: The visitor center is 1 mile north of Sharpsburg on S.R. 65. 🍂 HOURS: Daily 8:30–6 Memorial Day through Labor Day; 8:30–5 rest of year. 🍂 ADMISSION: Free 🍂 TELEPHONE: (301) 432-5124.

BALTIMORE

BASILICA OF THE ASSUMPTION

Irish settlers early found their way to Maryland, attracted by the religious tolerance of this colony. The colony's founders, the Calvert family, were not Irish, but they were Roman Catholics and their title of nobility, the Barony of Baltimore, was in the Irish peerage. It was not enlightenment but self-interest—most British monarchs were Protes-tant—that provoked the Calverts to make their colony the most tolerant of all religious faiths.

As early as 1684, a county of New Ireland was organized in what is now Cecil and Harford counties. This territory included the settlements of New Connaught, New Leinster, and New Munster, and there were place-names that included Cork, Clare, Limerick, and Wexford.

In 1817, the Irish of Maryland were sufficiently numerous to organize a Hibernian Society "to do all acts, matters, and things as are or shall be necessary for the purpose of affording charitable assistance and advice to such emigrants from or natives of Ireland arriving at or residing in any part of Maryland." The demand for labor on such projects as the Chesapeake and Ohio Canal was so great that in 1827 the port of Baltimore appropriated $260,000 to bring Irish laborers to Baltimore, entrusting the choice of the emigrants to the Hibernian Society.

The Carrolls were the most important Irish Catholic family in the American colonies before the Revolution. The first of them had come to the area that is now Maryland in 1688, during the reign of the last Catholic king of England, James II. "We derive our descent from princes," a member of the family wrote later, "and until the Revolution (of 1688), notwithstanding our sufferings under Elizabeth and Cromwell, we were in affluent circumstances and respected."

John Carroll, born in Upper Marlboro, Maryland, in 1735, was a member of this distinguished clan. At age 12, he was enrolled along with his cousin, Charles Carroll of Carrollton, in the Jesuit school (see Maryland). Destined early for the priesthood, he went to France for study and was ordained a Jesuit priest around 1767.

He returned to the United States in 1775, accurately gauging from England that revolution was near. Although an ardent patriot and supporter of his cousin Charles, John remained true to his clerical duties and took little active part in the Revolution.

One exception was the congressional mission to Quebec in 1776. John Carroll accompanied his cousin, as well as Benjamin Franklin, in an effort to convince the Catholic French-Canadians to join the revolution. The British, however, had secured French-Canadian cooperation by assuring them of tolerance for their language and religion. The Quebecois, as a result, felt little sympathy for the mostly Protestant Americans and the mission was a failure.

The Catholic church was not a welcome presence in the American colonies before the outbreak of hostilities. (The British had even forbade the construction of Catholic churches.) The war severed the American Catholic church's links with the vicar-apostolic in London, from which it was governed, and the organization was largely in chaos. There were about 30,000 Catholics total in the 13 colonies at the time.

John Carroll was determined to right this situation once the war ended. He wrote a "Plan of Reorganization" and pushed for its adoption by the fledgling American Catholic church. In 1785, he was named prefect-apostolic by Pope Pius VI, and in order to head off some scheming by French church authorities to take jurisdiction over the American church, he was named the first Roman Catholic bishop of the United States. He was consecrated on August 15, 1790.

The year before, Carroll had founded Georgetown College on the banks of the Potomac so that young American candidates for the priesthood would not have to travel to Europe for their ecclesiastical training, as he had had to do. He also laid the cornerstone of St. Peter's, Barclay Street in New York City and settled simmering resentments between Irish and German Catholics in Philadelphia.

His great project, however, was to erect the first cathedral in the United States. He began raising money in 1795, but not until 1806 was the cornerstone laid, and not until 1821, six years after Bishop Carroll's death, was the edifice finally completed.

Carroll had invited Benjamin Latrobe, the eminent architect, to examine plans for the basilica, which had been drawn up by another architect. Latrobe rejected them and suggested substituting a design of his own. Carroll agreed and Latrobe undertook the work for free, in keeping with his custom of designing churches for free.

The structure has three domes, the largest of which is 72-feet in diameter, and a barrel vault. The domes were built of stone and supported by piers and arches that give a play of shapes to the interior.

Carroll was elevated to archbishop in 1808, and even though he was not in favor of the War of 1812, he loyally supported the country's war policy and ordered a *Te Deum* sung in all churches upon the failure of the British assault on Baltimore.

Baltimore remained an important, though no longer preeminent, Catholic See after the Irish Famine immigration. Although Baltimore was a destination for some Irish immigrants at that time, it was no match for New York, Boston, or, to a lesser extent, Philadelphia. Because Baltimore was caught between North and South, the archbishop there had to deal with a more diverse population.

William V. Shannon, in his book *The American Irish,* speculates that perhaps this is why Baltimore produced the first prelate in the American church who could be called a liberal: James Cardinal Gibbons. Born in Baltimore in 1834, Gibbons was taken to Ireland at age 3 and returned to the United States at age 13. After the Civil War, at the tender age of 34, he was dispatched to North Carolina as "the boy bishop." After four years there and five years in Richmond, Virginia, also a city where Catholics were thin on the ground, he succeeded to the archbishopric in Baltimore.

Gibbons was the second American cardinal, receiving his red hat after that of James Cardinal McCloskey of New York. Gibbons, however, represented a more liberal strain of Catholicism than McCloskey or his predecessor, Archbishop John Hughes (*see* Emmitsburg, Maryland).

Gibbons enjoyed such secular pastimes as cards and horse racing (often placing bets through intermediaries). Unlike Hughes and the conservative prelates, who sought to build a completely separate and parallel Catholic social infrastructure of schools, hospitals, and fraternal organizations, Gibbons did not mind if Catholics mixed with nonbelievers in social settings.

Gibbons's great test was the growing labor union movement, which the church had first condemned as smacking of Freemasonry. He was under strong pressure to condemn the Knights of Labor. He refused and negotiated hard in Rome to avoid any such condemnation. He appealed to the Curia's sense of pragmatism. "To lose the heart of the people would be a misfortune for which the friendship of the few rich and powerful would be no compensation," he said.

Gibbons won his point, and no condemnation came forth from Rome. That the Knights of Labor later declined and disintegrated was of no moment. Gibbons had held the door of the church open to the great mass of working Catholics, unlike the church in France and Italy, where it cut itself off from them.

Gibbons reigned over Baltimore for four decades. He died in 1921.

❧ **EXHIBITS:** The nine stained glass windows are considered among the finest in the United States. Cardinal Gibbons' red hat hangs from the arches to the left of the altar. ❧ **LOCATION:** Cathedral and Mulberry Sts. ❧ **HOURS:** Monday–Friday 7–3:30; Saturday–Sunday 7–6:30; Guided tours are available on the second and fourth Sundays of each month and begin around noon. ❧ **ADMISSION:** Free, but donations appreciated. ❧ **TELEPHONE:** (410) 727-3564.

B & O RAILROAD MUSEUM

The Baltimore and Ohio was not the nation's first railroad, as is frequently stated. The Granite Railway, built in Quincy, Massachusetts, went into operation in 1826, a year before the B & O was chartered.

The B & O, however, was the first railroad to schedule regular steam passenger service. The man behind the B & O was George Brown, a Scotch-Irishman who was born in Ballymena, county Antrim, Ireland, in 1787. Brown's father, Alexander Brown, was one of the first millionaires in the United States.

The elder Brown was one of the pioneers of the linen trade in late 18th-century Belfast and brought his knowledge (along with a stock of Irish linen) with him to the United States in 1800. From this modest beginning, Alexander Brown built his Baltimore-based business into a worldwide import-export, banking, and shipping empire that was one of great business ventures of the 19th century.

George Brown had initially been left behind in Ireland with his brothers John and James when Alexander immigrated to America. They followed in 1802 and eventually joined Alexander Brown and Sons. (John and James eventually founded the Wall Street brokerage firm Brown Brothers & Company, now Brown Brothers Harriman.)

On February 12, 1827, George Brown gathered 25 leading citizens of Baltimore to discuss the best way of reviving Baltimore's port, which was suffering because of the recent completion of the Erie Canal and other water routes west. It was at this meeting that the plan for the Baltimore and Ohio Railroad was conceived, and stock subscriptions were let a little over a month later on March 20. Brown was made treasurer of the new company and, with his father, virtually supervised the construction, which began on July 4, 1828. Passenger service commenced in 1830.

Brown declined to take any compensation until 1834. In that year, his father died and he was forced to take on the responsibility of managing his father's far-flung business empire. As a result, he severed his ties with the B & O, which went on to become one of the most important railroads in American history. Brown remained active in Baltimore's civic affairs and in the local Presbyterian church, however. He was president of the first systematized charitable organization, the House of Refuge. He died in 1859.

❧ EXHIBITS: The largest railroad museum in the country, the 37-acre outdoor/indoor museum has an unparalleled collection of locomotives, train models, and telegraph and telephone apparatus. Included is a replica of the famed 1830 steam engine *Tom Thumb*. Also on display is the silver spade used by 93-year old Charles Carroll of Carrollton to begin construction of the railway in 1830. ❧ LOCATION: Entered through the old Mt. Clare Station off Poppleton St. at 901 W. Pratt St. ❧ HOURS: Daily 10–5. ❧ ADMISSION: $5 adults; seniors $4; children $3. ❧ TELEPHONE: (410) 752-2490.

CARROLL MANSION

Charles Carroll's education was very similar to that of his cousin John. Both men attended the Jesuit school at Bohemian Manor on the Eastern Shore. (*See* Warwick, Maryland.) Both also went to the College de St. Omer in France afterward. But whereas John settled on an ecclesiastical career, Charles opted for the life of a man of property. His father gave title to the family estates in Frederick County known as Carrollton Manor to young Charles when the latter returned from Europe in 1766.

Debarred from participating in Maryland's public life because of his Roman Catholicism (Maryland was more tolerant of Catholics than the other colonies, but not *that* tolerant), Carroll took little part in politics before the revolution. He emerged, however, as the author of a series of newspaper articles in 1773 pseudonymously signed "First Citizen" that addressed the rancorous issue of the tax to support the Established Anglican Church. Carroll thus became something of Maryland's first citizen. He quickly found himself a member of the local Committee of Correspondence and drawn into revolutionary politics.

Although he was not yet a member of the Continental Congress, all eyes fell on Charles Carroll when Congress sought to draw the Canadian colonies, particularly Catholic, French-speaking Quebec, into league with the 13 American colonies. Accompanied by Benjamin Franklin, Samuel Chase, and his cousin John, Carroll set out on the arduous journey to Montreal in February 1776. The mission was foredoomed to failure, however. The Catholic Quebecois were not in a revolutionary mood. And they were not especially eager to join with one dominated by English-speaking Protestants, the French-speaking, Roman Catholic Charles Carroll notwithstanding.

Back in Maryland by spring, Carroll was instrumental in shepherding through the Maryland legislature a resolution calling for separation from England. Elected to the Continental Congress on July 4, 1776, he appended his name to the Declaration of Independence on August 2. He also helped draw up the Maryland state constitution and its bill of rights. Courageously, he opposed the confiscation of British property in the state, saying it was symptomatic of the kind of tyranny the nation was rebelling against.

Elected to the Constitutional Convention in 1787, Carroll declined to serve, although he recommended ratification of the Constitution. He served for three years as one of Maryland's first U.S. senators.

After leaving the state senate in 1800, Carroll retired from public life, concentrating on developing his estates. He turned the first spade of earth for the Baltimore and Ohio Railroad in 1828 and sat on the board of the Chesapeake and Ohio Canal Company Upon his death in 1832, he was probably the wealthiest man in the United States and revered by all as the last surviving link with the nation's founding.

ᐧ EXHIBITS: The first floor displays Carroll's office, complete with a safe and protected by an iron door. A winding staircase leads to the formal rooms on the second floor. ᐧ LOCATION: The Carroll Mansion is part of the Baltimore City Life Museums at 800 East Lombard St., 2 blocks north of the Inner Harbor. ᐧ HOURS: Tuesday–Saturday 10–5, Sunday 12–5 Memorial Day through Labor Day; Tuesday–Saturday 10–4, Sunday 12–4 rest of year. ᐧ ADMISSION: $5 adults; $3.50 for students and military personnel with I.D.; children $2. ᐧ TELEPHONE: (410) 396-3523.

FT. MCHENRY

The fort whose bombardment inspired Francis Scott Key to write "The Star Spangled Banner" was named for James McHenry, secretary of war under Presidents Washington and Adams from 1796 to 1800.

McHenry was Scotch-Irish, born in Ballymena, county Antrim, in 1753. At age 18, he joined the great Scotch-Irish exodus to the American colonies, settling in Philadelphia and studying medicine under the great physician and patriot Benjamin Rush.

Like most of the Scotch-Irish, McHenry was fiercely anti-British. (*See* Kings Mountain, South Carolina, for more on the Scotch-Irish.) He volunteered for military duty in 1775 and was assigned to the medical staff. After a period in captivity, he was exchanged and eventually appointed secretary to George Washington. He ceased practicing medicine and his political career began its rise. He also served with and became great friends with the Marquis de Lafayette.

McHenry would eventually serve in the Continental Congress, the Maryland state legislature, and the constitutional convention that drafted the United States Constitution. In January 1796, he was the fourth choice for the post of secretary of war, retaining the post into the new Adams administration.

His period under President Adams was not happy, however. Adams began suspecting McHenry of secretly supporting Alexander Hamilton against him. In May 1800, Adams forced his resignation from the cabinet, and a congressional investigation of McHenry's tenure ensued. Nothing was found, and McHenry retired to his farm near Baltimore.

Construction began on the fort that bears McHenry's name in 1798 and was completed three years after McHenry left office. Ironically, McHenry opposed the War of 1812, although his son volunteered for the defense of Ft. McHenry.

The British bombardment of the fort on September 13–14, 1814, was preparatory to a planned British landing at Baltimore. The fort was unable to answer the storm of British shells because its guns did not have the range to reach the British ships. Nevertheless, the fort held out and Key, aboard a ship anchored in the harbor negotiating for the release of an American prisoner, was inspired to pen the four verses to what has become America's national anthem. McHenry died in 1816.

&. **EXHIBITS:** There is a 15-minute film on the fort's history and the writing of "The Star Spangled Banner." &. **LOCATION:** From I-95, take exit 55 (Key Highway/Ft. McHenry Monument) and follow the blue and green signs on Key Highway to Lawrence Street. Turn left onto Lawrence Street and then left on East Fort Avenue. &. **HOURS:** Daily 8–8 June through Labor Day; 8–5 daily rest of year. &. **ADMISSION:** $2 adults; over 62 and under 17 free. &. **TELEPHONE:** (410) 962-4299.

HOMEWOOD

Charles Carroll of Carrollton built this splendid mansion for his only son, Charles Jr., upon the latter's wedding in 1801. The house cost $40,000, an enormous sum in those days.

Unfortunately, Homewood turned out to be an unhappy abode. Charles Jr. was an alcoholic and could not control his drinking, to the despair of the rest of his family. His nephew wrote to a relative, "we can't get him to shoot himself, so we must bear with this degradation still longer." His wife, Harriet, and the four children could stand no more and moved out in 1816. Charles Jr. died in 1826, six years before his long-lived father.

❧ **EXHIBITS:** The house has been restored to its early 19th century splendor. It contains much of the original furniture, silver, and porcelain. ❧ **LOCATION:** 3400 N. Charles St., part of the campus of Johns Hopkins University. ❧ **HOURS:** Tuesday–Saturday 11–3; Sunday noon–3. ❧ **ADMISSION:** $5 adults; seniors $4; children $2.50. ❧ **TELEPHONE:** (410) 516-5589.

ELLICOTT CITY

B & O RAILROAD STATION MUSEUM

This was the first terminus of Irish immigrant George Brown's B & O Railroad (*see* Baltimore, Maryland). Ellicott City was the first destination of the fabled locomotive *Tom Thumb*.

❧ **EXHIBITS:** Steam engines and train models are on display, ❧ **LOCATION:** Maryland Avenue and Main Street. ❧ **HOURS:** Wednesday–Monday 11–4 Memorial Day through Labor Day. Friday–Monday 11–4 rest of year. ❧ **ADMISSION:** $3 adults; $2 seniors; $1 children. ❧ **TELEPHONE:** (410) 461-1944.

EMMITSBURG

JOHN HUGHES CABIN AND MT. ST. MARY'S COLLEGE

John Hughes did not appear marked out for greatness when he settled in this area with his Irish immigrant father around 1817. Patrick Hughes had been an impoverished tenant farmer in county Tyrone when John was born in 1797.

Although the family tried hard to keep John, the second of four sons, in school, the harshness of life in Ireland at the end of the Napoleonic Wars forced them to put John in the fields with his brothers and sisters. Patrick Hughes emigrated in 1816 accompanied by his eldest son, also Patrick, and they settled in the area around Chambersburg, Pennsylvania. John followed a year later and the rest of the family soon afterward.

The father and his sons worked in various pursuits: farm labor, road building, quarrying, and gardening. It was while working in the Emmitsburg area that John became firm in his resolve to enter the priesthood. Two priests, Frs. John DuBois and Simon Brute, both refugees from the French Revolution, had established Mount St. Mary's College in Emmitsburg in 1808. Young Hughes asked to be admitted as a seminarian, but the two priests turned him down. This Irish day laborer did not look like promising material.

By legend, Hughes appealed to Mother Elizabeth Seton, later the first canonized American saint, and she interceded with the priests to secure Hughes's admission. There is no documentary evidence of Mother Seton's intervention, however.

Whatever the reason, DuBois and Brute decided to admit Hughes as a kind of probationary student. He was hired as a gardener and groundskeeper, in exchange for which he would receive room, board, and informal instruction.

Hughes went to work, studying theology in every spare moment between his gardening duties. One day, according to Hughes's biographer, Father DuBois came upon Hughes studying while he was supposed to be eating dinner. The priest relented and Hughes was admitted as a regular student in 1820. He was ordained six years later and assigned to St. Augustine's Church in Philadelphia (*see* Philadelphia, Pennsylvania).

Hughes matured quickly into a political as well as ecclesiastical force in Philadelphia. Anti-Irish and anti-Catholic feelings were strong, and Hughes did not hesitate to challenge Protestant clergymen in dueling articles in popular periodicals and even on public platforms. This easily made him the most prominent priest in Philadelphia and a clear candidate for higher church office.

He got his chance in 1838. A priest for only 12 years, he was named coadjutor-bishop of New York under his mentor, Bishop John DuBois. The latter was felled by a stroke only two months after Hughes's arrival, however, and the leadership of the sprawling diocese, which stretched all the way to northern New England at that time, devolved upon the young Hughes. He thus embarked on his controversial 22-year reign in the nation's largest city. (*See* St. Patrick's Cathedral, New York, New York.)

• EXHIBITS: Hughes lived in the cabin while working as a gardener in 1820. The cabin is generally not open to visitors. • LOCATION: 3 miles south of Emmitsburg on U.S. 15. • TELEPHONE: (301) 447-6122.

ROCKVILLE

CEMETERY OF ST. MARY'S CATHOLIC CHURCH

Two decades of hard living lay behind F. Scott Fitzgerald in 1940. His sojourn as a scriptwriter in Hollywood during the 1930s had gone badly. He was drinking heavily and hadn't written a novel in seven years. He was attempting a comeback as a novelist when he suffered a heart attack in November 1940. A month later, on December 21, 1940, he suffered a second heart attack, this one fatal. He was only 44. The novel, *The Last Tycoon*, was eventually finished by Edmund Wilson.

Fitzgerald had expressed the wish to be buried beside his parents in St. Mary's Cemetery in Rockville, Maryland. As Fitzgerald was one of the country's leading apostates from Roman Catholicism, however, the local bishop refused permission and the author was buried instead in Rockville Union Cemetery.

By 1975, however, the theological winds had shifted and the Irish-American author and his insane wife, Zelda, were permitted to rest in the family plot. A reburial service was held on November 7, 1974, attended by the couple's daughter, Scotty Lanahan Smith. (*See* Montgomery, Alabama and St. Paul, Minnesota.)

🍂 EXHIBITS: On Fitzgerald's gravestone is inscribed a quotation from *The Great Gatsby*: "So we beat on boats against the current, borne back ceaselessly into the past." 🍂 LOCATION: 600 Veirs Mill Rd. 🍂 HOURS: Dawn to dusk. 🍂 ADMISSION: Free 🍂 TELEPHONE: (301) 424-5550.

SILVER SPRING

GEORGE MEANY LABOR ARCHIVES

The architect of the great labor confederation known as the AFL-CIO and the leading spokesman for American organized labor for 24 years, George Meany was born in the Bronx, a grandson of Irish immigrants. This excerpt from his 1976 address to the American-Irish Historical Society is probably the best summary of his background, motivations, and philosophy:

> Tonight, you honor a grandson of the Meanys of (county) West Meath. They came to these shores in the 1850s and had established a line of reasonably competent and successful plumbers—until I was drawn off into other pursuits. . . .
> I grew up among the Irish of St. Luke's parish in a household where Ireland and its troubles and history were subjects of daily discussion. I found

out, for instance, that my grandfather (my mother's father) was the champion cross-country runner in his native county, Longford. There can be no doubt on this, he told me so himself. I recall also his fruitless efforts to teach the children of the family to speak Gaelic. . . .

And while the early development of the American trade union movement was brought about by people of varied ethnic backgrounds, it cannot be denied that there again the American Irish made a significant contribution. . . .

Now it may be true that the Irish rose to leadership in American labor because of their inherited flair for language and love of the spoken word—but I like to think they were equally spurred by the deep, centuries old indignation which injustice stirred in them. They had been schooled in justice, freedom, equality and human dignity—and where they found those things absent, they rose to do battle. . . .

The yearning for freedom—the insistence on human dignity—are forever enshrined as part of the Irish character. Similarly, they are the wellspring of the American trade union movement. Oh yes, we spend lots of time negotiating for wages and hours and working conditions but these are simply the material manifestations of the achievement of worker dignity. The basis of our trade union movement, and the reason it continues strong, is that men and women see in it the vehicle for enduring recognition of their human dignity. They see it—correctly—as the device through which they can band together to help themselves and help one another assert their dignity and improve their lot and that of their children. . . .

The lessons I learned in the Bronx and the lessons I learned as the son of Irish forebears have stayed with me through the years. The love of God, family and country and the dedication to a freedom based upon the dignity of the individual has been a valid guidepost all my life."

Few who knew him would dispute any of this self-description. A high school dropout, Meany entered the union movement—he remembered it exactly—on January 10, 1917. He was inducted into Plumbers Union Local 463 in the Bronx at age 22.

Although Meany's plumber father was relatively comfortable as a skilled craftsman (though by no means well-off), he opposed his son's desire to follow in his footsteps. The elder Meany never made clear the reasons for his opposition, other than telling his son that plumbing was "awfully hard work." But Mike Meany was a union plumber, of course, and George later said that it was probably the atmosphere of union camaraderie as much as anything that inspired him to get into work that would get him into the trade union movement.

Meany wasn't exaggerating when he spoke of the Irish as founders of the labor movement, for the American Federation of Labor (AFL) was largely an Irish creation. Samuel Gompers, its famed president, was of Dutch-Jewish extraction. But below Gompers, the ranks were heavily Irish.

The largest AFL-affiliated union in the early part of the century, for instance, was the Brotherhood of Carpenters, whose longtime secretary-treasurer was Peter J. Maguire. "PJ," a son of Irish immigrants, is widely

AFL-CIO
president
(1955–79)
George Meany.
(AFL-CIO)

credited as the "father of Labor Day," first proposing the idea in 1882. Unlike Jewish trade unionists, many of whom were socialists or communists, the Irish tended away from socialism, at least partly because the Catholic church strongly condemned it. The Irish-dominated AFL tended to press for better pay and working conditions, unlike the more radical Congress of Industrial Organizations (CIO), many of whose members wanted wholesale changes in society.

Meany fit the AFL's bread-and-butter trade unionism like a glove. The movement, not plumbing or fixtures, would become his life's work. By the early 1920s, he was the union local's business agent and organizer. He steadily worked his way up the union ladder, to the presidency of the New York State Federation of Labor, to secretary-treasurer of the national AFL in 1940, to the presidency of the latter organization in 1952. Meany was the motivating force behind the momentous merger, three years later, with the industrial workers of the CIO.

Although not as radical as Walter and Victor Reuther of the United Auto Workers, for instance, Meany nevertheless was a man ahead of his time in many respects. He could not abide racism and insisted that the separate black and white locals around the country merge into single units. He also refused to tolerate crooks, expelling the mob-tainted Teamsters from the AFL-CIO, despite their huge contribution in dues and manpower.

Meany had two lodestars in his public career: first was pushing for the passage of progressive social legislation for all citizens, not just union members. He helped enact Social Security, Medicare and Medicaid, fair labor standards laws, and many, many others.

The other aspect of his life's work was a fierce anti-Communism, which he believed was the greatest foe of the working man. Sometimes, this passion led him into mistakes—he supported the Vietnam War without reservation until the bitter end—but he devoted a great deal of time, money, and effort toward supporting free trade unionists behind the Iron Curtain and elsewhere. This began bearing fruit just eight months after his death in January 1980, with the birth of the Solidarity trade union movement in Poland. Meany would no doubt have been pleased at the ultimate collapse of the Soviet Union.

&. **EXHIBITS:** The archives house many letters, documents, photographs, and memorabilia of George Meany as well as the labor movement in general. &. **LOCATION:** 10000 New Hampshire Ave. &. **HOURS:** Daily 9–5. &. **ADMISSION:** None. &. **TELEPHONE:** (301) 431-6400.

TANEYTOWN

ANTRIM

This beautiful antebellum mansion was built by Andrew Ege in 1844 as a wedding gift for his daughter and named for Ege's native county in Ireland. Perched among the rolling hills near Taneytown, Antrim was originally the center for a 450-acre plantation that became so noted for its self-sufficiency that it was said the residents never had to leave the grounds.

Antrim has recently been reborn as a bed and breakfast, with the house and outbuildings beautifully restored.

&. **LOCATION:** 30 Trevanion Rd. &. **ADMISSION:** None. &. **TELEPHONE:** (800) 858-1844.

WARWICK

ST. FRANCIS XAVIER AND OLD BOHEMIA MISSION

Constructed in 1704, this church is one of the oldest Catholic buildings in the country. The Jesuit order founded an academy here, probably the first Roman Catholic boys' school in the present-day United States, and among its distinguished pupils were the cousins Charles Carroll of Carrollton the only Catholic to sign the Declaration of Independence, and John Carroll, the First American Catholic bishop. (*See* Annapolis, Maryland; Baltimore, Maryland.)

🍋 EXHIBITS: Mass is said here only four times a year, on the third Sundays in April, May, September and October. There is a small museum and bookshop that is open 12–3 on Sundays in the summer. 🍋 LOCATION: On S.R. 282, west of Warwick.

MASSACHUSETTS

BELLEVUE APARTMENTS

 This unprepossessing apartment house was John F. Kennedy's home as a Massachusetts politician. The Bellevue Apartments was the sight of many a late-night strategy session in early Kennedy campaigns. Here, the candidate would confer with such trusted members of the "Irish Mafia" as Kenneth O'Donnell and David Powers.

In his memoir, *Johnny, We Hardly Knew Ye,* the late Kenneth O'Donnell recalled that when he retrieved the late president's wallet on the night of the assassination, he found in it the president's driver's license, bearing the address 130 Bowdoin St.

❧ EXHIBITS: The building is privately owned and not open to the public. ❧ LOCATION: 130 Bowdoin St., on Beacon Hill in central Boston. The street runs parallel to the Massachusetts State House on its east side. The building is on the eastern side of the street, just a few steps north of Beacon Street.

BOSTON COMMON

There are several sites relating to the Irish and Irish-Americans in and around Boston Common, the nation's oldest public park.

Behind the visitor information kiosk on Tremont Street is a granite memorial by John Paramino to Wexford-born Commodore John Barry, the first American to achieve the rank of commodore and the man widely credited as "The father of the American Navy." (*See* Philadelphia, Pennsylvania.)

A little farther along, just behind the Boston Massacre Memorial (*see* next entry), is the Parkman bandstand. On April 30, 1927, Eamon De Valera addressed a large crowd here on the last stop of a cross-country

Parkman bandstand in Boston Common.

fund-raising tour, one of many he made before finally becoming prime minister of the Irish Free State in 1932. After he finished speaking, the enthusiastic crowd accompanied him to Commonwealth pier, where he boarded a ship for his return to Ireland.

At the corner of Park and Beacon streets, just across the street from the front steps of the Massachusetts State House, is the bas-relief memorial to Col. Robert Gould Shaw and his all-black 54th Massachusetts Volunteers, the troops immortalized in the film *Glory*. The moving monument is the work of Augustus Saint Gaudens, the Franco-Irish-American sculptor born in Dublin in 1848. (*See* Plainfield, New Hampshire.)

Almost directly across the street from the Shaw memorial, on the grounds of the state house, is the new statue of Pres. John Fitzgerald Kennedy, the work of Isabel Mellvain. It shows him in a classic Kennedy pose, right hand in jacket pocket, striding forward.

Another sculptor with Irish roots whose work graces the Common is Martin Milmore, who was born in Sligo in 1844 and died only 39 years later. He did, however, manage to complete the Soldiers and Sailors Memorial, which stands on the Common and honors all Americans who fought in the Civil War.

Not technically a part of Boston Common, but very close to it, is the Public Garden, just across Charles Street. "The Public Garden is a monument to the master landscape architect William Dooge, a native of County Laois, who was Superintendent of Common and Public Grounds from 1878 until his death in 1906," writes James Ford in his "Irish Walking Tour of Boston." "He was the one who introduced the flower beds in the Public Garden. Here it is surely apt to borrow the classic quote: 'If you seek a monument, look about you.'"

Another Civil War memorial is the statue of Irish-born Col. Thomas Cass, located along the Boylston Street side of the Public Garden. Cass raised and led the largely Irish 9th Massachusetts Volunteers. He died leading his regiment at the Battle of Malvern Hill in 1862.

A footnote: Check out the Founder's Memorial on the Beacon Street side of Boston Common. The sculpture depicts William Blaxton, widely credited as the first white settler of what was then known as Shawmut, greeting John Winthrop and other early settlers of Boston, to their new home. Erected by Boston Brahmins on the city's tricentenary in 1930, Mayor James Michael Curley couldn't resist the temptation to play a big joke on his Brahmin tormentors. The very English Blaxton's face is said to bear a uncanny resemblance to the Celtic features of you-know-who. The squinting visitor will have to decide for him or herself.

ｉｌ **LOCATION:** Boston Common and the Public Garden are in the middle of downtown Boston, bounded by Park, Tremont, Boylston, Arlington, and Beacon Streets. ｉｌ **HOURS:** Dawn to dusk. ｉｌ **ADMISSION:** Free

BOSTON MASSACRE MEMORIAL

Living as we do in a century in which hundreds and even thousands of people are routinely massacred with scarcely anyone giving it a second thought, the Boston Massacre was pretty weak beer by comparison. All told, five were killed by British troops in front of the Old State House (then the Town House) on that wintry night in 1770. But for patriot agitator Samuel Adams, it was all he needed to get the colonists whipped up for the eventual showdown with the British that came five years later.

The precise circumstances surrounding what took place on the night of March 5, 1770, are still in dispute, but one of the men killed was Patrick Carr, an Irish immigrant.

The troops had been sent to Boston to suppress rioting caused by the passage in 1768 of the Townsend Acts, a series of revenue-raising measures imposed three years earlier on the unwilling colonists. Unrepresented in the British Parliament at Westminster, the colonists cared little that the money was supposed to pay for troops to protect them from raids by the French and the Indians. They saw the taxes simply as a burden imposed by a distant tyranny, of which the soldiers were the most visible symbol.

Contemporary accounts say that a series of fire alarm bells is what brought groups of men out of the taverns and into the streets that night. A mob soon surrounded a single soldier, who was standing with his back to the town house building. The British commander, Capt. Thomas Preston (an Anglo-Irishman), marched down with a group of reinforcements to where the lone soldier was standing.

The Boston Massacre Memorial stands just blocks from where the actual event took place on March 5, 1770.

The sight of more troops only enraged the mob further. A chunk of ice was thrown and a soldier lost his footing. Whether he deliberately fired his musket or it went off accidentally is unknown. Either way, his comrades immediately began firing pointblank into the crowd, leaving Carr and four others dead or dying on the pavement. Six were wounded.

Carr was to play one last role in the drama, one from beyond the grave. At the soldiers' trial, a doctor who treated Carr during the four days he lingered between life and death claimed on the witness stand that Carr believed the soldiers had fired in self-defense. The testimony was critical in helping win acquittals for Capt. Preston and six of his men. Two were convicted of the lesser charge of manslaughter, branded, and released.

Samuel Adams quickly made it known that Carr was a Roman Catholic, hoping this fact would lead mostly Protestant Boston to question the value of his last words. The soldiers' defense, however, was led by Samuel Adams's cousin, John, and Josiah Quincy, Jr., both lawyers with impeccable patriot credentials.

Nevertheless, Samuel Adams had no trouble exploiting the massacre politically. (Paul Revere had an idealized engraving of the event on sale in only three weeks.) With the taxes widely defied and the presence of the troops provoking so much opposition, the Townsend Acts were swiftly repealed—except for the levy on tea. In time, that would become another bone of contention.

Carr, along with the other victims of the massacre, was buried in the Old Granary Burial Ground on Tremont Street. The bronze and granite monument was erected on Boston Common in 1888, over considerable opposition from some elements of Brahmin opinion, who were reluctant to honor these ruffians. John Boyle O'Reilly, however, lobbied hard for the monument in the pages of the *Boston Pilot* and was a featured speaker at the dedication.

❧ EXHIBITS: The sites are part of the Freedom Trail, a walking tour of major historical places in downtown Boston. Information and maps can be obtained at the information kiosk on the Tremont Street side of the Common, or at the National Park Service office at 15 State St. ❧ LOCATION: All three sites are very close to one another in downtown Boston. A cobblestone circle in the middle of State Street in front of the Old State House marks the massacre site. The Old Granary Burial Ground is on Tremont Street 2 blocks west. The memorial is on Tremont Street 2 blocks south. ❧ HOURS: Dawn to dusk. ❧ ADMISSION: None.

CARDINAL CUSHING MEMORIAL PARK

 The turning point in young Dick Cushing's life came as he was exhorting a crowd from the tailgate of a wagon to vote for a friend who was running for the state legislature. Just as Cushing was reaching the climax of his address, Father Mortimer F. Twomey, the parish priest, appeared on the scene. Flushed with anger, the priest muscled his way through the crowd and pulled the young college student down from the wagon. Twomey kicked Cushing hard in the seat of his pants and exclaimed, "Make up your mind; either you're going to be a priest or a politician!" Recounting this anecdote later in life from his vantage point as a famous and powerful prince of the Church, Cardinal Cushing said he decided to become a priest "so I could be both."

Indeed, Cardinal Cushing became as famous for his political machinations (both within the church and without) and his longtime association with the Kennedy clan as for his ecclesiastical pronouncements. It was Cushing's predecessor as archbishop of Boston, William Cardinal O'Connell, who set the standard for politically active American prelates. "When I ask you to do anything, trust me and do it," O'Connell said on one occasion.

The Irish of Boston, for the most part, obeyed. They looked to their priests and the church as a bulwark against the hostility they encountered in their new country and against the harshness of urban life. A priest was something like an absolute monarch who was pretty much free to run his parish as he saw fit, provided his books balanced. As for an archbishop, well, in the absence of the pope in far-off Rome, he was as close to being God's representative on earth as it was possible to be.

Overt involvement in politics was usually confined to issues of family, sex, or morality, but occasional forays into other issues also took place. In 1924, for instance, Cardinal O'Connell campaigned against a proposed amendment to the U.S. Constitution banning child labor. "It is Socialistic, as it puts the State above the Parents," O'Connell thundered. The amendment was defeated.

Cushing succeeded O'Connell in 1944, and very much carried on this politically active tradition. Cushing's vigorous campaign against a proposal by the Yankee Republican legislature to legalize the sale of contraceptives helped elect a Democratic state house of representatives for the first time in the history of the commonwealth.

In 1966, Cushing told a stunned Hubert H. Humphrey that he, Cushing, was responsible for helping John F. Kennedy defeat Humphrey in the critical 1960 West Virginia primary, a defeat that knocked the Minnesotan out of the presidential race. "I'll tell you who elected Jack Kennedy," Cushing said. "It was his father, Joe, and me, right here in this room." He had helped to pick which Protestant ministers in the overwhelmingly Protestant state would receive $100 to $500 "contributions." "It's good for the Lord. It's good for the church. It's good for preacher, and it's good for the candidate," the cardinal chuckled.

Richard Cushing was the third native-born son of Irish immigrants to hold the office of archbishop of Boston. He was born in South Boston on August 24, 1895. He was the third of five children (two sons, three daughters) born to Patrick and Mary (Dahill) Cushing. Patrick Cushing, a native of county Cork, was a blacksmith who repaired wheels for the Boston Elevated Street Railway system, being paid $18 a day and not infrequently working seven-day weeks. Mary Dahill was a native of county Waterford. At Boston College High School, a Catholic institution, Richard Cushing excelled at baseball. Many said he might have turned pro had not debate and public speaking interested him more.

After about two years at Boston College itself, Cushing made the decision to enter the priesthood, and he was ordained in 1921. He spent almost all of his career in and around the Boston archdiocese. In 1922, he began his long association with the Society for the Propagation of the Faith, the purpose of which is to raise funds to support overseas missions. He worked full-time for the society (and honed his already considerable skills as a fund-raiser) until his elevation to the position of auxiliary bishop of Boston in 1939. It was said that American soldiers in the South Pacific sometimes found the natives unusually helpful, "because you come from the place of Father Cushing."

Universal brotherhood was a major theme of Cushing's prelacy. He never ceased speaking against racial or ethnic prejudice, long before it was popular to do so. "When a Catholic fails to take a stand against racial prejudice or intolerance," he said in a famous statement on the matter, "he is a slacker in the army of the church militant." He also was a strong advocate of ecumenism, preaching in such previously unheard of places (for a Catholic leader) as Jewish synagogues and Masonic temples.

It was probably his relationship with the Kennedy family, however, that brought Cushing the most fame. He had first come to know Joseph P. Kennedy, Sr., during his fund-raising days for the Society for the Propagation of the Faith. He delivered what seemed to many an interminable invocation at John F. Kennedy's inauguration. But the nation was touched 35 months later, when the old man's voice broke during the president's funeral mass as he beseeched the angels to carry his beloved Jack to heaven.

Cardinal Cushing died November 2, 1970, just a few months after retiring as archbishop.

❧ **EXHIBITS:** The park features a bust of Cardinal Cushing by James Rosati. ❧ **LOCATION:** A small park was dedicated to the cardinal's memory in 1981 at the corner of Congress and New Chardon Sts., just west of Boston City Hall. The cardinal's birthplace, at 808 E. Third St. in South Boston, is marked by a plaque. (Not open to the public.) ❧ **HOURS:** Dawn to dusk. ❧ **ADMISSION:** None.

COPLEY SQUARE, TRINITY CHURCH

This excellent open space in the center of Boston was named for John Singleton Copley (*see* Copley Studio, elsewhere in this chapter). The south side of the square is dominated by the massive glass sheath of the John Hancock Tower, the tallest building in New England. Directly in front of the tower is Trinity Church. Here, on January 5, 1904, a Boston girl named Mary Osgood married a young Englishman named Erskine Childers. As a wedding present, Mr. Osgood bought the couple a yacht, the *Asgard*. A decade later, the little boat would sail into the pages of Irish history.

Childers was one of those odd characters so beloved by the Irish: a man who, for few apparent reasons, attached himself passionately to the cause of Irish independence. The son of a British civil servant, Childers worked for a time as a House of Commons clerk. He also dabbled in creative writing. His spy thriller, *The Riddle of the Sands*, caused an international sensation when it was published in 1903, postulating as it did a German naval invasion of Britain.

But it was to Germany that Childers and other Irish patriots turned for weapons in 1914. Protestant Ulstermen had begun arming themselves that year as an Irish home rule bill finally wound its way toward passage at Westminster. "Home rule means Rome rule!" was their slogan, and they were determined to resist, by force of arms if necessary, incorporation into any Catholic-dominated united Ireland.

Not wanting to be caught unprepared in the event of a clash, Childers procured 1,500 rifles in Germany for the Irish Volunteers and the Irish Citizen Army, the two main pro-independence groups. He loaded them aboard the *Asgard* and skillfully ferried the precious cargo undetected across the North and Irish seas. The arms were landed at Howth, near Dublin, on July 26, 1914. Many of these weapons were eventually used in the 1916 Easter Rising.

Childers put his literary skills to good use, becoming one of the most effective propagandists for the Republican cause. When the British government finally opened independence negotiations in 1921, Childers served as secretary to the Irish delegation. He repudiated the treaty that was eventually signed, however, and in the Civil War that followed Childers sided with the Republicans against the pro-treaty Free State government.

Captured in possession of a small revolver Michael Collins had once given him, Childers was charged with taking up arms against the government and sentenced to death. His was the first of 77 such fratricidal executions that revulsed the nation in 1922–23.

His disgrace did not last, however. The son born of the marriage that began at Trinity Church, also Erskine Childers, was elected president of the Republic of Ireland in 1978.

❧ **EXHIBITS:** Trinity Church is one of the most architecturally distinguished churches in a city filled with architecturally distinguished churches. Free tours can be arranged by appointment. ❧ **LOCATION:** 206 Clarendon St., Copley Square. ❧ **HOURS:** Monday–Saturday, 8–6, Sunday 8–7:30. ❧ **ADMISSION:** Donations welcome. ❧ **TELEPHONE:** (617) 536-0944.

DEER ISLAND

Ask a modern-day resident of Boston about Deer Island and he or she will instantly think "sewage," because that is the location for the Boston municipal water treatment plant. That is a shame, because beginning in 1847—as the trickle of Irish immigrants became a flood tide with the beginning of the Great Hunger (*see* Great Hunger Memorial, elsewhere in this chapter), Deer Island served as a detention center for sickly immigrants, almost all of them Irish. No one knows just how many immigrants died and were buried here in unmarked graves, but estimates range up to 3,000.

Local Irish-American groups have recently begun raising funds to establish a visitor center on the island to recall its tragic past.

❧ **LOCATION:** Deer Island is separated from the rest of Boston by Boston Harbor. It can be reached from the northern suburb of Winthrop. Drive south along Shirley Street in Winthrop until the road crosses over onto Deer Island. ❧ **HOURS:** Dawn to dusk. ❧ **TELEPHONE:** The island is maintained by the Massachusetts Waste Recovery Authority. A tour of the water treatment facilities is available by calling (617) 241-6057.

DOYLE'S CAFE

Doyle's is a century-old monument to those two great Irish American passions: hospitality and politics. Television is a rarity at Doyle's, turned on only at presidential inaugurals, Boston mayoral election nights, and (maybe) the World Series. If you want to watch television, you can stay home or go someplace else. Doyle's is a place for serious conversation, preferably about politics.

The cafe is a monument to the Irish politicians who have dominated this city for decades. Each Boston mayor (all Irish) since 1930—James Michael Curley, Maurice Tobin, John B. Hynes, John Collins, Kevin White and Raymond Flynn—has a booth dedicated to him. And though the current mayor, Frank Mennino, is of Italian descent, he is definitely a favorite at Doyle's. He once represented the neighborhood in the city council and is still a regular. Before Pres. Clinton appointed him U.S. ambassador to the Vatican in 1993, Mayor Flynn used Doyle's virtually as a City Hall annex, regularly stopping by to hoist a few and join in the raucous choruses of Irish rebel songs with the crowd at the bar.

Boston is a much more multiethnic city than it was in years past, but the Irish vote can still be crucial. One of the stories you're likely to hear at Doyle's is that of John D. O'Bryant, who ran for school board in the mid-1970s. He plastered Irish neighborhoods with green signs that urged people to "Vote for O'Bryant." The signs carried no pictures of the candidate, however, since he was black. He won.

⊱ **EXHIBITS:** The walls are a parade of framed newspaper headlines, old campaign posters, and photographs of generations of Boston Irish politicians, some famous, some infamous, some forgotten. ⊱ **LOCATION:** 3484 Washington St., in the Jamaica Plain section of Boston. ⊱ **HOURS:** Daily. ⊱ **TELEPHONE:** (617) 524-2345.

EDWIN O'CONNOR APARTMENT HOUSE

Edwin O'Connor thought that calling it a "political novel" would damage his book's chances. He couldn't have been more wrong. Although hardly a great work of literature, *The Last Hurrah* unquestionably stands as a superior example of 20th-century American fiction and made O'Connor's reputation. A *roman à clef,* the book chronicles the last campaign of Frank Skeffington, an aging political boss whose resemblance to James Michael Curley was purely intentional.

O'Connor was third-generation Irish, born in the declining industrial city of Woonsocket, Rhode Island, in 1919. His father was a well-established doctor who had trained at both Harvard and Johns Hopkins. His mother was a public school teacher. After wartime service in the Coast Guard, young Edwin took a job as an announcer at a Boston radio station, while working fitfully on a novel about a famous radio announcer. *The Oracle* was published in 1951 to poor reviews and little commercial success.

O'Connor wasn't discouraged, however, and he looked about for a large canvas on which to paint. His eye fell upon Curley, whom he had interviewed on the radio several times. "I would like to do for the Irish in America what Faulkner did for the South," he told a friend. "He later said, I wanted to do a novel on the whole Irish-American business. What the Irish got in America, they got through politics; so, of course, I had to use a political framework."

Critics differ as to how well he succeeded. Published in 1956, *The Last Hurrah* comes across today as something of a period piece, loaded down with many long, talky passages punctuated by flashes of wit and insight. The narrator, Skeffington's midwestern-bred nephew Adam, is too naive to be credible. Yet, this is made up for by the fully drawn portrait of

Home of Irish-American novelist Edwin O'Connor.

Skeffington himself, who functions not merely as a political leader but also as a tribal chieftain. Warm, garrulous, generous, and with just a touch of badness in him, Skeffington is an unforgettable character.

The novel was a great critical and commercial success and was made into a movie starring Spencer Tracy and directed by John Ford. Curley's immediate reaction was to sue O'Connor, but friends prevailed upon him not to do so, for the novel was doing more to rehabilitate Curley's tattered reputation than any lawsuit could. Indeed, Curley "dined out on" *The Last Hurrah* for the remaining two years of his life, embracing Frank Skeffington's story wholly as his own.

O'Connor went on to other successes, winning the Pulitzer Prize in 1961 for *The Edge of Sadness,* a novel tackling the then-taboo subject of an alcoholic priest. He also wrote a play, *I Was Dancing,* which was produced in 1964.

Unlike other Irish-American writers such as F. Scott Fitzgerald and John O'Hara, who became full-blown rebels against their background, O'Connor celebrated his Irish-American roots and mined them for material. Indeed, he attended mass and took Holy Communion seven days a week until his untimely death in 1968, at only 49 years of age.

❧ EXHIBITS: The house is privately owned and not open to the public. ❧ LOCATION: O'Connor's small apartment where he worked on *The Last Hurrah* was at No. 10 Marlborough St., in Boston's Back Bay neighborhood. After its success, he moved into plusher digs at 46 Beacon St.

GREAT HUNGER MEMORIAL

No event has had so great an impact on the Irish people and on Irish America as the Great Hunger (or Potato Famine) of 1845–49. In its emotional scarring, it has been compared with the experience the Jews endured in the "final solution." Indeed, not a few Irish and Irish-American historians have made that comparison explicitly, saying the famine was a deliberately engineered plot by the English ruling class to wipe out the Irish.

What happened in Ireland in those days is indeed a dark story, and while the British government was certainly guilty of criminal negligence, its inactivity is probably explicable more as a result of ideological narrowness and indifference rather than murderous intent.

This subtle distinction, of course, scarcely mattered to the suffering Irish, only a few thousand of whom actually died of starvation, with tens of thousands dying of diseases to which they became vulnerable through malnutrition. For those who didn't die, the emigration ship was the only alternative. By the hundreds of thousands, the Irish emigrated, carrying away with them a bitter hatred for Great Britain. That hatred, nursed along by their children and grandchildren in the New World, complicates Anglo-American relations to this very day.

The potato is probably not native to Ireland. Legend has it that Sir Walter Raleigh planted the first potatoes soon after he returned from Virginia in the 16th century. By the 1840s, however, the potato had become the staple food of the Irish diet, grown on a small plot of land for the farmer and his family. The rest of the fields were taken up with cereal crops, almost all of which usually had to be sold to pay the landlord's rent.

The population of Ireland in 1840, the year of the first reliable census, was an incredible eight million, nearly double that of today, and almost all were engaged in agriculture. With so many people dependent on a single crop, disaster was inevitable if anything were to disrupt it. In 1845, something did: the potato blight.

At first, no one knew what was the cause of the diseased plants. Everything was blamed: the rain, the sleet, the moon, cow dung, even lightning. In fact, the cause was a killer fungus, then still unknown: *Phytophthora infestans.* The disease struck not only every county in Ireland, but England as well. There was no famine in England, however, since the population there was sufficiently well-off to be able to switch to other foods.

Not so in Ireland. In county Mayo in the far west, 90 percent of the population was wholly dependent on the potato for survival. It was much the same elsewhere. The government in London was not totally indifferent to the situation, appointing as it did a commission of relief and arranging for corn to be imported from the United States. But the government, blinded by its fixation on the free market and free trade, refused to give the food to the people and insisted they had to buy it. Although the price was cheap, few in Ireland could afford to buy food at *any* price. That was why they grew their own.

And while many landlords were sympathetic and did not insist on the payment of rent during the calamity, many others were pitiless and took back land for nonpayment. The sight of poor, starving people being evicted from their homes was burned deeply into many Irish hearts.

During the four years of the famine, hundreds of thousands left while hundreds of thousands of others died. Census figures give some indication of the scale of the disaster: the natural rate of increase would have raised Ireland's 1840 population to a little over 9 million by 1850. The actual count found only 6.5 million.

Three quarters of the emigrants went to the United States, making it the ultimate repository of hope for Irish nationalists. Some settled in England, others in Canada and as far as Australia.

Important as it was, there are few memorials to the victims of the Great Hunger, almost as if the Irish would prefer to forget it. The only one in the United States was dedicated in 1993 by Boston Mayor Raymond Flynn, who was soon named by President Clinton U.S. ambassador to the Holy See.

   EXHIBITS: The stone now in place is temporary, to be replaced by a permanent marker sometime in 1995.   **LOCATION:** The memorial stone is located at the Atlantic Avenue end of the Faneuil Hall Marketplace, near the entrance arch.   **HOURS:** Dawn to Dusk.

JAMES MICHAEL CURLEY HOUSE

On November 7, 1949, James Michael Curley received 126,000 votes for reelection as mayor of Boston, 10,000 votes more than he had ever received before. The only problem was, his opponent, John

Hynes, got 12,000 more. Curley would make two more runs for mayor of Boston, but 1949 would prove his "last hurrah." After 50 years in politics, including four terms as mayor (and a couple of terms inside a jailhouse), he had held his last elective office.

Controversy still swirls over whether Curley was a crook or a saint. Certainly he was a man of contradictions. He had little formal education, but enjoyed reading Shakespeare and other classics. Politically, he lionized the rough-hewn Irish working man, yet campaigned wearing sharply tailored suits and a plush raccoon coat. Of his tenement youth he spoke often, yet he lived in the baronial style of an English lord. He unquestionably had considerable administrative talent, yet presided over some of the most corrupt and slipshod municipal and state governance America has ever seen.

"The Purple Shamrock"—so called for his combination of regal bearing and powerful ethnic identification—was born in Boston of Irish immigrant parents on November 20, 1874. Fatherless at age 10, he and his brothers foraged for coal at the local dump while their mother scrubbed floors downtown. Walking down an alley with an uncle one day, Curley spied some coins in the dust. As he bent to pick them up, his uncle kneed him in the groin and took the coins for himself. "Life was grim on this corned beef and cabbage Riviera," he noted soberly in his memoirs.

Dropping out of school in the eighth grade, Curley pondered a career as a fire fighter or some other civil service occupation, but soon settled on politics as the best way to advance himself. Running his first race for Boston Common Council at 24, Curley didn't think he could lose. He did, however, and was determined not to let it happen again. The next year, he won, but not after considerable fisticuffs with his opponents.

He went on to hold a succession of offices: common councilman, alderman, state representative. But it was the mayoralty, with its vast potential for patronage, that he coveted. When John F. Fitzgerald (see Rose Fitzgerald Kennedy Birthplace, Boston, Massachusetts) reneged on what Curley thought was a promise not to seek reelection in 1914, Curley threatened to expose Fitzgerald's rumored affair with "Toodles" Ryan. Fitzgerald changed his mind again and did not seek reelection after all. Curley won city hall for the first time.

Curley was a builder. In his four unsuccessive terms in city hall (the Yankee-dominated state legislature, in a specific effort to short-circuit Curley's career, forbade Boston mayors to succeed themselves), he poured millions into swimming pools, parks, and, especially, Boston City Hospital. His favorite sobriquet was "the Mayor of the Poor."

Because he could not serve successive terms in office, Curley became the forerunner of a modern-day phenomenon: the political entrepreneur. He simply ran for whatever office was available, living off accumul campaign contributions in periods of enforced idleness. Altogether, he lost five races for mayor of Boston, two for governor, and one for U.S. senator.

Win or lose, however, the legend of James Michael grew inexorably. In 1932, he was barred from the Massachusetts delegation to the Democratic National Convention for the crime of backing the patrician and very Protestant Franklin D. Roosevelt over humbly born and Irish Catholic Al Smith. Curley, however, magically materialized on the floor as "Jaime Miguel Curleo," leader of the Puerto Rican delegation!

For all the sentimentality that surrounds Curley today, there was a dark side to the legend. Curley had an interest in keeping his flock boiling with resentment and dependent on his patronage. His stock-in-trade was fomenting hostility between the Boston Irish and the Yankee descendants of the original settlers from England with whom they shared the city and the state. "Waving the shamrock" incessantly, he deliberately magnified, distorted, and often simply invented supposed slights and in the process elevated what had been simmering hostility to the level of a blood feud.

The cost of Curleyism for Boston's growth and development was high. By taxing the (mostly Yankee) property owners heavily and selling tax abatements in exchange for campaign contributions, he discouraged growth and investment and encouraged flight to the suburbs. While Curley was by no means solely responsible, there can be no question that Boston at the end of the Curley era was a city with a much bleaker future than it had been at the beginning.

Curley's first jail term was in 1904, when he served 60 days for taking a postal examination for a needy but dull-witted constituent. Few of his supporters held this against him; indeed, he bragged about it in all his subsequent "waving the shamrock" campaigns.

His second jail term, however, was a more serious matter. During World War II, and while serving what would be his last term as mayor, Curley lent his name to a company that fraudulently claimed it could help land war contracts. The evidence was so damning that not even Roosevelt dared quash the prosecution. Curley served five miserable months in jail before Pres. Truman freed him just before Thanksgiving 1947.

Those five months were enough to finish Curley politically, for he lost his reelection bid in 1949 and two more efforts to regain the office he enjoyed above all others. "If they love me so much," he muttered to an aide ~~owd cheered him during one of his last campaigns, "why won't the ˡ~es vote for me?" Late in life, however, Curley's reputation when he found himself re-created as the thinly disguised ık Skeffington, the aging political boss in Edwin ɔ6 novel *The Last Hurrah* (*see* Edwin O'Connor Apart- ɔoston, Massachusetts).

Proud of his Irish heritage, James Curley emblazoned the shutters of his home with green shamrocks.

Curley didn't have long to enjoy his new found fame, however. Almost penniless because of several bad business ventures, he died November 12, 1958, eight days short of his 84th birthday.

For a man who made his career bashing "rich Yankees," Curley certainly had a taste for living like one. On March 17, 1915, the first St. Patrick's Day of his first mayoralty, construction began on the house that would symbolize "Curleyism" for generations of Bostonians. The mayor was always cagey about just where he got the money to build the 21-room mansion overlooking the Fenway in Boston's exclusive "Green Necklace," but build it he did.

By modern standards, the interior is opulent, with its chandeliers and Italian marble fireplaces. Curley called it his "place of repose." It was a long way from the corned beef and cabbage Riviera.

❧ EXHIBITS: The house has been owned by the city of Boston since 1988 (which is appropriate, since the city probably paid for it 10 times over). It is maintained for special events and not normally open to the public. The interior, however, can be viewed by appointment. Call the city Real Property Division at (617) 635-4105.

Also, there are two statues of Curley in a small park behind the new Boston City Hall, adjacent to Faneuil Hall. Dedicated in 1980, they show him in two familiar poses, sitting on a park bench and standing erect, as if to ask for a the vote of a passerby.

&a LOCATION: The Curley house, with its distinctive shamrock-decorated shutters, is located at 350 Jamaicaway at Moraine St.

JAMES FAMILY HOME

 The Jameses can almost certainly lay claim to being the most intellectually distinguished family America has ever produced. Henry's novels—*The Europeans, The Bostonians, Washington Square* — rank with the best of any American novelist (or of any novelist, for that matter). His brother, William, was one of the founders of psychology and developed his own, very American school of philosophy known as "pragmatism." Their troubled sister, Alice, wrote a brilliant *Diary* that was published after her early death.

The founder of the American branch of the family was the grandfather of these remarkable grandchildren. Also named William James, he was a Protestant from Bailieborough, county Cavan. He arrived in America in 1789, married a woman of Scotch-Irish descent, and quickly made his fortune in business. His success allowed his son, Henry Sr., and grandchildren the leisure to pursue intellectual careers.

The family was conscious of its Irish roots. Henry Jr. visited Ireland three times during his long residence in London, but stayed only briefly each time, repelled by the grinding poverty he found there. Alice also maintained a lively interest in Irish affairs and strongly supported Charles Stewart Parnell's Home Rule campaign. She was furious, however, when—after being named as the respondent in the notorious Kitty O'Shea divorce trial—"the uncrowned king of Ireland" refused to bow to political reality and resign the leadership of the Irish National party. Parnell's stance shattered all hope of achieving home rule in the 19th century. Of his sister, Henry Jr. wrote in his diary: "She really was an Irish woman."

After the death of his wife Mary in 1882, Henry Sr. and Alice moved into this house on Beacon Hill, where they lived for four years. Henry Jr. also did some writing here, working on a dramatization of his 1878 novel *Daisy Miller.*

&a EXHIBITS: The house is privately owned and not open to the public. &a LOCATION: 131 Mt. Vernon St., in the Beacon Hill section of Boston.

JOHN F. KENNEDY LIBRARY
AND MUSEUM

Kennedy was elected president by one of the thinnest margins in history, barely 100,000 votes. (And more than a few Republicans muttered that many of those came from the graveyards of Mayor Richard Daley's Chicago.) To millions of Irish-Americans, however, an inch was as good as a mile. In John Fitzgerald Kennedy, the United States had its first Irish Catholic president.

Historians have for decades vainly scoured Boston immigration records to discover precisely when Patrick Kennedy, John F. Kennedy's great-grandfather, actually landed in this country. That he started life in a two-room cottage in county Wexford, emigrated during the famine, and arrived sometime between 1848 and 1850 are about the only facts not in dispute.

From the beginning of the 1840s, the port of arrival for immigrants to Boston was Noddle's Island, a locale that eludes present-day researchers viewing maps of Boston Harbor. Noddle's Island in fact no longer exists, having been long ago attached to the mainland by landfill and disappearing under the concrete and asphalt of what is now East Boston. In time, East Boston would become the epicenter of Kennedy political power in the city.

The 25-year-old immigrant married a colleen named Bridget Murphy, and the couple produced three daughters and one son. The latter, also named Patrick, was born January 8, 1858, and was quickly nicknamed "P.J." Barely a year later, however, the elder Patrick, who worked mostly as a barrel maker, was felled by cholera at age 35.

It was P.J. who first displayed the twin attributes that were to make the Kennedys into America's First Family: a flair for making money combined with political ambition. From his meager wages as a dockhand, he saved enough to buy a tavern in East Boston. From this humble beginning, he soon invested his profits with sufficient skill to become a wholesale liquor distributor and partner in two other saloons.

It is no coincidence that many successful Irish politicians were also saloon owners. In the days when only men voted and social services were meager or nonexistent, the saloon rivaled the church as the focus of community life and place of refuge in troubled times. Patrick Kennedy turned his saloon into what one observer described as a "midget-welfare state." The gratitude thus earned came in handy when Kennedy sought and won a seat in the state house of representatives in 1886. His marriage a year later to Mary Hickey, daughter of a socially prominent Irish-American family, also set the Kennedy pattern for marrying "up."

In 1892, Patrick moved to the state senate in 1892 (where he made the acquaintance of another young state senator named John F. "Honey Fitz" Fitzgerald). But after winning one more term, he stepped down to further tend his business interests and never held public office again. That did not mean he quit politics, however. Far from it. Wielding power behind the scenes, he remained one of the most politically influential men in Boston for many years.

P.J.'s son Joseph took after his father, and his life became a never-ending effort to better himself and win acceptance from "society." He endlessly ingratiated himself with those who could help him while ruthlessly cutting down anyone he even imagined was standing in his way. He attended Harvard College in a day when Catholics were thin on the ground there. Shortly after graduation, in what was to be the first of many business coups, he became one of the country's youngest bank presidents by engineering the takeover of the Columbia Trust Company, which his father had helped found.

This small bank became the foundation stone for the multimillion-dollar business empire that would one day propel the Kennedys to the White House. As a consort, he chose John Fitzgerald's daughter Rose, another shrewd bit of Kennedy matchmaking. (*See* Rose Fitzgerald Kennedy Birthplace.)

Not even the most determined Kennedy family hagiographers (and there are many) now deny the marriage very quickly became a sham from a romantic point of view. Nevertheless, Rose did the duty expected of a Catholic mother in those days and produced nine children, four boys and five girls.

When Joe Jr. was killed in World War II, Joe Sr. immediately thrust his political plans onto his second oldest son, John, or Jack as he was known to family and friends. His heroic war record as commander of the PT-109, along with his father's limitless financial resources, enabled Jack to win a seat in Congress in 1946 over several other, better-known candidates. And he bucked the Republican tide to unseat Sen. Henry Cabot Lodge, Jr., in 1952. It was sweet revenge for the family, for Lodge's grandfather had defeated "Honey Fitz" for the same Senate seat 36 years earlier.

American society has changed so much since 1960 that it's hard to imagine today what a breakthrough John F. Kennedy's election as president represented for American Catholics in general and Irish Catholics in particular.

In 1960, Roman Catholics—of whom the Irish were the largest and most visible portion—were still a very distinct subgroup in American society. The reforms of the Second Vatican Council were still two years away. Catholics continued to worship in a long-dead language that few of *them* even understood. They abstained from eating meat on Fridays. Their families tended to be larger than those of Protestant Americans, and they frequently sent their children to Catholic rather than public schools, from kindergarten straight through college.

As political scientist Michael Barone has astutely pointed out, however, it was precisely because Kennedy did *not* fit the negative stereotype associated with Irish Catholics that he was the perfect Irish Catholic candidate. He was educated at Choate and Harvard; he married (however imperfectly) a beautiful and charming woman of aristocratic background (marrying "up" again); he was the father—at the time of the campaign—of only one child; he was a decided Anglophile possessed of a cultured-sounding and vaguely British accent; and his father's fortune freed him of any taint of ward boss corruption. "He was," Barone writes in his book *Our Country,* "what (someone said) every Irish Catholic woman wanted her grandson to be."

For all the anomalies in his biography, however, Kennedy was unmistakably Irish enough to more than satisfy his core constituency—and alarm a few others. Many Irish-Americans still nursed bitter memories of the vicious baiting Al Smith had taken in the 1928 election for his Catholicism. Kennedy's treatment was gentler, but he still felt compelled to confront the religious issue head-on.

He did it in a famous speech to Protestant ministers in Houston on September 12, 1960. "I am not the Catholic candidate for president," Kennedy insisted, somewhat defensively. "I am the Democratic party's candidate for president, who happens to be a Catholic." Kennedy went on to promise he would resign if he ever perceived a conflict between his religion and his duty as president. The speech achieved its intended purpose, and the religious issue largely faded away.

Kennedy steered well clear of religious controversy during his time in office. (He even refused to genuflect and kiss the ring of Pope Paul VI when they met in 1963.) Still, he realized it would not do for him to be seen ignoring his religion completely, and he began attending Sunday mass regularly, something he rarely did before he became president.

Even while he was in office, Kennedy took a keen interest in his future presidential library and museum, even visiting Boston on one occasion to scout possible locations. Originally slated for construction near Harvard University, community opposition to the anticipated hordes of tourists effectively forced the library to find another site. The University of Massachusetts at Boston finally came through with the offer of the present location at Columbia Point.

The site turned out to be more appropriate than anyone could have imagined. The waves crashing against the seawall remind visitors of the Kennedys' longtime association with sailing and the sea. The building also overlooks the entrance to Boston Harbor, through which the president's Kennedy and Fitzgerald ancestors passed through into the New World.

❧ **EXHIBITS:** The museum chronicles all aspects of the lives of John and Robert F. Kennedy. The museum has just undergone extensive renovation and was reopened in the fall of 1993. One of the new exhibits traces the Irish ancestry of the Kennedy family, correcting a much-criticized omission when the museum was first opened. ❧ **LOCATION:** The complex is located on the campus of the University of Massachusetts at Columbia

Point in the Dorchester section of Boston. Take exit 15 off of Route 3/I-93 and follow signs. By public transit, take the MBTA Red Line to the JFK/ UMass station and take the shuttle bus, which runs every half hour on the hour and half hour. &. HOURS: 9–5 daily. Closed federal holidays. &. ADMISSION: $4.50 adults; children under 16 free. &. TELEPHONE: (617) 929-4523.

JOHN SINGLETON COPLEY STUDIO SITE

One of the premier painters of the late 18th and early 19th centuries, John Singleton Copley was the son of Irish parents. His father, described in family records as a tobacconist, was from Limerick, his mother from Clare. They married in Ireland before immigrating to the United States around 1736. The painter's own birth date is uncertain, but it was around 1737–38 in Boston.

The family had a precocity for drawing and young John settled on a career as an artist well before he was out of his teens. Before he was 30, he had firmly established himself in Boston as a portrait painter and had even won fame abroad after a highly successful London exhibition in 1766. The income he earned was extraordinary for the time, enabling him to make a good marriage to a socially prominent Boston woman and buy land on Beacon Hill.

Up to that point, Copley had resisted entreaties from Benjamin West and others that he travel to Europe, which was considered the only fit place for an artist to refine his skills. By 1774, however, the political situation in Boston was heating up. While Copley himself was largely indifferent to all subjects save his art, his family connections were Loyalist. (His father-in-law was the consignee for the tea dumped in Boston Harbor for the tea party.) He found it prudent in 1774 to sail for London.

There, he established himself for the rest of his life, with almost as much success as he had enjoyed in Boston. It was in London that he completed most of his best-known works, many on British historical subjects, including "The Arrest of Five Members of the Commons by Charles I," "The Siege of Gibraltar," and "The Death of Major Pierson."

Though his son, John Singleton Copley, Jr., later became lord chancellor of England and was correct Lord Lyndhurst, the father remained a proud American. In 1782, after hearing King George III's speech formally recognizing American independence, Copley slyly painted the Stars and Stripes into the background of one of his portraits.

The Napoleonic War, however, ended Copley's string of good luck. Commissions were hard to come by, and he feared he was losing the sharpness he had enjoyed in his youth. He died, debt-ridden, in 1815.

Copley had continued to own his house and farm in Boston long after decamping to London. Around 1800, he had sold the property to a group of speculators and for the rest of his life complained that he had been cheated on the price, though he seems to have received considerably in excess of what he paid.

❧ LOCATION: Copley's home and studio are long gone. The former site is today marked with a plaque attached to the side of the exclusive Somerset Club at 42 Beacon St.

JOHN BOYLE O'REILLY MEMORIAL

"The most distinguished Irishman in America," wrote *Harper's Weekly* in its obituary of John Boyle O'Reilly in 1890. The description was probably not an exaggeration, for in his varied career as a journalist, poet, soldier, and unwilling guest in Her Majesty's prisons, O'Reilly became the foremost spokesman for Ireland and Irish causes in late 19th century America.

O'Reilly's remarkable career would have taxed the imagination of a fiction writer. He was born in 1844 near Drogheda, where his father owned a small school. Early on, he was attracted to journalism, spending four years as an apprentice on a local newspaper in Drogheda before moving on to the Preston *Guardian* in England for three years. He returned home in 1863 and enlisted in the 10th Hussars (nearly one-third of the British army at that time was Irish).

Almost immediately, however, he joined the secret Fenian Society and began actively promoting Irish nationalism among his fellow soldiers. Arrested with much of the rest of the Fenian movement in 1866, he was court-martialed, found guilty, and sentenced to death. The sentence was almost immediately commuted to one of life imprisonment, however, and subsequently to 20 years' penal servitude. After 2 years' solitary confinement in England, he and 62 other Irish nationalist prisoners were deported to the penal colonies in Western Australia.

Upon arrival on January 10, 1868, he was tagged "Imperial Convict No. 9843." Not for a moment, however, did O'Reilly give a thought to quietly serving out his sentence. He quickly befriended a sympathetic priest, and the prelate arranged for the prisoner's passage aboard an American whaling vessel called the *Gazelle*. Making his break on February 18, 1869, O'Reilly spent several harrowing days in the bush, hiding from British patrols. Eventually he made contact with the crew of the *Gazelle* and was rowed out to the vessel. After a few more narrow escapes (including a short period of living dangerously in England), he landed at Philadelphia on November 23, 1869. He was one of only a handful of prisoners ever to successfully escape from Down Under.

O'Reilly's genius for making fast friends served him well in his new country. Returning to his first vocation as a journalist, he found employment on the *Boston Pilot,* which was rapidly developing its reputation as the foremost "Irish" newspaper in America. O'Reilly won notice for his reporting on the ill-fated Fenian raid on Canada from St. Albans, Vermont, in 1871. (*See* Sheldon, Vermont.) He also began to publish poetry, his first volume appearing in 1873.

His time as a prisoner, however, seared him for the rest of his life. "My memory of that dreadful routine of hard labor and enforced silence in the imperial prisons . . . makes me shudder, even after 20 years. It is regulated inhumanity. It destroys many; it improves none."

One of his best poems, "Released—January, 1878," was written upon the release from British prisons of three of his fellow Fenians, imprisoned since 1866:

> *The years of their doom have*
> *slowly sped*
> *Their limbs are withered—*
> *their ties are riven*
> *Their children are scattered,*
> *their friends are dead*
> *But the prisons are open—*
> *the "crime" forgiven.*

Buying the *Pilot* in 1876, O'Reilly used it as a platform to agitate, not only for Irish Home Rule, but for the rights of oppressed people everywhere, including such *very* unfashionable causes as the rights of Indians and black Americans. Alarmed by the passage of Jim Crow laws in the South shortly before his own death, O'Reilly wrote one of his strongest editorials: "The black man in the South must face the inevitable, soon or late, and the inevitable is—defend yourself."

A strong Democrat, O'Reilly nevertheless refused all entreaties to run for office himself. He did not lose his taste for taking direct action in the cause of liberty, however. In 1876, he chartered a whaling vessel to Australia and freed six fellow prisoners from the torture he himself had escaped six years earlier. (*See* New Bedford, Massachusetts.)

His premature death in 1890 was an occasion for mourning throughout the Irish-American community. A popular appeal to raise a memorial to him had little trouble finding subscribers. The *Boston Pilot* soldiers on today as the official organ of the Boston Catholic archdiocese.

&☙ **EXHIBITS:** The memorial features a bronze bust surrounded by chains, flanked on either side by a marble screen.   &☙ **LOCATION:** The memorial to John Boyle O'Reilly, the work of Daniel Chester French (who did the statue of Lincoln at the Lincoln Memorial), stands in the Boston Fenway at the western end of Boylston St. It was dedicated in 1896.   &☙ **HOURS:** Dawn to dusk.   &☙ **ADMISSION:** None.

LOUIS SULLIVAN BIRTHPLACE

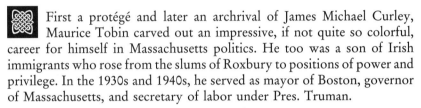 The Irish-American architect who is usually considered to be the father of "modernism" in American architecture was born in Boston in 1856 of an Irish immigrant father and a Swiss-born mother. (*See* Chicago, Illinois.)

On September 3, 1946, the Boston Society of Architects and the Massachusetts State Association of Architects placed a bronze plaque at the door of No. 22 Bennet Street to mark his birth site.

🦋 **EXHIBITS:** The house is privately owned and not open to the public. 🦋 **LOCATION:** Bennet St. is in the shadow of the ultramodern New England Medical Center. Most of the original buildings are now gone.

MAURICE TOBIN STATUE

First a protégé and later an archrival of James Michael Curley, Maurice Tobin carved out an impressive, if not quite so colorful, career for himself in Massachusetts politics. He too was a son of Irish immigrants who rose from the slums of Roxbury to positions of power and privilege. In the 1930s and 1940s, he served as mayor of Boston, governor of Massachusetts, and secretary of labor under Pres. Truman.

🦋 **LOCATION:** Tobin's statue stands on the Esplanade along the Charles River, near the Hatch Shell. 🦋 **HOURS:** Dawn to dusk. 🦋 **ADMISSION:** None.

OLD CITY HALL

Built in 1865, this six-story French Provincial structure was the seat of Boston's mayors for 104 years, until Kevin White moved the city government to the nearby (and less distinguished) new City Hall in 1969.

This was the building where James Michael Curley and his army of "Fedoras" (as his hangers-on were known) presided over Boston for a total of 16 years. Just inside the front entrance, surrounding the inner main doorway, are listed the names of all the Boston mayors who served here, with the predominance of Irish surnames being unmistakable.

🦋 **EXHIBITS:** The building was converted into restaurant and office space after the city government vacated it, so there are no exhibits or other evidence of the political dramas that took place here. 🦋 **LOCATION:** 41–45 School St. 🦋 **HOURS:** Maison Robert, the excellent French restaurant on the first floor, is open 11:30–2:30 and 5:30–9:30 Mondays–Fridays, Saturdays till 10. 🦋 **ADMISSION:** Free 🦋 **TELEPHONE:** Maison Robert: (617) 227-3370.

Boston's city hall until 1969, this distinguished building is now home to a restaurant.

PATRICK COLLINS MEMORIAL

The enmity between the Protestant Boston Yankees and the Irish Catholic immigrants in Boston has become so legendary that it's hard to believe that it wasn't always so. Indeed, much of the hostility is a 20th-century phenomenon, largely created by James Michael Curley's "waving the shamrock" in his numerous campaigns (*see* James Michael Curley House, elsewhere in this chapter).

Patrick Collins was the second Irish mayor Boston ever had (Hugh O'Brien was the first, elected in 1885) and a man highly leery of the political tactics of the ambitious young alderman from Roxbury. Born in Fermoy, county Cork in 1844 and brought to the United States as an infant, Patrick Collins quit grade school to become an apprentice to an upholsterer. He had higher ambitions, however, and by sheer self-discipline and determination, he acquired a college degree and graduated from Harvard Law School at age 23.

Collins cultivated an image as a "gentleman" and sought acceptance into refined Boston society, a goal he largely achieved. He was politically active as a Democrat of a reformist bent (he became the first Irishman ever elected to the Massachusetts state senate in 1876) and became a friend of President Grover Cleveland. In the second Cleveland administration, Collins served as consul general in London and he strongly opposed the radical economic policies of William Jennings Bryan and the Populists.

Collins firmly believed the Irish had to "assimilate" into American society if they were to succeed. In a speech supporting the candidacy of Brahmin Charles Francis Adams for governor, he set forth his ideas on the place of ethnic and religious differences in politics: "I denounce any man or body of men who seek to perpetuate divisions of races or religions in our midst. . . . I love the land of my birth but in American politics I know no race or color, nor creed. Let me say that there are no Irish votes among us. There are Irish-born citizens . . . but the moment the seal of the court was impressed on our papers we ceased to be foreigners and became Americans."

Collins served only three years as Boston's mayor, from 1902 until his health began failing and he died suddenly in 1905. In honor of the man who sought to bridge the gap between Yankee and Irish in Boston, President Charles Eliot of Harvard led the campaign to raise $26,000 to commission the statue of Collins that stands today along the mall on Commonwealth Avenue in Boston. It was dedicated in 1908.

& **LOCATION:** The granite and bronze monument, the work of Henry H. & Theo A. Kitson, is on Commonwealth Avenue between Berkeley and Clarendon streets. Also, just a block east, at No. 76 Commonwealth Ave., lived Hugh O'Brien, Boston's first Irish Catholic mayor. & **HOURS:** Dawn to dusk.

ROSE FITZGERALD KENNEDY
BIRTHPLACE

"There is one thing I want you all to remember," Rose Fitzgerald Kennedy told an assembly of her surviving children, grandchildren, and great-grandchildren on her birthday a few years ago. "You are not just Kennedys. You are Fitzgeralds, too."

The just-deceased family matriarch can be forgiven that bit of chauvinistic pride. Given how utterly her late husband had shoved her own family into the background during their marriage, some might say it was overdue. Indeed, so determined was Joe Kennedy to make his in-laws nonpersons that even he often failed to recognize them. While hosting a lavish luncheon at the Mayflower Hotel on the day of his son's inauguration, he pointed to a gaggle of Fitzgerald relatives who were helping themselves to the buffet. "Just who *are* all these freeloaders?" he demanded of an aide.

But the Fitzgerald connection was almost as valuable in the making of John F. Kennedy's career as that of his father's side of the family. James Michael Curley, running for his fourth term as mayor, was one of the few who thought the young war veteran had a shot at winning a seat in Congress in 1946. "With two names like Fitzgerald and Kennedy, how could he lose?" he asked.

Most newly married men hope their first child will be a son. Not John F. Fitzgerald. One of nine boys in his own family, he was thrilled when his wife, Josie, gave birth to a baby daughter on the steaming summer night of July 22, 1890. They named the daughter Rose, and despite the birth of three sons and two more daughters, she forever remained the apple of her father's eye. Young Joe Kennedy had to work hard to win her over her father's objections.

Like his future son-in-law's grandfather, John F. Fitzgerald's grandfather Thomas came from county Wexford during the potato famine. Though he started in America as a farm laborer, Thomas, like P.J. Kennedy, had entrepreneurial talents and soon opened a grocery and liquor store in Boston's North End, which was then a solidly Irish neighborhood.

One of twelve children (two sisters had died in childhood), John F. Fitzgerald was born in the North End in 1863. Though neither the oldest nor the tallest, he became a natural athlete and leader. When his father died in John's first year at Harvard Medical School, he dropped out to care for his brothers, taking a job as a clerk in the Customs House.

He didn't stay long, however. Within a few years, he had launched himself into the real estate and insurance businesses, where his gift for gab, which was to earn him the nickname "Honey Fitz," helped him to roaring success. By the time Rose was born, there were already lace curtains on the windows and her father was finding politics more interesting than insurance. In rapid succession, he was elected city councilman, state senator, congressman, and, finally, Boston's mayor from 1905 to 1914.

Rose had a privileged upbringing, wearing the finest clothes, traveling abroad frequently, and attending the best schools. When she was ready for marriage and motherhood, her father could scarcely stand young Joe Kennedy, refusing even to let him into the house. When Rose was adamant, however, her father finally relented. He conveyed his disapproval, however, by making her wedding a very small, low-key affair, taking place in Cardinal William O'Connell's private chapel.

For all of Joe Kennedy's efforts to downplay the Fitzgerald contribution, however, most recent scholarship gives Rose Kennedy much more credit than she has heretofore received for the family's success. She was, after all, the parent who was present in the house most of the time. In the process, she passed on many of the hints Honey Fitz had given her as a child: how to stand up straight for photographers, how to greet people warmly, how to remember names. All these skills stood them in good stead later when they stepped onto the political stage.

Near the birthplace is the small, one-acre Rose Fitzgerald Kennedy Garden, with a black granite fountain encircled by pink granite. On the base is inscribed a quote from Mrs. Kennedy: "If God were to take away all his blessings and leave me but one gift, I would ask for faith."

🐚 EXHIBITS: The family lived in the building (which they owned) for seven years. There is a commemorative plaque next to the front door. Otherwise, the building is privately owned and not open to the public. 🐚 LOCATION: 4 Garden Court St., in the now mostly Italian North End of Boston. Follow Hanover St., the main street of the North End, turn right on Fleet St., and Garden Court St. is the first street on your right.

SHELTON HALL

"I knew it, I knew it!" Eugene O'Neill is said to have thundered on his deathbed. "Born in a hotel room—goddamn it—and dying in a hotel room!"

The Irish-American playwright and Nobel Prize–winner lived on both the East and West coasts during his long and peripatetic career. (*See* Danville, California and New London, Connecticut.) He returned to the East Coast from California in 1942, living with his tempestuous wife Carlotta, in a big house in Marblehead. In 1951, they both suffered nervous breakdowns and separated.

O'Neill, also suffering from Parkinson's disease and in an advanced state of physical and mental decline, moved to Boston to be closer to his doctor. He lived in Suite 401 of what was then the Shelton Hotel, struggling to finish a cycle of twelve great tragedies. The disease, however, left him unable to write. The writer spent two unhappy years here before his death on November 27, 1953.

⬝ EXHIBITS: The dormitory is private property and not open to the public. ⬝ LOCATION: 93 Bay State Rd. The former hotel, which dates from 1923, is now Shelton Hall of Boston University.

SOUTH BOSTON

If there is a more famous Irish neighborhood in the United States, it would be hard to find. "Southie" has been home to Irish-Americans almost from the first days of the potato famine. And unlike so many Irish neighborhoods in other cities across America, the Irish never left Southie. The neat streets, lined with wooden "triple-deckers," remain home to many second-, third-, and even fourth-generation Irish-Americans (as well as a new generation of illegal aliens) who self-consciously continue to identify with their heritage. Some buildings are even daubed with pro-IRA graffiti and murals that would not be out of place in West Belfast.

The area's string of Irish luck began on March 17, 1776, when Gen. George Washington won his first victory over the British here by emplacing artillery on what is now Dorchester Heights. The besieged British troops under Lord Howe, realizing that Washington's cannon made their situation untenable, were forced to evacuate the city. A year later, to commemorate the event, George Washington made "St. Patrick" the password of the Continental Army for March 17. The 115-foot-tall Dorchester Heights Memorial was dedicated on March 17, 1902.

South Boston was first settled shortly after Boston's founding in 1630. A bridge was built from the main part of the city in 1805 and the area began to develop as a shipping and industrial district. Housing was cheap and jobs plentiful, so it is not surprising that the poor Irish immigrants chose to settle here.

The first thing to learn about South Boston is that it isn't—south, that is. Jutting into Boston Harbor east of downtown, Southie and its approximately 30,000 people are located on a spit of land separated from the rest of the city by an expressway. This isolation, combined with the neighborhood's ethnic homogeneity, has bred an almost tribal sense of identity among its residents. It was this clannishness that exploded onto national television screens in 1975 with the crisis known to everyone in the area simply as "busing."

Federal District Judge Arthur Garrity had declared Boston's public schools to be segregated by race, and he ordered black schoolchildren to be bused to schools in white neighborhoods such as South Boston, and vice versa. Enraged residents of Southie took to the streets, stoning school buses and beating their passengers. The enduring image of the crisis was of a black man being attacked in front of Boston City Hall by a white protester carrying an American flag.

Kevin White, the Irish-American mayor, was denounced as "Mayor Black" for his calm appeals to implement the court order. (The crisis abruptly ended his ill-disguised national political ambitions.) Judge Garrity, despite his own Irish ancestry, was derisively dismissed as a "hoper," defined as "an Irishman who goes to bed hoping to wake up a Yankee." Sen. Edward Kennedy was pelted with tomatoes and rotten fruit when he made an appeal for calm.

Although the crisis caused many to stereotype South Boston as an enclave of unreconstructed bigots, in reality the situation was far more complicated. It was bitterly noted that Judge Garrity sent his own children to expensive private schools, and that many of those most haughtily denouncing Southie as a den of racists themselves lived in distant suburbs, unaffected by the court order. South Boston residents couldn't understand how busing black children clear across town into a strange neighborhood was supposed to help them learn better. The skeptics were largely proved right in later years, and busing has since been abandoned just about everywhere it has been tried, including Boston.

South Boston became slightly less homogeneous in the 1980s, with a sprinkling of blacks and Hispanics moving in as well as upscale professionals. By and large, however, South Boston continues to exist as if in an ethnic time warp, one of the last concentrations of Irish-Americans in urban America.

& LOCATION: South Boston can be reached by crossing either the Sumner Street Bridge (near the Boston Tea Party Ship) or the Broadway Bridge (Broadway subway stop).

ST. STEPHEN'S CHURCH

Just around the corner from the Rose Fitzgerald Kennedy Birthplace (*see* earlier entry), St. Stephen's Church was the parish church of the Fitzgerald family and baby Rose was baptized here, in 1995, her funeral was also held here). The only Charles Bullfinch church still standing in Boston, St. Stephen's was originally built for a Protestant congregation and was known as New North Church. The Catholic church took it over when the North End neighborhood became overwhelmingly Irish. Richard Cardinal Cushing led a major restoration effort in the mid-1960s to return the church to its original condition.

St. Stephen's Church, located in Boston's North End.

❧ LOCATION: 401 Hanover St., in Boston's North End. ❧ HOURS: Monday–Friday, 8–4, Saturday 10–6. Call for Sunday mass schedule. ❧ ADMISSION: Free, though a small donation is requested. ❧ TELEPHONE: (617) 523-1230.

BROOKLINE

JOHN F. KENNEDY NATIONAL HISTORIC SITE

The newly married Mr. and Mrs. Joseph P. Kennedy moved into this modest home on a quiet side street in suburban Brookline just after they returned from their honeymoon at the Greenbrier Resort in West Virginia in 1914. It would be the last modest home they ever lived in.

Joe and Rose Kennedy's first home, and the birthplace of John F. Kennedy in 1917.

Joe Kennedy was still in debt from his takeover of Columbia Trust at the time of his marriage, and he had to borrow the $2,000 down payment on the $6,000 home. The halls of the house were narrow and the rooms small. But when it was dedicated as a national historic site in 1969, Rose Kennedy remembered it fondly. "We were very happy here," she told the assembled crowd in the street. "And although we did not know about the days ahead, we were optimistic about the future."

Jack was born here May 29, 1917, two years after Joe Jr., followed by Rosemary in 1919 and Kathleen in 1920. All except Joe Jr. were born in a second-floor bedroom near the window "to give the doctor plenty of light." Eunice, Patricia, and Robert were born after the family moved to a larger, more elegant house down the street. Jean and Edward arrived after the family moved to New York.

In 1966, the Kennedy family reacquired the old place and set about restoring it to its original condition as much as possible, with Jack's bassinet and some of his childhood toys. The house is today maintained by the National Park Service.

❧ **EXHIBITS:** The house contains much Kennedy family memorabilia, and a guided tour is available. ❧ **LOCATION:** 83 Beals St., Brookline. Robert was born nearby at 131 Naples Rd. A map is available from the desk at the Kennedy Historic Site that will guide you to the later residence, which is privately owned and not open to the public. ❧ **HOURS:** Seven days a week, 10–4:30. Closed Thanksgiving, Christmas, and New Year's Day. ❧ **ADMISSION:** $4 adults; children under 16 free. ❧ **TELEPHONE:** (617) 566-7937.

COHASSET

ST. JOHN'S MEMORIAL

Emigration may have been an alternative to starvation in Ireland during the Great Hunger, but by no means did it ensure survival. Maritime technology had not advanced much beyond what it had been for centuries, and the crossing usually took at least seven weeks, sometimes ten, depending on the weather. With passengers crammed into aptly named "coffin ships," diseases such as scurvy and cholera were a constant threat, as was fire.

Most feared of all, of course, was a shipwreck. In 1847, the *Exmouth*, out of Derry, foundered off the coast of Scotland, with only 3 survivors out of 251 passengers. Between 1847 and 1853, no less than 59 emigrant ships were lost before reaching America.

Saddest of all shipwrecks were those that not infrequently took place within sight of the passengers' destination. One of the most tragic of all was the *St. John* disaster.

In early September 1849, the last year of the Great Famine, 99 emigrants—50 from Galway and 49 from Clare—set out from Galway in the two-masted brig the *St. John*. They were leaving the ravages of the Great Hunger behind them and, they hoped, were on their way to start new lives in Boston.

They never made it. Just a mile offshore of this small town south of Boston Harbor, within sight of their goal, a sudden storm drove the ship aground on the submerged Grampus Ledge. Despite the heroic efforts of the Cohasset lifeboat crew, 88 of the passengers were lost. About half of the bodies recovered were never identified and were buried in a mass grave in the town cemetery.

One of the witnesses to the wreck of the *St. John* was the hermit of Walden Pond, Henry David Thoreau. In the first chapter of his book *Cape*

Cod, he gives a vivid account of the aftermath of the wreck. "All their plans and hopes burst like a bubble!" Thoreau lamented as he surveyed the bodies washed up along the shore. "Infants by the score dashed on the rocks by the enraged Atlantic! No, no!"

On May 20, 1914, the Ancient Order of Hibernians dedicated a 20-foot Celtic cross over the mass grave in Cohasset Central Cemetery in honor of the victims of the *St. John* and all the emigrants who never reached these shores.

❧ **EXHIBITS:** The Cohasset Historical Society, on Elm St. in the center of the village, maintains a maritime museum that displays the writing desk of the captain of the *St. John* and a few other artifacts that were retrieved from the wreck. ❧ **LOCATION:** Cohasset is approximately 25 miles south and east of Boston. From Boston, take Route 3 south to the Cohasset exit. Follow Sohier Street into the center of the village until it dead-ends at North Main Street. Turn left and almost immediately bear right onto Joy Place. Cohasset Central Cemetery will be on your right. The gate is sometimes locked, but the low stone walls surrounding it are easily stepped over. The large cross sits atop a hill near the main gate. ❧ **HOURS:** The cemetery is usually open from dawn to dusk. Museum hours variable. Call in advance. ❧ **ADMISSION:** None. ❧ **TELEPHONE:** (617) 383-6930.

EAST BROOKFIELD

CONNIE MACK BIRTHPLACE

"The grand old man" of professional baseball was born Cornelius McGillicuddy on December 22, 1862, in this modest house in East Brookfield, about halfway between Springfield and Worcester. Later, when he began his baseball career, he discovered his given name would not fit on a newspaper box score, so he took to calling himself what everyone had been calling him for years: "Connie Mack."

Mack's father, a famine immigrant, had settled in East Brookfield and gotten a job at the cotton mill there. When he was old enough, Mack worked in the mill, too, twelve hours a day, six days a week at 35 cents a day.

Despite the hellish conditions, Mack was almost nostalgic in later years about his time in the mill. All the boys had to rise early and work long hours, he said, and they received a whole hour for lunch, which gave him and his co-workers time to play ball.

Tall and thin to the point of being gaunt, Mack started out as the catcher on the town baseball team, in the days when catchers wore no protective equipment. He helped his East Brookfield team to the central Massachusetts championship.

Cap Anson, one of the early baseball greats, brought his team through the area for an exhibition game, and 20-year-old Mack, uncertain as to the direction his life would take, decided to give professional baseball a try. His mother was horrified, fearful of the rough reputation of many ball-players. Not to worry, Mack said. There was room for gentlemen in every profession, he said, and a gentleman he would be.

No one has ever found any evidence that he was anything but. Mack first played for the Meriden, Connecticut, team, earning the then-respectable salary of $90 a month. A year later, he played for Hartford, at $125 a month. His first effort at ownership ended in disaster when an investment in the Buffalo franchise cost him every cent he had. Nevertheless, he stayed in the game as a player and in 1894 became player-manager for the Pittsburgh franchise. Despite a respectable record, he was fired after two seasons, and at age 34 was widowed, out of work, and had three children to support.

It would have been hard to blame Mack for giving up on baseball at that point, but just then a minor league owner named Ben Johnson offered Mack the chance to manage Johnson's Milwaukee franchise. Mack leapt at the chance and managed Milwaukee for four years. When Johnson broke into the majors in 1900, he offered Mack the manager's position in Phila-delphia, which Mack agreed to take—in exchange for a 25 percent interest in the franchise. So that year, the Philadelphia Athletics played their very first game under the direction of Connie Mack. Over the next 50 years, they would play 7,876 more, including 43 in the World Series.

In terms of management style, Mack was utterly unlike his rival and fellow Irish-American, the New York Giants manager John McGraw, with whom Mack dominated the game for years. McGraw was a hard, domi-neering manager who expected the best from his players and let them know in no uncertain terms if they disappointed him. Mack, however, never forgot his promise to his mother about being a gentleman. The very image of dignified calm, he sat quietly in the dugout and never raised his voice or swore, no matter what happened on the field. He never wore a uniform, preferring well-tailored suits, bowler hats, and high, starched collars. He continued to wear the latter decades after they had gone out of style.

Mack had two golden eras with the A's. The first was before World War I, when his teams won three World Series, in 1910, 1911, and 1913. Then came a long dry spell that did not end until Mack acquired players like Ty Cobb and Tris Speaker and proceeded to win the 1929 and 1930 World Series, losing the 1931 series by a hair to the St. Louis Cardinals in the seventh game.

After 1931, however, Mack's teams went into eclipse again. Incredibly, he refused to retire, remaining in the dugout until the end of the 1950 season, on the eve of his 88th birthday, revered by the whole game as "the grand old man." He died, at age 93, in 1956, the year after his sons sold the team to Charles O. Finley, who moved it to Kansas City. (It later moved to Oakland, California.)

Connie Mack was a manager ahead of his time. On the scorecard that seemed perpetually fastened to his left hand during games, he took careful notes on the strengths and weaknesses of opposing players, and he briefed his pitchers and catchers on his findings during pregame meetings. He wanted particular pitches thrown to particular hitters at particular times.

Sometimes, however, the system backfired on Mack. Joe Dimaggio tells a story about how Louis "Bobo" Newsom had just joined the A's and was assigned to pitch against the Yankees the very same day. Mack asked Newsom if he knew how to pitch to each hitter. Newsom replied that he did, went out to the mound, and watched as Dimaggio promptly slammed one of his pitches over the outfield wall for a home run.

When Newsom got back to the dugout, Mack asked him what pitch Dimaggio had hit. "My fast ball, sir," Newsom replied. "Louis, don't ever throw Dimaggio another fast ball," Mack said. Throw him nothing but curves. You understand? Curves."

So the next time Dimaggio came up, Newsom threw him a steady series of curves. Dimaggio quickly read the pattern and wasted no time belting one of Newsom's curves clear over the stadium roof. As he circled the bases, the Yankee slugger recalled later, he heard Newsom shout across to his manager, "Mr. Mack, he hit yours farther than he hit mine!"

& EXHIBITS: The house is privately owned and not open to the public. &
LOCATION: The house is marked and stands at the corner of Maple and Main streets.

NEW BEDFORD

WHALING MUSEUM, CATALPA MEMORIAL

After his escape from an Australian penal colony in 1869, John Boyle O'Reilly (see O'Reilly Memorial, Boston, Massachusetts), did not forget his Fenian comrades left behind, sentenced to hard labor for life in the broiling sun of Western Australia. He immediately set about hatching a plan to free them and bring them to the United States.

It took him nearly seven years. Apparently deciding that if it worked once, it could work again, and O'Reilly settled on a whaling vessel as the

Part of the Catalpa exhibit at the Whaling Museum (left); and a granite marker commemorating the 100th anniversary of the rescue.

instrument of the prisoners' liberation. O'Reilly and a small group of co-conspirators raised money and hired the New Bedford whaler *Catalpa*, which was fitted out as if for a whaling voyage. The ship would not be a suspicious sight in the southeastern Indian Ocean adjacent to Western Australia, which was a rich whaling ground.

Captained by George Anthony, an adventurous New Bedford whaler, the *Catalpa* set sail in April 1875. The ship was crewed mostly by South Sea Islanders who knew nothing of their real mission. While the ship was making its way toward Australia, two Fenian leaders, John Breslin and Thomas Desmond, sailed from Los Angeles for Australia. They were to land in Freemantle to arrange the escape of the prisoners and their rendez-vous with the *Catalpa*.

By November, the two Fenian leaders were in Freemantle and had made contact with six surviving Fenian prisoners—Thomas Darragh, Martin Hogan, James Wilson, Thomas Hasset, Michael Harrington, and Richard Cranston. It took until the following April for the final arrangements to be made. The prisoners were to slip away from their work parties and meet Breslin, who would drive them in a carriage to Rockingham Beach. There, a whaleboat from the *Catalpa* was to pick them up and ferry them to the ship, which would be waiting in international waters offshore.

The plan worked perfectly until the escapees and the conspirators boarded the whaleboat. Foul weather blew them away from the *Catalpa;* and the party was forced to spend a lonely night tossed on the stormy sea. The next day, miraculously, they sighted the ship and began rowing toward it. At almost the same moment, however, a police cutter, by then alerted to the escape, quickly made the connection between the two vessels and began steering an interception course. A nail-biting race ensued, which the prisoners won by only minutes. Uncertain as to what course of action to take, the captain of the police cutter returned to Freemantle.

But the prisoners still were not home free. Enraged by the escape, the governor immediately ordered the gunboat *Georgette* sent in pursuit. A steamship, the British vessel had little difficulty overtaking the fleeing *Catalpa*. As the *Georgette* approached, the prisoners armed themselves and prepared to fight it out. They would rather have died than return to the living hell on shore.

The *Georgette* fired a shot across the *Catalpa's* bow and pulled alongside. Knowing full well he didn't stand a chance in an armed encounter, Capt. Anthony played his last, desperate card. Breaking out the Stars and Stripes, he ordered it hoisted from the mainmast.

"That's the American flag," he is supposed to have shouted across to the British captain. "I am on the high seas. My flag protects me. If you fire on this ship, you fire on the American flag."

The once-confident British captain now became uncertain. Wary of provoking an international incident, the *Georgette* proceeded to shadow the *Catalpa* for a time. After one more feeble attempt to bully Capt. Anthony, the British ship finally turned back to Freemantle. The Stars and Stripes had won the day. The prisoners arrived in New York on August 19, 1876.

᭞ **EXHIBITS:** An exhibit on the *Catalpa* adventure is on display at the museum, with many original photos and documents. A granite memorial to the *Catalpa* expedition was erected on the grounds of the Registry of Deeds Building in 1976, a few blocks from the Whaling Museum at the corner of Pack and 6th Sts. ᭞ **LOCATION:** The Whaling Museum is on Johnny Cake Hill, just south of U.S. 6, at the eastern end of the town. ᭞ **HOURS:** Monday to Saturday, 9–5, Sunday 1–5. ᭞ **ADMISSION:** $3.50 adults; $3.00 seniors; $2.50 children 6–14. ᭞ **TELEPHONE:** (508) 997-0046.

NEW HAMPSHIRE

PLAINFIELD

AUGUSTUS SAINT GAUDENS NATIONAL HISTORIC LANDMARK

"Aspet," the home of Augustus Saint Gaudens, is the only national historic site in the United States devoted to a visual artist. The man who would become America's greatest sculptor was born in 1848 in Dublin, the son of a French father and an Irish mother. Throughout his life, the Gallic and Gaelic strains fought within the artist, and produced works that were, and are, quintessentially American.

Saint Gaudens said that "no one ever succeeded in art unless born with an uncontrollable instinct toward it." Without question, Saint Gaudens had that instinct, though just how he came into possession of it is unclear. His forebears on his father's side were shoemakers for as long as anyone could remember. About his mother's side, less is known. According to Saint Gaudens's own *Reminiscences,* she was from county Longford and was the daughter of a plasterer. According to Burke Wilkinson, Saint Gaudens' most recent biographer, Mary McGuiness Saint Gaudens was a more low-key soul than her boastful husband, and young Augustus took her sensible advice at many critical points in his career.

Bernard Saint Gaudens learned the family trade in his hometown of Aspet, the namesake of the New Hampshire home, which is nestled in the French Pyrenees about 50 miles from Toulouse. He seems to have had wanderlust, however, and at some indeterminate point he decamped, first for London and then, by 1841, for Dublin. It was while working for an Irish shoemaker that he met Mary McGuiness and they later married. Two boys died in infancy before young Augustus was born on March 1, 1848, in a nondescript Dublin row house on Charlemont Street. The locale was barely two miles from the spot at the head of O'Connell Street where Augustus Saint Gaudens' memorial to Charles Stewart Parnell would be unveiled 63 years later.

At the time of Augustus' birth, the potato famine was in its third year. While the Saint Gaudenses did not appear to suffer greatly, the situation was no doubt depressing, and the family took ship for America six months after Augustus's birth.

First in Boston and later in New York, Augustus grew up into a handsome young man. His artistic inclination became apparent early on as he sat in his father's workshop making pen-and-ink sketches of the cobblers at work. By age 13, he was determined to become an artist. Fortunately, his father encouraged him and apprenticed the boy to several sculptors.

At age 19, he went to Paris for the European apprenticeship then considered essential for every aspiring American artist. He stayed in Paris until the Franco-Prussian War broke out in 1870, when he moved to Rome. There, he encountered Augusta Homer, the strong-willed daughter of an old, established Boston family who was also studying to be an artist but couldn't find an art school that took women students. Mr. Homer consented to the marriage of "Gus" and "Gussie," as they called each other, but would not let them marry until Augustus had secured a major commission that would show he had a future as an artist.

With that incentive driving him, Augustus moved with determination to secure a commission. In this respect, his timing was excellent. The Civil War had been over for nearly a decade, and a grateful nation was now prepared to begin erecting monuments to the heroes of that conflict. While in Rome, he heard of a competition being staged in New York for a memorial to Adm. David Glasgow Farragut, the hero of Mobile Bay, to be erected in Madison Square. Saint Gaudens sailed for New York, submitted his proposed design, and won the competition. His career was launched, and he married Gussie.

It was to be the first of many Civil War–related commissions. Saint Gaudens's sculptures have become so familiar they are literally part of the American landscape: Gen. William T. Sherman, being led to victory by an angel in front of New York's Plaza Hotel; Abraham Lincoln, his head bowed, one hand behind his back and the other clutching his lapel, in Chicago's Lincoln Park; the doomed Col. Robert Gould Shaw riding off to battle at the head of his all-black 54th Massachusetts Infantry; the haunting, shrouded woman in Rock Creek Cemetery in Washington, D.C., officially known as the Adams Memorial, but better known simply as Grief.

Saint Gaudens's sculptures broke free of convention. Farragut is shown not in a classically "heroic" pose, but standing foursquare, as if on the quarterdeck of his flagship with the wind flapping at his coat. The whole design struck a new and vital note.

Although Saint Gaudens tended to identify more with the French side of his heritage, flashes of "Irishness" were often observed in him. Biographer Burke Wilkinson says he possessed an openness and desire to please others more characteristic of the Irish than the French. To honor his Irish mother and the land of his birth, he hoped to make the statue of the Irish nationalist leader Charles Stewart Parnell in Dublin one of his finest. While the result is certainly more than adequate, Saint Gaudens was sick with the cancer that would kill him while he was working on the statue, and most critics do not consider it up to his previous standards.

Saint Gaudens arrived in New Hampshire in April 1885. A friend was hoping to assemble an "artists' colony" on the land he owned there and wanted Saint Gaudens to be the centerpiece of the action. No lover of nature, Saint Gaudens was skeptical but agreed to have a look. He and Gussie first saw the house, an abandoned tavern, on a gray, windy, northern New England day. Augustus thought it "so forbidding and relentless that one might have imagined a skeleton half hanging out the window, shrieking and dangling in the gale."

Gussie, however, thought the place had possibilities and convinced her husband. (Wilkinson speculates that one reason Augustus was so easily convinced was that he wanted a distant place where Gussie could go in summer so he could carry on an affair with a mistress in New York.) It soon became their summer home, and after Augustus was diagnosed with cancer in 1900, he made it his permanent home for the remaining seven years of his life.

❧ EXHIBITS: The home contains period furnishings from Saint Gaudens's residence there. The grounds, which host summer concerts and exhibitions, feature "the Old Studio" and "the Little Studio." Numerous busts and copies of earlier models of many of Saint Gaudens's most famous works are on display, as well as works by modern-day artists. A tour of the house is available. Saint Gaudens and the rest of his family are buried on the grounds as well. ❧ LOCATION: From the Lebanon exit off U.S. Route 89, turn south on Route 12A approximately 12 miles and follow signs. ❧ HOURS: Daily from Memorial Day through October. The buildings are open 8:30–4:30 and the grounds from 8 until dark. ❧ ADMISSION: Adults $2; children free. ❧ TELEPHONE: (603) 675-2175.

PORTSMOUTH

FORT CONSTITUTION

Lexington and Concord are remembered as the starting points of the American Revolution with the "shots heard 'round the world." But the first overt act of rebellion against the authority of the British

Crown actually took place here, five months earlier. On December 13, 1774, the New Hampshire Sons of Liberty attacked this installation, then known as Fort William and Mary, and seized nearly five tons of gunpowder.

The leader of the force was a local lawyer and militia commander named John Sullivan. His father, also John Sullivan, was born in county Limerick, and his mother, Margery Browne, was a native of county Cork. The parents had immigrated originally to what is now Maine in 1723. John is said to have bought Margery's freedom from an English landlord.

Sullivan's action, taken on Paul Revere's warning of a British threat, ensured that Portsmouth Harbor would remain in the hands of the revolutionaries. The gunpowder that was captured was quickly put to good use a few months later at the Battle of Bunker Hill.

Sullivan had a long and colorful revolutionary career. He was a member of the Continental Congress for a time, from which he received a commission as a brigadier general and left to take a field command with Washington's army. He saw action in the siege of Boston and the disastrous Battle of Long Island, in which he was captured. He was later exchanged for a British general and returned to his command. He led the right column of the Continental Army in the victory at Trenton on December 25–26, 1776.

Sullivan was a veteran of Valley Forge and later led a punitive expedition against the Iroquois in western New York State. The latter experience broke his health, and he was obliged to resign from the army in 1779. He then embarked on a political and judicial career, serving as attorney general of New Hampshire, assembly speaker, president (governor) of the state, and federal district judge. He died in 1795, only 54 years of age.

Although a brave soldier and competent political leader, Sullivan's temper made him many enemies and perhaps prevented him from rising even further. "Descriptions of Sullivan's character reveal traits typical of his Irish ancestry," reads a passage from his entry in the *Encyclopedia of American Biography.* "(H)e was brave, hot-headed, oversensitive, fond of display, generous to a fault, usually out of money, and a born political organizer."

❧ EXHIBITS: Little remains of the original fort except the base of the walls. The granite walls standing today date from the Civil War. ❧ LOCATION: Four miles east of Portsmouth on New Hampshire S.R. 1B in New Castle. ❧ HOURS: Dawn to dusk. ❧ ADMISSION: Free

N E W   J E R S E Y

AMERICAN LABOR
MUSEUM/BOTTO HOUSE

The Paterson silk strike paralyzed that industrial city in northern New Jersey for nearly six months in 1913. The mill owners, who controlled the Paterson city government, refused to allow the strikers to hold meetings. The nearby town of Haledon, however, had a socialist mayor. He allowed the workers and their union organizers to meet in his city at the home of an Italian laborer named Pietro Botto. Many of the biggest names in the radical wing of the American labor movement pitched in to help: Upton Sinclair, "Big Bill" Haywood, John ("Ten Days That Shook the World") Reed, and Elizabeth Gurley Flynn.

The striking workers of Paterson were ultimately forced to give in. But it was a major watershed for the American labor movement. While most Irish tended to steer clear of radical politics, a small but not insignificant number became actively involved in efforts to overthrow what they saw as an unjust economic system. Flynn, born with revolution in her blood, was one of these.

"My ancestors were immigrants and revolutionaries from the Emerald Isle. . . . There was an uprising in each generation in Ireland, and forefathers of mine were in every one of them," she wrote in her autobiography. "The awareness of being Irish came to us as small children, through plaintive song and heroic story. . . . As children, we drew in a burning hatred of British rule with our mother's milk. Until my father died, at over eighty, he never said *England* without adding 'God damn her!' Before I was ten, I knew of the great heroes—Robert Emmet, Wolfe Tone, Michael Davitt, Parnell, and Jeremiah O'Donovan Rossa."

Flynn gave her first "performance" in 1906 at the age of only 16. "It was in January last that she made her first appearance on the lecture platform and electrified her audience with her eloquence, her youth, and her loveliness," wrote novelist Theodore Dreiser of that first speech.

The American far left at that time was heavily dominated by Jews, Germans, Scandinavians, and other more identifiably "foreign" immigrant groups, a fact that almost inherently limited their appeal. The Irish were more "American" and thus often very effective as organizers. Flynn appeared on platforms with James Connolly, James Larkin, and other Irish labor radicals of the time. As Bob Callahan put it in his *Big Book of Irish-American Culture*, Flynn "was the Bernadette Devlin of her time."

ا**EXHIBITS:** Exhibits on the history of the American labor movement and on the everyday life of immigrant laborers. There is a display on Elizabeth Gurley Flynn and her role in the 1913 strike. ا **LOCATION:** 83 Norwood St. ا **HOURS:** Wednesday–Sunday 1–4. ا **ADMISSION:** $1.50 adults; under 12 free. ا **TELEPHONE:** (201) 595-7953.

JERSEY CITY

CITY HALL

"I am the law!" were the words that made Mayor Frank Hague (in)famous. His enemies seized upon them as evidence of political imperiousness, and although Hague didn't brook much opposition during his tenure as boss of Jersey City, a sober recalling of the circumstances reveals that Hague received a bum rap from history.

Two Irish youths wanted to change from day school to night school so they could work. The board of education, however, denied them working papers because the law stated they had to remain in day school. Hague slashed through the red tape and ordered that the working papers be issued. As he proudly recounted the incident before the Men's Club of Emory Church in Jersey City on November 10, 1937, when the school official told him, "That's the law," he replied, "Listen, here is the law. I am the law! These boys go to work."

Today, of course, the incident would be seen as the act of a public-spirited official pushing aside mindless bureaucracy for the benefit of his constituents. Thanks to Hague's already well-known reputation for high-handedness, however, the phrase quickly lost its context and was used against him.

Like many Irish-Americans who achieved fame in their endeavors, Hague had his mother to thank. Margaret Hague was described by those who knew her as "a bitch on wheels" and was without question the driving force in young Hague's life. (His father seems to have been something of a cipher.) She imbued him with an almost fanatical devotion to Irish-

Catholicism and a puritanical attitude that gave him his early image as a political reformer.

Indeed, Hague was noted for cleaning up Jersey City, which was a typically raucous waterfront town. In a single day during Hague's tenure as public safety commissioner, 125 police officers were tried for corruption, dereliction of duty, and other offenses. Hundreds of officers were demoted or dismissed. Hague replaced them with men of his own choosing and established a ruthless internal affairs division that kept a sharp eye on the force. He declared every one of the city's thousand or so saloons off-limits to women. (Hague himself did not drink.) He began an intensive campaign to clean up the city's sidewalks. All this got him elected mayor in 1917.

Hague was certainly very good at employing the "cemetery" vote and physical force when the electoral situation was sufficiently dire. But the basis of his control was patronage jobs for his supporters and the above-mentioned reforms. Hague ran a tight ship and was a man of considerable administrative ability. In the 1940s, after Republican-controlled state government had made poll watching a much more important business than it had been, Hague still triumphed with large majorities.

Hague's pride and joy, however, was the city's medical center, whose functions he supervised with fanatical zeal. There were plenty of questions surrounding the financing of its construction. (Critics called it the nation's first hospital "built of 100 percent solid steal.") But the citizens of Jersey City loved it. "Have your baby or your operation on Mayor Hague" was the saying.

Of course, Hague certainly did not forget his own needs. For three decades, he presided over his fiefdom. No one knows how much Hague plundered personally from the city's treasury, although toward the end of his career he admitted to a net worth of $8 million. (State investigators believed it was much higher.)

Hague's power was finally broken in November 1949 when his candidate lost the governorship. Hague himself had been out of the mayoralty for two years, passing the office to a nephew he hoped to use as a puppet. Thanks to a lawsuit filed by former city employees seeking to recover an estimated $15 million they had been forced to pay as dues to his machine over the years, Hague was essentially exiled from New Jersey. When he finally died on New Year's Day, 1956, his funeral was sparsely attended. There were a few who remembered, however. One woman held a sign that read, "God have mercy on his sinful, greedy soul."

◆ **EXHIBITS:** A portrait of Hague hangs in the city council chambers. ◆ **LOCATION:** Jersey City Hall is at 280 Grove St. in downtown Jersey City. The Medical Center still stands at Baldwin Avenue and Montgomery Street. ◆ **HOURS:** Monday–Friday, 9–4. ◆ **ADMISSION:** None. ◆ **TELEPHONE:** City clerk's office: (201) 547-5150.

Memorial to Dean McNulty, "the church builder."

DEAN MCNULTY

PATERSON

DEAN WILLIAM MCNULTY MEMORIAL AND CHURCH OF ST. JOHN THE BAPTIST

The Irish came early to Paterson, which Alexander Hamilton began developing as an industrial area in the 1790s because of the nearby Great Falls on the Passaic River. The Dutch and German farmers in the surrounding countryside had little desire to work in the dark, dangerous mills, so the mill owners began importing Irish laborers nearly a half-century before the potato famine.

The town itself is named for William Paterson, a native of county Antrim, signer of the Constitution and governor of New Jersey. Eventually, Paterson became a hotbed of union organizing among its heavily Irish workforce. (*See* Haledon, New Jersey.)

Paterson's industries attracted a great many Irish immigrants in the 19th century. Dean William McNulty, a native of Ballyshannon, county Down, was one of the greatest. Born in 1829, he immigrated to New York City in 1850 and graduated from Fordham University, being ordained a priest in 1857. Six years later he was appointed pastor of St. John's Parish in Paterson and immediately set about construction of the Church of St. John the Baptist. It was completed 14 years later, and today it is still distinguished by the tallest church steeple in Paterson.

But McNulty built many, many other churches throughout New Jersey. (He became known as "the church builder.") He also built schools, hospitals, orphanages, and homes for the aged. He died in 1922 at age 93. His funeral was recorded as probably the largest public gathering seen in northern New Jersey up to that time.

&· EXHIBITS: Dean McNulty's grave is in the churchyard at the right as you face the church. The bronze statue at the grave depicts him seated on a bench, head bent over, listening to a small boy typical of the children he loved. &· LOCATION: The church is at the corner of Main and Grand streets in downtown Paterson. &· HOURS: Dawn to dusk. &· ADMISSION: None. &· TELEPHONE: (201) 345-4070.

PATERSON MUSEUM

"A fantastic scheme of a civilian landsman!" exclaimed Secretary of the Navy George M. Robeson in 1875 when he was first heard about a New Jersey Irishman's idea for a warship that would travel *beneath* the sea. Capt. Edward Simpson told John Philip Holland that "it was very uphill work to put anything through in Washington." That indeed proved to be an understatement, but Holland was persistent, and his idea would revolutionize naval warfare forever.

Submarines were not a completely new idea in the decade after the Civil War. David Bushnell's stubby *Turtle*, a single-man, hand-crank-operated machine, attempted unsuccessfully to sink a British warship in New York harbor as far back as the American Revolution. Holland also certainly heard of the gallant but tragic Confederate submersible *Hunley*, which sank while making the first successful torpedo attack on a surface warship.

Holland was born in Liscannor Bay, county Clare around 1840, the son of coastguardsman. His education was elementary, but he became a fine self-taught draftsman and engineer. Early on he seems to have developed a fascination with submarines. He saw this as the one weapon capable of bringing low England's mighty navy, so she could be "retarded in her designs upon the other peoples of the world."

Holland secured work as a schoolteacher in Paterson soon after his arrival in the United States in 1872. He still devoted much of his free time, however, to designing submarines. A friend encouraged him to submit his design to the U.S. Navy in 1875, but he met with the rebuff described earlier. Holland then turned to a less reputable source of funding for his scheme: the Irish Republican Brotherhood, the Fenians.

The Fenian movement had splintered and gone into some eclipse after the failure of its 1866 invasion of Canada and the crushing of the movement in Ireland itself. By the 1870s, however, many of the leaders imprisoned in Ireland, such as Jeremiah O'Donovan Rossa, were released and made their way to the United States, where they resolved to renew the struggle to free their homeland.

After Holland successfully demonstrated a scale model of his craft to Fenian leaders at Coney Island, the movement set aside $6,000 from its "skirmishing fund" to construct "Boat No. 1," Holland's first working submarine. The first effort, in 1878, was a failure, with the 14-foot craft sinking to the bottom of the Passaic River because a worker had neglected to install two screws in the floor and water rushed in. (Fortunately, no one was aboard.)

Once the sub was raised, pumped out, and refloated, however, Holland took her on her first voyage in the same river. The sub dove and ran reasonably well, with Holland popping up smiling when the hatch was opened at the end of the voyage. The first modern submarine thus passed its supreme test: it had come back up. The Fenians thus invested more money for a larger, more powerful boat, one suitable for military operations.

The plan for using the submarine involved hiding it aboard a conventional steamship, which would then drop anchor near where some British warships were based. The submarine would then launch through a "sea door" and wreak havoc among the unsuspecting men-of-war. The submarine would then return to the "mother ship."

The practicality of this James Bond-like scheme given the technology available in the 19th century is open to question, but it eerily foreshadowed the kind of special operations submarine warfare that is now standard practice in the major navies of the world. After many delays, the new boat was launched into the Hudson River in May 1881. The source of Holland's financial backing was well known (Holland, however, would admit nothing), and a *New York Sun* reporter gave the submarine the only name it ever had: the *Fenian Ram.*

Holland had deduced that the ideal design for his craft was the shape of a dolphin. Indeed, the *Fenian Ram* looked like a floating cigar, tapered at both ends. Holland's deduction was absolutely correct, although it would

Dubbed the "Fenian Ram," John Holland's creation is now on display in the Paterson Museum.

not be until 1954 and the launching of the U.S. Navy's *Albacore* that his design would become the standard for submarines worldwide.

Just as the *Fenian Ram* was being perfected, however, the Fenians themselves were coming apart. One night in 1883, a group of dissidents stole the boat from its mooring place in New Jersey and towed it to New Haven, Connecticut, where they tried unsuccessfully to operate her. Frustrated, they abandoned the craft in an old brass factory. Holland never again bothered with his backers, nor they with him.

After years of trial and error and fruitlessly endeavoring to interest Washington officialdom, Holland finally had a sixth submarine commissioned by the navy in 1900. Unfortunately, the USS *Holland* was not the start of something big. The navy used the boat as a trainer before it was struck from the active list in 1910.

Holland never made any money from his invention. He fell out with his partners in the Electric Boat Company and failed in his effort to set up his own business. Toward the end of his life, Holland became horrified at the monstrous possibilities of his invention. He died on August 12, 1914, just before he would have seen his worst fears realized in the First World War.

  EXHIBITS: Both *Holland* I (the first submarine) and *Holland II* (the *Fenian Ram*) are on permanent display.   LOCATION: 2 Market St. at Spruce Street.   HOURS: Tuesday–Friday, 10–4; Saturday–Sunday, 12:30–4:30. Closed Mondays.   ADMISSION: Suggested donation $1.   TELEPHONE: (201) 881-3874.

N E W Y O R K

CHARTER DAY COMMEMORATION

Anyone who has read the novels of William Kennedy (*Ironweed, Billy Phelan's Greatest Game*) knows the New York State capital of Albany is a very Irish city. According to Kennedy's history of his home town, *O Albany!*, the Irish came first to dig the Erie Canal in 1818. They stayed on to man the labor-hungry foundries and cement factories of northern New York state.

And long after just about every other Irish big city political machine had gone the way of the horse and buggy, Albany's, under the leadership of local legend Daniel O'Connell, soldiered on. O'Connell was the undisputed political boss of Albany from 1921 until his death in 1977, a longer reign by far than those of Murphy in New York and, Curley in Boston, and Daley in Chicago. The machine still sputters on to some extent, although it has more competition these days.

It should not be surprising, therefore, that the man who started it all was Irish. On October 14, 1683, Thomas Dongan convened the first popular assembly, the forerunner of today's state legislature, in the colony of New York. That assembly framed a Charter of Liberties and Privileges that proclaimed religious freedom, the right to a trial by jury, and immunity from arbitrary arrest. Dongan's charter served as the basis for the New York State Constitution, and some elements were later incorporated in the United States Constitution.

Dongan was a privileged man. He was born in the manor house of Castletown, county Kildare, in 1634. He was the product of a distinguished Anglo-Irish family, although Dongan himself was raised a Catholic. The family were royalists in the English civil war, and when Cromwell arrived in Ireland in 1649, 15-year-old Thomas and his brother fled to

France. There, they joined the many "Wild Geese" (Irish who became mercenaries in just about every continental army in the 17th century).

While in the French army, Dongan made the acquaintance of the exiled James, duke of York, a fellow Catholic and the future King James II of England and Scotland. This connection served him well upon the restoration of the monarchy following Cromwell's death. In 1678, 29 years after he fled, James' brother, King Charles II, called Dongan home. After a stint as lieutenant governor of Tangier, Dongan was named a vice admiral in the Royal Navy and governor of the colony of New York, which James had received from his brother after British forces seized it from the Dutch in 1664.

The colony Dongan found upon his arrival was racked with disputes over taxes and enmity between the established Dutch settlers and the new English overlords. The intrigues of the French and their Indian allies also complicated matters.

Dongan's immediate task was to establish a recognized system of governance for the colony. To that end, he established a local assembly and organized elections for it. He granted charters for the colony of New York and, on July 22, 1686, chartered the city of Albany, located at the headwaters of the Hudson River on what was then the frontier.

After seeing what religious intolerance had done in his native Ireland and England, Dongan made establishment of religious freedom for all a top priority. This was a radical step for the time, and when colonists bridled at including Jews in this declaration, Dongan was forced to back down a bit. At the same time, however, he placed New York's small Jewish colony under his personal protection, allowing it to open a synagogue and worship freely.

Dongan's term as governor did not last long. Although King James II was a Catholic himself, he was acutely sensitive to Protestant feeling, and in 1687 felt compelled to remove Dongan and replace him with a Protestant. Instead of returning to England, Dongan settled on Long Island. It was just as well. James was overthrown barely a year later in the Glorious Revolution.

Anti-Catholic fever gripped England and the colonies in the months and years immediately following James's overthrow. Papist plots were thought to be everywhere, and Dongan found himself suspected of being at the heart of all manner of conspiracies. A warrant was soon out for his arrest, but he escaped to the dubious safety of England in 1691.

There, he repeatedly and unsuccessfully petitioned for payment of back salary owed him as governor.

Naturally, the government of William and Mary thought itself extremely generous to merely let Dongan remain at liberty, and he received nothing. Upon the death of his brother William in 1698, Thomas Dongan became earl of Limerick. The title was an empty honor, however, since the family estates in Ireland had long since been seized. He died virtually penniless in 1715.

There are only a few traces of Thomas Dongan left in today's New York State. On Staten Island, there are the neighborhoods of Castleton, named for his estate, and Dongan Hills. There is also a Dongan Street. In Albany, American Legion Post 1610 erected a small marker to commemorate him in 1976.

But every July, on the Saturday closest to July 22, the city of Albany celebrates Charter Day with bands, floats, and marchers to commemorate Gov. Thomas Dongan and his farseeing charter.

❧ EXHIBITS: Dongan's charter for the city of Albany is in the custody of the Albany County Hall of Records, where it is occasionally on display. It can be viewed privately by special arrangement with the Records Management Office. The date of the Charter Day celebration changes each year, usually occurring on the Saturday closest to July 22. Call the mayor's office for exact date, (518) 434-5100. ❧ LOCATION: Albany County Hall of Records, 250 South Pearl St., Albany, NY 12202. ❧ HOURS: 9–5. ❧ ADMISSION: Free ❧ TELEPHONE: (518) 447-4500.

EAST DURHAM

IRISH-AMERICAN HERITAGE MUSEUM

In all of the United States and Canada, this is the only private, nonprofit museum dedicated exclusively to the history and culture of the Irish in America. Located in a completely renovated 1850s farmhouse, the museum contains more than 2,000 square feet of gallery space and presents exhibits, readings, and lectures in Irish and Irish-American history, poetry, art, music, dance, and Gaelic language.

Founded in 1988 with the help of a state grant and chartered by the board of regents of the state of New York, the museum has been rapidly building its collection of photographs, prints, artworks, musical instruments, and period clothing. The museum's headquarters is located in Albany, and an archives has been established at the College of Saint Rose near Albany.

East Durham is an appropriate site for the museum. Although the Catskill resorts are usually associated in the public imagination with Jewish-Americans, the Irish are a strong presence as well, and Greene County has long billed itself as "Ireland's 33rd County." The first Irish in any numbers probably came to this area in the 1920s, possibly to manufacture bootleg liquor during Prohibition.

Over the years, resorts such as the Shamrock House and the O'Neill House have provided inexpensive vacations not far from home for generations of Irish-American working-class families from New York City and elsewhere.

❧ EXHIBITS: Call ahead for current exhibits. The museum's shop offers articles and publications related to exhibits and Irish history and culture. ❧ LOCATION: The museum is on Route 145, East Durham, in the Catskills resort area. Museum headquarters are located at 19 Clinton Ave., in the Albany Arts District. The museum's archive is located at the College of Saint Rose. ❧ HOURS: Memorial Day to Labor Day, Tuesday–Sunday, 10–4. Labor Day to Columbus Day, Friday–Sunday, 10–4. Other times, call for an appointment. ❧ ADMISSION: $3.50 adults; $2 for senior citizens and children under 12; $9 for families. ❧ TELEPHONE: East Durham: (518) 634-7497; Albany: (518) 432-6598.

JOHNSTOWN

JOHNSON HALL STATE HISTORIC SITE

As late as the middle of the 18th century, New York was far and away the least developed of the major English colonies in the New World. With a total population of only 80,000 (compared with 275,000 in Virginia and 180,000 in Massachusetts), it was only the sixth largest among the 13 colonies. Also, almost all of that population was centered in New York City. The Hudson Valley was occupied by the vast estates of Dutch patroon families (such as the Roosevelts). West of Albany, the land stretched away toward Lake Erie in vast wilderness, populated mostly by the strong Iroquois confederacy.

It was into this forbidding landscape that 22-year-old William Johnson plunged in 1737. Johnson's mother, Anne Warren, was the daughter of an important Protestant landowning family in county Meath. His father, however, was a Catholic tenant farmer on the estate. Young Johnson, according to historian James H. Tully, Jr.,

> realized early he was not being treated as well as his Warren cousins in the family manor; it took no unusual power to discern that the only people who could remain Catholic in the British Empire were peasants, priests and martyrs. He, accordingly, abandoned his Catholic faith, retained a vague belief in God, and outwardly adopted the precepts of the Church of England.

It must have been a smart move at the time, for young Johnson was almost immediately invited by his wealthy uncle Peter Warren to manage the latter's new estates in the Mohawk River valley of New York. Upon arrival, he immediately established a trading post.

Tully speculates that perhaps it was Johnson's own memories of mistreatment in Ireland that caused him to place a very high value on fair dealing with the Indians. When among them, he adopted Indian dress, observed their customs, and learned their language. As a consequence, he established not only good trading relations with the natives but also strong bonds of friendship with many of their leaders.

Johnson did not stay under his uncle's employ for long. Investing his profits in land purchases, he soon became the largest landowner in the Mohawk Valley, his good relations with the Indians enabling him to purchase land on very favorable terms. In time, he became not merely a friend to the Indians but also a blood brother and full-fledged member of the Mohawk nation, the only white man who could speak at the longhouse council of the Iroquois confederation.

Johnson used his influence to good effect on behalf of British interests. He allied the Iroquois with the British against the encroachment of French interests in the Mohawk Valley. In September 1755, Johnson and his Indian allies, along with a few British soldiers, decisively defeated a French force at Lake George, finally securing the Mohawk and Hudson valley's against French encroachment. For his services, Johnson was made a baronet and was entitled to call himself "Sir."

Johnson's very success in opening the Mohawk Valley, however, worked against his efforts to build ties with the Indians. As more and more settlers arrived, clashes with the Indians became more frequent. It was in 1774, while endeavoring to mediate a difficult dispute, that Johnson collapsed and died of a stroke. He was only 59.

In 1763, Johnson had contracted with noted Boston architect Samuel Fuller to raise a house for himself that would befit his baronial title and position. The result was Johnson Hall, a wooden house designed to appear as if made of stone. Johnson acquired the latest books and furnishings and laid out formal gardens.

The result was certainly impressive. A visitor to Johnson Hall wrote, "Off the river about 14 miles back, Sir William Johnson has made a new Settlement and has built a very comfortable house, having a Good Garden and field, all cleared in an Absolute Forest. . . . At this place, he is generally crowded with Indians, mostly of the Five Nations. . . ."

Johnson appears never to have formally married. By Catherine Weisenberg, a German servant of a Dutch family, he had three children—John, Ann, and Mary. After Catherine's death in 1759, he began a liaison with Mary Brant, a full-blooded Mohawk woman, by whom he had eight children. Whether Joseph Brant, the noted Mohawk leader, was Johnson's son or his brother-in-law is uncertain. Joseph was raised in Johnson Hall as Mary's brother.

After Sir William's death, Sir John Johnson endeavored to carry on his father's work. He persuaded the Mohawks to remain loyal to the Crown rather than join the revolutionaries, and he and Joseph Brant led the Indians on a series of bloody raids in the Cherry and Schoharie valleys during the Revolutionary War. After the war, however, Sir John and all the remaining family members were obliged to flee to Canada.

The Johnson family paid the price for backing the wrong side, for Johnson Hall was confiscated as Tory property in 1779. It was used as a private residence until 1906, when New York State purchased it as a historic site.

Sir William Johnson was certainly far from typical of the Irish-American experience. But he did present, in a very exotic way, an early example of the Irish-American political boss.

&ª. EXHIBITS: The house is maintained very much as it was when Sir William was in residence. There are many exhibits and a house tour. &ª. LOCATION: Johnson Hall is part of the Saratoga-Capital District Region of the New York State Parks, Recreation and Historic Preservation Office. From the New York State Thruway, take Exit 28 (Fonda). Turn left on Riverside Dr., right across the Mohawk River into Fonda. Then left on Route 5, right on Route 30A to Johnstown. Then left onto E. Main St. (Route 29), right on N. Williams St., right on Hall Ave. &ª. HOURS: Mid-May to October, Wednesday–Saturday 10–5; Sunday 1–5. Open Memorial Day, Independence Day, and Labor Day. Call for winter hours. Group tours can be arranged. &ª. ADMISSION: Free &ª. TELEPHONE: (518) 762-8712.

N E W   Y O R K   C I T Y

AL SMITH HOUSE NATIONAL HISTORIC LANDMARK

"Let's look at the record!" was New York Gov. Al Smith's trademark response to criticism, and indeed, he did build an impressive record as four-term governor of what was then far and away the largest state in the Union. With his trademark brown derby and cigar, he cut a much more plebeian figure than the debonair Jimmy Walker, who was mayor for much of the time Smith was governor.

Except for the years he spent in Albany as governor, Smith was a lifelong Manhattan resident. The site of his birthplace at 174 South Sreet is now occupied by the Al Smith Houses, a public housing development. The tenement was in the shadow of the brooklyn Bridge, which was under construction in the early years of Smith's boyhood. "The bridge and I grew up together," he often said.

Some historians have enjoyed pointing out that Smith—for many the quintessential "Irish" New York politician—had a fairly thin Irish background. True, his father, also Alfred Emmanuel Smith, was of Italian ancestry on his father's side and German ancestry on his mother's. The younger Smith's maternal grandfather was an Irish Catholic tailor who married a woman of English Protestant stock.

But "Irish" identity has always been exceedingly elastic. Eamon De Valera (*see* Rochester, New York), of course, had a Spanish father and an Irish mother. William Smith O'Brien, one of the leaders of the abortive 1848 uprising, was a Harrow-educated Protestant and a member of Parliament for many years and had all the attributes of a stuffy Victorian gentleman. Erskine Childers, the IRA's great propagandist of the Irish War of Independence, was an Englishman. The fact is that Al Smith clearly chose to identify himself with his Irish ancestry and the public accepted him as such.

Smith started out in politics as an opponent of Tammany Hall. (His mentor was one of those saloon-keeper politicians so common in 19th-century America named Thomas Foley, after whom nearby Foley Square is named.) Smith later reconciled to Tammany, however, and served a distinguished career in the state Assembly, where he eventually became Speaker.

Smith made his name investigating the Triangle Shirt Waist Factory fire of 1911, a tragedy that killed 146 workers. Out of this disaster came an avalanche of progressive legislation, most of it shepherded through the legislature by Smith, that limited working hours and restricted sweat shops. The high profile he achieved from the investigation made him the natural Democratic candidate for governor in 1918. Bucking the national Republican tide, Smith won by 15,000 votes.

Smith would serve four two-year terms as the state's chief executive. (He was defeated in 1920 and returned in 1922.) Smith had little trouble securing the 1928 Democratic presidential nomination, the first Roman Catholic to receive a major party endorsement.

Smith's defeat that year is usually written up as a triumph of anti-Catholic bigotry and narrow-mindedness, and Smith himself was indeed shaken by the virulence of the attacks on his Catholicism. The true reason for his defeat, however, was Republican prosperity, then reaching its pre-Depression peak. Despite the fact that New York was one of the best-run states in the nation, Smith had few issues to use against Herbert Hoover. Smith's campaign was also disorganized and badly managed. He was crushed, receiving only 15 million votes to Hoover's 21.4 million.

Smith's later years were embittered. He ran unsuccessfully for the Democratic nomination in 1932 and feuded with the winner (and his successor as governor), Franklin D. Roosevelt. Later, he attacked the New Deal as socialistic, costing Smith much of his remaining public support. He died in 1944.

&& **EXHIBITS:** A plaque marks the 25 Oliver Street house. A statue of Smith stands not far away in Al Smith Park on Catherine St. It is by Charles Keck (who also did the Father Duffy Memorial) and was dedicated in 1945 just after Smith's death. It portrays Smith standing at a podium. On the base are inscribed the words of "The Sidewalks of New York," his political theme song. && **LOCATION:** The three-story brick row house at 25 Oliver Street, built in the late 1800s, served as Smith's home from 1909 until 1924. Earlier, he had resided across the street at 28 Oliver Street. Both houses remain privately owned and are not open to the public. && **HOURS:** Dawn to dusk. && **ADMISSION:** None.

AMERICAN IRISH HISTORICAL SOCIETY

"That the world may know" is the motto of this venerable institution, founded in 1897 in order to set the record straight on the history of the Irish in America.

At the time of the society's founding, the image of the Irish in the United States in histories written by "establishment" historians tended to be negative, to say the least. "In stereotype, the men were hod-carriers, the women servant girls, and the children raised up into a slum world of lawlessness, fighting saloons, and corrupt political machines," writes novelist Thomas Flanagan in his introduction to the book *The American Irish Revival: A Decade of The Recorder, 1974–1983.* "In a word, they were a people without a culture. . . ."

The society sought to correct that by sponsoring research into the contributions to American life of men and women of Irish ancestry, both Catholic and Protestant. (President Theodore Roosevelt, who had some distant Irish roots, was a member.)

The society continues to fulfill this mission, publishing its quarterly journal, *The Recorder.* It also regularly sponsors poetry readings, historical panels and maintains an excellent library of books and periodicals relating to Irish American history.

&& **EXHIBITS:** Changing exhibits and events. Call for information. && **LOCATION:** 911 5th Ave., across the street from the Metropolitan Museum of Art. && **HOURS:** 10:30–5:30 weekdays. (Ring the bell in front.) Call in advance to conduct research. && **ADMISSION:** None, but donations appreciated. Membership information is available. && **TELEPHONE:** (212) 288-2263.

*The American
Irish Historical
Society was
founded in 1897 to
establish and
preserve the
history of the Irish
in America.*

ELLIS ISLAND, CASTLE CLINTON, STATUE OF LIBERTY, SOUTH STREET SEAPORT

The Famine immigrants were not the first Irish to immigrate to what is now the United States. Small numbers of Irish-Catholics had arrived in the decades before the 1840s. Some, such as Commodore John Barry and Charles Carroll of Carrollton (*see* Philadelphia, Pennsylvania and Annapolis and Baltimore, Maryland, respectively) achieved prominence. Others were convicts, rebels, or other undesirable forcibly transported by the English authorities. Irish Presbyterians from Ulster had arrived in large numbers throughout the 18th century. Small numbers of other denominations, such as Quakers and Methodists, also found their way to the Americas.

Larger-scale immigration to the United States actually began in the 1830s. The Great Famine was just that—simply a larger famine than the

smaller-scale ones that had come in the previous decade. A cholera epidemic in the 1830s acted as a further spur to leave. (Ireland's population
still has not recovered from the effects of the Great Famine. In 1840, the
whole island of Ireland had around 8 million souls, compared with around
4 million today. *See* Boston, Massachusetts, for more on the famine.)

So bitter did many famine emigrants feel toward Britain's clumsy and
callous handling of the famine that they refused to refer to themselves as
"emigrants" but instead dubbed themselves "exiles." "God brought the
potato blight," went one popular saying, "but it was England that brought
the famine."

Although Irish immigration never again reached the heights seen during the famine, it remained steady through the rest of the 19th and into the
20th centuries. The "land war" and "little famines" of the 1870s and 1880s
turned many Irish tenant farmers out of their modest homes, as did
continuing political unrest. Emigration continued after the Second World
War until the 1965 immigration act essentially cut it off. The 1980s saw a
new wave of immigrants, this time illegal, arriving on America's shores.

About 250,000 Irish immigrants arrived in the United States between
1830 and 1840. Between 1840 and 1850, however, the famine swelled the
number to over 800,000. Boston was a popular port of arrival, since it
usually was the cheapest fare from Irish ports. And since Britain wanted to
encourage settlement of the English-speaking dominions beyond the seas,
many immigrants took advantage of subsidized fares to Canada, then
crossed the border into the United States. Since these immigrants were
listed as coming from Canada rather than Ireland, the actual number of
Irish immigrants arriving in the United States must have been larger than
the officials numbers indicate.

Immigration was an unorganized affair in the 1840s. Most of the
famine immigrants came ashore at what is now the South Street Seaport
development near the Brooklyn Bridge. There, the immigrants were at the
mercy of the many hucksters and con men who sought to take advantage of
the "greenhorns." Many Irish were unwittingly relieved of what small
money and possessions they had by these tricksters.

On August 3, 1855, however, the state of New York opened Castle
Garden, a former fort and public arena at the southern tip of Manhattan, as
the first true immigrant station in the country. Fenced off from the rest of
the Battery, it afforded the immigrants some protection from the riff-raff
the earlier generation had to contend with. Here, generally reliable information about boarding houses, train fares, and travel routes were available
to the newcomers, who were also given a general medical examination.
Between 1855 and 1889, more than eight million immigrants, two out of
every three persons entering the United States in those years, passed
through Castle Garden.

Opened in 1855, Castle Garden was the first true immigrant station in the United States.

As the number of immigrants increased, however, the federal government took jurisdiction over immigration away from the state and on January 1, 1892, a purpose-built immigration station was ready for use on Ellis Island in New York Harbor. Five years later, the wooden buildings burned to the ground, taking with them all the immigration records from 1855 to 1890.

Although Ellis Island is usually identified more closely with Jewish and Italian immigration, it was a 15-year-old Irish schoolgirl, Annie Moore, who was the first newcomer to be officially processed through the new station. Over its next 62 years of operation, Ellis Island would welcome nearly 5 million Irish men and woman through its gates.

The Statue of Liberty welcomed many of these immigrants to their new home, of course. The brainchild of French citizens who wished to recall the historic alliance with the United States, the statue was dedicated by Pres. Grover Cleveland on October 28, 1886.

One of the speakers on that day was John L. O'Sullivan, the son of an Irish immigrant. As editor of the *United States Magazine and Democratic Review* in the late 1830s and early 1840s, O'Sullivan is credited with coining the phrase "manifest destiny" to describe what many felt was America's ordained mission to rule over all of North America. He later served as American ambassador to Portugal, one of the first Irish-Americans to receive such an appointment.

“ **EXHIBITS:** South Street Seaport Museum features several old sailing ships that are open to the public, as well as changing museum exhibits. Castle Garden has a small museum with changing exhibits reflecting its many different functions through history. The base of the Statue of Liberty contains a Museum of Immigration, with each ethnic group having its own display. After years of neglect following its closing in 1954, Ellis Island was spectacularly restored in time for its centennial in 1992. A statue of Annie Moore has been placed there. (A duplicate has recently been placed at Cobh, county Cork, the port of embarkation for most emigrants from Ireland when it was known as Queenstown.) ᲖᲐ HOURS: Tickets for ferries are sold between 8:30 and 3:30. Call for ferry sailing times. South Street Seaport Museum is open 10–6 seven days a week. ᲖᲐ LOCATION: South Street Seaport, a shopping center/museum, is located in the waterfront, just south of the Brooklyn Bridge at South Street and Fulton Street Castle Garden is located in the Battery at the southern tip of Manhattan. Inside the old fort's walls, visitors can purchase tickets for a ferry to Liberty Island and Ellis Island. ᲖᲐ ADMISSION: Castle Garden: free; Liberty Island/Ellis Island: $7 adults; $5 seniors; $3 children. South Street Seaport Museum: $5 adults; $4 seniors; $3 children; $2 children. ᲖᲐ TELEPHONE: Castle Garden: (212) 344-7220; Liberty Island/Ellis Island: (212) 269-5755. South Street Seaport: (212) 669-9400. Big Onion tours regularly offers "Irish Ellis Island" tours. Call (212) 439-1090 for details.

FIFTH AVENUE

Every March 17, the "Queen of Avenues" hosts the world's largest and oldest St. Patrick's Day Parade. The first parade was recorded in 1779, when the Volunteers of Ireland, a Loyalist (or Tory) regiment in British service held a commemoration. According to its organizers, the Ancient Order of Hibernians, the parade has been held annually ever since, except for one or two cancellations due to exceptionally appalling weather.

For all the green hats, banners, bands and good-natured blarney, however, political controversy has always simmered just below the surface of this event. John Cardinal O'Connor absented himself from his customary place on the steps of St. Patrick's Cathedral in the late 1980s because the Hibernians had chosen as grand marshal a man alleged to have ties to the IRA. In 1991, Mayor David Dinkins dodged flying beer bottles and verbal abuse when he insisted on marching with a group of Irish-American homosexual rights activists. (A subsequent court decision said parade organizers had a right to ban the gay marchers.)

In recent years, New York has canceled such one-time staple events as the Labor Day Parade and the Veterans Day Parade due to lack of interest. Despite the fact that the Irish are no longer much of a factor in New York City politics, the St. Patrick's Day Parade seems unlikely to suffer any similar fate.

ᲖᲐ EXHIBITS: The green line that decorates the parade route every year requires 40 gallons of paint. ᲖᲐ LOCATION: Fifth Avenue, from 44th to 86th streets. ᲖᲐ HOURS: Parade steps off at 11 A.M. ᲖᲐ ADMISSION: Free

FIRE DEPARTMENT MUSEUM

In an earlier New York, civil service jobs were largely divided up by ethnicity. Italians "had" the Sanitation Department; Jews were dominant in the school system; and the Irish ran the police and fire departments. Of course, these demarcations were never hard and fast, even if the system's glory days, but in the public imagination, they held true. (*See* Police Academy Museum, New York City.)

❧ **EXHIBITS:** The Fire Department Museum is a comprehensive history of firefighting in New York City, with several beautifully restored old fire engines on display. ❧ **LOCATION:** 270 Spring St. ❧ **HOURS:** Monday–Friday 10–4. ❧ **ADMISSION:** Free ❧ **TELEPHONE:** (212) 691-1303

FIVE POINTS SITE

In the 1973 movie *The Sting,* con man Johnny Hooker (Robert Redford) attempts to worm his way into the confidence of Irishman Doyle Lonigan (Robert Shaw) by telling him that he, Hooker, was raised in New York, in "a place called Five Points." Hooker was raised in no such place, of course, though he knows Lonigan was. Modern movie audiences frequently don't understand the reference, but in late 19th and early 20th century New York, "Five Points" conjured up images of the worst slums imaginable.

In the early 1800s, Five Points was virtually a swamp, with a brewery nearby. The Irish immigrants flooding into the country at the nearby South Street Seaport made their homes here because they could afford little else. Later in the 19th century, gangs made up mostly of Irish immigrants terrorized the area, making it one of the most violent places in an already violent city. Tourists actually visited it to "see how the other half lives." Today, Five points is much quieter, standing in the shadow of the city's court complex, where the brewery once stood.

❧ **LOCATION:** The intersection of Baxter, Park, and Worth streets just behind the New York County Court House in Foley Square.

FATHER FRANCIS J. DUFFY MEMORIAL

The Canadian-born Francis J. Duffy achieved immortality as the chaplain of the famed "Fighting 69th" during its service in France during World War I. A lesser known aspect of his life was his service as pastor of Holy Cross Church on West 42nd St., which made him a friend and confidante of producers, directors, and actors, many of them non-Catholics.

Duffy's paternal grandfather immigrated to Cobourg, Ontario about 1845 from Carrickmacross, county Monaghan. His maternal grandparents, Thomas and Mary (Buckley) Ready came from counties Kings and Roscommon, respectively. Francis, born in 1971, was the third of 11 children born to Patrick Duffy and Mary Ready. Young Francis was early destined for the priesthood because his sickly nature made him unfit to work the long hours in the local woolen mills.

Ordained in 1896, Duffy moved his parents to New York two years later and he himself became a naturalized American citizen in 1902. He got his first taste of army life as the post chaplain among some soldiers stationed at Montauk Point during the Spanish-American War. He was serving as the pastor of Our Savior Parish in the Bronx when Cardinal Farley nominated him as chaplain of the "Fighting 69th" in 1912. This National Guard unit had been the pride of Irish New Yorkers since before the Civil War, when its commander, Michael Corcoran (see Richmond, Virginia) refused to parade the regiment for the visiting Prince of Wales. Four years later, Duffy accompanied the unit on its first overseas deployment, against the Mexican bandit Pancho Villa.

The real test for Father Duffy came a year later, however, when the United States entered World War I. Many Irish-Americans were opposed to American involvement in the war, which they saw as England's fight. Duffy toured the city, urging Irish immigrants and Irish-Americans to prove their Americanism, just as they had done in the Civil War, by fighting. "Don't join the 69th unless you want to be among the first to go to France," he hollered from a sound truck in the Bronx.

He wasn't exaggerating. The 69th, redesignated the 165th Regiment for organizational purposes, embarked on October 29, 1917, as part of the famed "Rainbow Division," drawn from units all across the country. The church hierarchy worried that contact with non-Catholics would be detrimental to the spiritual welfare of the Irish-Americans in the 69th, but Duffy wasn't concerned. "The way the Clergy of different churches got along together in peace and harmony in this division would be a scandal to pious minds," he wrote later.

Always in the thick of the fighting, Fr. Duffy became known as the "Iron Man" and "Front Line" Duffy. (He was gassed while at the front, an experience that did nothing for his frail health.) He was the confessor, confidant, and inspiration for all the men of the division, regardless of faith. He endeavored to get to know every soldier personally, and he grieved deeply at the high number of casualties.

Duffy returned from the war a hero: the Distinguished Service Cross and the Croix de Guerre with palm were among his decorations. He was in constant demand as a public speaker and to lend his name to worthy causes. For all his celebrity, however, he gave priority to his priestly duties, having been appointed pastor of Holy Cross in 1920. In addition to the

The inspiration behind the "Fighting 69th" unit, Father Francis Duffy.

famous and well-known, he also moved among the poor and the down-and-out in Times Square. "Why does God make sinners so nice?" was one of his many quips.

For all the rigors of his life, however, Father Duffy never got over the essentially frail nature of his health, and he died in 1932 of colitis, only 61 years of age. His military funeral at St. Patrick's Cathedral was a major event, attended by 25,000 mourners and featuring eulogies by New York Gov. Franklin D. Roosevelt and Pres. Herbert Hoover.

❧ **EXHIBITS:** The Duffy Memorial was erected five years after Duffy's death by a committee chaired by William "Wild Bill" Donovan, the famed former commander of the Fighting 69th and future head of the wartime Office of Strategic Services. It features a life-sized statue of the priest in his World War I "doughboy" uniform, and is the work of sculptor Charles Keck. ❧ **LOCATION:** Just a few feet north of the Cohan memorial (see next entry) in what is now known as Duffy Square, West 47th Street between Broadway and Seventh Avenue.

GEORGE M. COHAN MEMORIAL

"Vaudeville" was a combination of song, dance, animal, and acrobatic acts that served as the main form of American popular entertainment between roughly 1875 and the onset of the radio age in 1925. Jews there were aplenty in vaudeville. The Irish and the Irish-Americans, however, were no strangers to the vaudeville stage either. (*See* Jackie Gleason Theater, Miami Florida, for more on the Irish in vaudeville.)

The Four Cohans were among the most successful of vaudeville acts early in this century. Jeremiah John Cohan early on rejected the career of a harnessmaker that his father had planned for him in favor of one as a traveling performer. The father, born Michael Keohane in county Cork, simplified the spelling of the family name after arriving in this country in the 1840s.

Jerry, as the younger Cohan was known, married Nellie Costigan of Philadelphia and she became his theatrical partner. Their first child, a daughter, died in infancy. But Josephine, who became a talented dancer, soon came along. She, along with George Michael, born in 1878 in Providence, joined their parents on the stage. In his first appearance, baby George was carried onstage in his mother's arms in a sketch written by his father.

The family act was extremely successful, achieving top billing by the turn of the century. George, who had left school at an early age, matured quickly into a natural showman. His closing lines to the audience at the end of every performance, "My mother thanks you. My father thanks you. My sister thanks you. And I thank you," became famous. He published his first song ("Why Did Nellie Leave Her Home?") at the age of 16.

Cohan's first efforts at writing and directing shows were not successful. Once he became partners with Sam Harris, however, the duo became unstoppable. Their first effort, *Little Johnnie Jones*, about an American jockey accused of throwing the English Derby, featured "Give My Regards to Broadway" and "Yankee Doodle Boy," two songs which have since become American standards. *Forty five Minutes from Broadway* featured, not only the title song, but "Mary is a Grand Old Name." *George Washington Jr.* featured "You're a Grand Old Flag."

Cohan's main contribution to the theater, apart from his musical numbers, was the drive and energy of his shows, so different from the gooey melodramas that then dominated the American stage. Critics frequently panned his "flag-waving," but the audiences loved it.

For many Americans, in fact, Cohan was the typical Irish-American: a genial, friendly sort, always ready with a song or a quip, a person who, while unmistakably proud of his Irish ancestry, was nevertheless 110 percent American.

James Cagney as George M. Cohan in Yankee Doodle Dandy. (*Museum of Modern Art*)

It was therefore somewhat ironic that Cohan was immortalized on screen by James Cagney, a man with whom he actually had little in common aside from Irish background. Cagney achieved fame by representing the dark side of the Irish-American dream: the wise-cracking, pistol-packing gangster.

Although Cagney always hoped he would be remembered primarily for the kind of song-and-dance work he displayed in *Yankee Doodle Dandy* (1942), he was destined to be recalled as the tough guy of *Public Enemy* (1931) and *Angels With Dirty Faces* (1938).

Cagney's liberal politics in the late 1930s placed him under suspicion of being a Communist. The charge was ridiculous, but Cagney feared it was hurting his career. (He lost the role of Knute Rockne to Pat O'Brien in *Knute Rockne: All American* because Cagney had signed an anti-Franco petition during the Spanish Civil War. *See* South Bend, Indiana.) Cagney thought that appearing in the flag-waving Cohan spectacular would lift the cloud of suspicion, which it certainly did.

As for Cohan's career, after 1920, he found himself in eclipse. He took management's side in the bitter 1919 actors strike (which gave birth to the union Actors' Equity). Frustrated, Cohan vowed to retire from show business.

He relented a few years later, however, and returned to producing and directing, but without his former success. He enjoyed a revival in popularity in the 1930s, not as a songwriter, but as an actor in musicals and plays written by others. He played the genial father in his fellow Celt Eugene O'Neill's only comedy *Ah Wilderness!* and he successfully essayed the daring role of President Franklin D. Roosevelt in the 1937 production of *I'd Rather Be Right.*

Cohan's career was effectively at a close, however. Congress, mindful of approaching war, presented him with a special gold medal in 1940 in commemoration of "You're a Grand Old Flag," his most popular song. He lived just long enough to see himself immortalized in "Yankee Doodle Dandy," a movie he greatly enjoyed.

&⮞ EXHIBITS: The statue of Cohan, which overlooks the Broadway he did so much to help create, is the work of sculptor George Lober and was erected in 1959. &⮞ LOCATION: West 46th and Broadway in Times Square. &⮞ HOURS: Dawn to dusk. &⮞ ADMISSION: Free

JIMMY WALKER HOME

The name Jimmy Walker conjures up images of flappers, men wearing expensive pinstripe suits with wide lapels and wide-brimmed Trilby hats. He was mayor for only six years, from 1926 to 1932, but in that short time, he made an indelible impression. A "night mayor," he seemed to spend more time in swanky nightclubs with Broadway showgirls than in his office in city hall attending to the public's business. And the city loved him for it.

Like so many other successful Irish-American politicians, Walker had a politically active father. William Henry "Billy" Walker was a native of Kilkenny, A carpenter, he came to New York in 1857, opened a lumber yard and became involved in Democratic politics. Eventually, the elder Walker was elected an alderman and later a state assemblyman. James, born in 1881, was the second son and the second of nine children that would be born to Billy and Ellen Walker.

Billy early on wanted Jimmy to go into politics, but his son was an indifferent student and preferred, of all things, writing songs. "Will You Love Me in December as You Do in May" was probably Jimmy Walker's best known composition.

Eventually, however, Billy Walker's pressure became strong enough for young Jimmy, at the age of 30, to get into the world of politics. The flamboyant style he made famous, however, demonstrated beyond doubt that he was a man whose heart remained in show business.

After serving his father as a district captain, Walker won election to the state assembly in 1909 and moved up to the state Senate in 1914. There, he attached himself to such rising stars of the Progressive wing of the Tammany Hall machine as Alfred E. Smith and Robert F. Wagner. He sponsored legislation instituting a 48-hour work week for women and minors employed in industry; a uniform gas-rate law, repealed the prohibitions on Sunday baseball and fixed the length of boxing matches at 15 rounds.

This record was creditable enough for him to secure the Democratic nomination for mayor in 1925 and he won handily. In a country enraptured with F. Scott Fitzgerald's stories of "the Jazz Age," Walker was made to order. "Beau James" and "Gentleman Jimmy," as he was known, loved leading parades, throwing out the first pitch at baseball games, appearing at the opening nights of Broadway shows and the like. His scarcely concealed affair with Betty Compton, the English-born daughter of an American wool millionaire, also lent spice to the legend.

But it was not all play and no work, for Walker's time in office was astonishingly productive. Construction began on the Triborough Bridge, the Queens-Midtown Tunnel, the West Side Highway, and a new subway line. The city's public hospitals were brought under a single administration. He handily won reelection in 1929 (over no less than Fiorello LaGuardia), despite charges of corruption and mismanagement.

Walker's past, however, began to catch up with him in 1930. As the Depression deepened, Walker's antics no longer appeared quite so funny and a state legislative commission found massive corruption and chaos in the Walker administration. Walker felt compelled to resign on September 1, 1932. The next day, he sailed for Europe.

Walker returned from his self-imposed exile three years later. He immediately secured a position as assistant counsel to the New York State Transit Commission, showing he still had powerful friends. His first wife had divorced him shortly after his resignation and Walker married Betty Compton in France. They were divorced in 1941 and she died three years later.

The death of his second wife seems to have awakened Walker's nascent spirituality. In a speech shortly before his death, Walker said "The glamour of other days I have found to be worthless tinsel, and all the allure of the world just so much seduction and deception. I now have found in religion and repentance the happiness and joy that I sought elsewhere in vain." His funeral at St. Patrick's Cathedral was a major event.

🍂 EXHIBITS: The Walker family moved into this solid three-story brownstone in 1886, five years after Jimmy's birth. It remained Jimmy's home through his mayoralty until 1934. The house is privately owned and not open to the public, though the traditional "lamps of honor," marking a mayor's residence, are on the front newel posts outside. 🍂 LOCATION: 6 St. Luke's Place, between Hudson Street and 7th Avenue.

POLICE ACADEMY MUSEUM

One of the most beloved and ubiquitous characters of American stage and screen, the Irish New York cop has become a part of American national folklore. Law enforcement in the Big Apple indeed owes a great debt to the Irish, who, at one point in the late 19th century, constituted almost 100 percent of the force.

Sociologists have speculated for years about why the Irish were attracted to low-paying civil service jobs rather than engaging in entrepreneurial activity, such as the Jews and the Italians. Perhaps the harshness of their previous life on the land, along with 19th-century England's well-known worship of the business culture, turned the Irish off to these pursuits and they sought security instead.

Irish-born officers had largely disappeared from the New York police department by the 1980s, following the virtual cut-off of immigration in 1965. The sons and grandsons (and yes, daughters and granddaughters) of Irish-born officers are still well represented in the ranks, however, as a glance at their uniform name tags will attest. And now that the immigration laws have been loosened up a bit, perhaps some Irish brogues might yet be heard in the city's precinct houses again.

🍂 EXHIBITS: The Police Academy Museum is one of the most comprehensive collections of police history on display anywhere. Exhibits range from the earliest police radios to the sophisticated equipment of today's SWAT team officers. A tour of the academy facilities is available, which includes the museum. 🍂 LOCATION: 235 E. 20th St., between Second and Third avenues. 🍂 HOURS: 9–3, Monday–Friday. 🍂 ADMISSION: Free 🍂 TELEPHONE: (212) 477-9753.

ST. JAMES CHURCH

By tradition, this brownstone Greek Revival church was the site in 1836 of the first meeting of the American branch of the Ancient Order of Hibernians (AOH), the most enduring of Irish-American fraternal organizations.

Ireland had a long history of secret societies, simply by virtue of the fact that openly anti-British organizations were not permitted. Shadowy

St. James Church, where the Ancient Order of Hibernians was founded in the early 1800s.

groups calling themselves "the Defenders" and "the Ribbonmen" roamed the Irish countryside at night in the 18th and early 19th centuries, terrorizing rack-renting landlords who evicted poor tenants.

As the number of Irish immigrants increased in the United States in the 1830s and nativist sentiment grew among Protestants, the Irish-Americans found need for mutual protection organizations in their new country as well. The early AOH was apparently such a secret society on the early model. Not until 1851, it seems, was the name "Ancient Order of Hibernians" used publicly.

Of the early activities of the AOH in the United States, little is known because reliable records have not survived. In the papers that incorporated the organization in the state of New York in 1853, the Hibernians listed themselves as a "society for benevolent and charitable purposes." They were a little bit more, however. A year later, the Hibernians saved Old St. Patrick's Cathedral from being burned by a nativist mob.

One of the great achievements of the AOH was to eliminate the intense, often violent, rivalry between Irishmen from different counties. It is hard to recall now, but there was a time when Irish people viewed themselves more as "Corkmen" or "Kerrymen" than as "Irishmen." John T. Ridge, in his excellent history of the society, *Erin's Sons in America* (1986), notes that such differences frequently exploded into violence on construction sites and the like. The AOH, by stressing a common Irish identity, did much to end such internecine strife.

Although the Hibernians as an organization did not actively involve itself in the various 19th century plots to overthrow British rule in Ireland, AOH members were frequently involved with the groups that did so, such as the Fenians and later, the Clan na Gael. Relations between the AOH and the clan, however, later became embittered over differing views on how to achieve Irish independence.

Today, the AOH is best known for organizing the annual St. Patrick's Day Parade on Fifth Avenue, a role that has recently embroiled the organization in controversy. During the administration of Mayor David Dinkins, organized homosexual rights groups insisted on marching in the parade over the vehement objection of the AOH and the New York Catholic Archdiocese. After a court fight of several years, the AOH won a federal court ruling that the parade constituted a free exercise of speech and religion that the city could not regulate.

&. **EXHIBITS:** A plaque outside the church's front entrance commemorates the founding meeting of the AOH. Another plaque at the school recalls Al Smith's attendance. &. **LOCATION:** Church at 32 James St. Rectory at 23 Oliver St. St. James School, where Gov. Al Smith (*see* elsewhere in this section) received his formal education, is at 37 St. James Pl. In 1986 the street was renamed "Ancient Order of Hibernians" Place. &. **ADMISSION:** Donations appreciated. &. **TELEPHONE:** (212) 233-0161.

ST. PATRICK'S CATHEDRAL

It is not the largest cathedral in the United States, or even in New York City. (The Episcopal Cathedral of St. John the Divine on Riverside Drive enjoys both distinctions.) But mention "the cathedral" to just about any New Yorker, regardless of nationality, and he will know immediately you are referring to St. Patrick's. It remains the spiritual heart, not only of Irish New York, but, in many ways, the city as a whole.

That was the intent of the man who built it, the great Archbishop John Hughes. When St. Patrick's was completed in 1879, many Irish complained that it was too far uptown to be reached conveniently and some dubbed it "Hughes' Folly." (The main line of settlement in those days ended around present-day 42nd Street.)

But Hughes, a far-sighted man for all his fabled conservatism, chose his site with care. He knew the city would grow up around his new church. And when it did, he wanted the church on Fifth Avenue, the premier street in America's premier city. He intended his cathedral as a statement: that Roman Catholicism, particularly Ireland's own very distinctive brand of it, had "arrived" on the American scene and intended to stay. (*See* Emmitsburg, Maryland for more on Hughes's early life.)

The then-Diocese of New York was in dire financial and organizational straits when Hughes arrived as coadjutor bishop with right of succession in 1838. He found a growing flock of mostly Irish and German immigrants struggling to come to terms with life in their new land. Although he did not formally become bishop until four years later, Hughes knew action could not be postponed, He immediately seized control of the diocese, paying off its debts and warding off the Protestant concept of "trusteeism," whereby congregations themselves owned their churches. Thus, he struck a blow for centralization of authority in the hands of the church, and, not incidentally, his own.

As the Great Famine swelled the number of Irish arriving every year in New York, Hughes came increasingly to be seen by the Irish-Americans as their champion and spokesman. He vigorously opposed the anti-immigrant Know-Nothing Party and campaigned unsuccessfully for state support of Catholic education. His failure in the latter effort caused him to embark upon the formation of New York's parochial school system.

While no one was more active in famine relief and other good works he deemed beneficial for Irish immigrants, Hughes was firm in his belief that the Irish-Americans should be concerned first and foremost with the affairs of their adopted country. For the Young Ireland movement of Smith O'Brien and Thomas Francis Meagher, he had only contempt. He urged that his flock ignore the radical pro-independence newspapers then circulating in New York, such as Thomas D'Arcy McGee's *Nation* and John Mitchel's *Citizen.* (*See* Ottawa, Ontario and Hampton, Virginia, respectively.)

Hughes played a substantial role in the Civil War, supporting the Union cause. Hughes often communicated with the Lincoln administration through William Seward, Lincoln's Secretary of State and a former governor of New York who had supported Hughes' efforts to gain public monies for Catholic schools. As a result, Hughes became an unofficial envoy for the Union effort in the capitals of Europe, including the Holy See.

Undoubtedly his greatest service to the war effort, however, came during the July 1863 draft riots in New York. Packed into some of the worst slum housing in the world, lukewarm at best in their attitude toward the war and facing the prospect of competition for jobs with freed black slaves, the Irish of New York were ripe for rebellion when the Federal

*St. Patrick's
Cathedral, the
spiritual heart of
New York City.*

government announced the beginning of conscription to fill the depleted
Union ranks in the third summer of the war.

The conscription act was not one of the more inspired pieces of
legislation in American history. It was riddled with exemptions and loop-
holes that the well-off and well-connected could take advantage of. When
the first lots were drawn on Saturday, July 11, the list was disproportionately made up of Irish names. Immigrant men gathered in the taverns to
grumble. It didn't take long for the conversation to turn to violence.

It began on Monday, July 13, with the destruction of several federal
offices. The violence soon spread throughout the city. No black was safe
and the Colored Orphan Asylum was burned to the ground. A total of 105
people were definitely killed in the riot (not the thousands claimed in many
accounts).

Although contemporary newspaper accounts tended to portray the
rioters as exclusively Irish, recent research has established that the mobs

were perhaps only two-thirds Irish. Most of the police endeavoring to suppress the rioting were also Irish.

At the behest of city and state authorities, Archbishop Hughes addressed the rioters from the balcony of his residence on Madison Avenue. He displayed great sympathy for the men and declined to call them rioters. But he urged that the crowds return to their homes and comply with the new law. Hughes's words worked better than nightsticks and bayonets. The riot was over. Hughes died less than a year later.

The war undoubtedly cast a shadow over what Hughes considered his greatest work: the building of St. Patrick's Cathedral. New York had been raised to an archdiocese in 1850 with Hughes as archbishop. It was around this time that he began thinking about the construction of "a cathedral of suitable magnificence" for the city of New York.

Up to that time, the seat of the bishop had been at "Old" St. Patrick's Cathedral on Prince and Mott streets. downtown. (On April 17, 1875, Archbishop John McCloskey was installed there as the first American cardinal.) But this church, venerable though it was, was far too small for the burgeoning archdiocese. Hughes wanted something much, much grander.

The new cathedral, designed by James Renwick, incorporated design styles from German, French, and Italian church architecture, a mixture that has caused architecture critics to turn up their noses at St. Patrick's. Where it counts, however, public affection, the cathedral succeeds magnificently.

St. Patrick's is visited annually by thousands of tourists and figures prominently in every St. Patrick's Day Parade, as the incumbent archbishop and other dignitaries review the parade from the front steps.

❧ EXHIBITS: Many statues and memorials adorn the interior, including busts commemorating visits to the cathedral by Popes Pius XII, Paul VI and John Paul II. ❧ LOCATION: 5th Avenue between E. 50th and E. 51st streets. ❧ HOURS: Call for Mass schedule and hours. ❧ ADMISSION: Free, but donations appreciated. ❧ TELEPHONE: (212) 753-2261.

ST. PAUL'S CHAPEL

This well-known place of worship (it is believed to be the oldest continuously used public building in New York City and the only extant colonial-era church) on lower Broadway near the Financial District has many, many connections with early American history. The service of Thanksgiving after George Washington's first inauguration as president on Wall Street was held here. It also is the final resting place of several well-known early Irish-Americans.

Richard Montgomery, the son of an Anglo-Irish member of the British parliament, was born in Dublin in 1738 and chose for himself a military

One of the oldest public buildings in New York City is St. Paul's Church on Broadway.

career. After serving with the British forces in the French and Indian Wars, he settled in New York, where he married the daughter of Robert Livingston and began to identify with the colonies as tensions rose with the mother country. In June 1775, the Continental Congress appointed him a brigadier general, an appointment he accepted after much agonized soul-searching.

Montgomery didn't have a long career, unfortunately. Leading American forces into Canada later that year, he achieved much initial success, despite leading a ragged, near-mutinous army. After capturing Montreal, he moved on the British capital at Quebec City. With the enlistments of most of his men set to expire on New Year's Day, Montgomery organized a futile attack in a snowstorm on New Year's Eve, during which he was shot and killed. He thus became the first American general officer to be killed in action.

There is a memorial here to Thomas Addis Emmet, the older brother of the better-known Robert Emmet, who was hanged by the British in 1803 and made from the dock the immortal demand that his epitaph not be written until Ireland was free. (It remains unwritten.)

The Emmet brothers had a privileged upbringing in Ireland. Their father, another Robert Emmet, was the court physician to his cousin, Lord Temple, the viceroy of Ireland. Thomas Addis, born in 1764, was trained as a physician as well, but switched to a legal career when his elder brother, Christopher, a well-known lawyer, died prematurely.

Thomas Addis Emmet, along with Wolfe Tone, was an early leader of the United Irishmen, the first (and so far only) organization to truly unite Protestant and Catholic Irishmen in opposition to British rule. (The Ulster Presbyterians at that time were almost as repressed as the Catholics because of the opposition of both to the established Church of Ireland.) Their insurrection in 1798, however, was a fiasco, betrayed by informers from within. Emmet was arrested and forced into exile in 1802. After unsuccessfully seeking to interest Napoleon in invading Ireland, he sailed for the United States in 1804.

Emmet's romantic reputation preceded him to New York and he was greeted enthusiastically by the partisans of President Thomas Jefferson. Requirements for the practice of law in New York State were specially waived for him and he soon built a thriving practice, much of it defending escaped slaves and immigrants in trouble with the law. He also served as president of the Irish Emigrant Association.

In 1812, he accepted appointment as attorney general of New York, but resisted all entreaties that he seek higher office. When he died in 1827, both Congress and the state legislature adjourned as a mark of respect.

❧ **EXHIBITS:** General Montgomery's remains were moved to St. Paul's in 1818. Although his gravestone is at St. Paul's, T. A. Emmet's body somehow found its's way to St. Mark's-in-the-Bowery Church at East 10th Street and 2nd Avenue, on the northwest corner. His flat grave marker, with name and relevant dates, lies just to the left of the prominent Peter Stuyvesant memorial at the right of the front gate. Guided tours are available. ☙ LOCATION: Broadway and Fulton streets, near the financial district. ☙ HOURS: 7–4 daily. ☙ ADMISSION: Free, but donations appreciated. ☙ TELEPHONE: (212) 602-0874.

69TH REGIMENT ARMORY

This massive complex was completed in 1906 as the headquarters of one of the most famous military units in American history, "the Fighting 69th" of the New York National Guard.

The 69th was raised in 1851 as the successor unit to the 9th Regiment. It seems the New York state authorities were uneasy that so many Irish had joined the 9th in an effort to gain military training in order to eventually liberate Ireland. The Irish, however, simply began joining the 69th instead. (The 9th was later re-raised by Irish-Americans and accepted into New York service.)

The 69th Regiment first achieved national notice in 1859, when its colonel, Michael Corcoran, refused to parade the regiment for the Prince of Wales (the future King Edward VII), while the latter was on a visit to New York. Corcoran said he could not ask Irish-born men to parade for a "the son of a sovereign, under whose rule Ireland was left a desert and her best sons exiled or banished." Corcoran was ordered court-martialed as a result.

The attack on Ft. Sumter brought an immediate end to the proceedings. The need for Irish trigger-pullers in the ranks was too great to put their hero in prison. The Corcoran connection meant that the 69th was the favorite unit of Irish New Yorkers, which it has remained to this day. The 69th was among the first regiments to rally to the Union cause and there were said to be five Irish volunteers for each vacancy in the regiment. It fought bravely in the first battle of the war, the disastrous engagement at Bull Run, where Corcoran was captured. (*See* Richmond, Virginia for more on Corcoran's experience as a captive and his subsequent commands.)

The 69th was re-recruited and reconstituted as the First Regiment of the Irish Brigade, commanded by Thomas Francis Meagher. Along with the 63rd and 88th New York regiments and the 28th Massachusetts and the 116th Pennsylvania, it fought as part of the brigade in every major engagement in the eastern theater of the Civil War. (*See* Antietam, Maryland and Fredericksburg and Richmond, Virginia for information on specific actions.)

James Cagney and Alan Hale in the 1940 film, The Fighting 69th. *(Museum of Modern Art)*

The swan song of the 69th as an identifiably "ethnic" unit was the First World War, where it fought as part of the famed "Rainbow Division." The army top brass didn't want National Guard units with famed histories such as the 69th "overshadowing" the draftees who were then filling the ranks of the "regular" army. As a result, the 69th was renumbered the 165th Infantry.

The changing ethnic nature of the unit (and of New York) is also reflected in the names of its Medal of Honor winners. Once World War II is reached, the list of Irish names abruptly stops at Alejandro Ruiz. Although now an ethnically mixed National Guard unit, the 69th retains its Irish connection by leading the St. Patrick's Day parade up Fifth Avenue every year with the Irish wolfhound mascots that give the unit its motto: "Gentle When Stroked, Fierce When Provoked."

& EXHIBITS: Four display cases on the history of the regiment from the
Civil War to World War II. Many battle flags on display also, including the
so-called Prince of Wales flag.   & LOCATION: 68 Lexington Ave., between East 25 and East 26 Streets.   & HOURS: Monday–Friday 8–4.   &
ADMISSION: Free   & TELEPHONE: (212) 532-6013.

TAMMANY HALL

Tammany Hall. The words conjure up images of men in black
fedoras smoking big cigars in back rooms while they made the
corrupt political deals that would guide one of the world's great cities.
Tammany Hall as a political organization existed before the Irish came to
these shores in large numbers. (Some early Irish Tammanians helped elect
Thomas Addis Emmet, brother of the executed Irish patriot, attorney
general of New York early in the 19th century.)

The Irish came to the United States with a live political tradition.
Daniel O'Connell's drive for Catholic emancipation brought about the
formation of Catholic Associations around Ireland to lobby for its passage.
Around the time of the famine emigration, a majority of the island was also
conversant in English, an unintentionally invaluable asset when the Irish
entered political life.

The golden era of Irish control of Tammany Hall was roughly from
1874 to pre-World War I. "There is probably no other location where
Celtic control was so complete," writes George Reedy in his study of
Irish-American urban politics *From the Ward to the White House.* "And,
in addition, no other place where power was so centralized."

Given this last fact, it is ironic that the Tammany Society was founded
in 1789 by New York citizens opposed to centralization of the United
States government under the Constitution. (The name came from a semi-
legendary chief of the Delaware Indians.) The period of Hibernian control
began in 1874 with the fall of the infamous Scottish-American William
"Boss" Tweed and his replacement by a succession of three remarkable
leaders: "Honest John" Kelly, Richard Croker and Charles Murphy.

Kelly did not wholly live up to his nickname, but compared with what
had gone before, he was clean as a hound's tooth. He was a religious man,
so much so that his expressions of it often made his associates uncomfortable. It was Kelly who transformed Tammany Hall from simply a vehicle
for graft to early social services agency, designed to help recent immigrants
and their families adjust to the often harsh life in their new country.

He succeeded magnificently. Anyone who needed anything—a job,
food, clothes for the children, an operation—could get it by consulting his
local precinct captain. Get it, that is, if he was a reliable machine supporter.
While Tammany Hall could and did stuff ballot boxes on a regular basis, the

reality is that there were many more voters who willingly and enthusiastically cast their votes for machine candidates. In a world of hostile corporations and distant, callous elites, the machine often seemed to be the only institution (aside from the Church) that cared about the immigrant Irish.

Not that the machine had things all its own way, however, even in its heyday. In 1913, John Purroy Mitchel, grandson of Irish patriot John Mitchel (see Hampton, Virginia and Charleston, South Carolina), defeated the Tammany candidate to be elected mayor of New York on a reform slate. Mitchel served only one, albeit successful, term and was killed in a aircraft training accident in 1918 after enlisting in the Air Corps in World War I.

Charles Murphy, who had ruled Tammany for two decades, died in 1924. He was the last of the really powerful machine chieftains in New York City. Although Tammany retained much of its power for another 20 years, the end of World War II brought about a decline. Franklin D. Roosevelt's New Deal transferred responsibility for a citizen's economic well-being from the city ward boss to the national government. The Irish lost control in the 1950s to the Italians under Carmine DeSapio, who, in turn, was deposed by an up-and-comer named Edward I. Koch.

Tammany's primary role thus was eclipsed. The Democratic organization is still very much alive in New York City, of course, but its power is mostly confined to judicial patronage. It is just a shadow of its Celtic past.

🍀 EXHIBITS: The building that was Tammany Hall's last headquarters is now a theater and office building. It is owned by the International Ladies Garment Workers Union (ILGWU). 🍀 LOCATION: 100 E. 17th St., off Union Square.

THOMAS MOORE MEMORIAL

Thomas Moore lived most of his life in England, but when Irish New Yorkers were seeking a cultural figure of their own to immortalize in Central Park, they unhesitatingly chose Moore, whose Irish Melodies helped ease the pain of exile for many an emigrant.

Moore, the son of a Dublin grocer, was born in 1779 and registered as a Protestant to gain a prestigious education at Trinity College, Dublin. Although a friend of Robert Emmet, he shunned the United Irishmen and went to live in England in 1800, where he studied law and sought to gain entrance into "society." Starting in 1807 and continuing for another 27 years, however, he began publishing his Irish Melodies.

The songs, for the most part, are sentimental evocations of Ireland's landscape and her past. The best known include "The Harp That Once Through Tara's Halls," "Come Back Paddy Reilly," "Flow On, Thou Shining River," and "Come Rest in This Bosom." These songs, with few

Thomas Moore's
Irish Melodies
soothed the soul of
many an Irish
emigrant.

hints of the hard, sad life that caused most of them to flee, were frequently sung by Irish emigrants around the fireside late at night to conjure up fond memories of "the old country" and allow young people who had never seen it to imagine what it might be like.

Moore's melodies were influential far beyond Irish-Americans, however. Musicologist Charles Hamm has demonstrated that Stephen Foster, the quintessential "American" composer of the 19th century, was strongly influenced by Moore's songs in producing his own work.

The Moore bust is one of many "ethnic" cultural figures memorialized in this area of the park. (Scottish-Americans, for instance, erected statues of Robert Burns and Sir Walter Scott.) In the late 19th century, city authorities banned ethnic gatherings in the park for fear of political disturbances, so these monuments to cultural figures were considered something of a substitute.

❧ **EXHIBITS:** The bronze sculpture, mounted on a granite pedestal simply marked "Moore," was erected by the Friendly Sons of St. Patrick Society and is the work of sculptor Dennis B. Sheahan. It was dedicated May 28, 1880, and was recently cleaned and restored. ❧ **LOCATION:** Just inside the entrance to Central Park at West 59th Street and Fifth Avenue, near the pond. ❧ **HOURS:** Dawn to dusk. ❧ **ADMISSION:** None.

VICTOR HERBERT MEMORIAL

The composer of such well-known light operettas as *Babes in Toyland* was born in Dublin in 1859, the grandson of the Irish novelist Samuel Lover. At age 7, however, the musically gifted youth was packed off to Germany to study the cello. He became so refined at this instrument that in 1882 he won first chair in Richard Strauss's orchestra in Vienna.

It was as a composer and conductor, however, that he was to achieve his greatest fame. Arriving in America in 1886, he quickly became associate conductor of the music festivals at Worcester, Massachusetts, and then conductor of the Pittsburgh Symphony Orchestra. In 1904, he founded Victor Herbert's New York orchestra and began composing the light Gilbert and Sullivan–style operettas that made him famous.

Throughout his career, Herbert stayed in touch with events in his native land and he was active in both the Friendly Sons of St. Patrick and the Sons of Irish Freedom. Before his death in 1924, he was instrumental in the formation of the American Society of Composers, Authors and Publishers, which sought to prevent the new medium of radio from broadcasting copyrighted music without compensating the composer.

❧ **EXHIBITS:** The bust, bronze on a granite base, was erected in 1927 by the American Society of Composers, Authors and Publishers. The sculptor was Edmond G. Quinn. ❧ **LOCATION:** The bust is located opposite the bandstand near the East 72nd Street entrance to Central Park. Herbert often conducted at the bandstand in his capacity as bandmaster of the 22nd Regiment, New York National Guard. ❧ **HOURS:** Dawn to dusk. ❧ **ADMISSION:** Free

WOODSIDE

Irish neighborhoods once dotted New York's landscape. The Lower East Side had the notorious Five Points slum. Later came Hell's Kitchen, between 30th and 57th streets on the West Side. (An Irish-dominated gang, the notorious Westies, was active there into the 1980s until the FBI smashed it.) There was another Irish enclave around the mostly German neighborhood of Yorkville in the east 70s. The Bronx was also heavily Irish.

Mostly, they are gone now, victims of Irish-American flight to the suburbs in the years after World War II. Pockets remain, however, and Woodside in Queens is one. Surrounded by cemeteries and connected to Manhattan by the "El," it is a neighborhood that retains its distinctive character. Although the older generation is gone now, second and third generations of Irish-Americans have made their homes here. So do some of the new generation of Irish illegal immigrants who have made their way to the Big Apple. (Bainbridge Avenue in the Bronx, however, is where most of these new Irish live.)

The semidetached homes on neat streets shelter many police, firefighters and other city workers. Although the Hispanic presence has been increasing in recent years, it is still possible to roam the streets and see stores with names such as "Shamrock Moving and Storage," "Kelly's," and other evidence that this is one of the few Celtic islands left in polyglot New York City.

⅋ LOCATION: Woodside is bounded on the west by New Calvary Cemetery, on the south by Mt. Zion Cemetery and on the east by the old railroad tracks of the New York Connecting Railway. Roosevelt Avenue is the main commercial street. Take the IRT number 7 train to 61st Avenue.

PLATTSBURGH

MACDONOUGH MEMORIAL

The War of 1812 is the only one in American history where naval events dominate our memory, and for good reason: until Andrew Jackson won the Battle of New Orleans, the progress of the war on land was generally disastrous for American arms (Washington, D.C. for example, was captured and burned).

Two of the greatest naval victories of that war were won far from salt water, however, and both had men of Irish descent in command on the American side: Oliver Hazard Perry won the Battle of Lake Erie and Thomas Macdonough won the Battle of Lake Champlain.

Macdonough was born in Trap (now Macdonough), Delaware. His father, also named Thomas, was a physician. His grandfather, James, a Protestant, emigrated from county Kildare about 1730. The younger Thomas was born New Year's Eve, 1783, and entered the navy as a midshipman when he was age 17, making his first cruise that year in the West Indies during the undeclared naval war with France.

The next few years saw him engaged in the Barbary wars in the Mediterranean, participating in several of the most famous actions of that war, including Capt. Stephen Decatur's daring raid to burn the captured *Philadelphia*. In 1805, he became first officer of the *Enterprise* and later filled the same position on the *Syren*. In January 1807, he received the permanent rank of lieutenant.

In October 1806, Macdonough was ordered to Middletown, Connecticut to assist Capt. Isaac Hull in the construction of some gunboats. This was an exceedingly important experience that held him in good stead eight years later on Lake Champlain, when he had to build a fleet literally from scratch.

Macdonough left the navy shortly thereafter for the merchant service, frustrated at the slow rate of promotion. Once war broke out in 1812, however, he volunteered to return to active service. After briefly taking command of the naval station at Portland, Maine, he was ordered to Lake Champlain.

The importance of the lake lay its position astride the main invasion route to Albany from British bases in Canada (*see* Saratoga, New York). Control of the lake would allow the British to either transport troops by ship or prevent Vermont-based American forces from attacking a land force.

Bad luck hit Macdonough as the 1813 sailing season opened. Through the poor judgment of one of his officers, the British captured two of his vessels and their experienced crews. With both ships now under the Union Jack, the British had naval superiority on the lake. They swiftly took advantage of this situation, raiding unopposed throughout much of the summer.

Fortunately, however, Macdonough was blessed with a timid, unimaginative opponent in Sir George Prevost, the British governor-general of Canada, who singularly failed to press home his advantage. Thanks to Prevost's vacillation, Macdonough was able to begin construction of a new fleet unmolested, which would be ready to sail in 1814.

Over the winter, Macdonough constructed the 26-gun *Saratoga* and the 20-gun *Eagle*, together superior to anything the British had on the lake. With this formidable force at his command, it was now Macdonough and the Americans' turn to dominate the lake. The British hastily constructed more ships of their own to meet the new threat, but this took most of the summer. Fearing the onset of winter, Prevost pressed the British naval commander to attack before his ships were ready. When the battle came on the morning of September 11, 1814, it proved to be no contest.

Macdonough showed he had learned well his naval tactics. Positioning his ships so that the British could not get a fair wind, and swinging his own ships around on their anchor chains so they could fire both broadsides instead of only one, Macdonough raked and pummeled the British. In a matter of a few hours, it was over, with every major British warship in American hands. The British force on land, under the incompetent command of Prevost, was also swiftly routed.

The battle had important consequences. The American peace delegation, under the quarrelsome leadership of John Quincy Adams and Henry Clay, was on the verge of agreeing to harsh British peace terms after the burning of Washington. Lake Champlain changed all that. "This unfortunate adventure on Lake Champlain," wrote Colonial Secretary Lord Bathurst, "has changed utterly the atmosphere of the negotiations." Peace terms were agreed to and signed on Christmas Eve, 1814.

The Macdonough Memorial is an obelisk that commemorates the battle fought on the lake below. Today, as a visitor gazes at the many pleasure craft gliding quietly across the still waters of the lake, it's hard to conceive of the events of that desperate summer of 1814.

& LOCATION: The Macdonough Memorial is located in front of Plattsburgh City Hall. Take U.S. 87 north to Plattsburgh, exit 87. Follow Cornelia Street east all the way to the lake. The memorial will be in front of you.

ROCHESTER

CATHERINE DE VALERA GRAVESITE

Eamon de Valera, the man who certainly has the best claim to the title "the father of modern Ireland," was born in New York City. Indeed, his American birth might well have helped save his life when he found himself under sentence of death for his leadership role in the 1916 Easter Rising.

On October 2, 1879, Catherine Coll of Knockmore Townland, near Bruree, county Limerick, landed in New York "tired and nearly penniless," fleeing from a one-room, mud-walled, thatched cabin in an Ireland where "famine threatened once more." Indeed, a partial failure of the potato crop in 1878 had raised the specter of a return of the conditions of the 1840s, with mass starvation, mass evictions, and mass emigration.

Catherine Coll was age 23 when she landed in New York. Her father, Patrick Coll, a farm laborer, had died five years earlier. She grew up amid the horrors of the "land war" between impoverished Irish peasants and their rent-racking landlords. Although she and her family were not among the poorest of the poor, conditions were certainly unpleasant and the future appeared bleak. It is scarcely surprising that emigration seemed the only real way out.

The lot of a young, unmarried Irish woman in New York was usually that of domestic servant and nanny, widely known among the established Americans who employed them as "Bridgets." Catherine Coll was no exception. It was while working for a well-off French immigrant family called the Girauds that she met Vivion de Valera, a Spaniard who gave music lessons to the Giraud children.

There is now considerable debate about the veracity of the account de Valera gave throughout his life as to his origins. He maintained that his parents were married in St. Patrick's Church in what is now Jersey City, New Jersey, on September 19, 1881. In his 1993 biography *De Valera: Long Fellow, Long Shadow,* Irish journalist Tim Pat Coogan says his research turned up no evidence of a marriage, either in church or state records. The birth and baptismal certificates of the future president of the Irish nationalist republican provisional government are of no help in clarifying the issue.

Certainly, de Valera was dogged throughout his political career by rumors that he was illegitimate, a serious stigma in strongly Catholic Ireland. Indeed, one version had it that his mother was already pregnant when she sailed for New York. The latter can almost certainly be discounted, but illegitimacy would go a long way toward explaining the odd turn events took after the boy's birth.

Vivion de Valera vanishes from the story very quickly after the birth of young Edward (who changed his name to the Gaelic spelling when he entered public life). The family lore states that Vivion's health began to fail soon after his son's birth on October 14, 1882 and, on doctor's orders, he went to Denver (or possibly Minneapolis), where he is supposed to have died in November 1884.

But why didn't his wife and young son accompany him? Why the uncertainty about his place of death? Coogan speculates that it is possible Vivion simply deserted young Kate well before he is said to have gone west. That might explain the boy's birth in the Nursery and Child's Hospital, which stood on Lexington Avenue between 51st and 52nd streets. Coogan says the facility was for "destitute, abandoned children, children whose parents were away, and orphans"—hardly a place a woman would choose to have a child, however modest her means, if she had an alternative.

Catherine de Valera's behavior is also hard to explain. Most Irish mothers would have moved heaven and earth to stay near their only child (and a son especially), yet she quickly placed the boy in the care of a Mrs. Doyle, who was also from Bruree. De Valera said later his earliest memory of his mother was of a woman dressed in black who came occasionally to visit. Then, in April 1885, she sent the boy to Ireland accompanied by her brother Edward, who had immigrated but decided to return.

While their relations later in life were by all accounts cordial, this apparent rejection by his mother and the death or abandonment by his father must have mystified young Edward. These are experiences, as Coogan notes, that "either break or toughened a man." Clearly, they toughened young de Valera for the trials, both actual and metaphorical, that lay ahead.

Catherine de Valera stayed on in America, eventually marrying Charles Wheelwright, an Englishman who was not even a Catholic, who worked as a livery driver for a wealthy family in this upstate New York city. She made no effort, however, to bring her son back to the new family home.

After his arrival in Ireland, Catherine de Valera saw her increasingly famous son only occasionally. When he was sentenced to death in May 1916, however, she swung into action. She called attention to her son's American birth and produced his birth and baptismal certificates to prove it. (How could the British try an American citizen for treason?)

At his trial, however, de Valera made no effort to invoke his American citizenship in order to avoid the death sentence. But the British government, which was endeavoring to entice the United States into the First World War, had no wish to needlessly antagonize American public opinion. For these and other reasons, de Valera was spared.

Mother and son saw each other more in the teens and twenties, when he would visit her on his periodic trips to the United States to raise funds and win political support. She lived quietly in Rochester until her death in 1932 at age 76.

⮞ **EXHIBITS:** The grave is located in Section 12 South, the second row from the end. The tombstone reads "Wheelwright" in large letters at the top. Between the name "Catherine" and the relevant dates is carved the name "de Valera" in small type. The Wheelwrights lived in an unmarked and privately owned wooden frame house at No. 18 Brighton St. ⮞ **LOCATION:** Holy Sepulchre Cemetery, 2461 Lake Ave., just north of downtown Rochester. ⮞ **HOURS:** 9–4 daily. ⮞ **ADMISSION:** Free ⮞ **TELEPHONE:** Cemetery office: (716) 458-4110.

PATRICK O'RORKE MEMORIAL

One observer called Patrick O'Rorke "the ideal of a soldier and a gentleman." Another commented favorably that "there was nothing of the wild Irishman about him." Many of his contemporaries expected him to rise to high rank in the Union army, perhaps even to command it one day. It was not to be. Patrick O'Rorke's young life was cut short by a Confederate bullet at Gettysburg—but not before he and his 140th New

York Regiment had saved the Union line from destruction at the moment of supreme crisis for the army and the nation it served.

Born March 28, 1836, in county Cavan, Ireland, O'Rorke was brought to the United States by his parents when he was barely a year old. The family eventually settled in Rochester, which had had a substantial Irish population since Irish laborers had helped construct the Erie Canal. Patrick was the eldest of four boys and three girls.

O'Rorke was a good student and won a scholarship to Rochester University, but his mother refused to allow him to attend because of the school's Protestant affiliation. O'Rorke was about to be apprenticed to a marble cutter when his name was put before Congressman John Williams as a candidate for a vacancy at the United States Military Academy at West Point. O'Rorke was accepted and did well, ultimately becoming first captain of the corps of cadets and graduating first in his class in June 1861.

Only two months before, of course, Fort Sumter had been fired upon and the Civil War had begun. O'Rorke entered the Corps of Engineers, the army's elite, and reported to Washington, D.C., where the young green lieutenant helped drill newly arrived recruits.

The next year and a half were busy, with O'Rorke seeing action at Bull Run, Port Royal, and Fort Pulaski. It was while on leave in Rochester to marry his childhood sweetheart in July 1862 that he was offered the colonelcy of a newly forming local regiment, the 140th New York. At age 26, he was one of the youngest commanding officers in the army.

The 140th served honorably throughout the fall and early winter of 1862–63, being present at Fredericksburg, though not engaged. It saw action at Chancellorsville and in the Wilderness. O'Rorke distinguished himself and even won temporary command of a brigade. By July 2, 1863, however, O'Rorke was back with the 140th New York, and the regiment found itself near a small crossroads town in south-central Pennsylvania called Gettysburg.

For most of this the second day of the battle, the 140th was held back in reserve. But as the afternoon wore on, a crisis erupted on the Union left flank. Gen. Dan Sickles had disobeyed orders and deployed his men in an open area in front of the main Union line that came to be called the Wheatfield. Under heavy rebel attack, Sickles needed reinforcement badly. The entire V Corps, of which the 140th was a part, was called forward.

Just then, however, Gen. Gouverneur Warren, the chief engineer of the Army of the Potomac, noticed that a nearby hill, known locally as Little Round Top, was all but undefended. If the Confederates could seize that position and place artillery on the summit, they could rake the entire Union line with shot and shell. Disaster seemed imminent.

Warren first located Col. Strong Vincent and the four regiments under his command, and they swiftly occupied the top of the hill, beating the

Confederates to it by only minutes. General Warren realized, however, that far more troops would be needed if Little Round Top were to be held. He galloped off in search of reinforcements.

Warren, a New Yorker who, by coincidence, had commanded the 140th briefly prior to O'Rorke, encountered the Irishman and his men on their way to help Sickles and immediately directed them to Little Round Top. O'Rorke protested they already had orders.

"Never mind that, Paddy," Warren shouted as he galloped off again. "Bring them up on the double-quick and don't stop for anything, I'll take the responsibility."

O'Rorke did as Warren asked, quickly followed by the other three regiments in the brigade, and not a moment too soon. The slopes of Little Round Top were already thick with gunsmoke as the scratch Union force commanded by Col. Joshua Lawrence Chamberlain battled desperately to hold off superior Confederate numbers. "The men . . . fought as if the outcome of the battle, and with it the war, depended on their valor, as indeed perhaps it did," wrote historian Shelby Foote of the fighting on Little Round Top. "The blood stood in puddles in some places on the rocks."

There was no time for parade ground tactics as the 140th scrambled to the crest. Some Confederates had broken past the sagging Union lines and were racing for the summit. O'Rorke quickly swung down off his horse, drew his sabre, and shouted, "Down this way, boys!" Running headlong at the advancing Confederates, O'Rorke turned around and shouted, "Here they are, men. Commence firing!" At that precise moment, a Confederate bullet shattered O'Rorke's neck. He died instantly and fell among the rocks.

O'Rorke had done his duty, however. His men surged past the body of their fallen colonel and repelled the rebel charge. Little Round Top, and perhaps the Union cause with it, was saved.

Originally buried on the field, O'Rorke's body was taken back to Rochester a few weeks after the battle. His funeral procession was watched by thousands in the streets. His final resting place, beneath a Celtic cross at the top of a small hill, is in Holy Sepulchre Cemetery (*see* previous entry).

In 1889, the veterans of the 140th dedicated a monument to their fallen chief at the summit of Little Round Top, near the spot where he had fallen (*see* Gettysburg, Pennsylvania). In 1990, however, Irish-Americans in Rochester conceived the idea of a memorial to O'Rorke in his hometown. Funds were raised and a bust of O'Rorke was unveiled in 1992 in the city's historic High Falls district. The colonel's uniform, along with other personal effects, are displayed by the Rochester Historical Society.

&. **EXHIBITS:** The bust of O'Rorke is flanked by two large museum-quality panels detailing the colonel's life and life in Rochester during the

Civil War. ❧ LOCATION: The bust is on the second floor of the High Falls development in the Brown's Race Historic District between Platt and State Sts. in downtown Rochester. Rochester Historical Society is at 485 East Ave. ❧ HOURS: High Falls: variable but usually seven days a week. Call in advance. Historical Society: Monday–Friday, 10–4. ❧ ADMISSION: Free ❧ TELEPHONE: High Falls: (716) 325-2030; Historical Society: (716) 271-2705.

SARATOGA

SARATOGA NATIONAL HISTORICAL PARK

There is no way of knowing exactly how many Irish-Americans fought in the Revolution, but a glance at the rosters of American regiments reveals many Irish surnames. One who won fame at Saratoga was Timothy Murphy.

Saratoga is the name collectively given to two separate battles fought on September 19 and October 7, 1777. Many historians consider it the turning point of the Revolutionary War, for the punishing blow the rebel army inflicted on the British greatly heartened the rebels. It also convinced many previously wary colonists to openly join the patriot cause. Even more important, it convinced the French government to back the upstart colonists with troops and money, which went a long way toward ensuring the eventual American success.

Murphy's parents were from county Donegal. They emigrated and settled in New Jersey sometime around 1750, and their son was born around March 1751. The family soon moved westward into Pennsylvania, land that was then still the frontier. The best fed were the best shots, and simply staying alive required the ability to match wits with nature and the Indians. By all accounts, Murphy grew into a superb marksman and backwoodsman.

When the American colonists took up arms against the British in early 1775, Murphy joined up with Col. William Thompson's famed Battalion of Pennsylvania Riflemen, the direct linear ancestor of today's United States Army. (Thompson himself was born in county Meath.)

Murphy and his comrades got around, for records show they participated in the siege of Boston, the crossing of the Delaware, and the Christmas Day Battle of Trenton in 1776. In June 1777, just as British Gen. John "Gentleman Johnny" Burgoyne and his army were beginning their trek south from Canada, Washington ordered the formation of a regiment of sharpshooters under Col. Daniel Morgan of Virginia. Murphy was posted to this unit.

Burgoyne aimed to link up with other British armies coming from the west and south and so cut off New England from the rest of the colonies. Both parts of the rebellious colonies could then be crushed in turn.

The plan went awry, however, when Col. Barry St. Leger, leading the army coming from the west, was badly beaten at Oriskany and Ft. Stanwix. General Howe, who was supposed to be coming north from New York City, never even got started, eventually moving south instead of north and capturing Philadelphia. In view of what happened later, it was an empty prize.

For Burgoyne, cut off deep in enemy territory and with winter fast approaching, the wisest course would have been to retreat to Canada. But he was a soldier, and he chose instead to fight it out.

In a sharp battle at Freeman's Farm on September 19, Burgoyne battered the Americans badly, but at high cost to his own forces. After another month spent waiting vainly for reinforcement, he decided to make one last effort.

On October 7, Burgoyne led 1500 of his best troops in a probing attack on the patriot line. Gen. Horatio Gates, the American commander, ordered his sharpshooters into action. "Order on Morgan to begin the game," he said.

Morgan needed little encouragement. He and his riflemen mauled the British right flank, which was under the command of Gen. Simon Fraser, a Scotsman who was a courageous and competent commander. Inspired by Fraser, the British continued the attack.

Benedict Arnold (not yet a traitor) spotted Fraser on his great grey horse and saw an opportunity. Samuel Woodruff, an American volunteer, described what happened next: "Knowing the military character and efficiency of that officer, Arnold called to Morgan, "That officer upon a grey horse is of himself a host, and must be disposed of—direct the attention of some of the sharpshooters amongst your riflemen to him." Morgan, nodding assent, went over to his riflemen. Pointing at Fraser, he said, "That gallant officer is General Fraser. I admire him, but it is necessary that he should die. Do your duty."

Murphy, who was equipped with a unique Swiss weapon with double barrels, is then reported to have climbed a nearby tree. His first two shots barely missed the general, grazing his horse first on the tail and then on the main. But taking deadly aim, Murphy didn't miss a third time and wounded Fraser mortally in the abdomen. Murphy then turned his attention to Sir Francis Clark, Burgoyne's aide-de-camp, and killed him also.

Murphy's marksmanship had immediate effects. Burgoyne, already despairing of victory, abandoned it altogether upon seeing Fraser fall. The British fell back to their camp and ten days later, on October 17,

Burgoyne surrendered his entire army, an event unprecedented in British military annals.

Murphy stayed with the army through the difficult winter at Valley Forge. Later in the war, he was sent to the Schoharie Valley, not far from Saratoga, to help defend this vital agricultural region from Indian raids led by Sir John Johnson (see Johnstown, New York). Murphy eventually settled in the area, dying in 1818. He was eulogized as "the Strong Man of Schoharie County" and is buried beneath an impressive monument in nearby Middleburgh Cemetery.

The Ancient Order of Hibernians erected a memorial to Murphy on the Saratoga battlefield in 1913, situated near where the fatal shots were supposed to have been fired. Sixteen years later, Gov. Franklin D. Roosevelt visited the battlefield and paid tribute to Murphy and his great feat.

✦ EXHIBITS: The seven-foot tall granite monument to Murphy is located in the section of the battlefield called the Barber Wheatfield, which is the fifth stop on the self-guided tour available at the visitor center. ✦ LOCATION: Saratoga National Historical Park is about 30 miles north of Albany, New York. Take Route 4 from Albany to Stillwater and follow the signs to the park's main entrance, which is about 3 miles north of Stillwater. ✦ HOURS: The visitor center is open daily except Thanksgiving, Christmas, and New Year's Day. The park roads are open to traffic from early April to November 30, weather permitting. ✦ ADMISSION: $4.50. ✦ TELEPHONE: (518) 664-9821.

SYRACUSE

ERIE CANAL MUSEUM

A man named Canvass White led the campaign to recruit Irish immigrant labor to construct the Erie Canal through upstate New York. The canal was the brainchild of Gov. DeWitt Clinton, himself a descendant of Irish immigrants.

While in England on a canal inspection tour in 1817–18, White became acquainted with an experienced canal construction engineer, an Irishman (the English used Irish immigrants to build their canals and later their railroads) from Tipperary named J. J. McShane. White persuaded McShane and his maintenance team to come to America and work on the Erie. White had little difficulty finding hundreds of brawny young Irishmen to come to America to work under McShane.

Hiring agents for the canal waited at the docks in New York as the ships landed. Many Irish laborers had scarcely set foot in New York before they were placed on another ship for the journey to the headwaters of the Hudson to take up their new jobs.

Lionel Wyld, a canal historian at the University of Buffalo 1984, had this to say about the Irish laborers:

> The Irish have come in for perhaps more than their share of the ribbing as foofoos (non-native canal workers) on the canal as well as off of it, but they were, by and large, well-respected as the backbone of canal construction. Imported largely to serve as laborers, the Irish proved to be the greatest of boons in digging the Ditch. They turned "Clinton's folly" into the Great Western Canal. Few people could stand the conditions which the Irish laborers tolerated. Local inhabitants, Pennsylvania Dutch, and Negroes from the South were all tried, but the Irish bogtrotters always proved the best of the lot. They had stamina and they had grit. Some of the Irish, such as Paddy Ryan of prize-fighting fame, made names for themselves after they left the canal behind; but the bulk of the Irish made their contribution as diggers and construction help. And among other qualities, they had a sense of humor. . . .

Upstate residents, most of them of Yankee stock, were highly apprehensive of their new neighbors. "Mohawks and Senecas we have survived," wrote an Oneida County housewife, "but these strange folk look fitter for crime than for honest work. I misdoubt that we shall find ourselves murdered in our beds one fine morning."

In fact, there was little to fear. While the Irish fought regularly amongst themselves, there were remarkably few cases of looting or crime against the local inhabitants. Sometimes, it was the New World that threw a scare into "the wild Irish": one diarist reported that the appearance of a snake in camp one night sent dozens of Irish laborers fleeing for their lives. (Snakes, of course, were unknown in Ireland.)

The role of manual laborer was a new one for most of the immigrants. It is one of the oddities of the Irish immigrant experience that, even though most of them had been farmers and farm laborers in the old country, few were attracted to agriculture in the United States, perhaps because the memory of farming in Ireland was so unpleasant.

Although the Irish started out as simple laborers, historian James H. Tully reports that many quickly found ways to move up the ladder to become not only foremen but subcontractors as well. In his book *To the Golden Door*, author George Potter had this to say:

> The canal produced a class of Irish contractors and subcontractors. The canal commissioners early concluded that the most politic way of proceeding with the work was to parcel out contracts for small sections to responsible bidders rather than concentrate it in the hands of a monopoly or a few large contractors. Ambitious Irishmen bid for sections, varying from forty rods to three miles, and since the state of New York advanced sums for a contractor to set up with teams, implements, provisions and other essentials and covered monthly payrolls, the Irish canal contractor was born along the route of the Erie.

Once the canal was finished in 1825, the Irish didn't disappear. They stayed and took advantage of the prosperity it brought to upstate New York as it opened up the American Midwest to settlement and trade. To this day, many people with Irish surnames are to be found in the cities strung out along the old canal route—Rochester, Syracuse, Utica, Rome, and Albany.

EXHIBITS: Indoor and outdoor exhibits detail the construction of the canal, with many references to the largely Irish laborers who dug it. **LOCATION:** Weighlock Building, Erie Boulevard East and Montgomery Street, Syracuse. **HOURS:** Daily, 9–5. Closed holidays. **ADMISSION:** Free **TELEPHONE:** (315) 471-0593.

TROY

JAMES CONNOLLY MEMORIAL

To the Irish and the Irish-Americans, the image was an indelible one: badly wounded in the fighting at the General Post Office (H.Q. of the 1916 Easter Rising, in Dublin), James Connolly was unable to stand before the firing squad to which he had been condemned as one of the insurrection's principal leaders. His Majesty's justice, however, was not to be denied. Connolly, founder and leader of the Irish Transport and General Workers Union and commander of the Irish Citizen Army, had to face it propped up in a wooden chair.

So much romance and myth has grown up around Connolly's dramatic death that it has tended to obscure the rest of his life, most of which was taken up with left-wing revolutionary politics. Indeed, his death is in many ways a contradiction of much that went before it. A Marxist and fervent believer in the brotherhood of all men under international socialism, Connolly died a martyr to Irish nationalism.

Born in Edinburgh, Scotland, of Irish immigrant parents, Connolly joined the British army at age 14. Some scholars believe he spent at least part of his service in Ireland, which might have shaped his future political development. Certainly he became politically active almost immediately upon his separation from the army in 1889 (whether by discharge or desertion is unclear).

Connolly had little contact with Ireland up to this point. It was in Scotland that he learned the art of public speaking (his English was Scottish-accented for most of his life) and political organizing. After fitful employment and standing unsuccessfully for the Edinburgh Town Council, Connolly was faced with the issue of how he would support a wife and growing family that by then included three children.

His wife, Lillie, whom he had met on a visit to Dublin, issued an appeal for employment on his behalf in a socialist newspaper. It was answered by the Socialist Club of Dublin, which invited Connolly to become its secretary. In 1896, he left Edinburgh for his new post.

Connolly quickly founded the Irish Socialist Republican party, and made a successful tour of the United States in 1902. Upon his return to Dublin, however, he became caught up in one of the many doctrinal splits and disagreements that characterize socialist politics. Frustrated, he decided to immigrate to the United States. He settled in this industrial city in upstate New York soon after his arrival in September 1902 because a cousin named Margaret Hume and her husband lived there.

While in Troy, Connolly secured unlikely employment as an insurance agent. His family had by then grown to include five daughters and an infant son. But when Connolly went to meet them at Ellis Island in New York a year or so after his own arrival, he received a shock: 13-year-old Mona had died in a fire accident just before the family sailed. The dazed Lillie had to go on ahead with the remaining five children.

Barely was the family settled in Troy, when an economic downturn caused Connolly to lose his insurance job. The Connollys left Troy in 1905 to settle in Newark, New Jersey, where James found work in the Singer Sewing Machine factory.

Connolly stayed in the United States another five years, founding the Irish Socialist Federation and editing its journal, *The Harp.* But he kept up with political news back in Ireland and in 1910 secured an invitation to return to Dublin as organizer for the newly formed Socialist party of Ireland.

Connolly's politics became more and more bound up with the nationalism issue as events gathered momentum in the years before the First World War. He came to believe that true working-class politics could not begin until Irish independence had been secured. Connolly soon became involved with James Larkin's Irish Transport and General Workers Union (ITGWU) and, in 1913, played a central role in the famous Dublin transport lockout, a pivotal event in Irish labor history.

The failure of labor to achieve recognition during the lockout, however, along with the failure of workers throughout Europe to resist the outbreak of the First World War, undermined nearly 25 years of political certainty for Connolly. Socialist internationalism increasingly gave way to nationalism. Irish nationalists, however, were suspicious of him, since he had previously showed little active interest in their cause. Nevertheless, he took command of the small, labor-dominated Irish Citizen Army and was one of the most aggressive advocates of the 1916 Easter Rising.

In military terms, the rising was a failure. An expected arms delivery from Germany was captured. Some nationalist leaders got cold feet at the last moment and tried to call off the uprising. Orders were given, counter-manded, and countermanded again. As a result, turnout among the volunteers on Easter Monday, April 24, 1916, was spotty at best. The insurgents also discovered they were none too popular with much of the population at large. Many had relatives in the trenches in France and did not sympathize with an uprising during wartime.

With barely 1,000 men (and some women) in arms, Connolly, Edward de Valera (*see* Rochester, New York), and the other leaders went ahead with their plan to seize various strong points in Dublin. The principal rallying point was Liberty Hall, headquarters of Connolly and Larkins's ITGWU. Connolly then marched his men to their chosen headquarters, the General Post Office (GPO) in central Dublin.

The unequal battle raged all week. Although more volunteers joined the rebels during the uprising, the British were able to pour more men and guns into the action than the rebels could have dreamed of. By Friday night, artillery fire had reduced the GPO to a flaming hulk, and Connolly, poet Padraic Pearse, and the rest of the garrison had to evacuate their headquarters. Connolly, wounded in the ankle earlier in the fighting, had to be carried on a stretcher on this desperate journey through the flaming streets.

After the surrender the next day, Connolly was taken to a hospital that had been set up in Dublin Castle, ironically, the seat of British rule in Ireland. He was court-martialed in his hospital bed and sentenced to death. In the early hours of May 12, 1916, the invalid Connolly was bundled into an ambulance, driven to nearby Kilmainham Jail, propped in his chair, and shot.

Although it failed utterly in its military objectives and its short-term political goals, the 1916 Rising, within a few years, became the centerpiece of 20th-century Irish nationalist mythology. The executed leaders added their names to the already long list of martyrs to the cause of Irish independence. Their fate became a rallying cry for resistance to British rule and helped bring about the final showdown that won independence for the Irish Free State in 1921.

🏵 EXHIBITS: The monument was built with funds raised by local trade unionists to commemorate Connolly's two years in Troy. It was unveiled in 1986. 🏵 LOCATION: The Connolly memorial consists of a bust sculpted by Irish artist Paula O'Sullivan, mounted atop a granite base. It stands in Riverside Park in Troy, along River St., just north of Troy City Hall, adjacent to the monument to "Uncle Sam" Wilson. 🏵 HOURS: Dawn to dusk.

ONTARIO

OTTAWA

THE ASSASSINATION OF THOMAS D'ARCY MCGEE

On a continent populated with colorful Irish politicians, D'Arcy McGee was certainly one of the most singular. Starting out as an Irish nationalist of impeccable credentials, McGee eventually did a 180-degree turn later in life, becoming a champion of the British Empire and one of the leading forces behind Canadian Confederation. Those positions would cost him his life.

McGee was born along the shores of Carlingford Loch in county Louth in 1825. His formal education was scant, but his mother had a love of books and a hedgerow schoolmaster appreciated the boy's intelligence and drilled him in basic subjects. Young Thomas had a rebel pedigree, for virtually all the male members of his family on both sides had participated in the United Irishmen rising of 1798. Thus, from an early age, the young man drank deep at the well of Irish nationalist mythology.

Like so many others, McGee decided to emigrate when his father died, leaving Ireland in the company of his sister Dorcas in 1842 for Providence, Rhode Island, where they had an aunt. In America he honed his skills as a newspaperman and was back in Ireland just three years later working on *The Nation*, the newspaper of the growing Young Ireland movement, which was modeled on Mazzini's nationalist Young Italy movement.

The uprising that McGee and others helped spark in Ireland in 1848, however, met with far less success than those in France and Germany the same year. With a price of nearly $1500 on his head, D'Arcy McGee fled first to Scotland. After he was recognized in the streets of Glasgow, however, he went south to England, from which he managed to reach the remote west of Ireland. Disguised as a priest, he boarded a ship at Derry and escaped to New York.

Once in the United States, McGee continued his agitations, founding the *New York Nation* and later, the *American Celt*. But disputes with colleagues and other Irish-American leaders, including the all-powerful Archbishop John Hughes of New York, caused him to pull up stakes in 1857 and move to Montreal. The latter was a city riven by differences between English-speaking Protestants and French-speaking Catholics. And its small but growing Irish community was looking for leadership.

McGee set up his own newspaper, *The New Era* and changed his politics completely, lashing out at Republicans and Fenian efforts to establish an Irish Republic in Canada. "The British provinces of North America are not necessarily miserable and unhabitable because the British flag flies at Quebec," he wrote. By 1865, he was a member of Parliament and secretary of agriculture.

His advocacy of Confederation fell on more receptive ears after the failed Fenian invasion of 1866, especially in the isolated Maritime Provinces closest to the United States. McGee argued that if Canadian disunity led to Fenian successes in the future, then the United States would be tempted to take advantage of the situation and make war on Canada (which, of course, is exactly what the Fenians were counting on).

The House of Commons rose after midnight on April 7, 1868. McGee, a week short of his 43rd birthday, had just given a well-received speech. Having shepherded Confederation through the year before, he seemed set for yet more political triumphs. On his way home that night, however, walking through the gaslit dampness of Sparks St. to his rooms in Mrs. Trotter's boarding house, he was ambushed by an assassin just as he inserted his key into the lock to let himself in. Shot in the neck by a single bullet, McGee was pronounced dead at the scene. He is, to date, the only Canadian politician ever to have been assassinated.

The crime was widely blamed on McGee's Fenian adversaries. Patrick Whelan, an Irish-Canadian, was arrested and charged with the murder, although he insisted he was innocent and denied belonging to the Fenians. Nevertheless, he was convicted on the basis of highly circumstantial evidence and hanged. McGee's true assassins remain unknown.

&. **EXHIBITS:** A plaque marking the spot is located on Sparks St., which is today a pedestrian mall. Some of McGee's personal effects, including a plaster cast taken of his hand after his death, are kept in the Bytown Museum, off Wellington Street at the Ottawa Locks. There is also a statue of him, in oratorical pose, near the Library on Parliament Hill. &. **LOCATION:** McGee was murdered outside his rooming house at 71 Sparks St. in Ottawa, near the Parliament buildings. &. **HOURS:** Bytown Museum is open Monday and Wednesday–Saturday 10–4, Sunday 2–5, mid-May to mid-October. Monday–Friday 10–4, April 1 through mid-May and mid-October through November 30. Other times by appointment. &.

ADMISSION: C$2.25. Seniors and children C$1. Ages 6–14, .50. Family rate
C$5.50. & TELEPHONE: (613) 234-4570.

RIDGEWAY

RIDGEWAY BATTLEFIELD

The Fenian invasion of Canada in June 1866 is, at best, a modest
footnote in American history. The effort by several thousand Irish-
Americans to conquer British Canada and hold it hostage for Ireland's
independence is usually dismissed as a hare-brained, comic opera affair
doomed to inevitable failure.

Closer examination, however, reveals that it was a far more serious
effort, with a greater chance of success than is usually acknowledged by
historians. Certainly the Canadians took it seriously: the Fenian invasion
was the motive event that gave birth to the present-day Canadian Confederation.

The Fenian invasion had its roots in the Irish potato famine of the
1840s, which brought so many Irish immigrants streaming to the United
States, many nursing a bitter hatred for Ireland's British overseers. Some
were determined to use their new home as a base for the eventual establishment of an Irish republic.

To that end, the Irish Republican Brotherhood, soon renamed the
Fenians (after a race of mythical Celtic warriors), were founded in 1858,
with branches in both the United States and, secretly, in Ireland.

The movement received a great shot in the arm from the outbreak of
the American Civil War in 1861. The Union naval blockade of Southern
ports deprived British industry of the cotton it needed for its mills. This
factor, along with several naval incidents, put great strain on Anglo-
American relations. At the same time, tens of thousands of Irish served in
the Union army, gaining military experience that the Fenian leaders hoped
could be put to use in liberating the homeland.

The Fenians in Ireland, however, had been dealt some serious setbacks
by 1865. In that year, the movement's newspaper was suppressed and some
of its leaders arrested. The American movement split into two rival camps.
One favored continuing the original plan and encouraging a rising in the
mother country. The other argued that since a successful revolt in Ireland
was probably impossible for the moment, more unconventional means
were required.

The latter argued for an invasion of Canada. Such a course, they
believed, might very well embroil the United States and Great Britain in a
war, which would divert British military resources from Ireland and so

Located in a cabin on the edge of the original battlefield is the Ridgeway Battlefield Museum.

increase chances for a successful rebellion there. Even if the Anglo-American war did not take place, but the invasion were successful, Canada could then be bartered for Ireland's independence.

American political conditions in 1865–66 gave the Fenians heart. Fear of alienating the Irish vote in the approaching 1866 elections made U.S. political leaders wary of taking any action against the increasingly open Fenian drilling and organizing. Also, Anglo-American relations remained frosty over a number of unresolved issues left by the Civil War, and the presence of a bellicose Fenian movement in the United States was a useful lever for the U.S. government.

At the same time, huge numbers of Irish-American Civil War veterans were being discharged and many were allowed to keep their weapons or purchase them for a nominal sum. Thomas Sweeny, who had fought in the Civil War as a major general, was appointed the Fenian commander-in-chief.

Sweeny's plan was not unsound. The idea was to draw the main British forces away from their bases in Quebec by diversionary attacks in Ontario, while the main Fenian force of about 16,000 men moved across the Vermont border to seize Quebec.

With a large, well-equipped army, the plan might have had a chance. The instrument at hand, however, was inadequate to the task. While volunteers were many and frequently experienced, they had no training in operating together as an army. Artillery, ammunition and even adequate food were lacking. The sympathy of the U.S government was simply assumed. The support the invaders expected to find among Irish-Canadians did not take into account the fact that many of the latter were completely unsympathetic Ulster Protestants.

Nevertheless, the Fenians began crossing the Niagara River for the diversionary feint shortly after midnight on June 1, 1866. About 1000 men under Col. John O'Neill (see O'Neill, Nebraska) were tasked with securing a bridgehead on the Canadian side for a much larger follow-up force that was assembling in Buffalo.

A Civil War veteran, O'Neill was a skilled, experienced commander, not the blundering amateur some have accused him of being. Throughout the three-day operation, he coolly assessed the situation at each turn, correctly anticipated his enemy's movements and deployed such forces as he possessed to meet them. He also managed the not inconsiderable feat of keeping good order and discipline in his army throughout, with no looting or pillage of the surrounding countryside.

Kept apprised of the Fenian buildup by their consul in Buffalo, the British authorities were prepared and lost no time dispatching two columns of British regulars and Canadian militia to deal with the invasion. O'Neill decided to strike first. He targeted the weaker of the two columns, which was detraining near the Ontario village of Ridgeway, about 10 miles west of Fort Erie. Early on the morning of June 2, as the Canadians marched northwards to join up with the second column, they fell into O'Neill's well-laid ambush.

Caught by surprise, the Canadians fell back in a disarray that one observer likened to the Union's retreat from Bull Run in 1861. Despite a tremendous amount of firing, casualties on both sides were relatively light: the Canadians suffered about 10 killed and 37 wounded and the Fenians eight killed and 16 wounded.

Despite this success, O'Neill knew he couldn't hold out long without reinforcements. He fell back on nearby Fort Erie and, after one more sharp skirmish with Canadian forces, withdrew most of his troops to the American side on June 3. U.S. military forces, finally alerted to the commotion, detained most of the Fenians. Still sensitive to Irish political sympathies, however, the U.S. government simply offered each man free transportation to his home and made apologies to the British government.

The Battle of Ridgeway was the high noon of the Fenian movement. A few days later, an advance guard of the "main force" made a half-hearted crossing of the Vermont-Quebec border, but ended up retreating or surrendering after British and Canadian forces appeared on the scene. Though further raids took place as late as 1871 (see Sheldon, Vermont), the Fenians were spent as a serious military threat to the British Empire. The movement staggered on until the mid-1880s, when it faded away altogether.

Americans quickly forgot about the Fenians and their invasion, but Canadians were deeply shocked, not only by the raid itself, but the lenient treatment of the invaders by the U.S. government. Ironically, the nationalism the Fenians ended up stoking most effectively was Canadian. The idea of confederating the Canadian provinces had been kicking around for some time, but the Fenian raids had demonstrated the urgency of presenting a united Canadian front against the colossus to the south. Canadian Confederation was a reality barely thirteen months after the Fenians were repulsed.

❧ EXHIBITS: The museum is housed in a cabin that stood on the edge of the battlefield during the encounter. The cabin's living quarters are restored to their 1866 condition. Two galleries contain interpretive displays and illustrations of the Fenian incursion. ❧ LOCATION: The Ridgeway Battlefield Museum is located on Highway 3 (Garrison Road), just east of Ridge Road in the town of Ridgeway. ❧ HOURS: Museum open from mid-June through Labor Day, Tuesday–Saturday, 12:30–5. ❧ ADMISSION: C$2 adults; C$1 for children. ❧ TELEPHONE: There is no telephone at the museum itself. Call Fort Erie Museum Board (416) 894-5322 for further information.

PENNSYLVANIA

ALLENTOWN

GEORGE TAYLOR HOUSE AND PARK

George Taylor was one of three men of Irish birth who signed the Declaration of Independence. About his early life, little is known, other than that He was born in the north of Ireland and must have sprung from a good family, for he had some education and means when he arrived in Philadelphia at age 20 in 1736.

He found work as a clerk in an iron foundry in Chester County and soon rose to become manager. Around 1754, he and a partner acquired an interest in a blast furnace in Bucks County, and for the rest of his life this was where his business interests largely lay. His political career, however, was made in Allentown in Northampton County.

He must have won the respect of his neighbors, for he was elected every year for five years, starting in 1764, to the provincial assembly, where he bitterly resisted further encroachments of royal rule from London. After a period of political inactivity that lasted about four years, he reappeared on the scene in 1774, and two years later was appointed a delegate to the Continental Congress on July 20, as a replacement for another Pennsylvanian who had refused to sign the Declaration of Independence. Taylor signed on August 2 or thereabouts. (Most of the signatures were added after July 4.)

Taylor seems to have taken little interest in the Continental Congress after signing the Declaration, however, and he resigned shortly thereafter. His health began deteriorating sometime in 1777 and he retired from public life, dying February 23, 1781.

⚜ **EXHIBITS:** The museum contains period furnishings and some of Taylor's personal possessions and memorabilia. Guided tours are available. ⚜ **LOCATION:** 4 miles north, of Allentown, off U.S. 22, at Front and Poplar streets, in Catasuqua. ⚜ **HOURS:** From June through October the house

George Taylor,
Irish-born delegate
to the Continental
Congress who
signed the
Declaration of
Independence.
(Lehigh County Historical
Society)

is open Saturdays and Sundays. Other times by appointment. ❧
ADMISSION: Free ❧ TELEPHONE: (610) 435-4664.

BRYN MAWR

HARRITON HOUSE

From 1774 to 1789, Charles Thomson served as the secretary to the Continental Congress, which adopted the Declaration of Independence. In addition to keeping the records, it was his duty to read the Declaration of Independence before the Congress and to notify George Washington of his election to the presidency.

Thomson was born of Scotch-Irish stock in Maghera, county Derry, on November 29, 1729. His mother died when he was 10 years of age, and his father, who emigrated along with his six children, died within sight of

American shores. Charles and his orphaned siblings were put ashore at New Castle, Delaware.

He appears to have recovered quickly from these blows, however, entering a well-known private academy and becoming a schoolmaster himself after graduation. It was while he was teaching in Philadelphia that he became acquainted with Benjamin Franklin, who helped turn his attention from teaching to commerce. Thomson proved a quick learner, becoming a wealthy merchant in a relatively short time. His reputation for fairness and integrity extended even to the Delaware Indians, who chose him as a mediator during treaty negotiations and made him a full-fledged member of the tribe, with an Indian name translated as "one who speaks truth."

Like most successful businessmen, Thomson chafed under the increasing British economic regulation after the French and Indian War and was in the forefront of opposition to the Crown on most matters in Philadelphia. He was instrumental in calling the Continental Congress, but thanks to intrigues among his political enemies, he was denied a seat as a delegate. His friendship with John and Samuel Adams, however, secured Thomson the crucial job of congressional secretary.

For the next 15 years, Thomson sat at the secretary's desk, faithfully recording the proceedings. Delegates and presiding officers came and went, but Thomson went on and on, beholding the birth of the new nation in its completeness as did no other man. Thomson is also credited with designing the Great Seal of the United States.

His final act was to notify George Washington of his election as president, but Thomson was deeply disappointed that be was given no role in the inauguration ceremonies, nor was he offered a position in the new administration.

Thomson thus retired here to "Harriton," spending the rest of his life translating the Holy Scriptures and writing commentaries on them. Although urged to write his memoirs, he refused, regarding his knowledge of the Congress's proceedings as "a sacred trust."

❧ **EXHIBITS:** Built in 1704, the house has some of Thomson's original furnishings and has been restored as nearly as possible to its appearance when he lived there. The grounds are pleasant and picnickers are welcome. ❧ **LOCATION:** 1½ miles north of U.S. 30 on Morris Ave., then 1½ miles west on Old Guelph Rd., then north on Harriton Rd. to entrance. ❧ **HOURS:** Wednesday–Saturday 10–4. Other times by appointment. ❧ **ADMISSION:** $2; students with ID free. ❧ **TELEPHONE:** (610) 525-0201.

CARLISLE

GRAVE OF COLONEL WILLIAM THOMSON

The U.S. Army originated, of course, with the citizen militias that formed in the several colonies in the early to middle 1770s. These units were useful for conducting "hit-and-run" raids against British positions or columns in the initial stages of the conflict. To win the war against the well-drilled British regulars, however, foreign advisers such as Lafayette and von Steuben transformed the militias into the Continental Army, the forerunner of today's U.S. Army.

The first unit to call itself a unit of the Continental Army was Thomson's Pennsylvania Rifle Battalion, formed in central Pennsylvania during the summer of 1775. The men of Thomson's unit were the first to consider themselves to be fighting not simply for Pennsylvania but for all of the American colonies when they marched off to Boston.

The Pennsylvanians were not an "Irish" unit *per se*, but they had a strong Irish representation. Their commander, William Thomson, was born in county Meath in 1736, immigrated to Pennsylvania, and settled on a farm near Carlisle, where he became a surveyor and justice of the peace. Thomson's second-in-command was Lt. Col. Edward Hand, who was born in Clyduff, county Laois.

Thanks to research done in the 1980's, by Col. William V. Kennedy, at one time a member of the U.S. Army Reserve, we now know that a high percentage of Thomson's men were Irish-born or of Irish descent and included both Protestants and Catholics. According to Kennedy, 361 of the 731 members gave Ireland as their place of birth. Of the remainder, 171 listed Irish surnames, indicating Irish descent. There was also a substantial contingent of men born in Germany and England.

Thompson's 1st Continental (Pennsylvania) Regiment was present at both Bunker Hill and Yorktown, seeing much action in between as well. Its men were renowned for their hardiness and the deadly effectiveness of their Pennsylvania long rifles.

Unfortunately, the U.S. Army was sadly negligent of Thomson as his men for decades. Both Thomson and Hand are buried in the Old Carlisle Graveyard at the back gate of what is now the U.S. Army War College, and at one time their graves were overgrown and untended. In October 1985, however, the Military Order of the World Wars held a ceremony to commemorate restoration of the gravesites, complete with fifes, drums, and Colonial era reenactors. Thomson, Hand, and their men at last received the tribute that had been denied them.

   EXHIBITS: Molly Pitcher, the famous woman who manned the gun after her husband was killed at the Battle of Monmouth, and who some authori-

ties believe was Irish or of Irish descent, is also buried in the cemetery. &
LOCATION: The cemetery is on East South Street in Carlisle, near the rear
entrance to the Army War College. & HOURS: Dawn to dusk. &
ADMISSION: Free & TELEPHONE: Further information can be obtained
by calling the Army War College Museum: (717) 245-3152.

GETTYSBURG

GETTYSBURG NATIONAL MILITARY PARK

Over the centuries, the Irish have developed a unique reputation as
fighting men, both with their fists and more sophisticated weapons.
It is not surprising, then, that the Irish were everywhere in the American
Civil War, on both sides and in all ranks, from lowly privates to high-
ranking commanders.

The largest, bloodiest, and probably most decisive battle of the Civil
War, Gettysburg, also featured more Irish connections than virtually
any other.

Robert E. Lee had invaded the north in an effort to relieve Union
pressure on Virginia and the threatened Confederate bastion of Vicksburg
on the Mississippi. The battle began on the morning on July 1, when
dismounted federal cavalry under the overall command of Maj. General
John Buford engaged the leading elements of the advancing Confederate
force. One of Buford's brigades was commanded by Col. William Gamble,
who was born in county Tyrone. Another brigade was under the command
of Col. Thomas Devin, who was born in New York of Irish immigrant
parents.

Although they took heavy casualties, Buford's troopers successfully
held off the rebel advance long enough to allow the Union I Corps, under
the command of Irish-American Maj. Gen. John Reynolds, to arrive on the
scene. Reynolds was felled by a musket ball as he was rallying the Iron
Brigade. The latter unit, although a "western" outfit from Wisconsin,
Michigan, and Indiana, contained many Irish soldiers. One, Pvt. Patrick
Maloney of the 2nd Wisconsin, had the honor of capturing and escorting to
the rear Confederate Brig. Gen. James J. Archer, the first of Lee's top
commanders to suffer the indignity of capture.

There were Irish on the Confederate side as well. One heavily Irish
outfit, a Mississippi unit called the 6th Montgomery Guards, was captured
attempting to circumvent the Union lines through an unfinished railway
cut. Not far away was Maj. Gen. Robert Emmet Rodes, named for the Irish
patriot. Only 34 years old, Rodes was a Virginia-born Alabamian, a
graduate of the Virginia Military Institute and protege of Thomas "Stonewall" Jackson, who had been killed at Chancellorsville only two months

Gettysburg National Military Park is populated with numerous memorials including, left, Col. Patrick O'Rorke Memorial and, right, a memorial to Col. Patrick Kelly's Second Brigade.

earlier. Rodes, along with his subordinate, an Alabama colonel named Edward A. O'Neal, tried vainly to smash the barb of the Union "fishhook" defense line.

The Union's Irish Brigade, now under the command of Col. Patrick Kelly since Thomas Francis Meagher's resignation following Fredericksburg, arrived at Gettysburg early on the second day of the battle after a forced march of 34 miles—one of the longest of any infantry unit in the war. By this time, however, after heavy losses at Antietam, Fredericksburg, and Chancellorsville, it was a brigade in name only, numbering barely 530 effectives, with "regiments" hardly larger than companies.

Nevertheless, the Irish Brigade did not waver. Assigned to support General Dan Sickles's hard-pressed III Corps in the Wheatfield, the brigade was halted by Father William Corby, chaplain of the 88th New York Regiment (and future president of Notre Dame University). Mounting a nearby boulder, the priest enunciated the ancient benediction of the Catholic church; *Eqo te absolvo.* The scene, one of the most famous in the rich lore of the Civil War, has been immortalized in painting, sculpture, and, most recently, on celluloid, having been depicted in Turner Broadcasting's superb 1993 film *Gettysburg.*

After receiving their chaplain's blessing, the Irish Brigade attended to the business at hand, charging into the Wheatfield and suffering a casualty rate of nearly 50 percent in devastating fighting at close quarters in the broiling July heat. With 214 men killed or wounded, the original Irish Brigade was all but wiped out at Gettysburg, though another one was raised later in the war.

Other Irishmen performing heroically that day included county Cavan–born Col. Patrick Henry O'Rorke on Little Round Top. (*See* Rochester, New York.) Opposing the Irish Brigade on the Confederate side in the Wheatfield was county Westmeath-born Capt. James Reilly's battery of six guns from North Carolina. Cpl. James Casey, who was serving with the 99th Pennsylvania under General Sickles, was killed trying to destroy muskets scattered over the battlefield.

The climax of the battle came on the third day with Pickett's Charge, one of the most gallant and foolhardy actions of the war. Lee, in a very uncharacteristic maneuver, sought to bull his way straight through the Union line at its center. The 15,000 Confederates making Pickett's Charge included many Irish-Americans. Willie Mitchel, son of Young Irelander and Southern newspaper editor John Mitchel (*see* Charleston, South Carolina and Hampton, Virginia), was badly wounded. Capt. John Dooley, brother of James H. Dooley (*see* Richmond, Virginia), marched with the heavily Irish Company C of the Montgomery Guards and was wounded in both thighs.

Dooley was hit just a few yards short of the Union lines, very possibly by a gun fired by Battery B of the First New York Light Artillery, serviced by James McKay Rorty. A county Donegal man, Rorty had enlisted in the 69th New York at the start of the war, was captured at the first Battle at Bull Run, but escaped and made his way back to Union lines. He was assigned to Battery B only the night before, and was killed in the repulse of Pickett's Charge.

As the remnants of Pickett's Charge scrambled up the slope toward the low stone wall that formed the Angle at the center of the Union line, the Confederates found themselves facing yet another Irish regiment at the summit. The 69th Pennsylvania, under the command of Col. Dennis O'Kane, received the full fury of the Confederate charge and repulsed it with heavy casualties at the place that came to be known as the "high water mark" of Confederate success. Colonel O'Kane was killed in the action.

Monuments are everywhere on the Gettysburg battlefield, including ones to just about every unit mentioned above.

(1) *The Irish Brigade Memorial.* Located on Sickles Ave., the Loop, near where the brigade charged at the Wheatfield. Dedicated to the three New York regiments that constituted the brigade—the 63rd, 69th, and 88th—the memorial is one of the most moving on the battlefield. Sculpted by William Rudolph O'Donovan, a Southerner of Irish extraction, the monument is a tall Celtic cross with a mourning Irish wolfhound at its base. It was dedicated July 2, 1888, exactly 25 years after the battle.

(2) *The 28th Massachusetts Infantry Memorial.* Not far from the Irish Brigade memorial is this eagle-topped monument to one of its non-New York units. The Irish identity of the 28th is evident from the Irish harp

The Irish Brigade Memorial stands stoically on the Gettysburg battlefield.

carved on the left face of the memorial and the Gaelic war cry *Faugh a ballaugh!* (Clear the way!).

(3) Near the previous two memorials on Sickles Ave. is *The 116th Pennsylvania Infantry Memorial.* Also a part of the Irish Brigade, this memorial is the most unusual on the battlefield. Normally, a Civil War regiment consisted of 10 companies of 100 officers and men, making 1,000 total. By the time of Gettysburg, only 142 men were left to march into battle as the 116th Pennsylvania. By the end of the second day of the battle, scarcely 100 were still fit for action.

It was this hard core that was determined to remember their fallen colleagues in a unique manner. Loyalty, bravery, devotion, and courage are the features of most Civil War memorials. The 116th's memorial, however, simply shows a solitary soldier, shot through the head, lying alone and forgotten on a desolate battlefield. It conveys, in a simple, yet powerful way, that death is the only victor in war.

Memorial to the
69th Pennsylvania
Infantry.

(4) *Father William Corby Portrait Statue* located on South Hancock Ave. near the intersection with United States Ave., this statue honors not only the famed chaplain of the 88th New York Infantry of the Irish Brigade but all of the hundreds of chaplains who served on both sides at Gettysburg.

The statue, erected in 1910, shows the priest with his hand raised in benediction. The boulder on which the statue stands is reputed to be the same one from which he actually delivered the blessing. A replica of the statue stands at Notre Dame University (where the irreverent and football-minded students have dubbed the statue of their late president "Fair Catch Corby").

(5) *O'Rorke Memorial.* This monument to Col. Patrick O'Rorke is one of several that graces the summit of Little Round Top. O'Rorke's nose is shiny because rubbing it is said to bring good luck. (*See* Rochester, New York, for the full story of O'Rorke at Gettysburg.)

(6) At the summit of Cemetery Hill is a memorial to James McKay Rorty and Battery B.

(7) At the Angle, where the climax of the battle took place on July 3, stands the obelisk-shaped memorial to Col. Dennis O'Kane's *69th Pennsylvania Infantry*. It is easily identifiable by the Irish harp inscribed near the top.

The visitor center contains an excellent selection of books on the battle and the story of the monuments. Not far from the visitor center is the Irish Brigade Shop, a gift store that specializes in books, prints, flags, and other memorabilia related to the Irish Brigade and Irish units in the war.

❧ LOCATION: 37 miles southwest of Harrisburg, off U.S. Highway 15. ❧ HOURS: Daily, 8–5. Closed New Year's, Thanksgiving and Christmas. ❧ ADMISSION: A guided tour of the battlefield in your car with a certified battlefield guide is highly recommended and costs $20. ❧ TELEPHONE: Visitor center: (717) 334-1124.

HAZELTON

ECKLEY MINER'S VILLAGE

Most of the Irish who came to these rugged hills in northeastern Pennsylvania had but one significant possession: muscle power. The industry that needed them was coal mining, which fed the hungry blast furnaces of the Industrial Revolution in America. Not surprisingly, the miners found themselves treated as little more than cogs in a vast machine, working long hours under extremely dangerous, often lethal conditions. When ordinary grievance procedures were found wanting, some of them, it appears, took to more direct methods of expressing their dissatisfaction.

Historians still can't agree on whether there really was an organization called the Molly Maguires, or whether it was a convenient fiction invented by the coal companies to justify hanging some union organizer "troublemakers." Many people believed there was such an organization, however, including Sir Arthur Conan Doyle, who sent Sherlock Holmes to battle the group in his novel *The Valley of Fear*. (*See* Jim Thorpe, Pennsylvania, for more on the Molly Maguires trials.)

Eckley is a restoration of a typical village occupied by mostly Irish miners during the area's heyday. (Coal was said to have been discovered here in 1818 when a deer knocked over a rock, revealing a rich vein of anthracite coal).

The village shows the cramped, unforgiving life of the miner. Keep in mind when you look at these small huts that families with seven or eight children lived in them. Miners also cursed their fate in song:

There's one thing I'll tell you and
don't you forget.
That your back with the droppers is all
wringing wet,
Your clothes they are soaking; your
shoes are wet through,
Oh! Never be a miner whatever you do.

Eckley was mostly abandoned until 1968, when Paramount Pictures restored it and used it to film the Sean Connery-Richard Harris feature film *The Molly Maguires.*

⠂⠢⠄ EXHIBITS: A guide is available at the visitor center. The restored town has 58 buildings, including typical miners' housing and several churches, which are open to the public. Several mining families still live here in a "living museum." ⠂⠢⠄ LOCATION: Off Route 940 in Eckley. ⠂⠢⠄ HOURS: Monday–Saturday 9–5, Sunday 12–5. ⠂⠢⠄ ADMISSION: $3 adults; $2 seniors; $1 children. ⠂⠢⠄ TELEPHONE:(717) 875-4708.

JIM THORPE

MOLLY MAGUIRE TRIALS

There were scarcely 1,500 men digging coal in northeastern Pennsylvania in the 1830s. But as industrialization gathered steam—literally—the demand for the black stuff soared. By the 1840s, there were nearly 10,000 coal miners and on the eve of the Civil War, over 20,000. By 1870, the number had swelled to 50,000.

Since this explosion of manpower also coincided with the influx of Irish immigrants, it is not surprising that at least a third of the new miners were Irish. They were certainly the largest single ethnic group in the mines, for few native-born Americans were willing (or sufficiently desperate) to risk an early death in the mine shafts for the low wages paid.

It is scarcely possible to describe for a 20th-century reader the horrors that passed for working conditions in the coal mines of mid-19th-century Pennsylvania. Safety precautions were virtually nonexistent, as was any form of governmental regulation. Flooded shafts and cave-ins were frequent and much feared occurrences. And for those who didn't die violently, an early death from black lung disease was almost a certainty, since the air in the shafts was thick with coal dust stirred up by the mining activity. In exchange for taking all these risks, miners worked for pathetically low wages, often less than a dollar for a 14–16-hour day.

Many of the mine owners were of English or Welsh descent, and they often appointed Welshmen or Scotsmen to supervisory positions in the pits. The Irish thus found to their chagrin that they had not left the old English power structure behind in Ireland, as they had imagined.

The origins of the Molly Maguires, assuming that such an organization existed, is as cloudy as the rest of their history. The Mollies supposedly began as an anti-landlord organization among poor tenant farmers and was named after one of their heroines. The organization was imported to the United States during immigration and became active in the coalfields in the early 1860s.

The subject of the Mollies has become so encrusted with legend and sensationalism that today it is impossible to separate fact from fiction. Terror was supposed to be the group's chief weapon, and they used it to impose a code of silence on their members and the rest of the population every bit as effective as the Sicilian *omertà*. Exceptionally brutal overseers were singled out for murder or mutilation. Mine property could be destroyed or dynamited. Suspected informers simply disappeared.

Many have cited the high rate of crime—142 unsolved murders in Schuylkill County between 1862 and 1877—as proof of the Mollies' existence. Studies of Pennsylvania and other mining regions, however, show a very high rate of crime in almost every mining community, even those with few Irish. Clearly, the lawlessness in the valleys cannot be exclusively attributed to Molly Maguire activity.

The Mollies first came to wider public attention during the Civil War. In 1863, President Lincoln enacted a law requiring conscription for the Union forces, but allowed many to opt out if they could pay $300 to a substitute. Most of the Irish miners had scarcely seen so much money in their entire lives, let alone had it to buy a substitute. "A rich man's war but a poor man's fight!" became the battle cry of those resisting conscription, among whom the Irish were prominent.

President Lincoln was anxious that the flow of coal to Northern war industries not be interrupted, so he refrained from taking violent action against the draft-resisting Irish of Pennsylvania and their reputed secret organization. While the Mollies are said to have continued their reign of terror after the war, crime statistics assembled by historian Walter Coleman in his book *The Molly Maguire Riots* indicate the period from 1870 to 1874 was relatively quiescent.

A series of murders beginning in 1875, however, shattered the mine owners' complacency about the Mollies. They called in renowned detective Allan Pinkerton and his agency to deal with the Mollies once and for all.

In his fascinating book *A Molly Maguire Story*, Patrick Campbell, an Irish-American journalist and descendant of one of the hanged men, posits an alternative theory for the sudden renewed concern about the Mollies on the part of the mine owners. The coal mine and railroad owners were seeking to establish a cartel to completely control the mining and distribution of coal in America. The recalcitrant Irish mine workers and their union were, the owners thought, all that stood in their way. Thus, it was necessary to destroy the local Ancient Order of Hibernians (AOH), which the mine owners believed functioned as a legitimizing front for the union and the Mollies.

Interestingly, the sudden upsurge of violent crime in 1875 also coincided with the arrival in the area of one Jim McKenna. McKenna was later revealed to be an Irish-American named James McParland, an undercover detective for the Pinkerton Agency. McParland, who either instigated or took advantage of the series of murders, almost single-handedly sent 20 alleged Molly Maguires to the gallows with his testimony.

Two major trials were held, one in Pottsville and the other here at Jim Thorpe, which was then called Mauch Chunk. The proceedings were a sham—the entire prosecution team were cronies or actual employees of Asa Packer and other railroad and coal moguls in the area. The judge was selected by Packer. Irish residents were systematically excluded from the juries that heard the cases, their places taken by German-Americans, many of whom scarcely had a command of English and who often held anti-Irish attitudes.

In an orgy of organized bloodlust, 10 men were hanged on the same day, June 21, 1877. Six of the executions took place in neighboring Pottsville, and four in the Carbon County Jail in Mauch Chunk. Over the next two years, 10 more men were hanged. Whether the Molly Maguires existed or not, they largely faded into the history books after the executions.

Ironically, all the conspiring to monopolize the coal industry was for naught. New labor disturbances, this time led by Scottish, Welsh, and German miners, broke out soon after the trials and the economic downturn of 1878 shattered the owners' hope of a coal mining cartel.

One fact is indisputable: the 20 men hanged were railroaded, even by the standards of the time. The prosecution witnesses were unreliable and, with the exception of the impeccably smooth McParland, forgetful or contradictory in their own testimony or in regard to one another's statements. In *A Molly Maguires Story*, Campbell uncovers some strong circumstantial evidence that McParland was handsomely compensated for his testimony, the detective's protestations to the contrary notwithstanding. In the more than a century since, the trials, no one has ever produced any convincing evidence that an organization known as the Molly Maguires actually existed.

For their partisans, the ultimate proof that the accused men were innocent is literally written on the wall of the Carbon County Jail. Alec Campbell, a county Donegal native, was charged with being an accessory to the murder of John Jones, a mine company official. Campbell consistently denied his guilt, and on the morning of his execution, rubbed his

Carbon County
Courthouse, scene
of the Molly
Maguire trials.

hand in the dust of his cell and planted it firmly on the cell wall, leaving an imprint. "There is the proof of my words," he is supposed to have said. "That mark of mine will never be wiped out. There it will remain forever to shame the county that is hanging an innocent man." Despite the efforts of successive generations of sheriffs to remove it, the handprint is still on the cell wall.

In a December 1993 "retrial" held on the same spot as the original trial, a Carbon County jury reheard the testimony, with the part of the defendants and prosecutors played by actors and actresses. After deliberating 45 minutes, they returned with a verdict of "not guilty."

The Carbon County Jail is located on West Broadway at the top of the hill that dominates the town. In 1931, the sheriff's office closed the jail to tourists, who came to gape at the handprint in Alec Campbell's cell. Since the jail is still in use as a penal institution, it remains closed to the public.

The courthouse, at the foot of West Broadway, is the third on the site and is not the one in which the accused Mollies were tried. Nevertheless, the existing courtroom is almost identical to the one in which the trials took place, and it is here that the courtroom scenes for 1970 Sean Connery/ Richard Harris vehicle *The Molly Maguires* was filmed. Visitors can inspect the courtroom during business hours.

The Jim Thorpe visitor center, located in a former railroad station in the center of town, contains much local information and a display area on local history, including the Molly Maguire trials and the filming of the movie.

Also worth a look is the Asa Packer mansion overlooking the courthouse. Packer was the owner of the Lehigh Valley Railroad and one of the prime movers in the effort to hang the alleged Molly Maguires. His opulent home shows where the money made from the sweat of the Irish miners went. Packer died suddenly just two years after the trials, his widow died a year after him, and his two sons died the year after that, putting an end to the Packer family name and bankrupting the company. Some Irish believed it was divine justice.

&⅄• LOCATION: The town of Jim Thorpe is located on Pennsylvania Route 209 in east-central Pennsylvania. &⅄• HOURS: Visitor center open Monday–Friday 9:30–4:30; weekends and holidays 10–5. Courthouse hours Monday–Friday 9–4, closed weekends and holidays. Packer mansion open Memorial Day through mid-October 12–4:30. &⅄• ADMISSION: Packer Mansion: adults $4; children $2. Other sites free. &⅄• TELEPHONE: Visitor center: (717) 325-3673; Packer Mansion: (717) 325-3229.

LANCASTER

WHEATLAND

President James Buchanan's father, also James Buchanan, was a Scotch-Irish immigrant who left Ramleton, county Donegal, in 1783. His son was the 15th president and inarguably one of the worst in American history. While almost any president would have found the Civil War difficult to prevent, Buchanan was singularly lethargic in seeking to head off the conflict as tensions rose to the boiling point during his single term between 1857 and 1861.

Buchanan, a dour Presbyterian who had held so many public offices his nickname was "the old Public Functionary," was chosen for the Democratic nomination in 1856 primarily because he had been out of the country for the previous five years serving as ambassador to Britain and Russia. He thus had played no part in the Kansas-Nebraska quarrel or

Wheatland, James Buchanan's home for 20 years.

other debates that had riven the country throughout the 1850s and had no enemies.

Buchanan tried desperately to straddle the widening chasm over slavery, refusing to endorse "coercion" of the South while at the same time refusing to condone secession. His dithering made the election of Republican Abraham Lincoln in 1860 inevitable.

After the expiration of his term, Buchanan retired to Wheatland, which he had owned since 1848, to live and write his memoirs, and he died here in 1868. Confederate troops entertained hopes of capturing him there during their 1863 invasion of Pennsylvania, hopes that were thwarted down the road at Gettysburg.

❧ EXHIBITS: The 17-room mansion is maintained as it was when the bachelor Buchanan lived here. Original furnishings and personal possessions are on display. ❧ LOCATION: 1120 Marietta Ave. in Lancaster. ❧ HOURS: Open daily April 1–November 30, 10–4:30. ❧ ADMISSION: Adults $4.50; seniors $4; students $3.75; children $1.75. ❧ TELEPHONE: (717) 392-8721.

PHILADELPHIA

BALCH INSTITUTE FOR ETHNIC STUDIES

The Balch Institute maintains a library and museum dedicated to the study of the influence of different ethnic groups on American history, not only in Philadelphia and Pennsylvania but nationally.

The museum contains a changing display of the letters, diaries, photographs, and clothing of American ethnic groups, including the Irish. The library contains numerous books and documents. Dennis Clark, the late scholar of the Irish in Philadelphia, who just before his death in 1993 had agreed to become an adviser to this project, was long associated with the Balch Institute and helped build its large Irish collection.

❧ LOCATION: 18 S. 7th St. ❧ HOURS: Museum open Monday–Saturday, 10–4; Library 9–5. ❧ ADMISSION: Donation requested. ❧ TELEPHONE: (215) 925-8090.

INDEPENDENCE HALL

Three men of Irish birth signed the Declaration of Independence: Matthew Thornton (1714–1803) of New Hampshire and two men from Pennsylvania, George Taylor (1716–1781) (*see* Allentown, Pennsylvania) and James Smith (1719–1806).

In addition, several other men of Irish descent also signed: Edward Rutledge and Thomas Lynch of South Carolina; Thomas McKean and George Read of Delaware, and Charles Carroll of Maryland, who was also the only Roman Catholic signer. (*See* Annapolis and Baltimore, Maryland.)

The convention that hammered out the U.S. Constitution in 1787 was also written here. Thomas Fitzsimons of Pennsylvania was the only Irish-born signer of that document. (*See* Old St. Mary's Church, Philadelphia, Pennsylvania.)

❧ EXHIBITS: The Assembly Room is restored to look as it did when the Founding Fathers met here between 1775 and 1787. The inkwell used to sign the Declaration is here as well as the "Rising Sun" chair George Washington used during the Constitutional Convention.

Also, a statue of Commodore John Barry, the Wexford-born naval commander considered by many "the father of the U.S. Navy," stands on the grounds in front of the hall. The work of sculptor Samuel Murray, it was a gift to the city from the Friendly Sons of St. Patrick, of which Barry was a member. It was erected in 1907 at a cost of $10,000. (*See* Old St. Mary's Church, Philadelphia, Penn.).

❧ LOCATION: Between 5th and 6th streets on Chestnut Street in Independence Square in downtown Philadelphia. ❧ HOURS: Daily, 9–5. Longer hours in summer. ❧ ADMISSION: Free ❧ TELEPHONE: (215) 597-8974.

KELLY HOUSE AND MEMORIAL

The Kellys, for all their wealth, were definitely not members of Philadelphia's high society. They didn't even count for much in the "lace curtain" world of Irish high society. But it was Jack Kelly, the self-

John B. Kelly Olympic Memorial (left); and Kelly with his famous daughter, Grace.
(right, Museum of Modern Art)

made millionaire grandson of a poor Irish immigrant, who won an Olympic gold medal for himself and saw his daughter become first an Academy Award-winning Hollywood movie star, and then a very real princess.

Jack Kelly was the grandson of John Henry Kelly, an Irish pig farmer who emigrated in the late 1860s, a generation after the famine. By the second generation, the family had achieved a level of prosperity and young Jack Kelly took up sculling, a sport in which a rower propels himself through the water in an almost-paper-thin boat. All through the teens, except for his World War I service, he practiced the sport fanatically, setting his sites on winning the Diamond Sculls at England's Henley Regatta, the world's most prestigious sculling meet.

Just three days before the meet, however, Kelly was informed his application had been rejected. Officially, it was because there was some question about his amateur status, but Kelly was convinced the real reason was rank prejudice against Irish-Americans by snobbish Englishmen. Kelly's revenge was sweet a few months later: he took the Olympic gold medal at the Antwerp Olympics, defeating Jack Beresford, the Henley champion.

Kelly made his money in the building trade. "Kelly for Brickwork" became a well-known Philadelphia advertising slogan. Although later research has shown that Jack's brother Charles was the businessman in the family and was the one really responsible for making most of the money, Jack Kelly was a millionaire many times over before the 1920s were out. In 1935, he came heartbreakingly close to being elected mayor of Philadelphia.

Jack married Margaret Majer, daughter of a German family and a Lutheran who converted to Catholicism to marry Jack. They had three daughters and one son. Grace, the third eldest, who was born in 1929, was

The Kelly house resides in the Germantown section of Philadelphia.

the odd one out. She was sickly and something of an intellectual in a physically rambunctious clan. Like her uncle, Pulitzer Prize-winning playwright George Kelly, she was drawn to arts and the theater (much to her father's chagrin, since he disliked his brother).

But Grace was determined in her own way and pursued an acting career over her parents' objections. Her first Broadway role came in 1949 as Raymond Massey's daughter in *The Father*. Her Hollywood debut came two years later with a small part in *Fourteen Hours*. Her breakthrough role, however, was as the Quaker wife opposite Gary Cooper in 1952's *High Noon*.

After *High Noon*, it was a dizzying series of successes for Grace, many with Alfred Hitchcock (who pined secretly—and vainly—for her love). Her career climaxed with the 1954 film *The Country Girl,* for which she won an Academy Award as best actress.

All the time, Grace was considered one of the world's most eligible women, and it was while she was on a European trip in 1954 that she met Prince Ranier, ruler of the microstate of Monaco, on a publicity stunt arranged by *Paris-Match* magazine. Their engagement was announced at a raucous press conference in the Kelly home in Philadelphia on January 6, 1955, and the two were married in April. Jack Kelly was less than thrilled when the prince's retainers informed him that a dowry of $2 million or so would be acceptable. Kelly grumbled, but he paid up.

It was the end of Grace's acting career, much to her later regret, and accounts differ as to how happy her marriage was. Grace's two daughters, Caroline and Stephanie, gave her no end of troubles, though Prince Albert came close to being as ideal a son as a mother could want. Grace died of a stroke at the wheel of her car near Monaco on September 13, 1982.

❧ **EXHIBITS:** The house is privately owned and not open to the public. The Kelly Monument was erected in 1965. ❧ **LOCATION:** The Kelly house, built of distinctive Kelly redbrick, is at 3901 Henry Ave., at the intersection with Coulter Street, in the Germantown section of Philadelphia. To reach the memorial to John Kelly, follow Midvale Avenue south to where it dead-ends at Kelly Drive and turn left (south). Follow Kelly Dr. approximately 1 mile to the distinctive Kelly Memorial, depicting Jack Kelly in his Olympic rowing scull, which will be in a small park on your right by the river's edge near the rowing grandstands. There is a parking lot next door.

MARINE CORPS MEMORIAL MUSEUM

In the lore of the U.S. Marine Corps, the famed fighting force was first recruited in a barroom on the Philadelphia waterfront known as Tun's Tavern, which was owned by an Irish immigrant or Irish-American named Mullen (or Mullan). Although some Marine Corps historians are skeptical of the tale, it endures nevertheless. This small museum, located in a restored 1791 building, commemorates the early history of the corps in Philadelphia and in early American wars.

❧ **EXHIBITS:** One of the exhibits is a diorama portraying Tun's Tavern and Mullen. Over the years, there have been various proposals to re-create the tavern itself as a museum, but these have come to nothing. The former site is now buried beneath an expressway. ❧ **LOCATION:** On Chestnut Street, between 3rd and 4th streets. ❧ **HOURS:** Daily, 9–5. ❧ **ADMISSION:** Free ❧ **TELEPHONE:** (215) 597-8974.

OLD ST. MARY'S CHURCH

Founded in 1763, St. Mary's was the principal Roman Catholic church in Philadelphia during the revolutionary period. Many notable Irish-Americans of the time are buried in the churchyard at the rear.

Probably the best known is Commodore John Barry, whose statue stands behind Independence Hall. Although the U.S. Navy generally plumps for Scottish-born John Paul Jones as its founder, a good case can be made that the county Wexford-born Barry is the "father of the American navy."

Barry appears to have gone to sea early, for he settled in Philadelphia in 1760, at only 15 years of age. Philadelphia at that time rivaled Boston as the busiest seaport and trading center of the American colonies, and Barry was quick to get in on the action, becoming wealthy as a trader and shipmaster. Naturally, he resented the British efforts to regulate and tax American trade, and he was an early enthusiast for rebellion.

*The outside of Old
St. Mary's Church
in Philadelphia.*

After offering his services to the Continental Congress, Barry was given command of the brig *Lexington,* which on April 17, 1776, captured the British tender *Edward,* the first capture ever of a British warship by a regularly commissioned American cruiser.

The rest of Barry's career was just as illustrious. Although Philadelphia was occupied by the British in 1777 and the U.S. ships were bottled up by British forces in the lower Delaware River, Barry still managed to carry out successful raids on British shipping on the river and capture supplies destined for the British occupation forces. He even joined Washington's army for a time and served in the Trenton campaign with distinction.

In 1794, Barry was named senior captain (in effect, overall commander) of U.S. naval forces to combat Algerian piracy. He also served in the undeclared naval war with France in 1798–99. When he died in 1803, he was still on active service as the highest-ranking officer in the navy.

Grave of John Barry, considered the father of the American Navy.

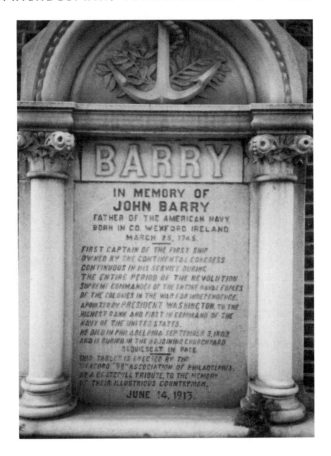

Barry was conscious of his Irish roots and was a founder and officer of the Friendly Sons of St. Patrick, one of the first Irish-American fraternal organizations.

Also buried here is Stephen Moylan, a county Cork native who served as George Washington's aide-de-camp in the Revolution. Because of the British penal laws that endeavored to suppress Roman Catholics, Moylan's merchant father was forced to dispatch his son to Paris in order for him to be educated in the Catholic faith. After a time in Portugal, he settled in Philadelphia in 1768, where he rose to wealth and prestige. In 1771, he became the first president of the Friendly Sons of St. Patrick.

Moylan came to Washington's attention through John Dickinson (who refused to sign the Declaration of Independence, but later helped write and signed the Constitution), who recommended Moylan to the general as a "zealous patriot." Moylan used his wealth to outfit several privateer vessels, which did considerable damage to British shipping.

Although he angled for a diplomatic assignment, Moylan was named Washington's aide in March 1776. Three months later, Congress named him quartermaster general of the army with a mandate to straighten out the chaotic supply system, a task that proved beyond him. He was removed from his post after a congressional investigation.

Moylan remained with the army, mostly in cavalry posts, though his hot temper repeatedly landed him in hot water. He clashed with Casimir Pulaski, the Polish officer commanding the American cavalry, and he was court-martialed for his conduct in October 1777. He was acquitted, however, and continued serving, despite Pulaski's protests. On the field, Moylan was a dashing figure, recalling his Irish ancestry by wearing a coat of bright green material. In 1796, he was again elected president of the Friendly Sons of St. Patrick. He died in 1811.

Dublin-born Mathew Carey had only a rudimentary education, but that didn't stop him from becoming one of the most prominent newspaper publishers in early America.

Carey got an early start as a troublemaker. In 1779, at age 19, became enraged at the wrongs done to Catholics and published an anonymous pamphlet detailing the abuses. The pamphlet was cited in both the Lords and the Commons as evidence of the treasonable attitudes held by Catholics, and a price of 40 pounds was placed on the head of the author. Carey's family took the precaution of packing him off to Paris, where he became acquainted with Benjamin Franklin, who was serving as the American ambassador. Franklin had a small printing shop in Paris, where Carey learned his future trade. Through Franklin, he also met the Marquis de Lafayette, who sounded him out on the political situation in Ireland.

In 1783, Carey's father set up his son as proprietor of the *Volunteer's Journal*, a paper meant to defend Ireland against English depredations. The paper's brief history, in Carey's words, "was enthusiastic and violent." The paper was held responsible for generating a demonstration against the Duke of Rutland, the lord lieutenant of Ireland, outside Daly's Theater. Carey soon found himself in jail for a short period, and after his release he escaped aboard a ship bound for Philadelphia dressed as a woman.

Arriving in the fall of 1784 with little money and no friends, Carey was delighted to reencounter Lafayette and dined with the general at his home. The Frenchman pressed $400 on the young Irishman, which the latter used to start his first American newspaper, the *Pennsylvania Herald*. Carey would repay the debt in 1824, when the general returned to the United States in straightened circumstances.

After many publishing ventures, Carey achieved a certain prosperity in the early 1790s and founded the Hibernian Society for the relief of poor Irish immigrants. He also achieved some note as an amateur economist, writing in favor of the need for trade protectionism. He became one of the

Grave of Thomas Fitzsimons, the only Irishman to sign the U.S. Constitution.

city's most prominent citizens, and his funeral in 1839 was described by contemporaries as one of the best attended in Philadelphia history up to that time.

The early life of Thomas Fitzsimons (or Fitzsimins—he used both spellings) is cloudy. Other than that he was born in Ireland around 1741 and arrived in Philadelphia sometime before he was age 21, little is known. His wife, Catherine Meade, was a great-aunt of Gen. George G. Meade, the victor of Gettysburg.

Fitzsimons was another of the merchant-rebels of Philadelphia, backing the revolutionary cause with hard cash, outfitting militia units and ships. He served in the Congress elected under the Articles of Confederation, as well as served several terms in the state legislature. A Federalist, he identified closely with Alexander Hamilton. He signed the U.S. Constitution, was elected to the first Congress, and served three terms until his defeat in 1794. He retired to private life and died in 1811.

Also buried in the churchyard is Michael Bouvier, an ancestor of Jacqueline Bouvier Kennedy Onassis (*see* Newport, Rhode Island).

❧ EXHIBITS: The plain exterior conceals a richly ornamented interior with an elaborate high altar and a Victorian Crucifixion scene. All the graves are in the rear churchyard and are clearly marked with plaques as well as tombstones. ❧ LOCATION: 252 S. Fourth St., not far from Independence Hall. ❧ HOURS: Guided tours are available 11:30–4 on Sunday. Call for church hours other times. The churchyard is open to the public during daylight hours. ❧ ADMISSION: Churchyard free. Donations appreciated for church. ❧ TELEPHONE: (215) 923-7930.

PENN'S LANDING

William Penn was an English Quaker, but he had significant Irish connections. In fact, almost everything that impelled him later on in life—conversion to Quakerism, his imprisonment for his faith and subsequent commitment to religious freedom—took place during his residence in Ireland.

Penn's father was an admiral in the Royal Navy, a staunch professor of the established Church of England, and a pillar of the English ruling class. Admiral Penn arrived in Ireland in the mid-1600s, after his family had been granted lands in the Irish "colony" by Cromwell's government in England.

The admiral owned Macroom Castle in county Cork. (His wife's family had owned an estate farther north, part of which is now located beneath the runways of Shannon Airport.) It was at Macroom that the 12-year-old William first encountered an itinerant Quaker preacher named Thomas Loe. It was Loe who would utterly change the course of Penn's life.

A few years later, Penn encountered Loe again, this time in county Cork, and after hearing the preacher speak, Penn was so moved he converted on the spot. The year was 1667, however, and religious tolerance was definitely not in the air. Penn and 18 other Quakers (or "Friends" as they are also known) were promptly thrown in jail under a 1661 statute prohibiting worship by Anabaptists and Quakers.

Penn's experience in this English jail in Ireland had the most profound consequences, both for him personally and for the future of the United States, for it impressed upon him the need for religious tolerance. Penn's influential father secured his son's release in fairly short order, but angrily demanded he return to England. It was on this voyage that he seems first to have considered the idea of America as a haven for persecuted Quakers. With his Irish-born secretary, James Logan, Penn accomplished just that in 1681.

Ireland thus played a key role in the life of the man who would found one of the great states of the American Union. The spirit of religious tolerance born in that jailhouse in county Cork took root in Pennsylvania and was the reason this colony attracted so many Irish Catholics in its early years.

❧ **EXHIBITS:** The 37-acre development contains a museum, a sculpture garden, and several historic ships. ❧ **LOCATION:** Penn's Landing, on the Delaware River between Market and Spruce streets, is built on the site where Penn and his Irish-born secretary, James Logan, landed in 1682. ❧ **HOURS:** Variable. Call for information. ❧ **ADMISSION:** Different exhibits have different admission fees. Call for information. ❧ **TELEPHONE:** (215) 629-3200 or 629-6237.

ST. AUGUSTINE'S CHURCH AND
ST. MICHAEL'S CHURCH

Small numbers of Catholic Irish immigrants had already made Philadelphia their home before the cholera epidemic and the potato famine of the 1830s and 1840s, because Quaker Pennsylvania was one of the colonies most tolerant—though still wary—of Catholicism.

More numerous were the Presbyterian Scotch-Irish, who had emigrated to the American colonies from the north of Ireland in large numbers in the years before the Revolution. When large numbers of Irish Catholics began arriving in Philadelphia in the early decades of the 19th century, antagonism between the two Gaelic races flared into one of the first major incidents of urban rioting in American history.

The Irish Catholics were the first large immigrant group with customs and religious beliefs substantially different from those of the Anglo Protestant majority. They didn't eat meat on Fridays, they worshiped in a long-dead language that not even many of the immigrants themselves understood, their clergy were celibate, and many of the new arrivals spoke the strange Gaelic tongue, which was totally unrelated to any language familiar to the natives. And their political influence was growing with the docking of every new immigrant ship.

Not surprisingly, this state of affairs aroused bitterness and opposition, particularly among the established "native Americans." The American Protestant Association was formed in Philadelphia in 1842 and carried out a campaign of vilification against Roman Catholicism. The same year, Archbishop Francis P. Kenrick sought to have Catholic schoolchildren exempted from having to read from the King James Version of the Bible, enraging the Protestants further.

For two years, these resentments smoldered. Then, on May 3, 1844, angry Catholics broke up an open-air meeting of Scotch-Irish at Second and Master streets in the Kensington section of Philadelphia. Three days later, another meeting at Second and American streets ended in a pitched battle and the death of Patrick Fisher, a Protestant of Irish background. By the end of the day on May 6, three more deaths were recorded.

The street fighting resumed with renewed fury the next day, leaving six Scotch-Irish dead. A Protestant mob, in retaliation, burned the Hibernia Hose House and a number of dwellings in the vicinity of Second and Master streets. St. Michael's Church, at Second and Jefferson, was burned to the ground the same day, along with an adjoining school run by Catholic nuns.

The bloodshed went on for three days and nights, and didn't end until the state militia was mobilized. The troops, however, were unable to prevent the burning of St. Augustine's Church at Fourth Street, below Vine. A total of 16 deaths on both sides were recorded, along with innumerable injuries and dozens of Irish Catholic homes burned or damaged.

Two months later, the Southwark neighborhood was similarly convulsed. In this riot, a rumor spread that Catholics were stocking arms in churches, and a Protestant mob menaced the Church of St. Philip Dé Neri on Queen Street. But the church, heavily guarded by militiamen, escaped damage.

The Philadelphia riot has often been cited as one of the first examples of anti-Catholic *"Know-Nothingism"* in the United States. (The "Know Nothings" were an anti-immigrant political party). The truth is probably a bit more complicated. Digby Baltzell, a scholar of the riots, cites as proof that the clash was largely an inter-Irish affair the fact that only Irish Catholic churches were burned, while those frequented by German Catholics were left untouched. This conclusion is supported by the late Dennis Clark, the eminent historian of the Irish in the city, in his book *The Irish in Philadelphia.*

Both St. Augustine's and St. Michael's were subsequently rebuilt much as they appear today. And the Cathedral of Saints Peter and Paul, begun in 1846, it was deliberately designed with no ground floor windows, so as to avoid tempting future mobs of rock throwers.

❧ LOCATION: St. Augustine's is located on Fourth St., just below Vine St. St. Michael's is located at Second and Jefferson streets. The Church of St. Philip Dé Neri is at 220–228 Queen St. The Cathedral of Saints Peter and Paul is at 18th St. and Benjamin Franklin Pkwy. ❧ HOURS: Call for mass schedule. Other times, inquire at church offices about seeing the interiors. ❧ ADMISSION: None, but donations appreciated. ❧ TELEPHONE: St. Augustine's: (215) 627-1838; St. Michael's: (215) 739-2358; St. Philip De' Neri: (215) 468-1922; Cathedral of Saints Peter and Paul: (215) 561-1313.

STENTON

There is a persistent story told about the voyage of William Penn and Armagh-born James Logan to their new home in the American colonies. In mid-voyage, their ship was supposedly attacked by pirates. Logan participated energetically in the defense of the ship while Penn, holding to his Quaker pacifist beliefs, retired below to his cabin while the fight raged above. After the pirates had been repelled, Penn upbraided his assistant for his aggressive behavior. Logan didn't flinch: "I being thy servant, why did thee not order me to come down?"

Although the anecdote may well be apocryphal, it is illustrative of the different attitudes and policies of the two men. Logan was not a strictly professing Quaker and believed self-defense to be justified. Later, he suggested that Quakers who could not vote funds for legitimate self-defense purposes ought not seek election to the legislature.

A native of Lurgan, county Armagh, Logan's father was a schoolmaster and a Scottish emigrant. Thanks to his father, young James was learned in Latin, Greek, and Hebrew before he was 13. In England around 1699, he made the acquaintance of William Penn and so impressed him that Penn asked him to become his secretary. He was to remain a confidential adviser to Penn and Penn's children and grandchildren for over half a century.

Logan built this house on more than 500 acres in 1728 and named it for his father's birthplace in Scotland. Since negotiating with the Indians was a major part of his career as one of the leading men of the colony, the Indians frequently camped on the grounds of the house. Later, it became headquarters for both George Washington and Lord Howe, the British commander, during the American Revolution.

❧ EXHIBITS: The house is furnished with fine examples of period furnishings and exhibits on the life of James Logan. ❧ LOCATION: 18th and Windrim streets, in the Germantown area of Philadelphia. ❧ HOURS: Tuesday–Saturday 1–4, March 30–Dec. 31. ❧ ADMISSION: $3 adults; seniors and students with ID $2. ❧ TELEPHONE: (215) 329-7312.

PITTSBURGH

THE IRISH ROOM—THE UNIVERSITY OF PITTSBURGH

The 42-story Cathedral of Learning at the University of Pittsburgh sports a 3-story Commons Room, which is surrounded by 23 "nationality rooms." The Irish Room is a gift of the Republic of Ireland and is made of stone. During the Christmas holidays, the rooms are decorated with the holiday themes of the country.

❧ EXHIBITS: A weekend is the best time for a visit, as the nationality rooms are used as classrooms during the week. ❧ LOCATION: 5th and Parkman Aves. ❧ HOURS: Monday–Saturday 9:30–3; Sunday 11–3. ❧ ADMISSION: $2; $1 for seniors. Guided tours are available. ❧ TELEPHONE: (412) 624-6000.

STATE COLLEGE

JOHN O'HARA STUDY

"I go through cheap shame when the O'Hara side gets too close for comfort," wrote the young John O'Hara to the other great American novelist who wrestled with his Irish identity, F. Scott Fitzgerald.

The O'Haras weren't coal miners, unlike so many Irish in the Schuylkill County town of Pottsville. Michael O'Hara, the author's grandfather, came from Ireland as a child during the famine. He later served as an officer in the Civil War and came to Pottsville to inform the parents of one of his men that their son had died. He liked that area and decided to stay, eventually achieving modest prosperity as a building contractor. He was able to send one of his sons, Patrick, to the University of Pennsylvania, from which he obtained his medical degree. Patrick O'Hara's son, the future novelist, was born in 1905.

As his letter to Fitzgerald shows, John O'Hara tended to identify more with the socially elevated, Anglo-Protestant elites in Pottsville than with the more proletarian Irish. At the same time, he resented the way the Protestants held the Irish to be a natural serving class. All his life, O'Hara yearned to be accepted by the "better class of person" he felt was exemplified by his (non-Irish) mother. This is evident in O'Hara's fiction. His Irish characters are almost invariably literary versions of the "stage Irishman," or crude reprobates.

Harry Reilly, for instance, is the social-climbing Irishman of O'Hara's first success, *Appointment in Samarra*. Reilly's pretensions so irritate the novel's protagonist, the Waspy Julian English (not too subtle here), that the latter violently throws a glass of whiskey in Reilly's face. A famous line spoken by Jimmy Molloy in *Butterfield 8* could well have been spoken by O'Hara himself:

> *I want to tell you something about myself that will help explain to you a lot of things about me. You might as well hear it now. First of all, I am a Mick. I wear Brooks Brothers clothes and I don't eat salad with a spoon and I probably could play five-goal polo in two years, but I am a Mick. Still a Mick.*

O'Hara achieved great fame and considerable wealth as a novelist and screenwriter, although critics tended to be lukewarm about the value of his work. Many of his books, including *Butterfield 8* and *Ten North Frederick*, were turned into highly successful films. In the end, he never resolved the conflict within himself about whether the Irish ought to be assimilated into American society or remain distinctly outside it, but he never stopped trying. He died in 1970.

❧ EXHIBITS: O'Hara's study in Princeton, N.J., was carefully dismantled by his widow after his death and reconstructed here. It is meant, according to the librarian, "to be recognizable to John O'Hara if he were suddenly to reappear today." ❧ LOCATION: The Pattee Library at Pennsylvania State University. ❧ HOURS: Library open Monday–Friday 8–5, Saturdays 9–1. O'Hara study can be viewed by appointment only however. Several of O'Hara's manuscripts, including *Appointment in Samarra*, are on display. ❧ ADMISSION: Free ❧ TELEPHONE: (814) 865-1793.

The monument to Irish-born Medal of Honor winners is nestled in the Medal of Honor Grove at Valley Forge.

VALLEY FORGE

FREEDOM'S FOUNDATION AT VALLEY FORGE

Although the members of the party known as "Andrews Raiders" are usually credited with being the first recipients of the congressional Medal of Honor in 1863, the first action for which a Medal of Honor was awarded took place almost two years earlier. The honoree was Patrick Irwin, an Irish immigrant who received the nation's highest award for gallantry when he led a rescue party through hostile Indian territory in 1861. Irwin didn't actually receive his medal, however, until nearly three decades after the event.

Since then, 202 men of Irish birth have received this coveted award, far and away the largest such immigrant group. That doesn't count, of course, the many Americans of Irish descent who have also received the medal.

The names of the Irish-born Medal of Honor winners are carved on an obelisk in the Medal of Honor Grove here at Freedom's Foundation at Valley Forge, a private organization founded in 1949. The obelisk was erected by the Ancient Order of Hibernians.

❧ **EXHIBITS:** The memorial, in Connemara marble, is recognizable because of the Irish harp inscribed on the surface. Tours of the grounds are available by appointment. ❧ **LOCATION:** On Pennsylvania Route 23, just past the Valley Forge National Historical Park. ❧ **HOURS:** Monday–Friday, 9–5. ❧ **ADMISSION:** Free ❧ **TELEPHONE:** (215) 933-8825.

Q U E B E C

GROSSE ISLE

In 1832, a cholera epidemic swept Europe. Ireland was particularly hard-hit and the first major wave of emigration to the New World began in that year, more than a decade before the Great Famine. Many of the emigrants headed for Canada, in part because of subsidized fares provided by a British government eager to encourage settlement of the English-speaking dominions.

Many Irish, of course, had no intention of staying in British-controlled Canada. Rather, they hoped simply to use it as a way station before crossing the border south to their real destination, the United States. Many never made it.

In 1832, the British authorities established an immigrant quarantine station on Grosse Isle (Big Island) in the St. Lawrence River, 30 miles below Quebec City. The idea was to intercept infected immigrants before they could spread the disease into Canadian cities. The station, however, was soon overwhelmed with sickly, half-starved immigrants, many of whom died in the hundreds soon after reaching their supposed place of refuge. Efforts at quarantine failed and cholera soon began raging in Canada's cities.

Fifteen years later came the height of Famine immigration and, once again, Grosse Isle was caught completely unprepared. French-Canadians began referring to the place as L'Ile des Irlandais" (The Island of the Irish), or, less happily, "The Island of Death."

No one knows how many Irish died and were buried in the unmarked graves on Grosse Isle, but many thousands would be a partial estimate. (Henry Ford's grandmother was reputed to have been one of them.) Enough survived and stayed in Canada, however, to create a prosperous Irish-American community. As a result, many French-Canadian politicians sport such un-French names as Claude Ryan, Pierre-Marc Johnson and, of course, Brian Mulroney.

In 1897, the local chapter of the Ancient Order of Hibernians began raising money to erect a memorial to the victims. The 40-foot-high Celtic Cross was unveiled in 1909, on the highest point on the island. Grosse Isle has recently been restored and is now part of the Canadian national park system.

🍂 **EXHIBITS:** The Celtic Cross monument dominates the island. Many buildings are in the process of being restored. 🍂 **LOCATION:** Grosse Isle is near the town of Montmagny, on the south shore of the St. Lawrence River, about 30 miles downriver from Quebec City. 🍂 **HOURS:** Half-day tours are available at 9, 10:30 and 1:15 mid-June through late September. Full day tours are available Wednesday and Saturday at 9. 🍂 **ADMISSION:** Full day tour is C$40,50 adults; C$20.25 for children ages 4 to 15; The half-day tour is C$30 adults; C$15 children. 🍂 **TELEPHONE:** (418) 259-2140 or (418) 622-2566.

Rhode Island

MIDDLETOWN

WHITEHALL FARM

Bishop George Berkeley, the Anglo-Irish philosopher and prelate, believed he had a mission in life to found a great university. The site he chose was Bermuda, and this small farm in Rhode Island was where Berkeley and his family waited for three years, in vain as it turned out, for the British Parliament to appropriate the money.

The family Berkeley (pronounced "barkly") was born into on March 12, 1685, at Dysart Castle near Kilkenny was well-to-do for the time. At the age of 10 he was sent to Kilkenny College, which even then was over 150 years old and which remains to this day one of the leading private schools in Ireland. (Jonathan Swift, later a lifelong friend of Berkeley's, had been there before him.)

Berkeley went on to Trinity College, Dublin, where he would eventually spend 24 years, teaching classics, logic, theology, and Hebrew. Although Berkeley's family had probably arrived in Ireland only about 20 years before his birth, he considered himself Irish, using the phrase "we Irishmen" many times in his letters and diaries.

It was while he was at Trinity that Berkeley began to develop his philosophy of immaterialism. In rapid succession, he published a series of philosophical works: *An essay towards a New Theory of Vision* (1709) is certainly one of his greatest and is considered a classic by psychologists as well as philosophers. At the time, the world was being introduced to new means of vision, such as eyeglasses, microscopes, and telescopes. Berkeley believed a new theory of vision was needed, and he distinguished between what we actually see, and what we infer or think we see. It is almost universally considered a pioneering work on perception.

Berkeley's writings won him fame and he traveled widely in the first quarter of the 18th century, first to England, then to France and Italy. The

Whitehall Farm, home of Bishop George Berkeley.

early stirrings of the Industrial Revolution and trade with the Americas was raising living standards everywhere, but Berkeley worried about the spiritual consequences. He considered Europe to be in a state of moral decay and dreamed of starting anew in the New World. The scheme he conceived grew into a passion that would grip him for nearly a decade.

His vision of a new university was one in which he would educate "the youth of our plantations" as well as "young American Savages" (Indians). The site he chose was the island of Bermuda, whose location halfway between the northern and southern colonies would make it convenient. He also cherished its isolation, which would provide few distractions for the faculty or the students.

Some thought the scheme mad, but Berkeley's prestige won important converts. Jonathan Swift endorsed the idea, as did the archbishop of Canterbury, the duke of Newcastle, and many others. Berkeley eventually sold his idea to King George I and Parliament, which promised to back him with a grant of 20,000 pounds.

Confident his money would soon be forthcoming, Dean Berkeley (he had been ordained in the Church of Ireland in 1709) sailed for the colonies. His plan was to buy a farm where produce could be raised to supply the proposed St. Paul's University. He arrived in Newport on January 23, 1729.

Berkeley's reputation had preceded him, and word of his arrival caused the local pastor to immediately end his service with a blessing and lead the entire congregation down to the wharf to greet the philosopher.

Newly married and with a growing family, Berkeley purchased a 96-acre farm in the nearby village of Middletown to supply the needs of the proposed college. He built a comfortable farmhouse that still stands and named it Whitehall Farm after Parliament's London address. (Perhaps he thought the flattery would hurry Parliament into sending along his money.)

Berkeley stayed a little over two years, increasingly in despair at ever receiving his 20,000 pounds. Although he frequently preached at Trinity Church in Newport, he resisted local entreaties to become the first bishop in the colonies.

When Prime Minister Sir Robert Walpole made it clear the money would not be forthcoming, Berkeley abandoned his dream. He donated Whitehall Farm to the struggling College of New Haven (Yale University) and returned to Ireland, where he became bishop of Cloyne in county Cork. He died while on a visit to Oxford in 1753.

Although certainly not an Irish nationalist in the modern sense of the word, Berkeley's writings show him to be well versed in economics, and he frequently called attention to the wretched conditions of the people in his see. Eamon de Valera (*see* Rochester, New York) sometimes quoted Berkeley, and the Irish Republic issued a postage stamp commemorating him on the 300th anniversary of his birth in 1985.

Although Berkeley never realized his dream of founding a great university, his influence on the development of higher education in America was strong. It was for this reason that when the University of California was looking for a name for its premier institution that they chose to honor this Irish clergyman by naming it after him.

&• EXHIBITS: The furnishings are of the period when Berkeley resided at Whitehall, though not originals. There is a small gift shop.   &•
LOCATION: Whitehall Farm is located on Berkeley Ave. between Wyatt Rd. and Green End Ave. in the village of Middletown, which is three miles north of Newport.   &• HOURS: Open daily July 1 through Labor Day, 10–5. Other times by appointment.   &• ADMISSION: Adults $3; $1 for children.   &• TELEPHONE: (401) 846-3116 or (401) 847-7951.

NEWPORT

HAMMERSMITH FARM AND
ST. MARY'S CHURCH

Hammersmith Farm was the 28-room summer "cottage" of the Auchincloss family and is one of many grand mansions that overlook Narragansett Bay in Newport. It was here that the wedding reception took place for Sen. John Fitzgerald Kennedy of Massachusetts and Jacqueline Lee Bouvier after their marriage at St. Mary's Church in downtown Newport on September 12, 1953. Later, during the Kennedy presidency, it served as the "summer White House."

*St. Mary's Church
saw the marriage
of John F.
Kennedy and
Jacqueline Bouvier
on September 12,
1953.*

Jacqueline had spent much of her childhood at Hammersmith. Her mother, Janet Norton Lee, had married John Vernon Bouvier III, and Jackie was born July 28, 1929. Janet, daughter of an Irish family that had made a modest fortune, had nevertheless married "up." The Bouviers had had wealth and position for several generations. Janet Bouvier's husband, came undone soon after Jacqueline's birth, however, losing most of his money in the Wall Street crash of 1929.

Bouvier did manage to recoup somewhat, until the newly formed Securities and Exchange Commission (SEC) banned the stock manipulations in which he had previously specialized. The chairman of the SEC was one Joseph P. Kennedy, Sr., who had profited handsomely from many of the same questionable transactions he was now outlawing. Jack Bouvier never forgave Kennedy.

Another blow to Jack's pride was the marriage of Janet to Hugh D. Auchincloss after her divorce from Jack in 1935. The wealthy Auchinclosses could give young Jackie and her sister, Lee, everything they ever wanted, a situation with which Jack could not hope to compete.

During Kennedy's three years as president, Hammersmith Farm came to be known as "the summer White House."

The wedding of Jackie to the heir of his bitter foe, Joseph Kennedy, needless to say, turned out to be more than Jack could bear. He passed out drunk in his room at the Viking Hotel and missed the ceremony entirely.

Herbert S. Parmet, in his book *Jack: The Struggles of John F. Kennedy*, described the wedding as having "the aura of a royal affair." Twelve hundred guests were in attendance under a huge striped tent that was set up on the lawn, which rolled from the house down to the sea. The bride and groom spent two hours in the receiving line greeting guests. The couple wasted little time, however; barely three hours after the ceremony, they flew off to their honeymoon in Acapulco.

They were to return often, however. During Kennedy's three summers as president, Hammersmith was known as the "summer White House." In her grandmother Rose's guestbook, young Caroline Kennedy scribbled, "Hammersmith is beautiful all year round. My favorite house anywhere."

&· EXHIBITS: The house was donated to the nation by the Auchincloss family and opened to the public in 1978. It contains many photographs and mementos of the Auchincloss family and much Kennedy family memorabilia, including the office Kennedy used as president when he was at Hammersmith. A guided tour is available. &· LOCATION: Hammersmith Farm is located on Ocean Drive in Newport. From New York, take I-95 north to Rhode Island exit 3 (Route 138) and follow signs for Newport Bridge. Once in Newport, follow the signs for Ocean Drive and Ft. Adams State Park. Hammersmith is next to Ft. Adams. &· HOURS: Open daily April–October. Spring and fall hours 10–5; summer hours 10–7. &· ADMISSION: Adults $5; children under 16 free. Group rates available by calling in advance. &· TELEPHONE: (401) 846-0420.

IRISH SERVANT PLAQUE

The Kennedys might have felt at home at Hammersmith Farm, but only a few years before their arrival, the only Irish-Catholics in Newport cleaned the floors and looked after the children.

In the late 19th century, a very high proportion of Irish immigrants, as many as a quarter (mostly women, but many men also), were employed as domestic servants. They were widely known among their employers as "Bridgets," their toil is what made life in these opulent mansions possible.

After their 12–hour days, the servants would gather down near the oceanside for socializing and relaxation.

❧ **EXHIBITS:** A plaque marks the location. ❧ **LOCATION:** At the beginning of Cliff Walk, near the end of Memorial Boulevard, a few minutes from downtown Newport.

NAVAL WAR COLLEGE

By 1890, the last of the Indian wars had come to an end and the U.S. Bureau of the Census declared the frontier closed. "Manifest Destiny" was finally a reality. "Whether they will or no," wrote the president of the newly established Naval War College in the pages of the *Atlantic Monthly* that same year, "Americans must now begin to look outward."

The writer was Capt. Alfred Thayer Mahan, who was described by Barbara Tuchman in her book *The Proud Tower* as "a quiet, thin-lipped naval officer with one of the most forceful minds of his time." Mahan had assigned himself the role of being "a voice to speak constantly of our external interests." Mahan's writings were to provide the intellectual muzzle velocity behind an America about to take its first tentative steps onto the world stage.

Mahan was eminently equipped for the role he was to play. His father, Thomas Mahan, was born in 1802 in New York City of Irish parents who had fled their homeland after the failed uprising of 1798. His academic brilliance became evident early on and he won appointment to West Point. Graduating first in his class, he almost immediately went to France for more advanced study.

Upon his return in 1830, Mahon was appointed to the West Point faculty as a professor of civil and military engineering, where he remained until his death in 1871. He became the author of such books as *Complete Treatise on Field Fortifications* and *Course of Civil Engineering,* which became standard military texts for decades to come. Thomas Mahan was a mentor to many of the best-known commanders on both sides in the Civil War.

Mahan's son Alfred felt the call of the sea, however, and graduated from Annapolis in 1859. He spent the Civil War on blockade duty off the

Southern coast and the 20 years after the war on routine cruises and patrols. He used his time profitably, however, studying not merely naval strategy and tactics but also the theory and history of naval power.

On the basis of this work, he was appointed lecturer at the newly established Naval War College in Newport in 1885. A year later, Mahan, by then a captain, was appointed president of the institution.

Mahan's great insight was that the nation that had control of the sea had control of the situation. To modern-day audiences, this might seem obvious, and it indeed seemed obvious to many at the time. But Mahan was the first to articulate what nations had been doing all along. In a series of lectures given at the Naval War College in 1887, Mahan expounded on the theory that was to make him world famous and lift the U.S. Navy to its 20th-century level of global preeminence.

"(I)t struck me how different things might have been could Hannibal have invaded Italy by sea . . . or could he, after arrival, have been in free communication with Carthage by water," Mahan said later of the genesis of his insight. "All at once, I realized that control of the sea was an historic factor which had never been systematically appreciated and expounded."

Although it took three years to find a publisher, *The Influence of Sea Power Upon History* —his 1887 lectures in book form—hit the world like a thunderclap when it was published in 1890. Theodore Roosevelt, who had already written his own history of sea power in the War of 1812, read it "straight through," pronounced the work "a naval classic," and declared himself converted. When he became president a decade later, Roosevelt used Mahan's work as the basis for his transformation of the U.S. Navy from little more than a coastal defense force to an oceangoing, worldwide fleet.

Roosevelt was scarcely the only world leader who took Mahan and his ideas seriously. Dispatched to Europe to command the European station, Mahan was received with great fanfare, dining with Queen Victoria and receiving honorary degrees from both Oxford and Cambridge in the same week. But his most enthusiastic admirer was Germany's Kaiser Wilhelm II, who invited him to dinner aboard his yacht. The kaiser already was nursing the idea of a great German fleet, and Mahan's ideas only gave him further impetus. Mahan died in 1914, before he could see the full results of what he had written come to pass.

❧ **EXHIBITS:** The museum contains many exhibits related to Mahan, including the desk on which he wrote his greatest work. ❧ **LOCATION:** The Naval War College is on Coasters Harbor Island in Newport. The museum is located in Founders Hall, which was the original home of the Naval War College when it was established in 1884. ❧ **HOURS:** Monday–Friday, 10–4, Saturday and Sunday 12–4, June through September. Monday–Friday, 10–4 rest of the year. ❧ **ADMISSION:** Free ❧ **TELEPHONE:** (401) 841-4052.

VERMONT

CHESTER ALAN ARTHUR BIRTHPLACE

One of President Chester Alan Arthur's few claims to fame was that he was the only American president never to have won elective office in his own right at any level. The "gentleman boss" of the New York Republican party, he was always a behind-the-scenes operator.

The future president's father, William Arthur, was a Baptist clergyman. The elder Arthur had actually emigrated from county Antrim to Canada a few years before settling in this small farming community in northern Vermont. (The family later moved to New York.) Chester was born October 5, 1830. Later, Arthur's political enemies started a rumor that he had actually been born in Canada, adopted the name and birth date of a younger brother who died as an infant, and was therefore ineligible to serve as president. This scarcely credible story, however, had no supporting evidence.

Arthur became a lawyer and an ardent abolitionist. He delighted in taking the cases of fugitive slaves. In one case that won him national attention, he won the freedom of six slaves whose Virginia owner mistakenly believed he could transport them through the free state of New York. He won $500 in damages for a Negro woman named Lizzie Jennings who had been thrown off a New York streetcar because of her color.

Active in the new Republican party, Arthur was appointed acting quartermaster general to help supply the volunteer troops who were mustering throughout the huge state. In this capacity, he received the rank of brigadier general, and even though he never got anywhere near the fighting front, he used the title "General" for the rest of his life.

Maintaining his party activity, Arthur was rewarded in 1871 with probably the juiciest patronage plum in American politics. President Grant appointed him collector of the port of New York. In addition to controlling the appointment of nearly 1,000 employees in the customs house, the post offered the opportunity for virtually unlimited graft and rake-offs from customs duties. Arthur became quite well off as collector, a job he held for eight years, and became noted throughout New York society for his sartorial splendor.

Arthur lost his post after a falling out with Pres. Rutherford B. Hayes in 1879. A year later, Arthur was leading the Stalwart faction that endeavored to return Ulysses S. Grant to the White House for a third term. Frustrated when the nomination went to James A. Garfield instead, Arthur was given the number two spot (which everyone considered a meaningless post) to ensure Stalwart support in the general election campaign.

All that changed when President Garfield was shot by a deranged office seeker just three months after becoming president in 1881. Garfield lingered through the summer, not dying until September. Arthur had resolutely refused to declare the president incapacitated and assume the powers of the office himself. He was sworn in at his New York home after being informed of Garfield's death.

"Chet Arthur President of the United States! Good God!" was the assessment of a leading Republican when he heard the news. Few expected much from the political boss-turned-president, but Arthur surprised everyone by proposing civil service reform in his first message to Congress.

Arthur's motives, however, were probably less pure than they seemed. He was no doubt influenced by the sight of huge numbers of Democratic-voting immigrants—Jewish as well as Catholic Irish—pouring into New York. A civil service system would lock educated Republicans into their jobs and, hopefully, keep illiterate immigrants out, at least for awhile.

Arthur was one of the few presidents denied renomination by his party. He returned to his law practice in New York in 1885, but was dead barely a year later, at only 56 years of age.

&a· EXHIBITS: The Vermont Division for Historic Preservation reconstructed the original clapboard house in 1954 from an old photograph. The house contains period furnishings and exhibits relating to Arthur's life and presidency. &a· LOCATION: Fairfield is in the far northern part of Vermont, near the Canadian border. From St. Albans, take Route 36 7 miles north to Fairfield and turn left at the village. About 1 mile north of the village, bear right and follow the road 4–5 miles. The historic site is the first house on the right after the road becomes gravel. The route is marked by signs. &a· HOURS: Open June 1 through early October, 9–5, Wednesday–Sunday. &a· ADMISSION: Adults $1; children under 14 free. &a· TELEPHONE: (802) 933-8362.

SHELDON

FENIAN RAIDS MARKER

Northern Vermont was the base for Fenian raids into British Canada in both 1866 and 1871. The secret society hoped to hold British Canada "hostage" for Ireland's freedom.

Although the Fenian invasion of 1866 achieved its greatest success in Ontario under Col. John O'Neill at the Battle of Ridgeway, the Niagara operation was meant only as a feint. It was from northern Vermont that the main blow was supposed to have been struck. The objective was the capture of Montreal and Quebec City, which the Fenians hoped would force Britain to negotiate terms of Irish independence, or where an Irish republican government-in-exile could be established.

Mustering in the nearby town of St. Albans, a Fenian army made up of several thousand Irish-American Civil War veterans gathered under the command of Samuel Spear, who had attained the rank of brigadier general in the Civil War.

Three days after O'Neill's successful, but unsupported, raid came to an end in Niagara, and while thousands of Torontonians were attending the funeral of the militiamen killed at Ridgeway, Spear and his men crossed the border and raised the green standard at Pigeon Hill, Quebec. In great contrast to O'Neill's disciplined force, Spear's men plundered the countryside shamelessly.

The alarm was quickly raised, however, and the next day a force of Canadian militia and British regulars moved into the area. Following a brief skirmish, the Fenians retreated back into Vermont, where Spear and his staff surrendered voluntarily to waiting American authorities. Most of the Fenian foot soldiers were quickly released on the condition they return directly to their homes.

The 1866 invasion was the high noon of the Fenian movement, although the dream of liberating Ireland through Canada did not die for some time. Four years later, Col. John O'Neill, the victor of Ridgeway, journeyed to Vermont to lead a second attempt. Unfortunately, his force was even smaller and less well organized and equipped than the 1866 effort and one of his closest confidants turned out to be a British spy. O'Neill and his force were routed near the Quebec village of Eccles Hill.

Arrested and imprisoned, O'Neill spent several months in jail until his political friends secured his release via a presidential pardon. Although he had promised to refrain from such actions in the future, O'Neill tried one more time a year later, this time on the Minnesota-Manitoba frontier. He hoped to join forces with the Canadian Rebel Louis Riel but met with as little success as before. O'Neill then settled down to found the town of O'Neill, Nebraska. (*See* O'Neill, Nebraska and Ridgeway, Ontario.)

&a **LOCATION:** A marker recalling the Fenian activity in this area was recently placed by the state historical society on a bridge spanning the Black River along S.R. 105, just west of the intersection with S.R. 78 in the village of Sheldon.

WASHINGTON D.C.

GEORGETOWN UNIVERSITY

In the middle of the 18th century, Georgetown was the only settlement of any description along this stretch of the Potomac River. A collection of taverns, wharves, and warehouses, it owed its existence to that great Maryland and Virginia commodity, tobacco.

It was here that the Irish-American bishop John Carroll chose to establish his Jesuit school for young men, so that American candidates for the priesthood would not have to make the hazardous crossing to Europe to study. It helped that the wealthy Carroll family owned much of the land in the area. (*See* Baltimore, Maryland, for more on Carroll.)

The bronze statue of a seated Carroll became fair game for student pranksters because the sculptor had thoughtfully left an open space beneath the bishop's chair. Chamberpots soon began appearing in the space, to the dismay of school authorities. So, in a spirit of practicality, the sculptor was asked to add a stack of bronze books.

Just behind the Carroll statue and in front of the Healy building are two cannons. These were on board the *Ark* and the *Dove,* the two ships that brought the first Catholic settlers to Maryland in 1634.

The two cannons played a small role in the bitter presidential campaign of 1928, in which Irish-American Al Smith was baited mercilessly for his Catholicism. Supposedly, Alabama Sen. "Cotton Tom" Heflin charged that the two cannons were aimed at the Capitol dome and would be used to intimidate Congress in the event of a Smith victory. If that was the case, then Smith's aim was off, since the dome of the Shrine of the Immaculate Conception would have been in more danger.

The Healy Building is named for one of Georgetown's most interesting figures, Father Patrick F. Healy, its 29th president. Appointed acting president in 1871, he earned the post on a permanent basis because of his drive and energy. He overhauled the curriculum and reorganized the medical and law schools. He was also determined to upgrade the physical

The statue of founder John Carroll, once fodder for student pranksters, welcomes students to Georgetown University.

plant, opening the massive structure that became known as the Healy Building in 1879.

For these reasons, Father Healy is sometimes thought of as Georgetown's "second founder." A native of Georgia, he attended Holy Cross College in Worcester, Massachusetts, and received his theological and postgraduate training in Europe (at Louvain University in Belgium).

He also was black. Although his father was an Irish immigrant who had married a freed slave woman, Healy was considered a slave under Georgia law. In 1865 he became the first black in America to hold a Ph.D. and the first black to head a major, predominantly white university.

❧ **EXHIBITS:** The statue of Bishop John Carroll sits near the entrance. Tours are available. ❧ **LOCATION:** Entrance is at 37th and O streets. ❧ **HOURS:** Dawn to dusk. ❧ **ADMISSION:** Free ❧ **TELEPHONE:** (202) 687-3600.

KENNEDY HOMES

 During his terms in the House and the Senate John F. Kennedy had several homes in the Washington, D.C., area. They are all located within a few blocks of one another in the Georgetown neighborhood.

3271 P Street, NW. The newly wed Sen. and Mrs. John F. Kennedy lived in this house for about a year just after Kennedy was elected to the Senate in 1953.

3307 N Street, NW. The Kennedys purchased the house in 1957 and occupied it during the 1960 presidential campaign. This was the house at which cabinet appointees were introduced to the nation from the front steps during the interval between Kennedy's election and his inauguration.

Worried about the charges of nepotism that would inevitably follow the announcement of brother Robert's selection as attorney general, JFK joked that he was tempted to open the door some night at 3 A.M. and whisper, "It's Bobby."

3017 N Street. Immediately after the trauma of JFK's assassination, Jacqueline Kennedy and her young family had to face up to a practical problem: the houses they had owned before had been sold and they had no family home to which to return after vacating the White House (which they did not do until mid-December). Democratic fixture Averell Harriman came to the rescue and offered his well-known Georgetown home at 3038 N Street as a temporary residence. After a short stay, the widow and her two children moved to this house.

Unfortunately, the family's residence here was not happy. Tourists and papparazzi stood outside gawking at all hours of the day and night, hoping for a glimpse of the grieving family. Finally, Mrs. Kennedy packed up her belongings and moved to a New York apartment.

Also, The Kennedy Center for the Performing Arts on the Washington waterfront is the official national memorial to John F. Kennedy.

❧ **EXHIBITS:** All of the houses listed here remain private residences and are not open to the public. Mounted on the side wall of the house at 3307 N Street is a plaque placed by the members of the Washington press corps in thanks for the kindness and hospitality the press received from the Kennedy family.

MATHEW BRADY STUDIO

The father of America's most famous 19th-century photographer was from Ireland. That much seems certain. About the rest of the details of Mathew B. Brady's background, early life, and other influences on his work, however, we know almost nothing. He wrote no memoirs, few letters, and kept no diary. Indeed, Brady himself sometimes seemed to know little about his background, since the spelling of his first name was admittedly eccentric and he claimed to have no idea what his middle initial "B" stood for.

In an interview late in life with the journalist George Alfred Townsend, Brady said he was born in Warren County in upstate New York and that his father was "an Irishman." He said nothing of his mother's identity and background. His schooling was meager and he early became interested in drawing. William Page, the portrait painter, encouraged young Brady to become an artist and later introduced him to Samuel F. B. Morse. Brady was fascinated by the newly developing art of photography, however, and he soon began experimenting with the new art form.

As technical improvements in photographic equipment followed rapidly, Brady established a studio at the corner of Broadway and Fulton streets in New York. He was an instant success, with his studio visited by thousands. In the first photographic competitions, Brady's portraits consistently took first place.

Throughout the 1840s and 1850s, Brady's fame grew, and his studio, soon relocated to a more fashionable address uptown, became a required stop for any notable visiting the city. "Photograph by Brady" was fast becoming a mark of excellence in the young field.

The Brady National Photographic Gallery opened on Pennsylvania Avenue between the White House and the Capitol in 1858. Upon the outbreak of the Civil War, Brady's immediate instinct was to accompany the Union armies and chronicle the fighting. "[A] spirit in my feet said 'Go' and I went," he said. The result was the first war to be chronicled in detail through photographs.

Accompanied by his assistants Alexander Gardner and Timothy O'Sullivan, Brady and his camera followed the Army of the Potomac to numerous battlefields. In between battles, they snapped portraits the soldiers could send home to their loved ones. Brady's September 1862 exhibition at his New York studio, "The Dead of Antietam," broke new ground. For the first time, the true nature of war, stripped of its romanticism, was displayed to a civilian population. "If he has not brought bodies and laid them in our dooryards and along streets," wrote the *New York Times* of the exhibit, "he has done something very like it."

He continued to take portraits throughout the war. Just about everyone of any note in wartime Washington posed before his camera in this studio. President Lincoln sat for several memorable portraits, including one just days before his death. The Lincoln portraits in particular show Brady's uncanny ability to capture the character as well as the likeness of his subjects.

Although the war made Mathew Brady even more famous, it did not make him rich. Indeed, he suffered financial reverses during the war, and

Mathew Brady Studios once occupied the upper floors of this recently renovated building on Pennsylvania Avenue.

the Panic of 1873 virtually bankrupted him. Two years later, the government purchased 2,000 of his Civil War photographs as a permanent collection, but almost all this money was used paying off his debts. He spent his last years in relative poverty. After being hit by a carriage in the streets of Washington in 1895, he never really recovered, dying early the next year.

Remarkably, Brady managed his feats of photographic genius while being (secretly) very nearly blind. Many of his photographs were actually taken by assistants.

 EXHIBITS: The building, recently renovated, is now occupied by the Washington lobbying offices of Sears Roebuck & Co. It is not open to the public. LOCATION: The four-story brick building at 627 Pennsylvania Ave., NW, was built in 1855. The studios were on the upper floors.

NURSING SISTERS MEMORIAL

A Civil War field hospital was no place for the fainthearted. A war fought using 18th-century field tactics with Industrial Age weapons produced fearsome wounds that medical science was ill prepared to cope with. Amputation of wounded limbs was frequent and rough, and sanitary principles, often imperfectly understood at best, were frequently nonexistent.

The stories of Dorothea Dix (who banned Catholics from her nursing corps), Clara Barton, and the U.S. Sanitary Commission in aid of wounded soldiers are well known of course. Less well known is the story of the Catholic sisters and nuns—most of them Irish, but some German—who nursed the wounded of both sides throughout the conflict.

"They served in every capacity," writes Jean Heimberger Candido in her article "Sisters and Nuns Who Were Nurses During the Civil War," (1993) probably the best single source on the subject. "Hospital administrators, surgical nurses, apothecaries, cooks, dieticians, laundresses, anesthetists, and morale officers. It is not remarkable that over 600 nuns served; if there were more to be had, the numbers would have been higher."

In fact, the Catholic nuns were among the first to go to the aid of the wounded. Brig. Gen. Robert A. Anderson, the hero of Ft. Sumter, had just been named commander of the Union Department of Kentucky, his native state, when he dispatched a letter to Bishop John Spaulding of Louisville, requesting the presence of nursing sisters at the front:

> The Sisters of Charity will nurse the wounded under the direction of army surgeons without any intermediate authority or interference whatever. Everything necessary for the lodging and nursing of the wounded, and the sick will be supplied to them without putting them to expense; they giving their services gratuitously. So far, the circumstances will allow, they shall receive every facility for attending to religious and devotional exercises.
>
> Robert Anderson
> Brig. Genl., U.S. Army

In response, Bishop Spaulding dispatched Sr. Columba Carroll, Mother Superior of St. Vincent's Academy in Union County, Kentucky, along with 23 sisters, to Louisville. There, they were assigned to a "hospital," which in fact had been home to several large manufacturing plants and was without heat, cots, or the most rudimentary medical facilities. It was a foretaste of what was to come.

Washington and Richmond reached an agreement that the nursing sisters would be allowed to pass through the lines. In the summer of 1861, a small group of sisters from St. Vincent de Paul of Emmitsburg, Maryland, went south to Richmond's Infirmary of St. Francis to treat Confederate wounded and Union prisoners.

When the sisters arrived, the makeshift hospital was not yet ready and a terrible stench permeated the building. A search turned up a pair of rotting amputated limbs. They were disposed of with dispatch. Sister Blanche Rooney noted that "yesterday, a man was buried with three legs."

The care received from the sisters was so loving and of such high quality that the Union officers raised $50 for a contribution to the Richmond orphanage.

A few days after the Battle of Gettysburg, sisters from the same order left Emmitsburg and headed north to the battlefield, where the wounded and dying still lay unattended where they had fallen. At the same time, the Sisters of Charity of Vicksburg, who had tended to the Confederate wounded throughout the long siege of that city, were attending to their duties in the squalid, makeshift hospitals that had been hacked out of the earth.

And of course there were casualties such as Sr. Philomena Kenny, mourned simply by the terse epithet "died in service." The Sisters of the Holy Cross buried Sister Fidelis (Bridget Lawler) and Sister Elise (Unity O'Brien).

"Of all the forms of charity and benevolence seen in the crowded wards of the hospitals, those of some Catholic Sisters were among the most efficient," wrote Abraham Lincoln. "I never knew whence they came or what was the name of the order. More lovely than anything I had ever seen in art, so long devoted to illustrations of love, mercy and charity, are the pictures that remain of these modest sisters going on their errands of mercy among the suffering and the dying."

❧ **EXHIBITS:** The marble and brass monument was erected by the Ladies Auxiliary of the Ancient Order of Hibernians and was unveiled on September 20, 1924. Just across from the memorial on Rhode Island Avenue stands St. Matthew's Cathedral, the seat of the Catholic Archdiocese of Washington and the site of President Kennedy's funeral mass in 1963. ❧ **LOCATION:** The intersection of Connecticut and Rhode Island avenues and M Street, NW, in downtown Washington, D.C. ❧ **HOURS:** Dawn to dusk. ❧ **ADMISSION:** Free

ROBERT EMMET STATUE

This statue of the executed Irish patriot, identical to the ones in San Francisco (*see* entry), Emmetsburg, Iowa (*see* entry), and Dublin, was cast from a mold by Irish-born sculptor Jerome Connor. This example was erected at its current site near the embassy of the Republic of Ireland in 1966, in commemoration of the 50th anniversary of the Easter Rising of 1916. (*See* New York, New York, for more on Emmet and his brother, Thomas Addis Emmet.)

❧ **EXHIBITS:** The statue shows Emmet making his famed speech from the dock during trial in 1803. His hand is outstretched as if pleading. A small reproduction is in the Woodrow Wilson House a few hundred feet down S Street. ❧ **LOCATION:** The triangle of land bounded by Massachusetts Avenue, 24th Street and S Street, NW. ❧ **HOURS:** Dawn to dusk. ❧ **ADMISSION:** Free

SHERIDAN CIRCLE

Gen. Phillip H. Sheridan ended the Civil War as one of the great heroes of the Union cause, standing just below the lofty pedestal occupied by Ulysses S. Grant and William T. Sherman. "Little Phil"—he stood only 5'5" tall—was the son of Irish immigrants and was probably born in Albany, New York, although some accounts say he might have been born on the ship that brought his parents to the United States. (*See* Somerset, Ohio and Middletown, Virginia for more on Sheridan's background and campaigns.)

Sheridan was a West Point graduate, receiving his commission a year later than normal, in 1852, since he was suspended for a year after threatening a fellow cadet with a bayonet. During the Civil War, he found himself in various commands, distinguishing himself by often winning small victories in otherwise losing campaigns.

He came to Gen. U. S. Grant's attention in the fall of 1863, after Sheridan's men made a wild charge up Missionary Ridge during the Battle of Chattanooga and defeated the Confederate forces under Gen. Braxton Bragg. When Grant was appointed to command all Union armies, he brought the diminutive cavalryman with him, appointing Sheridan to command all federal cavalry forces.

It was a daunting assignment, for up to 1864 the Union cavalry had been something of a joke. Dashing Southern cavaliers like General J. E. B. Stuart literally ran rings around their Northern opponents. Sheridan was resolved to change all that.

Within a month of taking command in April 1864, Sheridan was ready. Detaching himself from the Army of the Potomac, he set out on a daring raid on Richmond, proceeding south at a deliberate pace, almost daring Stuart to attack him. The two forces met north of Richmond at a crossroads called Yellow Tavern. There, the Union troopers achieved victory, along with the grim bonus of the death of Stuart.

The meteoric rise of "Little Phil" was attributable to "2 traits he himself recognized," says the *Historical Times Illustrated Encyclopedia of the Civil War*, "a willingness to take the offensive whenever possible and as aggressively as possible, and a willingness to exploit every edge over an opponent."

Sheridan's greatest achievement, however, was his campaign in the Shenandoah Valley in late 1864. His orders were to destroy everything in that fertile land that could conceivably be of use to the Confederacy and to seal both ends. Sheridan accomplished this task with brutal efficiency, burning houses and barns and crops with little regard to the political allegiances of their owners. Almost single-handedly, he turned defeat into victory at Cedar Creek on October 19, 1864. He was also present at Appomattox.

There was little rest for Sheridan after the war, however. He missed the big victory parade in Washington because he was immediately dispatched to the Mexican border, where tensions were running high with the French-backed government of Emperor Maximillian. He later served as Reconstruction military governor of Texas and Louisiana. His harsh policies, however, caused his removal after just six months, and he was sent west to fight Indians.

He apparently never said the great line attributed to him, that "the only good Indian is a dead Indian." It was more along the lines of "The only good Indian I ever saw was dead." The sentiment, however, was unmistakable and was used by friends and enemies alike. His career on the Plains was more controversial than his Civil War period. Sheridan was roundly criticized by many for claiming victories in "battles" that critics said were little more than massacres.

None of this negative comment halted his progression up the military ladder, however. He was promoted to lieutenant general in 1869 after William T. Sherman was promoted full general and commander of the army following Grant's election as president. Sheridan was advanced to commander in chief of the army in 1884 after Sherman's retirement. Sheridan died four years later.

As with Grant and Sherman, statues of Sheridan dot the countryside. One stands in little Somerset, Ohio, where he grew up, and another in front of the New York State Capitol building in Albany, where he believed he was born. The best known, however, stands in Sheridan Circle in Washington, D.C., at the entrance to the capital's "Embassy Row."

The statue, unveiled with great ceremony the day before Thanksgiving 1908, was one of the first great works by the Danish-American sculptor Gutzon Borglum, who went on to design Mt. Rushmore. The statue, 12 feet long, 8 feet wide, and 14 feet high, is different from the many other equestrian statues in Washington. Instead of depicting a dignified rider atop a gently trotting mount, it shows Sheridan and his horse "Rienzi" in arrested motion. The general seems to shouting something unprintable at his fleeing troops on the road from Cedar Creek.

Sheridan's widow and three spinster daughters moved from their home on Rhode Island Avenue to a house just across the street from the statue at 2551 Massachusetts Avenue. Every morning, so the story goes, the three daughters would open their bedroom window and call across to the statue, "Good morning, Papa!"

ᴥ LOCATION: Sheridan Circle is located at Massachusetts Avenue between Q and R streets, NW.

UNITED STATES CAPITOL

Irish-born James Shields's career was more colorful than it was noteworthy for great accomplishments. Two things, however, ensured that he would become one of the most memorialized of Irish-Americans. First, he was the only man in American history to serve as a United States senator from three different states (Illinois, Minnesota, and

Missouri). Second, he was the only Union officer to inflict defeat on Thomas J. "Stonewall" Jackson, at the Battle of Kernstown, Virginia, on March 23, 1862. (Jackson, however, returned the favor to Shields at Port Republic on June 9 and never tasted defeat again.)

The former House of Representatives chamber in the U.S. Capitol was converted into Statuary Hall after the House moved to its new chamber in 1857. Every state was invited to contribute statues of two distinguished citizens. Illinois chose Shields, along with the man with whom he very nearly fought a duel and who subsequently became his close friend, Abraham Lincoln. (*See* St. Paul, Minnesota and Carrollton, Missouri.)

♣ EXHIBITS: Statuary Hall is located in the House wing of the Capitol. It is part of the guided tour. ♣ LOCATION: The Capitol is located along First Street NE/SE, between Constitution and Independence avenues. ♣ HOURS: Daily 9–8, Memorial Day through Labor Day; 9–4:30 rest of year. ♣ ADMISSION: None. ♣ TELEPHONE: (202) 224-3121.

WALSH-MCLEAN HOUSE/EMBASSY OF INDONESIA

Tom Walsh was an Irishman with a vision of striking it rich out West. He succeeded, but the subsequent fate of many of his family members led some to wonder if providence had not exacted an awful price for it.

A native of Clonmel, county Tipperary, Walsh immigrated to America in 1869 at age 19. He worked for a while as a carpenter in Massachusetts, but soon figured he wasn't going to get rich that way and decided to go looking for gold. He very quickly had an opportunity to buy an interest in the Homestake Mine, which he turned down. That proved a mistake. The Homestake subsequently brought in over $300 million. One of the lucky investors was George Hearst, father of William Randolph Hearst.

Walsh refused to be discouraged, however, wandering around towns such as Leadville, Colorado (*see* entry) in search of another promising opportunity. In Leadville he found the beginnings of one. Exploring an abandoned mining camp west of the town one day, he had the soil analyzed and discovered that it contained a large quantity of silver. He bought the area for next to nothing and within a few months had taken out $75,000 worth of silver.

But the really big strike came at Ouray, Colorado. In a camp barely nine miles from his home, he discovered gold. After a quarter of a century of looking, Tom Walsh was finally a rich man.

And he wanted everyone to know it. Walsh immediately moved his family to Washington, D.C., partly because he figured a *nouveau riche* like himself would find it easier to crack "society" there than in Boston, New

York, or Philadelphia. He built this huge stone fortress embedded with chunks of real gold for the then-huge sum of $1 million. It was the largest house in the capital at that time.

Unfortunately, Walsh was not to enjoy his wealth in peace. Even before he became rich, Carrie Bell Reed Walsh, his wife, had begun showing signs of mental instability. Nevertheless, Walsh indulged his wife and young daughter Evelyn with everything that money could buy: furs, jewels, clothes, and much else besides. When young Evelyn complained about having to walk to school, for instance, her father immediately presented her with horses and a coach, along with a uniformed driver.

Young Evelyn married Edward "Ned" McLean, the son of the publisher of the *Washington Post*. Their honeymoon was probably one of the most fantastic in history, costing over $200,000 in pre-World War I dollars. And even then, the couple returned home from Europe with a fistful of unpaid bills.

With her taste for expensive jewels, it was probably inevitable that Evelyn would eventually acquire, for $154,000, the most famous jewel in the world: the blue, 44½-carat Hope Diamond.

Her mother was alarmed, being well aware of the diamond's reputation for bringing bad luck to its owners. It had reportedly belonged to Marie Antoinette. Another owner was said to have leapt to his death from a cliff. A third went down with a ship at sea after disposing of the diamond. Evelyn wasn't too concerned, but she did take the Hope to a priest to have the curse "exorcised." Supposedly, at the moment of the blessing, a flash of lightning crossed the sky and clap of thunder rolled.

Two years after Tom Walsh moved into his new house in 1903, his son Vinson was killed in a freak auto accident. The loss wounded him deeply and seemed to sap him of his own will to live. He died after a protracted bout with cancer in 1909.

Meanwhile, Evelyn and her husband sank into a nightmare haze of drugs and alcohol. The couple's son, also named Vinson, was himself killed in an auto wreck at age 20. Their daughter later committed suicide with an overdose of sleeping pills. Ned was ruined when he became caught up in the Teapot Dome scandal with Edward L. Doheny (*see* Los Angeles, California).

All the while Evelyn refused to believe in the curse of the Hope Diamond. She died of alcoholism, drug addiction, and malnutrition, the drugs having finally destroyed her appetite for solid food.

Curse or no curse, the family decided to dispose of the gem after Evelyn's death. It now resides in the Smithsonian Institution, where it can be seen (but not touched!) in the Museum of Natural History.

&· **EXHIBITS:** The building now houses the Embassy of Indonesia. It is not open to the public. &· **LOCATION:** The Walsh-McLean mansion is at 2020 Massachusetts Ave., NW.

THE WHITE HOUSE

Pierre L'Enfant, the Frenchman who designed the capital city, had originally envisaged a grand palace for the president, five stories tall and with many rooms. George Washington, a patrician planter from Virginia, was enthusiastic. The more egalitarian-minded Thomas Jefferson, however, had different ideas. Eventually, Jefferson won out, prevailing upon Washington to hold a competition to select a design.

The winner was James Hoban, a 30-year-old native of Dublin who had immigrated to the newly independent United States around 1782. Although Hoban had studied architectural drawing at the Dublin Society and had won a prize for his early work on "brackets, stairs, roofs, etc.," he had no other formal training as an architect or builder. Nevertheless, he was skilled at both, and an ad published in Philadelphia on May 25, 1785, advertised his services to "Any Gentleman Who wishes to build in an elegant style. . . ." He lived for a time in South Carolina, where he designed the state capitol building at Columbia (*see* Columbia, South Carolina).

Although Hoban also submitted designs for the new Capitol building, none of his drawings for that project survive. On July 17, 1792, he was awarded the commission for designing the President's House, as George Washington referred to it. (Officially, it was known throughout the 19th century as the Executive Mansion and colloquially as the White House, because the soft sandstone exterior had to be whitewashed almost immediately after construction. The latter term became official during the term of Pres. Theodore Roosevelt.)

What strikes most visitors who see it for the first time is the building's smallness and simplicity, especially compared with the palaces and seats of government of Europe. This is exactly the effect Jefferson desired and the reason Hoban's design was accepted. (Some designs had plans for a throne room!) And except for the addition of the low, unobtrusive East and West wings, the house today remains almost exactly as he designed it.

During his student days in Dublin, Hoban undoubtedly knew Leinster House, the present-day seat of the Irish Parliament. The resemblance between the White House and Leinster House is unmistakable. The engaged Ionic columns, the main north pediment, and the alternating curved and triangular over-window pediments are all virtually identical to those of Leinster House.

Hoban continued to work on the White House and was active in civic affairs until his death in 1831. He helped rebuild the house after it was

With no formal training as an architect, Irishman James Hoban designed the simple, yet gracious, White House.

burned by the British in the War of 1812. In 1824, Hoban added the distinctively rounded South Portico (based on that of the Chateau de Rastignac in Perigord, France). The North Portico was added in 1829.

Washington was the only president never to have lived in the great mansion. John Adams and his wife, Abigail, moved into the unfinished building in 1800. Since then, it has sheltered nine presidents who were of Irish descent through the direct paternal line: Andrew Jackson, James K. Polk, James Buchanan, Chester Alan Arthur, William McKinley, Woodrow Wilson, John F. Kennedy, Richard Nixon and Ronald Reagan.

🙠 **EXHIBITS:** A tour of the public rooms is available. 🙠 **LOCATION:** 1600 Pennsylvania Ave., NW, in the heart of downtown Washington, D.C. 🙠 **HOURS:** Tuesday–Saturday 10–noon. 🙠 **ADMISSION:** Tickets are required during the height of the tourist season between mid-March and mid-September. Tickets for specific tours at specific times are distributed at the booth on the Ellipse at E and 16th sts. starting at 8 A.M. on the day of the tour. They are distributed on a first-come, first-served basis and you should arrive early. 🙠 **TELEPHONE:** (202) 456-7041.

WOODROW WILSON HOUSE

Although the 28th president occasionally made reference to his Irish roots in St. Patrick's Day speeches and the like, the fact is few Irish-Americans were pleased with Woodrow Wilson. After winning election as governor of New Jersey in 1910, he ruthlessly turned on the mostly Irish bosses who helped elect him. And after he became president, they were embittered by his pro-British policies during and after the First World War.

The stately Woodrow Wilson House, where Wilson lived until his death in 1924.

Described once by the British ambassador to Washington as "by descent an Orangeman and by education a Presbyterian," Wilson was a decided Anglophile in his outlook. ("Orangeman" is the name often applied to Scotch-Irish Presbyterians.) A political science professor by training, Wilson's writings show a strong affinity for the Westminster-style of parliamentary democracy over the American system of checks and balances.

He also had little sympathy for those he called "hyphenated Americans." In dedicating a memorial to John Barry, the Irish-born revolutionary war naval hero, Wilson called him an Irishman "whose heart crossed the Atlantic with him." This naturally outraged many Irish-Americans, and several bitter articles appeared in Irish newspapers pointedly noting that thousands of Irishmen died in the Civil War to save the Union that Wilson's Southern ancestors sought to break up. (Wilson, however, saw himself as an American president, first and foremost).

Interestingly, the Irish had a strong friend at Wilson's right hand in Joseph Patrick Tumulty, Wilson's private secretary. He attached himself to Wilson during the latter's first campaign for governor and remained with him at the White House. Tumulty adored his chief, cheerfully doing the work of six men to stay by Wilson's side. Yet, Wilson several times was on the verge of firing him and, in the end, permanently cold-shouldered his Irish protégé over a minor political flare-up.

When the United States entered World War I on Britain's side, there was considerable consternation among Irish-Americans that Wilson had not first secured a promise of postwar independence for Ireland. In fact, just four days after the declaration of war, Wilson had sent a note to the British government raising this issue. He had also privately rebuked Britain for its ruthless suppression of the 1916 Easter Uprising.

The pressures of the war and the ensuing peace conference, however, caused Wilson to put the Irish issue on the back burner. Wilson needed British support for his plan for a League of Nations that would help prevent wars in the future.

Most Catholic Irish-Americans were highly suspicious of the league and the whole Treaty of Versailles in general, however. They were especially upset that the league would give full voting membership to Britain's dominions of Canada, Australia, New Zealand, and South Africa. To the Irish-Americans, it seemed like Wilson had fallen into a typically clever British trap.

Wilson's alienation of the Irish-Americans cost him dearly. Sen. Henry Cabot Lodge, Wilson's main antagonist in the treaty debate, was able to use his opposition to Wilson to build bridges to the previously hostile Boston Irish community. After the treaty was defeated, Republican presidential candidate Warren G. Harding made unprecedented inroads in Irish neighborhoods in the urban Northeast, carrying both Boston and New York by healthy margins.

Wilson was the only president to remain in Washington after his term of office expired. He used his Nobel Peace Prize money to purchase this handsome mansion on S Street and lived here, debilitated by a stroke, until his death in 1924. (*See* also Columbia, South Carolina, and Staunton, Virginia.)

❧ **Exhibits:** The house contains the Wilsons' furnishings and many personal belongings. One of the items on display is a miniature of the Robert Emmet statue that stands just down the street (Wilson had unveiled the San Francisco version of the statue). ❧ **Location:** 2340 S St., NW, near Embassy Row. ❧ **Hours:** Tuesday–Sunday 10–4. ❧ **Admission:** $4 adults; $2.50 for seniors, children, and students. ❧ **Telephone:** (202) 387-4062.

ALABAMA

ARKANSAS

FLORIDA

GEORGIA

KENTUCKY

LOUISIANA

MISSISSIPPI

NORTH CAROLINA

SOUTH CAROLINA

TENNESSEE

VIRGINIA

St. Patrick's Church in New Orleans. See page 243.

S O U T H E A S T

ALABAMA

1 Horseshoe Bend National Military Park, Daviston
2 Ryan Park, Mobile
3 F. Scott and Zelda Fitzgerald Museum, Montgomery
4 Knox House, Montgomery

ARKANSAS

5 Patrick Cleburne Memorial and Gravesite, Helena

FLORIDA

6 The Jackie Gleason Theater of the Performing Arts, Miami Beach
7 Olustee State Historic Site, Olustee
8 Fort George Park, Pensacola

GEORGIA

9 Taylor-Grady House, Athens
10 Atlanta-Fulton County Public Library, Atlanta
11 Church of the Immaculate Conception/Fr. O'Reilly Memorial, Atlanta
12 Dillard Russell Library at Georgia College, Milledgeville
13 Cathedral of St. John the Baptist, Savannah
14 Emmet Park, Savannah
15 Siege of Savannah, Savannah

KENTUCKY

16 Frankfort Cemetery, Frankfort
17 Brennan House, Louisville
18 Locust Grove, Louisville

LOUISIANA

19 Houmas House, Burnside
20 Chalmette Battlefield, New Orleans
21 Gallier House and Gallier Hall, New Orleans
22 Irish Channel, New Orleans
23 "Margaret" Statue, New Orleans
24 New Basin Canal Park, New Orleans
25 St. Patrick's Church, New Orleans

MISSISSIPPI

26 Fr. Ryan House, Biloxi
27 Sullivan-Kilrain Fight Site, Hattiesburg
28 Vicksburg National Battlefield Park, Vicksburg

NORTH CAROLINA

29 Historic Edenton, Edenton
30 Grave of Thomas Burke, Hillsborough
31 Liberty Hall, Kenansville
32 Battle of Moore's Creek Bridge, Moore's Creek
33 James K. Polk Memorial State Historic Site, Pineville
34 Andrew Jackson Birthplace, Waxhaw

SOUTH CAROLINA

35 The Cathedral of St. John the Baptist, Charleston
36 Hibernian Hall, Charleston
37 Magnolia Cemetery, Charleston
38 St. Lawrence Cemetery, Charleston
39 St. Mary's Church, Charleston
40 Fort Hill, Clemson
41 Hampton-Preston Mansion, Columbia
42 James F. Byrnes Home, Columbia
43 Old State House Marker, Columbia
44 Woodrow Wilson Boyhood Home, Columbia
45 Kings Mountain National Military Park, Kings Mountain

TENNESSEE

46 James K. Polk Ancestral Home, Columbia
47 Ft. Donelson National Battlefield, Dover
48 Oak Hill Cemetery, Erin
49 Carnton Plantation and the Carter House, Franklin
50 The Hermitage, Nashville
51 State Capitol, Nashville

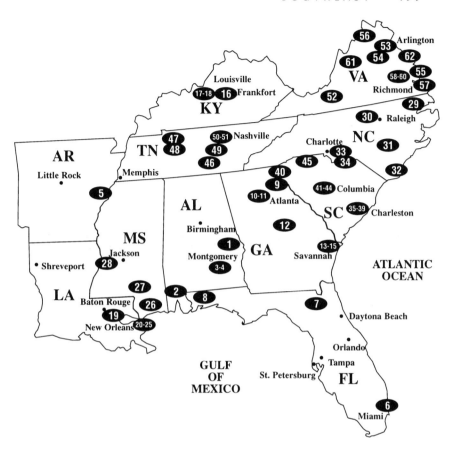

VIRGINIA

52 Avoca, Altavista
53 Arlington National Cemetery/
   Custis-Lee Mansion, Arlington
54 Fredericksburg and Spotsylvania
   National Military Park,
   Fredericksburg
55 Fort Monroe, Hampton Park
56 Cedar Creek Battlefield/Belle

Grove Plantation, Middletown
57 Fr. Ryan House Marker, Norfolk
58 Libby Prison Site, Richmond
59 Maymont, Richmond
60 Richmond National Battlefield
   Park, Richmond
61 Woodrow Wilson Birthplace and
   Museum, Staunton
62 Yorktown Battlefield, Williamsburg

ALABAMA

DAVISTON

HORSESHOE BEND NATIONAL MILITARY PARK

The narrow peninsula formed by one of the bends in the Talapoosa River in eastern Alabama was, in early 1814, the site of a stronghold established by the Creek Indians. The Indians were determined to resist further white encroachment and built a strong bastion. They believed their position to be unassailable.

On the morning of March 27, 1814, General Andrew Jackson and his frontiersmen would prove them wrong in one of the fiercest, most decisive battles in the history of the Indian Wars.

The war began in August 1813, when a Creek war party attacked Ft. Mims on the banks of the lower Alabama River 20 miles north of Mobile. An incredible 553 white soldiers and settlers were brutally massacred. The enraged state of Tennessee immediately called out its militia and asked Major General Andrew Jackson to command.

Jackson, the son of Irish immigrants, was by this time a prominent figure in Tennessee, though little known elsewhere. He accepted the assignment and marched south into what is now Alabama. He met the Creeks first at the Battles of Tallushatchee and Talladega, defeating them handily and inflicting heavy casualties. The Indians retreated to their horseshoe-shaped fortress on the Talapoosa.

Jackson attacked on the morning of March 27. After several hours of ineffective cannon fire, Jackson ordered his men to storm the Indian barricade frontally. The wild Tennesseans obeyed, and succeeded in scaling the walls and getting inside. For nearly five hours, ferocious hand-to-hand combat raged. The ultimate outcome, however, was never in doubt. By nightfall, the Americans were in possession of the fort, 800 Creek warriors lay dead, along with 49 Tennesseans.

The Treaty of Fort Jackson ended the war and the Creeks were forced to cede all their land, which includes most of the present-day state of Alabama. Jackson promptly became nationally famous and, combined with his victory nine months later at New Orleans, set him on the road to the White House.

❧ EXHIBITS: Indian relics and military weapons are displayed in the museum. A self-guided battlefield tour is available. ❧ LOCATION: Approximately 95 miles southeast of Birmingham, Alabama. Take U.S. 280 from Birmingham to Dadeville, then drive 12 miles north on S.R. 49 to the park. ❧ HOURS: Park open daily 8–5; museum 9–5. ❧ ADMISSION: None. ❧ TELEPHONE: (205) 234-7111.

MOBILE

RYAN PARK

 The states of the former Confederacy were devastated, physically and psychologically, in the immediate aftermath of the Civil War. Harsh Reconstruction policies imposed from distant Washington rubbed raw. Many Southerners, who were for the most part strongly religious people, also wondered if their defeat on the battlefield had not been willed by God, and that they were somehow being divinely punished for the sin of slavery.

Into this dispirited atmosphere came a poem, "The Conquered Banner," which appeared in the *Freeman's Journal* on May 19, 1866. Its beautiful, pathetic verses, quickly set to the music of an old hymn, were soon being sung in schools and churches throughout the South. Its closing stanza reads thus:

> *Furl that Banner, softly, slowly!*
> *Treat it gently—it is holy -*
> *For it droops above the dead.*
> *Touch it not—unfold it never,*
> *Let it droop there, furled forever,*
> *For its people's hopes are dead!*

The legend of "the Lost Cause" had been born. This spiritual succor for the mostly Baptist and Presbyterian South came from an unlikely source: an Irish-American Roman Catholic priest. There is dispute over precisely when and where Abram Ryan was born. He himself claimed to have been born in Ireland (though some sources claim it was Hagerstown, Maryland, and others Norfolk, Virginia) in 1838 or 1839. His parents, Matthew and Mary (Coughlin) Ryan, came from Clonmell, county Limerick, to Norfolk, Virginia, sometime in the 1830s.

Ryan was a mystical, deeply spiritual young man and he gravitated early toward the priesthood. He studied under the Vincentian Fathers at Niagara University in Niagara Falls, New York, and entered their order in 1854. After teaching for a time in Niagara Falls, he went to Cape Girardeau, Missouri, in the heart of Confederate-leaning southeastern Missouri. Upon the outbreak of war, he did not hesitate to cast aside his teaching career and seek a commission in the Confederate army. Unsuccessful, he attached himself to the Confederate forces as a chaplain, ministering to the wounded and dying of all faiths on many battlefields.

Ryan left a deep impression on almost all who met him. With black hair reaching almost to his shoulders, his expression seemed perpetually sad and his manner almost otherworldly. His Celtic mysticism deepened after his younger brother was killed serving in the Confederate army. Ryan then made his first stab at poetry, publishing "In Memory of My Brother" and "In Memoriam."

The publication of "The Conquered Banner," however, brought Ryan fame throughout the South. In a burst of inspiration, he followed it with "The Sword of Robert Lee," "The Lost Cause," "Gather the Sacred Dust," "March of the Deathless Dead," and numerous other tributes to the Confederacy and the men who fought for it.

Although the term "the Lost Cause" was popularized by journalist Edward Alfred Pollard, who published a book in 1866 with the same title, Ryan soon earned the nickname "the poet-priest of the Confederacy" and became the leading apologist for the Southern cause of secession. The main tenets of the Lost Cause were that the South tried peaceably to dissolve a tyrannical Union and was ruthlessly crushed by superior arms, numbers, and firepower. A blissful, pastoral way of life was stamped out by harsh industrialism and materialism.

Of course, this portrait left out a great deal, and former slaves largely paid the price for the Lost Cause ideology in the form of Jim Crow laws and lynching. Psychologically, however, the Lost Cause helped white Southerners give meaning to their sacrifices and make sense of the war they had just fought and lost. The echoes of the Lost Cause are occasionally still heard in the South today.

Ryan got around a great deal in the years after the war. He lived in Biloxi, Mississippi (*see* that entry), where he became quite friendly with former Confederate President Jefferson Davis. He edited a newspaper called *The Pacificator* while assigned to St. Patrick's Church in Augusta, Georgia. He also pastored churches in New Orleans; Nashville, Knoxville, and Clarksville, Tennessee; Macon, Georgia; and finally, St. Mary's Church in Mobile, Alabama.

In his last years, he made frequent lecture tours of the rest of the United States, as well as Canada and Mexico, raising funds for the relief of

Southern widows and orphans. He remained bitter toward the North, however, until 1878, when Northerners gave generously to the victims of a cholera epidemic in the South. Touched by this outpouring of sympathy for former enemies, Ryan wrote his poem "Reunited," to proclaim forgiveness between North and South.

His poems were collected and published in 1879 as *Father Ryan's Poems* and sold well, going through several editions. His death in 1886 was an occasion for mourning throughout the region. In 1912, the *Mobile Register* sponsored a drive to erect a suitable memorial to the man who helped give the South back its dignity. Thousands of Southern schoolchildren contributed pennies and dimes. The statue now stands in Ryan Park in downtown Mobile.

᨜ **EXHIBITS:** A statue of Father Ryan, unveiled July 13, 1913, stands in the middle of the park. The statue was recently cleaned and refurbished. ᨜ **LOCATION:** Ryan Park is a triangular park bounded by Spring Hill Avenue and Bayou and St. Michael Streets in downtown Mobile. ᨜ **HOURS:** Dawn to dusk. ᨜ **ADMISSION:** Free

MONTGOMERY

F. SCOTT AND ZELDA FITZGERALD MUSEUM

Francis Scott Key Fitzgerald was a cocky, self-assured young lieutenant with the 67th Infantry, stationed at Camp Sheridan, Alabama, when he met the 17-year-old Zelda Sayre at a dance at the Montgomery Country Club. Within two years, in 1920, they were married amid the splendor of St. Patrick's Cathedral in New York City.

Together, the novelist and his socialite wife became the defining symbol of what was dubbed "the Jazz Age." By the time of the Great Depression, however, they had become an anachronism, with Scott drowning himself in alcohol and Zelda confined to a mental institution.

F. Scott Fitzgerald was a rebel against his Irish background. Indeed, in a letter to the critic Edmund Wilson, who had cited Fitzgerald's Irishness as a key to his success, the novelist even tried—absurdly—to deny it altogether. "(It is) as if his Irishness and his connections with the Southern gentry were mutually exclusive," writes James R. Mellow in *Invented Lives: F. Scott and Zelda Fitzgerald* (1984).

Fitzgerald's mother, Mary McQuillan Fitzgerald, was the daughter of Irish immigrant parents. ("Straight 1850 potato famine Irish," Scott later wrote disdainfully.) His father was Irish on his father's side. His father's mother, by contrast, was descended from a long line of Maryland legislators and officials. Francis Scott Key, author of "The Star-Spangled Banner," was a distant ancestor. This was what Fitzgerald considered the "respectable" side of the family.

Being Irish and middle class "depresses me inordinately," Fitzgerald wrote later to a friend. "I mean gives me a sort of hollow, sheerless pain. Half of my ancestors came from just such an Irish strata or perhaps a lower one."

Try as he might to escape it, however, Fitzgerald was to remain a prisoner of his Irish roots, always fearful that they meant he somehow did not "measure up" in the eyes of Protestant America. Irish characters pop up in Fitzgerald's novels. The beautiful and cultured Beatrice O'Hara is the mother of Amory Blaine, the hero of Fitzgerald's first published novel, *This Side of Paradise* (1920), and seems to be an idealized version of the mother Fitzgerald wished he had. Also appearing in the novel is Monsignor Darcy, a kind of mother/father figure to Blaine.

Things were not going well for the Fitzgeralds when they arrived in Montgomery from Paris in October 1931 and rented this house. The Depression had set in and Zelda was in and out of sanitariums. The situation was not improved when the politically naive author jauntily declared his attraction to communism in an interview published in the local newspaper the day after their arrival.

During the six months or so they lived here, Scott worked on finishing *Tender Is the Night* (1934). Zelda, as therapy for her deepening insanity, began writing a novel herself, which her husband's publisher brought out as *Save Me the Waltz*. It received damaging reviews, however, and did not sell well.

Scott spent the rest of the 1930s trying to make his fortune in Hollywood as a scriptwriter, with little success. (His only screen credit was *Three Comrades*, starring Robert Young.) He was working on a novel, *The Last Tycoon*, which was later finished by Edmund Wilson, at the time of his death in 1940. (*See also* St. Paul, Minnesota.)

🐚 **EXHIBITS:** F. Scott Fitzgerald manuscripts and memorabilia. Many of the exhibits relate to Zelda Fitzgerald, who was born and raised in Montgomery. 🐚 **LOCATION:** 919 Felder Ave. 🐚 **HOURS:** Wednesday–Friday 10–2; Saturday–Sunday 1–5 🐚 **ADMISSION:** None, but donations appreciated. 🐚 **TELEPHONE:** (205) 264-4222.

KNOX HOUSE

The most elegant antebellum home in Montgomery was built by William Knox, who was born in Strabane, county Derry, in 1800. He immigrated to the United States in the 1820s and moved to Montgomery a decade later. Although born a Methodist, Knox later converted to Roman Catholicism and became an ardent advocate of secession.

Knox's marriage to Anna Octavia, the well-born daughter of a revolutionary war officer, set him on his way toward becoming one of Montgomery's leading citizens. He established the Central Bank of Alabama (whose building still stands at the corner of Dexter Avenue and Court Square), which made the very first deposit into the treasury of the newly formed Confederate States of America in 1861. He also built the residence on Lee and Bibb streets that later became the First White House of the Confederacy.

Knox built this house around 1848, engaging architect Stephen Decatur Button, who also designed the Georgia State House at Milledgeville and the Alabama State House in Montgomery. The cost of the house, $50,000, was an enormous sum at the time. The Alabama State House, by comparison, cost $60,000 in 1851.

The Knox house was a center of activity during the Civil War, with Mrs. Knox organizing a ladies' association to render services to the Confederacy. William Knox died in 1869.

❧ **EXHIBITS:** The Knox house now houses a public relations firm called Reid and O'Donahue. Staff members will be happy to show visitors the interior. Call ahead. First White House of the Confederacy contains period furnishings.   ❧ **LOCATION:** 419 S. Perry St. (Use entrance on South Lawrence Street on other side of the building.) First White House of the Confederacy is on Washington Avenue just across from the state capitol.   ❧ **TELEPHONE:** Reid and O'Donahue; (205) 263-7812; First White House of the Confederacy; (205) 242-1861.   ❧ **HOURS:** Reid and O'Donahue: 8:30–5; First White House of the Confederacy: Monday–Friday 8–4:30; Saturday–Sunday 9–4.   ❧ **ADMISSION:** Donations appreciated.

ARKANSAS

PATRICK CLEBURNE MEMORIAL AND GRAVESITE

Civil War historian Shelby Foote called him "the finest division commander on either side in the Civil War." Robert E. Lee eulogized him as "a meteor shining from a clouded sky." His men called him "Irish Pat" and "the Stonewall Jackson of the West." Yet, Patrick Ronayne Cleburne never rose above the rank of major general in the Confederate army. Like many Irishmen, particularly soldiers, Pat Cleburne was a man who knew his own mind and was not afraid to speak it.

Cleburne was a Cork man, born on St. Patrick's Day, 1828, of Protestant stock. His father was a physician, and young Patrick received an above-average education. He sat the examination for entry into Trinity College, Dublin, where he intended to study pharmacy. He failed the examination, however, and, too humiliated to face his father, enlisted in the British army instead.

For the three years he served in the 41st Regiment of Foot, Cleburne learned the art of soldiering and impressed his superiors, who offered to promote him. Cleburne, however, decided not to remain with the British army, purchased his discharge, and, with a brother and sister, sailed for America in 1849.

Relatively few Irish settled in the South. New Orleans, however, was a major port of entry, and that is where Pat Cleburne and his family made landfall. The Cleburnes soon moved to Cincinnati, where the brother and sister settled. Patrick, however, had a yearning to go west and strike it rich. He headed back down south to the then-booming Mississippi River town of Helena, Arkansas.

Without a friend in the state, Cleburne turned to pharmacy to get himself started, but began studying law in his spare time, eventually qualifying for the bar. Although socially shy, he made friends and showed he also knew how to take care of himself. As he and another lawyer were on their way to lunch one day, they were set upon by a group of "country people" who endeavored to waylay them. Cleburne and the other lawyer drew their revolvers and left two of their assailants dead and the other wounded. Cleburne himself was badly wounded in the incident, but he recovered and established that he was not a man to be trifled with.

As war edged closer, Cleburne left his neighbors in no doubt where he stood on secession. "I am with the South in life or death, victory or defeat," he wrote in a letter to his brother. Though he "cared nothing" for slaves or slavery, the Southerners, he said, "have been my friends and have stood by me on all occasions."

When Ft. Sumter was fired upon, Cleburne enlisted as a private soldier in the 1st Arkansas Regiment. His previous military experience, however, stood him in good stead and he was quickly elected a captain by his men and soon found himself catapulted into overall command.

Cleburne's military career was confined to the "western" theater of operations, which actually was Tennessee and Kentucky, as opposed to the better-known Virginia theater. At Shiloh in the spring of 1862, he first came to the attention of Gen. Braxton Bragg and was placed in command of a brigade. Cleburne commanded from the front, leading his men with a slashing audacity and determination that was notable in an army where those qualities were not in short supply.

At Perryville, Cleburne skillfully covered the Confederate army's withdrawal and was promoted to the rank of major general and placed in command of a division. His blue-white battle flag, with crossed cannons on a white moon, was known and feared by Union troops throughout the area. Cleburne went from triumph to triumph, excelling in battlefield command in an army that, in contrast with the brilliant campaigns of Lee and Jackson in the Virginia theater, was plagued by defeat and high-command intrigue.

"Cleaburne [sic] is young, ardent, exceedingly gallant, but sufficiently prudent," was Bragg's assessment. "He is a fine drill officer and has the admiration of his command, as a soldier and as a gentleman."

Cleburne performed superbly at the Battle of Missionary Ridge in November 1863, where his division repelled four of Sherman's while, once again, covering a Confederate withdrawal. Gloom enveloped the Army of Tennessee as defeat increasingly seemed inevitable.

The problem, as Cleburne saw it, was numbers. The North, with its huge pool of unmobilized manpower, could absorb heavy losses of men and materiel and make them good. The South, where virtually every available white male had already been mobilized, had no such luxury. "The

Confederacy had one last string in its bow," writes James M. McPherson in *Battle Cry of Freedom,* "a black string."

In January 1864, Cleburne dropped his bombshell. The South should mobilize a slave army and send it into battle, promising freedom to every slave who proved loyal to the Confederacy. "Slavery, from being one of our chief sources of strength at the commencement of the war, has now become, from a military point of view, one of our chief sources of weakness," Cleburne wrote in his proposal. The North was fighting to free the slaves, he argued, thus making the slaves their allies. Black troops were now fighting for the North. This threatened "the loss of all we now hold most sacred—slaves and all other personal property, lands, homesteads, liberty, justice, safety, pride, manhood." To save all the rest of these precious possessions, he said, the South must be prepared to sacrifice the first.

It seems likely that Cleburne's Irish birth—combined with his unmatched fighting record—made him perhaps the only Confederate commander who could actually make such a proposal. Since he was not steeped in the intricate tangle of Southern traditions, customs, and taboos surrounding the "peculiar institution" of slavery, he could not see the deep waters into which he was wading.

"A monstrous proposition," raged one of Cleburne's fellow division commanders. A corps commander said it was "at war with my social, moral and political principles." Although 12 brigade and regimental commanders eventually endorsed Cleburne's idea, the opposition it engendered was far too massive to be overcome. It wasn't until March 1865, when the military situation was beyond salvation, that Jefferson Davis signed an order implementing Cleburne's idea. By that time, however, its originator had been dead six months.

Contemporaries are rarely kind to men with bold ideas, and Cleburne was no exception. The damage to the Irishman's career was substantial. Once on an apparently unstoppable ride to the highest ranks, Cleburne's upward movement stalled after his call to mobilize slaves. He was repeatedly passed over for promotion while more junior officers were placed in command over him. Mutterings about his foreign birth and associations with what was thought to be the "wrong" people in the faction-riddled Army of Tennessee grew louder.

If Cleburne was bitter, he did not allow his disappointment to show in his battlefield performance. Disdaining the normal practice of division commanders directing the action from the rear, Cleburne continued to lead from the front. His recklessness proved fatal, for it was while leading another charge 10 months later that he was felled in the massacre that was the Battle of Franklin (*see* Franklin, Tennessee). He was only 36 years old.

General Patrick Cleburne rallies his troops at the Battle of Franklin, November 30, 1864. (Courtesy of Rick Reeves)

Cleburne's official disgrace did not extend to his men or the public at large in the Confederacy, however. After the war, counties were named for him in Arkansas, Texas, and Alabama. There was even a steamboat on the Mississippi for a time called *The Pat Cleburne.*

Cleburne never returned to Helena after he left in the spring of 1861. But the townsfolk were eager to honor their most famous son, and in May 1891, Cleburne's body was exhumed from its resting place on the field at Franklin and brought back to Helena with great pomp and ceremony. A 25-foot-tall granite obelisk was erected over his grave in the Confederate Cemetery, carved with the details of his career and the names of his victories.

❧ **EXHIBITS:** The Confederate Cemetery is operated as an adjunct to Maple Hill Cemetery on North Holly Street in Helena. ❧ **LOCATION:** Helena is in eastern Arkansas, built on a bluff overlooking the Mississippi River about 60 miles south of Memphis. Take Route 61 through Missis-

sippi from Memphis to Route 243 across the river and into Helena. ☺
HOURS: Daylight hours. ☺ ADMISSION: Free ☺ TELEPHONE: The
cemetery can be difficult to find. It is recommended you stop by the
Helena Chamber of Commerce at 111 Hickory Hill Drive in central
Helena, where you can obtain a map and directions. Chamber of Com-
merce: (501) 338-8327.

FL O R I D A

THE JACKIE GLEASON THEATER OF THE PERFORMING ARTS

To be in vaudeville, "you just had to be born," said the great Irish-American radio comic Fred Allen, who was born John F. Sullivan in Boston. Like blacks and Jews, the Irish found themselves caricatured and stereotyped on the stage. More than a few Irish performers themselves contributed to the image of the "stage Irishman,"—decked out all in green and wishing "top o' the mornin'" to one and all—but then, show business beat digging canals for a living.

The Irish dominated vaudeville during its heyday, roughly between 1875 and 1925. There were Ed Gallagher and Al Shean. ("Positively, Mr. Gallagher?" "Absolutely, Mr. Shean!" was their classic exchange.) Eddie Harrigan and Tony Hart constituted the original "Mulligan Guard Troupe." "The Three Keatons" featured young James Francis Keaton, who was known in the family as "Buster" before he was even eight years old. And of course, there were the four Cohans (*see* George M. Cohan Memorial, New York, New York).

Unfortunately, there is virtually nothing tangible that recalls these pioneers of early entertainment. This theater, which the city of Miami Beach built to house "The Jackie Gleason Show" in the 1960s, is perhaps the closest there is to a memorial to the man universally known as "The Great One."

Jackie Gleason cut his teeth in show business during the waning days of vaudeville in the late 1920s and early 1930s, both as a performer and as an emcee. In the classic "Honeymooners" series and later in "The Jackie Gleason Show," he brought vaudeville to television and continued a great Irish-American tradition of stage comedy.

Jackie Gleason with his father, Herbert, who abandoned the family a few months after this photo was taken. (Museum of Modern Art)

Jackie Gleason called himself Irish on both sides. His father, Herbert, appears to have been an Irish-American who worked as a clerk in an insurance company. In true vaudeville style, however, Herbert Gleason abandoned the family just 10 days before Christmas in 1925. Jackie was only eight, and no one ever saw Herbert again. Jackie's mother, Mae Kelly Gleason, was Irish-born and without question the major influence on the future comedian.

She married Herbert around the turn of the century when she was only 15 and he a decade her senior. A religious woman to the point of mysticism, she had a morbid distrust of doctors, perhaps because they were unable to save her other child, Jackie's older brother, Clemence, from death at 14 in 1919. Herbert had insisted on naming the couple's second son after himself, so he was christened Herbert John. His mother, and everyone else, however, called him Jack or Jackie.

Mae held tightly to her surviving son, especially after Herbert left. She kept him cooped up in the house, away from the neighborhood kids and the germ-filled streets that she feared would infect and kill Jackie. "He saw her as the epitome of lace-curtain Irish," a friend recalled later of Jackie's memories of his mother. She was "afraid he would fall in with the wrong elements" and was an "obsessively sheltering figure."

Nevertheless, Jackie found outlets for his natural tendency to perform, cracking wise to the teachers in school and becoming a sharp pool player. (The latter stood him in good stead later when he played Minnesota Fats alongside Paul Newman in *The Hustler,* for which Jackie was nominated for an Oscar as best supporting actor.)

After his mother died of complications from a skin disease while Jackie was still in his teens, he left Brooklyn for good with 36 cents to his name. Arriving in Hollywood, he played supporting roles in six pictures and honed his act on stage in nightclubs. His big break came when he was hired to headline at Slapsy Maxie's nightspot in Hollywood. The clientele was heavily from the movie community, and Jackie became known to a wider crowd that could advance his career.

Jackie made several excellent movies in addition to *The Hustler,* such as *Requiem for a Heavyweight* and *Gigot,* the latter in which he played a tenderhearted French mute. He also won a Tony award for his Broadway performance in the light comedy *Take Me Along.* But it was his television work that would make him famous.

It began in earnest with a chance to star in CBS's "Cavalcade of Stars" in 1950. All but one of his famous characters were born soon thereafter: Joe the Bartender, Reggie Van Gleason III, the Poor Soul, Charlie the Loudmouth, and Rudy the Repairman. Gleason also showed himself a master of the difficult art of physical comedy, flapping his arms as he boomed, "And awaaaay we go!"; taking a long sip from a cup and saucer, looking straight into the camera, and saying with a satisfied grin, "How sweeeet it is. . . ."

His Ralph Kramden character was born a few years later when Gleason decided he wanted to do a husband-and-wife sketch. "He's a loudmouth and she's a shrew, but they love each other," was how Gleason described it.

"The Honeymooners" itself ran for only a single season in 1955–56. It involved the lives of Ralph Kramden, a $62-a-week bus driver, his wife, Alice, and their friends, sewer worker Ed Norton and his wife, Trixie. "The Classic 39" episodes have since become a cult favorite. Many people have seen every episode numerous times in reruns, yet they still laugh uproariously at every gag, no matter how familiar.

For all the laughs, though, there was a serious side to the show, for it depicted a world that many working-class Americans, most definitely including Irish-Americans, could identify with. Ralph and Alice's bare flat, decorated only with a table and some chairs, a balky sink, a bureau into which everything was thrown, an old-style ice box and lacking even a telephone, was a very real depiction of the type of place where Jackie had spent his own childhood. He even gave the Kramdens one of his actual old addresses, 358 Chauncey Street, in the Bushwick section.

And even though the episodes had happy endings, with every fight resolving itself in a clutch with Ralph declaring, "Baby, you're the greatest," it is hard to escape the essentially dead-end nature of Ralph and Alice's lives. All of Ralph's schemes to better their condition come to naught and they end up back where they started. There was a nervous edge to a lot of the laughter.

By the end of the 1950s, Jackie Gleason's moon face—and huge frame (nearly 300 pounds at his heaviest)—was one of the best known in America. Only Lucille Ball rivaled him in terms of television popularity. Somewhere along the line, Orson Welles dubbed him The Great One, a moniker Gleason unabashedly adopted as his own.

In 1964, Gleason uprooted his entire 200-member entourage and moved the production of his television show from New York to Florida. The reason was simple: Gleason loved golf and wanted to play all year round, something he couldn't do in chilly New York. (He also didn't mind that the Florida location would force the CBS brass to get on a plane if they wanted to see him, which would give him more freedom.)

After the end of his television series, Jackie Gleason made numerous movies, most of them forgettable fluff such as *Smokey and the Bandit* with Burt Reynolds. He died of prostate cancer in 1987.

Gleason never forgot his roots or the effect that they had on him. "Both my parents were Irish," he told an interviewer long after he had become a sensation. "Sometimes, I feel guilty about living it up. The fleshpots! Delightful hedonism and all that.... At one time I studied the other religions thinking the answer might lie there. But every time I came back to Catholicism, the religion I was born into. At least with Catholicism, I know where I stand—among the sinners. Faith is to be placed in God."

What was the secret of his success? More than a few people have attributed it to Gleason's marvelous ability as an improviser. He could always come up with a witty line at the right time. When Milton Berle was performing in a nightclub one night, he noticed the portly Gleason sitting in the audience. "Look," Berle said, "I see two of my favorite comedians, Jackie Gleason!" Unfazed, Gleason shot back, "I wish you were *one* of mine."

❧ **LOCATION:** 1700 Washington Ave. and 17th Street. ❧ **HOURS:** Box office: 10–5 Monday–Friday; closed weekends except for performances.
❧ **ADMISSION:** Call for ticket prices. ❧ **TELEPHONE:** (305) 673-7300.

OLUSTEE

OLUSTEE STATE HISTORIC SITE

The largest Civil War battle fought in Florida took place here on February 20, 1864. It was a Confederate victory, and the credit belongs to Brig. Gen. Joseph Finegan, commander of the Department of East Florida and an Irish native.

The auguries were not good for the Union forces from the beginning of the Florida campaign, which had its roots in the crassest of political motives. Treasury Secretary Salmon P. Chase, entertaining dreams of displacing Lincoln as the Republican presidential candidate that summer, heard that Union loyalists in Florida would support him for the nomination if a pro-Union provisional government could be established there. Chase's supporters brought Union Maj. Gen. Quincy A. Gillmore into the plot, and he authorized the dispatch of Union forces into Florida.

After landing at Jacksonville on February 7, 1864, a 5,500-strong Union force—including a large contingent of black troops—marched across northern Florida. Along the way, they freed slaves, burned the mansions of the slave masters, seized supplies, and generally spread panic among the local residents.

Confederate forces were thin on the ground in this area of the South, which was far from the main fighting fronts. Brig. Gen. Finegan, however, did not spend his time bemoaning lack of resources. He gathered together a scratch force of two infantry brigades that eventually numbered over 6,000 and concentrated them near Olustee, a railroad junction that he correctly guessed was the objective of the Union forces.

Born at Clones on November 17, 1814, Finegan immigrated to the United States because of the famine in Ireland and settled in Florida, where he owned a lumber mill at Jacksonville. Later, he moved to Fernandina, where he practiced law and became involved in railroad construction. An ardent proponent of secession, he was a delegate to the state's secession convention, and Gov. John Milton appointed the fiery Irishman head of all Confederate military affairs pertaining to Florida.

Finegan handled his forces at Olustee with great skill. Deploying his men behind improvised fortifications at first, Finegan grew impatient with the wary approach of the Union commander, Gen. Truman Seymour. He thus dispatched one of his two brigades to engage the Union forces first. After four and a half hours of hard combat, the bluecoats broke and retreated, eventually returning to their base at Jacksonville.

Finegan was hailed for his victory and received a rare "Thanks of the Confederate Congress" for his action. There was some criticism, however, that he failed to pursue the Union force and achieve its complete destruction or capture it.

Nevertheless, Finegan's aggressiveness was noted and three months after Olustee he was transferred to the main cockpit of the war, Virginia. At Cold Harbor, troops under his command plugged a vital gap. They performed similar "fire brigade" functions during the long siege of the Petersburg campaign. Heavy casualties and the increasingly desperate military situation, however, caused a high desertion rate in his command. Two weeks before Appomattox, Finegan was transferred back to Florida, where he ended the war.

After the war, Finegan resumed his business interests and won election to the state senate. He died in Rutledge, Florida, in 1885.

&✿ **EXHIBITS:** There is a museum and a walking tour of the battlefield. &✿ **LOCATION:** Olustee State Historic Site is 42 miles west of Jacksonville and 3 miles east of the town of Olustee on U.S. 90. &✿ **HOURS:** 9–5 daily. Museum: Thursday–Sunday only. &✿ **ADMISSION:** Free &✿ **TELEPHONE:** (904) 752-3866.

PENSACOLA

FORT GEORGE PARK

France was America's best-known ally in the War of Independence, but Spain was allied with the new United States as well. And just as "Wild Geese" Irish troops (Irish refugees who enlisted in the armies of England's Catholic enemies) fought with the French armies (*see* Middlebury, Connecticut), Irish also fought under Spain's colors as well.

The Gulf Coast campaign of 1780–81 is almost forgotten today, even by those who consider themselves students of the American Revolution. Spain had lost Florida (which then included southern Alabama, Mississippi, and eastern Louisiana) to Britain in 1763 as its penalty for being on the losing side with France in the Seven Years' War. During the Revolution, northern Florida became a refuge for Tories driven out of the southern colonies. The Spanish government saw the American war as an opportunity to reclaim its lost colony and dispatched an expedition.

British forces at Mobile surrendered to the dashing Spanish commander, Gen. Bernardo de Galvez, on March 14, 1780. The young Spanish victor promptly began planning to seize British West Florida, the capital of which was at Pensacola.

The British, under Gen. John Campbell, were well aware the Spanish were coming and worked feverishly to improve Pensacola's defenses, particularly Fort George. Although they had a year to prepare (a storm drove back the first Spanish invasion fleet), a lucky hit on the fort's powder

A color sergeant and private hold the flag of Regimento de Hibernia, which took Pensacola from the British in 1781. (Ann Brown Military Collection, Brown University Library)

magazine by a Spanish shell on May 8, 1781, precipitated the fort's surrender.

The massive explosion of the powder magazine tore through the fort's main redoubt, killing 85 of the British defenders outright. A Spanish assault soon gained the works and General Campbell realized he was in an untenable position. Hostages were exchanged to ensure compliance with the truce while surrender terms were negotiated. The Spanish held Lieutenant Meggs of the 60th Regiment while the British held Lieutenant Kenney of the Regimento de Hibernia, which was part of the besieging Spanish force.

The Regimento de Hibernia was one of three regiments of exiled Irish soldiers that constituted the Spanish army's Irish Brigade, the others being the Irlanda and the Ultonia (Ulster). Originally organized and outfitted by exiled Irish nobles, the regiments were taken into Spanish service in 1709 and served throughout the confused dynastic struggles that preoccupied European royalty throughout the 18th century.

The Regimento de Hibernia, however, was arguably the most famous of the three. (Descendants of its officers remain part of Spain's military elite to this day.) For its gallant stand at the gates of Naples in 1744, where it lost 40 officers and hundreds of men in a delaying action that enabled the king of Naples to escape attacking Austrian forces, the Spanish king allowed it to bear on its colors the motto *La Columna Irlanda* (The Pillar of Ireland).

Col. Arturo O'Neill (later a lieutenant general), was in command of the 600 men of the Hibernia at Pensacola. Lt. T. O'Dunn was killed early in the siege by a British raiding party. In tribute to the Hispano-Irishman's courage, the British buried him with full military honors.

Colonel O'Neill was named governor of West Florida following the British surrender, and William O'Kelly, one of O'Neill's officers, succeeded him as commanding officer of the regiment. Later, Capt. Carlos Howard ("possessed of Irish charm and a silver tongue" in the words of a Spanish official) of the Regimento de Hibernia was dispatched with part of the regiment to deal with gangs of desperadoes in eastern Florida. Along with Colonel O'Kelly, they took the Castillo de San Marcos in St. Augustine from the British in July 1784 and restored Spanish rule.

Although it is little known, the Spanish campaign in the Gulf had important consequences. It tied up British land and naval power during the crucial months before the decisive battle at Yorktown (*see* Williamsburg, Virginia). It ensured that Florida was in Spanish, not British, hands at the end of the revolutionary war. A hostile Florida might have meant all manner of problems in the early years of the American Republic. It might have made a critical difference during the War of 1812.

The Spanish-Irish regiments continued in Spanish service throughout the Napoleonic Wars, fighting, ironically, on the British side during the Peninsular War. All three regiments were disbanded in 1818, after 109 years under the Spanish Crown.

❧ **LOCATION:** Excavated remains of the British fortifications can be seen in Ft. George Park, at Polofax and LaRua streets. ❧ **HOURS:** Dawn to dusk. ❧ **ADMISSION:** Free

GEORGIA

TAYLOR-GRADY HOUSE

A soldier and cotton merchant, Gen. Robert Taylor was born of Scotch-Irish stock in Cookstown, county Tyrone, on New Year's Day 1787. He and his entire family immigrated to the American colonies in the 1790s, landing in Savannah, where they had relatives.

Most of what is known about Taylor's life is taken from his obituary. (He died in 1859.) He went into business with his father at age 14, and 11 years later was made a full partner in the firm of Taylor, Davies and Taylor in Savannah.

Taylor married "up." Harriet Caroline Jones was of an aristocratic family from Beaufort, South Carolina. They had three sons, two of whom did not survive childhood. In 1821, just five years after their wedding, Harriet died.

Taylor became quite well established during this time, and he was a very active member of the Hibernian Society of Savannah. He remarried in 1827 and had three more sons by his second wife.

The family moved from Savannah to Athens around 1837 in order that Taylor's sons could attend the University of Georgia. He built a grand house, which burned to the ground just after it was completed. The present house was rebuilt in the winter and spring of 1838–39.

The 1850 census showed General Taylor (he had been commissioned a brigadier general in the state militia) to be a planter worth $200,000, an enormous sum in those days, and owner of land in five counties. Taylor died in 1859 after one of his feet was crushed under a moving train at Madison, Georgia.

The house was sold in 1863 to William Sammons Grady for $50,000 (Confederate currency). William Grady was the father of Henry Grady, later famous as the proprietor of the *Atlanta Constitution* and the leading spokesman for the "New South" in the 1890s. Although Grady was also presumably an Irish-American (his family name was O'Grady originally), there is no documentation of his ancestry beyond the mid-1700s, when his family was in North Carolina.

ᴥ **EXHIBITS:** The house contains a portrait of Taylor, as well as a copy of his will and other exhibits. ᴥ **LOCATION:** 634 Prince Ave. ᴥ **HOURS:** Monday–Friday 10–3:30. ᴥ **ADMISSION:** $2.50 ᴥ **TELEPHONE:** (706) 549-8688.

ATLANTA

ATLANTA-FULTON COUNTY PUBLIC LIBRARY

There hasn't been a phenomenon quite like Margaret Mitchell's *Gone With the Wind* in the years since it was published in 1936. It sold a million copies in its first six months (in the depths of the Great Depression), won for its author a Pulitzer Prize, and was converted by David O. Selznick into what many people consider the greatest film of all time. Incredibly, the book returned to the *New York Times* best-seller list five decades after its original publication.

The book very nearly didn't get published at all. Although young Margaret Mitchell had wanted to be a writer since her teenage years, she had labored on the enormous manuscript in secret, telling little about it, even to her closest friends. When she was introduced to Harold Latham, an editor at Macmillan who had been prompted by a mutual friend to ask Mitchell about her novel, she denied having written one. It was only after much agonized soul-searching that she finally turned it over to him.

Latham was instantly enthusiastic, as was the rest of the Macmillan house. *Gone With the Wind* was a sweeping love story set against the backdrop of the Civil War. For Southerners, it became a part of "the Lost Cause" legend, a hymn to a way of life misunderstood by outsiders. This interpretation was not to Mitchell's liking, however, according to biographer Darden Asbury Pyron. Mitchell, Pyron said, had intended the book as a repudiation of the "moonlight and magnolias" school of Southern romance.

One reason Margaret Mitchell could describe that world so well, perhaps, was because she herself was an outsider in the South. Like Flannery O'Connor (*see* Milledgeville, Georgia), Margaret Mitchell was Catholic on both sides of her family. The Irish in her was on her mother's side, and it was the most powerful influence on her work.

Margaret Mitchell's maternal great-grandfather was county Tipperary–born Phillip Fitzgerald. Almost as soon as he came into the world in 1798, however, his family fled to France for supporting Wolfe Tone's uprising that year. In his early twenties he departed for America, landing first in Charleston, which already had a small but important Irish community.

Phillip Fitzgerald moved around the backcountry of the South, finally chancing upon the small settlement of Irish Catholics at Locust Grove in Taliaferro County (which had been one of the stopping points of Flannery O'Connor's ancestors as well). There, at about age 40, he married a woman 20 years his junior named Eleanor McGahan. They eventually had seven daughters, and by 1854, Fitzgerald owned 3,000 acres and 35 slaves.

Many thought Fitzgerald's acquisitiveness was the cause of his being "cursed" with daughters, but curse or not, one of them married John Stephens, a native of King's County (now county Offaly). Stephens reinforced his father-in-law's cultural and intellectual legacy on the family, as well as made its fortune.

Stephens was an ambitious, driven man who earned a bachelor's degree from Hiawassee College in Tennessee in 1856. After service as a captain in the Ninth Georgia Regiment in the Civil War, he thrived as a merchant, earning $200 a month in gold. Going into partnership with another Irishman, John Flynn, Stephens went into the hardware and grocery business, eventually branching out into land speculation, construction, and property development. He became quite well-off.

"These two Irishmen helped shape the most fundamental stuff of Margaret Mitchell's imagination," writes Pyron in his biography of the writer, *Southern Daughter* (1991).

No less remarkable was Stephen's wife and Fitzgerald's daughter, Anne Fitzgerald Stephens. A strong-willed woman, she alone among Phillip Fitzgerald's daughters successfully resisted a convent education. In the Civil War, she showed the same spunk. She not only "walked through the whole Yankee army to get to the Federal general's tent," she secured protection for her home, and Union army rations besides. This feisty woman, Margaret Mitchell's grandmother, served as the inspiration for Scarlett O'Hara. Although Mitchell always denied any connection between her family history and her fiction, there is no shortage of resemblances. Irishness suffuses both the book and the film, a fact that gets remarkably little attention.

Pyron notes both similarities and important differences between Mitchell's actual family history and the O'Haras of Tara. Scarlett's father, Gerald O'Hara, is a rough-hewn, uncultured, semi-illiterate man, very much unlike the learned and highly numerate Phillip Fitzgerald and John Stephens.

Mitchell also downplayed her own ancestors' power and position. "They were both Irishmen born and proud of it and prouder still of being southerners and would have withered any relative who tried to put on a dog," she wrote. "I'm afraid they were so proud of what they were that they'd have thought any putting on the dog was gilding the lily and any way, they left that to the post-war noveaux riche who had to carry a lot of dog because they had nothing else to carry."

Whatever Margaret Mitchell thought of her ancestors, they certainly affected her work. "Pa, you talk like an Irishman," Scarlett says to her father early in the novel. In a scene repeated in the film, Gerald O'Hara tells his daughter to treasure the land, for it is the only thing that lasts. Tara, the plantation named for the ancient seat of the high kings of Ireland (who presided over Ireland early in the Christian era), is the spiritual center of the novel. It is the place to which Scarlett returns to renew her strength after Rhett Butler leaves her.

The success of both the book and the movie made Margaret Mitchell famous worldwide. Mitchell died when she was struck by a taxi in downtown Atlanta on August 11, 1949, just a few months shy of her 48th birthday.

* **EXHIBITS:** The Margaret Mitchell Room displays memorabilia and exhibits relating to *Gone With the Wind*, both the novel and the film. * **LOCATION:** 1 Margaret Mitchell Sq. Across the street is Margaret Mitchell Park. Where the Georgia-Pacific skyscraper now stands was the site of the Loew's Grand Theater, which premiered *Gone With the Wind* in 1939. * **HOURS:** Monday 9–6; Tuesday–Thursday 9–8; Friday–Saturday 10–5; Sunday 2–6. * **ADMISSION:** Free * **TELEPHONE:** (404) 730-1700.

CHURCH OF THE IMMACULATE CONCEPTION AND FATHER O'REILLY MEMORIAL

Union forces began burning Atlanta on the night of November 15, 1864. Just 10 weeks earlier, Gen. William Tecumseh Sherman had captured the city after a brilliant campaign. Now he was about to leave it behind, ungarrisoned, and he and his army were about to embark on a march that would win them fame in military history and bitterness in the memory of Southerners forever.

A foundry, an oil refinery, and a freight warehouse were the first buildings to be fired. Two Michigan regiments had used improvised battering rams to knock down the huge stone roundhouse that was the heart of Atlanta's railway system. Although Sherman had ordered the sparing of nonmilitary targets, such as churches and private homes, Union soldiers frequently disobeyed.

One man watching the flames with rising anger was county Cavan–born Fr. Thomas O'Reilly, pastor of the Church of the Immaculate Conception. The railroads that had brought Sherman to Atlanta had been hewn out of the wilderness largely by Irish Catholic immigrants. The first entry in the records of the parish was a baptism on August 9, 1846. It probably took place in a member's home, since there was no church yet and the parish was served by missionary priests from the Savannah diocese.

Work on a permanent wooden church began in 1848 as waves of famine immigrants coming up from the port of Savannah swelled the Irish Catholic population of Atlanta. That was the church that Father O'Reilly now sought to save from the flames.

During the siege and later during the occupation of the city by Union forces, O'Reilly established himself as a figure who could be trusted by both sides. He ministered to the wounded and dying, regardless of whether they wore blue or gray. After the city fell to Sherman's forces, he celebrated the Mass for the many Catholics, most of them Irish, in the Union army.

As Union troops began throwing firebombs on November 15, however, Father O'Reilly decided to act. Approaching Sherman through Gen. Henry W. Slocum, O'Reilly delivered his famous warning: "If you burn the Catholic Church, all Catholics in the ranks of the Union Army will mutiny." This was no idle threat, for in those days priests possessed authority with their flocks that is hard to imagine today. And given the large number of Irish Catholics in Sherman's army, O'Reilly had to be taken seriously.

So Immaculate Conception, scarred and scorched though it was by shellfire and nearby flames, survived the burning of Atlanta. And thanks to the Irish-born priest's efforts, so did St. Philip's Episcopal, Trinity Methodist, Second Baptist, and Central Presbyterian Churches, as well as Atlanta's City Hall. By the next day, with most of Atlanta in ashes, these structures were just about all that was left standing as Sherman's army moved off on its march to the sea.

O'Reilly continued in charge of the parish and supervised the construction of the present Church of the Immaculate Conception, which was completed in 1873. The priest did not live to see its completion, however. He died, probably of tuberculosis, in 1872 at age 41.

Another interesting aspect of the life of this church is the annual service of the Irish Horse Traders every April 28. The first of these families were thought to be of Gypsy origin, but in fact were probably Irish "travelers" or "tinkers." They settled in Washington, D.C., in the early 1850s and set up a livery stable. Others followed and eventually eight of these large, extended trading "families" were established in the United

Atlanta commemorates Thomas O'Reilly's heroic efforts during the siege of Atlanta. Shown here is the unveiling of the Fr. O'Reilly memorial in 1945.

(Atlanta Historical Society)

States: the Rileys, McNamaras, Carrolls, Sherlocks, Garmans, Costellos, Dartys, and O'Haras.

One of these bands, led by Pat O'Hara, established headquarters at Nashville, but the group soon changed its collective mind and headed for Atlanta, which was growing and expanding as the headquarters of the "New South." Using their profits from horse trading and wagon sales to buy property, the families became quite prosperous as the city grew.

Later, most of the traders moved on, but the burial of John McNamara, the leader of one clan, in Oakland Cemetery in 1881 established Atlanta as the central meeting point of the clans. When Oakland was full, the clans bought lots in West View Cemetery. The graves are elaborate affairs, with intricate stone carvings. One of the most notable is the grave of John Sherlock in West View, which carries photographs of himself and his wife engraved on porcelain and inserted into the stone.

🢡 **EXHIBITS:** The church contains the grave of Father O'Reilly. A guided tour is available. In 1945, the Atlanta Historical Society erected a memorial commemorating O'Reilly's heroism on the grounds of Atlanta's City Hall. It is around the corner from the church on Mitchell Street, between Central and Washington Streets. 🢡 **LOCATION:** Immaculate Conception is at 48 Martin Luther King Jr. Dr. at Central Avenue. Oakland Cemetery is on Fair Street between South Boulevard and Oakland Avenue. West View is at Gordon Road and Mozely Drive. 🢡 **HOURS:** Church office: 9–5 daily. Cemeteries: dawn to dusk. City Hall: 8:30–6 daily. 🢡 **ADMISSION:** None, but donations appreciated. 🢡 **TELEPHONE:** Immaculate Conception: (404) 521-1866; West View Cemetery: (404) 755-6611; Oakland Cemetery: (404) 658-6019; Atlanta City Hall: (404) 330-6000.

MILLEDGEVILLE

DILLARD RUSSELL LIBRARY AT GEORGIA COLLEGE

Mary Flannery O'Connor lived only 39 years (1925–1964) before succumbing to the disease lupus, which had also killed her beloved father. During that time she produced two slim novels, *Wise Blood* (1953) and *The Violent Bear It Away* (1960), as well as two collections of short stories, *A Good Man Is Hard to Find and Other Stories* (1955) and *Everything That Rises Must Converge* (published posthumously, in 1965). They were enough, however, to ensure her position as one of the foremost American writers of the 20th century.

O'Connor's mother's family, the Clines and the Treanors, were substantial landowners in this part of Georgia. Along with the O'Connors of Savannah, they were Roman Catholics, of whom there were few in this part of the United States. Most of the Irish in Georgia tended to be Presbyterian Scotch-Irish.

O'Connor's roots here were very deep. Her great-great-grandfather, Patrick Harty, arrived in Georgia in 1824 from county Tipperary, settling in Locust Grove in Taliafero County, the first substantial settlement of Catholics in a state never very friendly to that faith. (*See* Savannah, Georgia). Harty's daughter Johanna married Hugh Donnelly Treanor, also a native of Tipperary, in 1848.

On her father's side, Patrick Cline, the author's great-grandfather, arrived in Savannah as a famine immigrant from county Roscommon. He must have been a man of some education, for he secured a position as a Latin teacher at the Richmond Academy. In any event, he lived only three years after his arrival in his new country. Patrick's son Peter, however, did well in business and had several stores. Carl Vinson, who later became the legendary chairman of the House Armed Services Committee, had his first job as a "cash boy" in Peter Cline's store.

Edward O'Connor Jr., the author's father, was a descendant of Patrick O'Connor, who had been born sometime in the 1830s and came to Savannah with his brother in the period immediately after the Civil War. Patrick was a wheelwright who eventually opened a prosperous livery stable. Edward attended Catholic schools as a boy and met and married Regina Cline. They became the parents of the girl they christened Mary Flannery O'Connor. (She dropped the "Mary" for professional reasons.)

Edward O'Connor was a real estate agent, but never seemed to have the same zest for business as his forebears, according to Sally Fitzgerald ("Root and Branch: O'Connor of Georgia," *Georgia Historical Quarterly*, 1980). He was a World War I veteran who took his duties with the American Legion seriously. (He was elected state commander in 1936.) In

Flannery O'Connor's works frequently drew upon her Irish Catholic upbringing. (Flannery O'Connor Collection, Ina Dillard Russell Library, Georgia College)

1938, however, he contracted the degenerative disease lupus that eventually killed his daughter.

Flannery O'Connor was educated in Catholic schools until she was 12 and later attended Georgia State College for Women. Except for a brief period of time in the North, she lived and worked the rest of her life in Milledgeville.

The death of her father sent Flannery O'Connor into a deeply serious search of her religious faith, which became essential to her life and work. Some observers have suggested that O'Connor's Jansenist Catholicism in an essentially hostile region helped armor her against critics who were frequently uncomprehending of her work.

In 1946, after graduating from Georgia State College for Women, she sold her first story, *The Geranium*, to *Accent* magazine. Her career began its ascent until, in 1950, she was struck with lupus. The disease, however, had become more manageable in the years since her father's death and she was able to live a very nearly normal life for a time. During this time, she began collecting peacocks, the birds that have become associated with her in the mind of the public.

O'Connor's fiction is suffused with her religious sensibility, derived from her Irish Catholic background. Some critics have been uncomprehending of her frequently grotesque imagery, but she developed a loyal following among the reading public that has endured in the more than 30 years since her death.

"She complained in one of her letters that the trouble with most writers these days was that they weren't *from* anywhere," Sally Fitzgerald says of O'Connor. "By contrast, Flannery, who in her lifetime was sometimes referred to locally as 'Miss Regina's daughter who writes,' and who is now an author of international repute, was not only *from* Georgia, she was a part of it."

ᐓ **EXHIBITS:** Furnishings and manuscripts from the writer's nearby home are on display, and other materials can be viewed on request. Also, "Andalusia," the home where Flannery O'Connor lived, is just northwest of Milledgeville on U.S. 441. The house is on the National Register of Historic Places, but it is not open to the public. ᐓ **HOURS:** 8–5 daily. ᐓ **ADMISSION:** Free ᐓ **TELEPHONE:** (912) 234-8054.

SAVANNAH

CATHEDRAL OF ST. JOHN THE BAPTIST

"Catholics as such were pointedly excluded (from Georgia)—along with rum, lawyers, and blacks—from the first colonists to arrive . . . the only religious group so interdicted," notes Sally Fitzgerald in a *Georgia Historical Quarterly* article on Flannery O'Connor's background, ("Root and Branch: O'Connor of Georgia," 1980). The article serves as a useful guide to the history of Catholicism in Georgia, especially that of the Irish Catholics.

Fear of popish plots was still powerful in England (where the exiled Catholic Stuarts were still claimants to the British throne), and this suspicion was also strong in the colonies. The effort to keep Catholics out in the early years was apparently fairly successful. Fitzgerald could find a handful of references to Irish surnames in the colony, but these people apparently sought not to call attention to their Catholicism, if in fact they were Catholics.

One of the first recorded instances of Irish landing in Georgia was in the 1740s. An early history of Georgia chastised James Oglethorpe, the colony's founder, for admitting a boatload of 40 "Irish convicts" to the colony. The earl of Egmont, however, said this was untrue. They were not convicts, he noted, but simply immigrants who had found their way to the wrong port. Oglethorpe, by nature a generous and tolerant man, disregarded the prohibition on Catholics in the name of mercy.

Nevertheless, fear and hatred of Catholics remained widespread. Florida was still under the control of Catholic Spain, and many Indians who had been converted to Catholicism by Spanish missionaries lived in Georgia. Catholic immigrants, it was feared, would join with these forces to threaten the colony. Even John Wesley, the founder of Methodism, was slandered as a secret Roman Catholic when he fell out with the local power structure.

The regulations were relaxed a bit once the Crown took over the colony in 1752, and some Irish Catholics began to trickle into Georgia. A colony was established at Locust Grove around 1790, and the first Catholic church was erected there (see Milledgeville, Georgia).

The first Catholic church in Savannah was erected in 1799 as the city developed into a port of entry for Irish immigrants. It was named for St. John the Baptist, perhaps because the still-fearful Catholics thought it sounded nonthreatening. The first two pastors were French, but the third was a Father O'Neill.

By 1812 the Irish population had burgeoned so sufficiently that the Hibernian Society of Savannah was founded. One of the society's earliest projects was to provide aid for the many Irish who had been imported to dig the Ogeechee Canal.

Savannah became a diocese in 1850, as famine immigrants swelled its Catholic population. The building of a cathedral was spearheaded by John Flannery, an ancestor and the namesake of Flannery O'Connor. A famine immigrant, he arrived in Savannah in 1854 at age 19 after three years in first Charleston and later Atlanta. He eventually founded the John Flannery Company and became one of Savannah's most prominent businessmen.

The cathedral was completed in the mid-1870s but burned in 1898. John Flannery chaired the committee that oversaw the building of the current structure, which was completed early in this century.

🐚 LOCATION: Harris and Abercorn streets. 🐚 HOURS: 9–5 daily. 🐚 ADMISSION: None, but donations appreciated. 🐚 TELEPHONE: (912) 233-4709.

EMMET PARK

Few would dispute that New York has the world's largest St. Patrick's Day parade, but who has the second-largest? None of the usual suspects. Instead, it's right here in Savannah, or at least that's what the locals claim. Every March 17th, this very proper southern city dons the

green and becomes one of the most Irish cities in the world, commemorating its past as one of the major ports of entry for Irish immigrants to the
southern United States.

Emmet Park, of course, was named for Robert Emmet, the Irish
patriot who was executed for his part in organizing the 1798 uprising
against British rule. (*See* Robert Emmet Statue, San Francisco, California.)

✿ LOCATION: Emmet Park is between Bay Street and Factor's Walk on
Savannah's waterfront.

SIEGE OF SAVANNAH

The 1779 siege of Savannah is not one of the more glorious chapters
in the American Revolution. The British had captured Savannah the
year before, and the Americans were determined to take it back with
French help.

Thirty-three French ships, carrying 4,000 French and American troops
appeared off the Georgia coast in early September, achieving total surprise.
The French commander, Adm. Count Charles-Hector Theodat d'Estaing,
landed his troops on the night of September 11–12 and approached Savannah on September 16. After the garrison refused a demand to surrender,
d'Estaing commenced a siege.

The Franco-American forces included Count Casimir Pulaski and 200
of his cavalrymen. The French forces also included the Regiment de Dillon,
commanded by Count Arthur Dillon, which was a part of the fabled
French Irish Brigade (*see* Middlebury, Connecticut). The strength of the
regiment at Savannah was 450 all ranks.

The assault, on October 9, was a fiasco. The Regiment de Dillon was to
move secretly from the northwest and follow a route through a swamp that
would enable it to turn the enemy's right flank. Unfortunately, the regiment became lost in the swamp, and when it emerged, it found itself in full
view of the defenders' guns. The regiment's attack was a forlorn hope, and
50 officers and men were killed.

At the same time, the main assault on Spring Hill redoubt failed.
Pulaski, the Polish cavalry commander was mortally wounded and the
allied forces lost an incredible 800 men, a full 20 percent of the total force.
Amid mutual recriminations, d'Estaing sailed away, and Benjamin Lincoln, the American commander, withdrew to Charleston. Nothing was
gained, and the failure at Savannah emboldened the British to seize
Charleston soon afterward.

A footnote: one of the fatal casualties that day was Sgt. William Jasper,
the hero of Ft. Moultrie, South Carolina, who had raised the flag after it
had been shot away by a British shell on June 28, 1776. As a result, Jasper

became one of the most famous heroes of the American Revolution, celebrated in story and song and with many place-names in his honor.

Many Irish have claimed Jasper as one of their own. Unfortunately, so much myth and half-truth surrounds Jasper's legend and his background is so obscure that no reliable claim can be made for his ancestry. (Some historians insist Jasper was of German descent!) There is a memorial to Jasper in the midst of Madison Square in the heart of Savannah, the only tangible reminder of the siege of Savannah.

🐟 LOCATION: The site of Spring Hill redoubt was just south of where the Savannah visitor center stands today at 301 Martin Luther King Jr. Blvd. The site is unmarked, but visitor center staff are happy to point it out and provide other information. Jasper's statue is in the middle of Madison Square. 🐟 HOURS: Visitor center: Monday–Friday 8:30–5; Saturday–Sunday 9–5. 🐟 TELEPHONE: (912) 944-0455.

K E N T U C K Y

FRANKFORT CEMETERY

Theodore O'Hara is primarily remembered for a single poem, "The Bivouac of the Dead," certain lines of which are carved on military tombstones and war memorials across the United States. The most frequently quoted lines are these:

> On Fame's eternal camping-ground
> Their silent tents are spread
> And Glory guards, with solemn round
> The bivouac of the dead.

O'Hara was born in the United States on February 11, 1820. His father, Kane (or Kean) O'Hara along with his three brothers, had been implicated in Lord Edward Fitzgerald's United Irishmen uprising of 1798. The whole family fled Ireland for the United States, where Kane secured employment in Kentucky as a schoolteacher.

Theodore received a college education at St. Joseph's in Bardstown and prepared for life as an attorney. (He made the acquaintance of a fellow future lawyer named John C. Breckinridge, who eventually became vice-president of the United States under James Buchanan and a Confederate general.)

O'Hara found life as a paper-pusher indescribably boring, however, and he took work as a newspaperman for *The Yeoman*.

The outbreak of the Mexican War, however, set him on his lifelong course as a soldier and adventurer. He served with distinction in several battles and returned home a major. Restless after the end of the war, he became involved with a mercenary scheme to invade Cuba, where he was badly wounded and narrowly avoided capture by the Spanish authorities.

The coming of the Civil War saw O'Hara back in the saddle again, this time as a Confederate officer. He served on the staff of Gen. Albert Sidney Johnston and in several other posts until the war ended.

O'Hara wrote "The Bivouac of the Dead" in 1847 in commemoration of the reburial at Frankfort Cemetery of those Kentuckians who died at the Battle of Buena Vista in the Mexican War. O'Hara himself died in Alabama in 1867. In 1874, however, his body was exhumed and reburied in Frankfort Cemetery, alongside the men he had commemorated.

&⋅ EXHIBITS: O'Hara's impressive monument is located in Section 17. &⋅ LOCATION: 215 E. Main St., ½ mile east of Frankfort on U.S. 60/460. &⋅ HOURS: 8 A.M.–dusk. &⋅ ADMISSION: Free &⋅ TELEPHONE: (606) 873-5711.

LOUISVILLE

BRENNAN HOUSE

Louisville in the years before the Civil War was a volatile place, filling up with Irish immigrants fleeing the famine and German immigrants fleeing political turmoil in their homeland. The city also had a fairly large number of free blacks. The anti-immigrant Know-Nothing party was active and dangerous.

The Irish came to the growing city of Louisville to perform the manual jobs characteristic of most of the early immigrants. They helped dig the Portland Canal and build the Louisville and Nashville Railroad and worked in the slaughterhouses. Butchertown and Limerick were the names given to the two neighborhoods dominated by Irish immigrants.

The ethnic animosities boiled over in what became known as Bloody Monday, on August 6, 1855. As is the norm with riots, no one can say precisely how it started, but the Know-Nothings (who called themselves the American party) were endeavoring to prevent the Irish from voting in that day's elections. A melee erupted in the voting lines, with gunfire being exchanged. St. Martin's Catholic Church was saved only by the intervention of the mayor. Catholic neighborhoods and businesses were put to the torch. At least one priest was killed by a stone-throwing mob while on his way to give the last rites to a dying parishioner.

Thomas Brennan was born in Clogremon, county Laoighis, around 1839. He arrived in New Orleans in the care of his grandmother at age 3. Educated in Louisville, the boy grew up to be a tinkerer and blossomed into a talented inventor, eventually winning 27 first prizes for his inventions, including two at the 1893 Chicago World's Fair. He also held numerous patents.

Brennan helped build the first locomotive for the Louisville and Nashville, and he was co-owner of the Brennan and Company Southwestern Agricultural Works, which produced seed-drilling equipment and other farm machinery. Naturally, he became quite wealthy in the process and retired from business in 1897 to travel the world. His obituaries describe him as "a true Irishman" who maintained great affection for his native land and an active interest in Irish affairs until his death.

This opulent, Italianate Victorian house was built in 1868. Brennan bought it in 1884 and lived here until his death in 1914. Although Brennan and his wife, Anna, had eight children, all of them died without any children of their own, and the last Brennan to live here died in 1969. The house was bequeathed to the city of Louisville.

The house contains many notable furnishings, such as the carved solid walnut Centennial bedroom suite, which won first prize at the 1876 Philadelphia Exposition. Numerous family portraits line the walls.

* **EXHIBITS:** In addition, the house contains a portrait of Thomas Brennan, a Bohemian glass chandelier, a carved Bedford limestone mantle, and many other pieces accumulated by the Brennans in their years of worldwide travel. * **LOCATION:** 631 S. 5th St. * **HOURS:** 10–3:30 Monday, Wednesday, and Friday; 1–3:30 Saturday. * **ADMISSION:** $3 adults; $2 for seniors, children, and military personnel with ID. * **TELEPHONE:** (502) 540-5145.

LOCUST GROVE

This house was built by William Croghan Sr., who had come to Philadelphia from Ireland at age 17 in 1769. Little is known of the Croghan family's background in Ireland, but they appear to have been Episcopalians. The man William Croghan was coming to join, George Croghan, his Irish-born uncle, was already making a name for himself on the frontier as a scout, land speculator, and intermediary between the British authorities and the Indians.

George Croghan was born in county Roscommon around 1710 and arrived in Philadelphia around 1741. He established himself near present-day Carlisle, learning the Delaware and Iroquois languages and acquainting himself with their customs and habits.

None of this, of course, was done with simple charity or public service in mind. George Croghan very much wanted to be a rich man, and his complex land dealings from the 1750s through the 1770s earned him an unsavory reputation in some quarters. He unwisely engaged in a feud with George Washington over various land deals, in which Washington came out on top.

During the Revolution, George Croghan was unfairly accused of being a Tory and was acquitted, but his business operations were ruined and he died a virtual pauper in 1782. His journals, however, constitute one of the most important records of life on the early frontier, and he was undoubtedly one of the most important British Indian agents of the time.

George's nephew, William Croghan, led a somewhat more sedate, though still very interesting life. Enlisting in the British forces in 1771, he switched sides in 1775 and was commissioned captain in the Eighth Virginia Regiment of the Continental Army. After seeing action with Washington's army around New York and New Jersey, William was captured when the British took Charleston. One of his fellow captured officers, Jonathan Clark, was the elder brother of George Rogers Clark, the hero of the American Revolution in the West. Thus began a lifelong relationship between the Croghan and the Clark families.

William married Lucy Clark, the sister of Jonathan and George Rogers, in 1789. After the Revolution, the Clark family had made the dangerous journey to the Kentucky Territory, which George Rogers believed offered richer soil than Virginia. William became George Rogers's surveying partner, and they soon had a thriving shipping business on the Ohio River.

William and Lucy began construction of Locust Grove in 1790, the year after their marriage. Eight of the couple's children survived into adulthood. The rest of William's life, until his death in 1822, was marked by community service and continued economic success. In 1792, he was a delegate to the state constitutional convention. Kentucky was admitted to the Union in 1792.

George Rogers Clark, after losing his leg in an accident in 1809, came to live at Locust Grove with his sister and brother-in-law. His death in 1818 was an occasion for statewide mourning. William Clark, the younger brother of George Rogers, set out from Louisville in 1803 with his partner, Meriwether Lewis, on their famed journey of western exploration.

❧ **EXHIBITS:** The house contains original and period furnishings. A visitor center has a 10-minute film on the house's restoration. ❧ **LOCATION:** 561 Blankenbaker Ln. ❧ **HOURS:** Monday–Saturday 10–4:30; Sunday 1:30–4:30. ❧ **ADMISSION:** $3 adults; $2.50 seniors; $1 children. ❧ **TELEPHONE:** (502) 897-9845.

L O U I S I A N A

HOUMAS HOUSE

The prosperous port of New Orleans attracted many business-minded people in the late 18th and early 19th centuries, including many Scotch-Irish and Anglo-Irish. Prior to the famine immigration, most of these non-Catholic Irish referred to themselves simply as "Irish," adding the hyphen only later in order to distinguish themselves from the newer immigrants. Many of them, however, were as virulently anti-British as the Catholics.

One of the most prominent of these early New Orleans Irish was Daniel Clark. Born in county Sligo in 1766, Clark claimed to be descended from the ancient high kings who presided over Ireland early in the Christian era. An uncle urged him to come to New Orleans, which Clark did in 1786. Working closely with the Spanish government, he built up a fortune for himself.

With the coming of American rule, Clark was elected territorial delegate to Congress. He also had some involvement with Aaron Burr's shadowy efforts to establish an empire for himself in what was then the Southwest. It was the dispute over the disposition of Clark's estate at the time of his death in 1813, however, that made his name a legend in American legal studies. The case lasted 65 years, went through 30 separate trials, and was appealed to the state supreme court five times and the U.S. Supreme Court no less than 17 times.

Another early Irish immigrant was Oliver Pollock, sometimes referred to as "the unsung hero of the American Revolution." Born in Coleraine, county Derry, to a Scotch-Irish family in 1737, he and two brothers and a nephew immigrated with their father to Philadelphia, a major Scotch-Irish destination. The rest of the party eventually located in Carlisle, but Oliver became a merchant in Philadelphia.

Rich in history and beauty, Houmas House has been featured in a number of Hollywood motion pictures. (Courtesy of Houmas House)

It was on a trip to Cuba that he encountered Don Alejandro O'Reilly who was on his way to suppress the anti-Spanish uprising in New Orleans. Pollock relocated to New Orleans and established himself by provisioning O'Reilly's food short forces. The Spanish-Irish general reciprocated by granting Pollock exclusive trading rights along the Mississippi. Pollock very quickly became one of the richest men in the New World. Some credit him with inventing the dollar sign ($).

With Spain and France both cheering on the American revolutionaries, the anti-British Pollock had no difficulty buying 10,000 pounds of gunpowder from the Spanish armory in New Orleans and shipping it to George Washington's army. He was one of the most generous contributors to the American cause, even to the point of actually bankrupting himself. Although he eventually rebuilt his fortunes, he died in 1823 in such complete obscurity that no one to this day knows where his grave lies.

Unfortunately, there are virtually no memorials to these Irish merchants of early Louisiana. The closest thing is this plantation house, which was built around 1840 by the Preston family on land partly owned by Daniel Clark. In 1858, they sold it to John Burnside. The latter's background is obscure. He always claimed to have been born in Belfast, Ireland, and that he was orphaned at an early age. At some point, he immigrated first to Virginia and later to Louisiana, where he made a fortune in real estate speculation.

Burnside had barely moved to Houmas House (named for a local Indian tribe) when the Civil War literally arrived at his front door in the form of Union officers eager to take the house for their headquarters. Thinking quickly, Burnside pointed out that, since he was legally a British subject, his house was not subject to seizure as war booty. This argument held up and the house remained his property until his death in 1881. The nearby village was also named for Burnside.

Because of its architectural splendor and because it escaped damage in the war, Houmas House has won favor with Hollywood directors as the "typical" Southern plantation. It was featured in the 1965 Bette Davis/Joan Crawford cult horror film *Hush, Hush, Sweet Charlotte*.

❧ EXHIBITS: The house contains many original and period furnishings as well as a stunning three-story spiral staircase. The formal gardens have been extensively used in film and television. ❧ LOCATION: 942 River Rd. ❧ HOURS: Guided tours daily 10–5, February through October; 10–4 rest of the year. ❧ ADMISSION: $7 adults. ❧ TELEPHONE: (504) 473-7841.

NEW ORLEANS

CHALMETTE BATTLEFIELD

Peace had already been concluded between Britain and the United States when the final battle of the War of 1812 took place here just outside New Orleans. The Treaty of Ghent ending the war was signed on Christmas Eve of 1814, but word had not yet arrived in the United States when the battle occurred on January 8, 1815. The Battle of New Orleans, therefore, was by no means decisive, but it became a legend in American history anyway.

The British troops were battle-hardened regulars, veterans of the wars against Napoleon. The 4,000 Americans, by contrast, were a motley aggregation of regular troops, pirates from Jean Lafitte's band, Cajun backwoodsmen, civilian New Orleans residents, and even a regiment of free blacks. All were under the inspiring command of Gen. Andrew Jackson. The smashing victory was a tonic to a dispirited nation that had experienced mostly defeats up to this point. It also helped propel Jackson into the White House 13 years later.

There are several Irish connections to this most famous of American battles. Jackson, was the son of Presbyterian Irish emigrant parents from Carrickfergus in county Antrim (*see* The Hermitage, Nashville, Tennessee). His counterpart at New Orleans, Gen. Edward Michael Pakenham, was, like his brother-in-law, the duke of Wellington, of Anglo-Irish stock. Pakenham's collateral descendants today include the earl of Longford, the British Labour party politician, and Thomas Pakenham, the distinguished military historian.

After Pakenham was cut down on the field attempting to rally his flagging forces, command passed to Maj. Gen. John Keane, also an Anglo-Irishman, born at Belmont, county Waterford. Although badly wounded, Keane survived the action.

The land on which much of the battle was fought was owned by Augustin Francois de Macarty, whose home served as Jackson's headquarters during the battle. (It burned in 1902.)

Macarty was a descendant of the first two important Irish settlers in the area, Jean Jaques de Macary and Barthelemy Daniel de Macarty, who were the sons of Bartholomew McCarthy, who fled Ireland for France after the final defeat of the Stuarts in 1691. He entered the French naval service, eventually rising to command the Department of Rochefort, and de-anglicized his name to Macarty.

The sons of Batholomew McCarthy were both born in France and were serving with the French marines when they arrived in New Orleans in 1732. Both married French women and came to prominence in the Louisiana colony. Jean-Jaques married a wealthy widow and had five children. Two of his sons returned to France to serve Louis XVI. The younger son, however, returned to New Orleans, married, and himself had two sons. The eldest, Augustin Francois de Macarty, was the owner of the estate on which the battle was fought and was eventually elected mayor of New Orleans.

Also located on the battlefield site is Beauregard House, which was designed by the renowned Irish-born architect James Gallier, Sr. (*see* next entry).

&. **EXHIBITS:** A visitor center has exhibits and an audiovisual display on the battle. Rangers provide interpretive talks, and self-guided tours are available. &. **LOCATION:** About 6 miles south of the French Quarter in New Orleans on S.R. 46. &. **HOURS:** Daily 8–5. &. **ADMISSION:** Free &. **TELEPHONE:** (504) 589-4430.

GALLIER HALL AND GALLIER HOUSE

Early Irish immigrants to New Orleans were not the huddled masses who came later, but were often men of education and some position and wealth. James Gallier, Sr., was such a man. An Anglo-Irishman, Gallier was born at Ravensdale, county Louth, in 1798. The family name was originally Gallagher, but he apparently frenchified it before his

An architectural marvel when built in 1857, Gallier House has recently been restored to its original splendor.

arrival in the French-speaking colony. Gallier, "the father of Greek Revival architecture" in New Orleans, and his son, James Jr., became the Irish-Americans with the most lasting imprint on their adopted city.

James Sr. designed Gallier Hall, which served as New Orleans's city hall (and was the headquarters for the Union forces during the Civil War occupation) between 1852 and 1957. Considered one of the finest examples of Greek Revival architecture in the United States, the building is now used to host receptions and other civic functions. Confederate Pres. Jefferson Davis, who died and was buried in New Orleans, lay in state here in 1889. Gallier was also called in to design New Orleans's St. Patrick's Cathedral (*see* entry farther on).

Gallier traveled extensively in his later years, and he was ultimately lost at sea in a shipwreck off Cape Hatteras, North Carolina. His son, James Gallier, Jr., was born in 1827. He became best known for his design of the grand French Opera House that stood on the corner of Bourbon and

Toulouse streets between 1858 and 1919, when it was destroyed by fire. His Bank of America building can still be seen at 111 Exchange Place.

Gallier Jr. did not forget his own needs or those of his family, however. In 1857, he began work on an elegant townhouse at the edge of the famed Vieux Carre for himself, his Creole wife, Aglae, and their four small daughters.

The building, extraordinary for its time, showcased Gallier's genius as an architect. The kitchen had hot running water, as did a modern bathroom with flush toilet upstairs. Because ventilation was so crucial during the hot, muggy New Orleans summers, Gallier incorporated a skylight and ceiling vents.

Gallier lived in the house only a decade, dying at just 41 years of age in 1868. The house remained in his family until 1917, when it was sold. Now owned by Tulane University, Gallier House has been painstakingly restored to as near its original appearance as possible. The rooms are filled with original and period furnishings. Handwoven carpets, period French wallpaper, and hand-painted window shades complete the 19th-century look.

&. **EXHIBITS:** Gallier Hall contains the original mayor's office, furnished with original rococo revival tables and chairs. Gallier House contains numerous period furnishings, and portraits of both Galliers adorn the drawing room. &. **LOCATION:** Gallier Hall is at 545 St. Charles Ave. Gallier House is at 1118–1132 Royal St. &. **HOURS:** Call for Gallier Hall hours. Gallier House: Monday–Saturday 10–4:30. Guided tours available. &. **ADMISSION:** Gallier Hall free. Gallier House $4; $2 for seniors. &. **TELEPHONE:** Gallier Hall: (504) 586-4311; Gallier House: (504) 523-6722.

IRISH CHANNEL

The thousands of Catholic Irish who came pouring into New Orleans after the onset of the potato famine in 1845 got an even less enthusiastic welcome than they received in New York and Boston. New Orleans was pretty much built up by that time, so there was little vacant land. Housing was scarce, and slavery and a large population of black freedmen meant there were few menial jobs available. Working only sporadically or not at all, the Irish could not earn passage money to go north or west. "They were trapped in a city where they were unneeded," wrote Bethany Ewald Bultman in her book *New Orleans* (1994).

Nevertheless, the Irish persevered and carved out a place for themselves in Louisiana, many becoming dockhands on the developing waterfront, where ships loaded with cotton bales set out for Liverpool and returned carrying more Irish immigrants. The Irish dug many of the canals that lace the New Orleans area, with thousands dying of yellow fever in the semitropical climate (*see* New Basin Canal Park farther on).

This area just west of the concrete and steel mountain of today's Route 90 expressway became known as Irish Channel and was the major Irish ghetto of 19th-century New Orleans. The immigrants crowded into slums here, and they eventually became a political power as their numbers grew to rival the established French- and English-speaking "commercial" classes. By 1828, the Irish were holding the balance of political power, and they voted heavily for the Scotch-Irish Andrew Jackson that year.

Although the Irish have been pretty thoroughly assimilated in New Orleans, the city remains proud of its raucous St. Patrick's Day celebrations. (It is said the Irish receive special dispensation from the Lenten obligation.) There is a parade through downtown, and no prominent politician or businessman would dare miss mass at St. Patrick's Church (*see* entry farther on) on the big day.

🏵 **EXHIBITS:** Irish Channel visitors should be cautioned that the area has long since ceased to be Irish. Daylight visits are recommended and caution advised at all times. 🏵 **LOCATION:** The boundaries of Irish Channel are a matter of dispute, but the area is generally centered on the Camp Street/Magazine Street/Constance Street area west of Route 90. Parasol's Bar at 2533 Constance St. is a green-beer-and-leprechaun-type establishment. Over in the French Quarter is the bar that is widely considered the best Irish gathering spot in New Orleans, O'Flaherty's, at 524 Toulouse St. O'Flaherty's once hosted a museum of Louisiana Irish history on its second floor, but city red tape has prevented owner Dan O'Flaherty from maintaining it. 🏵 **TELEPHONE:** Parasol's: (504) 899-2054; O'Flaherty's: (504) 529-1317.

"MARGARET" STATUE

The first statue erected in the United States to honor a woman was to the memory of Margaret Gaffney Haughey (or Haughery), an Irish woman from county Cavan who became one of New Orleans's most beloved citizens.

Margaret arrived in Baltimore with her parents in 1818 at age 5. Orphaned four years later, she was raised by a family friend and at age 21 married Charles Haughey. The couple moved to New Orleans, where a daughter was born. Unfortunately, husband and daughter both died in fairly rapid succession, leaving Margaret alone and destitute.

She showed admirable pluck, however, devoting herself to helping the many orphaned children of New Orleans. By 1840, she had raised the funds to open St. Theresa's Asylum on Camp Street. In 1859, she became owner of a failing bakery and turned it around. Using the profits, she

With only the simple inscription "Margaret," this statue honors the memory of Margaret Gaffney Haughey.

opened more orphanages and asylums. By the time of her death in 1882, three asylums were operating on a sound footing thanks to her work—St. Vincent de Paul, the Female Orphan Asylum, and St. Elizabeth's.

Alexander Doyle, who also sculpted the statute of Robert E. Lee in Lee Circle, was commissioned to create a monument to this great woman. It stands today, rather forlorn, in a run-down park in Irish Channel, surrounded by barbed wire to protect it from vandals. The inscription on the base reads simply "Margaret."

🐌 **LOCATION:** The intersection of Camp, Prytania, and Clio streets, in Irish Channel. 🐌 **HOURS:** Dawn to dusk. 🐌 **ADMISSION:** Free

NEW BASIN CANAL PARK

 New Orleans began constructing a canal between Lake Pontchartrain and the French Quarter in 1832. Digging canals through the

mosquito-ridden swamps in the days before power tools was backbreaking labor that only the desperate would consider. The Irish were desperate. Black slaves were considered too valuable for a task with such a high mortality rate, so Irish immigrant labor was used instead.

The canal required six years to dig, and every indignity imaginable was heaped upon the laborers. Wages were pathetic and goods had to be purchased from the company store, where prices were almost twice as high as they were in town. To this day, no one can guess how many of the Irish laborers died during the construction. Estimates have run between a low of 8,000 and a high of 20,000. Many of those who died were simply buried where they fell alongside the canal. The prosperity of New Orleans owes much to these Irish laborers.

æ **EXHIBITS:** On November 4, 1990, a Celtic cross was erected by the Irish Cultural Society of New Orleans in memory of the Irish laborers who died digging the canal. A portion of the original canal survives in the park nearby. æ **LOCATION:** New Basin Canal Park is not an official park, so you won't find it on any map of New Orleans. Take I-10 to West End Boulevard exit and go north to Downs Street. æ **HOURS:** Dawn to dusk. æ **ADMISSION:** Free

ST. PATRICK'S CHURCH

Irish immigration to New Orleans in the 1830s caused the Catholic population of the city to swell. Up to that time, of course, most Catholics in the city were French, and the Irish immigrants had to hear mass in that language. St. Patrick's, founded in 1838, was the first English-speaking parish in the city. The design of the church, by James Gallier, Sr. (*see* earlier entry), was patterned after Yorkminster Cathedral in England.

æ **EXHIBITS:** A plaque outside the front door describes the church's history. æ **LOCATION:** 724 Camp St. æ **HOURS:** Church office: 9:15–3 weekdays. Ask to see interior. æ **ADMISSION:** None, but donations appreciated. æ **TELEPHONE:** (504) 525-4413.

MISSISSIPPI

BILOXI

FATHER RYAN HOUSE

Fr. Abram Ryan, "the poet-priest of the Confederacy" (*see* Mobile, Alabama), lived in this house during his residence in Biloxi off and on for 12 years after the Civil War, roughly between 1865 and 1877. During his time in Biloxi, he became quite friendly with former Confederate Pres. Jefferson Davis.

Father Ryan was well known as a militant Confederate and never hesitated to let anyone know it. In 1862, for instance, when New Orleans was occupied by Union forces, a cholera epidemic broke out. Ryan did not hesitate to go to the city to care for the victims. A rumor soon spread, however, that the priest had refused to give funeral rites to a dead Union soldier. Ryan was arrested and brought before Gen. Benjamin "Beast" Butler, the Union commander roundly detested by the city's residents.

"I am told you refused to bury a dead soldier because he was a Yankee," Butler said angrily.

"Why, I was never asked to bury him and never refused," the priest replied calmly. "The fact is, General, it would give me great pleasure to bury the whole lot of you." Butler leaned back in his chair at this bit of Celtic impertinence and roared with laughter.

While in residence here at this seaside house, Father Ryan worked on such poems as "Sea Rest" and "Sea Reverie."

Five years ago, Roseanne and Jefferson McKenney purchased the house and converted it into a bed and breakfast, restoring it as much as possible to its original condition during Father Ryan's residence.

❦ **EXHIBITS:** The house contains a portrait of Father Ryan, displays of his books and poems, as well as his restored writing desk. ❦ **LOCATION:** 1196 Beach Blvd. in Biloxi's historic district. ❦ **HOURS:** The McKenneys

are happy to give tours. Call in advance. ❧ **ADMISSION:** Free ❧
TELEPHONE: (601) 435-1189.

HATTIESBURG

SULLIVAN-KILRAIN FIGHT SITE

July 8, 1889, dawned hot and clear in Hattiesburg, but there was a buzz of excitement in the air that meant this would not be just another broiling Mississippi summer day. Down at the station, special trains from New Orleans were disgorging thousands of visitors, almost all of them men. They had come to watch John L. Sullivan, for 10 years the man who boasted he could whip any man in the world in a fight, defend his heavyweight title against challenger John L. "Jake" Kilrain.

The air of anticipation was particularly acute because the fight was to be held under so-called London rules: bare knuckles and an unlimited number of rounds, with the rounds lasting as long as both fighters remained standing. It would be, almost literally, a fight to the finish.

Those who find modern-day boxing appallingly violent and worthy of suppression would have been horrified at the 19th-century version. A bare-knuckles fight was a bloody, grueling spectacle that was an ordeal for both men. Broken ribs and fingers, shattered knuckles, torn tendons, and fractured limbs were commonplace. Fights were usually a winner-take-all arrangement. Sometimes a hat would be passed in the crowd for the loser, but only if he put on a good show.

Boxing thus had little appeal as a sport for most native-born American boys. Aside from the obvious dangers of the combat itself, many states and localities outlawed prizefighting, and prison stretches of up to two years were given. So it was left to immigrant groups with little to lose, such as the Irish, to supply the battlers for the ring.

To describe John L. Sullivan, "the Boston strong boy," as a sports idol would be an understatement. One observer, who was no fan, called him a "god." In those days when baseball was in its infancy and basketball, football, and hockey hadn't even been invented yet, boxing was the only real professional sport, and John L. Sullivan was its unquestioned king.

John Lawrence Sullivan's parents were Irish immigrants. He was born in the Irish ghetto of Roxbury, Massachusetts (now part of Boston), on October 15, 1858. His mother was a large, domineering woman who sought to push her son into the priesthood, but the wild young boy would have none of it. At age 19, he began boxing in Boston theaters on Saturday nights to earn a few dollars.

(These theater bouts, incidentally, were conducted under Marquess of Queensbury rules, with both men gloved and a limited number of rounds, each lasting three minutes. Sullivan, a consummate professional, always preferred these to the lack of discipline of "London" rules. His advocacy helped popularize the new rules and moved boxing a long way toward becoming a legitimate sport).

Marquess of Queensbury rules or no, Sullivan's style was anything but gentle. He sought to pummel his opponent with punches until the latter went down and didn't get up again. "When Sullivan struck me," one victim said, "I thought a telegraph pole had been shoved against me endwise."

Almost no one went three rounds with Sullivan without ending up on the seat of his pants, and Sullivan's fame as a fighter began to spread. He also acquired a manager, Billy Madden, who had a flair for public relations and advertising and was a major factor in Sullivan's success.

The fight that "made" Sullivan came on February 7, 1882, against Paddy Ryan, the reigning heavyweight champion. In a bare-knuckles brawl in Mississippi City, Mississippi, that lasted a comparatively short nine rounds, Sullivan knocked out Ryan and America had a new heavyweight champ.

After winning the title, no heavyweight champ ever reveled in it more. Traveling the country, Sullivan took on all comers, offering $1,000 to any man who could go four rounds with him. The fights were held in theaters, dance halls, armories, and any other place that could accommodate a crowd, but few collected on the bet. Sullivan's popularity soared, not only among the Irish but among Americans in general. He would today be described as a "crossover" superstar, and his popularity helped define the Irish-American identity. A popular song of the time went like this:

His colors are the Stars and Stripes,
He also wears the Green,
And he's the grandest slugger that
The ring has ever seen.
No fighter in the world can beat
Our true American,
The champion of all champions,
John L. Sullivan.

No one knows exactly how many fights Sullivan had, but it is estimated he knocked down around 200 opponents in his career. "The bigger they come, the harder they fall" was one of his quips. To make certain his title was truly a world one, he traveled to England and Australia, challenging all comers. Amazingly, given the ferocity of the sport at the time, he never killed anyone.

To be sure, Sullivan was not much of a role model for the youngsters who idolized him. His drinking was of heroic proportions (he once forfeited a sold-out match in Madison Square Garden because he was too

The bareknuckled brawl between Sullivan and Kilrain may have resulted in victory for Sullivan, but both men were arrested for staging an illegal bout at fight's end. (Bettmann Archive)

drunk to fight). His personal life was a shambles. He lived openly with a dance hall girl named Ann Livingston while keeping a wife in Boston. His income was enormous (he is estimated to have earned $1.2 million between 1882 and 1892), but he spent it as fast as he made it, mostly in bars.

When it came time to fight Kilrain in 1889, the promoters preferred New Orleans as a site, but boxing was technically illegal and the governor was opposed. Mississippi lumberman C. W. Rich offered his farm outside Hattiesburg as a site. Mississippi's governor was no more enthusiastic than Louisiana's, and tried to stop the trains with the National Guard. Nevertheless, the train carrying the fighters made it to Hattiesburg on July 7.

Sullivan was badly out of shape and had been drinking and eating just as irresponsibly as ever until two months beforehand, when his backers forced him, virtually at gunpoint, to give up drinking and start training. He did, losing 35 pounds. The morning of the fight, Sullivan appeared at the ring dressed in his traditional emerald green fighting tights and, except for a slightly protruding belly, looked fit. Kilrain looked worried.

The fight began at 10:15 A.M. on July 8, when the temperature was already over 100 degrees. Ringside seats were selling for $15, with seats in the stands selling for $10, a steep sum in those days. Water was 25 cents a ladle.

Rich bet $1,000 on Kilrain. Rich's wife, knowing her husband's habit of backing losers, immediately bet $1,000 on Sullivan.

The battle lasted an epic 75 rounds and went 2 hours and 16 minutes. Kilrain sought to tire the great John L. with defensive tactics, refusing to slug it out with Sullivan. He preferred to parry Sullivan's punches and try to wrestle him to the ground. "Why don't you fight?" snarled Sullivan at one point, but Kilrain kept up his defensive tactics. Sullivan was supposedly not good in a long match, and Kilrain was clearly playing for time.

The strategy, however, was a failure, for Sullivan soon began landing punches. "The blows could be heard for 75 yards," wrote one sportswriter who witnessed the event. Punches from Sullivan raised welts all along the left side of Kilrain's body. Sullivan had a scare in the 45th round, when he vomited up some brandy his handlers had mixed with tea. One writer commented that, knowing Sullivan, he probably upchucked the tea and kept the brandy.

But it was hopeless for Kilrain, who staggered around as if in a daze, taking blow after crashing blow from Sullivan. Somehow, he kept coming back for more, but it was useless. Finally, a doctor warned that Kilrain would die if the fight were not stopped. His manager threw in the towel, and Sullivan was still champion.

Afterward, both fighters were arrested for staging an illegal bout. Kilrain spent two months' "hard labor" under the benevolent eye of Rich. Sullivan paid a $500 fine, although legal bills for keeping him out of jail were around $18,000.

Sullivan said he was through with the ring and took up a lucrative career as an actor, touring the country and earning $1,000 a week. His spendthrift ways, however, soon drained his finances, and three years later he was forced to agree to fight "Gentleman Jim" Corbett.

The 1892 bout was Sullivan's last fight and the only one he ever lost. Overweight and out of shape, the great John L. stood little chance. Knocked out in the 21st round, he somehow got to his feet, raised his hand, and called for silence. "I fought once too often," he declared. "But I am glad that it was an American who licked me and that the championship stays in this country. I remain yours truly, John L. Sullivan."

At 31, John L. Sullivan was washed up as a fighter. His weight soared to 335 pounds and his drinking continued unabated. Then, one morning in March 1905, as he was coming off a bender, he simply declared he would never take another drink. And he never did, launching into a new career as a lecturer for the temperance movement. He died February 2, 1918, at only 59 years of age.

The Irish would continue to dominate the boxing world for almost 50 years after Sullivan finally retired. Irish-American champions such as Jack Dempsey and Gene Tunney dominated the ring in the 1920s. So prevalent was the Irish influence in boxing that many fighters without a drop of Irish blood adopted Irish-sounding "ring names," a practice that was denounced by the Ancient Order of Hibernians. Boxer Jack Sharkey, for example, was Lithuanian by birth.

Sullivan's early success, however, helped reshape the image of the Irishman in this country. No longer a loutish tough of dubious patriotism, he was a charming, rough-edged brawler who, while unmistakably Irish, nevertheless packed a two-fisted Americanism.

❧ **EXHIBITS:** A green historic marker commemorates the fight. ❧ **LOCATION:** The historical marker is at the intersection of Richburg Rd. and U.S. 11. The actual fight took place about 3 miles away at the corner of Richburg Road and Sandy Run Road. That sight is unmarked. ❧ **HOURS:** Dawn to dusk. ❧ **ADMISSION:** Free

VICKSBURG

VICKSBURG NATIONAL BATTLEFIELD PARK

Union military strategy in the Civil War had two primary goals: in the eastern, or Virginia, theater, the main target was the city of Richmond, capital of the Confederacy. In the western theater, it was the capture of the Mississippi River port of Vicksburg. Because Vicksburg was built on a high bluff overlooking the river, no Union naval or commercial traffic could traverse the river to or from New Orleans without having to run the gauntlet of the city's guns. Capture of Vicksburg would secure Union control of the Mississippi and cut the Confederacy in two.

The Union tried to take the city by naval bombardment in the summer of 1862. But despite a torrent of shot and shell, Adm. David Farragut concluded the city could only be taken by a land assault. Late in 1862, the rising Gen. Ulysses S. Grant was placed in command. In the spring of 1863, after a series a brilliant maneuvers, Grant's army had the Confederate forces, under Gen. John Pemberton, on the run through Mississippi, back toward the fortress city.

Pemberton made several abortive efforts to halt the Union advance short of Vicksburg. In a fierce action at Champions Hill, Mississippi, on May 16, the Confederates lost 4,000 men to the Union's 2,500. With Grant in hot pursuit and applying relentless pressure, Pemberton sought to make one more effort to halt the Federal forces, this time at the natural barrier of the Big Black River.

The position Pemberton had constructed at Big Black River was formidable, with cotton bales brought from nearby plantations to give the defenders cover and massed artillery that would make any frontal assault seemingly suicidal. Indeed, Grant had not wanted to attack the position at all. He preferred waiting for Gen. William Tecumseh Sherman, who was coming south on the other side of the river, to attack the position from the rear.

One man who was not willing to wait was Brig. Gen. Michael Kelly Lawler, a 49-year-old native of county Kildare and lately an Illinois farmer and friend of Grant's. Commanding a brigade of four regiments of Iowa and Wisconsin men, Lawler's motto was, If you see a head, hit it. He applied it to his own men as much as to the enemy. The year before, Lawler had been acquitted in a court martial on charges of imposing brutal discipline.

Perhaps hoping to remove the cloud that hung over his head, Lawler was determined to prove his worth, and Big Black River seemed as good a place as any to do it. Looping his sword belt over one shoulder because it wouldn't fit around his 250-pound girth and stripped to the waist because of the heat, Lawler stood up, unsheathed his sword, and ordered his men forward on the double.

"The most perilous and ludicrous charge I witnessed during the war" was the assessment of a war correspondent who watched Lawler's attack. The bayou was shoulder deep in places, but the bluecoats slogged on through withering Confederate fire. Somehow, most of them reached the other side and ran up the embankment with a yell. The rebels, astonished at the audacity of the charge, either fled or threw down their weapons and accepted captivity.

The rest of the Union force, following Lawler's example, attacked all the way down the line, causing the whole of the Confederate force to break and retreat toward Vicksburg, only 12 miles distant. The final tally was impressive. The Confederates suffered 1,751 dead, wounded, or captured, of which 1,200 were accounted for by Lawler's force alone. Eighteen field cannons were captured, and all at a cost of just 276 Union casualties.

Vicksburg itself would not fall for another six weeks, but Lawler's recklessness went a long way toward shortening the campaign. It certainly damaged the morale of Pemberton, who was dejected at the failure of his men to hold a position of such strength. "The affair of Big Black bridge was one which an ex-Confederate participant naturally dislikes to record," wrote a member of Pemberton's staff after the war.

After the surrender of Vicksburg, Lawler was transferred to administrative duties as a divisional commander in the Department of the Gulf, where he remained until the Confederate surrender. Promoted to major general in 1865, he mustered out of the army in 1866 and returned to his farm near Equality, Illinois, where he lived quietly until his death in 1882.

Of special interest is the part of the Vicksburg battlefield known as the Great Redoubt. Here, as happened on so many other Civil War battlefields, Irish-Americans fought Irish-Americans. The hill was defended on May 21, 1863, by the 21st and part of the 22nd Louisiana Volunteers, who were mostly Irish from New Orleans. The Union forces were led by the 7th Missouri Volunteers, a mostly Irish regiment that fought under a green banner.

A bronze bust on Vicksburg battlefield commemorates Union Brig. Gen. Michael K. Lawler.

❧ **EXHIBITS:** A bronze bust of General Lawler was erected on the Vicksburg battlefield in 1915. It is on Union Avenue, approximately 175 yards north of the Iowa memorial and not far from the park visitor center. ❧ **LOCATION:** The Big Black River battlefield is located on privately owned land and is not open to the public. Vicksburg National Military Park is entered on its eastern edge from U.S. 20. The 1,700-acre park completely surrounds the city of Vicksburg. ❧ **HOURS:** The visitor center is open daily 8–5. ❧ **ADMISSION:** $4 per private vehicle; $2 per person if entering by bus. Seniors and children under 17 free. ❧ **TELEPHONE:** (601) 636-0583.

NORTH CAROLINA

EDENTON

HISTORIC EDENTON

Who was the first Irish-American? It's a subject of considerable debate and not a little bit of blarney. St. Brendan the Navigator, of course, is reputed to have reached the area that is now Newfoundland in the distant mists of time. Whether or not that story is true, Irish monks did indeed settle as far west as Iceland sometime around 700 A.D.

Claims have been made for a William Ayers or Eris, a Galwayman who is said to have sailed with Columbus on his 1492 voyage. Certainly, Columbus was familiar with Ireland, for he had stopped there on previous voyages to take on fresh water. So it is at least possible he might have had an Irish crewman.

The best claimant for first Irishman within the boundaries of the present-day United States, however, is probably a man who made his reputation near what is now Edenton, North Carolina. William D. Griffin, in *The Book of Irish Americans* (1990), quotes a 1586 diary entry from Capt. Ralph Lane that says, "An Irishman serving me, one Edward Nugent, volunteered to kill Pemisapan, king of the Indians. We met him returning out of the woods with Pemisapan's head in his hands, and the Indians ceased their raids against the British camp."

❦ **EXHIBITS:** A self-guided walking tour and a guided tour of Edenton, one of the oldest towns in North America, are available. ❦ **LOCATION:** The visitor center is at 108 N. Broad St. ❦ **HOURS:** Monday–Saturday 9–5; Sunday 1–5, April through October. Tuesday–Saturday 10–4; Sunday 1–4 rest of year. ❦ **ADMISSION:** Guided tour $5; children and students $2.50; family rate $12. ❦ **TELEPHONE:** (919) 482-2637.

HILLSBOROUGH

GRAVE OF THOMAS BURKE

North Carolinians were a dispirited lot in the summer of 1781, suffering as they were from the depredations of Cornwallis's invading British army. The arrival of the Continental Army the year before didn't bring much solace. It was commanded by the incompetent Horatio Gates, who allowed his troops to take whatever supplies they required from local civilians without compensation. (Gates was relieved after he lived up to his reputation by losing the disastrous Battle of Camden in South Carolina in August 1780.)

In June of the difficult year 1781, Thomas Burke was elected governor of North Carolina. He was a native of county Galway, and his parents were aristocrats of Norman-French descent. Little is known for certain of his early life. The future governor was born around 1744 and probably attended Dublin University. After an unspecified dispute with his parents, he left Ireland for Virginia, where he first practiced medicine. He gave that up for a legal career, however, because, he said, it "promised more profit, and yet, much less anxiety than medicine."

In 1771, he relocated to Hillsborough in Orange County, North Carolina, where he opened a law practice and became active in anti-Royalist politics. He named his home outside Hillsborough Tyanquin, after his parents' estate in Ireland.

Burke was extremely active in organizing opposition to the British Crown in North Carolina, which is scarcely surprising, since Anglo-Irishmen of his station in life back home in Ireland were agitating for more independence from London at exactly the same time. He was elected to the provincial congresses, which met at Halifax.

It was at these sessions of the state congress that Burke made his greatest contributions. He helped frame the Test Act and also helped draft an appeal to the people to resist British authority. He was a member of the committee that unanimously adopted a resolution empowering North Carolina's delegates to the Continental Congress to seek support among the delegates from the other colonies for independence from Great Britain.

Burke was a member of the congress's "radical" faction. That is, he strongly believed in popular sovereignty, annual elections, the separation of powers within the government, and the separation of church and state. Much of this agenda was subsequently enshrined in the North Carolina Constitution. His prominence in these deliberations won him election to the Continental Congress in December 1776, where he served until his election as governor.

North Carolina had been largely spared the ravages of war up until Burke took office in June 1781. The arrival of Cornwallis and his men,

Thomas Burke, elected governor of North Carolina in 1781. (North Carolina Department of Cultural Resources, Archives & Records Section)

however, put an end to that situation. Burke realized vigorous action was needed and he didn't brook much opposition. Troops and supplies had to be raised quickly, and Burke soon found himself in conflict with the state board of war. The outcome of that dispute established him firmly as the supreme executive authority in the state.

So effective was Burke, in fact, that the local Tories decided to kidnap him. A Tory raid on Hillsborough on September 12, 1781, succeeded in this effort, and he was held prisoner at both Wilmington and Charleston.

In those days, the normal procedure for a prisoner was to await "parole," that is, be formally exchanged for another captive, before returning to his own lines. Burke's status as a high-ranking civilian, however, meant the negotiations surrounding his exchange were bitter and protracted. After an assassination attempt, in which two companions were killed, Burke jumped parole and fled back to American lines, resuming his duties as governor.

This was considered an extreme breach of military protocol, and many feared it would bring reprisal on other American prisoners still in British hands. Although Burke was cleared by an investigation of the General Assembly, he did not seek reelection as governor.

The strain of captivity, combined with the end of his public career and the break-up of his marriage, caused Burke to sink into depression and seek the solace of drink. His health broke, and he died at Tyanquin in December 1783, not even 40 years old.

❧ EXHIBITS: Burke's grave, on the grounds of his farm, was for many years marked only by a pile of stones. In 1923, however, a group of summer school students at the University of North Carolina in Chapel Hill undertook to place a proper marker on the grave. In 1944, the Sons of the American Revolution erected a large inscribed granite stone at the site and in 1973 added a bronze plaque bolted to a small footstone. The grave is located in a field off Governor Burke Rd., about three-quarters of a mile east of Highway 57. ❧ LOCATION: Hillsborough is located in north-central North Carolina just off Interstates 80 and 40 on the Colonial Heritage Scenic Byway, not far from Chapel Hill. ❧ HOURS: Dawn to dusk. ❧ ADMISSION: Free

KENANSVILLE

LIBERTY HALL

The Kenan family of eastern North Carolina was of Scotch-Irish descent. Thomas Kenan's place of birth is uncertain, although it was somewhere in Scotland or Ireland around 1700. Kenan's family was probably based in county Armagh, where he married his wife. The couple emigrated from Ireland to the port of Wilmington, North Carolina, in 1730.

Once in his new country, Kenan lost no time setting himself up as a man of means. He acquired lands in this area on the Turkey Branch River. "The Kenan family has been described as a race of gentlemen, highly esteemed, and always prominently identified with questions concerning the public welfare," writes Blanche Humphrey Abee in *Colonists of Carolina*. "Thomas Kenan was a man of considerable means and prominence and took an active part in public affairs."

Kenan served as a member of the colonial legislature and in the militia. He and his wife had eight children. He died in 1765.

A grandson, Thomas Kenan II, built Liberty Hall and served in Congress for a time. The house remained in the family until 1964, when the

Kenan descendants opened it as a museum commemorating their ancestors. The town was named in honor of the family in 1818.

  EXHIBITS: Many of the furnishings are original. A 12-minute videotape relates the story of the house and the Kenan family.   **LOCATION:** On South Main Street in Kenansville.   **HOURS:** Tuesday–Saturday 1–4; Sunday 2–4.   **ADMISSION:** $4 adults; $2 for children.   **TELEPHONE:** (919) 284-3431.

MOORE'S CREEK

BATTLE OF MOORE'S CREEK BRIDGE

Word of Lexington, Concord, Moore's Creek Bridge and Bunker Hill electrified patriot sentiment in the Carolinas. Within a few months, royal governor Josiah Martin had fled, a provincial congress was organized, and a patriot militia was drilling for war.

But no more than half of North Carolina, historians believe, could be thought firmly in the rebel camp. There were large numbers of Tories, prominently including Scottish Highlanders. The latter, who were led by Donald McDonald, a veteran of Culloden Moor, had come to the Americas after the failure of Bonnie Prince Charlie's 1745–46 uprising. They were motivated, not so much by loyalty to King George III, as by detestation of the Scotch-Irish, who formed the core of the patriot forces in North Carolina.

The Highlanders began marching toward the port of Wilmington to join Governor Martin, who had taken refuge aboard a British warship anchored in the Cape Fear River. The patriot forces moved to intercept them at Moore's Creek Bridge, about 20 miles outside Wilmington.

The patriot force was under the command of Colonel (later General) James Moore. He was a descendant of Rory O'More (1620–52), the primary instigator of the Irish rebellion of 1641. By the time he had settled in at Moore's Creek Bridge, Moore had 1,500 men, compared with about 1,000 Highlanders on the Tory side.

On the misty morning of February 27, 1776, the Highlanders found their way blocked at the bridge. Unwisely, their commander, Col. Donald McLeod, who had taken over for the ill Donald McDonald, decided to try a frontal assault.

The Highlander force was led by 80 men wielding broadswords and marching to the music of wailing bagpipes. These tactics worked as well as they had at Culloden, which is to say not very well at all. Colonel Moore had entrenched his forces solidly behind embankments and had support from artillery. Patriot fire raked the ranks of the Highlanders and McLeod was killed within a few paces of the rebel earthworks. Overall, however, casualties were not high, for the Highlanders quickly realized the odds against them and retreated.

Small as it was, the action at Moore's Creek Bridge had big consequences, for it secured the Carolinas against British attack for nearly four years. As for Colonel Moore, his action brought him promotion to the rank of brigadier general three days after his victory at the bridge, and he was appointed commander in chief of all patriot forces in North Carolina. Little more than a year later, however, he died of a myterious stomach ailment. A promising commander, he was only 40 years of age.

❧ **EXHIBITS:** A visitor center contains audiovisual displays and exhibits that explain the battle. ❧ **LOCATION:** About 20 miles northwest of Wilmington and 4 miles west of U.S. 421 on S.R. 210 near the town of Currie. ❧ **HOURS:** Daily 9–5; Saturday–Sunday 8–6, May 30 through September 5. ❧ **ADMISSION:** Free ❧ **TELEPHONE:** (910) 283-5591.

PINEVILLE

JAMES K. POLK MEMORIAL STATE HISTORIC SITE

James K. Polk is one of the nine American presidents who were of Irish descent through the direct paternal line. Polk, the 11th president, (1844–48), was the great-great-great-grandson of Robert Polk of county Donegal. Robert Polk immigrated to Maryland around 1690, fairly early for the Scotch-Irish. The family name was originally Pollok, but at some point was contracted to Polk.

Born November 2, 1795, Polk and his family relocated to the new territory of Tennessee when he was 11. He returned to North Carolina to attend the university and qualified to practice as a lawyer. This led him into politics, and he served seven terms in the House of Representatives between 1824 and 1838, the last four as Speaker. He served a term as governor of Tennessee before being nominated as the first dark horse presidential candidate in 1844. He was elected as a Jacksonian Democrat and served a single term.

Although he is little remembered today, some historians believe Polk deserves to be recalled as one of America's greatest presidents. Under his administration, the United States successfully fought and won the Mexican War, which increased the U.S. land area by nearly two-thirds. It also fulfilled the country's "manifest destiny" to stretch from "sea to shining sea." (*See* James K. Polk Ancestral Home, Columbia, Tennessee.)

❧ **EXHIBITS:** A 25-minute film recounts Polk's life. Guided tours of the restored houses are offered. ❧ **LOCATION:** ½ mile south of Pineville on U.S. 521. ❧ **HOURS:** Monday–Saturday 9–5; Sunday 1–5 April through October. Tuesday–Saturday 10–4; Sunday 1–4 rest of year. ❧ **ADMISSION:** Free ❧ **TELEPHONE:** (704) 889-7145.

WAXHAW

ANDREW JACKSON BIRTHPLACE

Where was the seventh president of the United States born? The man himself always claimed it was South Carolina, but, after his death, research indicated the site might have been in North Carolina. Certainly it was in the area known as the Old Waxhaw Settlement, which is a few miles southwest of present-day Waxhaw, North Carolina.

Jackson's parents hailed from Carrickfergus, county Antrim, not far from present-day Belfast. The president was not related to Thomas Jonathan "Stonewall" Jackson of Civil War fame, but church records uncovered in Ireland indicate the ancestors of the two famous men might have been neighbors at one point.

The Jacksons were part of the "Great Migration" of Scotch-Irish settlers to the American colonies between 1717 and the onset of the American Revolution (*see* Kings Mountain, South Carolina). The Jacksons arrived in America, probably in Pennsylvania, around 1765. They eventually made their way to North Carolina, however, which was already an area of considerable Scotch-Irish settlement.

Andrew Jackson, Sr., did not live long after arriving in his new country. Tradition has it that he strained himself lifting a log in early March 1767 and died a few hours later. His wife, Elizabeth "Betty" Hutchinson Jackson, was expecting their third child in a matter of days. She named her new son Andrew after his father. (*See* The Hermitage, Nashville, Tennessee, for more on Jackson's life and career.)

❧ **EXHIBITS:** Efforts to locate the foundations of the Jackson cabin over the years have been unsuccessful. Every June, a play, *Listen and Remember*, which recounts the story of the Jackson family, is presented in an outdoor amphitheater. ❧ **LOCATION:** A few miles southwest of Waxhaw, North Carolina. ❧ **TELEPHONE:** Call Waxhaw Chamber of Commerce for more information: (704) 843-5598.

SOUTH CAROLINA

CATHEDRAL OF ST. JOHN THE BAPTIST

The first Irish migrants to find their way into what is now the Deep South were those who in the 1680s and 1690s fled Barbados, whence Cromwell had banished many of them after his brutal repressions three decades earlier. Throughout the 18th century, many thousands of Irish found their way to the Carolinas as indentured servants, individual immigrants, or as convicts.

This was the world in which the 28-year-old newly ordained Father Patrick Neeson Lynch found himself in 1845 Charleston. He had been born at Clones in Ireland and was brought to South Carolina by his parents when he was but a year old. Returning to Charleston after his ordination in Rome, he became rector of St. Mary's Church in 1845, rector of the cathedral in 1847, and vicar-general of the diocese three years later. The death of the incumbent bishop eight years after that elevated him to the See.

Not only was Lynch notable for being a strong administrator, he was also a forceful preacher and writer, editing the *United States Catholic Miscellany*. His first major challenge was public opposition to the construction of an Ursuline academy in the city. (Lynch's sister, Baptista, was an Ursuline mother superior. *See* Columbia, South Carolina.) This was a potentially explosive situation (an Ursuline convent had been burned by a Boston mob in 1836). Nevertheless, Lynch saw the academy built without violence. With 10,000 communicants on the eve of the Civil War, Lynch reported favorably on the situation of the diocese at the ninth council of the province at Baltimore in 1858.

The war, of course, proved Lynch's greatest challenge. An ardent Confederate, he celebrated the breakup of the Union with a special mass in the cathedral. President Jefferson Davis chose him in 1863 to serve as a courier between Richmond and Pope Pius IX. Davis's message expressed the Confederacy's desire for peace and, not incidentally, asked the pontiff to somehow cajole the North into not using Irish immigrants to feed its war effort against the Confederacy.

The pontiff replied December 8, 1863, saying, "May it please God at the same time to make the other peoples of America and their rulers, reflecting seriously how terrible is civil war, and what calamities it engenders, listen to the inspirations of a calmer spirit, and adopt resolutely the part of peace."

This statement was widely interpreted in the South as an endorsement of Confederate government policy, a notion the Holy See was quick to disclaim. Lynch's mission, to achieve diplomatic recognition of the Confederacy by the papacy, thus came to naught.

Lynch was forced to watch from abroad as Sherman's army marched relentlessly through the Carolinas, burning and destroying a good deal of church property as he went. After the war, Lynch appealed to Secretary of War Edwin Stanton for permission to return to his diocese, citing his effort to improve the lot of Union prisoners of war. Lynch's request was granted.

The Charleston to which Lynch returned had been reduced to ashes, and the few priests were discouraged and demoralized. Lynch, however, refused to give up and immediately embarked on a tour of the North, raising funds for the reconstruction of his diocese and Charleston in general. His work to reconcile North and South became so widely known and respected that he was called "the ambassador of good will." He presided over the reconstruction of the cathedral and died in Charleston in 1882.

⮾ **EXHIBITS:** Bishop Lynch's tomb is in the cathedral crypt. ⮾ **LOCATION:** Broad and Legare sts. ⮾ **HOURS:** Church office open Monday–Saturday 8:30–12, 1–5. ⮾ **ADMISSION:** None, but donations appreciated. ⮾ **TELEPHONE:** (803) 724-8395.

HIBERNIAN HALL

Thirty-eight years before the foundation of the Ancient Order of Hibernians (AOH) in 1836, the Hibernian Society of Charleston was formed to assist new immigrants to the United States. Interestingly, the Hibernian Society from the beginning made no distinctions based on religion (unlike the strongly Catholic AOH). In a tradition that has continued from the society's founding, the presidency alternates every two years between a Catholic and a Protestant. The society, however, has never had a religious requirement of any kind for membership. Many Jews have been members.

A pamphlet published at the time of the society's founding states its goals as "fraternal intercourse, convivial relaxation and charity exhibited in the form of relief to the Irish immigrant."

Father Simon O'Gallagher was the society's first president, but most of its early leaders appear to have been Ulster Protestants. ("Scotch-Irish" was unknown at this time, and most emigrants from the north of Ireland simply called themselves "Irish.")

This seemingly anomalous situation becomes more readily explicable when one realizes that the Ulster Protestant Irish at that time did not hold the strongly pro-British views characteristic of today's Northern Ireland Protestants. Indeed, some of the founders of the Hibernian Society had fled to the New World because they had participated in Wolfe Tone's unsuccessful 1798 uprising against the British.

Presbyterians made common cause with their Catholic neighbors in that rising because the former were almost as oppressed as the latter. Both groups were forced to pay taxes to support the established Anglican church. In the American Revolution, the Scotch-Irish, almost unanimously, supported the patriot cause (*see* Kings Mountain, South Carolina).

The prosperity of the society is evident by the grand Greek Revival hall that was completed in 1841. It was designed by Thomas Walker, who had also worked on the U.S. Capitol in Washington. The similarity in design is clear, especially in the rotunda in the interior.

The hall was damaged in the Civil War but not burned, unlike so much of Charleston. It became a refuge for the city's war-battered residents, regardless of religion or background. Because so many of the city's churches had been destroyed, different denominations held their services in different rooms of the building. For the only time in its history, the society suspended its St. Patrick's Day feasting and was forced to sell some its substantial whiskey supply to meet expenses.

The society's fortunes varied over the years. At one time, it was reputedly down to 50 dues-paying members. The struggle for Irish independence, however, brought about a revival, and Eamon De Valera (*see* Rochester, New York) visited the hall. Presidents Harry Truman and Gerald Ford both attended St. Patrick's Day dinners. In addition to the St. Patrick's Day festivities, the hall is also the site of the St. Cecilia Day Ball, one of the most exclusive social events in Charleston.

Today, the Hibernian Society of Charleston is thriving again. The hall has been refurbished, and the waiting list for membership, which is limited to 550, is said to be more than a decade long.

&. **EXHIBITS:** Portraits of past presidents and display cases containing artifacts and exhibits relating to the history of the hall and the Irish in Charleston. &. **LOCATION:** 105 Meeting St. &. **HOURS:** Variable. Call in advance. &. **ADMISSION:** Free &. **TELEPHONE:** (803) 723-4752.

MAGNOLIA CEMETERY

Capt. John C. Mitchel, C.S.A., was the eldest son of John Mitchel, the Irish independence advocate and Confederate newspaper editor and writer. While the father wrote blistering anti-Union articles and editorials for the Richmond newspapers, the sons took more direct action, enlisting in Confederate service.

The younger Mitchel was born in Newry, county Down, in 1838, a decade before his father's banishment to Tasmania for anti-British writings in the *United Irishman.* The Mitchel family was allowed to go into exile together, however, and they escaped to the United States.

The elder Mitchel was a strong Southern partisan, so it was natural that his sons would take up arms in defense of the Confederacy. John C. Mitchel received his commission as a second lieutenant in the First South Carolina Artillery Regiment in late March or early April of 1861, making him quite possibly the first foreign-born man to receive a Confederate commission.

His first duty station was Ft. Moultrie, where he assisted in the bombardment of Ft. Sumter at the beginning of the war. (Ft. Moultrie is located on Sullivan's Island, which is named after Capt. Florence O'Sullivan, the sea captain who brought some of the first Irish immigrants to Charleston.)

Lieutenant Mitchel had various postings around the Charleston area for the next two years, assisting in the capture of one of the Union gunboats that for almost the entire war sought to blockade the port.

In July 1863, however, the Union made a determined effort to capture South Carolina's largest city. The plan involved seizing Battery Wagner on Morris Island on the south side of Charleston Harbor. Mitchel, by then a captain, was in command of the south end of Morris Island.

For all of young Mitchel's efforts, however, he could not prevent Union forces from overrunning the south end of the island. Union troops now had a beachhead, and Confederate forces were forced to evacuate Battery Wagner on September 6, 1863. (One of the early, unsuccessful attacks on the battery was made by the famed 54th Massachusetts Colored Infantry, as dramatized in the film *Glory.*)

This failure, however, was not a blot on young Mitchel's record, and on May 4, 1863, he was given the critical command of Ft. Sumter, being promoted to the rank of acting colonel over several more senior officers. Sumter received more attention from the Union forces than its military value perhaps warranted. But the psychological imperative of holding the fort against the Union placed a heavy burden of responsibility upon the shoulders of its young commander.

The grave of Captain John C. Mitchel in Magnolia Cemetery.

Early in July, Union guns from the newly captured Battery Wagner and other points around Charleston opened up on Ft. Sumter. About 1 P.M. on July 20, the 14th day of the cannonade, Captain Mitchel ascended the steps to the fort's parapets in order to inspect the enemy's dispositions around the fort. He wanted to gather information for his daily report, which was delivered to headquarters on shore each night by dispatch boat.

"The commander was not unduly exposing himself," writes John Johnson in *The Defense of Charleston Harbor*, "but while engaged with his glass a mortar shell of the largest kind rose in the air, and, descending well to the westward of the fort, as if about to strike the wharf, burst at an altitude of some eighty feet above the water. The commander continued his observation . . . until suddenly struck to the ground by a large piece of the shell, wounding him with great laceration to the left hip."

The wound was mortal, and Mitchel lingered for four hours before dying in the hospital at Ft. Sumter. Some accounts say his last words were "I die willingly for South Carolina, but oh it was for Ireland!" Others, however, say he was asked if there was anything that could be done for him. The dying Mitchel is supposed to have responded simply, "Nothing, except to pray for me."

For Mitchel's father, his oldest son's death was a heavy blow, coming almost exactly a year after 17-year-old Willie, the color-bearer of his regiment, fell in Pickett's Charge at Gettysburg. (The middle son, James, had been badly wounded at Chancellorsville and was subsequently posted to the staff of Confederate Gen. James B. Gordon. He was the father of John Purroy Mitchel, later mayor of New York City during World War I.)

These losses no doubt deepened John Mitchel's feelings of bitterness toward the North, feelings that would lead, as in Ireland, to a prison cell for expressing them.

&. **EXHIBITS:** Fifty years after his death, admirers erected around Mitchel's grave a replica of the ramparts of Ft. Sumter. &. **LOCATION:** Magnolia Cemetery is located on Old Meeting Road, at the base of Cunnington Avenue. &. **HOURS:** 8–5 daily. &. **ADMISSION:** Free &. **TELEPHONE:** (803) 722-8638.

ST. LAWRENCE CEMETERY

 On September 28, 1798, the following advertisement appeared in the Charleston *City Gazette and Daily Advertiser:*

> A meeting of the IRISH VOLUNTEERS, is requested at the THATCHED CABIN, Meeting-street, THIS DAY, the 28th instant, at half past six P.M. on business of importance to the company. By order of the Captain.
>
> September 28
JAMES SWEENEY,
Secretary

The exact date of the founding of the South Carolina militia company known as the Irish Volunteers is uncertain, but from the wording of the above advertisement, it had obviously been in existence for some time. The Irish had been coming into Charleston in the late 1700s, and a group of Irishmen had begun celebrating St. Patrick's Day at least as early as 1798. The Thatched Cabin was a tavern said to have been located on the northeast corner of Meeting and Chalmers streets.

Frequent notices of meetings appear in the Charleston *City Gazette and Daily Advertiser* throughout 1799, with O'Brien Smith, (very likely the same man who later served in Congress) and James Sweeney (or Sweeny, as it was sometimes spelled) continuing as the secretary. The company posted a notice of its St. Patrick's Day celebration in 1800. The names of the committee members organizing the event were listed as William McCormick, Daniel McGivern, B. Mulligan, and James McKernan.

The Irish Volunteers were organized as the 2nd Company, 1st Battalion, 28th South Carolina Volunteers. Although the South Carolina militia, including the Irish Volunteers, offered their services during the War of 1812, the federal government chose not to avail itself. Press reports show the company continued to have monthly meetings in Charleston throughout the war, broken up by some coastal patrolling.

The Irish Volunteers rallied to the state's cause during the 1832–33 nullification crisis, even shifting the notices of their meetings from the pro-Jackson *Daily Advertiser* to the pro-Calhoun *Charleston Mercury.* But of course, secession did not come for another three decades.

Next came service in the Seminole War in Florida in 1836. The company saw several actions against the Indians and sustained one fatal casualty. "Upon the whole, while there was no dangerous service, it was hard and rough" was one contemporary assessment of the deployment to Florida.

The Irish Volunteers appear not to have been activated for the Mexican War, but they saw service in the Civil War. Unfortunately, the records of the company were lost or destroyed, and no accurate account of their participation in that conflict can be pieced together.

🐚 EXHIBITS: A memorial was erected to the company in the cemetery in 1878. It is the towering shaft standing in the midst of a traffic circle in front of you as you enter the cemetery's main gate. 🐚 LOCATION: 60 Hughuenin Ave. at Meeting St., next to Magnolia Cemetery (*see* previous entry). 🐚 HOURS: Office 8–3; Cemetery 8–6 in summer; 8–5 in winter. 🐚 ADMISSION: Free 🐚 TELEPHONE: (803) 723-8228.

ST. MARY'S CHURCH

The first Catholic mass in Charleston was said in secret in the home of an Irish immigrant family. The celebrant was an Italian priest whose ship was delayed while taking him to South America. The year was 1785, and although the British were gone, Catholics were debarred from participating in the civic life of South Carolina and could not practice their religion openly.

Because of the hostility toward Roman Catholics and the consequent shortage of priests, many Irish Catholic immigrants in the South eventually abandoned their Catholicism and embraced Protestantism. It is therefore not unusual to find throughout the southern and western United States people with unmistakably Irish surnames who worship at Presbyterian and Methodist churches.

Within just a few years of that first secret mass, however, there were enough open Catholics in Charleston to establish a parish. This was done in 1789 and the pastor was Fr. Matthew Ryan, an Irish native. For a time, services were still held in private homes, but later in 1789, a ramshackle Methodist meetinghouse on this site was purchased.

The meetinghouse was replaced with a brick structure in 1806. When this burned in 1838, the present building replaced it. Although services were held in the new building, in those days churches could not be consecrated until they were paid for. Consecration, therefore, did not officially take place until 1901!

🐚 EXHIBITS: Church contains many religious paintings. 🐚 LOCATION: 89 Hasell St. 🐚 HOURS: Daily, 7–4:30. 🐚 ADMISSION: None, but donations appreciated. 🐚 TELEPHONE: (803) 722-7696.

CLEMSON

FORT HILL

The South's leading citizen-champion in the decades before the Civil War, John Caldwell Calhoun was the son of an Irish immigrant. Patrick Calhoun was born in county Donegal in 1727 and immigrated to the American colonies while still a young boy. The family was part of the "Great Migration" of Scotch-Irish that took place between 1717 and the outbreak of the revolutionary war (*see* Kings Mountain, South Carolina).

Like so many other Scotch-Irish, the Calhouns arrived in America via Philadelphia and settled in the fertile land of Augusta County, Virginia. The statesman was vague as to why his family decamped from southwestern Virginia for South Carolina, but said that the move took place in 1756. Of course, at the same time, many Scotch-Irish were doing exactly the same thing. Population pressures in their original settlement areas in Pennsylvania and Virginia were pushing up land prices, and land was available for the asking on the Carolina mountain frontier.

Biographer Irving H. Bartlett notes that Calhoun was careful never to allow his personal life to interfere with his public life, but he maintained a keen interest in his family background. In his memoirs, Calhoun could scarcely avoid noting the great debt he owed his rough-and-ready father, who became something of a legend in his own right on the American frontier.

Calhoun told the story of the day in 1760, 22 years before his own birth, when Patrick Calhoun and 13 other settlers—including Patrick's mother and sister—fell into an Indian ambush near their cabin. John's grandmother was killed, the aunt kidnapped. Patrick also told the tale of how he had outdueled an Indian chief in the forest by putting his hat on the end of a stick and drawing the Indian's fire.

Patrick Calhoun became a surveyor and eventually acquired a farm of 1,200 acres. His prosperity and "strong man" reputation made Patrick Calhoun a leading candidate for political office. In 1768, he was elected to the legislature, where he would serve for 30 years.

The future champion of slavery and states' rights clearly imbibed much of his future political thought from his father, who was strongly conservative and suspicious of change for its own sake.

The younger Calhoun held many offices in his long career: U.S. representative, secretary of war, vice-president under Andrew Jackson (from which office he resigned in 1832, unable to stomach Jackson any longer), U.S. senator, and secretary of state under James K. Polk.

But it was with slavery that John Calhoun's name would forever be identified. Before 1830, there is little evidence he thought much about it. Like his father, John Calhoun was a slaveholder who believed the institution utterly natural and efforts to change or abolish it as fringe thinking. The rising national debate in the 1830s, however, forced Calhoun to think systematically about slavery and devise ways to defend it, which he did as ably as anyone else probably could have done.

Calhoun realized that arguments about slavery being a "necessary evil," which many Southerners had used up to that point, would not be satisfactory. Instead, he devised an argument that slavery was a positive good for the nation as a whole. A servile black underclass meant there was no white underclass in the South, as there was in the North.

"I hold then that there never has yet existed a wealthy and civilized society in which one portion of the community did not in point of fact live off the labor of another," he thundered on the floor of the Senate in 1837. "There is and always has been in an advanced stage of wealth and civilization a conflict between labor and capital. The condition of society in the South exempts us from the disorders and dangers resulting from this conflict."

For all his efforts, of course, Calhoun could not halt the rising tide of antislavery fervor in the North. He still cherished the idea he might become president, however, and to that end joined the Irish Immigrant Society of New York and in other ways sought to call attention to his Irish ancestry.

Interestingly, one of the things that might have cost Calhoun the presidency had little to do with slavery or politics. The notorious "Eaton Affair" began shortly after Jackson's election in 1828, when Sen. John Henry Eaton married a lovely and (some said) less-than-virtuous widow, Margaret "Peggy" O'Neale. She was the daughter of a local taverner and was, as her name suggests, of Irish ancestry.

Eaton was named secretary of war in the new cabinet by Jackson, and the ladies of Washington society, mortified at the thought of having to treat the new Mrs. Eaton as an equal, promptly ostracized the couple socially. Jackson loyally backed Eaton, as did Secretary of State Martin Van Buren. The campaign against the couple, however, was led by the wife of the new vice-president, John C. Calhoun.

Incredibly, the affair dragged on for two and a half years, climaxing finally in 1831 with the implosion of the cabinet. Eaton and Van Buren resigned in order to give Jackson a free hand to clear out his cabinet. Three other cabinet members were fired.

The whole affair, needless to say, transfixed the country. Americans tend to be a forgiving lot where matters of the heart are concerned, and Eaton and his wife won considerable sympathy. Few forgot that it was

Calhoun's wife who had led the campaign against the Eatons, and he suffered politically while Van Buren went on to be elected president.

Upon Calhoun's death in 1850, many abolitionists found themselves with mixed feelings. They had hated his defense of slavery, to be sure, but they admired his daring, energy, and unwillingness to compromise what he considered basic principles. In Calhoun, they truly had a worthy opponent.

& EXHIBITS: Calhoun bought the house shortly after he resigned as vice-president in 1832. It contains many original furnishings belonging to Calhoun and his son-in-law Thomas G. Clemson, who founded the university bearing his name on the grounds of Calhoun's former plantation. & LOCATION: At the center of the Clemson University campus, which is about 11 miles west of I-85 exit 19B on U.S. 76. & HOURS: Monday–Saturday 10–5; Sunday 2–5. & ADMISSION: None, but donations appreciated. & TELEPHONE: (803) 656-4789.

COLUMBIA

HAMPTON-PRESTON MANSION

General William Tecumseh Sherman was sitting on a log next to General Oliver O. Howard on the morning of February 17, 1865, surveying the city of Columbia, South Carolina. "It's no small thing to march into the heart of an enemy's country and take his capital," Sherman said. According to an observer, his tone was not one of boastfulness, but one of "deep and evident satisfaction."

Four months earlier, Sherman and his army had burned Atlanta and left it behind, commencing an epic march that would lead them to Savannah, then north into the Carolinas. They burned and destroyed almost everything that could conceivably be of military use to the Confederacy, and a good deal that was not.

Confederate forces had abandoned Columbia earlier, and Sherman and Howard were merely contemplating how they would march in. A messenger, however, brought them a note from within the city. Sister Baptista Lynch, the mother superior of the Ursuline convent in Columbia, appealed for the general's protection.

The sister's note explained she had once been a schoolmate of Sherman's sister and had taught Sherman's daughter Minnie in Ohio. Something she tactfully did not tell him was that she was also the sister of Bishop Patrick N. Lynch, the firebrand pro-Confederate prelate of Charleston (*see* Charleston, South Carolina). The general, however, folded the note and handed it to his brother-in-law, Colonel Charles Ewing. "See this woman and tell her we'll destroy no private property."

Despite this reassurance, the sisters and the 60 young schoolgirls under their charge watched apprehensively as federal troops occupied the city. Sister Baptista sent an aged priest to seek out Sherman's headquarters and remind him of his pledge. The priest returned later in the afternoon with another reassurance the convent would not be disturbed.

Sherman, of course, had been through this before in Atlanta, when Fr. Thomas O'Reilly threatened to excommunicate every Catholic soldier in Sherman's army if the Church of the Immaculate Conception was harmed in any way (*see* Atlanta, Georgia). Fr. O'Reilly succeeded in saving his church. It would be a different story for the sisters of Columbia.

A few hours after the priest had returned, a young Irish-American cavalry officer, Major Thomas Fitzgibbon, appeared at the door of the convent. He was there to offer his protection, he said, "as an individual." Sister Baptista told him of Sherman's promise.

"This is a doomed city," Fitzgibbon told the mother superior. "The whole army knows it. I doubt that a house will be left standing."

Following this disturbing encounter, Sister Baptista sent yet another messenger to Sherman's headquarters asking for a reiteration of his pledge of safety for the convent and its occupants. For the third time, Sherman reiterated his pledge.

It is still a matter of dispute just how the fire that consumed Columbia started. As they retreated, the Confederate troops had set fire to several bales of cotton and some warehouses, but the fires appeared to be under control for most of February 17. Then, as dusk approached, the sparks apparently spread and a high wind began whipping the flames. Around the same time, Union troops discovered a local distillery and began helping themselves to the contents. Thousands of drunken soldiers thus hindered any efforts at fire fighting.

As the wall of flame advanced toward the Ursuline convent, Sister Baptista appealed to Sherman once more, and for the fourth time he responded that the convent would be safe.

That seemed more and more doubtful as the blocks between the convent and fire were consumed. Finally, a Father O'Connell decided they had to prepare for the worst. The sisters got their young charges together, and, their belongings wrapped in small bundles, they were instructed on what to do if they had to abandon the building. The youngest girl was 5 years old, and many were under age 10.

Father O'Connell tried to remove the Host from the altar, but the sisters asked that it remain in the sanctuary until the last possible moment. Flames were now visible through the convent shutters, and a final benediction was said. At that precise moment, a group of drunken soldiers burst through the door. Taking this as their cue to leave, the band of nuns and girl students, led by Father O'Connell, stepped into the glowing street "with the precision of a military band."

"Not a cry, not a moan" was how one witness described the scene later. "The roaring of the fires, the scorching flames on either side . . . did not create the least disorder. That majestic figure of the Mother Superior in the graceful black habit of the Ursuline order. . . . The long line of anxious, white young faces of the school girls."

Not long afterward, the flames took hold of the Ursuline convent, and its wooden roof crashed in embers. Around 3 A.M. , according to Burke Davis's *Sherman's March* (1980), the cross atop the structure finally toppled and fell to the ground.

The party took refuge in a nearby church. Sherman himself appeared later to finally meet the woman he had communicated with up to this point only through messengers. Raised a Catholic himself, Sherman was apologetic and tried to explain the fire had gotten out of control. Sister Baptista, however, retained her composed dignity and firmly told the general he had broken his promise.

Chewing on his omnipresent cigar, there was little else Sherman could do than offer the nuns another abode. He told them to take any house remaining in the city. Sister Baptista testily reminded him that none of the houses in the city were Sherman's to give, but, yielding to pragmatism, the nun agreed.

Later in the day, Sister Baptista settled on the house of John S. Preston as her temporary base. Union General John Logan, however, was already using it as his headquarters and was planning to burn it to the ground the next day when the army moved on.

Nevertheless, the mother superior was insistent, and Sherman, eager not to break another promise, turned the house over to the nuns, thus sparing the mansion from destruction.

❧ **EXHIBITS:** A plaque outside the house commemorates the presence of the Ursuline sisters. Exhibits inside relate the story of their presence. ❧ **LOCATION:** 1615 Blanding St. at Henderson St. ❧ **HOURS:** Tuesday–Saturday 10:15–3:15; Sunday 1:15–4:15. ❧ **ADMISSION:** $3 adults; $1.50 for seniors, children, and military with I.D. ❧ **TELEPHONE:** (803) 252-1770.

JAMES F. BYRNES HOME

The man President Franklin D. Roosevelt called "the assistant president" had a long and controversial career in South Carolina and national politics, and his Irish ancestry no doubt helped him in his chosen profession. But when it came to achieving his greatest ambition, the presidency for himself, Byrnes's ethnicity proved his greatest handicap.

Byrnes's parents were Irish immigrants. As was the case with so many Irish-American politicos, his father died when he was only a boy. His mother, Elizabeth McSweeney Byrnes, supported the family as a dressmaker.

At 14, James, or Jimmy as he was known, left school to work as a law clerk in a Charleston firm for $2 a week. With his mother's help, he learned shorthand and passed an exam for a court stenographer's job in Aiken, South Carolina. While serving as the official court reporter for the state's second circuit for eight years, Byrnes studied law in his spare time. He passed the bar in 1908 and in the same year bought the Aiken newspaper, *The Journal and Review,* and became its editor.

But Byrnes's passion was for a political career, and he was elected solicitor (district attorney) for the second circuit in that same remarkable year of achievement, 1908. Two years later, Byrnes thought he spotted a political opening and ran for Congress, in his own words "on nothing but gall and gall." He won by 57 votes.

It was in his second term in the House that Byrnes first became acquainted with President Wilson's bright young assistant secretary of the navy, Franklin D. Roosevelt. The two remained in close contact, and Byrnes, who had been elected to the U.S. Senate in 1930, became a key supporter of Roosevelt's during the New Deal. So useful was the South Carolinian in the Senate that after Supreme Court Justice James Clark McReynolds resigned from the court early in 1941, Roosevelt waited six months before announcing Byrnes as his successor.

Byrnes was a reluctant justice, however. "My country's at war and I want to be in it," he said after Pearl Harbor. "I don't think I can stand the abstractions of jurisprudence at a time like this." After serving only 16 months on the court, he resigned to take a more active role in the war effort.

Roosevelt had no trouble finding work for his friend. First as director of the Office of Economic Stabilization and later as director of the Office of War Mobilization, Byrnes was a key man in the prosecution of the war. As the president himself put it when Byrnes took up his new duties, "I want you to act as a judge and I will let it be known that your decision is my decision and that there is no appeal. For all practical purposes, you will be assistant president."

Byrnes took on an important role in foreign policy as well, accompanying Roosevelt to the Yalta Conference early in 1945. President Harry Truman appointed Byrnes secretary of state later that year, and he played an important role in resisting Soviet demands at the Potsdam Conference.

Byrnes's innate conservatism on domestic issues, however, opened a rift between him and the more liberal Truman, and Byrnes resigned in 1947.

Perhaps another reason Byrnes gave up a lifetime appointment to the Supreme Court was that he still had higher political ambitions for himself. In both 1940 and again in 1944, Roosevelt strongly considered his friend for the vice-presidency. Had he gotten it the second time (as Byrnes fully expected he would), he and not Harry Truman would have become president after Roosevelt's death.

Two things frustrated Byrnes's ambitions, however. As a Southerner, he was unofficially "barred" from holding national office because of the continuing policy of racial segregation (of which Byrnes was a supporter) in the South.

Perhaps Roosevelt could have overridden this objection had it not been for one more problem. Byrnes had been raised a Catholic but had converted to Episcopalianism before entering politics. Thus, anti-Catholic Southerners tended to be suspicious of him because of the faith of his birth, while at the same time Irish, Italian, and Polish voters in the North would have been incensed at the idea of voting for a man who had abandoned their faith. Much as Roosevelt wanted Byrnes, he could see no way around these problems.

After three years in private life, Byrnes returned to the political arena as governor of South Carolina, winning election on a states' rights and school segregation ticket. He served a single term before retiring for good.

Byrnes bought this house in 1955, after leaving the governorship. During his term in office, he also lived in the white stucco Governor's Mansion at Richland and Lincoln streets in Columbia. His previous homes in Charleston and Aiken no longer stand. He died in 1972.

❧ **EXHIBITS:** The house is owned by the McKissick Museum, but is not currently open to the public. ❧ **LOCATION:** 12 Heathwood Circle.

OLD STATE HOUSE MARKER

 James Hoban, the Dublin-born architect, came to South Carolina in the late 1780s to design plantation homes for wealthy planters. While he was engaged on these projects, he designed the first state house for South Carolina in 1790. After he completed that commission, he went north to where the new capital city was rising on the banks of the Potomac and won the competition to design the President's House, which later became better known as the White House (*see* Washington D.C.).

Hoban's original state house lasted until 1855, when it was thought to be too small for the growing needs of the state government and construction began on the current structure.

&. **EXHIBITS:** A granite marker on the west side of the grounds marks the site of Hoban's state house. &. **LOCATION:** Gervais St. between Assembly and Sumter Sts. &. **HOURS:** Dawn to dusk. &. **ADMISSION:** Free &. **TELEPHONE:** State House: (803) 734-9146.

WOODROW WILSON BOYHOOD HOME

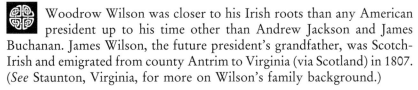 Woodrow Wilson was closer to his Irish roots than any American president up to his time other than Andrew Jackson and James Buchanan. James Wilson, the future president's grandfather, was Scotch-Irish and emigrated from county Antrim to Virginia (via Scotland) in 1807. (*See* Staunton, Virginia, for more on Wilson's family background.)

Although he occasionally made reference to his Irish roots in St. Patrick's Day speeches, Wilson's closest associates thought the dour, severe Scottish side of his nature much more pronounced.

Wilson's father was a Presbyterian minister and the family moved frequently. They lived here for three years, between 1872 and 1875.

&. **EXHIBITS:** The house contains exhibits and period furnishings, as well as the bed in which the future president was born. &. **LOCATION:** 1705 Hampton St. &. **HOURS:** Tuesday–Saturday 10:15–3:15; Sunday 1:15–4:15. &. **ADMISSION:** $3 adults; $1.50 for children and seniors. &. **TELEPHONE:** (803) 252-1770.

KINGS MOUNTAIN

KINGS MOUNTAIN NATIONAL MILITARY PARK

The hills of western North and South Carolina had been mostly quiet during the nearly six years of war before 1780. In that year, however, British forces invaded the southern American colonies, capturing Charleston and advancing deeper into the interior, which was populated by people widely known as "the over-mountain men" or simply "the mountain men."

Who were these people? By and large, they were Scotch-Irish settlers who had come to this area in the what historian James G. Leyburn called "the Great Migration" from Ulster to the Americas in the early to middle eighteenth century. The ancestors of these people had been "planted" in Ulster by King James I of England and King James VI of Scotland a century before in an effort to pacify the restless and rebellious (and mostly Catholic) island to the west.

The colony was successful, in the eyes of England. Attracted by cheap lands usually seized from their Catholic owners, Scottish farmers established themselves most heavily in the fertile lands east of the Bann River, in counties Antrim and Down. One of the other attractions was that leases on Ulster land ran for 31 years, considerably longer than leases in Scotland.

The government in London, however, began pursuing policies that seemed designed to antagonize the very colonists they had planted. The Woolens Act of 1699 protected English woolen goods from competition at the expense of woolens made in the north of Ireland. The evolution of the linen industry helped compensate for this somewhat, but the economy of Ulster had been damaged severely.

The first great exodus from Ulster to America, in 1717, however, was provoked by the practice of "rack-renting." On paper, rack-renting made sense. After a tenant farmer's lease expired, there were many other applicants for the tenant's land, so the landlord put the lease up for bid. The human consequence, however, was that many tenant farmers simply lost their land to higher bidders. Ironically, many of the bidders themselves were soon forced to head for America after discovering they could not pay the rents they had contracted for. A succession of droughts and frosts during this period also pushed people to emigrate.

The passage of the 1703 Test Act, which required all officeholders in Ireland to be members of the Established Church of England, hurt the Presbyterians badly. It was used unscrupulously by many English officials to place Presbyterians on the same level as Roman Catholics. Many ministers were turned out of their pulpits, and Presbyterians lost their offices in government and the military.

The Carolinas and Pennsylvania were the major areas of settlement for these people, who referred to themselves as "Irish." ("Scotch-Irish" came into widespread use only after the famine immigration.) Estimates of the number of Ulstermen who immigrated to America between 1717 and the beginning of the Revolution varies between 200,000 and 300,000.

The people who settled the piedmont of North and South Carolina in the 1750s came for a variety of reasons. Land prices in Pennsylvania and the Shenandoah Valley of Virginia—two previous Scotch-Irish destinations—were rising along with the population. The valley acted almost like a funnel, pouring one of the greatest internal migrations of people in American history into the nearly empty areas of the western Carolinas.

So when Major Patrick Ferguson of Lord Cornwallis's force in the Carolinas sent a message to these people in September 1780 to submit to the king or risk seeing their land "laid waste with fire and sword," the reaction can be imagined. The Scotch-Irish mountain men, already ill-disposed toward the British, decided the best way to protect themselves from Ferguson was to get him before he got them.

The mountain men were not only patriotic, they were an extremely tough lot. Henry "Light-Horse Harry" Lee, in his war memoirs, described the volunteers as "a hardy race of men, who were familiar with the horse and rifle, were stout, active, patient under privation, and brave. Irregular in their movements, and unaccustomed to restraint, they delighted in the fury of action, but pined under the servitude and inactivity of camp."

Kings Mountain was a very small battlefield area, a ridge about 600 yards long shaped somewhat like a canoe paddle with a short handle. Ferguson was camped on the "paddle" end of the summit and, for some reason, failed to fortify his position with breastworks or other emplacements, relying instead on the rugged slopes leading to the summit to protect him from attack. Worse, his 900 men were mostly Tory militiamen, trained to fight as British regulars, in ranks firing volleys. This would be of no help against an enemy accustomed to fighting from cover.

The rebels, by this time 1,800 strong, attacked on October 7, achieving almost complete surprise. For most of the day, Ferguson led his men well, driving the rebels back several times with bayonet charges. But the differences in tactics and equipment soon began to show, and the Tories were pushed back into a corner of the ridgeline. Ferguson refused all counsel to surrender and, mounted on his great white charger, instead lead a "forlorn hope" charge at the rebel lines. He died in a hail of rebel rifle fire, and the surrender of the rest of the force came quickly thereafter.

The mountain men, however, were not content with merely obtaining the Tories' surrender. Enraged by the brutality of previous British raids on their homes, and none too happy that their neighbors had sided with the British, the mountain men systematically shot down many of the surrendering Tories, even those without weapons. While perhaps understandable in the context of the moment, such behavior did not do credit to the patriot cause.

The impact of Kings Mountain on the overall conduct of the war, however, was out of all proportion to the size of the engagement. Cornwallis, alarmed at the wipeout of Ferguson's entire force, feared a large rebel army was now advancing on his headquarters at Charlotte. He immediately ordered a retreat and the British offensive in the Carolinas came to an end. Sir Henry Clinton, the British commander in North America, later said that Kings Mountain was "the first link in a chain of evils that followed each other in regular succession until they at last ended in the total loss of America."

❧ EXHIBITS: Markers and monuments dot the battlefield. A visitor center provides a map for a self-guided tour. ❧ LOCATION: Just off I-85, just south of the town of Kings Mountain, N.C. ❧ HOURS: Daily, 9–6, Memorial Day through Labor Day; 9–5 rest of year. ❧ ADMISSION: Free ❧ TELEPHONE: (803) 936-7921.

TENNESSEE

JAMES K. POLK ANCESTRAL HOME

Some historians regard James Knox Polk, the 11th president, as one of America's greatest chief executives. Hard to believe? Consider: during his single term in office from 1844 to 1848, the United States expanded its territory by two-thirds, adding the Oregon Territory, annexing Texas, and seizing all Mexican provinces above 31 degrees north latitude. The nation now extended from sea to shining sea, thus fulfilling its "manifest destiny." Not bad for an "obscure" president.

Polk, whose great-great grandfather emigrated from county Donegal in 1690 (*see* Pineville, North Carolina), was a protege and supporter of Andrew Jackson, although the earnest and hardworking Polk lacked his mentor's charisma and stamina. After service in Congress (where he was elected Speaker) and as governor of Tennessee, Polk was truly a dark horse when the Democrats nominated him for president in 1844. He handily defeated Whig Henry Clay in November.

Despite the tremendous success of American arms in the war with Mexico, the results of the war did not immediately bring the United States the hoped-for benefits. The issue of whether or not slavery would be permitted in the newly acquired territories almost instantly began tearing at the fabric of the nation. The inability to resolve this burning issue, of course, led to the Civil War.

Polk was one of nine U.S. presidents who were of Irish origin through the direct paternal line.

  EXHIBITS: The house contains original furnishings from the White House, personal memorabilia, and Mrs. Polk's inaugural gown.   **LOCATION:** Two blocks west on U.S. 43/412 at 301 W. 7th St.   **HOURS:** Monday–Saturday 9–5; Sunday 1–5.   **ADMISSION:** Adults $2.50; seniors $2; children $1.   **TELEPHONE:** (615) 388-2354.

DOVER

FT. DONELSON NATIONAL BATTLEFIELD

Irish and Irish-Americans fought in substantial numbers on both sides in the Civil War. The North had its Irish Brigade, of course, plus other predominantly Irish units, such as the 69th Pennsylvania, which won glory at Gettysburg, and the 23rd Illinois, which held off a vastly superior Confederate force at Lexington, Missouri, until forced to surrender.

Most of the Irish units on the Confederate side consisted heavily of Scotch-Irish Presbyterians and Anglo-Irish Episcopalians, as opposed to the highly visible Catholic Irish who predominated in the North. There were Catholics, however, in such units as the 24th Georgia, which helped mow down the Irish Brigade at Fredericksburg and was commanded by Col. Robert McMillan, a native of county Antrim. There was also the 6th Louisiana, which recruited among the Catholic Irish stevedores of New Orleans.

Only one Confederate regiment fought under a green battle flag, however, and that was the 10th Tennessee Volunteer Infantry Regiment (Irish). Most of its men consisted of Catholic Irish railroad workers living in and around the Nashville area, although it had a fair number of Presbyterian and Episcopalian Irish as well. There was also a sprinkling of Germans.

The 10th Tennessee was the brainchild of Randal W. McGavock, a fourth-generation American of Scotch-Irish descent. Elected mayor of Nashville before the Civil War, McGavock had made it a point to cultivate the small but not insignificant Irish vote. Centered around the St. Patrick's Club of Nashville, its members called themselves "the Sons of Erin."

The coming of the Civil War found the Southern Irish in a peculiar position. Many of them were new to the country and reluctant to rise up in arms against its government. Others saw the Southern plantation owners as the social equivalent of the hated English aristocracy they had left behind in Ireland. Few could see themselves fighting to preserve that way of life.

McGavock had to get around this problem, and he found a solution. "The focus was Irish pride, the idea that the Irish men were as good as anyone when it came to toasting company spirit, banging on drums, blowing into bagpipes, parading around with flags and fighting the enemy," writes Ed Gleeson in his history of the 10th Tennessee, *Rebel Sons of Erin.* Thus was born the 10th Tennessee.

Military action in the western theater of operation in 1862 focused on the rivers of Tennessee and Kentucky. Ft. Donelson, on the Cumberland River, was a fort in name only, resembling more a stockade enclosing 15 acres of soldiers' huts and equipment. It had been hastily constructed by

Flag of the 10th Tennessee Infantry Regiment, known as the "Sons of Erin." (*Courtesy Tennessee State Museum. Photo by June Dorman.*)

the Confederates in the months before the battle, and the fort commander was Gen. John Floyd, who had lost West Virginia for the Confederacy.

Adding to the South's woes, the Union commander was an up-and-comer named Ulysses S. Grant, who had captured nearby Ft. Henry on February 6 and was determined to capture Donelson as well. The fall of both forts would virtually drive the Confederates from Tennessee.

Grant had boasted he would capture Ft. Donelson on February 8, but bad weather delayed his attack. On February 13, Grant began making probing attacks around the fort's defenses.

By remarkable coincidence, the 10th Tennessee found itself defending an area in the fort's defenses known by the locals as Erin Hollow, on the Confederate right. For the Sons of Erin, it was to be a fortuitous coincidence.

Union Gen. John A. McClernand, an ambitious Illinois politician who had earned Grant's mistrust, threw a frontal assault against the entrenched Confederate position at Erin Hollow early on the afternoon of February 13. The 10th Tennessee took the brunt of the attack and repelled it completely, with heavy loss to the Union 45th Illinois Regiment. Later, however, in a remarkable display of common humanity, the Irish of the 10th Tennessee joined the bluecoats in rescuing wounded Union soldiers from a raging fire that broke out on the field, started by exploding artillery rounds.

The Battle of Erin Hollow, however, was only a temporary respite for the defenders of Ft. Donelson. Ten thousand Union reinforcements arrived the next day, and the end came on February 16, after Floyd had ignominiously fled. Grant demanded the then-new terms of "unconditional surrender," which he got. Colonel McGavock of the Sons of Erin never forgave the "betrayal" at Ft. Donelson.

The story of the 10th Tennessee Volunteers as an organized regiment pretty much ends at Ft. Donelson. After that came captivity in Chicago, where Col. James Mulligan of the 23rd Illinois "Irish Brigade of the West" sought unsuccessfully to convert the force to the federal cause (*see* Lexington, Missouri). Most of the prisoners were returned to the South by the end of the year, and after that the unit fought as a small sharpshooter detachment in most of the battles in the western theater.

🍀 **EXHIBITS:** There is a 10-minute slide show on the battle. Erin Hollow is located just west of stop no. 8, a spot called French's Battery, on the self-guided battlefield tour. 🍀 **LOCATION:** The visitor center is on U.S. 79, 1½ miles west of the Cumberland River Bridge at Dover. 🍀 **HOURS:** Daily 8–4:30. 🍀 **ADMISSION:** Free. Tour tape is $3. 🍀 **TELEPHONE:** (615) 232-5706.

ERIN

OAK HILL CEMETERY

The most Irish county in America is not in New York or Massachusetts, but here in the hills and hollows of Tennessee. According to the 1990 census, 40.2 percent of the 7,000 inhabitants of Houston County claim Irish ancestry. That is the highest percentage of any county in the country.

Erin had its beginnings as a Scottish settlement, with a family called McMillan being the first recorded residents in the early 1850s. The coming of the Louisville and Nashville Railroad in the late 1850s, however, brought Irish muscle power to the area. According to legend, the name was given to the town because, in the slightly jaundiced words of the town's official history,

> ... a couple of Irish railroad workers took a wee drop too many one day and forthwith fell to fighting. The sight must have looked like home to the rest of the lads in the crew, and one of them let go with that ancient Irish rallying call, 'Erin go Bragh!' (Ireland forever!) From then on, for no better reason that we could unearth, the town was known as Erin.

A more benign version is that the green hills surrounding the area reminded the inhabitants of their native land.

Many of the Irish railroad workers moved on in the years after the railroad was built. In the early 1960s, however, there was a revival of interest in the town's past, and today it sponsors an annual St. Patrick's Day Parade.

❧ EXHIBITS: There is little that recalls Erin's Irish heritage, but Oak Hill Cemetery contains numerous weathered tombstones with names like Mahoney, McCarthy, McKinnon, and O'Connell. It is at the top of Jail House Rd., just past the county jail. ❧ LOCATION: Erin is located at the confluence of S.R.'s 13, 49, and 149. ❧ HOURS: Dawn to dusk. ❧ ADMISSION: Free ❧ TELEPHONE: Call Houston County Public Library for more information: (615) 289-3858.

FRANKLIN

CARNTON PLANTATION AND THE CARTER HOUSE

The war situation was becoming progressively dimmer for the Confederacy in the fall of 1864. Gen. Ulysses S. Grant, now the Union commander in chief, held Petersburg, Virginia, in a vise-like grip. And, despite the best efforts of Gen. John Bell Hood, the newly appointed commander of the Confederate Army of Tennessee, Atlanta had fallen to Sherman's Union forces on September 2. Atlanta was the rail hub of the Confederacy, and its fall was a heavy blow to the Southern cause.

Hood had replaced Gen. Joseph E. Johnston in the summer, the latter having lost the confidence of President Jefferson Davis. Davis's appointment of the impetuous Hood, however, was viewed warily by none other than Robert E. Lee, who thought Hood a bit too aggressive. Lee's fears were to be all too grimly borne out on the field at Franklin.

The man who almost certainly would have received the vote of most Confederate soldiers in the western theater of operations, had they been consulted, would have been Maj. Gen. Patrick Ronayne Cleburne (*see* Helena, Arkansas). Already known by his nicknames "Irish Pat" and "the Stonewall Jackson of the West," Cleburne had led his division fearlessly and flawlessly for over two years in battles in and around Tennessee. At Missionary Ridge, for instance, while the rest of the Confederate army crumbled, Cleburne rallied his division and held firm, protecting the army's rear as it retreated.

Why, then, was Cleburne not placed in command? Because Cleburne was, quite simply, much too practical a soldier and much too inexpert a politician. He saw quite clearly that, however brilliant his victories and however hard his men fought, the North could absorb its losses in men and materiel and make them good, while the South could not. Virtually every white Southern male who could carry a rifle was already in service. Without a new source of manpower, the South faced the prospect of being bled dry of its manpower.

There was only one potential source of trigger-pullers at the Confederacy's disposal: the slaves. In a secret meeting of the highest officers of the battered Army of Tennessee early in 1864, Cleburne boldly proposed offering the slaves freedom in exchange for picking up the rifle on the Confederacy's behalf. Cleburne reasoned such a move would strip the North of the moral high ground, allow Europe to enter the war on the Confederacy's side, and make a vast pool of military manpower available.

While some of his colleagues privately agreed with Cleburne, few would back him openly. In the South, where memories of Nat Turner's rebellion were still fresh, the thought of armed slaves was simply too radical to contemplate. Cleburne's idea met with instant and violent opposition from several generals, and Jefferson Davis ordered copies of Cleburne's proposal destroyed. Only one survived, and it did not see print for over three decades.

After that, Cleburne's seemingly unstoppable ascent hit a wall. He was conspicuously passed over for promotion several times. That he had not been a professional soldier before the war and his Irish birth also did not help him. The South thus chose not to make fullest use of the talents of the one man who conceivably could have held the West against the marauding armies of Sherman.

There was a ray of happiness for Cleburne amidst the gloom, however. Gen. W. J. Hardee asked Cleburne to be his best man at his wedding, and Cleburne found himself taken with the maid of honor, Sue Tarleton. The two were engaged in a whirlwind romance, and Cleburne returned to the Army of Tennessee with his spirits buoyed.

Sherman, however, was on the march, and Cleburne did his best to slow the inevitable Union advances. After the fall of Atlanta, Hood led the Army of Tennessee into northern Alabama, hoping to take it north into Tennessee, recapture that state for the Confederacy, and link up with Lee in Virginia.

It was an audacious plan, and in Cleburne's hands it might have succeeded. In Hood's, it did not stand a chance. Hood advanced north toward Nashville, maneuvering warily against Union Gen. John Schofield's forces. When a Union column managed to escape a trap Hood had laid for it at Spring Hill, the Confederate commander flew into a rage. Believing his army had lost its fighting edge, he was determined to "discipline" it.

The instrument of that discipline was to be the Battle of Franklin. On the afternoon of November 30, 1864, Hood ordered a suicidal frontal attack against Schofield's forces, which were solidly entrenched behind a line of earthworks. "Well General," said one of Cleburne's brigade commanders, Daniel C. Govan, when he received Hood's orders, "there will not be that many of us that get back to Arkansas."

"Well, Govan," Cleburne replied, "if we are to die, let us die like men."

Few would dispute that was exactly what Patrick Cleburne did. Early in the action, his borrowed horse was shot out from underneath him. An aide immediately dismounted and offered the general his own. Cleburne had just placed his foot in the stirrup when that horse, too, was killed. Just 80 yards from the Union earthworks, Cleburne elected to plunge ahead on foot. He was last seen disappearing into the smoke, waving his distinctive embroidered kepi above his head, when a Union minié ball found its mark. Shot just below the heart, Cleburne died moments later.

Another Confederate Irish-American general who fell that day was John Adams. A son of Irish immigrants to Tennessee, Adams seemed immune to danger as he spurred his horse through a whizzing storm of projectiles. "We looked to see him fall every minute," an amazed Union officer wrote later, "but luck seemed to be with him." Even Irish luck had its limits, however. As Adams's horse, "Old Charley," leapt the Union parapet, it crashed to earth, shot dead in mid-air. Adams, by that time riddled with bullets himself, fell beside him and with his last breath asked for a drink of water.

The massacre at Franklin beggared belief. No less than six Confederate generals were killed, the entire midcommand of the Army of Tennessee. The Confederates were repulsed with a loss of 6,250 men, a quarter of the army.

Cleburne was laid beside Adams and two other dead generals on the porch of Carnton Plantation in a grim tableau of the battle's cost. With Cleburne died any hope the Confederacy might have had of survival in the West.

🙚 **EXHIBITS:** Carnton Plantation is open while undergoing restoration; the Carter House contains Civil War relics and a video presentation on the Battle of Franklin. 🙚 **LOCATION:** Take exit 65 off I-65, drive 1½ miles west to the Mark Hatcher Bypass, then ¹⁄₁₂ mile south to state S.R. 431 and follow signs to Carnton Plantation; the Carter House is on Route 31 south of town. 🙚 **HOURS:** Carnton Plantation: Monday–Saturday 9–5; Sunday 1–5 April through October; Monday–Saturday 9–4; Sunday 1–4 rest of year. Carter House: Monday–Saturday 9–4; Sunday 1–4. 🙚 **ADMISSION:** Carnton Plantation: $4.50; over 65 $4; 3–12, $1.50. Carter House: $3; under 13 $1. 🙚 **TELEPHONE:** Carnton Plantation: (615) 794-0904; Carter House: (615) 791-1861.

NASHVILLE

THE HERMITAGE

Without question, Andrew Jackson was *the* dominating personality in the United States between the Revolution and the Civil War. His victory at New Orleans on January 8, 1815 (*see* Chalmette Battlefield, New Orleans, Louisiana), won him national fame and instantly made him a possible presidential candidate. His presidency between 1828 and 1836 was a crucible of American democracy, marking the dividing line between the aristocratic-dominated American government of the early Republic and the more plebeian politics of the later 19th century.

Jackson was the son of Scotch-Irish emigrants, weavers by trade, from the town of Carrickfergus, county Antrim, near Belfast. It was Jackson's mother, a spirited woman named Elizabeth Hutchinson, who nursed the dream of getting the family to America. She had been bewitched by the tales of Hugh Jackson, the senior Andrew Jackson's older brother, who, along with George Washington, had survived the slaughter of General Braddock's column and who became a renowned Indian fighter.

Hugh Jackson was preparing to return to America in 1765, and Andrew and Betty Jackson decided to go with him. At the last moment, however, Hugh's young wife decided she preferred life in Ireland to the unknown dangers of the American frontier and refused to go. Hugh would not leave without her, and most of the other 20 families in the party refused to go without Hugh. Andrew and Betty, however, were determined, and they went on ahead. The family, which by this time already numbered two sons, settled in the area called Waxhaw near the border of North and South Carolina (*see* Waxhaw, North Carolina).

Andrew Sr. did not last long in his adopted country. Betty was pregnant in March 1767 with their third child when Andrew strained himself while clearing land for their farm. Within a few hours he was dead. A few days later, a son was born and Betty named him Andrew Jr., after her dead husband.

Young Andrew's irascibility and aggressiveness showed early. "He was the only bully I ever met who was not also a coward," recalled one childhood acquaintance. His childhood was disagreeable to an extreme. His oldest brother, Hugh, was killed in 1779, and his other brother, Robert, died of disease contracted while both he and Andrew were confined in a British prison during the Revolution, even though both were mere lads. Betty Jackson died in 1781, leaving young Andrew alone in the world at age 14.

It is a tribute to Jackson's pluck and grit that he was determined to make his way and qualified as a lawyer, following an unsuccessful stint as a schoolteacher. He quickly found himself in Tennessee politics and was

The seventh president of the United States, Andrew Jackson.

(*Courtesy Gale International Portrait Gallery*)

elected to the state constitutional convention, where he fought hard, but unsuccessfully, to prevent a clause from being written into the state's basic law requiring a belief in God as a prerequisite to hold office.

Jackson built the Hermitage in 1804, the same year he resigned as a judge and retired to private life. He did acquire the command of the Tennessee state militia, however, and won fame at the Battle of Horseshoe Bend (*see* Horseshoe Bend, Alabama) in Alabama on March 27, 1814. It was his success there that led him to his command and victory at New Orleans 10 months later. The battle instantly placed him on the short list of presidential candidates. He came close in 1824, but finally snagged the prize in 1828.

Jackson's administration was one of the most important in American history. His frequent use of the veto—up to that point a rarely used power—helped strengthen the executive in relation to the legislature. He strongly defended the rights of the federal government over those of the states, the first rumblings of the conflict that would eventually erupt in the Civil War.

He also paid off the national debt and returned the surplus to the states. Suspicious of large financial institutions, he abolished the Bank of the United States and deposited U.S. tax receipts in state banks, the latter derided by Jackson's opponents as "pet banks."

Jackson's Scotch-Irish Presbyterian background was not unusual for his time and place, and he does not appear to have placed great emphasis on it. He did not ignore it altogether, however, for a certificate survives attesting to his membership in the Hibernian Society of Philadelphia. Some of his supporters also sought to use Jackson's Irish connection to win him votes in Irish neighborhoods, particularly in New Orleans.

The Hermitage was Jackson's retreat, before and after his period in the White House. It was damaged by fire in 1834, during his second term in office, and he subsequently rebuilt it. Jackson died here on June 8, 1845.

❧ **EXHIBITS:** Many original furnishings and personal effects. ❧ **LOCATION:** 12 miles east of Nashville via I-40E or I-65/24N to Old Hickory Boulevard/Hermitage exit. ❧ **HOURS:** Daily 9–5. ❧ **ADMISSION:** Adults $7; seniors $6.50; children $3.50. Free on January 8, Jackson's birthday. ❧ **TELEPHONE:** (615) 889-2941.

STATE CAPITOL

For all the success enjoyed by American arms and diplomacy during the single term of his administration, Pres. James K. Polk did not enjoy the burdens of office and the divisions engendered by the war with Mexico. He refused to seek reelection in 1848 and died just three months after leaving office. He and his wife are buried on the grounds of the Greek Revival state capitol.

❧ **EXHIBITS:** An equestrian statue of Andrew Jackson is also on the grounds. ❧ **LOCATION:** Capitol Plaza, on Charlotte Avenue. ❧ **HOURS:** Tuesday–Saturday 10–5; Sunday 1–5. ❧ **ADMISSION:** Free ❧ **TELEPHONE:** (615) 741-2692.

VIRGINIA

AVOCA

Clarence Thomas was fighting to save his nomination to the U.S. Supreme Court in October 1991 from allegations by Anita Hill that he had sexually harassed her. Appearing before the committee, the future justice accused the Senate Judiciary Committee of subjecting him to a "high-tech lynching." The emotion-packed charge seemed to stun the committee and turned the proceedings in Thomas's favor. He was confirmed.

Clearly, nearly two centuries after the term came into common use in America, the concept of "lynching"—especially in a racial context—still packs a powerful wallop. That would probably surprise the man who the practice is named after, however; he saw himself only as a patriot doing his duty whose actions had nothing to do with race at all.

Colonel Charles Lynch was named for his father, who ran away from school in Ireland while still a teenager and found himself an indentured servant in the Virginia colony in the early 1700s. Fortunately, his services were purchased by one Christopher Clark, whom history records as a kindly planter who raised the boy virtually as a son and whose daughter Lynch eventually married.

He received from Clark a tract of land along the James River to farm. The town of Lynchburg, named for the elder Lynch, now sits on that property. At the time of his death in 1753, Charles Lynch, Sr. was a member of the House of Burgesses and one of the most respected men in the colony.

The younger Charles Lynch was born in 1736 and was raised a Quaker, which was his mother's religion. The pacifist sect, however, became disturbed at Lynch's increasing belligerence toward British authority and expelled him from the society in 1776.

Avoca, the third homesite of Col. Charles Lynch, is a Virginia Historic Landmark.
(The Portrait Place)

A member of the House of Delegates and a friend of Thomas Jefferson's, Lynch played a key part in mobilizing Virginia's resources for war. In 1778, he was recommended for the post of colonel of militia, and in 1781 he joined Gen. Nathaniel Greene in North Carolina, where he participated in the Battle of Guilford Court House, a costly victory for the British.

But it was in his role as justice of the peace in frontier Bedford County that Lynch was to make his name. The breakdown of the old royal court system during the revolutionary disorder meant that judicial proceedings were conducted by extralegal courts. Lynch presided over one of these and became known for the swiftness of the proceedings in his court and the near-certainty of convictions, which were usually followed by whippings (not hangings).

In 1780, with Lord Cornwallis marching virtually unopposed just over the border in the Carolinas, Tory activity in Bedford County began increasing. Lynch and several compatriots acted swiftly. Tory suspects were arrested and brought to his home, Green Level (now Avoca). Contrary to popular belief, the defense was allowed to contest the charges and question witnesses. If acquitted, the defendant was allowed to go free with apologies. If convicted, however, he was strung by his thumbs from a walnut tree outside the house and given 39 lashes or beaten until he shouted "Liberty forever." No prisoner was hanged.

Two years later, the colonial assembly investigated the events in Bedford County in 1780 and ruled that, while the actions of Lynch and his compatriots "were not strictly warranted by the law," they were nevertheless "justifiable from the imminence of the danger."

"Lynch's law" and "lynching" have come to be irrevocably associated with the name of Charles Lynch. (The origin of the term might even have been earlier. In 1453, Charles FitzStephen Lynch, the lord mayor of Galway, hanged his own son for defrauding and killing strangers.)

Avoca is the third house to stand on this site. Lynch's Green Level burned in 1878, and a replacement house burned in 1900. This house was named Avoca by Lynch's descendants, after the mystical valley celebrated by Irish poet and songwriter Thomas Moore in his song "The Meeting of the Waters." The family bequeathed the house in 1982 to the town of Altavista, which has set about restoring it to its former glory.

⇜ **EXHIBITS:** The interior of the house has been beautifully restored with period furnishings and fixtures.   ⇜ **LOCATION:** 1514 Main St.   ⇜ **HOURS:** House open only from June through August. Thursday–Saturday 11–3; Sunday 1:30–4:30.   ⇜ **ADMISSION:** $5 adults; $4 for seniors and children.   ⇜ **TELEPHONE:** (804) 369-1076.

A R L I N G T O N

ARLINGTON NATIONAL CEMETERY/ CUSTIS-LEE MANSION

Even in the immediate shock and grief of the aftermath of President John F. Kennedy's assassination in Dallas in 1963, arrangements for the president's funeral had to be made. All of the presidents except for William Howard Taft (also buried in Arlington) and Woodrow Wilson were buried in their home states. Even President Lyndon B. Johnson assumed Kennedy would be buried in Massachusetts.

Defense Secretary Robert McNamara, however, had a different idea. He felt strongly that an ordinary burial site in the family plot was not appropriate for a grave that would likely be visited by many thousands of people. The day after the assassination, McNamara met with the superintendent of Arlington National Cemetery, who had selected three possible grave sites. The defense secretary was immediately drawn to the location right below Arlington House, overlooking the Potomac.

Attorney General Robert Kennedy was brought to the site later that day and agreed it was the right choice. The final decision, however, would rest with JFK's widow, Jacqueline Kennedy, who gave her consent later that afternoon.

The funeral rites for President Kennedy transfixed the nation and the world for four days. After the lying in state in the Capitol Rotunda and the funeral mass at St. Matthew's Cathedral in downtown Washington, the late president's flag-draped casket was borne to Arlington on the back of the same caisson that had carried Abraham Lincoln.

Nearly one million mourners lined the route to the cemetery. Among those present was President Eamon de Valera of the Republic of Ireland. Now 81 and almost completely blind, he refused to ride in a limousine to Arlington, preferring instead to walk vigorously, keeping a pace, his biographer says, that would have left a younger man gasping. (*See* Rochester, New York, for more on de Valera.)

At the graveside ceremonies, the pipes and drums of the Air Force band played for Kennedy one last lament, "Mist Covered Mountains." Cardinal Richard Cushing performed the last rites at graveside. President Kennedy had joined the nation's most honored dead.

Five years later, Robert Kennedy himself would join his brother at Arlington. It was during his 1968 bid for the presidency when RFK was assassinated by Palestinian immigrant Sirhan Sirhan just after a primary victory party in Los Angeles, California.

After heroic efforts by doctors to save his life, Robert Kennedy died early on June 6, leaving his wife, Ethel, pregnant with their eleventh child.

Although RFK had expressed the wish to be buried in Massachusetts, the family thought it appropriate that he rest near his brother in Arlington Cemetery. Buried with less pomp than JFK, Robert F. Kennedy was laid to rest beneath a simple stone cross a short distance from his brother's grave. In 1994, Jacqueline Kennedy Onassis was laid to rest next to her husband.

There are many other famed Irish-Americans buried in Arlington: William J. "Wild Bill" Donovan, a son of Irish immigrants who won the Medal of Honor commanding the "Fighting 69th" in France in World War I and headed the cloak-and-dagger Office of Strategic Services (OSS) in World War II; Audie Murphy (*see* Greenville, Texas), buried behind the Memorial Amphitheater; and Civil War General Phillip H. Sheridan (*see* Somerset, Ohio), to name just a few.

There is also another Irish connection at Arlington. George Washington Parke Custis was the adopted son of George Washington, the father-in-law of Robert E. Lee, and wasn't Irish at all. Yet, he was one of the strongest champions the Irish had in the United States in the early years of Irish immigration.

George Parke Custis was the son of John Parke Custis, Martha Washington's only son by her first marriage. Born in 1781, his father died of swamp fever when Custis was only six months old. When his mother remarried, Custis was accepted and raised by George Washington as if he were his own son.

He was 21 when Martha Washington died in 1802, just three years after the death of George Washington. Although Washington expected his foster son to follow him into military or public life, young George was more interested in agriculture. He took possession of 1,100 acres of land that his foster father had left him on the banks of the Potomac across from Washington D.C. and began farming.

He also began constructing the mansion that is now such a familiar landmark in the Washington area. In 1804, he married Mary Lee Fitzhugh, and four years later they had a daughter, also named Mary. She became the childhood sweetheart of a boy in the neighborhood named Robert E. Lee. Later, they would marry.

Custis was many things besides a planter. He encouraged scientific experimentation, composed songs and lyrics, and even took a stab at playwrighting.

"Most of all, however," writes Michael J. O'Neill in his biographical article on Custis in *The Irish American Revival*, "Custis was an orator in the grand tradition of the early 19th century and, over the years, he delivered innumerable speeches in support of innumerable causes—for political and religious liberties, for freedom for Poland, Greece and the countries of South America, for equal rights for all men."

Around 1826, Custis developed a special interest in Irish affairs. Daniel O'Connell's campaign for Catholic emancipation was going full tilt around that time, and Custis and a few like-minded friends called on all the "friends of civil and religious liberty" to rally at Washington City Hall "to express their sympathy for the people of Ireland and an earnest desire and hope for a speedy amelioration of their condition."

It was the beginning of something, for Custis devoted himself thereafter to the cause of the Irish, both in Ireland and in America. In his speech that day in 1826, he called attention to the Irish who had rallied to his foster father in the Revolution. "When our friendless standard was first unfurled for resistance, who were the strangers that first mustered round its staff?" he thundered. "And when it reeled in the fight, who more bravely sustained it than Erin's most generous sons?"

He made it clear he wasn't talking only about the Protestant Scotch-Irish, but Catholic Irish as well, a controversial stand in those days when anti-Catholic prejudice was powerful. "We were glad to receive the religionists of any creeds and found to our comfort, and to our independence too, that a Catholic arm could drive a bayonet on the foe, and a Catholic heart beat high for the liberties of our country. . . ."

Every year, until the day he died in 1857, Custis would be the featured speaker at the big St. Patrick's Day dinner in Washington. (He did skip one year, however, when a temperance faction had temporarily taken over the celebrations. He returned a year later, when drink was once again a part of the celebration.)

"It may not be in my day, but I trust in God when it shall be, though years after my mortal body shall have be laid in the bosom of our common mother, some Irish heart may come and, dropping a shamrock on my grave, cry, 'God bless him,'" he said on St. Patrick's Day 1844.

For a century after his death, Custis's desire was forgotten. But in 1956, a National Park Service historian named Murray H. Nelligan came across Custis's request and a tradition was born. Now, every St. Patrick's Day, members of the Friendly Sons of St. Patrick and the Ancient Order of Hibernians, accompanied by dignitaries from the Republic of Ireland Embassy, place a shamrock on the grave beside the obelisk behind Arlington House, and cry, "God bless him!"

⪧ **EXHIBITS:** Arlington National Cemetery is open to the public. The Custis-Lee Mansion contains furniture and mementos of the Custis family. ⪧ **LOCATION:** Directly across the Memorial Bridge from Washington, D.C. Washington Metrorail also has an Arlington Cemetery stop. ⪧ **HOURS:** Cemetery: 8–7 daily April through September; 8–5 rest of the year. Mansion: 9:30–6 daily April through September; 9:30–4:30 rest of year. ⪧ **ADMISSION:** Free. Tourmobile $2.75. ⪧ **TELEPHONE:** Cemetery: (703) 692-0931; Mansion: (703) 557-0613; Tourmobile (202) 554-5100.

FREDERICKSBURG

FREDERICKSBURG AND SPOTSYLVANIA NATIONAL MILITARY PARK

The Battle of Fredericksburg on December 13, 1862, ranks as one of the greatest acts of military incompetence in American history. Determined to push his way past Gen. Robert E. Lee's army and capture the Confederate capital at Richmond, Union General Ambrose E. Burnside ended up sacrificing thousands of his men in one pointless charge after another against a line of Confederates solidly entrenched four-deep behind a four-foot-high stone wall at the base of Marye's Heights. For Burnside's bullheaded stupidity, the Irish Brigade would pay a fearsome price.

Officially the Second Brigade of the First Division of the Union Army's II Corps, the Irish Brigade had already seen heavy fighting before reaching Fredericksburg. Originally 2,500 strong at the time of its organization by Brig. Gen. Thomas Francis Meagher in August 1861, it was down to around 1,200 effectives just 16 months later.

The brigade had taken heavy casualties in the Seven Days battles (*see* Richmond, Virginia) at the end of the Peninsular Campaign and had been badly bloodied at Antietam only three months before Fredericksburg. (*See* Antietam, Maryland, for more on that battle and the brigade's formation.)

Burnside had lost his opportunity at Fredericksburg long before the battle opened. He reluctantly accepted command of the Army of the Potomac from President Lincoln following Gen. George McClellan's lackluster performance at Antietam. Had Burnside moved swiftly, he might have been able to cross the Rappahannock and head for Richmond before Lee's battered army could return from Maryland. But delays and indecision allowed Lee to heavily fortify the heights outside Fredericksburg before Burnside began his advance.

December 13 dawned misty, gray, and cold. As the Irish Brigade marched through the streets of Fredericksburg, General Meagher ordered his men to put sprigs of green boxwood into their caps. Seeing this, a nearby band struck up "Garryowen." A Private Galway, an Irishman serving in the 8th Ohio Regiment, recalled later the sight of the Irish Brigade marching past, cheering and waving their caps with the little sprigs of green on them.

On the field before Marye's Heights, however, the situation was grim. The three brigades of Gen. William H. French's Third Division had gone first at around noon, and each was slaughtered in its turn by artillery and musket fire as it approached the stone wall. Gen. Winfield Scott Hancock's First Division of the II Corps, of which the Irish Brigade was a part, was slated to go in next.

The assault was suicidal, and there could not have been a man in the Irish Brigade who did not recognize it as such. The brigade watched as Gen. Samuel Zook's Third Brigade, First Division, vanished like wheat before a scythe in a blaze of musketry and grapeshot. Then came the order, "Irish Brigade, advance!"

The five regiments of the brigade—the 63rd, 69th, and 88th New York, the 28th Massachusetts, and the 116th Pennsylvania—broke out the national colors as well as their distinctive green battle flags. The latter were emblazoned with the brigade's Gaelic motto, *Riam Nar Druid o Shairn Lann* (Who never retreated from the clash of lances).

The Irish went forward at a rush, shouting "Erin go bragh!" ("Ireland forever!") and "Faugh a ballagh!" ("Clear the way!") Intense Confederate fire ripped holes in their ranks. The Irish plugged the gaps and kept running. The wounded of previous charges, lying on the ground, waved their caps and cheered the Irish as they ran past.

Maj. John Dwyer, an officer in the 63rd New York Regiment, described the action later:

> Canister shot, shrapnel and shell ploughed the ground all round this devoted brigade, but they faltered not; they rushed on to their doom. Arriving a few rods from the famous stone wall sheets of flame from thousands of muskets, withheld until this moment, assaulted them. Men fell in groups along the entire front of those five regiments, until nothing remained but skeletons of companies.

Irish courage was not enough. The bodies of Major William Horgan and Adjutant John R. Young, both of the 88th New York, were found 25 paces from the Confederate gun muzzles, the closest any Union soldiers had gotten to the stone wall that day. Color Sgt. William H. Tyrrell of the 116th Pennsylvania was shot down near the stone wall. To prevent the color from falling into enemy hands, Lt. Francis Quinlan braved Confederate fire to rescue it, rolling back down the hill to safety afterward.

In all, 545 men of the brigade fell before the stone wall that day, nearly a 50 percent casualty rate. Meagher survived the debacle, having somehow become separated from his command during the charge. (Unkind critics later murmured his absence was deliberate, although Meagher's unquestioned personal courage in other battles makes this seem unlikely.)

Later, Gen. Winfield Scott Hancock learned of the extent of the disaster when he saw three men of the Irish Brigade standing by themselves. He reproached them for not forming up with their company. One of the privates saluted and said, "General, we *are* a company."

"Never at Fontenoy, Albuera, or Waterloo was more courage displayed by the sons of Erin," wrote a by-no-means friendly correspondent for the *London Times,* who was observing from the Confederate positions. Robert E. Lee himself is said to have remarked of the Irish Brigade's conduct at Fredericksburg, "Never were men so brave."

As Ken Burns noted in his television series *The Civil War,* the great irony of Fredericksburg was that one of the Confederate units firing on the Irish Brigade that day was the 24th Georgia Regiment. A mostly Scotch-Irish unit, the 24th was raised in the counties north and east of Atlanta. It was commanded at Fredericksburg by Col. Robert McMillan, a native of county Antrim.

After a winter in quarters, the remnants of the Irish Brigade, along with the rest of the Army of the Potomac, prepared for the campaigning season as spring approached in 1863. The tremendous losses of the previous year, however, did nothing to dampen the spirits of the brigade, and their celebration of St. Patrick's Day in 1863 was one of the most memorable ever.

"There were sack races, pig chases, Irish jigs, reels and hornpipes, more fun because the quartermasters had brought in barrels of whiskey and rum," writes Ernest B. Furgurson in *Chancellorsville: The Souls of the Brave.* "The Irish Brigade erected a greasy thirty-foot pole with a thirty-day furlough and a twenty-dollar gold piece on top, and the man who could reach the prize could have it. One got within ten feet, then slid wailing to earth."

The merriment, which was attended by new Army of the Potomac commander Gen. Joseph Hooker as honored guest, was briefly interrupted by the threat of a Confederate raid. But the merriment went on until well past nightfall. "And then the next day the army groaned and went on, trying to recover from a day it would always remember and a winter it would rather forget," Furgurson wrote.

The Battle of Chancellorsville, however, which followed six weeks after St. Patrick's Day on May 2, was almost as great a disaster for the Army of the Potomac as Fredericksburg. The Irish Brigade was detailed to halt the pell-mell retreat of the Union army's XI Corps, shattered by Stonewall Jackson's brilliant flanking maneuver, but it could not stem the tide. Later, as Gen. Winfield Scott Hancock sought to prevent his artillery from falling into enemy hands, the Irish Brigade saved the guns of the 5th Maine Artillery.

After the disaster at Chancellorsville, the entire Irish Brigade had been reduced to about 500 men. Meagher demanded that the brigade be pulled out of the line in order to recruit replacements. This permission was refused, for the practice in the Union army was to raise new regiments rather than replenish the ranks of depleted ones. Meagher resigned his commission in protest. Although he later was restored to various posts with Sherman's army in Georgia, Meagher never commanded the brigade again.

After further losses at Gettysburg (see Gettysburg, Pennsylvania), the Irish Brigade engaged in heavy recruitment of replacements during the winter of 1863–64. Unlike the older, more mature volunteers of 1861, the new recruits were mostly boys still in their teens. In the spring of 1864, the brigade returned to this part of Virginia, "the cockpit of the war." And this time, there was a new army commander, Ulysses S. Grant.

Almost a year to the day after Chancellorsville came the action known as the Wilderness. In his official report, II Corps commander Winfield Scott Hancock wrote, "The Irish Brigade . . . attacked the enemy vigorously on his right and drove the line some distance. The Irish Brigade was heavily engaged, and although four-fifths of its members were recruits, it behaved with great steadiness and gallantry, losing largely in killed and wounded."

The fighting at the Wilderness produced one of the most dramatic episodes of the war for the brigade. The area had received little rainfall in the preceding weeks, and the woods were dry as tinder. The Irish Brigade was manning a breastwork of logs and dried branches when they began firing at approaching Confederates.

"The breastwork caught fire from the spent buck and ball cartridges, growing into a fiery wall 15 feet high," wrote Kevin E. O'Brien in *America's Civil War* magazine. "The Irishmen stood their ground, firing blind volley after blind volley through the barrier of flames until the Confederates withdrew."

Less than a week later commenced the running two-week fight that began at a quiet place called Spotsylvania Court House. The brigade was among the first to mount the Confederate defenses at the spot that became known in history as "the Bloody Angle."

"The One Hundred and Sixteenth (Pennsylvania) were among the first over the works," wrote St. Clair Mulholland in his history of the regiment, "and the colors of the regiment were in advance. . . . Lt. Fraley, of Company F, ran a Confederate color bearer through with his sword; a Confederate shot one of the men when almost within touch of his musket, then threw down his piece and called out 'I surrender,' but Dan Crawford of Company K, shot him dead." The fighting continued at Cold Harbor. (*See* Richmond, Virginia, for further information on Irish Brigade engagements.)

❧ **EXHIBITS:** There is a 12-minute movie on the battle of Fredericksburg. Although there are no actual memorials at either Fredericksburg or Chancellorsville, every December hundreds gather before the stone wall to recall the deeds of the Irish Brigade. The park service also maintains units at the Wilderness and Spotsylvania. ❧ **LOCATION:** The Fredericksburg visitor center is located on U.S. 1 (Lafayette Boulevard) in Fredericksburg. ❧ **HOURS:** Daily, 8:30–6:30, mid-June through Labor Day; Monday–Friday 9–5, Saturday–Sunday 9–6 April 1 through mid-June and day after Labor Day to October 31; Daily 9–5 rest of year. ❧ **ADMISSION:** Free ❧ **TELEPHONE:** (703) 373-4461.

HAMPTON

FT. MONROE

 In 1848, John Mitchel was arrested and imprisoned by British authorities in Ireland for "seditious" newspaper articles. In 1865, the U.S. government imprisoned him for exactly the same thing. John Mitchel sorely tried the patience of seemingly every government he ever lived under, whether it was British, Confederate, or Union.

Mitchel's route to Ft. Monroe began with his founding of the *United Irishman* in February 1848. Five years earlier, a new political movement had sprung up calling itself Young Ireland. It had split off from the mainstream of Daniel O'Connell's movement to repeal the union between Great Britain and Ireland. Mitchel and his confederates, who included future Union General Thomas Francis Meagher and balladeer Thomas Davis ("A Nation Once Again"), rejected O'Connell's strategy of nonviolent gradualism. As the famine tightened its grip on Ireland, they demanded violent action.

Like the great Irish nationalists Wolfe Tone and Robert Emmet of 1798 and 1803, Mitchel was a Protestant—the son of a Presbyterian minister from county Derry. Trained as a solicitor, Mitchel became active in Young Ireland in 1843 when he became disillusioned with O'Connell's "go slow" attitude. In 1845, he began writing for the *Nation,* the movement's publication.

But not even Young Ireland, it seems, could satisfy Mitchel's demand for action. In December 1847, he founded his own newspaper, the *United Irishman.* In its pages, he openly preached republicanism and armed insurrection. He, along with Meagher, was arrested in May 1848. The "rising," such as it was, was a fiasco and was quickly suppressed. (It had far-reaching implications, however, for the Fenian movement of mid-century flowed directly from it.)

Tried by a packed jury, Mitchel was sentenced to 14 years imprisonment and bundled off, first to Bermuda, then later to Tasmania (the notorious Van Dieman's Land). His family was permitted to join him, and together they dramatically escaped to the United States in 1853.

Arriving in San Francisco, he received a tumultuous welcome from the city's growing Irish population. Arriving in New York, he immediately conceived the idea for a newspaper and began publishing the *Citizen,* containing the same fire-breathing sentiments as the *United Irishman.* The *Citizen* was a success, quickly reaching a circulation of 50,000.

Sectional differences were tearing at the American fabric at this time, of course, and it was inevitable that Mitchel should take a position on slavery. In the conflict between the Abolitionists and the slave states, he thought he detected the same efforts as he saw in Ireland of one people to impose its will on another. He enthusiastically embraced the Southern cause and began violent attacks on abolitionists such as Henry Ward Beecher. The issue helped blunt the growth of the *Citizen.*

Mitchel thus determined to settle in the South. Giving up the *Citizen,* he bought a farm outside Knoxville, Tennessee, from which he commenced lecture tours and founded a new newspaper, the *Southern Citizen,* which lasted two years. After a sojourn in Paris, Mitchel returned to New York after the Civil War broke out. Making his way to Virginia, he took up the editorship of the *Richmond Examiner.* His three sons joined the Confederate army (*see* Charleston, South Carolina).

Initially a supporter of the Davis administration, Mitchel in 1864 turned against the Confederate president for what he saw as Davis's lack of sternness and willingness to retaliate for Northern acts. He moved to the *Richmond Exponent* —which took a harder line than the *Richmond Examiner*—as chief editorial writer. His life was darkened by the deaths of two of his sons, one in Pickett's Charge at Gettysburg, and the other at Ft. Sumter in South Carolina.

After Appomattox, Mitchel accompanied the Confederate government to Danville, but the Confederacy's cause was lost. He relocated back to New York and became the editor of the *Daily News,* which had been sympathetic to the South during the war. "I set myself at once to tell the truth about the Southern cause," he thundered in its pages, "to expose and explode the villainy of considering [devotion] to our Confederacy as a penitentiary offense and generally to denounce Mr. [Andrew] Johnson's [policy]."

Those sentiments, it can be imagined, did not sit well in the North, and he was warned several times by the civil authorities to be on his guard. Characteristically, these warnings only provoked Mitchel to ever higher levels of vitriolic comment. On June 14, he was arrested in his office without warrant or charge. He was placed aboard a ship and sent South to Ft. Monroe, where Jefferson Davis had already been imprisoned.

Mitchel's incarceration, even for a man who had already known prison, was difficult. For two months he was confined to his cell. He was plagued with asthma, which the damp cell aggravated, and his physical health was badly damaged. Although he lived another decade, he never really recovered from his four-and-a-half-month enforced stay at Ft. Monroe. Finally, with the help of influential Irish citizens, Mitchel was freed on October 26, 1864.

Mitchel spent the rest of his life in Paris, Richmond, and New York, at first working for the Fenian movement, but later, characteristically, criticizing it. In 1875, he returned to Ireland and was elected without opposition to a parliamentary seat in Westminster representing Tipperary. Forbidden to take his seat because of his conviction, he simply stood again and won. He had not long to savor this triumph, however, for he died only eight days later.

"He was not the first to have been the victim of oppression for daring to raise his voice nor was he the last," said Richmond newspaperman Raymond B. Bottom at the dedication of the Mitchel plaque at Ft. Monroe. "But what Mitchel did in defiance of oppression, in resisting any control of the right of speaking and writing, reproaches all of his craft who have cringed or who have wanted for the spirit to defend."

❧ **EXHIBITS:** The Casemate Museum contains historical displays about the role of the fort in the Civil War. Mitchel was held in Casemate no. 2, next to Jefferson Davis, the deposed president of the Confederacy. In 1951, the Virginia Press Association placed a plaque in Mitchel's memory on the exterior wall. ❧ **LOCATION:** Ft. Monroe is 3 miles south of downtown Hampton, just off I-64 at exit 143. ❧ **HOURS:** Daily 10:30–5. ❧ **ADMISSION:** Free ❧ **TELEPHONE:** (804) 727-3973.

MIDDLETOWN

CEDAR CREEK BATTLEFIELD/BELLE GROVE PLANTATION

Up from the South at the break of day,
Bringing to Winchester fresh dismay,
The affrighted air with a shudder bore,
Like a herald in haste to the chieftain's door,
The terrible grumble, rumble and roar,
Telling the battle was on once more,
And Sheridan twenty miles away.

Thus begins T. Buchanan Read's epic poem "Sheridan's Ride," which at one time virtually every Northern schoolchild had to know by heart. Actually, Sheridan was only 14 miles away when the Battle of Cedar Creek (Middletown to the South) broke on the morning of October 19, 1864. The actual distance scarcely mattered, however, for at the end of it, this son of Irish immigrants had won for himself a place in the pantheon of Union military heroes only just below that of Ulysses S. Grant and William T. Sherman.

The beautiful Shenandoah Valley of Virginia was probably the single most fought-over piece of ground in the entire Civil War. Stretching for 150 miles between the Allegheny Mountains on the west and the Blue Ridge Mountains on the east, the fertile lands of the valley supplied the Confederacy with much of its food and other supplies. In his brilliant Valley Campaign of 1862, Confederate general Thomas J. "Stonewall" Jackson established Confederate control over the area. Now, in the autumn of 1864, Union general Phillip H. Sheridan was under orders to take it back.

Sheridan was by no means the unanimous choice of the Union high command for the task of retaking the valley. Secretary of War Edwin Stanton thought the 33-year-old cavalry commander was too young, rash, and unpredictable. Ulysses S. Grant, however, liked these qualities and thought the diminutive cavalryman perfect for the job. Grant told "Little Phil" that his task was to "eat out Virginia clear and clean, so that crows flying over it for the balance of the season will have to carry their own provender with them."

For much of September and October, Sheridan did exactly that, burning houses, crops, barns, and anything else the Confederates could conceivably use. Little distinction was made between Confederate farmers and the many Union supporters in the valley. Descendants of the residents at the time refer to this period simply as "the Burning."

Opposing Sheridan was Confederate general Jubal Early, a typically dashing Southern officer who had recently staged spectacular raids on Washington, D.C., and Chambersburg, Pennsylvania. Outnumbered nearly three to one by Sheridan's forces, however, Early's veterans could do little other than harry and delay him.

On October 16, Sheridan left his headquarters at Belle Grove Plantation near Cedar Creek for a conference with Secretary of War Stanton in Washington. Expecting no activity until their commander's return, the Union troops settled into camp.

It was the opportunity Early had been waiting for. He achieved complete surprise with his attack on the morning of October 19. In no time, it seemed, three Union corps were reeling north of Middletown and the Confederates had captured 1,300 prisoners. The Southerners, however, hungry and short of equipment in this last year of the war, stopped to loot the wellstocked Union camp, allowing the bulk of the Federal army to escape.

Sheridan was on his way back from Washington. Eating breakfast with the troopers of the 17th Pennsylvania Cavalry regiment on the morning of the 19th, he became worried as the sporadic gunfire in the distance picked up in tempo and intensity. Mounting his big black charger "Rienzi," Sheridan began riding toward the gunfire. He soon encountered straggling Union soldiers and camp followers, who told him of the unfolding disaster at Cedar Creek.

Spurring his horse, Sheridan began his ride into history. Encountering dispirited Union soldiers, he shouted at them, "Turn back! Turn back! Sheridan's here!" Almost hypnotically, the Union troops stopped their retreat and began chanting their general's name, over and over. "Don't cheer me," he shouted, "fight, damn you, fight!"

And fight they did. The Union troops re-formed their lines and returned to Cedar Creek, surprising the Confederates, who were still busy looting the abandoned Union camp. The Union cavalry, commanded by Gen. George Armstrong Custer, smashed a hole in the Confederate line through which other units poured. Overwhelmed, the graybacks were forced to yield the field they had won only that morning.

Sheridan's ride that turned defeat into victory has been described as probably the greatest individual feat of personal battlefield leadership in the entire war. Militarily, the Union victory at Cedar Creek sealed the Shenandoah Valley forever to Confederate use and secured the Union against further attack from that direction.

"General Sheridan, when this particular war began," wrote President Abraham Lincoln in a note of congratulation, "I thought a cavalryman should be at least six feet, four inches high but I have changed my mind. Five feet four inches will do in a pinch." (*see* Somerset, Ohio and Washington, D.C., for more on Sheridan.)

❧ EXHIBITS: Guided tour of Belle Grove is available. Unfortunately, the battlefield is not a park, and none of the land is protected from development. The recently formed Cedar Creek Battlefield Foundation (CCBF) has been buying up land to preserve the site. A map allowing a self-guided tour of the battlefield is available. Annually, on the anniversary of the battle, the CCBF sponsors "Living History Days," in which reenactors re-create the battle. ☙ LOCATION: Cedar Creek Battlefield is in southwest-ern Virginia, not far from where Interstates 66 and 81 intersect. Belle Grove Plantation, which was Sheridan's headquarters, is 1 mile south of Middletown on U.S. 11, then ½ mile west on County Road 727. ☙ HOURS: Open March 15 through November 15. Monday–Saturday 10–4; Sunday 1–5. ☙ ADMISSION: $3.50 adults; $3 seniors; $2 children. ☙ TELEPHONE: Belle Grove Plantation: (703) 869-2028; Cedar Creek Battle-field Foundation: (703) 869-2064.

NORFOLK

FATHER RYAN HOUSE MARKER

Where was Father Abram Ryan born? In three U.S. censuses, "the poet-priest of the Confederacy" claimed to have been born in Ire-land. Other records, however, claim he was born around 1839 in Hagers-town, Maryland, where the family moved after landing at and living in Norfolk for a time. (*See* Mobile, Alabama and Biloxi, Mississippi for more on Ryan.)

☙ LOCATION: The Ryan family house is believed to have been located near the corner of Lafayette Street and Tidewater Drive. The city of Nor-folk has marked the northwest corner of the intersection with a plaque.

RICHMOND

LIBBY PRISON SITE

On November 9, 1861, Brig. Gen. John Winder, C.S.A., the Con-federate provost marshal at Richmond, received a dispatch from Confederate Secretary of War Judah P. Benjamin: "You are hereby instructed to choose by lot from among the prisoners of war, of the highest rank, one who is to be confined to a cell appropriated to convicted felons," the dispatch read. "And who is to be treated in all respects as if such convict, and to be held for execution in the same manner as may be adapted by the enemy for the execution of prisoner of war Smith, recently con-demned to death in Philadelphia."

Nowhere does Benjamin use the word "hostage," but that is exactly the fate he meant for the officer whose name would be chosen. Benjamin added that 13 more officers were also to be chosen, to be held in similar condition as the first. They were to be held in exchange for the safe return of 13 Confederate seamen condemned to death in Philadelphia.

What had prompted this orgy of hostage taking? President Lincoln, on April 19, 1861, had proclaimed a blockade of the coast of the southern United States. Few took him seriously at first, for the Union navy scarcely existed except on paper. To show he meant business, however, President Lincoln declared that anyone captured running the blockade would be treated not as a prisoner of war, but as a pirate. The penalty for piracy was death.

The new president didn't have long to wait for his first test. The *Jefferson Davis*, a privateer licensed by the Confederacy and commanded by Walter W. Smith, captured the *Enchantress*, a Federal vessel, off the coast of Delaware and seized $13,000 worth of cargo. Shortly thereafter, however, the U.S.S. *Albatross*, a warship, caught up with the *Jefferson Davis* and Smith surrendered without a fight. He and his crew were shipped to Philadelphia to await trial.

Although Smith and his crew were ably represented by Nathaniel Harrison, one of the country's most noted defense lawyers, it took only three days for them to be found guilty of piracy and sentenced to death. Appeals exhausted, Harrison sent a message to Confederate president Jefferson Davis, warning that his clients would surely be executed unless the Confederate president took action. The result was Benjamin's message to Winder.

A lottery was duly held to see who the unfortunate Union officer/hostage would be. "The lot fell upon Colonel Corcoran," the Southern newspapers reported.

Col. Michael J. Corcoran of the 69th New York State militia regiment was at that time probably the most famous prisoner of the war. When Ft. Sumter was fired upon, the Irish-born Corcoran was awaiting court-martial for refusing to parade his regiment for the visiting prince of Wales (the future King Edward VII).

The court-martial was forgotten when war broke out. With so many of the army's best officers having gone over to the Confederacy, experienced military leaders were in short supply in the North. Besides, Corcoran's act of defiance had made him a hero to Irish-Americans, and he would be needed for recruiting his fellow countrymen to the Union cause.

Corcoran was 33 when the war began. His father had been an officer in the British army, and the younger Corcoran himself had enlisted in the new Royal Irish Constabulary in 1845. The eviction from their homes of famine-starved tenants unable to pay their rents, however, revolted him and turned him against Britain. He resigned in 1849 and immigrated to America.

Libby Prison site in 1993. *("Libby Prison" by James L. McElhinney; oil on canvas 1993; Medical College of Virginia collection. Photo by Joseph Painter.)*

Corcoran soon enlisted in the 69th Regiment and rose to the rank of colonel within a decade. After the threat of court-martial was removed, he actively recruited Irish immigrants to fight for the Union cause. Unfortunately for Corcoran, he was captured in the fiasco that was the First Battle of Bull Run (Manassass) on July 21, 1861.

The large bag of Union prisoners taken at Bull Run meant the South would have to find accommodations for them. Two prisons were set aside for Union officers, Castle Pinckney in Charleston and Libby Prison in Richmond. (The infamous Andersonville in Georgia was for enlisted men.)

Libby Prison received its name from Libby & Son Ship Chandlers and Grocers, who used the building for a warehouse before it was taken over for use as a prison because its isolated location made it easy to guard. The three floors were divided into eight large rooms. While conditions were not as squalid as at Andersonville, life at Libby was still plenty tough. The prison was so crowded that the officers slept in squads on the hard floors, turning over as a unit upon the orders of an elected leader.

This was the prison to which Corcoran was taken after the first Battle of Bull Run. He later served in Castle Pinckney as well. Fortunately for Corcoran and his fellow hostages, tempers cooled and a compromise was struck that allowed for the eventual exchange of all the prisoners involved. Upon his release in August 1861, Corcoran was rewarded for his steadfastness with a brigadier general's star and a dinner with President Lincoln.

Corcoran returned to duty, organizing the Corcoran Legion, the most famous Irish unit of the war after Thomas Francis Meagher's Irish Brigade. Corcoran died in a fall from his horse on December 22, 1863.

& EXHIBITS: Two plaques, one placed jointly by the Sons of Confederate Veterans and the Sons of Union Veterans, are bolted to the flood control

wall at the foot of 20th Street.   ❧ LOCATION: The site of Libby Prison
is on Cary Street, at the foot of 20th Street, just outside downtown
Richmond. It is now occupied by an Army Corps of Engineers flood
control wall.

MAYMONT

 Large-scale Irish immigration to the United States began not during
the potato famine of the 1840s, as is commonly believed, but more
than a decade earlier, when a cholera epidemic swept Ireland. Many of the
immigrants of that time had some means, unlike those who came later, and
they and some of their descendants were often able to rise fairly quickly to
positions of wealth and prominence in their adopted country. The Dooley
family of Richmond, Virginia, is one such story.

James Dooley, born in Richmond on January 17, 1841, was the eldest
child to survive childhood of the nine born to John and Sarah Dooley,
natives of county Limerick, who immigrated to the U.S. in 1832. John
Dooley established himself as a hatter and furrier to Richmond's elite, and
he became a leader in the city's small Irish community. In the Civil War,
John Dooley organized and commanded the Montgomery Guards, a militia unit made up mostly of Irish Richmond residents that saw extensive
action on the Confederate side throughout the war (*see* Gettysburg, Pennsylvania).

Fresh out of Georgetown College (later University), James Dooley
also served in the Montgomery Guards, but was wounded and taken
prisoner in the Battle of Williamsburg during the Peninsular Campaign in
May 1862. After being exchanged three months later, he was commissioned
a lieutenant in the Ordinance Corps in Richmond, where he served
through the war. (Although he used the title "Major" for the rest of his life,
there is no evidence he ever officially held this rank.)

After the war, Dooley began the legal and business career that would
make him one of the richest men in Virginia. In 1869, he married Sallie
Mays, a woman from a prominent local family whose parents refused to
attend the ceremony, almost certainly because they objected to Dooley's
Catholicism.

Dooley became president of the Richmond and Danville Railroad and
organized the Seaboard Airline Railroad. He also controlled the Sloss-
Sheffield Steel and Iron Company, one of the largest steel producers in the
United States. He was also involved in banking and real estate, and his
efforts helped revive Richmond from the devastation it had suffered in
the war.

In 1886, Dooley purchased a 94-acre dairy farm along the James River
west of Richmond as the site for a new home that would reflect his growing

James Dooley, master of Maymont. (Maymont Foundation)

wealth. Four years later, Maymont, a name derived from his wife's maiden name, was a reality.

The 33-room Romanesque mansion is an extraordinary piece of Victorian excess. A turreted manse of sandstone, the house contains a great collection of porcelain, marble, gold, rosewood, and many items in the shape of swans, a bird that was a particular favorite of Mrs. Dooley's.

A childless couple, the Dooleys were generous with their wealth. James sat on the board of St. Joseph's Academy and Orphan Asylum for 50 years. He donated the money for two hospitals, an orphanage, and a public library. When a "mini-famine" struck Ireland in the 1880s, the Dooleys were in the forefront of organizing and funding relief efforts.

James Dooley died in 1922 of a stroke, and Mrs. Dooley died three years later. Upon her death, the house was donated to the city of Richmond and is now operated by the nonprofit Maymont Foundation.

The Maymont Mansion stands along the James River just west of Richmond.
(Maymont Foundation)

❧ **EXHIBITS:** The house preserves the Dooley's eclectic furniture collection (the master bedroom contains a bed in the shape of a swan). The gardens are splendidly landscaped in many different styles. ❧ **LOCATION:** Hampton Street and Pennsylvania Avenue. ❧ **HOURS:** April through October, 10–7 daily. November through March, 10–5. ❧ **ADMISSION:** Suggested donation: $3 for adults; $1 for children 12 and under. ❧ **TELEPHONE:** (804) 358-7166.

RICHMOND NATIONAL BATTLEFIELD PARK

Following the heavy fighting at the Wilderness and Spotsylvania, Ulysses S. Grant sought to outflank Robert E. Lee's army closer to Richmond. It was at the small town of Cold Harbor that he made what he later said was the biggest military mistake of his life.

Had Grant not felt sympathy for his exhausted, hard-fighting troops and given them a night's rest, he might have avoided the debacle that unfolded at 4:30 A.M. on June 3, 1864. Lee's army used the hours Grant had given his men to rest in order to fortify the area around Cold Harbor. By the time of the Union attack, the ground outside the town was probably better fortified than even Fredericksburg had been.

The Irish Brigade, as always part of the II Corps, was in the second wave at Cold Harbor, but still suffered badly. One of the heaviest blows was the mortal wounding of Col. Richard Byrne of the 28th Massachusetts, who was in command of the whole brigade at the time. He died after lingering a few days in the field hospital.

The area around Cold Harbor was familiar territory for the veterans of the brigade, for it had fought its first actions of the war here in the Seven Days battles that concluded the Penninsular Campaign of 1862.

The brigade first won distinction at Fair Oaks, then went on to fight at Gaines' Mill, Savage's Station, the Peach Orchard, White Oak Swamp, and Malvern Hill. At the latter, Pvt. Peter Rafferty won the Medal of Honor. Earlier, at Savage's Station, Maj. James Quinlan of the 88th New York also earned the nation's highest decoration when he captured a Confederate battery. The Seven Days proved costly for the brigade, however. It lost 700 men during the fighting.

Fighting beside the Irish Brigade at Cold Harbor was the Corcoran Legion, also known as the Irish Legion. After Col. Michael Corcoran was freed from Confederate Libby Prison (see Richmond, Virginia), he was given a brigadier general's star as a reward. With no command forthcoming, however, Corcoran returned to New York and raised one of his own.

Made up mostly of Irish immigrants, the Corcoran Legion eventually consisted of the 155th, 164th, 170th, and 184th New York regiments. Dispatched to the Virginia theater in late 1862, they defended Suffolk, Virginia, against Confederate general James Longstreet's forces. From July 1863 to May 1864, they were part of the garrison defending Washington, D.C. Corcoran died December 22, 1863, when he fell from his horse near Fairfax County Courthouse.

The Corcoran Legion was assigned to General Hancock's II Corps for the fighting at the Wilderness, Spotsylvania, and here at Cold Harbor. Along with the Irish Brigade, the legion suffered terribly at the latter. One of the legion's colonels, James McMahon of the 164th New York, managed to plant his regimental flag on the Confederate works before being riddled with rifle fire.

❦ **EXHIBITS:** The park preserves 10 sites on 768 acres throughout the Richmond area. Maps are available at the visitor center, and interpretive markers are located at most of the sites.   ❦ **LOCATION:** The visitor center is located at 3215 E. Broad St. in Richmond.   ❦ **HOURS:** 10–5 daily.   ❦ **ADMISSION:** Free   ❦ **TELEPHONE:** (804) 226-1981.

STAUNTON

WOODROW WILSON BIRTHPLACE AND MUSEUM

Woodrow Wilson, the 28th president and the grandson of an Irish immigrant, was probably closer to his Irish roots than any chief executive between Andrew Jackson and John F. Kennedy. Contrary to his image as a well-born American of old stock, Wilson's roots were not particularly deep in America and he was not from a particularly privileged environment.

Wilson was Scotch-Irish on his father's side. By the time of his grandfather James Wilson's arrival in America in 1807 at age 20, the great Scotch-Irish immigration wave to America was long past (*see* Kings Mountain, South Carolina). James Wilson is also described as being quite unlike the normally dour and reserved Scotch-Irish. "[He] carried himself with the exuberant self-confidence, the brash cheerfulness, traditionally associated with the Irish," writes August Heckscher in his biography *Woodrow Wilson.* "James Wilson behaved, indeed, very much as an immigrant was supposed to behave according to classic American theory. He worked harder than those already established, showed himself more enterprising and resourceful, and quickly won the rewards of his industry."

James Wilson started off as a newspaperman with the Philadelphia *Aurora,* published out of a printing office on the former site of Benjamin Franklin's house. His wife, Anne Adams, was also Scotch-Irish, having grown up in either county Antrim or county Down. She recalled that on a clear day she could see wash drying on the line across the water in Scotland.

In 1815, the couple moved to Steubenville, Ohio, part of the great westward trek that took place after the end of the War of 1812. They settled in Steubenville, where James lost no time becoming involved in politics. He was elected justice of the peace (which entitled him to be called "judge") and served a term in the state legislature. A Jeffersonian at the beginning, he later became enamored of the expansionist nationalism of Henry Clay.

The couple had 10 children. Two of the sons, identical twins, became generals in the Union army in the Civil War. The youngest son, Joseph Ruggles Wilson, who was born in 1822, became a churchman and was the father of Woodrow Wilson. After marrying Jessie Woodrow, a Scotswoman, Joseph was assigned to a Presbyterian pastorate in Staunton in 1855, where the future president was born a year later.

Woodrow Wilson himself was convinced, perhaps only for purposes of St. Patrick's Day politics, that somewhere along the line he had inherited Irish traits. "How else, he asked, could he explain those moods when his Scotch conscience seemed to be at rest and he experienced 'a most enjoyable irresponsibility'?" writes Hecksher in his biography. Of course, some of Wilson's associates in his later years thought the somber Scottish side of his personality had become dominant.

Certainly, in office, Wilson did not prove himself a great friend of Irish nationalism. For all his rhetoric about national "self-determination," Wilson was eager to avoid offending British sensibilities and did not press Ireland's cause at the Versailles Conference. (*see* Washington, D.C., for more on Wilson's political career.)

✒ **EXHIBITS:** The house contains seven galleries detailing Wilson's life and political achievements, including memorabilia of his years as president of Princeton University and of the United States.   ✒ **LOCATION:** Coalter and Frederick Sts.   ✒ **HOURS:** Daily 9–5, March through December; Monday–Saturday 9–5, Sunday 1–5 rest of year.   ✒ **ADMISSION:** Adults $6, seniors $5; students and military with ID $4.   ✒ **TELEPHONE:** (703) 885-0897.

WILLIAMSBURG

YORKTOWN BATTLEFIELD

One of the most famous paintings in American history is John Trumbull's portrayal of the surrender at Yorktown, which hangs in the rotunda of the U.S. Capitol in Washington, D.C. The 1781 victory of George Washington over British forces under Lord Cornwallis effectively secured American independence, although it would be nearly two years before peace was formally concluded.

Few of the thousands of tourists who troop past the painting every day, however, realize that the British officer in the center of the painting is not Lord Cornwallis at all. Indeed, the British commander was not present at the surrender ceremony. Pleading illness, though in truth perhaps simply too humiliated to do the deed himself, Cornwallis delegated the unpleasant task to his second-in-command, Major General Charles O'Hara. It is this officer, the scion of an old Irish military family, who figures in the painting.

O'Hara's family is said to have originated in county Sligo, though his grandfather was born in county Mayo. Both the grandfather and James O'Hara, Charles's father, served long military careers in the service of successive British monarchs, winning knighthoods and Irish peerages (along with a few parliamentary inquiries) along the way.

Charles O'Hara was his father's illegitimate son, born during James O'Hara's sojourn as Britain's ambassador to Portugal. Later, James O'Hara formed one of the first Irish Catholic units to serve under British command.

The son followed his father into the military, serving in a succession of posts with varying degrees of distinction. He arrived in the Americas in 1777 and was wounded leading the Grenadier Guards in the victorious but costly Battle of Guilford Court House in North Carolina. It was following this action that he was detailed to Cornwallis as the latter's executive officer, just in time to play his part in the largest surrender in British military history.

O'Hara continued his military career after Yorktown, though he didn't break his habit of being captured by famous men. At the siege of Toulon, he had the honor of being taken prisoner by an up-and-coming young artillery officer named Napoleon Bonaparte. He ended his days as governor of Gibraltar, dying in 1801.

❧ EXHIBITS: The last stop on the self-guided battlefield tour is Surrender Field, where O'Hara handed over his sword. The recipient was not George Washington. A stickler for proper protocol, the American commander insisted that O'Hara turn his sword over to Gen. Benjamin Lincoln, who was Washington's number two. The surrender ceremony is reenacted every October 19 by volunteers wearing period costumes and uniforms.
❧ LOCATION: The Yorktown Battlefield is approximately 60 miles southeast of Richmond. From Richmond, take I-64 to VA-199 (exit 57). Follow VA-199 north for 2 miles to Colonial Parkway, turn right and drive east to the Yorktown visitor center. ❧ HOURS: Dawn to dusk. ❧ ADMISSION: Free ❧ TELEPHONE: (804) 898-3400.

ILLINOIS

INDIANA

MICHIGAN

MINNESOTA

OHIO

WEST VIRGINIA

WISCONSIN

A view of the University of Notre Dame campus; home of the "Fighting Irish." See page 331. (The Chamber of Commerce of St. Joseph County)

ILLINOIS
1 Auditorium Building, Chicago
2 Bridgeport, Chicago
3 Fire Academy, Chicago
4 Irish-American Heritage Center, Chicago
5 St. Patrick's Church, Chicago
6 Washington Park, Chicago
7 Ronald Reagan Boyhood Home, Dixon
8 Vinegar Hill Museum and Lead Mine, Galena
9 Miner's Union Cemetery, Mt. Olive

INDIANA
10 James Whitcomb Riley Birthplace Museum, Greenfield
11 James Whitcomb Riley House, Indianapolis
12 University of Notre Dame, South Bend

MICHIGAN
13 Beaver Island
14 Irish Hills, St. Joseph Shrine, Brooklyn
15 Henry Ford Estate (Fairlane), Dearborn
16 Henry Ford Museum and Greenfield Village, Dearborn
17 Corktown, Detroit
18 Frank Murphy Boyhood Home, Harbor Beach
19 Shrine of the Little Flower, Royal Oak

MINNESOTA
20 Fr. Ireland Marker/Site of Connemara, Graceville
21 Nininger, Hastings
22 F. Scott Fitzgerald National Historic Site, St. Paul
23 Irish American Cultural Institute, St. Paul
24 Minnesota State Capitol, St. Paul
25 University of St. Thomas, St. Paul

OHIO
26 William McKinley National Memorial, Canton
27 Phillip Sheridan Statue, Somerset

WEST VIRGINIA
28 National Historic Park, Harpers Ferry
29 Blennerhassett Island/ Blennerhassett Museum, Parkersburg
30 Point Pleasant Monument State Park, Point Pleasant

WISCONSIN
31 Outagamie County Court House, Appleton
32 St. Patrick's Church, Erin Prairie

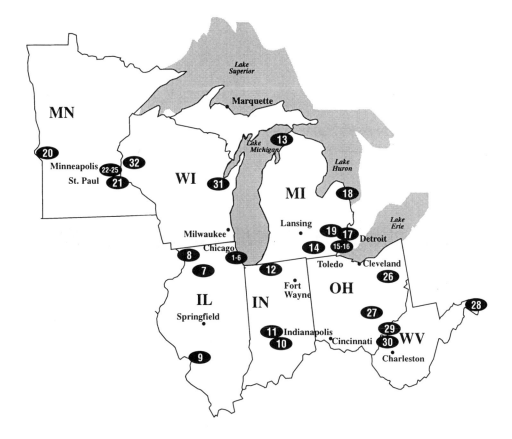

ILLINOIS

CHICAGO

AUDITORIUM BUILDING

"Form follows function," said Louis Henry Sullivan of the architect's art, and he followed it to become one of America's premier designers of buildings. He lived and worked mostly in Chicago, and the Auditorium Building is considered one of his finest works. His irascibility, however, made Sullivan an unpopular man in the profession during his lifetime and prevented him from achieving anything like the fame of his one-time employee Frank Lloyd Wright.

Sullivan described himself as "a mongrel," being of Irish ancestry on his father's side and French-German-Swiss ancestry on his mother's. Sullivan's family had an artistic bent. Patrick Sullivan, his father, was from county Cork and was a dancing instructor. He immigrated to Boston in 1847, where he married Adrienne List, who had recently arrived with her parents from Geneva. Louis was the couple's younger son and was born in 1856.

Sullivan and his father did not get along, according to the architect's memoirs. His father was "a free-mason and not even sure he was a Catholic or an Orangeman." Indifferent though their relationship might have been, young Louis "was the most Celtic of Celts, if there is such a thing," according to a biographical article on the architect by Adolf K. Placzek in *The Recorder,* the journal of the American-Irish Historical Society, "and if verbal brilliance, mercurial temperament and poetic passion are some of its hallmarks."

Raised on the Massachusetts farm belonging to his maternal grandparents, Sullivan early on appreciated the forms of nature. He entered the Massachusetts Institute of Technology in 1872 and subsequently served apprenticeships with architects in Philadelphia and Chicago. He went to Paris for a year in 1874, but returned to Chicago, which was recovering from the conflagration of 1871 and was in the process of transforming itself into one of the world's great cities.

Sullivan's fine draftsmanship set him apart from his peers, and in 1881 he formed Adler and Sullivan, a fruitful partnership with Dankmar Adler, a hard-nosed engineer who turned Sullivan's visions into reality. In 1886, they built the Auditorium Building, an architectural marvel that featured a 400-room hotel, a 17-story tower containing 136 offices, and a 4,200-seat opera house.

The high-rise building, however, is considered to be Sullivan's greatest contribution to architecture. The Wainwright Building in St. Louis a few years later was one of the world's first freestanding skyscrapers, along with the Guaranty Building in Buffalo, New York.

Sullivan's personal relationships were stormy, and the young Frank Lloyd Wright was fired from his position as a draftsman in 1893. Adler himself followed two years later, and even though Sullivan went on to design other buildings, his career now went into a long decline. Separated from his wife and drinking heavily, he died alone, virtually bankrupt, in a bleak Chicago hotel room in 1924.

"Form follows function" became virtually the motto of modernistic architecture, and the concept is frequently misunderstood. Sullivan did not believe in bland, formulaic architecture in which everything served a specific purpose and nothing more. For Sullivan, forms were derived from nature and should express themselves that way. As he explained in his *"Autobiography of an Idea"* (1924):

> Whether it be the sweeping eagle in his flight or the open apple-blossom, the toiling work-horse, the blithe swan, the branching oak, the winding stream at its base, the drifting clouds, over all the coursing sun, form ever follows function, and this is the law. Where function does not change, form does not change.

❧ **EXHIBITS:** The building has been substantially modified to serve the needs of Roosevelt University. Check in advance for events. ❧ **LOCATION:** Michigan Avenue at Congress Street ❧ **TELEPHONE:** (312) 341-3510. The Chicago Architectural Foundation conducts tours of the city that include the Auditorium Building. Call (312) 922-3432 for details.

BRIDGEPORT

If Irish Chicago has a beating heart and soul, it is Bridgeport, centered around Lowe, Union, and Halsted Avenues between 28th and 37th Streets. In recent years, it has produced three Chicago mayors: the legendary Richard J. Daley and his successor, the hapless Michael Bilandic, and the patriarch's son, Richard M. Daley. Innumerable lesser political lights hail from (and still live in) these narrow streets of modest, working-class homes.

The Irish first came to Bridgeport (then known as Lee's Place) in the 1830s to work on the Illinois and Michigan Canal, the waterway that would link the city to the Mississippi River and the South. Like many Irish neighborhoods, it was a fearful slum, with the inhabitants living in shanties and open sewers running through the streets. Other Chicago residents referred to the area derisively as Cabbagetown. (Maguane Park, at the corner of 30th and Halsted, was once the neighborhood cabbage patch.)

The area got its present name after the canal was finished and river boats plying the waterway were forced to unload their cargoes in the area in order to pass under the low-slung Ashland Avenue Bridge.

Bridgeport didn't remain an exclusively Irish neighborhood for long. Eastern European immigrants began pouring in after the Civil War to work in the growing stockyards. Although Hispanics are now a presence in Bridgeport, one ethnic group that never made it here was blacks. As recently as 1989, a mob of whites chased and beat two blacks who were deliberately dropped in the neighborhood by Chicago police.

Bridgeport was also immortalized by Finley Peter Dunne, the son of an Irish immigrant, through his character Martin Dooley, "a bachelor, saloonkeeper, and a Roscommon Irishman." "Mr. Dooley" made his first appearance in the *Chicago Evening Post* on October 7, 1893, and Dunne kept him going for over 20 years. The portrait that emerged of Bridgeport in Dunne's satire—written in a distinctive Irish patois—was the first fully realized urban ethnic community in American literature, according to Dunne expert Charles Fanning.

Politically, Bridgeport has always been a Democratic bastion, though in recent national and state elections Republicans have been winning support. The small house at 3536 South Lowe Avenue was the home of the man who for more than two decades was the most powerful ward commit-teeman in the United States. It was regularly visited, not only by local politicos, but by governors, senators, and even presidents, plus all who aspired to these lofty positions. The man was Richard J. Daley.

Daley lived his entire life on a single street here in Bridgeport. He raised his family in a house just a few doors down from the one where he had been born in 1902. And his funeral in 1976 was held at the same church in which he was baptized. City events were always scheduled so that Daley could return home every night for dinner with his family. Intensely conservative, Daley simply could not understand a man who would bring a family into the world and then refuse to support it.

Daley's father, Mike, a second-generation Irish-American, was a small, wiry man who perpetually wore a derby and worked as an agent for the Sheet Metal Workers Union, a job that inevitably involved him in ward

*Mayor Richard J.
Daley, ca. 1965.*

(Chicago Historical Society)

politics. The future mayor's mother, Lillian Dunne Daley, was eight years older than her husband when their only child was born. No shrinking shamrock, Lillian Daley was an early advocate of women's suffrage and frequently took her son on marches in downtown Chicago. She also doted on her son and passed on to him her practical way of getting things done, advice that he would remember fondly until the day he died.

Young Daley entered politics early. At age 12 he was doing odd jobs for the local 11th Ward Democratic organization. After graduating high school in 1918, he took a clerical job in the stockyards, but soon decided he needed more schooling to get ahead and began attending DePaul Law School at night. It took a decade before he was admitted to the Illinois bar.

All the while, Daley continued his steady ascent in Chicago politics. There were no shortcuts. You started at the bottom and you paid your dues. One of the instruments of his rise was the Hamburg Social Athletic Club (which, reflecting the changing neighborhood, had separate Irish, Lithuanian, and Croatian factions). A rough-and-ready crew, the Hamburgs not only canvassed neighborhoods and got out the vote but could also be counted on occasionally to act as "muscle" for the organization when it was required.

At age 21, Daley was working for 11th Ward City Councilman Joseph McDonough, who got the young man a job as a clerk in the city treasurer's office. Eventually, he rose to the highest administrative position in the city treasurer's office and won his first elective office, that of state representative, in 1936.

Daley moved up to the state senate a few years later, and after World War II became both county clerk and chairman of the of the all-powerful Cook County Democratic Committee. Upon election to the mayoralty in 1955, he insisted on retaining the party post. He now had untrammeled control of the city municipal and party patronage organizations.

Daley's rule was much misunderstood at the time and still is even today. Although referred to as a "boss," Daley's leadership style was far more consultative than authoritarian. Before making a major decision, Daley would check with all the power brokers within his organization to ensure everyone was satisfied. And while he certainly saw to it that friends got city jobs and contracts, he drew the line at blatant thievery. Daley's Chicago was not Boss Tweed's New York.

The result was a metropolis that proudly labeled itself "the city that works." Potholes were repaired, garbage was picked up, police came when they were called. Daley had little use for mayors such as New York's John V. Lindsey, who seemed to confuse the job with some kind of sociological mission.

Daley's greatest contribution in national politics was the controversial role he played in helping John F. Kennedy win the White House in 1960. Daley enthusiastically supported his fellow Irish-American and worked especially hard for his election. Kennedy ended up carrying Illinois by less than 9,000 votes, a victory many Republicans hinted was made possible by graveyard voting. However he did it, Daley was invited to spend the night at the White House early in Kennedy's term, and he was widely described as probably the second-most-powerful politician in America.

Daley's darkest hour, of course, came eight years later at the 1968 Democratic convention. Pres. Lyndon Johnson had deliberately chosen Chicago as the site of the convention because he feared trouble and knew the no-nonsense Daley could be counted on to contain it. Behind the scenes, Daley was urging Johnson to get out of Vietnam, but was determined to play the role of loyal soldier.

He succeeded all too well in the eyes of many. The Chicago police showed little restraint in keeping antiwar demonstrators from blocking the city's streets. The so-called battle of Telegraph Avenue was televised worldwide and so damaged the reputation of Daley in particular and

Chicago in general that not until 1996 was another major political convention scheduled for the Windy City.

Although three generations removed from "the auld sod," Daley was proof that Irish-Americans are often more Irish than the Irish themselves. He brought the St. Patrick's Day Parade downtown early in his mayoralty and began the tradition of dying the Chicago River green on the big day. He reveled in his role as tribal chieftain.

Daley was also noted for his colorful malapropisms. "The policeman isn't there to create disorder," he thundered memorably during the 1968 crisis, "the policeman is there to *preserve* disorder!"

Daley soldiered on into the 1970s, almost a living anachronism in the eyes of all but the thousands of Chicagoans who loved him. The worst blow to his pride came at the 1972 Democratic National Convention, when his delegation was prevented from taking their seats and an insurgent faction led by the Reverend Jesse Jackson was seated instead. Daley helped Jimmy Carter get to the White House in 1976, although Daley was luke-warm about the Georgian. Late in that year, Daley began suffering occasional chest pains and was visiting his doctor for a checkup just before Christmas when he suddenly collapsed and died.

Daley was buried from Nativity of Our Lord Church, his funeral attended by Vice-President Nelson Rockefeller and President-elect Jimmy Carter. The Shannon Rovers Pipe Band, with which he had always maintained a close relationship, played "Garryowen"—the mayor's favorite marching tune—at the funeral.

While an era appeared to have ended, the Daley dynasty returned to city hall in 1991 with the election of the mayor's son, Richard M. Daley, to his father's old job. Unfortunately for Bridgeport, however, the younger Daley soon vacated the neighborhood for a downtown condominium.

❧ EXHIBITS: Both houses are privately owned and not open to the public. ❧ LOCATION: Mayor Richard Daley's home, the one he occupied from 1939 until his death, stands at 3536 S. Lowe Ave. He was born not far away at 3502 S. Lowe. Nativity of Our Lord Roman Catholic Church is at 37th and Union sts. Also, visit Schaller's Pump, a lively, raucous saloon-restaurant at 3714 S. Halsted. It has for years served as the unofficial headquarters of the Daley machine and the 11th Ward Democrats. ❧ HOURS: Nativity of Our Lord parish office is open weekdays during business hours. Ask to see the interior. ❧ ADMISSION: None, but donations appreciated. ❧ TELEPHONE: Nativity of Our Lord Church: (312) 927-6263; Schaller's Pump: (312) 847-9378.

FIRE ACADEMY

The summer of 1871 in Chicago was an exceptionally dry one, with only five inches of rain falling between July and October. September had been especially bad, with scarcely an inch of rain. As a result, fires were frequent in the growing city, the structures of which were mostly wood and closely packed together.

A bad fire had broken out on Saturday night, October 7, in a planing mill on the West Side and proceeded to consume every building in a four-block area before it was brought under control early on Sunday morning. Exhausted firefighters flopped into their beds the next day. The *Chicago Tribune,* in a story about the Saturday fire, warned more prophetically than it could have known that the city was so dry "a spark might set a fire which could sweep from end to end of the city."

Of the Great Chicago Fire that began on that Sunday, October 8, the only fact not in dispute is that it started in the cowshed behind the home of Patrick O'Leary and his wife at 137 DeKoven Street. The O'Learys never ceased to deny that their cow had kicked over the coal-oil lantern that supposedly started the conflagration. Their son, James "Big Jim" O'Leary, who later became one of the city's most notorious gamblers, always claimed the fire had been started by neighborhood tramps catching a smoke near the barn.

That was indeed a common enough cause of fire at the time, but somehow the story about the clumsy bovine got started and never stopped. The O'Leary's cow probably became the most famous in history.

Patrick O'Leary, a laborer, had bought the house seven years earlier for $500 and rented out a portion of it to Patrick McLaughlin, a railroad worker, and his family. The McLaughlins were having a party on the night of October 8 in honor of Mrs. McLaughlin's brother, newly arrived from Ireland. The O'Learys had retired early.

Across the street, a neighbor named Daniel "Pegleg" Sullivan, a dray-man, was sitting on the boardwalk listening to the sounds of McLaughlin's fiddle around 9:30 P.M. when he noticed the first tongues of flame licking up from the O'Learys cowshed. He scrambled to his feet and began hobbling toward the barn shouting "Fire! Fire!" at the top of his lungs.

Through a series of tragic errors, the response by the fire department was initially slow, thus preventing any chance of containing the fire within the O'Learys' block. DeKoven Street quickly burned. By 11:30, the flames had leapt the Chicago River and began devouring the South Side and the downtown business district. By early Monday morning it was the turn of the North Side. The fire became so intense that the heat was felt in the town of Holland, 100 miles across Lake Michigan.

By the time it was over, four square miles of the city were in ashes, at least 250 people were dead, 18,000 buildings had been consumed, and

In an ironic twist, the O'Leary House, where the Great Chicago Fire began, was left standing after most of Chicago was destroyed. (Chicago Historical Society)

100,000 had been made homeless. The board of trade estimated the damage at $200 million, an almost inconceivable sum in those days.

Mrs. O'Leary always stoutly insisted she had nothing to do with the fire, and no one could ever prove the cow story. Anti-Irish illustrators, however, tended to portray the poor woman as a witchlike crone. And while the fire indeed leveled much of the city of Chicago, incredibly, the O'Leary house, in the backyard of which it all started, was somehow spared.

🐾 **EXHIBITS:** The Fire Academy is open to the public. In front, a bronze sculpture, *Pillar of Fire*, by Egon Weiner, marks the spot where the O'Leary barn stood. A memorial plaque is bolted to a wall inside. (A museum is in the planning stages.) The Chicago Historical Society contains many exhibits and artifacts relating to the fire of 1871. 🐾 **LOCATION:** 558 West DeKoven St., between W. Taylor and S. Jefferson sts. The Chicago Historical Society is at 1601 N. Clark St. 🐾 **HOURS:** Fire Academy: Monday–Friday 9–4; Historical Society: Monday–Saturday 9:30–4:30, Sunday noon–5. 🐾 **ADMISSION:** Historical Society: $3 adults, $2 for seniors and students, $1 ages 6–17; Fire academy: free. 🐾 **TELEPHONE:** Historical Society: (312) 642-4600. Fire Academy: (312) 747-7239.

IRISH-AMERICAN HERITAGE CENTER

This Gothic-style former college on Chicago's northwest side is gradually being transformed into a center of Irish culture and history. The site of conferences, theatrical productions, Gaelic language lessons, courses in harp and bagpipe music, and much else besides, the building also features a beautiful first-floor pub and dining area. The magnificent fireplace was built by a local volunteer. A library has opened, and there have already been several distinguished visitors, including Ireland's president, Mary Robinson.

&. **EXHIBITS:** Many exhibits on Ireland and Irish-American culture. Call in advance for events. &. **LOCATION:** 4626 N. Knox Ave. &. **HOURS:** Offices open Monday–Saturday, 9–4. &. **ADMISSION:** None, but donations appreciated. &. **TELEPHONE:** (312) 282-7035.

ST. PATRICK'S CHURCH

The survival of the O'Leary cottage in the Great Chicago Fire of 1871 was miraculous. Almost as miraculous was the sparing of Old St. Patrick's Church. Everything around the church lay in ruins, but the fire for some reason stopped at the church's steps. Divine intervention some parishioners say (although many other churches burned to the ground). As a result, St. Patrick's is the oldest church in Chicago and quite possibly the city's oldest public building.

St. Patrick's was dedicated Christmas Day 1856 and is built in a Romanesque style, with one tower Gothic and the other Byzantine, to represent the Catholic immigrants in the neighborhood who hailed from both Ireland and eastern Europe.

St. Patrick's was a pioneering church in many ways. The Irish who were flooding into Chicago in the 1850s had only the most rudimentary acquaintance with the parish system. In Ireland, priests frequently celebrated the Mass in the small, thatched cottages of the Irish countryside. The haphazard scheduling of services meant that churchgoing was not as regular in 19th-century Ireland as many now seem to believe.

St. Patrick's Church was brought to completion by Fr. Denis Dunne, one of those energetic parish priests who did so much to make the church the center of Irish immigrant life in the United States. A native of Timahoe, county Laoighis, Father Dunne was born in 1823, and his family immigrated to Canada soon thereafter. Young Dunne was ordained in 1848.

Arriving at St. Patrick's in 1854, he presided over the completion of the church, the liquidation of the parish debt, and the formation of a local St. Vincent De Paul Society, which helped establish Catholic schools and saw to the welfare of impoverished parishioners. This was one of the first church-led efforts to deal with the social problems plaguing inner cities even as early as the 1860s.

&. **EXHIBITS:** The church is well known for its stained glass windows representing the Irish saints Brigid, Columba, Brendan, Finbarr, and others. Also of interest is the window celebrating the memory of Terence MacSwiney, the imprisoned lord mayor of Cork, who died in Brixton Prison in London after 73 days on hunger strike in 1920. &. **LOCATION:**

718 W. Adams St. at Desplaines.   **HOURS:** Call to see church interior. **ADMISSION:** None, but donations appreciated.   **TELEPHONE:** (312) 782-6171.

WASHINGTON PARK

Altogether, James T. Farrell set eight of his novels of the Chicago Irish in and around this green expanse on the South Side of Chicago. Indeed, the author himself had grown up here. (He resolved to become a writer while living in the second-floor apartment at 5816 South Park Avenue.) Like Bridgeport, Washington Park was a community of immigrants unto itself. In addition to the park, the reference points were school, home, and church. This was the world into which Farrell was born as a second-generation Irish-American in 1904, and which he brought to life as the world of Studs Lonigan.

The Irish first began coming to this area in the years after the Civil War, but the growth really took place in the last years of the 19th century and the early years of the 20th. That was when "hardscrabble" Irish who had managed to get a foot on the lower rungs of economic advancement began moving from Bridgeport to the solid apartment houses of Washington Park.

Blacks began moving into the neighborhood around World War I, an event that resulted in tensions. Irish street gangs, including Richard Daley's Hamburg Social Athletic Club, staged street fights that sought to keep the blacks "in their place." The climax came in a 1919 riot, the first major race riot of the 20th century. It started when a young black boy crossed the invisible "fence" at the 31st Street beach and he was stoned to death. The Irish soon began to flee, however, and Washington Park today is a mostly black neighborhood.

Farrell was no sentimentalist. His novels are of the "realistic" school of American literature that includes such classics as Upton Sinclair's *The Jungle,* about the Chicago stockyards, and Theodore Dreiser's *Sister Carrie.* Unlike F. Scott Fitzgerald, who wrote about the rich, and John O'Hara, who wrote about the frustrated middle class, Farrell takes us into the world of the upwardly striving Irish-American working class, the so-called steam heat Irish. The time period is roughly between the turn of the century and the Great Depression.

Farrell's world is not that of the immigrants who "made it" into middle-class, assimilated, suburban respectability, but largely that of those who failed to do so. He gives the reader the casualties, those for whom the effort was too great, the drunks, the whores, the dropouts, the gangsters, as well as those who, while not poor, could not aspire to "lace curtain" status: the shoe salesmen, the house painters, the butchers.

Indeed, Studs Lonigan is not a product of the slums. As Farrell himself noted in later years, "Had I written *Studs Lonigan* as a story of the slums it would then have been easy for the reader falsely to place the motivation and causation of the story directly in economic roots. Such a placing of motivation would have obscured one of the most important meanings which I wanted to inculcate into my story. Here was a neighborhood several steps removed from the slums and dire economic want, and here was manifested a pervasive spiritual poverty."

This spiritual poverty did not arise from lack of religious presence. Quite the opposite, for priests are a substantial presence in Farrell's novels. Despite having reasonably normal parents who send him to mass and to parochial school and seek to set a good example, Studs hungers for something more, something only the streets can offer him. He yearns to be a "tough guy," somebody who is looked up to, and it is that hunger that proves his undoing.

Through three novels, *Young Lonigan* (1932), *The Young Manhood of Studs Lonigan* (1934), and *Judgement Day* (1935), the reader follows Lonigan through adolescence to a dull marriage and dead-end job, several failed attempts to reform, and finally, death at age 29. His father, Patrick Lonigan, loses his business in the Depression, along with his fancy home on the South Shore. It is a bleak, depressing tale.

The Studs Lonigan trilogy is the height of James T. Farrell's achievement, though by no means the end of his career. Some critics consider the other five "Washington Park" novels about Danny O'Neill, which followed the Lonigan books, to be a superior literary accomplishment.

Studs Lonigan, however, stands as the first serious literary attempt to deal with the Irish working-class experience in America. Writers such as James Jones and Norman Mailer acknowledged their debt to Farrell. Unfortunately, in the postwar years, Farrell's style of fiction went out of public favor, and he labored the rest of his life in the shadow of his earlier achievement. He died in 1979.

❧ LOCATION: Washington Park is bounded by 51st St. on the north and 60th St. on the south, Cottage Grove Ave. on the east and Martin Luther King Ave. on the west. Social activity in Farrell's youth centered around St. Anselm's Parish at 61st and Michigan Ave.   ❧ HOURS: All the time. Although the park remains much as it was and many areas are as Farrell described them, visitors are warned that the Washington Park area is not the safest in the city. Caution is advised.   ❧ ADMISSION: Free

DIXON

RONALD REAGAN BOYHOOD HOME

Republican presidents, it seems, are almost required to be of humble origin, preferably born in a small town. Ronald Wilson Reagan, the 40th president and the most recent to be of Irish ancestry, fit the bill well.

Reagan has always considered Dixon to be his hometown. (He was actually born in Tampico, Illinois.) "Dixon is part of me," he once said. It was in this small farming town of many churches and volunteer organizations that the sunny outlook he developed on life and the political philosophy he brought to the White House were shaped. His mother, Nelle Wilson Reagan, was a strongly religious woman involved in charitable endeavors. This helped shape Reagan's later views on welfare. He believed that people were always better off looking to someone like his mother rather than the government for help.

Although Reagan has described his childhood as "a Huck Finn idyll," that is clearly a rose-colored-glasses reminiscence. His father, Jack, worked mostly as a shoe salesman who dreamed of striking it rich, but was held back by what neighbors tactfully called "a powerful thirst." Ronald Reagan's older brother, Neil, always said that his father's drinking prevented him from achieving the business success he craved.

According to Lou Cannon, Reagan's best biographer, Jack Reagan was proud of his Irish ancestry and claimed descent from Brian Boru, the 11th-century warrior from whom innumerable Irish claim descent. Jack's great-grandfather, Michael O'Regan, left Ballyporeen, county Tipperary, during the potato famine and immigrated first to England and then America. While in England, he married an Irish woman named Katherine Mulcahy on October 31, 1852. In signing the register, he wrote his name "Reagan," dropping the "O" and adding an "a."

The family has a curious religious history. Jack Reagan, who was born in Illinois in 1883 and raised by his aunt after his parents died when he was a boy, was raised a Catholic, and he and Nelle were married in a Catholic church in 1904. Ronald Reagan's older brother, Neil, was baptized and remains a Catholic. Ronald, however, for unknown reasons, was not raised in that faith. Never particularly religious, he has always considered himself a Presbyterian.

The Reagans led a nomadic existence for the first decade or so after Ronald's birth in 1911, finally settling in Dixon in 1920. Although Dixon was a small town, Jack and Nelle Reagan were determined their boys would not be small-minded and encouraged them to read widely. Ronald Reagan's proudest story of his father told of the time when, while on a business trip, his father went to check into a hotel and the clerk told him he would like the place because it didn't accept Jews. Jack stormed out, saying the hotel probably wouldn't like Catholics either, and he spent a cold night in his car. Reagan said he learned to judge people as individuals, not as members of groups.

The Reagans remained in Dixon for the rest of the 1920s, with Ronald, or "Dutch" as he was known, attending the local high schools and eventually Eureka College. In 1931, Jack Reagan was fired from his job on Christmas Eve. The event was a tragedy and ended Jack's dreams of owning his own shoe store, but the elder Reagan threw himself into Franklin D. Roosevelt's campaign for president in 1932 and was rewarded by being made head of the local welfare office. The family thus ate regularly and young Reagan had his first political hero in FDR, whose politics he later turned against.

Reagan graduated from Eureka College with a degree in economics in 1932. He had played football at the college and had taken his first turn at acting in school plays. With the country in the pit of the Depression, job prospects were slim, but he eventually secured work as a radio sports announcer. His Irish "gift of gab" served him well in this role, since it frequently forced him to re-create for the listening public games he himself could not see but only read about on a Western Union ticker-tape.

But Reagan had dreams of becoming a Hollywood actor. In 1937, while on a trip to Los Angeles, a female friend introduced him to a Hollywood agent with whom she was acquainted. The agent instantly took a liking to the handsome young man, screen-tested him, and signed him to a $200-a-week contract with Warner Bros.

Although Reagan never became a really big star, his good looks and earnest manner won him a following. He rarely received poor notices, and his reputation in Hollywood was that of a hardworking, competent actor who could be relied upon to get the job done.

Reagan's foray into politics began in 1964 when he gave what is widely remembered as "the Speech," a nationally televised appeal in support of Republican Barry Goldwater's doomed presidential candidacy. Reagan's political views had been trending rightward for some time before this, and his endorsement of Goldwater brought him to the attention of Republican "kingmakers" looking for candidates. Reagan was nominated for governor two years later and, to the surprise of almost everyone, won handily. He arrived at the White House 14 years later.

&· **EXHIBITS:** The house has been restored and furnished as it was when the Reagan family lived here between 1920 and 1923. &· **LOCATION:** 816 S. Hennipin Ave. off Galena Ave. &· **HOURS:** Monday and Wednesday–Saturday 10–4; Sunday and holidays 1–4, March through November; Saturday 10–4, Sunday 1–4, rest of year. &· **ADMISSION:** Free &· **TELEPHONE:** (815) 288-3404.

GALENA

VINEGAR HILL MUSEUM AND LEAD MINE

Galena was once the world capital of lead mining. At one point in the mid-1850s, a total of 55 million pounds of the ore was taken out of the earth in this area. The whole countryside around the town is laced with the tunnels of abandoned mines.

John Furlong was one of the few survivors of the disastrous Battle of Vinegar Hill, the high point of the Irish rebellion of 1798. The battle, fought on high ground overlooking the town of Enniscorthy, county Wexford, pitted Irish armed with pikes against British with muskets and cannons. The Irish position was overrun and John Furlong and the few other survivors were captured. They were forcibly impressed into the British army.

Dispatched to Canada, Furlong became acquainted with French Canadians who had prospected in the territory now constituting Wisconsin and Illinois, particularly Julien Dubuque, who prospected for lead. Furlong and several comrades deserted and made their way to the eastern banks of the Mississippi to prospect for lead.

It wasn't until 1824, however, that Furlong and his friends really struck pay dirt. A rich vein of ore was discovered on some land he had purchased. They named the mine after the battle where they had been captured, and the Vinegar Hill lead mine was born.

The mine continued to produce ore several decades into the 20th century. John's great-great grandson Earl opened it to tourists in 1967 and great-great-great grandson Mark has continued the family tradition since 1986. Not far away is the old Irish cemetery (one had to be Irish to qualify for burial), where many early pioneers are buried.

❧ **EXHIBITS:** A 30-minute tour of the lead mine is offered. Artifacts and implements from mining days are on display. ❧ **LOCATION:** 8885 N. Three Pines Rd., 6 miles north of Galena on S.R. 84. ❧ **HOURS:** 9–5 daily, June through August; Weekends only, May, September, October; Closed rest of year. ❧ **ADMISSION:** $4 adults; $2 students. ❧ **TELEPHONE:** (815) 777-0855.

MT. OLIVE

MINERS' UNION CEMETERY

If George Meany (*see* Silver Spring, Maryland) represented the cooperative strain of Irish-American unionism that eventually became dominant in American labor relations, Mary Harris "Mother" Jones represented the confrontational side. Throughout the last half of her century-long life, the deceptively frail-looking woman in a black bonnet was present at seemingly every major labor dispute in the United States. And there was never any doubt about whose side she was on.

"She was a born crusader, a woman of action, fired by a fine zeal, a mother especially devoted to the miners," wrote trial lawyer Clarence Darrow in his famous introduction to her autobiography. "Wherever fights were fiercest and danger greatest, Mother Jones was present to aid and cheer. She had a strong sense of drama. She staged every detail of a contest. . . . Her personal non-resistance was far more powerful than any appeal to force."

Mary Harris came to the United States in 1835 at the age of five. Her father, Richard Harris, had immigrated to the United States alone and secured work as a railroad construction laborer, sending for his family after he had saved the passage money.

Young Mary did much of her growing up in Toronto, Canada, where her father's work had taken them. She received an above average education for a woman of her time, and she taught school for a time in a convent in Monroe, Michigan. After operating a dressmaking business for a time, she returned to teaching in Memphis, Tennessee, where she met and married her husband in 1861.

A life of quiet domesticity was not to be hers, however. Just six years after her marriage, her husband and all four children died in a yellow fever epidemic that swept Memphis. Devastated, she sought to start over again in Chicago, but lost everything she owned in the disastrous fire of 1871 (*see* Chicago, Illinois).

Perhaps in an effort to assuage her grief and loneliness, she began attending meetings of the Knights of Labor, an early labor organization. Her life was transformed, and she found a new purpose in helping achieve better pay and working conditions throughout the United States, especially for miners. She discovered she had a talent for public speaking, which she did in a distinctive high falsetto voice, and her speech was frequently littered with the picturesque terminology of the ordinary working man.

Her first big confrontation was the labor riots in Pittsburgh in 1877. She was present in Chicago at the time of the Haymarket riot of 1886 and in Birmingham during the American Railway Union strike of 1894.

As Clarence Darrow stated, Jones had a flair for drama. She also had what today would be called media savvy. She organized protests by striking miners' wives armed with mops and brooms. She led an army of children into New York in one of her many protests against child labor. She also traveled incognito to the sites of labor disputes in an effort to gather information on company efforts to repress union organizers. Her actual politics were somewhat hazy. Radical she certainly was, although she denied being a socialist.

She was jailed several times for her activities, with the most serious charge against her coming after the Copper Mine strike in Colorado in 1913, when she was convicted of conspiracy to commit murder by a kangaroo court set up by the state militia. A special investigation by the U.S. Senate, however, cleared her of any wrongdoing.

Mother Jones remained active into her nineties, speaking at a conference of the American Federation of Labor in 1923 at age 93. On her 100th birthday, she was interviewed for newsreel cameras and gave a lively talk. Six months later, however, she died of old age in Silver Spring, Maryland.

Her body was brought back to this coalfield cemetery for burial. The Reverend J. W. McGuire of Kankakee, Illinois, in a eulogy that was broadcast live over radio, said, "Wealthy coal operators and capitalists throughout the United States are breathing sighs of relief while toil-worn men and women are weeping tears of bitter grief. The reason for this contrast of relief and sorrow is apparent. Mother Jones is dead."

❧ **EXHIBITS:** A stone obelisk atop a three-step pedestal marks the grave of Mother Jones. ❧ **LOCATION:** The cemetery, a shrine of the American labor movement, is located on Lake St. on the northwestern limits of the town. ❧ **HOURS:** Dawn to dusk. ❧ **ADMISSION:** Free ❧ **TELEPHONE:** Town clerk's office: (217) 999-4261.

INDIANA

JAMES WHITCOMB RILEY
BIRTHPLACE MUSEUM

Was "the Hoosier poet" Irish? He claimed he was, and, according to biographer Peter Revell, "[Riley's] Irishness was a part of his public personality." At any rate, Riley's Irish ancestry, if any, was fairly remote.

Born in 1849, Riley became known for his homespun verse in the *Indianapolis Journal,* celebrating the simple pleasures of life in the Midwest. Though he is little read today, there is scarcely anyone—especially children—who would not recognize the characters of "Little Orphan Annie" or "The Raggedy Man."

The tour of the Riley birthplace includes the room of the young girl who boarded with the Rileys during the poet's childhood here and inspired the characters of Raggedy Ann, Raggedy Andy, and Little Orphan Annie.

Riley's father, Reuben, was a socially and politically prominent lawyer in pre–Civil War Indiana, being the youngest member of the state legislature at the time of his election in 1844. Reuben claimed that one of his grandfathers was "a proud Irishman." If this is indeed the case, it is the only evidence of Irish ancestry in the poet's bloodline. The name Riley appears to come from Riland, which was a Pennsylvania Dutch name. On his mother's side, Riley was of Welsh-Huguenot descent.

Another reason Reuben Riley might have claimed Irish ancestry was to help his law practice. Many immigrants passed through Greenfield on their way west, a good number of them Irish. Riley's claim of Irish ancestry helped him establish immediate confidence with these clients.

❧ **EXHIBITS:** The museum chronicles the life of Indiana's poet laureate, with photographs, mementos and exhibits. ❧ **LOCATION:** 250 W. Main St. ❧ **HOURS:** Monday–Saturday 10–4; Sunday 1–4, April 1 through

December 21. ❧ **ADMISSION:** $2 adults; senior citizens and children $1.50. ❧ **TELEPHONE:** (317) 462-8539.

INDIANAPOLIS

JAMES WHITCOMB RILEY HOUSE

Riley lived in this house from 1892 until his death from heat prostration in 1916. The author of "When the Frost is on the Punkin" was the innovator of the type of poetry critics call "the Midwestern pastoral," as contrasted with the "New England pastoral." It was while living here that Riley achieved his greatest fame as a newspaperman and lecturing poet.

❧ **EXHIBITS:** Many personal mementos, including the poet's pen, are on display. ❧ **LOCATION:** 528 Lockerbie St. ❧ **HOURS:** Tuesday–Saturday 10–4; Sunday 12–4. ❧ **ADMISSION:** $1 adults; children 25 cents. ❧ **TELEPHONE:** (317) 631-5885.

SOUTH BEND

UNIVERSITY OF NOTRE DAME

The origins of the University of Notre Dame are, as the name suggests, more French than Irish. It was a French priest named Edward Sorin who arrived in this area in 1842 to open a mission to the Potawatomi Indians and to start a school for secular students and for those studying for the priesthood. The university that resulted, marked by the famous golden dome on the main building, is now one of Indiana's biggest tourist attractions.

The waves of Irish immigration and the resulting domination of the American Catholic clergy and hierarchy by Irish-born and Irish-American priests made Notre Dame a kind of Irish-Catholic island in a mostly Protestant, Midwestern sea. Many Irish-Americans in the eastern cities who had never set eyes on the school nevertheless contributed to its scholarship funds and rooted for its sports teams, particularly football.

The origin of "the Fightin' (the official spelling) Irish" nickname is impossible to ascertain with certainty. Several people have claimed they were present when one person or another coined the phrase.

Sportswriters (and opposing fans) used several nicknames for the Notre Dame team in the early decades of the 20th century. "Hoosiers" and "Catholics" were among the kinder ones. "Papists," "Damn Micks," and

"Dirty Irish" were others. Sometimes, however, just plain "Irish" came to be used in many newspaper accounts.

"Eleven fighting Irishmen wrecked the Yost machine this afternoon," wrote the *Detroit Free Press* in its coverage of Notre Dame's 1909 victory over Michigan in one of the first known appearances of the nickname in print. In the years after World War I, "the Fighting Irish" nickname increased in popularity among the students, sometimes to the discomfort of the administration and the alumni, who feared for the school's image. One graduate wrote in to the *Scholastic,* the alumni newspaper, that the sobriquet was nonsensical because so many of Notre Dame's students were not Irish or of Irish descent. A flurry of letters followed from students, many of whom pointed out that "you don't have to be from Ireland to be Irish."

The students had a powerful supporter in Knute Rockne, a Norwegian, who knew exactly what they meant. "They're all Irish to me," the great coach said. "They have the Irish spirit, and that's what counts." In fact, a remarkably high percentage, about half, of the 340 varsity letter winners that Rockne coached had Irish surnames.

But it was Francis Wallace, who had started out as Rockne's undergraduate press agent and later became sports editor of the *New York Daily News,* who finally cemented "the Fightin' Irish" nickname in place for all time. After unsuccessful attempts to popularize some nonethnic nicknames, like "the Blue Comets," he began regularly referring to the team as "the Fighting Irish" in 1927.

Thanks to the mass circulation of the *New York Daily News* other newspapers and wire services began picking up on it. It was at this time that Notre Dame's administration, anxious to suppress all the other unkind nicknames, decided to throw its official weight behind "the Fighting Irish" as the team's nickname.

"The University authorities are in no way averse to the name 'Fighting Irish' as applied to our athletic teams," read a statement of university policy. "It seems to embody the kind of spirit that we like to see carried into effect by the various organizations that represent us on the athletic field."

Some feared that as Irish immigration tapered off and the faculty and student body became more and more heterogeneous, there might be pressure to change the nickname. If anything, however, pride in "the Fighting Irish" connection appears to have increased. Today, a student dressed as a leprechaun aggressively leads cheers at football games, and the "Fightin' Irish" nickname appears secure for all time.

A sidelight: Warner Bros. had originally intended to cast James Cagney in the lead role in its 1940 production of *Knute Rockne: All American.* Cagney, however, had signed a petition in support of the anti-

Knute Rockne (Pat O'Brien) offers sage advice to George Gipp (Ronald Reagan) in "Knute Rockne: All American." (Museum of Modern Art)

Catholic Loyalist government of Spain during the Spanish Civil War. The university administration, which approved all aspects of the filming, thus nixed Cagney as the star, and Pat O'Brien got the role instead.

․ **LOCATION:** Tours of the 1,250-acre main campus are led by students every weekday from mid-May to mid-August. Call for information. ․ **TELEPHONE:** (219) 239-7367.

MICHIGAN

BEAVER ISLAND

"Michigan's Emerald Isle" is situated in the middle of Lake Michigan, southwest of the Straits of Mackinac. If you really want to leave the madding crowd behind and get in touch with nature and some Irish history at the same time, Beaver Island is the best place this side of Ireland's Aran Islands.

Beaver Island (53 square miles, year-round population approximately 400) is the most isolated of all of Michigan's permanently inhabited islands, 18 miles and a two-hour ferry ride from the mainland at Charlevoix.

A thriving fishing community until the deadly sea lamprey made its appearance in the Great Lakes in 1950s, Beaver Island has been home to a mostly Irish population since the mid-1800s, when immigrants fleeing the potato famine began making their appearance.

The most turbulent period in the island's history began in 1847, when a sect of breakaway Mormons under the leadership of one Jesse James Strang arrived on the island. Strang, a brooding polygamist with a taste for enriching himself through "tithes" levied on his followers, proclaimed himself first a "saint" (St. James, the island's only hamlet, is named for him), and in 1850, "king."

His followers, numbering over 1,000 at one point, also elected him to the state legislature and the county commission. Needless to say, this kind of behavior did not sit well with the locals, resulting in the inconclusive Battle of Pine River, which took place on the mainland near Charlevoix in 1853. On June 16, 1856, Strang's authoritarian ways caught up with him and he was assassinated by a rebel from his own group.

In the same year, Thomas O'Donnell, an Irish immigrant, was contracted to help maintain the lighthouse on Beaver Island. He contacted relatives and fellow countrymen in Toronto and told them he had found a place that reminded him of Ireland. As the first Irish settlers began arriving, most of the Mormons began leaving to return to their original homes in Michigan and Ohio. The story that the Irish forcibly ejected the Mormons does not appear to have any basis in fact, and in recent years, Beaver Island residents have invited descendants of the Mormon settlers back for reunions.

The Irish hailed mostly from Arranmore, an island off the coast of county Donegal, and after the first group arrived in 1856, the Arranmore Irish just kept coming, on through the turn of the century. Numerous Gaelic place-names—Erin Motel, O'Donough Grocery, Donegal Bay— dot the island, and the telephone directory would not look out of place in Ireland. The island's chief watering hole—called the Shamrock, naturally—is the local gathering spot and often rings with raucous choruses of Irish folk songs.

Beaver Island is nothing if not secluded. There are many beautiful homes that are occupied by their owners only a few weeks a year and are available for rent the rest of the time. There are also miles of deserted beaches and wooded trails.

To get a real feel for the island's history, visitors are lucky to have Jim Willis, a native and the proprietor of Beaver Island Tours. He's there as the ferry docks and will take you to all the major sites: the Mormon Print Shop and Museum, the lighthouse, an old convent. In addition to history, he'll tell you all about the quirks of island life today, such as how the bank is open from 9 to 1 P.M. on Tuesdays and how the island has a single deputy sheriff, "who only gets busy when someone has a bit too much to drink at the Shamrock."

❧ EXHIBITS: Beaver Island Tours offers a 1-hour tour of the major historic sites on the island, including the small museum. Inquire at the ferry dock upon landing. ❧ LOCATION: Take I-75N to Route 33W, where it becomes Route 66, to Charlevoix. Follow signs for Beaver Island ferry. ❧ HOURS: Visiting Beaver Island requires some planning. During summer, ferries run twice a day, at 8:30 A.M. and 2:30 P.M. and irregularly the rest of the time. (There is no service at all between January and March.) ❧ ADMISSION: Round-trip ferry fare is $22 per person. Taking your car costs $75. Island Airways makes nonscheduled charter flights to the island for $25, one-way, per person. Tour cost is $6 for adults, $3 for children under 12. ❧ TELEPHONE: Beaver Island Boat Company: (616) 547-2311. Island Airways: (616) 448-2326. Call the Beaver Island Chamber of Commerce for details about cottage rentals and the small summer hotels: (616) 448-2505.

BROOKLYN

IRISH HILLS, ST. JOSEPH SHRINE

About an hour's drive southwest of Detroit is Michigan's Irish Hills region. The area was settled by famine immigrants, who found the emerald green hills and blue skies so similar to the land they left behind that they dubbed the region "the Ireland of the West." Ground for the first cabin was broken in 1852. Irish settlers donated five acres of land for the building of a church and construction of St. Joseph's Shrine, the spiritual heart of the Irish Hills, was begun two years later. The first mass was said in 1863.

A 1928 renovation quadrupled the seating capacity to 400 and the 1,600,000 mosaic tiles that adorn the ceiling were installed. The outdoor Way of the Cross was constructed, making the area a site of pilgrimage for Catholics throughout the Midwest.

⟡ **EXHIBITS:** A small gift shop is located on the shrine grounds. ⟡ **LOCATION:** From Detroit, take I-94 West to U.S. 12 near Ann Arbor. Take Route 59 North about five miles into Brooklyn. St. Joseph's is at 8743 U.S. Route 12, just outside Brooklyn. ⟡ **HOURS:** The Church is usually open during daylight hours. Call for mass schedule. ⟡ **ADMISSION:** Free ⟡ **TELEPHONE:** (517) 467-2183

DEARBORN

HENRY FORD ESTATE (FAIRLANE)

Henry Ford didn't go out of his way to advertise his Irish roots, but he didn't shy away from them either. Late in life, after he had become the world's richest man, Ford hired genealogists to search his background, not for evidence of noble birth, as many rich men did, but to see if there was anything that might explain his success and his accomplishments.

The search centered on Ireland. There, in the midst of the potato famine of 1847, John and Thomasina Ford, Henry's grandparents, were evicted from the estate of a rich Englishman near Bandon, county Cork, where they worked as tenant farmers. The couple's eldest son, a 21-year-old carpenter named William, convinced his parents there was no future in Ireland, even should the famine end. William, described by a biographer as "a man of medium height, with a great strength, gray agate eyes, and a serious demeanor," was undoubtedly the driving force in the family's decision to set out for America in the spring of that year.

The family, which trudged from Bandon to the port of Queenstown (now Cobh), passed thousands more like them, headed in the same direction. One hundred thousand had fled in 1846, the year a partial crop failure became total. Double that number left in each of the next four years. Between 1847 and 1854, nearly 1.2 million Irish would settle in the United States, nearly one in every seven of the prefamine Irish population.

There is still debate about the makeup of the Ford party, but it seems to have consisted of William, his parents, his brothers Henry and Samuel, and his sisters Rebecca, Jane, Nancy, and Mary. Tragedy struck during the voyage, when Thomasina Ford succumbed to illness. Some accounts say she died before the ship docked and was buried at sea. Others say she died and was buried, along with thousands of other potential Irish settlers, in a mass grave at the immigrant quarantine station on Quebec's Grosse Isle (*see* Montmagny, Canada).

The Fords were different from their fellow passengers in that they were Protestants rather than Catholics, descendants of English settlers from either Somersetshire or Essex who were settled in Ireland during the reign of Elizabeth I nearly 250 years before. They were sent to Ireland both to relieve overpopulation in England and Scotland and to pacify the rebellious Catholic Irish. The town from which the Fords hailed, Bandon, was constructed specifically as a Protestant bastion in a hostile, Catholic sea.

Also unlike most of their fellow passengers, the Fords had someone to go to in the New World. Fifteen years earlier, Samuel and George Ford, William's uncles, had emigrated and settled in the small village of Dearborn outside Detroit, where they were becoming prosperous. Their reports of the wonders of life in Michigan undoubtedly were a major factor in the family's decision to take ship.

"Michigan fever" gripped America soon after the completion of the Erie Canal (*see* Rochester, New York) in 1825. The canal opened up an enormous reservoir of cheap land in what is now the Midwest. (Little thought was given to the Indians already on it.) The near-simultaneous invention of the steamboat cut the journey from Buffalo to Detroit from a month to just 48 hours. Michigan became the gateway to the interior.

Upon arrival, John Ford, Henry Ford's grandfather, borrowed $350 and bought 80 acres of land. For more than a decade, William labored to clear his father's land and help pay off the debt by working as a carpenter for the Michigan Central Railroad. Occasionally, he also worked as a handyman for another local landowner and fellow Corkman named Patrick O'Hern (sometimes spelled "Ahearn"). In 1861, William married O'Hern's daughter Mary, and in 1863, their son Henry was born.

From a very young age, Henry knew he hated farm work and drove his father to distraction by his constant tinkering with watches and other mechanical objects. While still a boy, he built a small steam turbine near the fence of the schoolhouse, but the boiler exploded and a fragment injured a classmate. The fence burned down and an enraged William Ford had to pay to replace it. This fascination with gizmos, combined with his social shyness, marked Henry out as a "queer duck" in the neighborhood.

Henry ignored his father's pressure to become a farmer, however, and dropped out of school in the seventh grade, moving to Detroit. In 1888, he married Clara Bryant and secured a job as an engineer with the Detroit Edison Company. When not working or sleeping, he was tinkering with something in the shed behind the couple's house on Bagley Avenue. Ford had an idea for a gasoline-powered contraption that he hoped would do the work of a horse. He dubbed the machine the quadricycle, and on June 4, 1896, took the first spin around his neighborhood in Detroit.

Ford's was not the first car—far from it. Siegfried Marcus, a German Jew, had began experimenting in Vienna with carriages propelled by gasoline-powered combustion engines as early as 1873. Two German engineers, Gottlieb Daimler and Karl Benz, are generally credited with building the first true automobiles in the early 1890s.

Ford's genius lay in production, and in finding rich backers for his ideas. Prior to Ford, automobiles were virtually custom-made by artisan methods, one at a time. The process was slow and the product high-priced. Early on, Ford decided that had to change. "The way to make automobiles is to make one automobile like another automobile, to make them all alike, to make them come through the factory just alike, just as one pin is like another pin when it comes from pin factory," he said. "The proper system, as I have in mind, is to get the car to the people."

The result was the assembly line, and the car was the Model T, a light, durable machine that rolled onto the road for the first time in 1908. Built "in any color, so long as it's black," Ford's ultramodern Highland Park plant turned out 19,000 Model T's in 1910, 34,500 in 1911, and 78,440 in 1912.

The assembly line had its dark side, however. The long hours, the low pay, the monotonous repetition of simple tasks, all took their toll on the workers, who often quit after only a few weeks. Ford discovered that he was hiring and training nearly 1,000 workers for every 100 he retained. Something had to be done.

The something was the $5 day. Prodded by James Couzens, a company executive, Ford agreed to the then-unheard-of wage only after being convinced that it would be the greatest advertisement any company could have. He had no idea how right he was.

It's hard to recall today the impact the announcement of the $5 day had on America and the world on January 5, 1914. The next day, Ford's Highland Park plant was literally besieged by job seekers. Ford had to leave his office via a window. Jews living within the pale settlement in

Russia and Arabs from Mesopotamia headed for the boats. Reporters swarmed to Henry Ford's side, and the man who was not even listed in the 1913 edition of *Who's Who* almost overnight became a household name.

Ford's sudden fame meant that his house on Edison Street in Detroit became uninhabitable, surrounded as it was at all hours by job seekers and the curious. Ford decided to build a more secure mansion on 1,500 acres he had been painstakingly assembling along the Rouge River in Dearborn, the place where the Fords had first settled and achieved modest prosperity in their new country years before.

Ford hired Frank Lloyd Wright to design the new home, but was repelled by Wright's daring, modernistic approach. He changed architects and switched to a Scottish baronial style, resulting in an architecturally undistinguished pile that cost $2 million, a huge sum now and an extraordinary one then. He named the house Fairlane, after the street in county Cork on which his grandfather Patrick O'Hern had been born. (Fair Lane is today called Wolfe Tone Street, named for the leader of the 1798 uprising.)

Fairlane boasted such unheard-of amenities as a heated indoor swimming pool, a bowling alley, a $30,000 organ, and its own power plant, designed by Ford's friend Thomas Edison. Ford had a pond dug so that Clara could ice skate in the winter, as she had done while they were courting.

By the time Fairlane was completed, Henry Ford's interests were moving beyond the manufacturing of automobiles. Clara and their young son, Edsel, moved into the mansion without him just before Christmas 1914, while he was sailing his "peace ship" across the Atlantic in a quixotic effort to end World War I. Ford also ran for and narrowly lost a race for the U.S. Senate in 1918.

Ford lived at Fairlane the rest of his life, becoming increasingly crotchety and ill-tempered as the years went on. He refused to believe there could be a better car than the Model T and stubbornly insisted on retaining the design, even as the rest of the industry moved forward. By the end of World War II, Henry was senile and infirm, completely under the control of his security chief, Harry Bennett, who effectively ran the company. Realizing the magnitude of the disaster that would befall the economy if the company went under, Pres. Franklin D. Roosevelt arranged the early discharge from the navy of the patriarch's 26-year-old grandson, Henry II. Thanks almost wholly to young Henry's efforts, the Ford Motor Company survived.

In the first week of April 1947, a heavy spring downpour caused the Rouge River to flood. The water seeped into Thomas Edison's power plant, causing a short and cutting power to the big mansion. At 11:40 P.M. on April 7, by the flickering light of candles and a fireplace, 83-year-old

Henry Ford died. It was almost a century to the day since his father and grandfather had left Ireland.

& EXHIBITS: Unfortunately, a visitor to Fairlane today might have a hard time seeing how the Fords really lived, since the house has been much altered in the years since Henry Ford's death. (The University of Michigan today uses it as a conference center.) The true highlight of any visit to Fairlane, however, is the grounds. Nature was one of Ford's passions, and the hundreds of acres of forests and meadows that surround the house are much as Ford left them. A map of the grounds is available for 25 cents. Tours are conducted Monday through Saturday at 10, 11, 1, 2, and 3 and Sundays between 1 and 4:30 on the half-hour. Closed January 1 through April 1, except Sundays. & LOCATION: Off Evergreen Road between Michigan Avenue and Ford Road. Parking available at the visitor center. & ADMISSION: Adults $6; $5 for seniors and students; children 5 and under, free. & TELEPHONE: (313) 593-5500.

HENRY FORD MUSEUM AND GREENFIELD VILLAGE

Both of these institutions, great historical sites in every respect, grew out of Henry Ford's contradictory passions for technological improvement and preserving the lost America of his youth, an America his inventions did so much to change forever.

Greenfield Village is an outdoor museum that seeks to document the lives of ordinary Americans in the 18th, 19th, and early 20th centuries. Throughout the 1920s and 1930s, Ford personally sought out exhibits and spent millions of dollars expanding the collection. The exhibits include his own birthplace as well as the Bagley Avenue shed where he worked on the quadricycle. From East Orange, New Jersey, he had Thomas Edison's laboratory disassembled and rebuilt on the site, as he did the Wright brothers' bicycle shop in Dayton, Ohio.

The museum, located just a few yards from the village (separate admission charge) is gradually shedding its reputation as a disorganized agglomeration of Americana. The collections, many of which could be formidable museums in their own right, such as the steam engine and lighting collections, are now better organized and presented.

One of the grislier exhibits is the car in which another famous Irish-American, John F. Kennedy, was riding when he was assassinated in Dallas on November 22, 1963.

& LOCATION: On Village Rd, east off Oakwood Boulevard Take I-94W from Detroit to the Southfield Freeway and follow the signs for the village. & HOURS: Open daily, 9–5. Greenfield Village buildings closed January 1 through mid-March, but exteriors can be viewed with a ticket to Henry

Experience a slice of Americana at Henry Ford Museum. (Courtesy of the Henry Ford Museum and Greenfield Village)

Ford Museum.   ❧ ADMISSION: Adults $12.50; seniors $11.50; children 5–12 $6.25; under 5 free. A 2-day pass for both the museum and the village is $22 for adults, $11 for children.   ❧ TELEPHONE: (313) 271-1976.

DETROIT

CORKTOWN

Corktowners like to call theirs Detroit's oldest extant neighborhood, and their claim is probably as good as anyone else's. The neighborhood got its nickname, naturally, from county Cork, which supplied many of the early residents. (In those days, the Irish had not yet formed an "Irish" identity for themselves and tended to identify with the counties from which they hailed, rather than the country as a whole.)

The first substantial numbers of Irish immigrants arrived in Detroit in the 1830s, attracted by what even then was a growing industrial city. At first, they crowded into slums around the present-day downtown and near the river. As the population grew and became more prosperous, however, the Irish began to move west into the new homes they could afford. Most of Corktown's dwellings today were built in the middle to late 19th century.

Corktown today is a mixture of the charming and the shabby. Some young couples have moved into the magnificent old Queen Anne–style homes and renovated them. Others, unfortunately, have become victims of Detroit's pervasive urban blight.

Corktown's show street is Leverette, which you reach by turning south off of Michigan Avenue at 11th Street.

When the Irish first arrived in Detroit, the only Catholics in the area were French. If the Irish wanted to hear mass in English, they had to rise at a very early hour on Sunday. Dissatisfied, the Irish founded Holy Trinity Church in 1834. Originally located downtown, it was physically uprooted and moved to its present site at Porter and 6th streets in 1849, following the movement of the Irish population. It has been the spiritual heart of Corktown ever since.

The interior of the Gothic Revival structure has been beautifully restored, and outside is a fine plaza that is a local gathering place in warm weather. Although the regular congregation is now mostly Hispanic, the Irish return for mass every St. Patrick's Day prior to the parade in downtown Detroit.

Unfortunately, the future of Corktown now appears even more uncertain. If nearby Tiger Stadium is torn down, as appears likely, the neighborhood might not survive.

& **EXHIBITS:** The Corktown Citizen's District Council sponsors home tours the weekend after Mother's Day. Call (313) 962-5660 for information.   & **LOCATION:** Approximately 1 mile west of downtown Detroit, south of Michigan Avenue, between 6th and 14th streets.   & **HOURS:** Always open, though daylight hours are recommended. You can visit Holy Trinity for 10:30 A.M. mass on Sundays (in Spanish). Other times ask at the church office to see the interior.   & **ADMISSION:** Free   & **TELEPHONE:** Holy Trinity (313) 965-4450. Also worth a visit is the nearby Gaelic League of Detroit, 2068 Michigan Ave., (313) 964-8700.

HARBOR BEACH

FRANK MURPHY BOYHOOD HOME

Frank Murphy served as governor of Michigan for only two years, and he is all but forgotten in most of America today. But in union households, his name is still pronounced with something approaching reverence. For it was Murphy's refusal to use the National Guard to break the Flint sit-down strikes in 1937 that forced the recognition of the United Auto Workers (UAW) by General Motors. The rest of the auto industry eventually followed, paving the way for American workers to join the great American middle class in the years after World War II.

Frank Murphy was born in this simple wood frame house in Harbor Beach, on the tip of Michigan's "thumb." He did little to discourage family lore that his great-grandfather had been hanged by the British for anti-Crown activities, but Murphy biographer Sidney Fine says there is no documentation to support this.

True or not, the family's Irish nationalist credentials certainly are impressive. The governor's grandfather, William Francis Murphy, and his wife, Margaret, both of county Mayo, were famine immigrants, arriving in Canada in 1847. William entered the dairy business and became quite prosperous.

The couple's eldest son, John F., was Frank Murphy's father and was born two years after his parents arrived in Canada. At age 17, in June 1866, he became caught up in the Fenian invasion of Canada. (*See* Ridgeway, Ontario.)

"According to his own account," writes Sidney Fine, "he was sent to Buffalo by Fenian authorities and there found a force of about 30,000 Fenians. He recrossed the border in a party of 650 men who were under the erroneous impression that they were the advance guard of a much larger army."

While the group was foraging for food, they blundered into a detachment of British troops, and John and many of his comrades were captured. Owing to his youth, Canadian citizenship, and previously clean record, young John Murphy was released. He embarked on a legal career.

His Fenian background, however, was a definite liability to pursuing a career in Canada, and he decided to try his luck south of the border. Murphy received his law degree from the University of Michigan in 1881 and went to work in a Detroit law firm. Almost immediately, however, Murphy heard of the need for a lawyer in a small Michigan town then called Sand Beach. He arrived in late 1882 or early 1883 and stayed the rest of his life. Young Frank was born April 13, 1893.

The boy followed in his father's footsteps, receiving his law degree from the University of Michigan in 1914. Frank Murphy, however, was attracted by the big city and immediately commenced practicing law in Detroit, where he worked for 30 months before entering the army in World War I. To supplement his income, he sometimes worked in a mill. This is where he learned what life was like for ordinary workers and where he nursed a desire to help them improve their lot.

Upon his discharge from the army in 1919, Murphy embarked on what was to become a career in public service of almost uninterrupted success. He became chief assistant U.S. attorney for the Eastern District of Michigan, and in 1922 was elected a judge of Detroit Recorder's Court (a criminal court).

Murphy's hour struck, however, with the onset of the Great Depression. Detroit Mayor Charles Bowles was recalled in 1930 as a tidal wave of unemployment and unrest swept the city. Murphy resigned his judgeship, defeated four other candidates, and became mayor of Detroit. He easily won a full term in 1931.

Murphy became one of Franklin D. Roosevelt's earliest and most enthusiastic supporters. The president rewarded the mayor with appointment as governor of the Philippines in 1933, with a mandate to begin steering America's Asian colony toward selfgovernment. This he accomplished in 1935 with the election of a local legislature.

Worried about his own reelection, Roosevelt wanted Murphy to come home and run for governor in 1936. The president feared a third party movement headed by Father Charles Coughlin (*see* Royal Oak, Michigan) might sap Catholic votes from the Democratic ticket. The president needn't have feared. He won Michigan handily, while Murphy, ironically, barely squeaked into the governor's office.

Despite the narrowness of his victory, Murphy wasted no time enacting a statewide version of the New Deal, with liberalized unemployment and old-age insurance benefits, health care for the indigent, and an expanded mental health program. But his major test came just days after he entered office: the Flint sit-down strikes.

The 44-day strike began December 30, 1936. Prior to that time, if management sensed a strike was imminent, it would go to a friendly judge, who would issue an injunction banning the strike. Management would then lock out the workers and bring in "scabs" to replace them.

The infant UAW decided to thwart this tactic by physically occupying the auto plants in a "sit-down" strike. Court order or no, management would have to physically remove the strikers before replacements could be brought in, an operation that would certainly be difficult, bloody, and require the use of the state National Guard.

General Motors got its court order, but Murphy made it clear he would not enforce it. "As a last resort government may properly use and was prepared to use whatever force might be required to maintain its authority. But the government of Michigan was unwilling to employ force unnecessarily to dignify the law," Murphy said in a famous statewide radio address.

To secure the confidence and obedience of many thousands of men under the strain of a conflict of such vast proportions and strong emotions, without causing disaffection and distrust for the institutions of popular government, required methods vastly different from those a sheriff employs in dealing with an ordinary case of trespass.

GM thus had little choice but to settle with the Flint strikers, an event that provoked an outbreak of further sit-down strikes throughout the state, for which Murphy was much criticized. These events, along with his alienation of party leaders through his tendency to make appointments without consulting them, combined to defeat Murphy for reelection in 1938.

But his career was far from over. President Roosevelt remembered his old friend and named him attorney general of the United States in 1939, and then an associate justice of the Supreme Court in 1940.

It was in the latter capacity that Murphy showed loyalty had its limits. Always a believer in racial equality and civil liberties, Murphy was appalled by the roundup of Japanese Americans on the West Coast after Pearl Harbor. Denouncing this "legalization of racism," he was one of three justices who strongly dissented from the infamous *Korematsu v. United States* decision in 1944, which upheld the detention. Murphy served on the high court until his early death from a heart attack on July 19, 1949. He was buried in Harbor Beach.

A lifelong bachelor, Murphy used his Harbor Beach home as a base and repository for all the many artifacts he collected throughout his public life, and it has been turned into a museum commemorating his life and accomplishments.

Tended by faithful UAW retirees, the Murphy home looks much as it did when Frank and his brothers and sisters were growing up here early in the century.

&. **EXHIBITS:** The house is filled with photos of Murphy meeting with national and world leaders. The many crucifixes are evidence of his deep Catholic faith. There are also some interesting mementos he picked up while in the Philippines. &. **LOCATION:** From Detroit, take I-94E to Port Huron, where the highway becomes Route 24, hugging the shore of Lake Huron. Harbor beach is approximately 40 miles north of Port Huron. The museum is at 142 South Huron St. &. **HOURS:** Open mid-June through Labor Day, Monday through Saturday 10–5:30; Sunday 11–5. &. **ADMISSION:** Free &. **TELEPHONE:** (517) 479-9664.

R O Y A L   O A K

SHRINE OF THE LITTLE FLOWER

Irish America has produced many politically active priests. Few, however, were as active, or as notorious, as Father Charles E. Coughlin, the "radio priest" of the Depression era. Coughlin's radio broadcasts during the 1930s and early 1940s made him, for a time, one of the most powerful figures in the country and very probably the most controversial Catholic priest in American history.

Father Coughlin's hour-long sermons, begun in 1926 and delivered from the pulpit of this church in Detroit's northern suburbs, were carried by the CBS radio network. At the peak of his popularity in the mid-1930s, they were heard by as many as 40 million listeners. Crowds of as many as 25,000 would gather on Woodward Avenue outside the overflowing Shrine of the Little Flower Church to hear him.

At first, Father Coughlin's sermons were almost entirely religious in nature, but as the economic downturn of 1929 deepened into the Great Depression, his talks came to focus more and more on politics and economics. He denounced communism, "modern capitalism," and "the money changers on Wall Street."

An early and enthusiastic supporter of Franklin D. Roosevelt's and the New Deal, Coughlin soon turned against the president and began vitriolically attacking him, because, the priest said, "he recognized the atheistic, godless government of the Communists in Russia." Soon, the radio priest's Sunday afternoon talks had only the most tenuous connection with religion, becoming instead diatribes against not only Communists, but also Jews, the British and anyone else Coughlin considered an agent of Satan.

Shrine of the Little Flower on Woodward Avenue, just minutes from Detroit.

As the 1930s became the 1940s, however, the radio priest's influence waned. Despite vigorous campaigning, all candidates he supported in the 1936 election lost badly. His extravagant praise of Hitler and Mussolini alienated vast segments of his audience. After the United States entered World War II, the Justice Department threatened to charge Coughlin with sedition. The Catholic Archdiocese of Detroit moved first, suppressing Coughlin's magazine *Social Justice* and ordering the radio priest off the air.

"I could have bucked the government and won—the people would have supported me," Father Coughlin said after he was silenced. "But I didn't have the heart left, for my church had spoken. It was my duty to follow, for disobedience is a great sin."

Though no longer the "radio priest," Coughlin carried on as pastor of the church he built. An architectural marvel visible for miles, the Shrine of the Little Flower is the fruit of Coughlin's early broadcasts. He retired as pastor in 1966 and died in 1979, virtually forgotten.

Coughlin was born in Hamilton, Ontario, Canada, on October 25, 1891. His great-grandfather had emigrated from Ireland shortly before 1820 and was one of the many Irish laborers who helped dig the Erie Canal (*see* Rochester, New York). His father, Thomas Coughlin, had worked as a stoker on Great Lakes ore ships until he fell ill with typhoid. Determined not to return to the harsh life of a seaman, he settled in Hamilton, Ontario and found work as a church sexton. He met Amelia Mahoney, the woman who would become his wife, at church. They had one child, Charles.

Charles experienced the same conflict so many young, ambitious men of Irish descent faced in deciding between becoming a priest or a politician. He felt the call of the Church, but also enjoyed the give-and-take of debate and discussing current affairs. When he entered St. Basil's Seminary in Toronto in 1911, he was resolved to combine the calling of the priest with that of a political leader. He was ordained in the Basilian order in 1916 and assigned to teach at Assumption College in Windsor, Ontario, where he remained for a decade after his ordination.

Ironically, for all his later reputation as a hatemonger, Father Coughlin built the Shrine of the Little Flower as a weapon *against* hatred and bigotry. In 1926, the Detroit archdiocese, to which he had become affiliated, dispatched him to the small suburb of Royal Oak. There were only 26 Catholic families in the parish at the time, and they were drawing the attention of a very strong chapter of the Ku Klux Klan.

The Klan wasted little time greeting the new priest. Two months after he erected the ramshackle wooden structure that had been dubbed the Shrine of the Little Flower Church, the Klan burned a cross outside and left a note, "Move from Royal Oak." Never one to be easily intimidated, Father Coughlin instead told his parishioners, "Someday, we will build a church and raise its cross so high to the sky that neither man nor beast can burn it down."

He was as good as his word. A 100-foot granite tower forms a cross at the front of the church that depicts the Crucifixion of Christ. The sculpture of Christ that faces Woodward Avenue is 28 feet high and weighs nearly 10 tons. The tower was constructed between 1929 and 1933 at a cost of $300,000; the adjoining octagonal church, which seats 3,000, was completed in 1936.

The church was named for St. Therese of Lisieux, known as "the Little Flower of the Child Jesus." She died in a French convent in 1897 and was canonized in 1925. The Shrine of the Little Flower was the first church named in her honor.

← **EXHIBITS:** The church opened a heritage room in 1966, where memorabilia, photos, and artifacts are on display. Tours can be arranged by calling in advance. ← **LOCATION:** The Shrine of the Little Flower is on the northeastern corner of Woodward Avenue and 12 Mile Road in Royal

Oak. From Detroit, take I-75 north to I-696 west to the Woodward Avenue exit. Go north on Woodward approximately two miles. The church will be on your right. ❧ **HOURS:** Open daily. ❧ **ADMISSION:** None, but donations appreciated. ❧ **TELEPHONE:** (313) 541-4122.

MINNESOTA

FATHER IRELAND MARKER/SITE OF CONNEMARA

"The Irish of Minnesota performed two surprising feats," writes Ann Regan in her study of the Irish in Minnesota. "They established themselves as successful farmers in the southeastern counties on the Mississippi and Minnesota rivers and in settlements scattered across the state ... [and,] although outnumbered by their German neighbors, they stamped St. Paul, the state's capital, with an Irish label that was still attached in the 1980s."

According to the 1890 census, there were around 1.8 million Irish-born Americans, approximately one quarter of whom lived in the north central states between Ohio and the Dakotas. Half of those were to be found in northern and western Illinois, northeastern Iowa, southern Wisconsin, and southeastern Minnesota. Of these, Minnesota had the smallest Irish representation, with only about 1.4 percent of the Irish-born population of the entire country.

One of the enduring questions asked by scholars of the Irish in America is why an agricultural people in Ireland became an almost exclusively urban people in the United States. The reasons are not really hard to fathom, however.

Farming was not a happy experience for most of the Irish. High rents, small plots, and crop failures such as the potato blight made many anxious to avoid depending on the soil for a living. Industrial wages, low as they were, were higher than anything available in Ireland. Rural living also meant long trips to church and the company of fellow emigrants, a sacrifice most Irish were not willing to make.

The desperate conditions of the eastern slums, however, caused western Irish-Catholic prelates to consider settling the immigrants in a more wholesome rural setting. Irish "colonies" were established in scattered places throughout western New York State, Indiana, Wisconsin, Illinois, and Ohio.

Organized colonies, however, were usually less successful than settlements established through individual immigration of adventurous Irish families. Few Irish came directly to Minnesota. Most settled first in the eastern ports or in Canada, then settled once or twice more before arriving on the wild frontier of this isolated state.

Bishop (later Archbishop) John Ireland was one of those western churchmen determined to improve the lot of the Irish through farming. (*see* St. Paul, Minnesota, for more on Bishop Ireland.) Ireland was able to make his venture more successful than others because he had the foresight to become an agent for the St. Paul and Pacific Railroad. This allowed him to acquire land cheaply and without having to compete with speculators. The land was thus not beyond the range of many Irish.

Between 1876 and 1880, Ireland contracted for 369,000 acres in southeastern Minnesota. Eventually, there were nine colonies, many of them with names evocative of Ireland: Clontarf and DeGraff in Swift County; Adrian in Nobles County; Avoca, Iona, and Fulda in Murray County; Graceville in Big Stone County; and Minneota and Ghent in Lyon County.

Still, the minimum grub stake each family needed to see them through the first harsh Minnesota winter—$400—meant that few of the settlers were dirt-poor urban dwellers. Many were Irish who were already farming in New England or elsewhere in the east before migrating to Minnesota. Ireland also saw to it that churches were near all the new colonies.

Although the number of Irish attracted to the Great Plains never came close to expectations, historian William V. Shannon nevertheless called Bishop Ireland's efforts "the largest and most successful Catholic colonization program ever undertaken in the United States."

Bishop Ireland's successes, however, were very nearly overshadowed by the near disaster of the Connemara colony near Graceville. In 1880, Bishop Ireland accepted responsibility for settling a group of 309 Irish from the Connemara region of county Galway and placed them on land near Graceville.

Most of the settlers, however, had been fishermen or subsistence farmers in the old country and knew nothing of largescale wheat cultivation. Their suffering in the Minnesota winter attracted sensationalistic coverage from Minnesota and national newspapers, hampering efforts to recruit more Irish for the other, successful settlements.

Bishop Ireland's efforts to correct the erroneous impression that his colonies were failures met with only mixed success. "The Connemara families are 24 in number," he wrote in an exasperated letter to the *St. Paul Pioneer-Press.* "Around Graceville are 400 other Catholic families, mostly

Irish, and I beg the public, when Graceville is mentioned, to remember the latter rather than the former."

Bishop Ireland was eventually forced to dismantle Connemara and remove the population to railroad jobs in St. Paul. His biographer, however, characterized Ireland's feelings over Connemara as "the greatest grief of his life."

Nevertheless, the late archbishop would be pleased to know that all the towns he founded are still on the map. In 1976, the Minnesota Agricultural Society began to list the farms that had been in the same family for 100 years or more. They found that in the nine Minnesota counties with the heaviest concentrations of rural Irish, 13.7 percent of these long-held farms were in the hands of descendants of Irish settlers.

❧ **EXHIBITS:** A plaque commemorating Archbishop Ireland's founding of the town of Graceville and the other Irish settlements in the area is located on the north side of S.R. 28 on the western edge of the town. ❧ **LOCATION:** Graceville is located on S.R. 28 in western Minnesota. ❧ **HOURS:** Dawn to dusk. ❧ **ADMISSION:** Free ❧ **TELEPHONE:** Graceville city clerk's office: (612) 748-7911.

HASTINGS

NININGER

The United States was a country in transition in the 1890s. The agrarian old order was giving way to the new industrialism, a transformation that was causing great bitterness on the Plains as the family farm was caught in the squeeze. The result was the Populist party, and one of its leading voices was an Irish American with an eclectic career background named Ignatius Donnelly.

Donnelly's career hit its high point on July 4, 1892, when the platform of the Populist party, largely drafted by Donnelly, was read aloud before assembled delegates at the Coliseum in Omaha, Nebraska. "We meet in the midst of a nation brought to the verge of moral, political and financial ruin," it read. "Corruption dominates the ballot box, the legislatures, the Congress. . . . The newspapers are largely subsidized or muzzled, public opinion silenced, business prostrated, our homes covered with mortgages, labor impoverished, and the land concentrating in the hands of the capitalists. . . ."

Donnelly, a son of Irish immigrants who settled in Philadelphia, was a superb rabble-rouser. He was also a real estate developer, farmer, member of Congress, and best-selling author. And while he did many things, he could not, unfortunately, do any of them well enough to have his life truly considered a success. He did at times, however, seem almost to possess a crystal ball for seeing into future events.

Donnelly's father was a physician, and the son was well educated in Philadelphia schools. He read law as a young man in the chambers of Benjamin Harris Brewster, later attorney general of the United States. He grew bored with law, however, and in 1856 struck out for the West.

The frontier was well west of Minnesota by 1856, but it was close enough for a boy from Philadelphia. He had a mind to make a career in land speculation and kept a sharp eye out for development prospects. He thought he found what was he was looking for in the little community of Nininger, which was developing close to Hastings, Minnesota, on the Mississippi River.

It was an auspicious time for development in Minnesota. Still two years away from joining the Union, the territory was filling up fast. (The population increased from 40,000 to 120,000 between 1855 and 1857.) Working with a group of investors, Donnelly subdivided the land around Nininger (which was named for John Nininger, one of Donnelly's partners) into 6,800 lots, which went on sale for $6 apiece.

Donnelly put his considerable writing talents to work boosting the new settlement. He edited the *Emigrant Aid Journal,* a booster's sheet that advertised good land and good living in Nininger and elsewhere.

By the spring of 1857, Donnelly's scheme seemed to be working. Over 500 settlers had arrived, and two sawmills and two general stores had opened, as well as a druggist shop and a hotel. The price of a lot had risen to $100, and Donnelly's paper worth was estimated at close to $100,000. Donnelly had visions of being the founding father of a new metropolis on the Mississippi.

The land boom was, of course, a classic speculative bubble that soon burst. The Ohio Life Insurance and Trust Company closed its doors, an event that started a domino effect of collapsing banks. By 1858, not only had construction at Nininger ceased, but many residents actually disassembled their houses and moved into the more established community at Hastings. Donnelly's "wealth" vanished overnight and he found himself in debt. He had his first bad taste of the effect that the machinations of distant banks could have on ordinary people.

After trying farming for a time, Donnelly followed the traditional Irish path and turned to politics as an avocation. He had been a Democrat in Philadelphia, but joined the new Republican party because of its antislavery stance. He ran in 1859 for lieutenant governor and won. By all accounts he served faithfully, if flamboyantly, for two terms. When the Civil War broke out, Donnelly helped organize (but did not join) the First Minnesota Volunteers, a regiment that later became one of the most

*Poster promoting
emigration up the
Mississippi River to
Nininger, 1857.*

(*Minnesota Historical Society*)

famous of the war when it was all but wiped out in a suicidal charge at Gettysburg.

In 1862, Donnelly ran for Congress and won. But his abrasive style caused him to run afoul of Republican party politics, and he lost the party's nomination in 1868. He ran anyway as an independent, thus ensuring the election of a Democrat and cutting his ties to the GOP for good. He never held federal office again.

A bankrupt in real estate, a failure at farming, a washout in politics, Donnelly now decided to make his way as a writer and lecturer. Fortunately, his Irish gift for the word stood him in good stead and he did well, despite the fantastic aspects of his work. *The Great Cryptogram (1888)*, for instance, was an effort to prove Sir Francis Bacon "really" wrote Shakespeare's plays.

His great success, however, was *Caesar's Column (1890)*. It was clearly inspired by Edward Bellamy's 1887 novel *Looking Backward*. But while

Bellamy had looked 100 years into the future and seen an ideal world, Donnelly instead saw one divided between a corrupt plutocracy and a cynical, callous population. Donnelly intended the book as a populist warning about what great extremes of wealth and poverty could produce.

Although the plot is amateurish and heavy-handed, Donnelly foresaw modern problems such as air pollution, population pressures, and modern weapons (poison gas). His "ideal" state featured an eight-hour work day with two days off per week, a program of socialized medicine, no interest rates, and the death penalty for bribing a public official. (Not so wild after all, perhaps.)

Although he repeatedly insisted he was through with politics, Donnelly was among the first to suggest that farmers organize themselves as an interest group. Ultimately, he became one of the national figures in the Populist party and largely drafted its program, which included a graduated income tax, a free and secret ballot, direct election of U.S. senators, voter initiatives and referendums, and public ownership of railroads, telegraphs, and telephones.

Donnelly was certainly a man ahead of his time, and that was his curse. He died on New Year's Day 1901, believing "all my immense labor [was] for nothing." He could not know that his investment in Nininger would one day pay off, as the area effectively became a distant suburb of Minneapolis-St. Paul. Nininger was in the right place; but, like Donnelly, it was there too soon.

⤳ **EXHIBITS:** The former town hall is all that remains of the original Nininger settlement, although modern subdivisions are now sprouting in the area. ⤳ **LOCATION:** About 1½ miles north and west of Hastings on CR 42, also known as the Nininger Road. ⤳ **HOURS:** The building is closed and locked most of the time, but access can be arranged by calling ahead of time. ⤳ **ADMISSION:** Free ⤳ **TELEPHONE:** Hastings Area Chamber of Commerce: (612) 437-6775.

ST. PAUL

F. SCOTT FITZGERALD NATIONAL HISTORIC SITE

Mrs. James J. Hill, the wife of the richest man in St. Paul, walked into a bookstore in 1920 and said she had the perfect man to write a biography of Archbishop John Ireland (*see* University of St. Thomas, farther on). "They tell me there is a fine young Catholic writer who has just published a religious book, *This Side of Paradise*," she said excitedly.

The anecdote no doubt amused F. Scott Fitzgerald, who stood on the threshold of literary fame and was about to cut his ties to the faith in which he was raised. Fitzgerald's ambivalence about his Irish roots, combined with the (then) scandalous nature of his books and his lifestyle, are what have prevented Irish-Americans from clasping him to their bosom as one of their own.

Fitzgerald's Irish roots are authentic enough. "I am half-black Irish and half old American stock," he wrote in a famous letter to John O'Hara (*see* State College, Pennsylvania.) "The black Irish half of my family looked down upon the Maryland side of the family, who had, and really had, that certain series of reticence and obligations that go under the poor old shattered word 'breeding.' (modern form: 'inhibitions.')"

Indeed, in a turn of events opposite what is usually taken to be the case, it was the Irish side of the family that had the money. Phillip Francis McQuillan, Scott's grandfather on his mother's side, emigrated from county Fermanagh in 1843 and became a highly successful grocer in St. Paul, which had a substantial Irish community. Building up the business must have taken its toll, however, for Grandfather McQuillan died at just 43 years of age.

It was that McQuillan money that came to the family's rescue when Edward Fitzgerald, the novelist's father, failed utterly in business. Edward was Irish on his father's side. It was Edward Fitzgerald's mother who brought the Maryland gentry that the novelist treasured so highly (*see* Montgomery, Alabama).

The Fitzgeralds of St. Paul were thus "lace curtain" Irish, people who had "come up" by virtue of work (or Grandfather McQuillan's work, anyway) and had no other "pedigree." Fitzgerald was always uncomfortable with this situation, always thinking of himself as being close to the wealthy, Anglo-Protestant ruling class but never quite "good enough" to be a part of it. Of course, that very fact positioned him ideally to write about the moneyed class in a way no true insider ever could.

It is also not hard to see why Fitzgerald was eager to avoid being thought of as an "Irish" writer, for the image of the Irish in America was very much coarser then than it is now. Brogues, bars, Pat-and-Mike jokes, the "stage Irishman," and the like would not have made promising material for a literary career in the Jazz Age.

Irishness found its way into Fitzgerald's work in spite of the author—or perhaps because of him, much as he might be loathe to admit it. Many critics, such as the great Edmund Wilson, thought Fitzgerald's Irish background essential to an understanding of his work.

Stephan Talty, writing in the June 1987 issue of *Irish America*, discovered a previously overlooked review written by Fitzgerald. The book is *The Celt and the World*, a study of Irish patriotism written by Shane

Leslie, a good friend of Fitzgerald's and the son of a Catholic Anglo-Irish baronet. *"The Celt and the World* is a sort of bible of Irish patriotism," Fitzgerald wrote in the *Nassau Literary Review.* He continues,

> To an Irishman, the whole of the book is fascinating. It gives one an intense desire to see Ireland free at last to work out her own destiny under Home Rule. It gives one the idea that she would do it directly under the eyes of God and with so much purity and so many mistakes. It arouses a fascination with the mystical lore and legend of the island which 'can save others, but herself she cannot save.'

This review is one of the rare instances of Fitzgerald's apparently praising his Irish roots. It also shows he read the works of J. M. Synge, W. B. Yeats, Lady Gregory, and other contributors to the Irish literary renaissance of the early part of this century.

In his first novel, *This Side of Paradise,* Fitzgerald evokes several Irish themes. His alter ego in the book, Amory Blaine, is the son of "Beatrice O'Hara." One of the important characters is Monsignor Darcy, a thinly disguised rendition of Monsignor Fay, an influential presence during Fitzgerald's youth.

The Great Gatsby (1925) was a thinly disguised retelling of the story of his Grandfather McQuillan. The novel is populated by McCartys, Muldoons, Corrigans, and Fitzpatricks. One of the messages of the novel is that the Irish have "made it" in American society. It is also a savage portrait of the rich and their endless, pointless quest for total happiness.

The Fitzgeralds lived in several houses in St. Paul. The novelist's birthplace still stands at 481 Laurel Avenue and is a private residence. The house now known as the Fitzgerald National Historic Site was occupied by the family between 1918 and 1920. In the front bedroom on the third floor he wrote *This Side of Paradise.*

🔊 **EXHIBITS:** All of the St. Paul area Fitzgerald houses are privately owned and occupied. None are open to the public. 🔊 **LOCATION:** 599 Summit Ave. (Summit Terrace). He and Zelda also lived at 626 Goodrich Ave., where he wrote his second novel, *The Beautiful and the Damned.*

IRISH AMERICAN CULTURAL INSTITUTE

Founded in 1962 by Eoin and Jeanette McKiernan and by the late Patrick Butler, a St. Paul businessman and philanthropist, this institute is intended to propagate Irish culture and history in the United States and around the world.

Its programs include the "Irish Way," which introduces American high school students to a summer of study in Ireland. The institute also publishes *Eire-Ireland,* one of the leading journals of Irish studies, as well as *Ducas,* a lively newsletter that keeps its members informed on happenings within the organization. It also sponsors speakers, art exhibits, theater groups, and other cultural events associated with Ireland and the Irish.

  EXHIBITS: Call to use research facilities.   **LOCATION:** On the campus of the University of St. Thomas, 2115 Summit Ave.   **HOURS:** 9–5.   **ADMISSION:** None, but donations appreciated.   **TELE-PHONE:** (612) 962-6040.

MINNESOTA STATE CAPITOL

As the United States expanded westward in the 19th century, itiner-ant congressmen, elected from different districts and sometimes different states, were not unusual. Still, even by the colorful standards of Irish politicians in that era, James Shields had a uniquely varied career. Fluent in four languages, he served as a U.S. army general, a state auditor, a state supreme court justice, and a U.S. senator from three different states.

Shields was a native of county Tyrone, where he had a privileged upbringing and received a classical education. He immigrated to the United States in 1826 at age 16 and was early attracted to life on the frontier. He settled in Kaskaskia, Illinois, where he qualified as a lawyer and became active in Democratic party politics. His first taste of military life came in 1832 when he participated in the Black Hawk War.

Shields set his sights on politics and was elected to the state legislature in 1836. He was later elected state auditor and then a state supreme court justice. It was at this point that he got into a violent quarrel with a young Whig politician named Abraham Lincoln and challenged the future presi-dent to a duel. Fortunately, tempers cooled and the two men eventually became close friends.

The Mexican War allowed Shields to indulge his taste for military life, and his political connections ensured his appointment as a brigadier gen-eral. Later promoted to major general, he returned a modest war hero and won his first term in the U.S. Senate, serving from 1849 to 1855.

Shields failed to win reelection, however, and moved to the new state of Minnesota. Purchasing an interest in the town site of Faribault in 1855, Shields set about organizing the first rural Irish colony in the United States. He laid out what would eventually become the town of Shieldsville, attracted seven men from St. Paul, and started boosting the colony.

According to Ann Regan, Shields enjoyed considerable success. By 1856, 460 Irish-born Catholics were living in and around Shieldsville, and a church (St. Patrick's, naturally) was erected to serve their spiritual needs. In 1857, Shields won a U.S. Senate seat from Minnesota, but he failed to win reelection after serving just three years.

The coming of the Civil War brought out the soldier in Shields again, and he had no trouble securing a brigade command from his old friend Lincoln. After a promising start, in which he inflicted a tactical defeat on the then-little-known Confederate Gen. Thomas J. "Stonewall" Jackson at Kernstown on March 23, 1862, Shields's Civil War career was mostly undistinguished. Jackson also got his revenge six weeks later, when he defeated Shields at Port Republic, Virginia.

Shields resigned the from the army a year later and moved to San Francisco, where he worked as a railroad executive. He returned east after the war and settled in Missouri, where he resumed his political career. He ran unsuccessfully for Congress, but was elected to fill an unexpired term in the U.S. Senate in 1879. He died only a few months after becoming the only man ever to represent three different states in the Senate.

• **EXHIBITS:** The statue of Shields was commissioned when the capitol building was constructed in 1905. Shieldsville still exists, and some of Shields's descendants still live there today. Carrollton, Missouri (*see* entry), also has a statue of Shields. Illinois erected a statue of Shields in Statuary Hall in the U.S. Capitol in Washington, where he represents that state along with one of his good friends, Abraham Lincoln (*see* Washington, D.C.) • **LOCATION:** Aurora and Constitution Avenues. The statue is in the second-floor rotunda. • **HOURS:** Monday–Friday 9–5; Saturday 10–4; Sunday 1–4. • **ADMISSION:** Free • **TELEPHONE:** (612) 296-2881.

UNIVERSITY OF ST. THOMAS

"You will not ever be without voices that preach to you prudence," Archbishop John Ireland once told an audience. "As for me, I prefer to speak to you about action."

Those two sentences sum up well Archbishop Ireland's outlook. In the late 19th century, American Catholics—who were overwhelmingly Irish—were still uncertain of their place in American society. The hierarchy thus tended to be conservative, both politically and socially. John Ireland, however, was a rebel.

When most clergymen, like their parishioners, identified with the Democratic party, Ireland was a power amongst the Republicans. At a time when few Catholic clergymen objected if their parishioners (or themselves) imbibed a bit, Ireland was a fiery scourge of the liquor trade. He was noted for his house-to-house tours in the Irish slums of St. Paul, sending whiskey bottles flying out of windows when he found them. He would routinely walk into bars and ask the bartender for a contribution, and then sit down at the bar and seek to convince the man to give up his profession of "making widows and orphans."

Stained-glass-window memorial to Archbishop John Ireland in St. James Church.

(University of St. Thomas, St. Paul, MN)

A famine immigrant, Ireland was born in Kilkenny in 1838. His father, Richard, was a carpenter who early on decided the crowded cities of the East were not for him. After landing in Boston, he settled first in Burlington, Vermont, and then in Chicago. He then made his way to the Irish settlement around Galena, Illinois, and, finally, he went up the Mississippi by steamboat to the booming new town of St. Paul in 1852.

John Ireland early showed an aptitude for the priesthood, arguing strenuously with the Presbyterian minister on his milk delivery route. This was noticed by the St. Paul bishop Joseph Cretin, who selected the 14-year-old for study in France, a sign of an exceptionally promising young man. The bishop's confidence was well placed. When John returned eight years later, he was ready to be ordained a priest. Fourteen years after that, at the remarkably young age of 37, he was bishop of St. Paul.

It was the Civil War that made Ireland a Republican. It had broken out while he was still abroad, and he argued fiercely with some of his seminarians who were pro-Confederate. Minnesota was the first state in the nation to offer its sons for the Union cause, and Ireland immediately volunteered as a chaplain to the 5th Minnesota Regiment. He served with distinction until a fever he contracted at Vicksburg forced him to muster out and return to St. Paul. Ireland was a prominent figure in the Grand Army of the Republic, the Union veterans organization, for the rest of his life.

Ireland's outstanding intellectual contribution to American Catholic life, however, came at the Third Plenary Council of the Catholic Church in America, which opened in Baltimore on November 10, 1884. Choosing "The Catholic Church and Civil Society" as his topic, Ireland took on an issue that would remain explosive right up until John F. Kennedy ran for president: could good Catholics, with their loyalty to the pope, also be good Americans?

"There is no conflict between the Catholic Church and America," he declared. "I could not utter one syllable that would belie, however remotely, either the church or the republic, and when I assert, as I now solemnly do, that the principles of the church are in thorough harmony with the interests of the Republic, I know in the depths of my soul that I speak the truth."

For Catholics raised in the European tradition, where the state was either an ally of the church or its militant opponent, this was revolutionary rhetoric. A state that was neutral in the matter of its citizens' religious beliefs was novel in the Catholic experience. Ireland's oration began the long process of making American Catholics, especially the Irish, part of the American "mainstream."

Ireland was not alone in being repelled by the slum conditions in which so many Irish-Americans lived in the middle to late 19th century. Col. John O'Neill (*see* O'Neill, Nebraska) and Father Hore (*see* Wexford, Iowa) also sought to resettle Irish immigrants on the land and away from the cities. John Ireland ultimately established nine colonies on the Minnesota prairies, securing the land with his own money. These include the present-day towns of De Graff, Clontarf, Avoca, and Graceville (*see* Graceville, Minnesota). The idea did not take hold among the mass of Irish-Americans, however, most of whom resolutely remained city dwellers.

Ireland generated controversy almost everywhere he turned, it seemed, both within the church and without. In 1889, for instance, he kicked over the hornet's nest of religious instruction in the public schools.

Ireland was seeking to save the members of his flock from the burden of paying a "double tax"—one to support the Protestant-oriented state school system and the other to the parish school, where most Catholics sent their children.

Ireland proposed a compromise. The state would pay for secular instruction at parochial schools in which religious instruction would be carried out by the denomination concerned. He actually arranged to give his idea a trial run in two school districts in Minnesota, but was blocked because of militant Protestant opposition and divided church opinion. He responded by founding more parish schools than ever, including the school that is now the University of St. Thomas.

And, always, there was politics. Ireland's Republicanism was always viewed with some suspicion by his fellow prelates. "Pray hard for the country," he wrote to his friend Cardinal Gibbons just before the latter was to give a blessing at the Democratic National Convention. "Not so much for the party."

And though his party affiliation was certainly genuine, the fact is there was no Democratic party to speak of in Minnesota at that time. If Ireland was to have any political influence in his home state, he had little choice but to work with the Republicans. He became friends with Presidents William McKinley and Theodore Roosevelt, even though he opposed the Spanish American War and the diplomacy surrounding the building of the Panama Canal.

Like another activist priest, Fr. Peter Yorke in California, Ireland's doctrinal orthodoxy was unquestioned, yet his outspokenness made him numerous enemies within as well as outside the church. Elevated to archbishop in 1889, he was several times conspicuously passed over for a cardinal's red hat. He died in 1918.

& EXHIBITS: A statue of Archbishop Ireland has recently been erected and stands in the center of the campus. & LOCATION: The University of St. Thomas is at 2115 Summit Ave. in St. Paul. & HOURS: Dawn to dusk. & ADMISSION: Free & TELEPHONE: University information: (612) 962-5000.

OHIO

WILLIAM MCKINLEY NATIONAL MEMORIAL

William McKinley, who served as president from 1896 to 1901, was not one of America's most distinguished chief executives. If he is remembered at all today, it is because he became the third president in 36 years to be murdered by an assassin. The event, which brought Theodore Roosevelt to the Oval Office at the early age of 41, brought about the assignment of the Secret Service as permanent bodyguards for the chief executive.

McKinley was one of nine American presidents of Irish origin through the direct paternal line. One biographer, perhaps fancifully, traces the president's origin to McDuff, thane of Fife, whom Shakespeare has brandish Macbeth's head on a pike. Whether or not this is true, the president was certainly of Scotch-Irish ancestry. His first recorded ancestor in county Antrim was James MacKinlay (as the name was then spelled), who went to Ireland with William III and fought on his side in the Battle of the Boyne in 1690.

The earliest immigrant to America was David McKinley, a son of James, who was known as "David the Weaver" and was the great-great-great-great grandfather of the president. He settled in York County, Pennsylvania, where he purchased 316 acres of land overlooking the Susquehanna River. There does not appear to be any truth to the story that an uncle of the president was hanged for participating in the 1798 uprising of Catholics and Presbyterians against British rule.

Like so many late 19th-century politicians, McKinley got his start in the Civil War, serving in the 23rd Ohio Regiment (under the command of the man who would be his presidential predecessor, Rutherford B. Hayes). After the war, McKinley parlayed his war service into a career in Congress

The McKinley ancestral home in county Antrim, Ireland. (Stark County Historical Society)

and two terms as Ohio's governor. When he ran for president in 1896, it was the last "front porch" campaign in American political history.

As president, McKinley preached fidelity to the sound money of the gold standard, a high protective tariff (to keep industrialists happy), and expansion abroad. After the battleship *Maine* exploded in Havana harbor in 1898 under mysterious circumstances, McKinley declared war on Spain. The United States annexed Puerto Rico and the Philippines as a result.

Early in his second term, McKinley was greeting visitors at the Pan-American Exposition in Buffalo when he was approached by a young man with a handkerchief wrapped around his hand. Leon Czolgosz, a deranged anarchist, fired two quick shots from a derringer pistol. McKinley dropped. Czolgosz was tackled by bystanders (including a huge Negro porter). He later confessed to the crime and was executed.

McKinley made few references to his Irish roots politically, although he was not ignorant of the power of the large Irish Catholic community. In 1899, he invited Cardinal James Gibbons to say a prayer of thanksgiving at a public event commemorating the Spanish-American War. It was one of the first occasions on which a Roman Catholic prelate was invited to officiate at such an event.

&. **EXHIBITS:** The 26-acre complex is dedicated to the memory of the 25th president. The tomb of McKinley, his wife, and his children are on the grounds. &. **LOCATION:** 800 McKinley Monument Dr., NW, off I-77, exit 106. &. **HOURS:** Monday–Saturday 9–7; Sunday noon–7, Memorial Day through Labor Day; Monday–Saturday 9–5; Sunday noon–5, rest of year. &. **ADMISSION:** Free &. **TELEPHONE:** (216) 455-7043.

SOMERSET

PHILLIP SHERIDAN STATUE

Civil War hero Gen. Phillip Sheridan wasn't sure where he was actually born. *The Biographical Register of Officers and Graduates of the United States Military Academy* accepts Albany, New York, as the most likely place, although in truth it could have been anywhere between his parent's homestead in county Cavan in Ireland and this little town in Ohio, where the future general spent his childhood. Some accounts have him being born in Ireland itself, while others say it was on an immigrant ship on the way over. Even his date of birth, March 6, 1831, is in dispute.

Sheridan himself seems not to have cared particularly much. He considered himself an American, and that, simply, was that. He was the third of six children born to John and Mary Meenagh Sheridan, second cousins who had been tenant farmers on the Cherrymount estate in Cavan before heading for the New World.

John Sheridan's uncle, Thomas Gainor, had preceded them, settling in the New York State capital of Albany. Gainor had urged the family to move to America, painting a rosy picture of life there. Upon arrival, the Sheridans learned the truth and discovered there was little work to be had in the city. They went to Ohio because John figured he could get work helping build the new National Road that was then threading its way westward.

John soon worked his way up from common laborer to subcontractor, making a modestly comfortable, but by no means affluent, living. Somerset, a crossroads town south of Columbus, was something of a Catholic colony, boasting the oldest Catholic church in Ohio, the Church of St. Joseph. A prominent Catholic family in the area was the Ewings, who had a foster son named William Tecumseh Sherman, though there is no evidence the two future generals ever met as boys.

Young Phil early showed an aptitude for things military. He worshiped the town's lone surviving revolutionary war veteran, and, using a small sword a local tinsmith had fashioned for him, Sheridan would drill the local boys. Too young to join in the Mexican War, he became a local authority on the war. Few were surprised when Sheridan, despite his diminutive stature, went off to West Point in 1848.

Sheridan struggled to survive at West Point. His awkward physical appearance, lack of money, and Irish Catholicism made him something of an outcast. Potato famine immigrants were tumbling off the boat down in New York City, a fact that did not sit well with many of his more patrician classmates. "Sheridan was not long off the boat himself—literally or figuratively," writes Roy Morris, Jr. in *Sheridan: The Life and Wars of*

General Phil Sheridan. "And it may have been that his bristling Irishness acted as a goad to certain cadets."

Sheridan's Irish temper very nearly ended his career before it started. On September 9, 1851, at the beginning of his senior year at West Point, Cadet Sgt. William Terrill of Virginia began to berate Sheridan during a parade. Unable to take any more, Sheridan screamed, "God damn you sir, I'll run you through!" and lunged at Terrill with a fixed bayonet. Although there were no injuries, it was a shocking breach of discipline, and Sheridan got the rather lenient punishment of one year's suspension. He went back to Somerset for nine months and then returned to finish his last year, graduating in the bottom half of his class (*see* Virginia, and Washington, D.C.).

⅋ **EXHIBITS:** A statue of Sheridan by Carl Heber stands in the center of the town. ⅋ **LOCATION:** Somerset is 43 miles southeast of Columbus at the intersection of Routes 668 and 22.

WEST VIRGINIA

HARPERS FERRY

NATIONAL HISTORIC PARK

It was George Washington himself who decided to place an armory at the settlement that stood at the confluence of the Potomac and Shenandoah rivers, reasoning that the swift-running waters would provide power for the machines to turn out weapons. Congress voted to establish it in 1794. Seven years later, Harpers Ferry Arsenal was turning out weapons for Lewis and Clark to take with them on the fabled expedition to the Far West.

But it was events of the night of October 16, 1859, that would make Harpers Ferry famous across the nation. The surrounding hills, which George Washington thought would make the area secure, also appealed to John Brown. A radical abolitionist, Brown thought that a raid on this federal installation, located in what was still the slave state of Virginia, would be the match that would touch off a nationwide slave revolt.

The plan, foolhardy from the beginning, began to unravel almost at once. The first victim of the 21 raiders (5 of them black) was Heywood Shepherd, a Negro freedman who was the railroad station's baggagemaster. He was cut down in a hail of nervous gunfire in the first few moments.

Instead of rallying to his cause, as he had hoped, the local townsfolk angrily turned on Brown, cornering the small force in the armory's firehouse. In the siege, two of Brown's own sons were killed, and he was forced to abandon his plan to escape into the hills. On October 18, a force of U.S. Marines, under the command of Lt. Col. Robert E. Lee and Lt. J. E. B. Stuart, arrived on the scene.

Concerned for the lives of the 13 hostages Brown and his men were holding inside the firehouse, Lee determined that any storming party should use bayonets rather than bullets. Early on the morning of October 18, Stuart approached the firehouse under a white flag. Brown refused to surrender. Stuart then gave the signal to the 12-man storming party to batter down the door.

A breach in the door was made. Brown and his men were in the process of reloading when the first marines stormed in. One of Brown's men fired and killed Pvt. Luke Quinn, a 19-year-old Irish immigrant. Two of the raiders were killed. John Brown lived to stand trial and rally the nation against slavery before he was hanged at nearby Charles Town.

Harpers Ferry was burned to the ground by retreating Union troops two years after the raid to prevent the armory's capture by the Confederacy. Private Quinn was the only fatality suffered by U.S. forces in the incident at Harpers Ferry. As a result, some consider this young Irish immigrant marine to have been the first military casualty of the Civil War.

🌤 EXHIBITS: The entire town is something of a museum of pre–Civil War history. The National Park Service has embarked on a years-long project to re-create the town's appearance of 1859. The John Brown Monument, which stands near the B & O Railroad Station, marks the original site of the firehouse where Brown and his followers made their stand. 🌤 LOCATION: Harpers Ferry is about 70 miles northwest of Washington, D.C., by way of I-270 and U.S. 240. 🌤 HOURS: Daily, 8–5. 🌤 ADMISSION: Free 🌤 TELEPHONE: (304) 535-6029.

PARKERSBURG

BLENNERHASSETT ISLAND AND BLENNERHASSETT MUSEUM

Aaron Burr. His name still conjures up debates among historians. Was he a villain, or a misunderstood hero? Whatever the verdict of history, it is clear that he usually brought grief upon those who became too closely involved with him. One of those who learned the hard way was Harmann Blennerhassett.

The son of Conway Blennerhassett, a wealthy Anglo-Irish landowner, Harmann was born in 1765 in England, where his parents were on a trip. He was educated at Trinity College, Dublin, and was called to the Irish bar in 1790.

It was while on a trip to revolutionary Paris soon afterward, however, that Harmann became infatuated with republican ideals. He was, by all accounts, a cultured man with a flair for music and an interest in science. He was gifted, noted one observer, "with all sorts of sense except common sense." Falling out with his father, Harmann married Margaret Agnew and set out for America in 1796.

The idyllic Blennerhassett Mansion. (Courtesy of Blennerhassett Museum)

Taking a large part of his patrimony, Blennerhassett purchased a 500-acre island in the Ohio River in what then was still the state of Virginia. In 1800, he built a magnificent mansion for himself, with furniture and artworks imported from London and Paris.

The estate was something close to idyllic. "Until I go to my grave, I must bear remembrance to the beautiful Blennerhassett . . . this paradise," wrote English actor John Bernard after visiting the estate in the early 1800s.

Blennerhassett's idyll didn't last long however, for former Vice-President Aaron Burr showed up in 1805, on the run from a murder indictment for killing Alexander Hamilton in a duel the year before. Burr's smooth talk and vague proposals about carving out a new empire in the American Southwest appealed to the impetuous Blennerhassett, who seems to have grown bored in his rural isolation. The two met several times, and Blennerhassett Island soon became a center for Burr's activities.

All this commotion soon attracted the attention of the local authorities, and the Virginia State Militia raided the island on December 11, 1806. Blennerhassett had gotten wind of the impending sweep and had fled the night before, leaving his mansion to be sacked and looted by the militiamen.

Arrested along with Burr for treason, Blennerhassett was never brought to trial after the government failed to convict Burr. Although now a free man, creditors had seized his estate, and he never returned to the island. He became a planter for a time in Mississippi, practiced law in Montreal, and ultimately returned to Europe, dying in 1831 on the island of Guernsey. Efforts by his wife to recover their property failed.

The last remains of the mansion were destroyed by fire in 1811. The island was thus abandoned until archaeologists discovered the original foundations in the 1970s. Working carefully from drawings and historical documents, the house was painstakingly reconstructed. It is today a state park.

&. **EXHIBITS:** Guided tours of the island, which is rich in wildlife, are available. Horse-drawn wagon rides are also offered. Picnic facilities and food are available. The museum contains exhibits and a 10-minute film on the Blennerhassetts and their island. &. **LOCATION:** Blennerhassett Island is reached by a stern wheeler that leaves from the dock at 2nd and Ann streets in Parkersburg. The Blennerhassett Museum is at 2nd and Juliana streets. &. **HOURS:** Island: Tuesday–Sunday 10–5:30 May 2– Labor Day; Saturday–Sunday 10–5:30 rest of year. Museum: Tuesday– Sunday 9:30–5:30 May 2 through November 1; Tuesday–Saturday 11–5; Sunday 1–5 November 2 through December 31; Saturday 11–5; Sunday 1– 5 rest of year. &. **ADMISSION:** Ferry fare: $4, children $3; Horse and carriage fare: $3, children $2; Mansion tour: $2, children $1; Museum: $2, children $1. &. **TELEPHONE:** (304) 428-3000 or 1-800-225-5982.

POINT PLEASANT

POINT PLEASANT MONUMENT STATE PARK

Westward expansion in the early 1770s was putting pressure on the Indians in what is now West Virginia, and raids and attacks on settlers were increasing. Lord Dunmore, the royal governor of Virginia, began organizing a force to attack the Indians in 1774.

Of course, Dunmore might have had ulterior motives for his action. Anti-British sentiment was coming to a boil in Virginia, and he no doubt hoped the Indian threat would distract attention from the growing political crisis. Some accounts have even suggested he encouraged the Indians to rebel for precisely this reason.

Commanding the force made up of men from Virginia's southwestern counties was Andrew Lewis, who had been born in Ireland around 1720. Lewis's father, John, was a tenant farmer possibly of Welsh or Anglo-Norman ancestry. In classic Irish style, John Lewis had a dispute with his landlord, in which he ended up killing the man. A fugitive on the run, he arrived in America around 1732 and established himself near present-day Staunton, Virginia, which he helped to found.

Andrew Lewis became one of the colony's leading citizens, serving as a justice of the peace and a member of the House of Burgesses. He was a friend of George Washington's and was captured with him at Ft. Necessity during the French and Indian War. While living along the frontier, he built up a considerable reputation as both an Indian fighter and as an emissary to the Indian tribes. He was instrumental in the negotiation of several treaties. So he was a natural to command the expedition.

Lewis and his 1,100 men left Camp Union (now Lewisburg, West Va.) and marched in 19 days to Point Pleasant, a distance of 160 miles. Here they were attacked by the Shawnee Chief Cornstalk and his allies and a daylong battle ensued.

The fight, according to almost all accounts, was among the bloodiest and most savage ever seen in the Indian Wars up until that time. Lewis directed his men with skill and great personal courage. At the end of the day, the Indians retreated, leaving nearly 200 of their dead on the battle-field. Eighty-one Virginians were dead and about 140 wounded.

The victory, however, secured the frontier against Indian attack for nearly four years and opened the way for further westward expansion. Lewis was commissioned a brigadier general in the Continental Army on March 1, 1776, which Lewis considered a snub, having been led by Washington to expect a major generalship. The commander had to use all the persuasive powers at his disposal to soothe his friend's feelings and get him back into action.

Lewis took command of the U.S. forces at Williamsburg and drove Gov. Dunmore from the colony. His army rank, however, still rankled him and he abruptly resigned his commission on April 15, 1777, allegedly because of ill-health. He continued to serve in the state militia and in Gov. Thomas Jefferson's executive council until his death in 1781.

❧ EXHIBITS: An 84–foot tall granite monument marks the battlefield, at the base of which is a statue of a typical Virginia frontiersman of the time.
❧ LOCATION: Point Pleasant, said to have been named by George Washington himself when he surveyed the area in the 1740s, sits at the junction of the Ohio and Kanawha Rivers at the end of S.R. 35. ❧ HOURS: Dawn to dusk. ❧ ADMISSION: Free ❧ TELEPHONE: (304) 675–3330.

W I S C O N S I N

OUTAGAMIE COUNTY COURT HOUSE

"A Republican with a Democrat name can't lose in this state" was the cynical advice supposedly offered by a lawyer from Wisconsin's North Country to a young colleague named Joseph Raymond McCarthy. Cynical or not, it must have been sound, for within just seven years, McCarthy would rise from this courthouse in rural Wisconsin to the U.S. Senate. Less than a decade after that, he would be nationally famous—and soon enough—infamous.

Few Irish-Americans have had so profound an impact on American political life as Joseph McCarthy. His very name has been incorporated into the language—McCarthyism. The passions he aroused and the controversy that continues to surround him can still flare into arguments. His notoriety, however, has tended to obscure both his background and his early career, which was in many ways typical of Irish-American politicians.

McCarthy was born in Grand Chute, Wisconsin, in 1908. The area where he grew up was locally dubbed "the Irish settlement" because it was an island of Irish farmers in an area heavily populated by Germans and Swedes. McCarthy was three-quarters Irish. His mother, Bridget (Tierney) McCarthy was born in Ireland. His father, Timothy, had an Irish father and a German mother. Joseph was the fifth of seven children.

A youth of hard work on the farm convinced Joe he would not be happy as a farmer. He quit school at 14 and knocked around for awhile. Then, six years later, almost inexplicably, he suddenly returned to school and qualified for his high school diploma in only a year. He then worked his way through college and law school at the Jesuit-run Marquette College and qualified as a lawyer.

McCarthy was not a very good lawyer, and he dabbled in Democratic politics on the side. He ran unsuccessfully for district attorney in 1936, and then, three years later, another lawyer casually mentioned that he might run for a circuit court judgeship. In true sharp-elbows style, McCarthy himself declared for the seat the very next day.

McCarthy's first campaign set the tone for the rest of his political career. He ran a take-no-prisoners campaign against an aging incumbent, promising to clear the docket of backlogged cases, and made the first of many unsubstantiated charges. Nevertheless, he won.

The Outagamie Court House was McCarthy's base of operations during his period on the 10th Circuit Court. For all the outrageousness of the campaign, McCarthy kept his promise to clear the docket and he became well known for the speed of his trials, particularly divorces. He also continued to cut corners ethically, and in one case was censured by the state supreme court.

World War II provided McCarthy with the political break he was looking for. When another Wisconsin politician joined the navy, McCarthy joined the marine corps, because he thought it sounded more macho. Assigned to the South Pacific as the intelligence officer for an air squadron, McCarthy never heard a shot fired in anger. Nevertheless, he became famous as "Tail Gunner Joe" (sometimes campaigning in his marine corps uniform), and, this time running as a Republican, he won his Senate seat in 1946.

For four years, McCarthy served in relative obscurity. Then, looking for an issue on which to run for reelection in 1952, someone suggested to him communism. A young California congressman named Richard Nixon had won national fame as the pursuer of Alger Hiss, the State Department official who was convicted of perjury for denying he was a Soviet spy. It probably looked good to McCarthy, and the result was what became known as "the Wheeling speech" (for Wheeling, West Virginia, where it was delivered).

"I have in my hand a list of 205," McCarthy declaimed dramatically. "A list of names that were made known to the Secretary of State as being members of the Communist Party and who nevertheless are still working and shaping policy in the State Department."

Instead of doing what they ought to have done, which was ignore McCarthy and his charges, the Senate Democrats thought they could expose and ridicule him by undertaking an investigation. They did not reckon with McCarthy's natural instinct for theater.

William V. Shannon, in his excellent study *The American Irish* (1971), points out that only a roguish Irish-American politician like McCarthy could have carried off the show that unfolded over the next four years. "Where a more cautious man would have taken care not to overextend himself and would have embellished a central lie with edgings of fact, McCarthy, boldly and recklessly, followed one sweeping assertion with another still more breathtaking," Shannon said. "When disaster confronted him in the shape of a denial or convincing refutation, he responded lightheartedly, waggishly, almost frolicsomely, with some fresh invention or wild diversion."

How could the public have been so easily bewitched? McCarthy had several things going for him in addition to his own inventiveness. The fresh memory of the Alger Hiss case and the outbreak of the Korean War just a few months after the Wheeling speech made it seem plausible that there was treason in high places. McCarthy's earthy, sometimes crude personal manner may not have endeared him to the nation's elite but marked him out as a "regular guy" among the masses.

Irish-Americans were an important, though by no means exclusive, base of support for McCarthy. Polls consistently showed that self-described Catholics, of whom Irish-Americans were a very large part, had the most favorable view of McCarthy, while Jews had the least favorable.

Why? Clearly, many Irish-Americans viewed McCarthy, with his humble origins and rough-hewn image, as "one of us." Few Irish Catholics were represented in the upper ranks of the State Department or any of the other institutions McCarthy attacked. Pope Pius XII made anticommunism a hallmark of his papacy, thus lending a certain ecclesiastical legitimacy, in the eyes of many, to McCarthy's crusade.

In the end, of course, McCarthy went too far and took on the U.S. Army, an institution many ordinary Americans could indeed identify with. When he finally questioned the loyalty of a young associate of the counsel defending the army, Joseph Welch, the latter responded with his famous "at long last sir, have you no decency?" The televised hearings revealed his charges to be baseless and he was censured by the Senate. Although he sought to revive his crusade, his credibility was gone. McCarthy died, a broken man, on May 2, 1957.

Even after much of the country turned against him, however, many Appleton residents still recalled him fondly. A bust was commissioned and stands today in the courthouse where he once presided. Occasionally, the bust becomes a local political hot potato, with some residents petitioning for its removal. Even in death, Joseph Raymond McCarthy still stirs controversy.

❧ **EXHIBITS:** A bust of Senator McCarthy stands just outside the county clerk's office. He is buried in St. Mary's Cemetery, beneath a headstone bearing his name, relevant dates, and the simple inscription "United States Senator." ❧ **LOCATION:** The county courthouse is located at 320 S. Walnut in the center of Appleton. St. Mary's Cemetery is at 317 E. College St. ❧ **HOURS:** Courthouse open 8:30–6 Monday–Friday. The cemetery

is open during daylight hours seven days a week. ❧ **ADMISSION:** Free
❧ **TELEPHONE:** (414) 832-5131.

ERIN PRAIRIE

ST. PATRICK'S CHURCH

"In rural America," writes Margaret Fitzgerald and Joseph King in *The Uncounted Irish*, "the Irish were quieter than their big city kinsmen, but the fact of their pervasive presence is evident in the churches, the hospitals, the schools, the universities, the communities with distinctively Irish aspects, all over the rural West."

Erin Prairie on the plains of western Wisconsin is one such place. The Irish first arrived in this remote corner of Wisconsin before 1850, according to Fitzgerald and King By 1870, according to the U.S. Bureau of the Census, there were more than 200 Irish-born farmers in Erin Prairie alone. The first Irish in this area were fur traders. They were followed, in the 1840s, by lead miners, then railroaders and farmers.

Irish settlers had been in this area for several years before St. Patrick's Parish was organized in 1857. (Erin Prairie was recognized as the name of the area in 1853.) Priests said the first masses in the homes of parishioners. The building of a log church commenced in 1857, but was never completed. In 1860, a parishioner donated two acres of land, and a wood frame church was constructed on the site of the present structure. A permanent structure went up in 1869. The current structure was built in 1914.

❧ **LOCATION:** The church is located on County Trunk Road "G," approximately 9 miles east of New Richmond, Wisconsin. ❧ **HOURS:** Call to see interior. ❧ **ADMISSION:** None, but donations appreciated.
❧ **TELEPHONE:** (715) 796-2244.

IOWA

MISSOURI

NEBRASKA

OKLAHOMA

SOUTH DAKOTA

TEXAS

The Texas School Book Depository ca. 1963. See page 417. (Squire Haskins Photography)

GREAT PLAINS

IOWA
1　Robert Emmet Statue, Emmetsburg
2　Franklin County Historical Society, Hampton
3　Sullivan Park, Waterloo
4　Church of the Immaculate Conception, Wexford
5　John Wayne Birthplace, Winterset

MISSOURI
6　James Shields Statue and Gravesite, Carrollton
7　James Pendergast Statue, Kansas City
8　Battle of Lexington State Historic Site, Lexington
9　Mulanphy Park, St. Louis
10　O'Fallon St., St. Louis
11　Mark Twain National Forest/Irish Wilderness, Oregon County

NEBRASKA
12　Boys' Town, Omaha
13　Union Pacific Railroad Museum, Omaha
14　Holt County Historical Society, O'Neill

OKLAHOMA
15　The Murray-Lindsay Mansion, Lindsay

16　An Irish Town, Shamrock
17　Choctaw Nation Museum, Tuskahoma

SOUTH DAKOTA
18　Holy Rosary Mission, Pine Ridge

TEXAS
19　Irish Cultural House, Corpus Christi
20　The Sixth Floor, Dallas
21　Goliad State Historical Park, Goliad
22　Walworth Library/Audie Murphy Room, Greenville
23　San Jacinto Battleground State Historic Park, Houston
24　Fr. Miguel Muldoon Memorial, La Grange
25　Refugio County Museum, Refugio
26　Sabine Pass Battleground State Historic Park, Sabine Pass
27　The Alamo, San Antonio
28　Old San Patricio Court House, San Patricio
29　An Irish Town, Shamrock

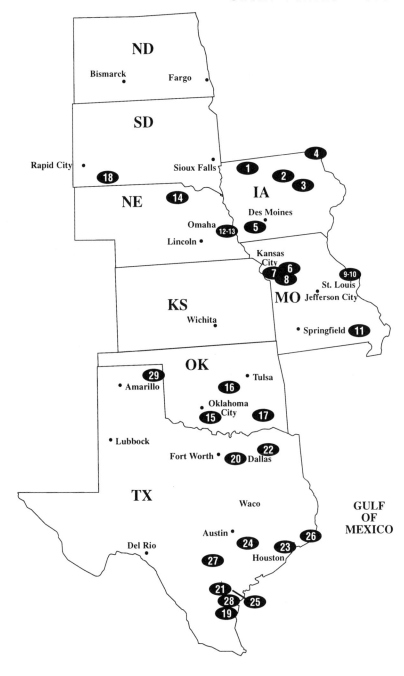

I O W A

ROBERT EMMET STATUE

Iowa is generally thought of as an Anglo-Saxon state in its ethnic makeup, and, indeed, in most census surveys, German and English come in first and second when people are asked to name their ancestry. A surprising third, however, are the Irish. In fact, Iowa ranks 11th among the states with the largest percentage of people claiming Irish ancestry.

Many individual Irish found their way onto the Great Plains in the migration that took place in the mid-19th century. Sometimes, however, the Irish migrated in groups, founding colonies on the vastness of the prairies. On the treeless plains, they were exposed to howling winds and snow in winter and broiling heat and the danger of tornados in summer. Many settlers described it as living on a "land ocean," exposed to the elements with nowhere to run if trouble struck.

What drove the Irish to abandon the eastern cities and risk life in such an environment? Some were repelled by the squalid conditions in which so many Irish immigrants lived in New York and Boston. Others wanted to escape the violence and brutality of the anti-immigrant Know-Nothing party, whose power rose along with the numbers of Irish immigrants in the 1850s. By 1880, Iowa had 44,061 Irish-born inhabitants.

An Irish colony was established in the area of Emmetsburg in north-west-central Iowa in 1856, and the town was incorporated two years later. It was one of several Irish settlements in the state, along with Wexford (*see* entry farther on). The town was named for Robert Emmet, the Irish Protestant patriot who played a small role in the 1798 uprising that sought to force Catholics and Protestants into a common Irish identity. Emmet was subsequently hanged by the British in 1803 for acts against the United Kingdom.

Emmetsburg was a center of Irish culture in Iowa for many years. The Ancient Order of Hibernians had an active division in the town that organized the annual St. Patrick's Day celebrations. But as the number of Irish-born settlers dwindled, so did enthusiasm for continuing the celebrations. During the hard years of the 1930s, they stopped altogether.

Then, in 1961, some local residents revived the St. Patrick's Day festivities. It is now a four-day celebration, presided over by an illustrious Irish politician brought to town for the occasion. In 1993, the guest dignitary was Gerard Collins, former minister for foreign affairs of the Irish Republic.

The statue of Robert Emmet that stands in the courthouse square of Emmetsburg has a colorful history. It is one of four that were cast from the same mold by Irish-born sculptor Jerome Connor. The other three are in Dublin, Washington, D.C. (*see* entry) and San Francisco (*see* entry).

Although the statue was delivered in 1919, disputes among the townspeople as to where it should be placed prevented it from being erected. So it spent most of its early existence in the basement of the town grocery store. The store owner, tired of the space it was taking up, sold the statue in the late 1930s to an Ancient Order of Hibernians chapter in Minnesota.

Emmetsburg, however, did not entirely forget about the statue, and interest in its fate revived when the town celebrated its centennial in 1958. A group of townspeople sought to negotiate for the statue's return to Iowa. Unable to come to terms with the Minnesotans, however, several residents simply stole the statue back. This time, there was no debate about placement. It was cemented down firmly in front of the county courthouse, where it remains today. A $10,000 restoration job was recently completed.

❧ **EXHIBITS:** The life-sized bronze statue of Robert Emmet, his hand outstretched in sorrow and appeal, stands before the county courthouse in the center of town. ❧ **LOCATION:** Emmetsburg is the seat of Palo Alto County in northwest-central Iowa. U.S. 18 runs through the center of town. ❧ **HOURS:** Dawn to dusk. ❧ **ADMISSION:** Free ❧ **TELEPHONE:** St. Patrick's Association: (712) 852-4326.

HAMPTON

FRANKLIN COUNTY HISTORICAL SOCIETY

Adm. William D. Leahy never went to sea in a combat command during the Second World War. Like his army counterpart, George C. Marshall, his wartime lot was to fill critical diplomatic and staff roles in Washington and abroad. In 1944, Pres. Franklin D. Roosevelt rewarded

Leahy for his services by promoting him to the five-star rank of fleet admiral, one of only 10 officers so honored in American history.

Leahy was born in this small town in Iowa (it was even smaller then) on May 6, 1875. His father, Michael Leahy, was a local lawyer who had served as a captain in a Wisconsin regiment during the Civil War. His paternal grandparents, Daniel and Mary (Egan) Leahy, emigrated from Ireland around 1836. Although the details are hazy, it seems likely that the admiral's father went west to Wisconsin and then to Iowa, where isolated Irish colonies had been established on the vast plains of these two states generally thought of as primarily German in their ethnic makeup.

Young William graduated from the Naval Academy in 1897 and promptly saw action in the Spanish-American War the next year. He held various administrative and sea commands before (apparently) climaxing his career with appointment to the navy's top job, chief of naval operations, in 1937. In that post, he supervised the massive naval rearmament program that President Roosevelt began in 1938.

Admiral Leahy retired from active duty in 1939, but President Roosevelt had taken a liking to him and appointed him governor of Puerto Rico, where he was generally popular as a conservative but open-minded administrator. After barely a year in that post, however, Roosevelt dispatched him on the extremely delicate task of U.S. ambassador to the Vichy French regime of Marshal Pétain. He managed to prevent Pétain from actively joining the Germans in their war effort, but he could achieve little else and returned home in 1941.

Leahy spent the rest of the war in the White House, functioning as Roosevelt's liaison with the armed forces and functioning as de facto chairman of the Joint Chiefs of Staff, a position that was not formally created until after the war.

Leahy visited this, his hometown, during the war. He was in Hampton visiting relatives and old friends on June 6, 1944, when the news broke of the Normandy invasion. What Leahy was hoping would be a quiet, sentimental journey became a very raucous one indeed.

✦ **EXHIBITS:** The museum contains photographs and personal memorabilia of Admiral Leahy. The Leahy birthplace was torn down in the 1970s. ✦ **LOCATION:** The Franklin County Historical Society is located on the county fairgrounds west of Hampton, on Highway 3 West. ✦ **HOURS:** During the summer, the museum is open Saturdays and Sundays 1–4; other times by appointment. ✦ **ADMISSION:** Free ✦ **TELEPHONE:** Hampton Chamber of Commerce (515) 456-5668.

WATERLOO

SULLIVAN PARK

Neither the U.S Navy nor their parents were happy when the five Sullivan brothers of Waterloo, Iowa, wanted to serve together aboard the cruiser U.S.S. *Juneau* early in 1942. The chances of an entire family being wiped out in a single disaster were too great.

The navy, however, was not blind to the morale-boosting possibilities of five brothers from an ethnic family in the American heartland serving together on the same ship. As for their parents, the brothers insisted they would fight as a unit, and, if necessary, they would die as a unit. Unfortunately, in one of the most publicized tragedies of the Second World War, that is exactly what happened.

Thomas Sullivan, the boys' father, was born in Harpers Ferry, Iowa, near the Wexford settlement (*see* next entry). His parents were emigrants from county Cork, and Tom ran away at age 16, chasing his childhood dream of becoming a cowboy. After swallowing enough cow dust to convince him it was not what he wanted, he went mining in Colorado before returning to Iowa to work on the Illinois Central Railroad.

In 1914, he married Alleta Abel, the daughter of a co-worker. Alleta was mostly of Irish ancestry, although she had some Scottish blood and one of her grandfathers was Jewish. "The household was typically Irish," writes Dan Kurzman in his history of the *Juneau* disaster, *Left to Die* (1994). "harboring all the joys and sins that eternally blessed or plagued Irish life anywhere."

The marriage produced five sons—George, Frank, Joseph (Red), Madison (Matt), and Albert—and a daughter, Genevieve. The eldest, George, became quite an accomplished amateur boxer, predictably earning the nickname "John L." All the children went to St. Mary's Catholic School, which still stands in Waterloo. Kurzman recounts the family took pride in its heritage, with the boys often signing "Danny Boy" and "When Irish Eyes are Smilin'" during their summer jaunts in the countryside around Waterloo.

The Depression hit hard in the farm belt, and George and Frank both joined the navy in 1937. On the day Pearl Harbor was attacked, the two elder brothers were home in Waterloo on Christmas leave. Their three brothers immediately decided to follow and join the navy too. "Well, I guess our minds are made up, aren't they fellows," George said. "And when we go in, we want to go in together. And if worse comes to worst, we'll all go down together."

The navy was reluctant, however. The five brothers walked into a recruiting station, marched straight up to an officer, and asked if he could promise they would all serve on the same ship together. If he could not,

The five Sullivan brothers, from left: Joseph (Red), Francis (Frank), Albert, Madison (Matt), and George. (Waterloo Courier)

they said, they would not enlist voluntarily. The officer was astounded, for it was apparently unprecedented for five brothers to serve together on the same ship. Navy policy was to split up families, so that if a ship went down, no more than one family member would be among the casualties.

The policy, however, had often been honored in the breach in the past, and the navy decided to bend its rules in the case of the four oldest boys, who were still bachelors. The youngest, Albert, however, was newly married with a baby son and thus exempt from service. More fist-pounding and letter writing followed, and the navy relented. Five brothers on the same ship would be great headlines and a powerful recruiting tool.

Just before leaving Iowa, however, the family heard that a neighborhood boy, Bill Ball, who was serving with his brother aboard the battleship *Arizona,* had been killed at Pearl Harbor. His brother was wounded.

The Sullivans' ship turned out to be the U.S.S. *Juneau,* a brand-new light cruiser just off the ways at the Brooklyn Navy Yard. Dispatched to the South Pacific in September 1942, the ship was to support the operations of the First Marine Division, which was then battling in a life-or-death struggle with the Japanese for possession of a spit of land called Guadalcanal.

November 13, 1942, was Friday the thirteenth, and there were 13 ships in Adm. Daniel Callaghan's task group that night, including the *Juneau.* These unlucky facts were not lost on many of the men aboard the American task force. Callaghan (*see* San Francisco, California) was a desk jockey who should not have been in command. Vice Adm. Norman Scott, his subordinate, had defeated the Japanese in a night battle a month earlier and was the ideal choice for the top job. But navy politics had won the day, and Callaghan—an Irish-American and former naval aide to Pres. Franklin D. Roosevelt—was in charge when the Japanese fleet came into sight.

A veteran later described the Battle of Friday the Thirteenth as "a barroom fight with the lights out." Admiral Callaghan might have improved the odds had he fired immediately upon sighting the unfamiliar Japanese ships in the distance, but he held back, waiting to be sure of his identification. Once the firing began, however, confusion reigned. The *San Francisco* hit the *Atlanta,* thinking it a Japanese vessel. The *Juneau* was badly hurt but still afloat when she pulled away from the combat zone later that night.

As the remnants of the U.S. fleet made their way back to base, however, a lurking Japanese submarine pumped a torpedo into the battered *Juneau,* causing the ship to explode, break in two, and sink almost immediately. Perhaps 140 of the ship's 700 crewmen ended up in the water, clinging to debris. Task force commander Capt. Gilbert Hoover, succeeding the dead Callaghan, made the decision not to risk the remains of his force in a search for survivors. While perhaps prudent under the circumstances, that decision led to his disgrace.

Now the ordeal of the *Juneau* survivors began. Attacked by sharks and maddened by thirst and the relentless tropical sun, the number of surviving men steadily dwindled. Even though several planes overflew the area of the sinking and reported the presence of survivors, no one back at base gave mounting a rescue effort a high priority. Even after Adm. William "Bull" Halsey himself ordered the men rescued, the response was oddly lethargic. Nearly a week after the sinking, only 10 men were still alive to tell the story of the final, harrowing days of the *Juneau's* crew.

And the Sullivan brothers? George and Albert were among the initial group of survivors, and although some witnesses claim that Joseph and Matt were also in the rafts at the beginning, this cannot be confirmed. George, the eldest, was also the last of the quintet to die. He spent days slipping in and out of hallucinations, pathetically calling out for his brothers before mindlessly leaping into the water to his doom.

In the wake of the disaster, the navy decided to hold firm to its policy of not allowing brothers to serve aboard the same vessel. Hollywood contributed to the legend with a (fairly mediocre) film, *The Fighting Sullivans.*

❧ **Exhibits:** The memorial in Sullivan Park consists of five anchors, commemorating the five brothers. There is also an exhibit on the brothers in the lobby of the convention center. ❧ **Location:** Sullivan Park is located in the neighborhood where the boys grew up, indeed, on the site of their boyhood home, which has since been torn down. The park is at E. 4th and Adams Streets. The Five Sullivan Brothers Convention Center is at W. 4th and Commercial. ❧ **Hours:** Park is open dawn to dusk. Call for convention center hours. ❧ **Admission:** Free ❧ **Telephone:** Waterloo Chamber of Commerce: (319) 233-8431.

WEXFORD

CHURCH OF THE IMMACULATE CONCEPTION

Refugees from the Great Hunger of the 1840s—a result of the 1845 potato crop failure—found their way to unlikely parts of the United States, such as this one in the far northeastern corner of Iowa. Here, Fr. Thomas Hore, a native of county Wexford, founded an Irish colony and named it after his native county in Ireland.

These, however, had to be sold to pay rent to English landlords in order to prevent eviction. As a result, there was great starvation and emigration, mostly to America. (*See* Boston, Massachusetts).

Hore went to the United States for the first time in 1820, when he was 24 years old and a newly ordained priest assigned to the diocese of Richmond, Virginia. After six years, however, his health began failing and he returned to Ireland. There, he recovered and embarked on a crusade of building new churches and founding new parishes. He probably did not expect ever to see America again, but then, he did not expect the potato blight that began in 1845 either.

At first, Wexford was not hard hit by the famine. Its economy did not depend on the potato and continued to produce good crops of grain, pork, and dairy products. But as the deadly disease roamed the soil in the rest of the country, Wexford soon began to feel the desperation of the rest of the country, as refugees began making their way toward the coasts looking to emigrate.

Emigration was neither cheap nor easy. The passage money to get aboard a ship was often more than most families could afford. And then there were departure taxes that the British administration levied on all emigrants. And all this took place before the hazards of the voyage itself and the uncertain reception awaiting them in their new country.

The Church of the Immaculate Conception, built of native stone, is located in the Parish of Wexford, and was founded in 1851 by Father Thomas Hore.

Father Hore witnessed all these hardships and was determined to do something, according to Margaret Fitzgerald and Joseph King in *The Uncounted Irish* (1990). He began contacting old friends still in America about organizing an emigration.

The first choice was Arkansas, where Father Hore had a friend in Bishop Andrew Byrne. In November 1850, Hore and 450 colonists sailed for New Orleans aboard the *Ticonderoga*. After five weeks, the group landed and then boarded a steamboat to take them upriver to Arkansas. Unfortunately, Arkansas had no land to spare for the immigrants. After a month, they reboarded a steamship, this time for St. Louis, where they waited while Hore scouted another possible location, this time in Iowa.

Fortunately, Father Hore found a sympathetic ear in Bishop Loras of Dubuque, who directed him to Allamakee County. There, Hore was able to obtain 3,000 acres cheaply. Unfortunately, by the time he returned to St. Louis, only a dozen or so families were still willing to accompany him, the rest opting to stay in the city or emigrate farther west to the goldfields of California. Undaunted, Hore brought his diminished flock to the banks of the upper Mississippi in March 1851, where they founded a colony and named it, unsurprisingly, Wexford.

Following a custom said to be common in Wexford, the new settlers named their church after the feast day of the saint on which it was founded.

Since that day happened to be April 23, 1851, this Irish church was given the unlikely name of St. George's, England's patron saint.

The name must not have been very popular, however. When a new church was built on the same site in 1870, it was rechristened the Church of the Immaculate Conception.

Father Hore stayed in Iowa six more years, founding churches and parishes throughout the area, just as he had done in Ireland. He left in 1857, fulfilling a lifelong wish to visit Rome and the Holy Land. Afterward, he returned to Wexford, Ireland, where he died in 1864.

&& **EXHIBITS:** A stained glass window, donated by the original settlers, is dedicated to Father Hore. && **LOCATION:** The church is located between the towns of Harpers Ferry and Lansing on Route X52, which runs along the Mississippi River. The church is about 8 miles south of Lansing and 5 miles north of Harpers Ferry. && **HOURS:** Variable. Call to see the interior. && **ADMISSION:** None, but donations appreciated. && **TELEPHONE:** (319) 586-2150.

WINTERSET

JOHN WAYNE BIRTHPLACE

For western movie fans the scene is unforgettable. The man appears in the distance before the approaching stagecoach. The camera is unfocused, and the figure, indistinct, is twirling a rifle over his head. Then, suddenly, in the very next shot, he fills the screen, head and shoulders, in sharp, clear focus. John Wayne, a.k.a. the Duke, makes his dramatic entrance as the Ringo Kid in the 1939 John Ford classic *Stagecoach.*

Stagecoach was not Wayne's first starring role, but it was the film that definitively lifted him out of the muck of B movies and bit parts that he had played throughout the 1930s. He made the most of it. The character of Ringo—the strong, independent, broad-shouldered, and quintessentially American hero—would become Wayne's hallmark. It set him on a 50-year career as one of the most consistently bankable stars in Hollywood history. His films grossed a total of more than $800 million, which, in constant dollars, remains a record for any star.

Wayne was mostly Scotch-Irish on his father's side and English Irish on his mother's. He was born in Winterset on May 26, 1907.

Wayne's great-great grandfather, Robert Morrison, was born November 29, 1782, in county Antrim, the son of John and Nancy de Scrogges Morrison. Robert was involved with the United Irishmen in the 1798 uprising (*See* Emmetsburg, Iowa) and made tracks for the New World after the rebellion failed. The family was involved mostly in farming, both

John Wayne (pictured with costar Clair Trevor) as the Ringo Kid, the role that propelled him to stardom in John Ford's Stagecoach (1930). (Museum of Modern Art)

in Ohio and Iowa. Clyde Leonard Morrison, Duke's father, was born in 1884. His mother, Mary Alberta (Molly) Brown, was of English and Irish ancestry (her father, Robert Emmet Brown, was named for the Irish revolutionary hero of 1803). She and Clyde were married in 1905.

The couple settled in Winterset, where Clyde worked as a pharmacy clerk. (Winterset was also used as the location for Norman Lear's 1971 comedy *Cold Turkey,* which has some excellent shots of the courthouse square. It is also the seat of Madison County, which is known for its covered bridges and is the setting for the best-selling 1993 novel *The Bridges of Madison County.*)

The future actor's boyhood was not happy. His father was shy and retiring by nature, while his mother was almost the stereotype of the Irish mother from hell that Maureen O'Hara satirized so splendidly in the film *Only the Lonely.* The couple quarreled a great deal, but there seems to be little doubt as to who ruled the household. Young Marion, who was nicknamed Duke after a big dog that he owned as a boy, frequently ran away from home.

Wayne always told interviewers that the family moved to California in 1914 because his father was in poor health. That seems to have been a cover story, for the fact is Clyde's drugstore in Iowa was failing and he badly needed a fresh start. The family settled on some land near the Mojave Desert and tried to make a go of farming again, but without much success.

Duke grew into a tall, strong young man. A football scholarship sent him to the University of Southern California, which he attended for two years until a shoulder injury ended his athletic career. While in college, he worked part-time in the prop department at Fox Studios, where he first met John Ford. The director took a shine to the brawny young man and put him in a few minor (*very* minor) roles in some of his early silent films. Wayne's first screen appearance, interestingly, had an Irish theme: *Hangman's House* (1928), which starred another Ford favorite, Victor McLaglen.

But Wayne didn't stay with Ford long. Raoul Walsh needed a star for a big western epic called *The Big Trail* he was making for the then-staggering sum of $3 million. Legend has it that Walsh spotted Wayne moving props on the Fox lot and offered him the role on the spot. Whatever the truth, Marion Morrison was clearly unsuitable as the moniker of a star and he was rechristened "John Wayne." The "Wayne" was after General "Mad Anthony" Wayne of revolutionary war fame, and "John" was chosen simply because, unlike Marion, it was a good, solid, masculine American name.

The new name did nothing to help the movie, however. *The Big Trail* flopped badly. As the Great Depression set in, Wayne went on to increasingly minor action films and westerns with ever less prestigious studios.

Wayne and Ford, however, continued to dance a cautious minuet, the latter never quite sure of Wayne's drawing power as a star. He was also suspicious of Wayne's loyalty; the director was very much a dictator who demanded unquestioned fealty from those who worked for him. Wayne's decision to make *The Big Trail* put him in Ford's doghouse for a decade.

Ford, however, had bought the rights to a short story called *Stagecoach to Lordsburg* and knew it had big potential as a movie. He had Wayne in mind for the lead role of the Ringo Kid and let Wayne know it. Ford kept Wayne on tenterhooks for several months, however, not only because the director wanted to keep Wayne in suspense, but also because he could not convince a studio to make a movie with an unproven star. Once Ford got the backing, however, neither he nor his star ever looked back.

In 14 more films, the men worked together and made motion picture history. *She Wore a Yellow Ribbon* (1949), *The Quiet Man* (1952), *The*

Searchers (1956), and *The Man Who Shot Liberty Valance* (1962) were among the greatest. Wayne also made great films without Ford. *Red River* (1948) and *Rio Bravo* (1958), both directed by Howard Hawks, were among his best performances. His image as the two-fisted American patriot was cemented by such war films as *The Fighting Seabees* (1944), *They Were Expendable* (1945), and *The Sands of Iwo Jima* (1949).

Wayne's courage was not merely cinematic. He had a cancerous lung removed in 1963 and had open-heart surgery in 1978. In 1979, however, the cancer flared up again, and this time he could fight no longer. A special congressional medal was struck in his honor, but a more intriguing remembrance was provided by the crowds of Americans who protested the taking of U.S. diplomats hostage in Tehran in November of that year. Mocking what they viewed as the docility of the Carter administration, many carried posters bearing the likeness of the just-deceased star.

It became chic among film critics to denigrate Wayne's acting ability, completely missing the point that he was such a good actor that he made it look easy. He also matured into a competent, if unspectacular, director. While his characters were rarely explicitly Irish, Irish-Americans certainly viewed him as one of their own. His strong, independent, yet charming demeanor—especially in *The Quiet Man*—came for many to symbolize the assimilated, yet still ethnically identifiable, first-generation Irish-American.

❧ **EXHIBITS:** Two of the four rooms in the house have been restored to their 1907 condition. Photographs and memorabilia are on display. ❧ **LOCATION:** 224 S. 2nd St. ❧ **HOURS:** Daily 10–5. ❧ **ADMISSION:** $2; seniors $1.75. ❧ **TELEPHONE:** (512) 462-1044.

MISSOURI

JAMES SHIELDS STATUE AND
GRAVE SITE

James Shields was a man who certainly got around. Born in county Tyrone in 1810, he was the only man in history to serve as a U.S. senator from three different states (Illinois, Minnesota, and Missouri). In addition, he also served as governor of the Oregon Territory and as a general in the U.S. Army in the Mexican and Civil Wars and had a business career in California (*see* Minneapolis, Minnesota and Washington, D.C.)

Shields migrated to Missouri in 1866. His Civil War career had started with great promise. On March 23, 1862, at the First Battle of Kernstown (Virginia), Shields became the only Union commander to inflict a defeat on the Confederate general Thomas J. "Stonewall" Jackson. Jackson, however, learned from his mistake and didn't make it again. Six weeks later, at Port Republic, Jackson sent Shields's troops in full flight from the field.

Shields resigned from the army in 1863 and went to California, where he held a railroad post. When he moved back east, he settled in Missouri and resumed his political activity. He ran unsuccessfully for Congress in 1872 and was elected to fill an unexpired term in the U.S. Senate in 1879. He died while on a speaking tour in Ottumwa, Iowa, after holding office for only two months.

🍎 **EXHIBITS:** The statue of Shields, by Frederick Cleveland Hibbard, was unveiled in 1914. There is also a bust of Shields over his grave site. 🍎 **LOCATION:** The seat of Carroll County, Carrollton is at the intersection of U.S. 65 and U.S. 24 in central Missouri. The statue of Shields stands on the east lawn of the Carroll County Courthouse in the center of town. He is buried in St. Mary's Cemetery, which is on the west side of U.S. 65 heading north, about a mile out of Carrollton. 🍎 **HOURS:** Dawn to dusk. 🍎 **ADMISSION:** Free

KANSAS CITY

JAMES PENDERGAST STATUE

"That's all there is to this boss business, friends," explained James Pendergast to The *New York Times* in what is probably the most succinct job description of an Irish political boss ever given. "You can't make 'em vote for you. I never coerced anybody in my life. Whenever you see a man bulldozing anybody, he don't last long. Still, I've been called a boss. All there is to it is having friends, doing things for people, and later they'll do things for you."

Well, James Pendergast certainly left a *few* things out in that description, but it came close to the truth. The Irish were never a majority in Kansas City, but thanks to James's, and later his son Thomas J.'s, organizing abilities, they ran the city's politics for decades. Harry Truman wasn't Irish himself, but he owed his political rise to the close relationship he had with the Pendergast machine; too close, many of his other political friends thought. When he arrived in Washington as a U.S. senator in 1935, he was derided by some as "the senator from Pendergast."

James Pendergast, also known as "Alderman Jim" to distinguish him from his numerous relatives, was a typical Irish-American success story. His parents were famine immigrants who migrated from Ohio to St. Joseph on the Missouri River north of Kansas City in 1857. St. Joseph was a major destination for Irish immigrants in mid-19th-century Missouri.

Pendergast relocated to Kansas City in 1876, a young man with plenty of ambition but no money. He took a job in a slaughterhouse and later in an iron foundry, both located in the West Bottoms section of Kansas City, a neighborhood that was also known as the Irish Patch. Around 500 Irish families were settled in West Bottoms in 1880, with about 400 settled in another Irish area called Old Town.

As early as 1872, Kansas City newspapers were reporting that the Irish controlled the city government. "The Irish control the Municipal Elections, and . . . the municipal offices, from Mayor to policeman as crumbs of their own table," wrote the anti-Irish *Kansas City Star* on St. Patrick's Day 1872. "The Irishman is an office seeker by birth; The German and Scandinavian is not. The American only partially so. Our city government has mainly been in the hands of the Irish for years."

If the Irish are natural office seekers, then James Pendergast had the genes. He saved his money from his various menial jobs, but he also had some fabled Irish luck. In 1881, after betting on a long-shot horse called Climax, he used the money he won to buy a combination hotel and saloon, which, naturally, he named the Climax. In time, Pendergast added more saloons, which, thanks to some backroom gambling operations, became highly profitable.

A rare photograph of Harry S Truman with Thomas "T. J." Pendergast at the 1936 Democratic Convention. Pictured left to right: Truman, Pendergast, James P. Aylward, James A. Farley, N. G. Robonsin, and David A. Fitzgerald. (Harry S Truman Library)

It is not a coincidence that so many Irish political bosses in so many cities were saloonkeepers. "In the nineteenth century, the saloon was something of a 'club' staffed by bartenders who acquired social follow-ings," writes George Reedy in *From the Ward to the White House: The Irish in American Politics* (1991). "It was not very difficult to translate this into political followings."

In 1892, Pendergast was elected an alderman from the First Ward, a position he would hold for 18 years, never losing an election. It was around this time people began to call him "boss," although he disliked it. He bore more than a passing resemblance to boxing hero John L. Sullivan, which did him no harm. He also had a flashing wit. When a bill was introduced in the state legislature that would ban anyone who owned a saloon from holding public office, he said it was clearly a measure designed to raise the reputation of saloonkeepers.

It was Alderman Jim's younger brother, Tom, however, who would become the truly famous Pendergast. Sixteen years Jim's junior, Tom, or T.J. as he was better known, was almost young enough to be the former's son. He took his brother's seat on the city council after Jim's death in 1911. Like Patrick Kennedy in Boston, however, T.J. preferred exercising power from behind the scenes. After serving four years, T.J. retired and never sought public office again.

Instead, he devoted his energies to building up the famed Pendergast machine. Only 5 feet 9 inches tall, T.J. was nevertheless powerfully built and could knock a man senseless with one blow. Yet he had a jauntiness and affability that made him hard to dislike. As a longtime reporter for the hostile *Kansas City Star* was forced to admit, once you met T.J. Pendergast, he was impossible to forget.

His admirers—and he had many—would be moved almost to tears in later years when they described his acts of kindness. When winter storms struck Kansas City, trucks would arrive in the neighborhoods with overcoats, coal, food—anything people might need. Many recalled how during the terrible influenza epidemic of 1918–1919, T.J. Pendergast, at great personal risk, went house to house on a personal inspection tour, seeing who needed help. And all he asked in return was a person's vote on election day.

His detractors, of course, painted a different picture. T.J. Pendergast saw politics far more as business opportunity than his brother Jim did. His Ready-Mixed Concrete Company was one of the first in the nation to make concrete in a plant and transport it to the building site in a truck. Ready-Mixed won a remarkable number of city and county contracts, of course. To those who said he used his political influence to obtain contracts, Pendergast would reply, "Well, yes. Why not? Aren't my products as good as any?"

Pendergast's greatest protégé, of course, was Harry Truman. Truman served with Pendergast's nephew, another James Pendergast, in the National Guard in World War I. When the latter was brought up on charges of negligence that resulted in a fatal explosion at Camp Doniphan in 1917, Lieutenant Truman ably defended young James and got the charges dropped.

Truman's unit was Battery D, whose members called themselves "the Wild Irish" the unit was made up heavily of Kansas City and Jackson County Irish-Americans. Although Truman had not a drop of Irish blood, his men loved and admired him as a fair, honest, and brave commander. When Truman went into politics after the war, the Wild Irish were a major part of his political base.

After the war, the Pendergasts were casting around for a candidate who could win the "country" vote in Jackson County, outside Kansas City, for one of the seats on the three-member county board. James Pendergast immediately suggested his friend and savior Harry Truman, whose haberdashery business was failing and who was in need of rescue. Truman, who had given thought to going into politics while in France during the war, immediately agreed. He won the election and never looked back.

Truman never forgot the debt he owed T.J. and James Pendergast. In his Senate office, he kept a picture of T.J. displayed prominently over the mantlepiece. Even after Pendergast was indicted in 1939, Truman stood by him. "Tom Pendergast has always been my friend and I don't desert a sinking ship," he told reporters who asked for his comment.

Later, when Pendergast died just a week after Truman was sworn in as vice-president in 1945, he unhesitatingly attended the funeral, which many thought outrageous behavior for a vice-president. Many others, however, saw the act as an admirable one for a man who had risen so high, yet refused to forget those who had helped him get there.

&. **EXHIBITS:** Erected by public subscription after Pendergast's death in 1911, the 10-foot-tall bronze statue stood in Mulkey Square until 1991. At that time, badly scarred by spray paint and vandalism, it was removed and restored to its original condition. It was rededicated at its present location in 1992. &. **LOCATION:** Case Park, which is bounded by I-35 on the west, 10th Street on the south, Jefferson Street on the east, and 8th Street on the north. &. **HOURS:** Dawn to dusk. &. **ADMISSION:** Free

LEXINGTON

BATTLE OF LEXINGTON STATE HISTORIC SITE

Rally! All Irishmen in favor of forming a regiment of Irish Volunteers to sustain the government . . . in arms through the present war, will rally at North Market Hall, this evening at 7½ o'clock. . . . For the honor of the Old Land, rally. Rally for the defense of the New. —April 20, 1861 Chicago Tribune

The number of men responding to this call to arms by James A. Mulligan totaled 325 by nightfall, and nearly 1,000 over the next three days. Ft. Sumter had surrendered only a week earlier, and President Lincoln had called for 75,000 volunteers to suppress the Southern "Insurrection." The Irish were eager to demonstrate their loyalty to their adopted country, which many Anglo-Protestants questioned. Many also hoped that their participation would somehow convince the U.S. government to pressure Great Britain into granting Irish independence.

Mulligan, who was born in Utica, New York, of Irish immigrant parents, was described as a spellbinding orator. He became commander of the 23rd Illinois Volunteer Regiment, which he christened "the Irish Brigade of the West," after the famous unit then forming in New York. Despite his grand ambitions, however, the "brigade" never was more than a single regiment in size.

Missouri was one of the major cockpits of conflict in the early days of the Civil War. A large and important border state with substantial numbers of both Union and Confederate sympathizers, Missouri was prized by both sides. Mulligan and his men, marching under a green banner as well as the Stars and Stripes, were quickly dispatched to this arena soon after being organized.

Confederate Maj. Gen. Sterling Price, leading a force of Missouri militia, was determined to rid Missouri of Union troops, and he won a victory over Union Gen. Nathaniel Lyon at Wilson's Creek on August 10. This sent Union forces reeling, and Price concentrated his attention on Lexington, the largest town between St. Louis and Kansas City.

The 23rd Illinois was part of the 2,800-strong Union garrison, which was under the overall command of Colonel Mulligan. Entrenched on the campus of the Masonic College just north of town, Mulligan had in his possession the great seal of the state and a million dollars in cash from the local bank. He was ordered to hold his position "at all hazards."

Price arrived outside Lexington on September 12 with 7,000 men, forcing the Union forces inside their prepared earthen ramparts. Mulligan's only hope lay in relief from Gen. John C. Fremont, "the Great Pathfinder of the West," who was in command in the state. However great a scout he might have been, however, Fremont was incompetent as a military commander, and no relief was forthcoming.

With pro-Confederate sympathizers swelling the ranks of the besiegers with every passing day, Mulligan's position was growing ever more desperate. He had been forced away from his only source of water and had lost control of the Anderson house, the only building in his possession. A relief column under Brig. Gen. Samuel Sturgis made a halfhearted effort to reach Mulligan and his thirsty troops, but Price had little difficulty shooing them away.

On the morning of the September 20, the Confederates began advancing, pushing big bales of hemp before them as mobile breastworks. A Confederate messenger arrived during a truce and requested surrender, an option Mulligan at first refused. Later in the day, however, as the fighting intensified and his men began passing out from thirst and heat exhaustion, Mulligan held a council of war with his officers and decided to surrender.

Although they were defeated, Mulligan and his men soon found their weeklong stand at Lexington had made them heroes. When the 23rd Illinois was re-formed a few months later, Congress authorized it to carry the name "Lexington" on its colors. Mulligan had inscribed, on his regular stationery, "Remember Lexington and Fontenoy." The latter, of course, was the famous battle fought in France in 1745 in which the Irish Brigade of the French army defeated the British Guards Brigade.

An 1861 sheet music cover for a song commemorating Mulligan's "Irish Brigade of the West." (Chicago Historical Society)

After returning to Chicago and while waiting to re-form his regiment, Mulligan found himself in command of a prisoner of war camp. Among the prisoners were men of the Irish 10th Tennessee Regiment, the only Confederate regiment to fight under a green banner. Mulligan paid special attention to the men of the 10th Tennessee, improving their rations and endeavoring to convert them to the Union cause, but without success (*see* Ft. Donelson, Tennessee).

Mulligan eventually rose to command the 2nd Division, Department of West Virginia. He was killed in action at the Third Battle of Winchester, Virginia, on September 19, 1864, almost three years to the day after his surrender at Lexington.

❧ EXHIBITS: Original earthworks are visible at the battlefield, which features explanatory markers. The Anderson House still stands and contains a museum with artifacts from the battle. A guided tour is available.

❧ LOCATION: About 50 miles east of Kansas City and four miles off

U.S. 24. ❧ HOURS: Monday–Saturday 8:30–4:30, Sunday noon–5:30, April 15–October 31. Anderson House: Monday–Saturday 10–4, Sunday noon–5, April 15–October 31; Monday–Saturday 10–4, Sunday noon–4 rest of year. ❧ ADMISSION: None for battlefield; $2 for Anderson House ($1.25 for children). ❧ TELEPHONE: (816) 259-4654.

ST. LOUIS

MULANPHY PARK

The land west of the Mississippi River changed hands several times between France and Spain in the 17th and 18th centuries (once even secretly). It became part of the United States in 1804 with the Louisiana Purchase. Missouri became the gateway for settlers moving farther west, and would remain so for the rest of the 19th century. Well before Missouri was admitted to the Union in 1821, the Irish had come to dominate life in St. Louis, which became, and would remain for many years, the most important city west of the river.

Irish were present in the St. Louis area from the days of Spanish and French rule. Michael C. O'Laughlin, in *Irish Settlers on the American Frontier* (1984), writes that Spanish officials recorded residents with names such as Cavenaght (Cavanagh), M. Mullen (McMullen), O'Bune (O'Bryan), and Sullivan (O'Sullivan). In 1790, the Spanish commandant in the area asked that a priest be sent and that he be "of the Irish nation." Fr. James Maxwell duly arrived and served the area for many years.

The first exclusively Irish settlements in Missouri were made in the last years of the 18th century in what is now Perry and St. Genevieve counties south of St. Louis. One of the earliest and most important Irish settlers during the American period was Joseph Charless. A native of county Westmeath, he found his way to St. Louis in 1807 after being employed for a time by Mathew Carey, the famed Irish publisher in Philadelphia (*see* Philadelphia, Pennsylvania).

Charless began publishing the *Louisville Gazette* (later the *Missouri Gazette*) the first newspaper west of the Mississippi, on November 24, 1807. He also published the first book west of the river and was a major figure in getting Missouri statehood in 1821. A participant in Wolfe Tone's abortive 1798 uprising of Protestants and Catholics against the British, Charless migrated to the United States for political reasons. His newspaper strongly opposed slavery, which was not a popular stand in a territory whose residents were then mostly Southern.

Many other Irish made successes of themselves in this frontier city. One of the greatest was John Mullanphy. Described as red-faced and weather-beaten, he was born in county Fermanagh in 1758, before St.

Louis itself was even founded. He became quite possibly the first million-aire west of the Mississippi.

As a Catholic in the years before Daniel O'Connell won emancipation for Catholics, Mullanphy could obtain little formal education. He read extensively in Dublin, however, where he lived above a bookshop. Leaving Ireland for France, he was commissioned an officer in the Irish Brigade of the French army and served with it until its dissolution during the French Revolution. He returned briefly to Ireland, where he married Elizabeth Browne of Youghal, county Waterford, and then struck out for America. In Baltimore for a time, he became close to Bishop John Carroll, the first American Catholic bishop (*see* Baltimore, Maryland).

After settling for a time in Kentucky, Mullanphy, his wife, and his four daughters headed for Missouri shortly after the Louisiana Purchase. Mullanphy lost little time plugging into the power structure, for he records that he was appointed an associate judge of the court of common pleas shortly after his arrival, one of the first such appointments under American rule.

Mullanphy's knowledge of French culture gave him an inside track on business opportunities in those early years, and he made the most of them. He established very nearly a corner on the cotton business in St. Louis, which became the basis for his wealth.

Mullanphy never forgot his Irish roots and was a great and generous contributor to Irish and other philanthropic causes. He established the first orphanages in St. Louis and the first hospital in Missouri. He became one of the largest landowners in Missouri, and Irish famine immigrants were allowed to settle on part of his estate in 1847, which was the beginning of the Kerry Patch, the largest Irish neighborhood in St. Louis.

John Mullanphy died in 1833, at age 64, but the family's contributions continued. Bryan Mullanphy, the millionaire's son, who had been sent to France for his education, served as mayor of St. Louis in the late 1840s at the height of the famine immigration. St. Louis became the nation's fifth-largest city at this time, and the younger Mullanphy worked hard to make the new arrivals as comfortable as possible, just as his father had done before.

"A man of great enterprise, foresight and judgement, he contributed more than any other individual to the building of St. Louis" was the eulogy of Mayor Darby for the elder Mullanphy.

&. **LOCATION:** Mullanphy Square Park is bounded by Mullanphy Street and Cass Avenue between 11th and 12th streets, not far from downtown St. Louis. &. **HOURS:** Dawn to dusk. &. **ADMISSION:** Free

O'FALLON ST.

The O'Fallons claimed to be of high-born descent from the O'Phelans, "the princes of the Desi," and one-time high kings of ancient Ireland. Certainly, Dr. James O'Fallon (he was born without the "O," which he added later) had high-flown ambitions. He never achieved them, but his sons made up for this deficiency.

James O'Fallon was born in Ireland and took his medical degree in Edinburgh. He arrived in North Carolina in 1774 to practice medicine and became fascinated by public affairs. He was an outspoken advocate of the revolution and was briefly jailed by the Tory Committee of Public Safety in Wilmington. He became a confidant of George Washington's and was ultimately appointed surgeon general of the Continental Army.

Unable to settle down after the war, O'Fallon became involved in various plots between the French, the Spanish, and the Americans in the Mississippi Valley. O'Fallon's murky plans sufficiently alarmed his old friend President Washington that the latter issued a public proclamation warning the western settlers to stay away from him. That was the coup de grace to O'Fallon's plans. His wife soon left him and his friends deserted him. So total was his abandonment that his time and place of death can only be guessed at, most likely early 1794.

O'Fallon's wife was the younger sister of the celebrated brothers George Rogers Clark and William Clark, the latter of Lewis and Clark fame (*see* Locust Grove, Louisville, Kentucky). William Clark looked after the education of John and Benjamin O'Fallon, born in 1791 and 1793, respectively, after their mother deserted their father. At age 20, John O'Fallon decided upon a military career.

It was an auspicious decision, for the United States was about to go to war again with Great Britain and there was much Indian fighting to be done. O'Fallon became aide-de-camp to Gen. William Henry Harrison and was seriously wounded at the famed battle of Tippecanoe.

Later, during the 1840 presidential campaign, Harrison came under attack for exaggerating his military record. Harrison appealed to O'Fallon, who provided a timely letter from St. Louis attesting to the general's courage under fire:

> I served under him (Harrison) during the greater part of the period he was in active service, near his person, commencing with the Tippecanoe expedition and continuing to its termination. . . . I can safely say that I never in my life saw a braver man in battle, one more collected, prompt and full of resources, than General William Henry Harrison.

The rumors were thus squelched and Harrison was duly elected president.

O'Fallon left the army in 1818 and headed for St. Louis with the frankly expressed ambition of making a lot of money. He succeeded. Working as a trader with the Indians and as a contractor with the army,

O'Fallon was soon doing quite well indeed. He wrote his mother that he was making money "at the rate of $1000 a month." He invested his profits in St. Louis real estate and eventually became one of the state's wealthiest citizens.

Elected to the state legislature in 1821, he eventually became the first president of the Ohio and Mississippi Railroad. He was commander of the Missouri militia and served as a visitor-examiner at West Point. He also served on the boards of banks and hotels.

But it is as a philanthropist that he is probably best remembered in St. Louis. He donated the grounds of St. Louis University and the O'Fallon Polytechnic Institute. He also built the dispensary and medical school of Washington University. He also helped build the First Methodist Church. (O'Fallon's ancestors were Catholic, but he himself was raised Protestant. Later descendants returned to the Catholic faith.)

"The fact is," wrote Abel Rathbone Corbin to O'Fallon in 1851, "you have done so much for religion, scientific and public purposes that it is difficult to make out a list of beneficiaries; not a fire company, not a library association, not a church, not anything but appeals to Col. O'Fallon in their hour of need."

O'Fallon's last great service to his city and state came during the Civil War. At age 70, O'Fallon stood strongly for the Union, and his towering presence in St. Louis did much to galvanize the Irish community there to the Northern cause. He died in 1865. O'Fallon Street in downtown St. Louis is named for him.

John O'Fallon's younger brother, Benjamin, became a well-known western explorer and fur trader. O'Fallon's Creek in Montana was named for him while still a boy by his uncle, William Clark.

❧ LOCATION: O'Fallon Street runs from Jefferson Avenue on the west to 2nd Street, on the Mississippi River, on the east.

OREGON COUNTY

MARK TWAIN NATIONAL FOREST/IRISH WILDERNESS

Throughout the 19th century, Irish priests and bishops in various states and cities dreamed of removing their parishioners from the degradation and poverty of the urban slums. Their goal was to resettle the Irish immigrants in an Edenic wilderness where they could support themselves on their own farms, become spiritually and morally renewed, and be far from the urban temptations of liquor and vice.

Almost all of these schemes came to naught. Although farmers in the old country, the Irish in America seemed determined to avoid a life on the land, even when they could own it themselves instead of paying rent to a landlord. The vagaries of the weather and bad memories kept the Irish close to the big urban centers, where even a poor wage at least had the virtue of being steady.

Bishops John Ireland of St. Paul (*see* Graceville, Minnesota) and Francis Fenwick of Boston both established colonies in the wilderness. So did Father John Hogan of St. John's Parish in the Kerry Patch neighborhood of St. Louis.

The Kerry Patch was originally a part of John Mullanphy's estate in St. Louis (*see* St. Louis, Missouri). He donated it to the wretched refugees from the potato famine who found their way to St. Louis from New Orleans as well as overland from the eastern cities. Like Five Points in New York and the West End in Boston, the Kerry Patch was a slum of the worst order, with huge numbers of Irish crowded together in terrible conditions. (Opinion differs as to the present-day boundaries of the Kerry Patch, but most agree that 14th Street and O'Fallon was pretty much the center.)

An Irish immigrant himself, Father Hogan was anxious to help his flock avoid spending their lives as railroad workers and domestic servants, two occupations that were heavily Irish and often forced husbands and wives to live apart. In 1857, he began scouting land in northern Missouri for his colony. But high prices and a distinctly unfriendly reception (an attempt on his life was narrowly thwarted by a Protestant preacher) caused him to look elsewhere.

He found what he was looking for in Oregon County, in the southern part of the state near the Arkansas border. The land was not ideal, but it could be used for grazing, orchards, and, with some work, perhaps other crops as well. By 1859, Father Hogan had settled 40 Irish families in his colony. More were coming, and a log cabin church was thriving.

"Maidens and wains married young, usually before 20 and often at 16, and their married life was remarkably virtuous and happy," Hogan wrote of his new colony. "The marriage dowry was usually a one-room log house. The young man was fortuned by his father with a yoke of oxen and a plow. The bride was dowered by her mother with a wealth of home-spun dresses and household fabrics of like manufacture. Timber from a neighboring sawmill was framed into furniture and the young couple was delighted with it."

Hogan's idyll didn't last long. The coming of the Civil War soon meant the surrounding woods were filled with raiders from both armies and freebooting "bushwhackers" loyal to no one but themselves. The raiders carried off crops and livestock and anything else they could carry, causing the settlers to seek safety in the cities from whence they had come. By the end of the war, there was nothing left of Hogan's dream.

Hogan's drive and energy were noticed, however, and he was eventually consecrated bishop of Kansas, where he leant his support to other colonization efforts.

Meanwhile, the wilderness where Father Hogan's short-lived colony had thrived was turned over to loggers, who damaged it severely in the latter half of the 19th century. Reforestation efforts began with the Civilian Conservation Corps in the 1930s, and today the Irish Wilderness is a 16,500-acre tract belonging to the much larger Mark Twain National Forest. It is closed to mechanized vehicles so that visitors can ride horses and hike its trails.

&ae; **EXHIBITS:** Unfortunately, nothing remains of the original settlement. &ae; **LOCATION:** East of the Eleven Points River in northeastern Oregon County. Take S.R. 160 about 45 miles west of West Bluff, Missouri. Then take County Route J north about 5 miles to the town of Wilderness. &ae; **HOURS:** Call for information on camping and other recreational activities. &ae; **TELEPHONE:** More information can be obtained from the Forest Supervisor, 401 Fairgrounds Rd., Rolla, Mo. 64501. (314) 364-4621.

NEBRASKA

BOYS' TOWN

Immortalized in the 1938 MGM film of the same name starring Spencer Tracy and Mickey Rooney (for which Tracey received a best actor Oscar), Boys' Town is still in existence and visitors are welcome.

Father Edward Flanagan, founder of the settlement for delinquent boys, was born in county Roscommon in 1886. Assigned to a parish in Nebraska, he at first opened a home for alcoholic men, but soon came to take an interest in the problems of boys who came from broken homes or had committed acts of juvenile delinquency. He became a fixture in the juvenile courts, insisting (optimistically, even then) that "there's no such thing as a bad boy." He sometimes persuaded judges to release the boys into his custody instead of sending them to jail.

Father Flanagan established Boys' Town with 5 boys in December 1917. By Christmas, he had 25. A month later, 50. By 1921, he and his charges had outgrown their original quarters and moved to a farm outside Omaha. To raise money, the boys formed a traveling circus, which performed around the state. In 1936, Boys' Town was incorporated as a separate municipality. Worldwide fame came with the movie two years later.

Father Flanagan ran the home until his death in Berlin, Germany, in 1948 while on a promotional tour for the U.S. government. His body was loaded aboard a C-47 Dakota and flown back to Omaha, where it lay in state at Boys' Town for two days. A private mass for Boys' Town students and faculty was held on May 21, followed by a public mass attended by 2,500 mourners.

It was Flanagan's wish that he be buried near his beloved "boys," so after the mass, six Boys' Town seniors carried the bronze coffin to the rear

Father Flanagan (Spencer Tracy) tries to straighten out juvenile delinquent Mickey Rooney in Boys' Town (1938). (Museum of Modern Art)

of the chapel. His tomb bears the words, "Father Flanagan, Founder of Boys' Town, Lover of Christ and Man."

Although Boys' Town faded into obscurity after Flanagan's death, it is still very much alive and has become more prominent recently. Girls were admitted in 1979, and the school operates a nationwide 24-hour toll-free hot line (1-800-448-3000) for troubled youth. It has also opened branches around the country.

In 1986, the U.S. Postal Service honored Boys' Town's founder with a stamp issued on the centennial of Father Flanagan's birth.

&. **EXHIBITS:** The story of Boys' Town is chronicled in the Hall of History. Flanagan's residence, which contains personal effects and memorabilia, is open to visitors. &. **HOURS:** 9–4:30 daily. &. **LOCATION:** 132nd Street and West Dodge Road. &. **ADMISSION:** None, but donations appreciated. &. **TELEPHONE:** (402) 498-1140.

UNION PACIFIC RAILROAD MUSEUM

On May 10, 1869, the golden spike was driven at Promontory Point, Utah, formally linking the Union Pacific and Central Pacific railroads. The event was witnessed by politicians, railroad officials, and lots of just plain railroad workers, a large proportion of whom were Irish immigrants.

William M. Jeffers, the son of one of the immigrant laborers, rose to become president of the Union Pacific from 1937 to 1946.

❧ **EXHIBITS:** The museum contains many exhibits on the building and history of the railroad. ❧ **LOCATION:** 1416 Dodge St., in the Union Pacific headquarters building. ❧ **HOURS:** 9–3 Monday–Friday; 9–12 Saturday. ❧ **ADMISSION:** Free ❧ **TELEPHONE:** (402) 271-5457.

O'NEILL

HOLT COUNTY HISTORICAL SOCIETY

Fourteen year-old John O'Neill left county Monaghan in the politically turbulent year of 1848. Politically aware beyond his years, he set sail with a bitter hatred of Great Britain and the way it ruled his native land. Irish freedom remained his passionate cause for the rest of his life.

After working in various odd jobs, O'Neill joined the U.S. Cavalry in 1857 for "the Mormon War." Once in Utah, however, he appears to have deserted and made his way to California, where he enlisted in another regiment. The start of the Civil War found him with the rank of sergeant.

O'Neill very quickly proved himself a natural soldier and leader of men. He was commissioned in December 1862 and distinguished himself in the actions at Glasgow, Kentucky, and at Buffington Bar. In December 1863, he was badly wounded. Believing he had been unfairly passed over for promotion, he resigned from his regiment and was appointed to the 17th Colored Cavalry Regiment. He resigned from the army, however, in 1864.

After a period as a government bureaucrat in Nashville, Tennessee, he became interested in the plan of the Fenians to invade Canada (*see* Ridgeway, Ontario). A talented and experienced commander, O'Neill defeated an Anglo-Canadian force at the Battle of Ridgeway on June 2, 1866, but withdrew back across the Niagara River when it became clear he could not expect reinforcements.

Twice more, O'Neill led invasions of Canada, in 1870 and 1871. After the failure of the 1870 attempt, he was sentenced to two years' imprisonment by the United States, but received a presidential pardon after serving only three months. In 1871, he and a few followers sought to join forces with Louis Riel's Metis Rebellion in Saskatchewan, but were quickly taken into custody by U.S. forces at the North Dakota border. He was tried but released.

O'Neill now gave up thoughts of securing Irish freedom by force and came up with the idea of creating Irish colonies throughout the United States and even the world. He was appalled at the living conditions of so many Irish in the slums of the eastern cities and thought it could be alleviated by settling the Irish on farms in the West.

"I have always believed," he wrote, "that the next best thing to giving the Irish people their freedom at home is to encourage such of them to come to this country, either from choice or from necessity, to take up lands and build homes in America."

The instrument at hand for O'Neill was the Homestead Act, passed in 1862. It promised free land to those who would agree to live on it and make improvements. O'Neill settled on Nebraska because it had millions of acres of land available for almost no money, which would attract poor eastern immigrants. The state also promised $600 and several lots within the town if he could bring immigrants to the area.

O'Neill returned to Pennsylvania and became a booster of the project among the Irish of Philadelphia and the coalfields, painting a glowing picture of life on the Great Plains. "Why are you content to work on public projects and at coal mining," he rhetorically asked prospective settlers, "when you might, in a few years, own farms of your own and become wealthy and influential people?"

Few took O'Neill up on his offer. As has been noted before, the Irish were terrified of life on the land following the potato blight. They preferred the comparative security of urban wage labor, even in terrible conditions, to taking their chances on the farm.

Nevertheless, on May 12, 1874, the first group of immigrants for "New Ireland" arrived at Omaha. After changing trains twice more, the group of 13 men, 2 women, and 5 children were still 110 miles from their destination. They had to go the rest of the way by stagecoach and wagon train.

The land they arrived in must not have looked promising (northern Nebraska, even in springtime, is not much to look at scenically). The treeless, grassy plains rolled away to the horizon every way a person looked. Because there was almost no timber in the area, the first houses were made of sod bricks cut from the prairie.

Prospects for the new town of O'Neill did not appear bright at first. The first harvests were meager, and a plague of grasshoppers ate all the seed for three years in a row. Many settlers left before the first winter, though many others arrived to replace them. Colonel O'Neill continued his boosterism in the east, attracting more settlers, but all the time battling tales of hardship that preceded him on his travels.

O'Neill might have become a ghost town had it not been for the gold strike in the Black Hills of South Dakota 250 miles north of O'Neill. The new town was the nearest settlement to the goldfields and became a hub for supplying provisions to the miners. Buildings went up and more settlers arrived. The railroad finally came in 1881 and O'Neill's days of living on the edge of nowhere were at last over.

Today, O'Neill has about 5,000 inhabitants, many of them descendants of the original settlers living on the original homesteads. Although the ethnicity of the town has diversified somewhat, O'Neill proudly bills itself "the Irish Capital of Nebraska" and throws a widely known St. Patrick's Day celebration.

O'Neill did not live to see the town that bears his name truly established, however. In November 1877, he suffered a slight stroke and his wife took him to a hospital in Omaha, where he died six weeks later.

❧ **EXHIBITS:** The society has many documents and artifacts relating to the history of the town and the area. ❧ **LOCATION:** The historical society is housed in the Kincaid Building. ❧ **HOURS:** Monday–Thursday 10–12, 1–4. ❧ **ADMISSION:** None, but donations appreciated. ❧ **TELEPHONE:** No phone at the museum. Call the Holt County Chamber of Commerce for information: (402) 336-2355.

OKLAHOMA

THE MURRAY-LINDSAY MANSION

The Irish tended to venture to out-of-the-way places such as Oklahoma as individuals rather than as part of a group, and in the 1870s and 1880s enterprising mixed-blood Indians and intermarried whites carved extensive ranches from Indian lands in the Chickasaw Nation. Two of these were Frank and Alzira Murray, who constructed a huge mansion at the center of their empire.

Frank Murray came from a well-off family in Ireland, although when he landed in New Orleans in the 1850s he was penniless. After drifting around the frontier for a few years, he met and married Alzira McCaughey in 1871. Alzira was a Choctaw Indian who had married a Capt. William Powell in 1868. Powell and Alzira had a daughter, Anita. Unfortunately, Powell died only two months after Anita's birth. In 1871, Alzira married Frank Murray, who was ambitious to make a name and fortune for himself.

The young couple and Anita moved to Paul's Valley on the western edge of the Chickasaw Nation, and from there they relocated to a spot they dubbed Erin Springs, about two miles south of the current town of Lindsay. Situated near the Washita River, their four-room cabin was on the stage line between Caddo and Ft. Sill, a busy road that carried freight and passengers between the railroad and the fort. Their nearest neighbors were more than 25 miles away.

The key to the Murrays' success was that, as an intermarried couple, they could legally improve and exploit Indian land. This loophole allowed Murray to build a vast ranching and farming empire, eventually encompassing more than 20,000 acres. They ran more than 26,000 head of cattle on this range and in one year reportedly harvested 400,000 bushels of corn.

With unlimited markets for beef and produce, the Murrays' farm prospered. To house their growing family (the couple had eight children) and to reflect their rising status, they began work on a grand house. The stone was quarried nearby and lumber was hauled in from Gainesville, Texas. Walls and partitions in the ground level were 18 inches thick and made of solid rock. The original building was a two-story square design with a full basement and attic. A wooden veranda extended across the front facade. When finished, it was one of the largest and most ornate houses in the entire territory, containing 15 rooms, 2 baths, and 4 fireplaces.

But it didn't last. In the drier 1880s, the business began sinking into debt, and Frank Murray died in 1892, leaving his wife and children to manage as best they could.

Alzira showed she was equal to the task. She drastically cut back expenses and reorganized the farm. Just as the family's fortunes were rebounding, however, the rules were changed and the family no longer had unlimited access to tribal lands. Nevertheless, Alzira diversified the family into banking and sawmill operations.

By 1902, the family situation had improved to the point where Alzira could afford to remodel the house. She installed a classical Greek-style portico and raised the roof to create room for more bedrooms. This is the house that is now open for all to see, a monument to Irish immigrants on the Great Plains and the ingenuity of Indians faced with adversity.

🥐 **EXHIBITS:** The house contains many original and period furnishings, along with photographs and mementos of the family. 🥐 **LOCATION:** The home is located approximately 2 miles south and ½ mile west of Lindsay. 🥐 **HOURS:** Open 1–5 except Mondays. 🥐 **ADMISSION:** None, but donations appreciated. 🥐 **TELEPHONE:** (405) 756-2019.

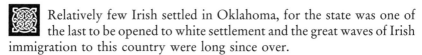

SHAMROCK

AN IRISH TOWN

Relatively few Irish settled in Oklahoma, for the state was one of the last to be opened to white settlement and the great waves of Irish immigration to this country were long since over.

The oil boom early in this century, however, brought some Irish adventurers to Oklahoma. Between 1912 and 1915, a Tulsa realtor named Edwin L. Dunn founded the town of Shamrock, which at the height of the fever for "black gold" boasted over 10,000 residents. Its streets have names like Cork and Tipperary, and its newspapers were called the *Blarney* and the *Brogue*.

Like many of the ghost towns of the West, however, the people left when the fever abated. Unlike many others, however, Shamrock refused to die completely. Today, the town has just 200 residents, although it still manages to put on a fairly lively St. Patrick's Day Parade.

&. **LOCATION:** On Highway 16 northeast of Oklahoma City, about halfway to Tulsa.

TUSKAHOMA

CHOCTAW NATION MUSEUM

The Great Hunger of 1845 to 1849, caused by the blight of the potato crop, was the greatest catastrophe ever suffered by the Irish people. Through a combination of laissez-faire economics and indifference to the Irish, British officialdom did little of any real consequence to relieve the suffering. Offers of help for the starving Irish came from some unlikely places, including the czar of Russia and the sultan of Turkey. Neither of these rulers, of course, was particularly noted for generosity toward his own subjects, and both were more eager to embarrass the British government than help the Irish.

Some of the unlikely donors, however, were quite genuine in their desire to help. Among these was the Choctaw Indian Nation of Oklahoma, a people who understood dispossession and fear. Little more than a decade earlier, the Choctaw, along with several other Indian tribes, had suffered through the Trail of Tears when they were forcibly removed from their ancestral lands in Mississippi. Half the Choctaw Nation is estimated to have perished on their way to the strange and unfamiliar area Congress designated "the Indian Territory," which later became the state of Oklahoma.

In November 1845, British Prime Minister Sir Robert Peel purchased $100,000 worth of Indian corn and shipped it to Cork and Limerick in an effort to relieve the starvation. Since an estimated $3 million worth of potatoes had been destroyed by the famine, however, it wasn't much of a gesture. Also, corn was an utterly alien food to the Irish, who knew not how to cook it and eat it. The Irish dubbed the resulting mess "Peel's brimstone," and this perhaps accounts for the dislike of corn by many Irish to this very day.

When Irish-American groups appealed to other Americans for funds to buy food for their starving countrymen, the appeal was heeded here in far-off Oklahoma. In 1847, the Choctaw Nation held a great meeting near Skullyville and raised $710 to send to the starving Irish.

❧ **EXHIBITS:** The museum contains several exhibits on the help the Choctaw Indians sent to the Irish in the Great Famine, including photos of Choctaws who visited Ireland recently to commemorate the event. Guided tours of the museum are available. ❧ **LOCATION:** The museum is north of U.S. 271 on a marked county road. Tuskahoma is about 30 miles east of the Indian Nation Turnpike by way of Oklahoma 43 and U.S. 271. ❧ **HOURS:** Monday–Friday, 8–4. Closed holidays. ❧ **ADMISSION:** None, but donations appreciated. ❧ **TELEPHONE:** (918) 569-4465.

SOUTH DAKOTA

PINE RIDGE

HOLY ROSARY MISSION

Not far from Holy Rosary Church lies Wounded Knee, site of a battle/massacre in 1890 that for many came to symbolize the injustices done to the American Indians by white settlers. The Irish, in spite of their own history of oppression, were rarely sympathetic to the Indians' plight, participating enthusiastically in the Indian Wars as cavalrymen and on the Great Plains as settlers. Hugh Gallagher, however, was a notable exception.

Gallagher was an Irish immigrant and Civil War veteran who settled in Indiana and became active in Democratic party politics. When Pres. Grover Cleveland was elected in 1884 after two and a half decades of Republican rule, Gallagher was in line for a patronage appointment and was named agent for the Oglala Sioux on the Pine Ridge reservation in what was then the Dakota Territory.

The once great Sioux nation was in its twilight by the time Gallagher arrived in November 1886. Sitting Bull was confined to a reservation and Crazy Horse had been killed. Red Cloud, the victor of Little Bighorn, knew that armed resistance was now quite pointless. "It was Red Cloud's task to seek, by his wits, the best compromise he could for his people," wrote William Hanlon in an article on Gallagher in *The Recorder* (1984), the journal of the American-Irish Historical Society.

Red Cloud's major concern was to bring the Jesuit order back to the Pine Ridge reservation to teach the Indian children. From the time of the great missionary Father DeSmet, the Indians had viewed "the blackrobes" as friends, and were wary of other denominations.

Roman Catholic missionaries had been barred from the reservations during the years of Republican rule, which favored Protestants. As a result, those Indians who had been converted to Catholicism by earlier missionaries were effectively prevented from practicing their faith. Gallagher saw to it that the situation came to end. "Father Jutz is here with a lay-brother to determine upon a site for the school," Gallagher wrote to his wife back in Indiana in 1887. "They are trying to secure a place that I showed them, distant some six miles from the agency. Red Cloud went out with them today to assist in negotiations for the place."

The school was opened in 1888 and quickly grew from 20 to over 100 pupils in its first year, largely because Gallagher allowed non-Catholic Indians to send their children to the Catholic school if they so desired. Later agents, however, did not follow Gallagher's open-minded example, which made the Indians bitter.

Gallagher's stay at Pine Ridge was short. Grover Cleveland was defeated for reelection in 1888, and by 1890, Gallagher had been replaced. The Indians could no more understand the workings of political patronage than they could understand the changes that were sweeping over them. William Hanlon speculates in his article, perhaps with considerable justice, that had the more understanding Hugh Gallagher still been in place a few months later, perhaps the Wounded Knee massacre in December 1890 might have been avoided.

❧ LOCATION: The Pine Ridge reservation covers nearly 5,000 square miles in southwestern North Dakota. It is reached by U.S. 18, about 110 miles southeast of Rapid City. The church is 5 miles north of the town, near White Clay Creek. There are historical markers on the site.

TEXAS

IRISH CULTURAL HOUSE

Corpus Christi really got its start in 1845 when Gen. Zachary Taylor's army landed there at the start of the United States' war with Mexico. Taylor's army contained many Irish Americans, and some returned to settle after Texas was annexed to the United States. Also, many Irish moved into the fast-developing town from the outlying Irish settlements at San Patricio and Refugio (*see* San Patricio, Texas, and Refugio, Texas).

According to John Brendan Flannery's definitive *The Irish Texans* (1980), the Corpus Christi area had a distinctly Irish flavor about it in the years after the Mexican War. A man named Charles Callihan edited the local newspaper, and of course there was politics. Irish-born officeholders included Richard Powers, elected to the first county commission, H. N. Barry, who was elected sheriff, and Edward Fitzgerald, who served as county clerk. The Irish dominated politics in the area for years.

In time, a 27-square-block area came to be known as "Irishtown," and was bounded by Twigg, Mesquite, and Brewster streets and the bay. The area was home to the city's Irish gentry as well as its working class and had its own volunteer fire unit, the Shamrock Hose Company. A church (St. Patrick's, of course), was completed in 1857.

Cornelius Cahill and his wife were among the early residents of Irishtown in the 1850s, having lived first in New York after emigrating from county Kerry. The family had originally been Gaelic speakers, and Mrs. Cahill even taught her black maidservant to say her prayers in the Irish language!

The city of Corpus Christi has sought to preserve its heritage by rebuilding old Irishtown as Heritage Park, commemorating the contributions of not only the Irish, but also the Dutch, the Moravians, and the

Formerly the Ward-McCampbell house, the Irish Cultural House now serves as the base for Irish-related activities in the Corpus Christi area.

many other nationalities that built up Corpus Christi. The Ward-McCampbell house, a 2½ story Victorian era Greek Revival structure, was moved from its original location at North Water Street and Fitzgerald to its present location at North Chaparral and Fitzgerald in 1984. It is now designated the Irish Cultural House and serves as the base for Irish-related activities in the Corpus Christi area.

🙈 **EXHIBITS:** The house contains original and period furnishings. Exhibits are being developed on the lives of the Irish in Corpus Christi's Irishtown. The house also contains a chapel dedicated to Bishop Drury, an Irish-American Catholic prelate in the area. 🙈 **LOCATION:** 1501 N. Chaparral Dr. 🙈 **HOURS:** 10–4:30 daily. 🙈 **ADMISSION:** None, but donations are appreciated. 🙈 **TELEPHONE:** (512) 883-9662.

DALLAS

THE SIXTH FLOOR

The trip to Texas was supposed to be the kickoff for Pres. John F. Kennedy's 1964 reelection campaign. Texas, a heavily Protestant state, was barely carried by the Roman Catholic Kennedy in 1960 with Vice-President Lyndon Johnson's help. The Texas Democratic party was roiled by factionalism, with Johnson, Sen. Ralph Yarborough, and Gov. John Connally all feuding for supremacy. Kennedy hoped his visit could smooth things over before the campaign began in earnest.

At 12:29 P.M. CST on November 22, Kennedy was riding next to his wife in an open limousine toward the Dallas Merchandise Trade Mart,

The Texas School Book Depository (left) and visitors at the "Sixth Floor" Kennedy exhibit (right).

where he was scheduled to be the luncheon speaker. As the car rounded the corner from Houston Street onto Elm in the shadow of the six story Texas School Book Depository, a shot was heard, followed quickly by a second. The president slumped over in his seat before a third shot struck him in the back of the head, mortally wounding him.

The shots appeared to come from an open window at the southeastern corner of the sixth floor of the depository building. Lee Harvey Oswald, an employee who was also an ex-Marine who had once defected to the Soviet Union and had failed at just about everything he had ever tried in life, was arrested in a theater a few hours later. In his pocket was a revolver later proved to have been used to murder Dallas police officer J. D. Tippett about 45 minutes after the attack on the president. Despite the numerous assassination conspiracy theories, this fact for many clinches Oswald's guilt as the president's assassin, for why would he shoot a police officer if he had nothing to hide?

The funeral rites, which captivated the nation on television for the next three days, were modeled on those for Abraham Lincoln. On Sunday, the president's lying-in-state in the Capitol rotunda was interrupted by the incredible news that Oswald himself had become the victim of an assassin, one Jack Ruby, a shady nightclub owner.

Kennedy was laid to rest in front of the Custis-Lee Mansion in Arlington National Cemetery (*see* Arlington, Virginia). On a visit not long before his death, Kennedy had told his wife, "I could stay up here forever."

❧ EXHIBITS: The "sniper's nest," from which Oswald is believed to have shot President Kennedy, is preserved as it was found on the day of the assassination. Numerous panels and video screens cover almost every aspect of John F. Kennedy's visit to Texas, his death, and its aftermath. ❧

LOCATION: The Sixth Floor is located in The old Texas School Book Depository at 411 Elm St. at the corner of Houston. 🐚 HOURS: 10–6, Sunday–Friday; 10–7 Saturday. 🐚 ADMISSION: $6 adults; seniors $3; children 6–18 $2, under 6 free. 🐚 TELEPHONE: (214) 653-6666.

GOLIAD

GOLIAD STATE HISTORICAL PARK

Three weeks after the fall of the Alamo (*see* San Antonio, Texas), on Santa Anna's direct orders, 407 captured Texas soldiers were marched out of the fort that once stood on this site and shot down in cold blood. "Remember Goliad" became as inspiring a slogan (if not as euphonious) as "Remember the Alamo" for the revenge-hungry Texans at the Battle of San Jacinto.

At least 47 Irish-born or Irish-surnamed Texans were among those killed at Goliad, and 16 of these were from the Refugio and San Patricio colonies. John Brendan Flannery (*The Irish Texans,* 1980) believes the actual number of Irish and Irish-American victims is almost certainly higher, since members of the New Orleans Greys, a volunteer unit that was at Goliad, contained many Irish-born men.

Twenty-eight Texans escaped the executioners and hid in the nearby woods. About 20 others were spared because they had ties to some of the Mexican officers. The latter included several Irish. Nicholas and John Fagan, Edward Perry, Anthony and John Sidick, and James Byrnes, for instance, were spared because they were neighbors of Mexican Capt. Carlos de la Garza. Andrew Boyle of San Patricio was saved by a Mexican officer who had received hospitality from Boyle's brother and sister.

🐚 EXHIBITS: Park headquarters features a multimedia presentation and artifacts from the massacre. 🐚 LOCATION: At the intersection of U.S. 59 and U.S. 77A. 🐚 HOURS: Daily 8–5. 🐚 ADMISSION: $3 per vehicle. 🐚 TELEPHONE: (512) 645-3405.

GREENVILLE

WALWORTH LIBRARY/AUDIE MURPHY ROOM

On January 26, 1945, the U.S. Army's Third Infantry Division was pressing the remains of Hitler's army back toward its homeland. Second Lt. Audie Murphy, acting commander of his depleted Company B, was ordered to hold a position in front of some woods. Out of the haze before them, however, loomed two companies of German troops, almost 600 strong, backed by six tanks. All Murphy and his men had were their rifles and two unimpressively armed tank destroyers.

No one would have blamed Murphy for abandoning the position and pulling back. Indeed, Murphy had already done more than his share of fighting, having won the Distinguished Service Cross, the Silver Star (with oak leaf cluster), the Bronze Star, the Purple Heart (wounded three times), and many others. Given that track record, though, there was only one course of action Murphy *could* take.

Ordering the rest of his men to fall back into the woods, Murphy stepped forward and emptied his carbine at the advancing German troops. Looking around, he caught sight of a machine gun mounted atop one of the tank destroyers, now burning furiously after being hit by a German shell earlier in the action.

Ignoring the likelihood that the tank destroyer would explode underneath him, Murphy leapt aboard, swung its machine gun toward the Germans and started firing. As he did so, he shouted instructions to the field artillery through a radio telephone while at the same time keeping up a steady patter of witty remarks. When asked if he was all right, for instance, Murphy replied, "I'm fine, sir. What are *your* postwar plans?"

After half an hour of Murphy's deadly accurate fire, the Germans pulled back with heavy casualties, and this young Irish-American had won his Medal of Honor, capping off the remarkable feat of winning every medal for gallantry the United States can bestow on a combat soldier, several of them more than once. Counting postwar decorations, Audie Murphy was entitled to wear 37 medals, making him the most decorated U.S. soldier of the Second World War. On the day he received his Medal of Honor, he was not yet 21 years of age.

Audie Murphy joined the army on his 18th birthday in June 1942, after being rejected by the marines because he was only five feet five and one-half inches tall. Murphy's Irish roots are cloudy. His paternal great-grandfather is said to have come from Ireland to New Orleans, then a major port of entry for Irish immigrants to the South. His grandfather, George Washington Murphy, fought in the Civil War on the Confederate side. Audie's mother's maiden name, Killian, was Irish. His father, Emmet Murphy, preferred to go by the name Pat and abandoned the family when Audie was a boy. Young Audie was forced to develop his marksmanship in order to put food on the family's table.

When he returned home after the war, the government propaganda machine held up the baby-faced soldier as the prototype of the ideal American hero. There were parades, speeches, and an appearance on the cover of *Life* magazine. The adulation, however, concealed weariness and depression. Audie's sister is said to have once had to rescue his medals from the trash, where he had thrown them in a fit of guilt over his own survival when so many of his friends had died.

It was another Irish-American, James Cagney, who first thought Murphy had potential as an actor. Thanks to Cagney, Murphy had a bit part in a 1948 war movie called *Beyond Glory.* His breakthrough role as a star was the 1951 Civil War epic *The Red Badge of Courage.* Four years later came the film version of his own autobiography, *To Hell and Back,* which was the biggest moneymaker in Universal Studios history up to that time.

Murphy went on to make some 40 other films, with moderate success. But there is no denying that life was mostly downhill for the young hero after the war. Many found him charming and generous, but he could also be quick-tempered and irresponsible. He went through several wives, had a few scrapes with the law, and gambled uncontrollably.

Murphy was trying to straighten out his life when he was killed in a North Carolina plane crash in 1971. He was buried in Arlington National Cemetery, in a plot near the Tomb of the Unknowns. His grave is so frequently visited that a special small path has been built to lead visitors to it.

"Audie Murphy's was not the kind of life that Americans like to emulate," wrote author Don Graham in his 1989 biography of Murphy, *No Name on the Bullet.* "From age twenty-one on, Audie Murphy's life was a postscript to battle."

❧ EXHIBITS: The centerpiece of the exhibit is an oil portrait of Audie Murphy commissioned by the local Veterans of Foreign Wars chapter in Greenville. Also on display are replicas of Murphy's medals, stills and posters from his movies and a first edition of his memoir, *To Hell and Back.* The library's collection also contains numerous research files on almost every aspect of Murphy's life and career. ❧ LOCATION: The W. Walworth Harrison Public Library is at 3716 Lee St. Also, on U.S. 69 north of Greenville just outside Celeste, there is a Texas state historical marker near Murphy's birthplace. ❧ HOURS: Monday–Thursday, Saturday 9:30–8:30; Friday 9:30–6; Sunday 1–6. ❧ ADMISSION: Free ❧ TELEPHONE: (903) 457-2992.

HOUSTON

SAN JACINTO BATTLEGROUND STATE HISTORIC PARK

Along with the Alamo, one of the most hallowed names in Texas military history is San Jacinto. In purely military terms, the action that took place on April 21, 1836, wasn't much of a battle, being over in just 20 minutes and with few casualties on the Texas side. The consequences, however, were staggering. Mexican Pres. Santa Anna was captured (after trying to escape disguised as a private soldier), an event that led to the withdrawal of Mexican forces from Texas and the latter's independence.

The battle that cemented Texas independence was fought on a piece of land known locally as McCormick's League. It was the property of an Irishman named McCormick who had left his native land in 1822 and settled with his wife, Peggy, and two sons on this flat land south of the present-day city of Houston. McCormick, however, had drowned in 1832, leaving his family to manage on their own.

Thus, Mrs. McCormick had her mind very much on practicalities when she confronted Gen. Sam Houston after the battle. Some accounts say the encounter took place immediately afterward, while Houston sat nursing his wounded foot under a tree. Others say it took place several days later. Whatever the chronology, Mrs. McCormick demanded to know who was going to clean up the mess on her land.

"Madam," Houston is said to have replied with patience, "do you not know your land will be famed in history?"

"To the devil with your glorious history!" Mrs. McCormick replied as she turned her horse away and headed back to her farmhouse.

& EXHIBITS: The 570-foot monument is made of reinforced concrete faced with Texas limestone. At the base is the San Jacinto Museum of Texas History. A multimedia show tells the story of the Texas War of Independence. & LOCATION: About 20 miles east of Houston on I-10, then follow signs. & HOURS: Daily 9–6; Observation deck open 10–5:30. & ADMISSION: None for battlefield; Slide show $3:50 adults; $3 seniors; children 12 and under $1. Observation deck fee $2.50; seniors $2; children 12 and under $1. & TELEPHONE: (713) 479-2421.

LA GRANGE

FATHER MIGUEL MULDOON MEMORIAL

In theory, all non-Spanish-speaking settlers in the Mexican province of Texas had to be Roman Catholic, which the Mexican authorities vainly hoped would ensure the settlers' loyalty. For this reason, Irish settlements in Texas were encouraged by the Mexican government (see San Patricio, Texas, and Refugio, Texas).

In practice, the religious requirement was frequently winked at, and settlers often produced records of bogus conversions in order to obtain land. Father Miguel Muldoon, the son of an Irish emigrant to Spain, frequently helped settlers obtain such "proof." This is no slur on the strength of his personal faith, which was unquestioned. He merely sought

The memorial to the "forgotten man of Texas history," Father Miguel Muldoon.

(The Institute of Texan Cultures, San Antonio, Texas)

to help the people he lived among as best he could, and he did obtain plenty of genuine conversions as well.

Father Muldoon entered the priesthood while in Spain, but he asked for assignment to the New World and arrived in Texas in 1823. He went to the frontier and took up residence in the colony established by Stephen Austin. "Muldoon, apparently of a friendly nature and jovial disposition, got along well with the Anglo colonists," writes John Brendan Flannery in *The Irish Texans* (1980). "They looked forward to his scheduled visits for baptisms and weddings."

As the number of non-Mexican colonists increased in the 1830s, however, tensions between them and the Mexican authorities began rising. Father Muldoon did his best to act as a mediator. In 1832, he helped draft a list of grievances that the colonists sent on to Mexico City. One of the major complaints was the customshouse at Anahuac, near present-day Port Arthur. Supplies and new colonists had to pass through this port of entry and were heavily taxed. Protests against the customshouse were becoming larger and more violent.

When some colonists were imprisoned at Anahuac, Muldoon accompanied the imprisoned men's neighbors, who came to demand their freedom. He even offered himself to the Mexican commander as a hostage in exchange for the imprisoned men. On another occasion, he went by himself to an Indian camp and secured the release of a kidnapped white woman. He also helped William H. Wharton, a Texas independence leader, escape from jail at Matamoros.

Muldoon became a good friend of Stephen Austin, and on a New Year's Day banquet in 1832, he rose and offered this toast:

> *May plow and harrow, spade and fack*
> *Remain the arms of Anahuac*
> *So that her rich and boundless plains*
> *May yearly yield all sorts of grains.*
> *May all religious discord fall*
> *And friendship be the creed of all.*
> *With tolerance your pastor views*
> *All sects of Christians, Turks and Jews.*
> *We now demand three rousing cheers*
> *Great Austin's health and pioneers.*

To this day, the term "Muldoon Catholic" is occasionally used in Texas to describe an ancestor whose Catholicism was simply a flag of convenience. A town in Fayette County was named for this well-loved and much-respected Irish-Catholic priest, whom Texas Pres. Sam Houston personally thanked for all he had done for the people of Texas. Nearly a hundred years later, a memorial was erected to "the forgotten man of Texas history."

& LOCATION: Approximately 5 miles south of La Grange on the east side of S.R. 77.   & HOURS: Dawn to dusk.   & ADMISSION: Free

REFUGIO

REFUGIO COUNTY MUSEUM

Conditions in Ireland were bleak in the 1830s. True, thanks to the efforts of Daniel O'Connell, Catholics had been "emancipated" in 1829, but few saw any practical improvement. Land was still firmly in the hands of an absentee British aristocracy. Memories of the 1798 uprising—in which Protestants and Catholics jointly sought to throw off British rule—and the brutal reprisals by Crown forces in its aftermath were still fresh, especially in county Wexford, where the rebellion had been strong. To these man-made burdens was added the cholera epidemic that began sweeping Ireland in 1832. Emigration seemed to many the only practical alternative to death or a life of peonage.

James Power was 10 years old when the doomed rebels of 1798 made their last stand at Vinegar Hill, not far from his home in Ballygarrett, county Wexford. In 1809, he left for Philadelphia and eventually wound up in New Orleans, where he opened a dry goods business. A few years later, he emigrated to Mexico, where he married a Mexican woman whose father had been involved in some early efforts to colonize the land that is now Texas.

Texas at that time was a wild, forbidding territory, inhabited by the fierce Comanche Indians and known only to a handful of brave settlers and missionary priests. Authorities in Mexico City, first Spanish and then Mexican, watched with trepidation as people from the newly formed United States began pushing westward. They feared that Texas would fill up with Anglo settlers who would eventually demand unification with the United States.

In partnership with another Irishman named James Hewetson, Power signed an *empresario* contract with the Mexican government on June 11, 1828. Under these agreements, the *empresario* would agree to find a certain number of settlers who met Mexican requirements (i.e., they were Catholic and would agree to become Mexican citizens). In return, the promoter would receive grants of over 40,000 acres. The two men had six years to fulfill their end of the bargain.

After several false starts, Power himself sailed to Ireland in 1833. He went to his old hometown of Ballygarrett, which he hadn't seen in 24 years. Relatives and friends were naturally astounded by his tales of life on the frontier and were interested in his plans to found a colony on the wide-open spaces of Texas. It would not be cheap, however: each adult would have to pay $30 passage money and provide his own farm implements and enough supplies to last a year. Still, it seemed like a better option than most had in Ireland, and Power had little difficulty signing up 250 families to accompany him.

Most of those hoping for a better life on the other side of the Atlantic were to be cruelly disappointed. Although most of the colonists eventually reached New Orleans, they were greeted by something they had hoped they had left behind: cholera. Many died or languished in hospitals. Others opted for the apparent safety and opportunity of New Orleans in preference to the unknown dangers of life in Texas.

Hoping he could get out of New Orleans before any more of his colonists fell ill or deserted, Power hurriedly chartered two ships for the last leg of the journey. Some kind of insurance scam was clearly afoot, for both captains apparently deliberately ran their ships aground within site of the Texas coast. No one died, but many farm implements and provisions were lost in the flooded holds.

Gravesite of Empresario James Power, Mt. Calvary Cemetery, Refugio, Texas.

Worse was to come. Before the colonists could be rowed to shore, cholera broke out again and the Mexican authorities forbade any landings. At least 250 more colonists died while aboard the stranded ships, and their bodies were dumped in the bay without ceremony.

At long last, Power succeeded in convincing the Mexicans to let the colonists be quarantined on dry land. His father-in-law helped get them released and on their way to Refugio (pronounced re-FURE-e-o), an isolated Spanish mission that would be the center of the new colony.

An estimated one-third of all those who set out from Ireland died before reaching their destination, including about half the adult men. The first titles were granted in August 1834. Today, it is not unusual to find O'Briens, Burkes, Kennedys, and other descendants of the original settlers still living in Refugio County. Some still have the original holdings that were granted to their ancestors over a century and a half ago.

Like most of the rest of the Irish colonists in Texas, Power ended up disappointing his hosts. He joined the Texas Revolution and signed both the Texas Declaration of Independence and the first state constitution when Texas joined the United States.

Nevertheless, Power had to spend his last years defending in court the legality of the land grants he had received from the Mexicans. He died

August 15, 1852. His body is buried under an impressive tombstone in Mt. Calvary Cemetery in Refugio.

In 1900, Mary Power Woodsworth, a granddaughter of the *empresario*, built an impressive house in Refugio and called it Ballygarrett, after her grandfather's hometown. The house still stands today, and even though it is boarded up and abandoned, it gives the visitor an idea of how grandly these Irish-Americans lived after they had done well so far from home.

& **EXHIBITS:** The museum contains displays on the Irish who settled Refugio, including some original clothing and weapons. Behind the museum is the home of John Linney, an Irish immigrant to Refugio, which the museum is restoring to its original condition. Also on display is the birth certificate of the most famous Irish-American son of Refugio—Texas Rangers all-star and certain baseball Hall of Famer Nolan Ryan. & **LOCATION:** The county museum is at 102 West St. Mt. Calvary Cemetery is at West Santiago and Pecan streets. Ballygarrett is the unmistakable yellow Victorian pile in the 200 block of Purisima Street. & **HOURS:** Tuesday–Saturday, 1–5. & **ADMISSION:** Free & **TELEPHONE:** (512) 526-5555.

SABINE PASS

SABINE PASS BATTLEGROUND STATE HISTORIC PARK

The fortunes of war were at a low ebb for the Confederacy in the late summer of 1863. Robert E. Lee had tasted defeat for the first time at Gettysburg on July 3, and the Mississippi River fortress of Vicksburg had fallen a day later, severing land communications between Texas and the rest of the Confederacy. The government of Jefferson Davis badly needed some good news from the battlefield. It was to be supplied by a flame-haired young Irish lieutenant and 47 Irish immigrant Texans under his command.

The Battle of Sabine Pass, located near Beaumont where the extreme eastern fringe of Texas meets the Gulf of Mexico and Louisiana, was a quick and frantic affair, lasting barely an hour. A Union force of 5,000 troops under the command of Gen. Nathaniel Banks sought to enter Texas by way of Sabine Pass. Their hope was to end blockade-running out of the area and capture the city of Houston, which, it was hoped, would effectively knock Texas out of the war.

There were diplomatic reasons for the expedition as well. Emperor Napoleon III of France was threatening to intervene in the war on the side of the Confederacy and had assembled a large army in Mexico. President Lincoln and his cabinet hoped that a major victory in Texas would dissuade the French from any adventuring.

On the Confederate side, Sabine Pass was guarded by Company F, First Regiment, Texas Heavy Artillery, C.S.A., also known as "the Davis Guards," stationed at a small emplacement called Fort Griffin. Its commander, Capt. Frederick Odlum, was frequently on duty in Sabine City or elsewhere, so the unit at the fort was under the effective command of Lt. Richard William "Dick" Dowling.

Dowling's background was scarcely typical of the Southern aristocrats that constituted the bulk of the Confederate officer corps. Nor were his men ordinary Confederate soldiers. A native of Tuam, county Galway, Dowling had come to New Orleans with his family in 1846 at 8. After his parents died in an epidemic in the 1850s, young Dick moved to Galveston and then to Houston, where he eventually opened a successful saloon. The woman Dowling eventually married was Annie Odlum, daughter of his company commander's brother. Dowling was a strong Catholic and was remembered as an active and well-liked parishioner.

The Davis Guards were originally a militia unit that had not exactly covered itself with glory during a Keystone Kops–style expedition to the Rio Grande early in the war. Predominantly Irish, the Davis Guards were made up of brawling, hard-drinking men straight off the docks and railroads of Houston and Galveston. If you treated them right, they would return the kindness, "but woe to you if you offended one," wrote a contemporary observer. "You would hear from him in true Irish style."

So wild and disorderly was the Rio Grande expedition that orders were issued for the disbandment of the Davis Guards for their "mutinous and disorderly conduct." The order was subsequently rescinded, however, and the Guards began training as artillerymen. The brush with disbandment seems to have shaped up their attitude, for they learned their new craft well and began hitting targets anchored in Sabine Pass with accuracy and regularity.

When Confederate Gen. John Magruder got wind of the sailing of the Union fleet, he warned Odlum against giving battle, which he feared would be "a useless sacrifice, with almost a certainty of defeat." Upon receiving this dispiriting message, Odlum appended his own postscript before sending it on to Dowling: "Use your own discretion about giving battle." Dowling asked his men for a show of hands. There was never any doubt about the outcome. "Victory or death was our motto," Dowling wrote later.

The Federal force arrived off Sabine Pass on the night of September 7. Thanks to confusion of orders and communications, a whole day was

A memorial to Lt.
Richard William
"Dick" Dowling
and his unit stands
in Sabine Pass,
Texas.

wasted, the element of surprise lost, and the attack postponed until the next afternoon.

Three Union gunboats, the *Sachem, Clifton,* and *Arizona,* were assigned the task of silencing any shore batteries before the troops were landed. Dowling and his men waited until the Union ships had closed to almost point-blank range, then opened up with a murderous fire. In just 45 minutes, the Southern Irish had fired 137 rounds with devastating effect, and lost not a single man. That afternoon, Dowling accepted the surrender of the grounded *Clifton,* and he and his 47 men took charge of nearly 400 Union prisoners. The rest of the Union force scurried back to New Orleans.

The Confederacy was ecstatic, with President Davis dubbing the action "the Thermopylae of the Civil War." The Confederate Congress passed a special "Thanks of Congress" to Dowling and his men, and a special award, "The Davis Guards Medal" (suspended from a green ribbon), was struck for distribution to the unit. It was the Confederacy's only national award for valor.

Dowling continued to serve after the battle and retired to Houston after the war to resume his saloon business. He is said to have founded the first oil company in Texas in 1866, but did not live to see anything come of it. He died in a yellow fever epidemic on September 23, 1867.

&◆& **EXHIBITS:** A statue of Lt. Dick Dowling stands atop a pedestal of pink Texas granite inscribed with the names of Dowling's men, an account of the action, and Jefferson Davis's tribute. &◆& **LOCATION:** About 15 miles south of Port Arthur on S.R. 87. &◆& **HOURS:** Dawn to dusk. &◆& **ADMISSION:** Free

SAN ANTONIO

THE ALAMO

Twelve Irish-born men, Catholic and Protestant, were among the 187 or so Texans who died on March 6, 1836, in the most famous siege in American history. In addition, there were 14 native-born Texans with Irish surnames among the doomed defenders of the old Spanish mission fort. Eight or nine of the Irish-born defenders were from the colonies at Refugio and San Patricio (*see* Refugio, Texas, and San Patricio, Texas).

People were praying here long before anyone started fighting here. The Mission San Antonio de Valero was built atop an old Indian holy place in 1718. The priests, who converted the local Indians to Catholicism, occupied the mission until 1793. It stood vacant into the early 1800s. Spanish troops from Mexico first fortified the building around this time and named it Pueblo del Alamo. It became a Mexican fort in 1821 when Mexico broke with Spain.

The Alamo was seized by the Texians (as they were initially known) in the opening stages of the Texas War of Independence in December 1835. Enraged, Santa Anna marched on the city in early 1836. The Texians, under Col. William Barret Travis and including former congressman Davy Crockett and the bedridden Jim Bowie, retired inside the fort, hurling defiance at Santa Anna and his men and hoping relief would arrive before the Mexican attack.

It was not to be. Santa Anna ordered that no quarter be given and no prisoners be taken. According to legend, Travis assembled his men and drew a line in the dust with his sword. Any man who crossed it was free to leave. None did. For 13 days, the defenders held out, until the Mexicans finally breached the defenses at the north wall at dawn on March 6. All the defenders died.

Santa Anna was determined that his harshness at the Alamo be remembered, and it was, but not in the way he hoped. Instead, "Remember the Alamo!" became a rallying cry for the young, dispirited Texas army. Santa Anna's two-and-a-half-week delay in laying siege to and taking the Alamo proved a mistake. Gen. Sam Houston was able to use the time to muster his forces for Santa Anna's final defeat at San Jacinto.

The Daughters of the Republic of Texas, who operate what they call "the Shrine," have recently begun honoring the Irish who gave their lives at the Alamo. In conjunction with the Harp and Shamrock Society of Texas, a wreath is laid annually at the old mission on St. Patrick's Day in memory of the Celtic soldiers who died for Texas independence.

❧ **EXHIBITS:** A video presentation and two museums chronicle the battle and Texas history. ❧ **LOCATION:** 100 Alamo Plaza, downtown, near the river. ❧ **HOURS:** Monday–Saturday 9–5:30; Sundays and holidays 10–5:30. ❧ **ADMISSION:** None, but donations appreciated. ❧ **TELEPHONE:** (210) 225-1391.

SAN PATRICIO

OLD SAN PATRICIO COURT HOUSE

The San Patricio colony had a somewhat less rocky start than the neighboring Refugio colony. Once again, *empresarios* were the trailblazers. In the case of San Patricio, they were John McMullen, born in Ireland in 1785, who relocated to Matamoros, Mexico, from Savannah, Georgia, in 1825, and his partner and son-in-law, James McGloin, who was born in county Sligo in 1799. Originally scheduled to board a ship for Australia, McGloin changed his mind at the last moment and decided to head for the United States instead. A good thing, too, since the Australian-bound ship sank without a trace.

The two met in Matamoros, where McMullen had a merchandising business, and McGloin married McMullen's stepdaughter. Lured by the prospect of large tracts of land available to successful *empresarios,* the two signed a contract to develop a colony along the banks of the Nueces River. Unlike Power and Hewetson of Refugio (*see* Refugio, Texas), who recruited their colonists directly from one part of Ireland, McMullen and McGloin canvassed Irish neighborhoods in New York and Philadelphia. As a result, the San Patricio colony was thought to be more open and less "clannish" than Refugio.

Life was far from peaceful in the politically turbulent Texas of the 1830s, however. It is not true, incidentally, that Texans were unanimously in favor of independence. Substantial numbers simply would have been content with the rights they had been promised under the Mexican Constitution—such as trial by jury and local autonomy—and were now being denied. Santa Anna, who had become president in 1830, was initially a proponent of conciliation. But a taste of power caused him to see the virtues of a strong centralized government, and he brutally repressed any opposition to his rule. One didn't have to be a seer to know that pleas for autonomy and tolerance were unlikely to get much of a hearing from him.

The Irish, by a very substantial majority, favored independence. They had not come all this way in order to exchange one tyranny for another. It is thus ironic that in many accounts the Irish have been put down as being pro-Mexican. A few no doubt were. A decade later, during the Mexican War, some Irish fought against the U.S. Army in the San Patricio Battalion, and, in a well-publicize incident, many were executed after being captured by Gen. (and future president) Zachary Taylor. These Irish had no connection with the Irish colonies in Texas, yet they were all tarred with the same brush.

By and large, the Irish were strong and unwavering supporters of Sam Houston and his fighters. And, as John Brendan Flannery notes in *The Irish Texans* (1980), "none paid a greater price" for their stand than the Irish. Enraged at the refusal of the Irish to keep their promises of loyalty, Santa Anna singled them out for particularly brutal reprisals.

Most of the fighting during the Texas War of Independence, in fact, took place in the vicinity of the two Irish colonies. The towns of San Patricio and Refugio were burned to the ground by Mexican forces and a major battle was fought at San Patricio. Even the supposedly friendly Texas forces—often made up of freebooting adventurers from outside the area—made off with cattle and livestock. In tribute to their sacrifice, Sam Houston decreed that the colony, then known by its full name of San Patricio de Hibernia, be the first county organized in the newly independent Texas Republic.

John McMullen came to a bad end. He left San Patricio in 1837 and was eventually murdered in San Antonio by persons unknown in 1853. McGloin, by contrast, continued to live in the colony he cofounded and devoted the rest of his life to making it prosper. After the Irish potato famine, he helped bring more Irish settlers to the area. His house near San Patricio is the only home built by an *empresario* that is still standing. He died June 19, 1856, and is buried in the town cemetery.

For all McGloin's efforts, however, San Patricio never really took off as a self-sustaining community. In 1886, the railroad bypassed it and the county seat was removed to Sinton. The 1919 hurricane was for many the final blow, destroying many of the remaining houses and buildings.

San Patricio today is little more than a settlement, with around 300 people. Nevertheless, in 1985 local residents banded together and rebuilt

The Old San Patricio County Courthouse was rebuilt in 1985.

the former county courthouse, using old photographs as a guide. A local museum was opened, and historic homes are in the process of being restored. The town's St. Patrick's Day celebration is among the most lively in Texas.

❧ **EXHIBITS:** Texas historic markers are placed at most of the above sites. The second floor of the courthouse—which now serves as the town hall—features the courtroom, restored as it appeared in the 19th century. The Old San Patricio Museum contains artifacts on the lives of the early Irish in San Patricio. ❧ **LOCATION:** The restored courthouse sits on the corner of S.R. 666 and McGloin Avenue, just north of the Nueces River. St. Patrick's Church, the Old San Patricio Museum, and the McKeown House are about a half-mile farther along S.R. 666. The McGloin House is at Round Lake about 5½ miles down Nopal Road, which begins just across Route 666 from St. Patrick's. (Stay on the asphalt roadway. Do not stray onto the gravel road.) ❧ **HOURS:** St. Patrick's Day is one of the few regularly scheduled times when the restored courthouse is open to the public. Town meetings are held on the first Monday of the month. The museum is open the first Sunday of every month. Other times call for an appointment. ❧ **ADMISSION:** Free ❧ **TELEPHONE:** Call Jack Lewis of the San Patricio Historical Society for further information and admittance: (512) 547-3432; or Mayor Lonnie Glasscock III: (512) 547-2256.

SHAMROCK

AN IRISH TOWN

A homesick Irish sheep farmer named George Nichels originally dubbed this tiny hamlet Shamrock in 1890. Few other Irish have ever actually lived in this small natural gas town on the high plains of the Texas panhandle, and there were several attempts over the years to change the name. But the town fathers decided years ago it was better to capitalize on the town's ethnic connection rather than fight it.

As a result, you don't have to travel all the way to Ireland to kiss the Blarney stone; a small sliver of the real thing was brought to Shamrock in 1959, embedded under glass, and placed in a park. The annual St. Patrick's Day Parade is the major annual event.

& **EXHIBITS:** The small stone encasing the sliver of the Blarney stone is located in Elmore Park. & **LOCATION:** On Interstate 40, approximately 27 miles west of the Oklahoma state line. & **HOURS:** Dawn to dusk. & **ADMISSION:** Free

ARIZONA

CALIFORNIA

COLORADO

IDAHO

MONTANA

NEVADA

NEW MEXICO

OREGON

UTAH

WASHINGTON

WYOMING

The former Hibernia National Bank headquarters. See page 465.

ARIZONA

1 William O. "Buckey" O'Neill Memorial, Prescott
2 Russ House, Tombstone
3 Arizona Historical Society, Tucson

CALIFORNIA

4 Bodie State Historic Park, Bodie
5 Tao House, Danville
6 Old St. Raymond's Church and Irish Heritage Park, Dublin
7 Concannon Winery, Livermore
8 Doheny Mansion, Los Angeles
9 William Mulholland Memorial Fountain and Mulholland Drive, Los Angeles
10 Reed Sawmill Restoration, Mill Valley
11 Town Named for Two Brothers, Murphys
12 Archbishop's Mansion, San Francisco
13 Broderick-Terry Duel Site, San Francisco
14 Chief Sullivan Fire House, San Francisco
15 Fr. Peter Yorke Way, San Francisco
16 Hibernia National Bank Building, San Francisco
17 James Flood Mansion (Pacific Union Club) and Fairmont Hotel, San Francisco
18 The *Jeremiah O'Brien*, San Francisco
19 Kate Kennedy School, San Francisco
20 Knights of the Red Branch Hall, San Francisco
21 Mechanics Monument, San Francisco
22 Mission Dolores, San Francisco
23 Nobbie Clark's Folly, San Francisco
24 O'Farrell Street, San Francisco
25 Phelan Building, San Francisco
26 Phillip Burton Memorial, San Francisco
27 Robert Emmet Statue, San Francisco
28 St. Patrick's Church, San Francisco
29 United Irish Cultural Center, San Francisco
30 Captain Thomas Fallon House, San Jose
31 St. Vincent's School for Boys, San Rafael
32 Villa Montalvo, Saratoga
33 Daniel O'Connell Memorial Bench, Sausalito
34 Ronald Reagan Presidential Library and Museum, Simi Valley
35 Donner Historic State Park, Truckee
36 Filoli Mansion, Woodside
37 Richard M. Nixon Presidential Library and Birthplace, Yorba Linda
38 O'Shaughnessy Dam, Yosemite

COLORADO

39 Molly Brown House Museum, Denver
40 An Irish Town, Leadville

IDAHO

41 O'Farrell's Cabin, Boise

MONTANA

42 Historic Anaconda, Anaconda
43 Marcus Daly Mansion, Hamilton
44 General Thomas Francis Meagher Equestrian Statue, Helena
45 Little Bighorn National Battlefield, Helena

NEVADA

46 City Named for an Irishman, Laughlin
47 Mackay Museum of Mines and Mackay Memorial, Reno
48 Mackay Mansion, Virginia City
49 St. Mary of the Mountains Church, Virginia City

NEW MEXICO

50 Ghost Ranch Living Museum, Abiquiu
51 Lincoln Courthouse Museum, Lincoln

OREGON

52 John McLoughlin House National Historic Site, Oregon City

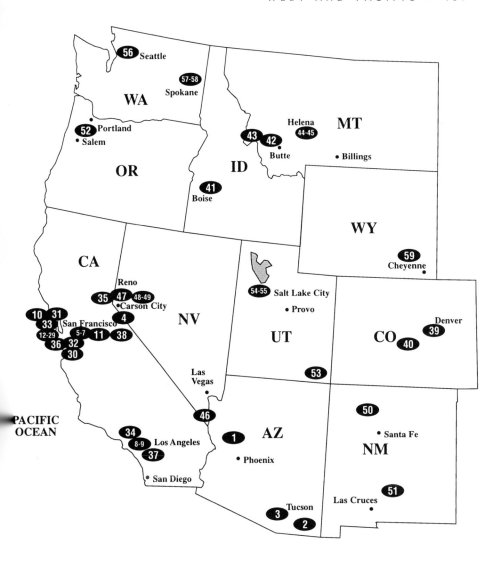

UTAH

53 Goulding's Trading Post and
   Lodge, Monument Valley
54 Governor's Mansion (Kearns
   Mansion), Salt Lake City
55 Col. Patrick Edward Connor
   Gravesite, Salt Lake City

WASHINGTON

56 Burke Museum, Seattle
57 Crosby Library, Spokane
58 Patsy Clark's Mansion, Spokane

WYOMING

59 Fort Laramie National Historic
   Site, Fort Laramie

ARIZONA

WILLIAM O. "BUCKEY" O'NEILL
MEMORIAL

The Spanish-American War of 1898 was a triumph of American pluck and daring over military logic and common sense. On paper, the United States did not stand a chance. On the day war with Spain was declared, April 21, 1898, the U.S. regular army consisted of just 2,143 officers and 26,040 enlisted men, most of them scattered in small posts across the American West. The same month, the Spanish military listed 196,820 troops garrisoning Cuba alone, of whom 155,000 were regulars. Thus, the United States would be forced to raise huge numbers of utterly raw troops and train them in great haste before active campaigning could begin.

One of the most eclectic units in an eclectic war was the First Volunteer Cavalry Regiment, or "the Rough Riders," as they came to be known. They were a mélange of Western cowboys and New York blue bloods straight out of the social register. In addition to their great commanders, Leonard Wood and Theodore Roosevelt, their ranks included Benjamin Franklin Daniels, the marshal of Dodge City; Bob Wrenn and Bill Larned, two of the nation's top tennis players; Dudley Dean, a famed quarterback for the Harvard football team; Craig Wadsworth, a star polo player; and many others.

But the unit that would become the Rough Riders was the brainchild of an Irish-American Arizona sheriff, newspaperman, lawyer, politician, gambler, and businessman named William O. "Buckey" O'Neill. He is supposed to have earned his nickname by his skill at the Indian game of faro, which involved a move called "bucking the tiger." There are countless stories about Buckey O'Neill, some of them no doubt true. But it was at a desolate place in Cuba called San Juan Hill that he would earn his greatest fame.

There is confusion about O'Neill's birthplace. A 1940 biography gives his place of birth as February 2, 1860, at St. Louis. The muster roll of the

William O. "Buckey" O'Neill circa 1898. (Sharlot Hall Museum Library/Archives, Prescott, Arizona)

Rough Riders, however, preserved in the National Archives, says, "38, 5'10½ in.; dark brown eyes, dark brown hair; born in Ireland, lawyer, joined April 29, Whipple Barracks; residence, Prescott, Arizona, married."

Whatever the truth, O'Neill was described by a contemporary as "strikingly Irish" in appearance with a persuasive voice and manner. His father had served with the Irish Brigade during the Civil War, and the son had been schooled in the nation's capital. He migrated west when he was barely 20 years old and is supposed to have arrived in Arizona in the garb of a Catholic priest. Stories about his daring multiplied quickly and he was twice elected sheriff of Yavapai County. A Populist Democrat, he ran unsuccessfully for Congress in 1896 but was elected mayor of Prescott a year later.

O'Neill made a fortune for himself in mining, newspapering, lawyering, and various other business pursuits. He was in the process of developing real estate in Phoenix when word came of the mysterious sinking of the

U.S. battleship *Maine* in Havana harbor. Without waiting for a formal declaration of war, O'Neill swung into action. Sen. Henry Cabot Lodge of Massachusetts, a war hawk, clipped a newspaper item datelined Prescott, Arizona, and sent it to Assistant Navy Secretary Theodore Roosevelt:

> As a result of the sinking of the *Maine* at Havana and the feeling that war is imminent, initial steps are being taken in this city to form the first regiment of the Arizona flying cavalry. . . . The personnel of the force will be made up principally of cowboys, all of whom are expert marksmen and skilled horsemen. . . . The plan was initiated and is being carried forward by Alexander O. Brodie, West Point graduate, and Mayor Wm. O. O'Neill of this city. . . .

Congress authorized the raising of three "cowboy" regiments made up of civilian volunteers from the western states and territories. Throughout the West, cowboys and ranchers poured into recruiting depots offering their services. On May 4, barely two weeks into the war, O'Neill and Brodie led more than 200 men in a parade through Prescott, the first volunteer troops organized for the war. The governor of the territory presented the unit with a mountain lion as a mascot.

O'Neill was blessed with the Irish "gift of gab," and his displays of erudition amazed his fellow Rough Riders, including Theodore Roosevelt. The latter noted in his diary how this rough-hewn western sheriff could lean over the rail of the troopship at sunset and quote from memory the poetry of Shelley, Browning, and Whitman. O'Neill also displayed a surprisingly tolerant and compassionate nature, even toward his foes. "They can't help being Spaniards any more than a skunk can help being a skunk. God made them that way," he said on the trip to Cuba.

O'Neill didn't have long to wait to display his physical courage, however. As the small boats carrying the first American troops ashore approached Cuba at Daiquirí, one that was carrying two troopers of the all-black 10th Cavalry Regiment overturned. O'Neill instantly dived in to save the two men, who were weighted down by their heavy equipment. His efforts proved futile, however, and both men drowned. The incident brought O'Neill his first national publicity, however, since it was witnessed by a reporter for the *New York World*, who sent an account of O'Neill's heroism home.

The San Juan Heights command the eastern approaches to Santiago, the major city in southeastern Cuba. The Spanish had fortified them heavily, but fortunately for the Americans, the Spanish commander had placed only a relatively small force in the fortifications.

The attack itself on July 1 was a complete shambles, with American artillery actually hitting American troops. The Spanish at first resisted fiercely, pinning down the American forces, and many of the untried American volunteers refused to go farther. Once a couple of Gatling guns were brought up, however, the Spaniards began fleeing their positions and the Americans sprinted up the hill to victory.

Nevertheless, as Geoffrey Regan acidly comments in his book *Great Military Disasters* (1987), "It must be rare in military history for an army to have performed as ineptly as the Americans did at San Juan Hill and still win the battle."

The victory was costly, however, and Buckey O'Neill was one of the casualties. Displaying not the slightest concern for his own safety, O'Neill strode up and down in front of his line of troops, calmly smoking a cigarette as bullets pierced the air all around him.

Cries for him to take cover came from the ranks. One of his sergeants screamed, "Captain, a bullet is sure to hit you!" O'Neill took the cigarette from his mouth, blew out a cloud of smoke, and smilingly shouted back, "Sergeant, the Spanish bullet isn't made that will kill me!" A moment later, a bullet struck him in the mouth and exited out the back of his neck. "The poetry-loving mayor passed into the great beyond before he hit the ground," wrote Virgil Carrington Jones in *The Rough Riders* (1971).

O'Neill was buried in Cuba, with many of the other Rough Riders killed there. His death hit Arizonans hard. The black residents of Phoenix, in appreciation of his efforts to save the two black troopers at Daiquirí, held a mass meeting and adopted a resolution lamenting his death. His widow was touched, commenting that her husband "was a friend of everybody, regardless of race or color."

An equestrian statue of O'Neill, executed by Solon Borglum, brother of Mt. Rushmore sculptor Gutzon Borglum, stands today in Court House Square in Prescott, an eternal reminder of this great Irish-American legend in the Far West.

❧ **LOCATION:** Prescott is the former territorial capital of Arizona and is now a resort area. It is located in the west-central part of the state off U.S. 89. ❧ **ADMISSION:** Free ❧ **TELEPHONE:** Prescott Chamber of Commerce: (602) 445-2000.

TOMBSTONE

RUSS HOUSE

Tombstone, "the town too tough to die," is probably the most famous Old West town of them all. The name came, not from the many shootouts that took place here, including the famed one at the O.K. Corral, but from someone's telling town founder Ed Shieffelin that "all you'll find out here is your tombstone."

But amid the Earps, the Clantons, Boot Hill, and the general rowdiness, there was a gentle Irishwoman who was an island of quiet hospitality. Her name was Nellie Cashman.

Nellie was born in Ireland, though exactly where and when is uncertain. She and her sister boarded a ship at Cobh (then Queenstown), county Cork, for Boston in 1844. They moved on to Washington, D.C., and eventually to San Francisco, following so many other Irish to see if they could get a piece of the prosperity of the western goldfields. Nellie also lived in such mining towns as Virginia City and Coeur d'Alene, Idaho. Along the way, she operated restaurants and rooming houses that catered to the miners in the area, many of whom were Irish.

Nellie came to Tombstone in 1879. She opened a grocery store in partnership with a local man, but later bought a restaurant/rooming house called the Russ House. She also owned a saloon, but she never entered it. Nellie was firmly against alcohol, and to this day it is not served in the restaurant that now bears her name.

In addition to her business, Nellie thought the town of Tombstone could do with a bit of spirituality and some decent health care, so in 1881 she brought three Sisters of Mercy to Tombstone to open a hospital. They founded St. Mary's, which was the first nonmilitary hospital in Arizona. (It still operates today.) Nellie was also largely responsible for founding Sacred Heart Church, the first Catholic church in the town.

Always a woman with a wanderlust, however, Nellie left Tombstone in the early 1890s and went to Africa for a time. In 1898, she returned to Arizona and opened a restaurant in Prescott. When gold was discovered in the Klondike, however, Nellie was off again, opening another restaurant in Dawson in northern Canada. Eventually, she settled in Victoria, on Vancouver Island, British Columbia, where she died on January 4, 1925.

⫸ **EXHIBITS:** There is a portrait of Nellie Cashman in the restaurant, and a pamphlet on her life is available. ⫸ **LOCATION:** The Russ House, is at 115 S. 5th St. in Tombstone. ⫸ **HOURS:** Call for operating hours. ⫸ **TELEPHONE:** (602) 457-2212.

TUCSON

ARIZONA HISTORICAL SOCIETY

They were the "other" Irish-Americans, the Hispano-Hibernian-Americans who served Spain in the construction of its empire in the New World as well as its former colonies once they gained independence. Though not nearly so numerous as the Irish who arrived in North America, the Hispanic Irish-Americans made significant contributions as well.

How did they get to Spain? The flight of the Catholic earls of Tyrone and Tyrconnell from Ireland in 1607 sealed Ireland's fate under Protestant English rule. Many Irish Catholics who had the means and the desire sought haven overseas in the Catholic lands that were England's sworn enemies, particularly France and Spain. Within seven years of the Flight of the Earls, there were 300 Irish seminary students in Spain and 3,000 Irish soldiers enlisted in Spanish regiments. Many, many more would follow over the next few centuries.

Some of these "Wild Geese" would rise to high rank in their adopted countries. Ambrose O'Higgins became viceroy of Peru, the highest-ranking official in all of New Spain. Col. Arturo O'Neill, commander of the Regimento de Hibernia, which took Pensacola from the British during the American Revolution in 1781 (see Pensacola, Florida), became Spanish governor of Florida. In the postcolonial era, of course, there was Bernardo O'Higgins, the father of Chile, and Adm. William Brown, father of the Argentine navy.

The city of Tucson, Arizona, owes its existence to one of these Wild Geese. Don Hugo Oconor was baptized Hugh O'Conor in the parish of St. Thomas in Dublin on Christmas Eve 1734, the second son of Daniel O'Conor and Margaret Ryan. The family claimed descent from Roderic O'Conor, the last high king of Ireland, but by the time of Hugh's birth, the family's once vast landholdings were reduced to a small estate in Clonalis, county Roscommon.

Hugh thus decided to make his way to Spain as a soldier in the service of the Spanish king, as his great-grandfather had done in the time of the Flight of the Earls. His military career would last 27 years and carry to him to battles and adventures on two continents.

Hugh O'Conor (or "Hugo Oconor," as the Spanish named him) rose swiftly through the ranks as his natural military ability became apparent. He commanded Spanish troops in the wars against England and Portugal in the late 1750s and early 1760s. He was transferred to Cuba, which Spain had taken back after a brief sojourn under English rule, and won notice for his ability to take raw recruits and whip them into fighting shape in record time.

Oconor seemed just the man the viceroy of New Spain (Mexico) was looking for in 1767 when he needed somebody to tackle the situation in the Interior Provinces of New Spain, which included present-day Texas, New Mexico, and Arizona. It was a daunting prospect. Spanish settlements in the area were coming under increasingly heavy attack from Apache Indians, who were themselves under pressure from the more powerful Comanches. Soldiers were poorly trained and equipped, and the viceroy suspected local commanders of embezzling army funds for their own use.

Appointed commandante inspector (in effect, governor) of the area, Oconor reorganized the situation from top to bottom. He closed indefensible outposts and organized a line of 22 presidios between Texas and California and sent out regular patrols that helped end the Apache raids.

He established a regular rank system and appointed a paymaster to see to it funds were properly disbursed and accounted for.

In four years in this demanding post, Oconor succeeded as well as could be expected and established relative peace. His red hair and beard made him notorious among the Indians he fought, who nicknamed him "Colonel Colorado." He paid for his vigorous action with his health, however, which suffered badly in the hot climate. In 1777, while serving as governor of the Yucatán, he fell ill and died, only 45 years of age.

The most enduring piece of Oconor's legacy, however, is the city of Tucson, Arizona. Tucson is one of the *presidios* Oconor established against Indian attacks. By tradition, Oconor is supposed to have traced out the line of the fort in the dust himself on a hot day in August 1775.

&. **EXHIBITS:** In August 1994, the museum established a major exhibit entitled "Hugo Oconor and the Irish Military Experience in New Spain." It utilizes artifacts, paintings, drawings, weapons, old maps, and documents from the society's collection, as well as from Spain. &. **LOCATION:** The Tucson Historical Society is near the entrance to the University of Arizona at 949 E. 2nd St. &. **HOURS:** Monday–Saturday 10–4; Sunday 12–4. &. **ADMISSION:** Free, but donations appreciated. &. **TELEPHONE:** (602) 628-5774.

CALIFORNIA

BODIE STATE HISTORIC PARK

The story of the Irish in the settling of the American West remains one of the richest untapped veins in American scholarship and one that is only now attracting the attention of academics. Perhaps because the Irish tended to come west as individuals rather than as whole communities, they tended to fade into the background, but they were very much here. The U.S. cavalry had a strong Irish representation within its ranks, and while the bulk of Irish immigrants stayed on the east coast, many individual Irish came west to try their hand at prospecting.

Bodie is now a preserved ghost town, but in its day it had a well-deserved reputation as one of the roughest gold mining towns in America. Nearly $100 million in ore was taken out of the surrounding hills in the 20 years or so that Bodie was a gold mining center.

The best study of Bodie, done by Prof. Roger McGrath of the University of California at Los Angeles (*Gunfighters, Highwaymen and Vigilantes: Violence on the Frontier*), makes note of the particular presence of the Irish in the town. "The Irish were irrepressible," he wrote. "They leaped out of the original source material with every bit of research I did."

In *The Uncounted Irish,* Margaret Fitzgerald and Joseph King note that of the 5,300 inhabitants of Bodie in 1880, the U.S. Census lists 850 as "Irish-born." Many of those listed as "American-born" or "Canadian-born" also had Irish surnames.

No less than 40 saloons graced the streets of this small town, and many had names like Gallagher's Shamrock Bar. It was in the Shamrock on June 1, 1879 that a blazing shootout took place between county Tyrone-born Alex "Big Alec" Nixon and one Tom McDonald. Big Alec came out the loser, shot in the side and dying two hours later.

The sheriffs in Bodie had names such as McQuade, O'Malley and Kerrigan. Sometimes it was hard to tell the lawmen and the gangsters apart. The Daly gang, a group of cutthroat Irish, were actually deputized for a time. They were all hanged, however, after a vigilance committee had enough of their bloody antics.

But one man who was undeniably on the right side of the law in Bodie was Patrick Reddy, who was probably the most famous trial lawyer west of the Mississippi in the latter half of the 19th century. Born in Woonsocket, R.I. of Irish parents from county Carlow, Reddy arrived in California in 1861 at the age of 22.

After a few years in the mining camps, he was forced to quit because he lost his left arm in a quarrel with another miner. Casting about for a profession that did not require two arms, he qualified as a lawyer. Setting up shop in Bodie in 1879, Reddy specialized in representing miners in claim-jumping cases and the like, often without fee. Even though he was born in the United States, Reddy had affected a lilting Irish brogue that he used to great effect on judges and juries.

Reddy founded the Bodie chapter of the Irish Land League and served a term as a state senator and as a delegate to the state constitutional convention. A friend of organized labor and advocate of the underdog, he was sought out by other lawyers for advice and by aspiring lawyers as a mentor. He died in San Francisco in 1900.

⮾ **EXHIBITS:** One hundred and seventy buildings are preserved here in what is described as a state of "arrested decay." That is, they will not be restored, but will not decay any further.   ⮾ **LOCATION:** The park is 20 miles southeast of Bridgeport via U.S. 396 and California state route 270. (The last three miles to the park are unpaved, and the park is frequently closed in winter.)   ⮾ **HOURS:** 9–7 during summer; 9–4 rest of year. ⮾ **ADMISSION:** $5 per vehicle.   ⮾ **TELEPHONE:** (619) 647-6445

DANVILLE

TAO HOUSE

Eugene O'Neill was a famous and newly wealthy playwright (he won the Nobel Prize for literature in 1936) when he and his wife Carlotta bought this house on the slopes of Mt. Diablo in Danville in the East Bay area. It was here that he began writing the "cycle" of 12 great tragedies that he hoped would cap his career. As it turned out, he finished only the first play, *A Touch of the Poet*, before he ceased writing altogether around 1943, as Parkinson's disease steadily robbed him of his gifts.

O'Neill had already changed the face of American drama by the time he moved into Tao (pronounced dow) House. American plays had been pretty dull going before O'Neill came along, featuring melodramatic set pieces, lots of dramatic gestures, and overwrought oratory. Young O'Neill had seen a bellyful of this kind of drama as he literally grew up backstage, watching his father, James, perform in his signature role as Edmond Dantes in *The Count of Monte Cristo.*

Once O'Neill got serious in the 1920s, however, the theater was transformed into a place of fire and brimstone, passion and anger, driven along by such then-unheard-of themes as incest, suicide, infanticide, and miscegenation. In *Strange Interlude* the characters spoke directly to the audience about their deepest thoughts and fears. This is now a standard technique, but was bold and innovative in 1928. In *The Great God Brown,* O'Neill brought back the ancient Greek use of masks to indicate emotion.

Irish characters are found throughout O'Neill's fiction. Bill Hogan, the pig farmer and shrewd Irish clown in *A Moon for the Misbegotten,* is one of O'Neill's most sharply drawn creations and was based on an Irishman named John Dolan whom he had known in New London. Cornelius Melody, the defeated but defiant "shanty" Irishman of *A Touch of the Poet,* is seen as a spokesman for O'Neill's own bitter feelings about how his family was snubbed by the "better" (i.e., Yankee) people of New London, Connecticut.

Although by no means a recluse—he and Carlotta frequently entertained guests—O'Neill found the isolation of Tao House ideal for his creative needs. Sealed off from any visitors by three separate sets of doors, O'Neill would often start early in the morning and work well into the night, sometimes developing several plays at once. Sometimes he took a break, swimming in the pool, walking with Carlotta, or listening to his extensive collection of jazz and blues records.

In addition to the uncompleted tragic cycle, O'Neill also wrote *The Iceman Cometh* at Tao House, as well as *Long Day's Journey Into Night,* which he refused to publish during his lifetime. The interlude at Tao House seems to have been the happiest, most contented period of O'Neill's boisterous life.

The onset of the Second World War, unfortunately, brought the idyll to an end. The unavailability of servants and O'Neill's fears of a Japanese invasion caused him and Carlotta to return to the East Coast in 1943. "We stayed at Tao House for six whole years," Carlotta recalled later on, "longer than we lived anywhere else."

& **EXHIBITS:** The house is furnished in the Oriental style the O'Neills favored when they lived here. A guided tour is included. & **LOCATION:** The house is 1½ miles west of the town at the end of privately owned Kuss Road. Because of neighborhood fears of heavy traffic, however, it is not

St. Raymond's Church was constructed with the help of the townspeople of Dublin.

possible to reach the house except in a National Park Service van that runs twice a day. Seating is limited and reservations a must. ❧ **HOURS:** Two tours a day are conducted, one at 10 and the other at 12:30, seven days a week, but hours are changeable. Call to find out van pickup point. ❧ **ADMISSION:** Free ❧ **TELEPHONE:** (510) 838-0249.

DUBLIN

OLD ST. RAYMOND'S CHURCH AND IRISH HERITAGE PARK

One sight of the green-and-white police cars tells you you're in Dublin, California, 40 miles east of San Francisco on the far side of the bay. Although the area is now an ethnic melting pot, and suburban

Marker in Irish Heritage Park honoring Tom Donlon.

high-tech sprawl has eliminated most of the original town, traces of Dublin's Irish heritage are still visible if the visitor knows where to look.

The best short account of Dublin is given in Fitzgerald and King's *The Uncounted Irish* (1990). The Irish were very numerous in rural California in the mid-19th century. Thirty-eight of fifty California counties reported a majority of its foreign-born residents were Irish. In the 1980 census, California was first in the nation in the number of residents who reported having "one specific" Irish ancestor.

The Dublin area was first settled in 1847 by two county Roscommon families, the Fallons and the Murrays, who avoided being trapped with the Donner party only because they chose to push on from Ft. Bridger with little rest. After a few years in what is now San Jose, Jeremiah Fallon and Michael Murray made enough money in the goldfields to purchase the land at the foot of Mt. Diablo that is now Dublin.

As in so many other places, a small settlement of Irish attracted others. Census records show families with such Irish surnames as Donlon, Horan, McGrath, and Flanagan settling in the new community.

Construction of St. Raymond's Church began in the late 1850s. Thirty-six of the forty-eight family names on the original donors' list are clearly Irish in origin. One tragedy accompanied its construction: Tom Donlon, who had pledged the then-large sum of $50 toward construction, fell from the roof and was killed. He was buried in the churchyard, and a street and school in Dublin today are named for him.

❧ **EXHIBITS:** The Irish Heritage Park is in the cemetery/churchyard at the rear of the church. In addition to the headstones themselves, plaques have been erected at the gravesites explaining the identity of the people buried here and their relationships to one another.

Next to the church is Murray's School, which is now maintained as a museum by the Dublin Historical Preservation Association. Just a short distance away, at 6680 Regional St., is Dublin's Howard Johnson's Hotel, where a heritage room on the early Irish history of the area is maintained.

&⪙ LOCATION: From San Francisco, cross the Bay Bridge and follow Route 580 to where it intersects with Route 680. Go north approximately 5 miles to Dublin. The distinctive white steeple of Old St. Raymond's Church is at 6600 Donlan Way. &⪙ HOURS: Hours for St. Raymond's and Murray's School Museum are irregular. Call for information. Heritage room in Howard Johnson's is open during regular business hours. &⪙ ADMISSION: Free &⪙ TELEPHONE: Murray's School (Dublin Historical Preservation Association): (510) 828-3377; Howard Johnson's (510) 828-7750.

LIVERMORE

CONCANNON WINERY

When Pres. Ronald Reagan stepped off the plane for his "homecoming" visit to Ireland in 1984, he presented Irish Prime Minister Garret Fitzgerald with a vintage bottle of Petite Sirah from the Concannon Vineyards in Livermore, California. The gesture thus proved that Irish immigrants succeeded in many endeavors in their new country besides politics.

James Concannon was an Irish-speaker from the Aran Islands who arrived in the Livermore area in 1883. At age 18 he had landed in 1865 in Boston, where he worked for a time in the Singer Sewing Machine factory. After many odd jobs and a return to the Arans to marry his sweetheart, James and his young family moved west, where he tried sheepherding for a time in Oregon and then worked as a traveling salesman. By 1883, he had accumulated enough capital to purchase the 47 acres in Livermore that today serve as the focus of the winery that bears his name.

James had taken the trouble to learn Spanish, which was still the language of many Californians, and from the friendships he formed he began to take an interest in viticulture. After some study at the University of California at Berkeley, he became convinced that the land and soil conditions in northern California were almost identical to those of the wine-growing regions in Europe. He began importing vines from France and elsewhere. This was by no means easy or inexpensive, since the cuttings took months to make the long, arduous journey to California, if they arrived at all.

Gradually, by trial and error, the Irish immigrant learned the complex trade of winemaking. His big break came when he obtained from his good friend Bishop Alemany of San Francisco the contract for providing the diocese with sacramental wine. It was this connection alone that later

Concannon is one of the oldest vineyard wineries in Livermore Valley. *(Courtesy of Concannon Winery)*

enabled the winery to survive the dark days of Prohibition, when almost all the other wineries in California were forced to close down.

James Concannon never forgot his Irish roots and always instilled a strong sense of ethnic identity in his children. The family always said their daily rosaries in Gaelic, and Thomas Concannon, a half-brother, eventually returned to Ireland and helped found the Gaelic League, which revived the ancient Irish language early in this century.

The Concannon Winery remains in operation today as the oldest continuously operating winery in the state. Although the family was forced to sell the business to outside investors in 1980, family members, particularly Jim Concannon, the founder's grandson, continue to be involved in its operations.

🍂 **EXHIBITS:** James Concannon's 1883 house now serves as the winery's headquarters. Staff are happy to show visitors around. And, of course, what would a winery be without a tasting room? 🍂 **LOCATION:** From the Bay Bridge take Route 580E to the North Livermore Avenue exit and turn right (south). Go about 3 miles until you reach Tesla Avenue. The winery is at 4590 Tesla. 🍂 **HOURS:** 9–5 Monday–Friday; 10–5 Saturdays and Sundays. 🍂 **ADMISSION:** Free 🍂 **TELEPHONE:** (510) 447-3760.

LOS ANGELES

DOHENY MANSION

 The mention of oil does not normally bring California to mind, but for years it has been one of the nation's major oil-producing states, after Texas and Oklahoma. Edward L. Doheny, the son of an Irish immigrant, was the man who struck oil in California, drilling his well in what is now Westlake Park in 1892.

Gold, not oil, was the first mineral Doheny sought. His father was a native of county Tipperary, and his mother, born in Newfoundland, was also of Irish heritage. They settled in Fond du Lac, Wisconsin. Almost as soon as young Doheny graduated from high school, he headed west to look for gold.

He found it in Arizona, but his failure to properly register his claim meant that he received little from the opening of the Cave Creek fields or the Wild Rye Creek district. Three years later, he was more careful when he struck gold in the Black Range of New Mexico and made a small fortune for himself.

Shortly after achieving this success, however, Doheny suffered an accident that landed him in the hospital with two broken legs. He used this period of enforced idleness to study law, and he qualified for the bar in New Mexico. He practiced for only a year, however. Bored, he dusted off his pick and shovel again and traveled the West in search of another big strike.

As he told the story in later years, he was in Los Angeles in 1892 when one day he noticed a passing wagon loaded with brea, a tarry black pitch that was used locally for fuel. Doheny's thoughts turned to the possibility there might be oil deposits in the area. He examined a brea-producing area near what is now Westlake Park and concluded that a large quantity of oil lay underneath the area. With a partner, he bought a lot and began drilling. The pair struck "black gold" almost immediately, and the California oil industry was born.

More big finds followed at Fullerton and Kern River valley, as well as in Mexico. Doheny ranked with John D. Rockefeller as one of the barons of the early oil industry.

But it was a political scandal that was to make Doheny nationally infamous and forever tar his name. His company leased from the Department of the Interior 30,000 acres known as the naval reserve oil lands in the Elk Horn district of Wyoming. The area became famous, however, as "Teapot Dome."

In exchange for the right of access to the oil, Doheny agreed to guarantee a supply of fuel for the navy and to construct the facilities to store it at such major naval bases as Pearl Harbor. Doheny sank millions into the project, constructing tank farms and pipelines to carry the oil.

Unfortunately, Doheny had had to provide Interior Secretary Albert Fall with roughly $400,000 in bribes in order to obtain the leases. Fall eventually went to jail, and Doheny lost his oil concession and virtually his entire investment. Ironically, Doheny's investment turned out to be extremely fortunate, for the fuel tanks he built were not attacked by the Japanese at Pearl Harbor, and it was that fuel that kept the U.S. Navy in the war during the dangerous six months before the Battle of Midway turned the tide.

None of that was apparent at the time, however, and Doheny had to accept considerable public opprobrium, though he avoided prosecution. He died in 1935.

The Doheny mansion was completed in 1900, but Doheny only bought it later on. It has been called by some the grandest residence ever built in California, Hearst Castle included. Damaged in a 1933 earthquake, it was rebuilt in a beautiful French rococo style.

❧ **EXHIBITS:** The house is now occupied by the Sisters of St. Joseph of Carandolet. ❧ **LOCATION:** 8 Chester Place, Los Angeles. ❧ **HOURS:** Tours can be arranged by appointment. ❧ **ADMISSION:** Donation requested. ❧ **TELEPHONE:** (213) 746-0405.

WILLIAM MULHOLLAND MEMORIAL FOUNTAIN AND MULHOLLAND DRIVE

For more than 200 miles, it snakes its way from the Owens Valley in Inyo County all the way to the San Fernando Valley, an intricate network of tunnels and aqueducts that even today ranks among the greatest engineering feats of modern times. When the Los Angeles Aqueduct was built, it was hailed as second only to the Panama Canal as an example of American engineering know-how, and the man who conceived and built it was proclaimed the "Goethals of the West" and "California's Greatest Man." He was William Mulholland, chief water engineer of Los Angeles, native of Ireland, and the man who, in a very real sense, "invented" Los Angeles as one of the great cities of the world.

In the decades since the aqueduct was built, some critics have impugned Mulholland's work, complaining that he and his associates "raped" the Owens Valley and ruthlessly took its water to slake the thirst of a parched Los Angeles and enrich himself and the city's establishment. There is an element of truth to this criticism, but for most people it is hard to look at what he brought forth and say that he did wrong.

In the first years of the 20th century, the small but growing city of Los Angeles had drawn its water from the Los Angeles River, not much more than a stream really. But as the population grew, water famines became more and more common, especially on hot summer days. At those times, Angelenos would often open their dry taps wide before going to bed, hoping their buckets would catch enough water to get them through the next day.

William Mulholland (left), and Mayor George Cryer of Los Angeles (right).

(UPI/Bettmann)

Clearly, this situation was intolerable if Los Angeles was to have a future as a great metropolis.

Enter William Mulholland. Born in Belfast in 1855, he ran away from home at age 14 to become an apprentice sailor. In five years at sea, he began developing the mechanical aptitude and self-education as an engineer with which he would later make his living. After various wanderings in Europe, the United States, and the West Indies, he arrived in Los Angeles in 1876, where he found employment as a ditchdigger with the Los Angeles City Water Company, which was struggling to provide water to the nascent city of 15,000.

It was here that he made the critical connection that would change his life and the course of Los Angeles history. He became friendly with Fred Eaton, the water company's chief superintendent. Eaton was soon elected city water engineer, and Mulholland replaced him as chief superintendent.

Eaton later went on to be elected mayor of Los Angeles and promote his Irish friend further.

The battle to build the aqueduct began in earnest in 1905, with the need for an election to sell bonds to pay for the massive project. To that end, Mulholland's Irish background was exceedingly useful to the aqueduct's boosters. His immigrant roots and "cut the bull" attitude were emphasized in friendly newspapers such as the *Los Angeles Times,* and his lilting brogue and flashing Irish wit were frequently employed when the pro-aqueduct forces needed a public speaker. "If you don't get the water now, you'll never need it," he said in one memorable statement. "Because the dead don't get thirsty." The bond issue passed by an incredible 10 to 1 margin.

On November 5, 1913, William Mulholland stood in an honored place on a stand near the Elizabeth Tunnel in the San Fernando Valley. A multitude of 40,000 had assembled to watch the opening of the floodgates. When Mulholland was introduced as "the builder of the aqueduct," the entire throng rose as one and cheered him for a long while. Nudged forward to the speaker's stand, he had no appropriate remarks prepared. Finally, he said, "This rude platform is an altar, and on it we are here consecrating this water supply and dedicating this aqueduct to you and your children and your children's children—for all time!"

Mulholland then stepped to a flagpole and raised the Stars and Stripes, a prearranged signal to the engineers at the top of the cascade to turn the great wheels and release the water. Mulholland and the crowd held their collective breath as the metal gates rose with ponderous slowness. At first, nothing seemed to happen. Then a trickle of water appeared and started down the spillway. It grew into a stream and finally a flood. Mulholland allowed himself a moment of release and laughed out loud. Then he turned to the crowd and spoke the words that made him famous: "There it is. Take it."

William Mulholland was now one of the first citizens of Los Angeles, living elegantly, though not extravagantly. (His estate was worth $700,000 at the time of his death, a substantial sum, though nowhere near what some of his associates in the building of the aqueduct managed to acquire.) Although repeatedly approached about running for mayor, he always declined, saying "I would rather give birth to a porcupine backwards than become mayor of Los Angeles."

Unfortunately, the story of William Mulholland does not have a happy ending. At three minutes before midnight on March 12, 1928, the St. Francis Dam, christened by Mulholland "the safest dam in the world," collapsed, sending a wall of water 10 stories high slamming down the Santa Clara Valley. The damage was beyond belief: a 65-mile-long swath of destruction was cut from the broken dam to the Pacific Ocean between Oxnard and Ventura. Whole towns were flattened; an estimated 450 people lay dead. It still ranks as the worst disaster in California history after the San Francisco earthquake.

A coroner's jury held Mulholland responsible for the disaster, although it declined to recommend prosecution. The panel left open the possibility the dam might have been dynamited as part of the "water wars" that were raging at the time and were dramatized in Roman Polanski's 1974 film *Chinatown*.

The true cause of the dam's failure has never been established, and despite considerable circumstantial evidence that sabotage might have been the cause, William Mulholland accepted full and complete responsibility. The man who had dedicated his life to building Los Angeles was now viewed by many as a villain. His last years were gloomy and depressing. He died in 1935.

&· LOCATION: William Mulholland's contribution to Los Angeles is memorialized, fittingly, by a water fountain. Dedicated August 1, 1940, it stands at Los Feliz Boulevard and Riverside Drive at the entrance to Griffith Park. In the western part of the city, from Hollywood to the Pacific Ocean, is the glorious 22-mile stretch of road known as Mulholland Drive. Opened in 1924, it offers spectacular vistas of the city and the Pacific Ocean.

MILL VALLEY

REED SAWMILL RESTORATION

This quaint town in the oh-so-mellow San Francisco suburb of Marin County, just across the Golden Gate Bridge from San Francisco, was named for the sawmill that Dublin native John Reed (or Read— he seems to have used both spellings) established here around 1836.

Reed was born in 1805 and arrived in Marin around 1826, when the entire area was still virtually an Edenic wilderness. He married well. His wife was Hilarita Sanchez, daughter of the commandante of the Presidio. As a wedding present, Reed received 7,845 acres, making him the first English-speaking settler to acquire land in Marin County.

All around Reed's property stood majestic redwood trees, and Reed's mind turned to how he could best harvest them at a profit. In the mid-1830s, he developed an ingenious water-powered sawmill. When the forty-niners arrived and the city across the bay boomed, Reed was ready to supply the lumber to construct, first their shacks, and then their homes. He became quite well off doing it.

&· EXHIBITS: There is an explanatory plaque near the old mill. A fine stand of redwoods surrounds the site, which is excellent for picnicking. &·

The remains of Reed Sawmill in Old Mill Park.

LOCATION: The remains of Reed's sawmill stand in Old Mill Park on Throckmorton Avenue in Mill Valley. ❧ **HOURS:** Dawn to dusk. ❧ **ADMISSION:** Free

MURPHYS

TOWN NAMED FOR TWO BROTHERS

This town in the heart of the California gold country was named for two brothers, Daniel and John Murphy, who were the sons of Martin Murphy, Sr., one of the giant figures of early California history.

The latter was born in county Wexford on November 23, 1785. Along with his wife and a large family that included several already-grown children, they immigrated to Quebec around 1820. There they stayed for about 20 years, but the harsh winters, short summers, and the continued fact of British rule did not make for a real home. After 20 years, the family pulled up stakes again and settled in St. Joseph, Missouri.

Tragedy struck almost immediately, however. The low-lying land attracted mosquitos, and that meant malaria. Martin Sr.'s wife soon died as did Martin Jr.'s youngest daughter. A local priest urged the family to seek a drier climate and a place where Catholics were welcomed and suggested they try California. Martin Murphy, Sr., now nearly 60, uprooted his family again.

Remarkably for those days, the party did not experience a single death along the trail and arrived in California intact. (Theirs was the first party to successfully take wagons and oxen over the Sierra Nevadas.) Thanks to some sharp dealing by Daniel and James Murphy—who had agreed to fight on the winning side in a local civil war—the Murphys received property in what is now Santa Clara County. Martin Murphy, Sr., acquired the vast Aquede La Cocho Rancho and lived the remaining 20 years of his life in patriarchal splendor, surrounded by his children, grandchildren, servants, flocks, and herds. The family became the largest landowners in Santa Clara County, owning a nearly continuous 30-mile stretch, 7 miles wide, from Sunnyvale to Gilroy.

Martin Murphy, Jr., built a grand home in Sunnyvale, but, unfortunately, it no longer exists. Although uneducated himself, he was a driving force in the establishment of the University of Santa Clara and the College of Notre Dame (no relation to the university in South Bend, Indiana). He also is credited with pioneering the growing of wheat in California and with bringing the citrus industry to the state.

Daniel and John Murphy set up shop in Calaveras County around 1848. They discovered a rich ore deposit that soon came to be known as "Murphy's Diggins" and, finally, just plain Murphys. After a few years, however, they returned to their family's holdings in Santa Clara County.

It was in Murphys that the notorious career of Juan Murietta is supposed to have started. The outlaw was an acquaintance of the Murphy family, and it was supposedly near Murphys that he and a friend were set upon by anti-Mexican gold prospectors, who beat Murietta and lynched his friend. This episode is supposed to have set Murietta on his spree of lawlessness. Many Irish, including the Murphys, saw Murietta as a victim of Anglo injustice, however, and often helped him evade the clutches of the law.

"The Murphys," wrote one anonymous journalist early in this century, "ruled like ancient Irish kings over California for half a century." The description is a little bit of an exaggeration, but not much of one.

&◆ EXHIBITS: Unfortunately, virtually nothing remains in Santa Clara County to recall the role of the Murphy family in the establishment of this part of California. In the town of Murphys, however, is the Old Timers Museum, which stands on Main Street and contains many exhibits and artifacts from the town's early days. Also, the Murphys Hotel has been restored. Its guests included Mark Twain and Pres. Ulysses S. Grant. &◆ LOCATION: The town of Murphys is in the hills of the Gold Country and can be reached via S.R. 4, about 10 miles east of Angel's Camp in Calaveras County. &◆ HOURS: Museum hours vary, but it is usually open most days during the week in summer and weekends only in winter. "If it don't look very busy, they shut it down," said the desk clerk at the Murphys Hotel. Things are informal out here. &◆ ADMISSION: Free &◆ TELEPHONE: Murphys Hotel: (209) 728-3444.

SAN FRANCISCO

ARCHBISHOP'S MANSION

Patrick W. Riordan was the second archbishop of San Francisco, but he was certainly the man who "made" the San Francisco archdiocese. His energetic fund-raising and construction of churches, hospitals, and schools left his *See* one of the richest in the United States at the time of his death. It is also notable that he accomplished this feat *twice*—having been forced to rebuild everything after the 1906 earthquake.

Riordan's parents emigrated from Ireland in 1840 or 1841, landing at Chatham, New Brunswick, which was then a major immigration station for the Irish. Patrick was born in August 1841, and the family moved to Chicago in 1848, where the boy began his preparations for the priesthood. He graduated from the then-new Notre Dame University in 1858.

After study in Paris and Rome, Riordan was ordained in 1865 and assigned to parishes in Illinois, where his abilities both as a preacher and an administrator were first noted. In what must have been an experience that later stood him in good stead after the earthquake, he helped rebuild devastated parishes in Chicago after the Great Fire of 1871.

The contacts Riordan made while studying in Rome did him no harm when the church decided the ailing Archbishop Alemany of San Francisco needed a young, energetic aide. He was named an auxiliary bishop in 1883, and no sooner had he arrived on the West Coast when Alemany decided to retire and return to his native Spain. At age 42, Riordan was one of the youngest archbishops in modern church history. He would reign for a full 30 years, until his death in 1914.

Riordan wasted no time developing the archdiocese. St. Mary's Cathedral was erected along with 40 other churches; St. Patrick's Seminary in Menlo Park was established; and several hospitals and old age homes were founded, along with special schools for deaf-mutes and other handicapped people. Under Riordan's leadership, the number of priests and communicants nearly doubled.

To be sure, all was not positive for Riordan. The earthquake damaged and destroyed many of the churches and other buildings under his stewardship, and the last years of his life were devoted largely to rebuilding efforts. Another cross he had to bear was the political controversialist Father Peter Yorke (*see* entry farther on), who often seemed determined to test how far he could push his superior.

❧ **EXHIBITS:** Archbishop Riordan built this sumptuous 15-room residence in 1904 (with not a little controversy about a churchman having so extravagant a residence). It is now a historic bed and breakfast that operates under the name Archbishop's Residence. Unfortunately, the mansion does not contain any exhibits or personal effects. ❧ **LOCATION:** 1000 Fulton Street at Alamo Square. ❧ **ADMISSION:** Free ❧ **TELEPHONE:** (415) 563-7872.

BRODERICK-TERRY DUEL SITE

When one thinks of San Francisco's ethnic groups, the first that usually springs to mind is the Italians. The Irish, however, were a presence in the city by the bay almost from the very start. Boston had to wait until 1887 for its first Irish mayor. New York's turn came even after that. San Francisco, however, had its first Irish mayor in 1867. David C. Broderick, the first Irish-Catholic in the U.S. Senate, hailed not from Massachusetts or New York, but California.

In January 1848, San Francisco was a town of 200 buildings and barely 1,000 people. Twenty-two years later, it was the 10th largest city in the country, with 150,000 inhabitants. Of that number, nearly 50 percent were foreign-born, and far and away the largest percentage of that group was Irish. If second-generation Irish are included, the number swells even further.

What attracted the Irish? The same thing that attracted everyone else in those years: gold. The eastern cities were swollen with Irish immigrants fleeing the potato famine, and the states with the largest Irish populations by far were New York, Massachusetts, and Pennsylvania. But the gold rush brought many adventurous souls west, either by wagon over the Sierra Nevada, or by ship via the Isthmus of Panama.

Needless to say, the Irish brought their flair for political activity with them. David C. Broderick was, in many ways, typical of the new San Francisco Irish. Broderick had been born in Washington, D.C., in 1820, shortly after his father arrived from Ireland. The elder Broderick, a stone-cutter by trade, had found work on the expanding U.S. Capitol building.

Young Broderick cut his political teeth in New York. Although apparently never a member of the Tammany organization, he studied its methods closely. Arriving in San Francisco in 1849 with the gold rush, he wasted little time replicating the Tammany structure in his adopted city (while making a small fortune in gold smelting on the side). Within months, he was elected to the state constitutional convention and had won the Democratic primary for a seat in the state senate with all but 28 votes out of nearly 2,500 cast. One of his loyal associates was William Walker, the mercenary who later staged his bizarre takeover of Nicaragua.

Broderick's organization, which came to be known as "Young Ireland," was born. By all accounts, they were a rough-and-ready crew. "You respectable people I can't depend on," Broderick told some of those who objected to the coarse nature of some of his associates. "You won't go down and face the revolvers of those fellows who stuff the ballot boxes or steal the tallylists, so I have to keep such material as I can get a hold of. I have to keep these fellows to aid me."

Broderick took his organizational skills to the legislature, and barely a year after his arrival was elected president of the state senate. He was making enemies as he advanced, however. His Roman Catholicism was a frequent target of attack. One verse composed by his political opponents went thus:

> Hail to the chief who in triumph advances,
> Noted for playing political "roots,"
> Who has broken the points of chivalry's lances,
> And 'lam'd' all the Roman men 'out of their boots.'
> Then the victor's wreath twine for him,
> Go the whole swine for him
> Who maketh our leaders his tools or toys;
> We all go of course for him,
> And shout till we're hoarse for him,
> Broderick, the chief of Bowery boys.

Nevertheless, election to the U.S. Senate—his highest ambition— came in 1857. His term would be cut short after only two years, however.

Like the rest of the nation, passions ran high in California in the years immediately preceding the outbreak of the Civil War. Although a Democrat, Broderick was a strong Union supporter who opposed slavery, and made his sympathies plain on the floor of the Senate.

When Sen. James Hammond of South Carolina made his infamous 1858 speech defending slavery and attacking the industrial workers of the North as "white slaves," Broderick rose to make a famous reply. Recalling his own roots, he said, "(S)ir, the class of society to whom I was born will control the destinies of this nation. If I were inclined to forget my connection with them, or to deny that I sprang from them, this chamber would not be the place in which I could do either. While I hold a seat here, I have but to look at the beautiful capitals adorning the pillasters supporting this roof to be reminded of my father's talent, and to see his handiwork."

Although a free state, California had many residents of Southern origin, and the state's adherence to the Union was not a forgone conclusion. One of the leaders of the pro-slavery Democrats was David S. Terry, chief justice of the state supreme court, who had been born in Kentucky and raised on a plantation.

Although Broderick did not dislike Terry personally (he once called him the only honest man on the state's high court), he was incensed when Terry declared in print that the Douglas to whom Broderick owed his allegiance was named, not Stephen, but Frederick, the black ex-slave and abolition campaigner. A duel was thus arranged for the morning of September 13, 1859.

A marker commemorates the Broderick-Terry Duel Site.

The best account of the duel is given by Jeremiah Lynch in his biography of Broderick, *Senator of the Fifties*. Terry had arranged beforehand the selection of pistols and was aware that one had a hair-trigger, which was liable to discharge the pistol without the trigger even having been pulled. Terry, naturally, saw to it that this faulty weapon ended up in the hands of Broderick. As Broderick elevated the pistol, it discharged prematurely, allowing Terry, who was a crack shot, to wound Broderick in the chest.

Although the wound was not initially believed to be mortal, Broderick nevertheless died three days later, an event that managed to shock even the jaded residents of San Francisco. It was the last legal duel in California; the practice was outlawed soon thereafter.

Terry's political connections ensured he would escape prosecution for the murder of Broderick. But his volatile temperament saw to it that he came to a violent end anyway.

The instrument of Broderick's posthumous revenge was a U.S. marshal named Neagle, who was acting as a bodyguard for U.S. Supreme Court Justice James Field after Terry had threatened Field's life because of an adverse ruling in an estate case. Terry had threatened to kill Field if the latter ever set foot in California again. Pres. Grover Cleveland in 1888 appointed Neagle to serve as Field's bodyguard when the justice next rode circuit in California.

As the train on which Neagle and Field were riding made its first stop in California, Terry was there to meet them, apparently intent on making good on his earlier pledge. Neagle drew first, however, killing Terry instantly.

The dead man's political friends had Neagle arrested and sought to have him tried for murder, but this time, their influence wasn't enough. In one of the most interesting cases ever decided by the Supreme Court (and one in which there was an understandable dose of self-interest), *In Re Neagle,* the high court ruled that the president did indeed possess the constitutional authority to send Neagle on his mission, and the marshal was freed from custody. The ruling broke new ground for presidential authority.

❧ **LOCATION:** The Broderick-Terry duel site sits almost exactly on the county line between San Francisco and San Mateo at the intersection of Lake Merced Boulevard and John Muir Drive. Take Lake Merced Boulevard south until you see an apartment complex called Lake Merced Hill at 1100 Lake Merced Blvd. The duel site is at the end of a cul-de-sac next to the apartment complex. A marker at the end of the cul-de-sac recalls the event. The car can be parked here, and if you walk about 50 yards farther on through a clump of trees next to a tennis court, another marker sits at the spot where Broderick fell.

CHIEF SULLIVAN FIRE HOUSE

Every year at 5:12 A.M. on April 18, a dwindling band of survivors of the 1906 San Francisco earthquake gather to tell their story of surviving the worst disaster in the city's history. Hollywood's image notwithstanding, the quake itself did relatively little of the damage. It was the fire, which burned for three days and nights afterward, that leveled three-quarters of the city. This was a disaster that San Francisco Fire Chief Dennis P. Sullivan was determined to head off, until the tragedy itself prevented him from doing so.

Like their East Coast counterparts, the San Francisco Police and Fire Departments were virtual Irish "fiefdoms" in the late 19th century. Sullivan, born in Boston of Irish parents in 1852 and chief of the San Francisco Fire Department since 1893, knew that a major earthquake was a possibility and tried to prepare for it as best he could. The city government, for the most part, ignored his requests for improved fire fighting equipment. Sullivan particularly wanted apparatus that could use salt water as well as fresh, since the chief (correctly) anticipated that the city's water lines would fail in any major tremor.

Sullivan was asleep in his apartment in this, the city's fire headquarters, the morning when his worst fears were to be realized. As the earth began to sway, the chimney of the California Hotel immediately next door collapsed and fell through the firehouse roof, pinning Sullivan in his bed. It took several hours to free the chief, who was so severely injured he could take no part in fighting the blazes that were now breaking out all across the city. Sullivan died of his injuries three days later.

Thus, the city's firefighters found themselves deprived of the knowledgeable leadership of their beloved chief at the most critical moment in San Francisco's history. Just as Sullivan predicted, fire hydrants throughout the city ran dry as water mains collapsed. The fire, unstoppable now, went on to devastate San Francisco, a disaster from which the city took almost a decade to recover.

🐚 **EXHIBITS:** A memorial plaque to Chief Dennis Sullivan, with a *bas relief* likeness of him, is bolted to the front of the firehouse. Be careful though! The building is still an active firehouse and the doors could swing open at any time if a fire alarm is pulled. The building is not open to the public. 🐚 **LOCATION:** 870 Bush Street at Kearny, near the financial district.

FATHER PETER YORKE WAY

This short street is San Francisco's only memorial to one of its most prominent men in the late 19th and early 20th centuries. Father Peter Yorke was known as "the labor priest" and became Irish-Catholicism's most outspoken advocate of organized labor and unofficial guardian of tribal loyalty. He was also a controversial (and frequently highly quotable) antagonist of James Duval Phelan (*see* Saratoga, California), who Yorke thought far too close to management interests. Yorke also thought Phelan (perhaps even more unforgivably for an Irish American politician) insufficiently zealous in the cause of Irish freedom from British dominion.

Father Yorke was born in Galway in 1864 and was educated for the priesthood in both Ireland and in the United States. He arrived in San Francisco in 1888 and, for a time, could do no wrong in the eyes of his superior, Archbishop Patrick Riordan (*see* Archbishop's Mansion, San Francisco, California). He was Riordan's personal secretary, chancellor of the archdiocese, and held the powerful position of editor of the *Catholic Monitor,* the archdiocesan newspaper and the longest continuously published newspaper in San Francisco.

Yorke knew what he was about and held nothing back. He insisted on total devotion to the cause of Irish independence, hatred of England, and unquestioned fealty to Catholic doctrine. (Phelan's kind words for former British Prime Minister William Gladstone did not help him in Yorke's eyes.) Yorke was credited with smashing the remnants of the American Protective Association (APA), the anti-Irish vigilante committee formed in the 1850s to "keep order" in the rowdy city. In reality, of course, the huge influx of Irish and other immigrants had much earlier written the obituary for the APA, but Yorke's resolute stand made him a hero in the eyes of the city's Irish population, as well as other ethnic groups.

Perhaps acclaim came too early for Yorke (he was only 30 years old when the APA was dissolved), for he began to show signs of an unstable personality that would soon cause Archbishop Patrick Riordan to put some distance between himself and his young protege. It certainly seemed to many that Yorke's vituperative attacks on the gentle Phelan seemed out of proportion to the latter's alleged misdeeds.

Yorke openly and strongly intervened in the 1898 governor's race and was credited (or blamed) for the incumbent's defeat. Riordan was finally forced to declare that the priest spoke for himself and not the archdiocese. For good measure, His Eminence then endorsed James Duval Phelan's reelection as mayor.

This was a stunning repudiation for Yorke. While the Irish-American community of San Francisco might love Yorke's fire and determination, they were not about to buck the archbishop's authority, and Phelan was duly reelected. Yorke got his revenge later, however, when he dubbed Phelan "Jimmy the Rag," because, he said, Phelan was as useful to the Irish as "a dishcloth on top of a pole." The epithet stuck, much to Phelan's distress.

In 1902, Riordan was compelled to remove Yorke as editor of the *Monitor.* Yorke simply founded his own newspaper, the *Leader,* which gave him unfettered outlet for his strongly held views. Yorke intervened prominently in the Teamsters' strike and the street railway strikes in 1906–07 and was seemingly everywhere during the relief efforts after the earthquake.

For all his political radicalism, Yorke insisted on holding firmly to Catholic teaching in religious matters. He was a highly educated man and a voracious reader who was fluent not only in English, but Gaelic, French, Spanish, Latin, and Greek as well. He was a powerfully built man with a strong voice, a fact which added greatly to his success as a stump speaker. At the time of his death in 1925, he had numerous friends and not a few enemies, but the latter certainly respected him for the forthright way he expressed himself.

❧ LOCATION: Father Peter Yorke Way is a small lane bounded by Franklin and Gough streets and Post and Geary streets.

HIBERNIA NATIONAL BANK BUILDING

When kidnap victim-turned-terrorist Patricia Hearst picked a bank to rob, it was a branch of the Hibernia National Bank (though not this branch). There is no evidence of any motivation other than money, but it did call national attention to this great banking institution founded by and for early Irish residents of California.

As the gold rush Irish in San Francisco became more prosperous, they began to establish institutions around which their community life revolved. In the case of the Irish, these are usually stereotyped as churches and parochial schools, but they also included banks and large companies.

By 1860 or so, reports R. A. Burchell in *The San Francisco Irish* (1980), the Irish were sufficiently well established to begin forming many associations and organizations. The most important of these was the Hibernia Savings and Loan Society, founded on April 12, 1859, by Irish-born John Sullivan, who arrived in California with the Murphy-Stevens party in 1844 (*see* Murphys, California). The first office was in an upstairs room on Jackson and Montgomery streets, with Sullivan as president and John McHugh as vice-president.

The society originally took deposits of $2.50 or more, remaining a stock company until 1864, when it became a mutual. By 1869, the society had 14,544 depositors and assets of over $10 million, making it half as large as its nearest rival. The institution catered strongly, though by no means exclusively, to the city's Irish community and served for many years as a symbol of Irish success in the fast-growing city.

Although the Hibernia Bank's name still appears on the exterior of this classic 1908 Greek Revival headquarters, the Hibernia no longer has an independent existence, having been absorbed into the Bank of America. In keeping with San Francisco's efforts to mix redevelopment with preservation, the old Hibernia Bank headquarters is now a police station.

& **EXHIBITS:** The exterior of the building has been maintained as it appeared in the bank's heyday. The interior is quite striking and worth a look. & **LOCATION:** 1 Jones Street, at the intersection of Market and McAlister. & **HOURS:** All the time (naturally). & **ADMISSION:** Free

JAMES FLOOD MANSION (PACIFIC UNION CLUB) AND FAIRMONT HOTEL

They were "the Irish Four"—James Flood, James Fair, William O'Brien, and John Mackay—the "silver kings" of California and Nevada. These four men—three Irish-born and one an Irish-American—together developed the most spectacular mining bonanza in the Western Hemisphere after the Mother Lode: Nevada's Comstock Lode.

It is estimated that the company the men formed eventually took nearly $140 million out of the ground in Nevada. In the 1870s, that was *real* money.

Flood was the Irish-American, born in New York of immigrant parents. By trade a carriage maker, he, like his future business partners, came

The former James Flood mansion is now home to the exclusive Pacific Union Club.

west to seek his fortune. Flood's first venture in San Francisco was a livery stable, which prospered for a time, but went bankrupt when the gold bubble finally burst around 1854.

He had become acquainted, however, with an Irish-born businessman named William O'Brien, who had spent time in New York after emigrating from county Laois during the famine. O'Brien had worked his way to San Francisco as a deckhand on a freighter, and when he stepped off the ship, a nearby stranger took such pity on the young Irishman's condition that he immediately bought him a new pair of shoes. Years later, when O'Brien was a multimillionaire, he sought, in vain, to find the Good Samaritan and reward him appropriately.

Flood and O'Brien both decided to go into business together as bar owners. Offering two drinks for a quarter instead of the then-customary one, they also served a free lunch with each purchase. The Auction Lunch, as their establishment was known, became wildly popular with San Francisco's growing business community. The two men made the acquaintance of many brokers and traders and became intrigued with the ways men could make quick riches. They sold the Auction Lunch at a handsome profit and opened a brokerage firm, Flood and O'Brien.

In 1864, the two men formed a partnership with Dublin native John Mackay (*see* Mackay Mansion, Virginia City, Nevada), and in 1868, with Belfast-born James Fair. The latter two had already made considerable money in Nevada mining, and they took in Flood and O'Brien as partners with everything agreed by handshake. Flood became president, O'Brien and Mackay trustees, and Fair, with his exceptional mining knowledge, became superintendent.

The firm's first venture was getting control of the bankrupt Hale and Norcross Mine from the Bank of California. This they did, and made it

Named for Irishman James Fair, the Fairmont Hotel was the first one on Nob Hill.

profitable. Using the money earned, they acquired 13 other mines in the Comstock Lode silver region of Nevada. (Comstock himself, as Western tradition seems to demand, ended up with nothing.) The partnership became fabulously profitable, pouring out as much as $500,000 a month per partner. They soon branched out into banking and other businesses and became even richer.

Unlike almost all the other mansions on Nob Hill, which were built of wood, Flood built this mansion—one of the great landmarks of San Francisco—in 1886 out of brownstone, because it reminded him of the houses in his native New York. This personal idiosyncracy is what saved the house from total destruction when fire swept the hill after the 1906 earthquake and consumed the wooden homes of his neighbors. According to legend, Flood had a full-time worker who did nothing but keep the bronze fence (now turned green) surrounding the building polished.

Flood declined to rebuild the mansion after the fire and moved to Pacific Heights, where two more Flood mansions were built. The Nob Hill mansion with its fire-blackened walls remained standing vacant for a time until the building was purchased by the Pacific Union Club with a bond subscription raised among its members. The club, the most exclusive men's club in the West, occupies the building to this day.

Across the street from the former Flood Mansion sits the hulking edifice of the Fairmont Hotel, named for James Fair by his daughter Theresa Alice (Tessie), who built it as the first hotel on Nob Hill. Fair spent much of his time in Nevada and served a term as U.S. senator from that state between 1880 and 1886. He invested his money heavily in San Francisco real estate, and at one point was reputed to have owned almost all the property under the city's growing financial district. He died in 1894.

Construction of the Fairmont Hotel began in 1902, but work proceeded slowly on the 600-room edifice, and Tessie sold the unfinished building in 1906. Just in time, as it turned out, for the earthquake/fire consumed the building entirely. Later, it was rebuilt as one of the grandest hotels on the West Coast.

* **EXHIBITS:** Unless you are the right sex and have a great deal of money and the proper connections, you will find getting inside the Pacific Union Club a tad difficult. You might have to content yourself with a picnic lunch in next-door Huntington Park, or tea across the street in the Fairmont. While at the Fairmont, take the elevator to the tower for the million-dollar view of the city. * **LOCATION:** The Pacific Union Club/Flood Mansion, is located on the northwest corner of California and Mason streets. The Fairmont Hotel is directly across the street on the northeast corner. The later mansions built by Flood and his son, James Leary Flood, are located at 2120 Broadway, now the exclusive Hamlin School, and a block away, at 2222 Broadway, now the Convent of the Sacred Heart High School. Flood also built the architecturally distinguished Flood Building at 870-98 Market St., between Ellis and Eddy streets. * **HOURS:** Fairmont Hotel open at all times. * **TELEPHONE:** Fairmont: (415) 772-5000.

THE JEREMIAH O'BRIEN

The United States built 2,751 "liberty ships" during World War II to carry troops and cargo to embattled American allies all over the world. The *Jeremiah O'Brien,* named for the Irish American naval hero of the revolutionary war (*see* Machias Bay, Maine), is the only fully operational liberty ship left in the world.

* **EXHIBITS:** During "steaming weekends" (usually the third weekend of every month), passengers can view the steam engines and the galley. A five-hour bay cruise, complete with buffet lunch, is available in May. * **LOCATION:** The ship is berthed at Ft. Mason. * **HOURS:** Monday–Friday 9–3; Saturday–Sunday 9–4. * **ADMISSION:** $3; seniors and children under 12 $1; families $5. * **TELEPHONE:** (415) 441-3101.

KATE KENNEDY SCHOOL

Equal pay for equal work became a rallying cry for American women in the 1970s. But nearly a century before, an Irish-born San Francisco schoolteacher made it an issue. And she got it enacted into law.

Kate Kennedy was a county Meath native, born in 1827 and raised in comparative comfort as the daughter of a prosperous farmer. She learned to read early and often read newspapers to illiterate neighbors. She started her teaching career early, educating her younger sisters during the desper-

*The U.S.S.
Jeremiah O'Brien.*

ate years of the Great Hunger (the Irish potato famine of the 1840s). The Kennedy girls' father had died in 1841, and when the famine came, they joined so many of their neighbors in the flight to America.

In New York, the Kennedy family found work in the overcrowded, unsafe garment industry sweatshops. Even so, Kate kept up her love of reading and studying. After gold was found, the Kennedy girls made the trek westward in search of better opportunities.

In 1856, Kennedy achieved her lifelong ambition and received her teaching certificate. A year later, she joined the fledgling San Francisco school system. In due course, her sisters followed her example.

After 10 years, Kennedy's competence was recognized and she was promoted to principal. She was shocked to discover, however, that although her responsibilities had increased, her pay had not, solely because she was a woman. Not about to keep her mouth shut, Kate Kennedy began lobbying the legislature to declare such discrimination illegal. She won the support of well-known women's rights activist Susan B. Anthony, and the legislature enacted Kennedy's proposal in 1874.

Kate Kennedy did not simply let it go at that, however. She became an outspoken advocate for groups such as the Knights of Labor, an early union that practiced sexual equality. She also supported Henry George, author of *Progress and Poverty* and a supporter of the Irish Land League. She was a regular speaker on the organized labor circuit and in 1886 stood unsuccessfully as labor's candidate for state superintendent of schools.

Needless to say, she made enemies as well as friends, and not a few of the former were on the San Francisco school board. After she lost the 1886 race, the school board crassly transferred her to a smaller school and cut her pay. When she refused the transfer, she was fired.

Kennedy sued. After three years of legal battles, the state supreme court vindicated Kennedy, in one of the first successful job discriminations suits in history.

The long years of fighting, however, apparently took their toll. Kate Kennedy died the day after St. Patrick's Day, 1890, just a few months after her judicial vindication. She is remembered, however, by the school system that once fired her: a public school in San Francisco's Mission District is named after her.

❧ **EXHIBITS:** Kate Kennedy's teaching certificate was framed inside the building for many years, until a modern educational phenomenon—vandalism—carried it off. The building is not open to the public. ❧ **LOCATION:** Kate Kennedy Children's Center is located at 1670 Noe St. in the Noe Valley section of San Francisco.

KNIGHTS OF THE RED BRANCH HALL

In *The San Francisco Irish* (1980), author R. A. Burchell tells of the huge gatherings the San Francisco Irish used to organize in the years after the Civil War. "The balls and picnics gave a chance for outings, meetings and gossip on the grandest scale," he writes. "In May of 1868, it was reported that 8,000 to 10,000 Savage wing Fenians went on a picnic to Belmont Park on the Peninsula by rail. Their line of carriages stretched for half a mile and was "headed by three or four engines, puffing and blowing like so many savage Fenians, eager for the fray."

With 25 years in the country and with many of them now war veterans, the Irish began forming associations to promote fellowship and their own political and economic interests. Along with the Clan na Gael, the Knights of the Red Branch is one of the oldest such Irish fraternal organization in San Francisco. Founded in 1869, the origin of the name is somewhat obscure, but is said to have been taken from the "Cycles" of the

Pictured is the temporary Knights of the Red Branch Hall used after the 1906 San Francisco fire and earthquake destroyed the original hall. (Courtesy of Sean Prendiville)

ancient Celtic Warrior Finn McCool (in which the Red Hand of Ulster also figures).

The Knights grew out of the wreckage of the Fenian movement in the late 1860s (*see* Ridgeway, Ontario). The failure of the invasions of Canada to secure Irish independence or an Irish-dominated republic on the North American continent split the Fenians into various mutually antagonistic factions. The Knights of the Red Branch (KRB) grew out of some factions and the Clan na Gael out of others. Thomas Desmond, one of the Fenians rescued by John Boyle O'Reilly (*see* New Bedford, Massachusetts), was a member of the KRB.

This is the fourth KRB hall and the third one on this site. The second hall burned to the ground during the 1906 earthquake and was replaced by a wooden, temporary hall. The current building dates from around 1909. The Knights are still technically in existence, although their membership is but a shadow of the former times, when thousands gathered to celebrate their Irishness under its banner.

❧ **EXHIBITS:** Unfortunately, the remains of the KRB have been forced to rent out much of their space to some very non-Irish groups and establishments to help keep up the hall. Bob Mandell's theatrical supply shop, a well-known San Francisco landmark, occupies the first floor, and various dance groups now rent out the main meeting hall for their rehearsals. You can check the bulletin boards inside, however, for information on KRB meetings. ❧ **LOCATION:** 1133 Mission St. ❧ **HOURS:** Very irregular. ❧ **ADMISSION:** Free

MECHANICS MONUMENT

In the 19th century, engineers were known as "mechanics" (for the obvious reason that the internal combustion engine had not yet been invented). One of San Francisco's great "mechanics" was Peter Donahue, a man with an impressive list of California firsts to his credit.

Peter Donahue was born in Glasgow, Scotland, to Irish parents in 1822. He was early introduced to mechanics, having gone to work in a factory at 9. After the family immigrated to New York, he continued to work in a factory, and when they moved to Paterson, New Jersey, he was apprenticed to Thomas Rogers, a locomotive builder, under whose tutelage Donahue became an expert machinist.

The high quality of his work became well known locally, and in 1845 he was employed to work on a gunboat under construction in New York harbor for the government of Peru. When the ship was completed, he decided to sail with her, and spent several years in Peru. In 1849, however, he heard of the gold strikes in California and promptly boarded a steamship and headed north.

While the steamship was still at sea, however, its engines malfunctioned and Donahue volunteered to fix them. This he did so expertly that the steamship line paid him the then-fantastic sum of $1,000 and offered him permanent employment.

But Donahue had come to California for gold and he headed out for the mother lode instead. Six months was enough to convince him he would not find riches panning in a river, and he returned to San Francisco, where he encountered his brother James. The two opened a blacksmith shop together and took in a third brother, Michael, when he arrived in California in 1850.

From this humble beginning came the Union Iron Works, which built Monitor-style ironclad warships for the Union navy in the Civil War. He sold the ironworks in 1864 and with $1 million capital founded a gasworks that was the first company to offer street lighting in the city. More important, he also founded the Omnibus street railway, the precursor to the famed cable cars that are San Francisco's signature.

Donahue had discovered that California offered many riches aside from gold. He founded the San Francisco–San Jose Railroad, and sold it later for $3.25 million. He also founded the San Francisco and North Pacific Railroad Company, which his eldest son, Mervyn, headed for many years.

Although often beseeched to run for office, Donahue always refused. He took an active part in civic affairs, however. His staunchly pro-Union sentiments at the outbreak of the Civil War carried considerable weight when, for a time, it was uncertain whether California would remain in the Union or secede and join the Confederacy.

*The Mechanics
Monument stands
in memory of
Peter Donahue.*

"He was a man of most genial and affectionate nature," wrote an anonymous obiturist. "He never forgot a friend or an act of kindness. He was especially attached to the people whom he had employed . . . so that among the artisans and laboring population of the city, he always enjoyed and deserved an exceptional popularity and influence." He died in 1875.

&. **EXHIBITS:** The Mechanics Memorial was commissioned in his father's memory by James Donahue. The statue, cast by famed California architect Douglas Tilden in 1894–95, shows three brawny mechanics, young, middle-aged, and elderly, attempting to force a huge mechanical punch through a plate of metal. A plaque commemorating the Donahue family is at the base. &. **LOCATION:** Market and Battery streets. &. **HOURS:** Dawn to dusk.

MISSION DOLORES

The large number of Irish flowing into San Francisco during the gold rush was not seen as an unmixed blessing, particularly by Anglo-Protestants with whom they were sharing the city. The Irish brought with them their sharp-elbow political tactics, and some Irish were no doubt scoundrels who would have been unwelcome in any community, even Wild West San Francisco. Crime ran rampant.

James P. Casey was apparently one of the latter. He had done a two-year stretch in New York's Sing-Sing Prison before he came west with the gold rush. Once in San Francisco, he became involved in politics and served as deputy county treasurer, as a member of the board of supervisors, and as an inspector of elections. He seems to have had a taste for violence and was involved in several shootings of political rivals and was not above helping stuff a few ballot boxes for his friend, Sen. David Broderick (*see* Broderick-Terry Duel Site, San Francisco, California).

Methods for keeping law and order were primitive at best in early San Francisco, and several "vigilance committees" were formed. "The personnel of the committee were men above the average," sniffed committee president William T. Coleman in later years. "They were selected for their worth, integrity and good standing in the community. . . . Politics, creed, nationality or profession were not considered, nor thought of." Perhaps, but it is a fact that most of the men on the committee were northern and western Protestants, while their victims were almost exclusively Irish and Catholic and allies of David Broderick.

The 1856 committee was the most deadly. Nativism was heating up as the Civil War approached, and the "good men" of the committee vowed to "clean up" their city. The spark that set them off was James P. Casey's murder—in broad daylight on Montgomery Street—of James King of William, the scalding editor of the *Evening Bulletin,* whom Casey believed had insulted his wife.

The committee was already enraged at the failure of a (mostly immigrant) jury to convict Charles Cora, an Italian, of the murder of a U.S. marshal. On the day of James King of William's funeral, both Cora and Casey were taken from their cells in the city jail and ended up dangling from the second-story windows of a building in Portsmouth Square. Two more Irishmen would be victims of the committee, while some 30 others were told to make themselves scarce or else risk sharing the fate of the others.

Casey and Cora were brought to be buried in the churchyard of Mission Dolores, the city's preeminent Catholic parish and the burial place of many early Irish settlers. The committee was disbanded later in the year. Distasteful as their methods were, the committee seems to have accomplished their purposes and restored some semblance of law and order to San Francisco.

❧ **EXHIBITS:** Toward the Dolores Street side of the cemetery lies the monument to James P. Casey, a tall, brown sandstone marker decorated with firemen's helmets at the corners and upside-down torches. (Casey was also a volunteer fireman.) Also buried here are Cora and another Vigilance Committee victim, James "Yankee" Sullivan. Numerous other headstones in the cemetery are carved with Irish names and places of birth, testifying to the heavily Irish nature of mid-19th-century San Francisco. ❧ **LOCATION:** Mission Dolores, or more accurately, the Mission of St. Francisco de Asisi, is located at 320 Dolores St. at 16th Street, in the Mission District. ❧ **HOURS:** Daily 9–4. ❧ **ADMISSION:** $1 donation. ❧ **TELEPHONE:** (415) 621-8203.

NOBBIE CLARK'S FOLLY

Nobbie Clark was an Irish immigrant who built this imposing Victorian pile in 1892, allegedly with savings accumulated from over 30 years as clerk to the San Francisco chief of police. The Irish yew trees planted around the house were brought from county Roscommon. The house was originally the center of a 17-acre farm.

❧ **EXHIBITS:** The house is subdivided into apartments now, but it is open for "haunted house" tours during the Halloween season. ❧ **LOCATION:** 250 Douglas St. at Casselli.

O'FARRELL STREET

Poll after poll consistently shows that a majority of Americans, if they had the choice, would most like to live in San Francisco. A visit makes it easy to see why: the hilly streets with colorfully painted houses clinging precariously to the sides make it a city almost created to be photographed. One of the men responsible for the city widely considered America's most beautiful and inviting was Jaspar O'Farrell, the Dublin-born engineer and city planner who laid out most of the city's best-known streets.

O'Farrell had nothing if not vision. He wrote a friend in 1847, when San Francisco was not much more than a small village, "I have no doubt of it (San Francisco) becoming one day, and not very distant, the Empire City of the Pacific."

O'Farrell came to what was then Yerba Buena in 1843, after two years as a member of an expedition surveying the western coast of South America. He was 26 years old, having been born in Dublin, where he had studied engineering.

Upon arrival, the local Mexican government offered O'Farrell employment as a surveyor, and he spent the next few years conducting surveys in what is today Marin and Sonoma counties. After California entered the Union in 1850, O'Farrell continued his work under the U.S. administration, receiving one parcel of land for every 20 he laid out. The land titles in Marin, San Francisco and Sonoma counties today are still based on O'Farrell's drawings.

Washington Bartlett, the first non-Hispanic mayor of San Francisco, engaged O'Farrell to lay out the streets for the growing city, which was now bustling as the center of the gold rush.

Immediately upon setting to work, O'Farrell discovered that the existing streets, instead of running on a true north-south grid, were off by about two degrees. His first task was to correct this error, and "O'Farrell's Swing" realigned the streets at right angles and brought the streets more in alignment with the city's many hills. (The present intersection of Kearny and Washington streets was the "pivot" of the "swing.") Fortunately for O'Farrell, there were few houses in the area at the time that would be disturbed.

O'Farrell wasn't so lucky on another occasion, however. Some citizens became irate when they found that O'Farrell's plan would cut streets right through their property. The planner came to a meeting to explain his reasons, but the gathering became ugly and there were some cries of "lynch him!" O'Farrell was forced to make his escape through a side door and sailed across the bay to Marin County until things quieted down and he could return to the city. He got his way on most of his decisions, however.

O'Farrell named most of San Francisco's well-known streets. Supposedly, Bush Street got its name when one of O'Farrell's assistants angrily demanded that O'Farrell pay him his overdue wages. Unable to pay at that moment (the planner received only $5 per lot surveyed), O'Farrell offered him immortality instead. He promptly scrawled Bush's name on one of the streets he was surveying at that time.

O'Farrell's greatest achievement, however, is unquestionably Market Street. Instead of having this main thoroughfare cut straight across the peninsula, as other planner's might have done, he followed the route that would connect the waterfront with the ancient Mission Dolores, ending at the dramatic vista of Twin Peaks. Unfortunately, his decision to make the blocks south of Market Street four times as large as those north of it meant the streets were unsuitable for residential development. By the early 1850s, "south of Market" became a euphemism for industrial and warehouse development.

O'Farrell's success in San Francisco assured him a lucrative living as a town planner. He eventually settled in Sonoma County, where he had a large house and lived with his wife and children, as well as his aged mother, whom he brought from Ireland. He served a term in the state senate from 1858 to 1862, when he lost a race for lieutenant governor. He died in 1875.

&⁓ **LOCATION:** O'Farrell Street is bounded by Geary Street on the north and Ellis Street on the south, Franklin Street on the west, and Market Street on the east.

PHELAN BUILDING

The impressive Phelan Building anchors Market Street at one of the city's great intersections. It is a fitting monument to James Phelan, Sr., father of James Duval Phelan (*see* Saratoga, California). The elder Phelan was one of the many Irish pioneers who helped transform California into one of the world's most unique and productive civilizations.

Phelan made his money in the gold rush, though not in the goldfields themselves. He was born in Ireland in county Queens (Laois or Leix). The year is uncertain, but 1821 seems to be the accepted date. Phelan himself seems to have cared little about the date. Starting points were irrelevant, he often said. It was destinations that mattered.

Phelan's father had started a business soon after arriving in New York in 1827. The business failed after a time, however, and James, the middle of three brothers, quit school to find work. In the ashes of a family tragedy, however, were sown the seeds of one of the great success stories of California and America.

The only work James could find was as a $5-a-week clerk in a grocery store. Although certainly not lucrative, the work enabled him to see up close how business was done, lessons which would prove invaluable later on. He was in Cincinnati in 1846, running a thriving dry goods business, when he heard the word of gold in California. Unlike so many others, who sold everything they had and went west as quickly as possible, Phelan planned his move carefully. He would make his, money not by panning for gold, but by selling needed goods to others who were panning for gold.

To that end, he sold his assets in Cincinnati and bought a large consignment of nails, tacks, paper, cooking utensils, and anything else that could conceivably be sold to miners. He divided the cargo among three ships, so as to guard against piracy or shipwreck, and sailed to California himself via Panama, while much of the cargo went around Cape Horn.

He very nearly didn't make it. A malaria epidemic was raging in Panama and Phelan very nearly succumbed. Fortunately, he recovered and entered a lottery for a ticket on the next available ship north. He won, and even managed to sell part of his cargo to the ship's captain at a profit and upgraded his accommodation to a cabin as part of the deal.

Once in San Francisco, James Phelan continued his cautious ways and they paid handsome dividends. He easily sold out the stock he had placed on the other ships and reinvested the profits in banking, insurance, construction, and, especially, land development. In 1883, he constructed the impressive five-story Phelan Building at Market and O'Farrell. Even to-day, the Phelan Building is one of San Francisco's great landmarks, but back then it was an incredible statement of wealth and power.

All did not go well, however. James' elder brother and junior business partner, Michael, was not nearly so cautious or successful. When James went east to prepare to marry Alice Kelly, daughter of a wealthy and established Irish family, he received word that San Francisco newspapers were printing cartoons of his brother carousing at Irish Mary's Pleasure House. The debts run up through Michael's dissolute lifestyle very nearly destroyed the Phelan company. James had to return to San Francisco and straighten things out before he could go east and claim Alice as his bride.

James and Alice raised three children in an atmosphere reflecting their Irish roots. In the *Legacy of a Native Son* (1993), historians James P. Walsh and Timothy O'Keefe note that priests were frequent guests at dinner and conversation often revolved around Ireland and Irish affairs.

In 1882, at age 61, Phelan's thoughts turned to Panama once again and the thought of digging a canal. Phelan formed a partnership with several other men and built a huge mechanical digger that Phelan thought could dredge the canal. The idea failed, but Phelan was among the first to think transoceanic canal was a possibility. Phelan died in 1892.

* **EXHIBITS:** A bust of James Phelan graces the lobby inside the Market Street entrance. The building burned in the 1906 earthquake, but has since been fully restored. * **LOCATION:** The block bounded by Market, Grant, and O'Farrell streets. * **HOURS:** Open during regular business hours, Monday–Friday. * **ADMISSION:** Free

PHILLIP BURTON MEMORIAL

U.S. Rep. Phillip Burton, who served in Congress from 1964 until his sudden death in 1983, was one of the giants of the modern House of Representatives. "When I came to the House, they told me Phil Burton was tough as nails," recalls former Republican U.S. Rep. Mickey Edwards in his book *Behind Enemy Lines* (1984). "I soon discovered they were wrong. They don't make nails that tough."

A fighter for liberal causes, Phil Burton pushed through legislation that made it possible for strikers to qualify for food stamps, and he greatly loosened the eligibility requirements for food stamps in such American territories as Puerto Rico and Guam. In 1975, he missed being elected House majority leader (and presumptive Speaker) by a single vote.

Phil, along with his brother John, who also served in Congress from 1974 to 1982, were wholly Irish on his mother's side and of mixed Irish-German ancestry on his father's side. Both brothers acknowledged the influence their Irish heritage had on their political careers, which goes to

Not far from Fisherman's Wharf is the statue of U.S. Representative Phillip Burton.

show that even in this day of assimilation, the Irish can still be found shaking things up in California politics.

The statue of Phillip Burton was erected on the grounds of Ft. Mason, not far from Fisherman's Wharf, several years after his death. It shows Burton in a customary pose, tousle-haired and striding forward. Out of the right jacket of the his suit pocket sticks a sheet of paper on which is written an earthy summary of his political philosophy.

&a LOCATION: The grounds of Ft. Mason, near Fisherman's Wharf. &a HOURS: Dawn to dusk. &a ADMISSION: Free

ROBERT EMMET STATUE

Another of James Duval Phelan's contributions to San Francisco is this memorial to the Irish patriot executed by the British in 1803

The statue of Irish patriot Robert Emmet stands proudly in Golden Gate Park.

ROBERT EMMET

IRISH PATRIOT
EXECUTED IN DUBLIN
SEPT. 20, 1803
AGED 25 YEARS

(*see* Saratoga, California; Emmetsburg, Iowa; St. Paul's Chapel, New York, New York; Robert Emmet Statue, Washington, D.C.).

Phelan was still smarting under the attacks of Father Peter Yorke (*see* Father Peter Yorke Way, San Francisco, California) and wanted to burnish his Irish credentials by the gift of this statue. (He also donated the one standing in Washington, D.C.) Eamon de Valera (*see* Rochester, New York), who was on one of his periodic fund-raising trips in the United States, unveiled the statue on July 20, 1919.

Father Yorke was not impressed. He said Phelan could not hide his insufficiently militant Irish nationalist credentials behind all the statues in the park.

❧ **EXHIBITS:** Emmet's dramatic speech from the dock, in which he asked that his epitaph not be written until Ireland was free, is read here every year on September 20, the anniversary of his execution. ❧ **LOCATION:** Outside the Academy of Sciences Building in Golden Gate Park.

St. Patrick's Church.

ST. PATRICK'S CHURCH

The church now sits in the shadow of the enormous George Moscone Convention Center, and the congregation is mostly Filipino, but St. Patrick's is without question an *Irish* church.

The interior glows with green Connemara marble, and the stained glass windows celebrate all of Ireland's 32 counties and her canonized saints.

The church, along with a parochial school, was constructed in 1851 by Father John Maginnis as the first Irish parish in what had been a Spanish and Mexican city up to that time.

❧ LOCATION: 756 Mission St. ❧ HOURS: Call for hours. ❧ ADMISSION: Free, but donations appreciated. ❧ TELEPHONE: (415) 661-2700.

UNITED IRISH CULTURAL CENTER

This building is the center of the Irish-American community in San Francisco. The library contains an extensive collection of books and newspapers related to Ireland and the Irish-Americans. The dining and drinking facilities also are excellent.

☙ **EXHIBITS:** Poetry readings, lectures, and discussion groups on Irish and Irish-American themes are frequently sponsored here. Call for events information. ☙ **LOCATION:** 2700 45th Ave. ☙ **HOURS:** Hours variable. Call ahead. ☙ **ADMISSION:** Free ☙ **TELEPHONE:** (415) 661-2700.

SAN JOSE

CAPTAIN THOMAS FALLON HOUSE

Thomas Fallon was yet another of the Irish pioneers whose influence at critical points helped bring California into the Union. His reputation has been somewhat tarnished in recent years, but he was definitely a folk hero in his time and deserves to be remembered today.

Born in 1824, Fallon set out for Canada from Ireland as a young boy, and he was apprenticed to a saddle maker. Unable to conceive of such a humdrum existence, however, Fallon was more interested in the destinations of the men who sat in the saddles than the saddles themselves. He headed to Texas at age 18 and hitched up with some men who were marching to the Pacific. He arrived in what was then the Mexican province of *Alta California* in the spring of 1844.

He settled down in Santa Cruz and, to get started, returned to the trade of making saddles. However, the news of the "Bear Flag Revolt" reached him in June 1846, and Fallon's immediate instinct was, in his own words, "to raise a party and go and help them." Fallon declared himself a "captain" and had little trouble finding about 20 eager volunteers. They crossed the Santa Cruz mountains to what is now San Jose, where he and his small band had little trouble securing the surrender of the small Mexican garrison there. The outbreak of the Mexican War soon thereafter ensured California for the United States.

But the story of Thomas Fallon doesn't end there by a long shot. He married Carmelita Lodge, the half-Irish, half-Spanish daughter of one of the area's largest landowners, and he struck it rich in the gold rush, building a grand house for himself in Santa Cruz. After Carmelita's mother died, the family pulled up stakes and moved to Texas.

Tragedy awaited the family there, however, as three of the couple's children died. Moving back to California, Fallon began buying up property in Santa Clara County and San Jose, where he eventually was elected

Recently renovated, the Thomas Fallon House is planned to open as a museum.

mayor. It was while serving as mayor, in 1859, that he built this magnificent house, one of the finest in the area.

But Fallon's domestic life, never tranquil at the best of times, was roiled further when Carmelita divorced him and moved back to Santa Cruz. Fallon remarried in 1875. That marriage lasted only seven years until his second wife divorced him, too, and Fallon moved to San Francisco. There, he spent the last three years of his life, dying in 1885, just 60 years of age. Yet another woman had a breach of promise suit pending against Fallon at the time of his death, and settlement of his very large estate dragged on in the courts until the 1920s.

The house remained disused into the 1980s, when a kindergarten moved in for a time, and it later became a boarding house. Eventually, it was taken over as an Italian restaurant, catering to the city's growing Italian population. Recently, it was renovated, and plans are afoot to open it as a museum.

A statue of Fallon stood in San Jose for many years, but was taken down after the area's Mexican-American population protested. It seems that during his reign as mayor, Fallon pursued a strong anti-Mexican policy, excluding them from the city's civic life to the extent possible. Proposals to reerect it as part of the restoration of Fallon's house have met with strong opposition.

On the grounds of St. Vincent's School is this memorial to Don Timiteo Murphy.

❧ **EXHIBITS:** A historic marker details Fallon's life and career. Plans are in place to restore the house to the way it was when Fallon lived there. ❧ **LOCATION:** The Fallon house stands at 175 St. John St. in downtown San Jose.

SAN RAFAEL

ST. VINCENT'S SCHOOL FOR BOYS

This boarding school for troubled boys, run by the San Francisco archdiocese, is the only tangible legacy of Timothy Murphy, better known in these parts as Don Timiteo Murphy, for this 300-pound Irishman was held in great esteem by the early Spanish settlers. Like the Murphys farther south in the Santa Clara Valley (to whom he was no relation), Murphy was one of those Irish pioneers who came more than 6,000 miles from his homeland to make his fortune.

Murphy was from Enniscorthy, county Wexford, where he was born in 1800. Immigrating to Britain, a job in a meat-packing plant sent him to Peru, where the company was opening an office. In 1828, he went north to what was then known as *Alta California* (Upper California) and sought to establish a Monterey office, which did not work out. He struck out on his own as a trapper, however, and made the acquaintance of many influential Mexicans, who were still the law in this part of the world.

One of his friends was Mariano Vallejo, the governor, and in 1837 he appointed Murphy to run the San Rafael Mission in what is now Marin County and act as the agent for the 1,400 Indians there. He held this post until 1849.

Murphy was well liked by the Indians, although he employed them as hired hands on what was, technically, the Indians' land. His grand "abobe" in San Rafael (which no longer exists) was the center of a 21,000-acre farm and ranch and became a well-known place in the area for lavish entertaining.

Murphy died young in 1853. On his deathbed, he willed 217 acres of land to his good friend Archbishop Alemany of San Francisco for the construction of a school. St. Vincent's was founded two years later.

❧ EXHIBITS: A plaque commemorating Don Timiteo Murphy's role in founding the school is located in the courtyard in front of the main entrance. One of the school buildings is named for him. Visitors are welcome and tours can be arranged by calling ahead of time. ❧ LOCATION: Built in what is still a sylvan setting in what is now a mostly built-up area, St. Vincent's School for Boys is approached down a road under a grand procession of elm trees. Take Highway 101 to the St. Vincent's Drive exit and follow the signs. ❧ HOURS: 8–3 on weekdays. ❧ ADMISSION: Free ❧ TELEPHONE: (415) 507-2000.

SARATOGA

VILLA MONTALVO

James Duval Phelan was the only son of James Phelan, Sr., the Irish-born entrepreneur who constructed the Phelan Building (*see* San Francisco, California). The son, who never married, devoted his life to politics and the arts, however, rather than business, and this magnificent estate is his legacy.

James Duval Phelan was a worldly, sophisticated youth, very much unlike his no-nonsense father. When someone once asked the senior Phelan why he smoked five-cent cigars, while his son smoked one-dollar cigars, the older man replied brusquely, "I don't have a rich father."

But the son carried on the family name prominently and honorably for nearly 40 years after the patriarch's death in 1892. Running for mayor of San Francisco in 1897, James Duval Phelan assembled a curious coalition of Irish working-class voters who liked his heritage and upper-class San

Villa Montalvo, home of Irish-American philanthropist and politician James Duval Phelan.

Franciscans who liked his personal honesty even more. (The Phelan family was so rich, it seems, graft appeared pointless.)

Winning the first of three terms, Phelan overhauled the city charter and prosecuted corruption. His greatest achievement, however, was the beautification of what had been, up to that point, a pretty rough frontier town. Phelan was a major force in the "city beautiful" movement of the late 19th and early 20th centuries, and the wide boulevards, plazas, parks, and fountains that dot San Francisco today are largely his legacy. Phelan also served a single term as a Democrat in the U.S. Senate between 1914 and 1920.

When Phelan decided to build a country house, he chose this spot in the Santa Clara Valley. It offered him a refuge from the hustle and bustle of San Francisco, as well as near-perfect year-round weather. As a man of almost unlimited means, Phelan could afford the best, and Villa Montalvo is certainly among the most impressive of the estates built by the early California rich.

Phelan was the principal designer of the house, which is constructed in the style of a Spanish villa. Completed in 1912, the house is named for Garci Ordonez de Montalvo, the early sixteenth-century Spanish novelist who gave California its name. The grounds of the mansion are dominated by statues of griffins, the half-lion, half-eagle animals that guarded California's gold in Montalvo's romances. Phelan used them as a motif, the friendly guardians of his estate.

During his residence here, Phelan entertained lavishly and often, and the guest books show the wide range of his acquaintances: Franklin D. Roosevelt, Knute Rockne, John Barrymore, Alfred E. Smith, and many others. Phelan died here in 1930, having donated the estate to the people of California for the development of the visual and dramatic arts.

Also of interest is the Phelan mansion in San Francisco itself, an exact duplicate of Villa Montalvo. (This was because Phelan wanted to be able to find his way around in the dark no matter where he was, supposedly.) The house was built by Phelan after the 1906 earthquake destroyed the family's in-town residence. The house was mostly occupied, however, by Mary Phelan, James Duval's sister, who also never married.

ᕦ EXHIBITS: The house contains original furnishings and decorations purchased by James Phelan, plus an art gallery and open-air theater. The gardens surrounding the house, however, are the real attraction, with hundreds of species of birds and trees, prominently including the Irish yew. Call for schedule of exhibits and theatrical productions. The San Francisco home is not open to the public. ᕦ LOCATION: One-half mile southeast on California 9, then 1 mile southwest on Montalvo Rd. The Phelan mansion in San Francisco is at 2150 Washington St. ᕦ HOURS: Tours of the house are offered Thursdays and Saturdays at 10. The gardens are open Monday–Friday 8–5, Saturday and Sunday 9–5. ᕦ ADMISSION: Gardens are free. Tour is $5 for adults, $3 for children and seniors. ᕦ TELEPHONE: (408) 741-3421.

S A U S A L I T O

DANIEL O'CONNELL MEMORIAL BENCH

Every July, the world's wealthiest and most powerful men (and make no mistake, they are *men*) gather for two and a half weeks at a secluded "grove" in Sonoma County north of San Francisco. They are members of one of the world's most exclusive organizations, the famed Bohemian Club, and the occasion is their annual "encampment." Members are known to have included Richard Nixon, George Shultz, William F. Buckley, George Bush, Ronald Reagan, Henry Kissinger, and virtually every CEO of every major corporation you can think of. Some say the meeting is held to plan the takeover of the world. What a silly idea. These men *already* run the world.

No member has ever publicly revealed its secrets, but an encampment at the Bohemian Grove is said to include weird rituals designed to help these men unburden themselves of their daily worries. (Nude walks in the woods are supposed to be part of the cure.) Although it is now a refuge for the very cream of American society, the Bohemian Club actually sports humble origins among the poets and playwrights of post–Civil War San Francisco. One of the club's founders and early leaders was Daniel O'Connell, poet, Bohemian, Irishman.

A grand-nephew of his namesake, the Great Emancipator who finally wrested civil rights for Roman Catholics from a suspicious British Crown, O'Connell was born at the end of the famine in 1849. But the younger O'Connell was to make his mark in poetry and as a raconteur, not in the more serious world of Irish politics.

O'Connell's father was a prominent lawyer who took advantage of the new emancipation laws to get his son Dan a commission in the Royal Navy. O'Connell didn't stay long, however. After a visit to New York, he decided he liked the New World better than the Old, and he resigned his midshipman's position and hitched a ride on a ship headed 'round the Horn for California. It was 1868.

O'Connell had little difficulty landing teaching positions at various Catholic schools in California once the administrators realized the tall, strong, well-read youth before them was the grand-nephew of the great O'Connell himself. O'Connell's natural gift for making friends soon made him a well-known figure in San Francisco literary circles. He began calling himself a "bohemian," meaning a person little burdened by the normal cares of life but was always busy improving the mind and the body.

The "Bohemian Club" was O'Connell's suggestion for a name when he and several other area literary types met to form an association on February 20, 1872. For the next 27 years, O'Connell would serve as the club's Master of High Jinks and King of Munster, after the province in Ireland where he was born.

"His desire to spend money vastly exceeded his capacity to acquire it," writes Patrick Dowling of O'Connell in his superb book *California: The Irish Dream* (1989), "and he was consequently left without funds to publicize his work." O'Connell's indifference to normal concerns means that his literary canon is considerably less well known than its quality would otherwise merit.

O'Connell's money problems, however, appear to have come to an end when, in 1874, he married Anna Ashley, the daughter of a U.S. senator. They eventually had seven children and removed to a fine house in Sausalito, across San Francisco Bay in Marin County.

All the years of fast living, however, must have taken their toll and Dan O'Connell died on February 23, 1899, surrounded by his wife and children. His wake was held in the Bohemian Club's Green Room, and he was buried in Lone Mountain Cemetery next to William O'Brien of the Comstock Lode.

A few years later, the city of Sausalito erected in memory of their illustrious citizen a granite bench on a high promontory overlooking the bay that O'Connell loved. The words of O'Connell's poem *"The Chamber of Sleep,"* are inscribed upon it:

*Lower the portcullis softly, sentries placed on the wall; Let shadows of
quiet and sadness upon my palace fall
Softly draw my curtains . . . Let the world labor and weep-
My soul is safe environed by the walls of my chamber of
sleep.*

ᶻ& LOCATION: The corner of Bulkley and Harrison Avenues in Sausalito. ᶻ& HOURS: Dawn to dusk. ᶻ& ADMISSION: Free

SIMI VALLEY

RONALD REAGAN PRESIDENTIAL
LIBRARY AND MUSEUM

Nineteen eighty-four was an election year and President Ronald
Reagan was not blind to the political possibilities of a "homecoming" visit to the land of his ancestors. Although Reagan did not receive the
rapturous welcome that greeted John F. Kennedy on his trip over 20 years
earlier, the visit was certainly more of a success that Richard Nixon's
in 1970.

A few days before his celebrated journey to the beaches of Normandy
for the 40th anniversary of D-Day, President and Mrs. Reagan helicop-
tered into the small village of Ballyporeen in county Tipperary, from
which his great-grandfather, Michael Reagan, emigrated during the famine
around 1850.

While in Ballyporeen, the president was shown his greatgrandfather's
1929 baptismal certificate in the church where the baptism was performed.
(Reagan himself was raised a Protestant). The president also stopped into a
pub (now known as "The Ronald Reagan") and quaffed a beer with a
crowd of locals.

Unlike Nixon, who couldn't find a single Milhous in all of Ireland,
north or south, there were distant relatives of President Reagan's still
resident in the area. "(I) got a shock," the former president wrote later in
his memoirs. "They brought in a man in his middle twenties who caused
me to do a double take. It was amazing how much he and I resembled each
other—his eyes and hair, his whole facial structure resembled mine. Since
it had been over a century since my great-grandfather had left Ballyporeen
for America, it was an eerie experience."

Reagan also visited the cemetery where his ancestors had been buried
in paupers' graves and reflected on the great journey that had begun in that
small town. "Although I've never been a great one for introspection or
dwelling in the past," Reagan wrote, "as I looked down the narrow main
street of the little town from which an emigrant named Michael Reagan
had set out in pursuit of a dream, I had a flood of thoughts. . . . I thought of

President Reagan receives his family coat of arms from Irish prime minister Garrett Fitzgerald during his "homecoming" visit to Ireland, June 1984. (Courtesy Ronald Reagan Library)

Jack (Reagan's grandfather) and his Irish stories and the drive he'd always had to get ahead; I thought of my own childhood in Dixon, then leaving that small town for Hollywood and later Washington."

It is a matter of debate how much Reagan's Irishness helped his political career. Although the Irish-Americans are usually Democrats, Reagan had considerable support among many Irish Americans, who feared their part of the American dream might be slipping away under the ravages of inflation and high taxes. Reagan's popularity was always a mystery to his great antagonist, House Speaker Thomas P. "Tip" O'Neill.

However much the two men might have disliked each other politically, they both took pride in their heritage and always got on well personally. "Once the politics is over with," one observer commented of the relationship between the president and the Speaker, "it's just two old Irish pals swapping stories."

EXHIBITS: The Spanish Mission–style museum contains displays and memorabilia of President Reagan's life and accomplishments from birth to after his presidency. There is a replica of the Oval Office and a large section of the Berlin Wall, a tribute from the formerly divided city to the man who did so much to bring the Cold War to an end.   LOCATION: 40 Presidential Dr.   HOURS: Monday–Saturday 9–5; Sunday 12–5. Closed major holidays.   ADMISSION: $4 for adults; $2 for seniors; under 12 free.   TELEPHONE: (805) 522-8444.

TRUCKEE

DONNER HISTORIC STATE PARK

One of the most horrifying chapters in the history of the American West was the saga of the Donner party. Of the 87 people who set out to cross the Sierra Nevadas into California during the winter of 1846–47, only 48 were rescued after the party had spent four months trapped by snow drifts as deep as 22 feet. When food ran out, some of the survivors stayed alive until help came by eating the dead bodies of their fellow travelers. Irish-born Patrick Dolan, 40 years old and single, achieved the unhappy distinction of perhaps being the first deceased member of the party to be eaten.

The entire horrifying experience was chronicled by Patrick Breen, a county Carlow native who kept a diary throughout the ordeal. Breen, his wife, Margaret, and their seven children were the only Catholics in the party, which also included the Irish-born Protestant Reed family. The Breens, according to Joseph A. King's groundbreaking and important study of the event, *Winter of Entrapment* (1992), were more prudent than the others in husbanding their resources, and they survived intact.

Patrick Breen had immigrated to St. Thomas, Ontario, Canada, around 1828, where he married Margaret, whom he had known in Ireland. Six years later, they crossed over to the United States and settled first in Illinois, and later in Iowa. For reasons not precisely known, the Breens pulled up stakes in the spring of 1846 and headed for California.

The family headed west out of Independence, Missouri, accompanied by their friend Patrick Dolan. At a place called Little Sandy, which is now in Wyoming, a fateful decision was made to go to the left instead of the right. The left-hand route was supposedly a shortcut, but it led over more desolate terrain. The party was led by a 62-year-old Illinoisan named George Donner, and it became known as the Donner party.

The "shortcut" proved anything but. The band had to hack their way through the desolate Wasatch Mountains, and then cross the treeless, arid Great Salt Lake Desert, during which many of the oxen and cattle died, forcing the party to abandon some of their wagons. Indians began raiding the camp. Tempers grew short, and James Reed ended up knifing another man to death. Although many thought he had acted in self-defense, others thought he had overreacted, and he was forced to leave the party and go on alone. His wife and children, out of necessity, stayed with the others.

By late October, the party had reached the Truckee Meadow, a site now occupied by the city of Reno, Nevada. Charles Stanton, a bachelor who had gone ahead to obtain provisions, returned with seven pack mules loaded with meat and brought news of a difficult mountain crossing ahead. The party chose to rest for a week to build their strength. The delay proved fatal. By the time the party made camp on the shores of what is now Donner Lake, there was already an inch of snow on the ground. They tried to drive up toward the mountain pass, but the deepening snow forced them back toward the lake. The agony of the Donner party had begun.

The entire ordeal was recorded by Patrick Breen on a notebook he fashioned from eight sheets of paper, which he trimmed and folded to make a book of 32 sheets altogether. Every day, he took his pencil in hand, which must frequently have been almost frostbitten, to record the events going on around him. Eventually, he filled 29 of the 32 sheets between November 20, 1846, and March 1, 1847.

As Joseph A. King notes, the diary is a remarkable document for a man who might very well have been facing death. He is almost never critical of the other members of the party, even though many of them were jealous of the Breens for seeming to have more to eat than the others. It is also remarkably devoid of self-pity and never loses its hopeful attitude.

The Irish family was in the terrible moral position of having to decide whom to help and when to help them. Could food be shared if it meant the Breens' own children might go hungry? Apparently not. The Breens decided their own needs would come before anyone else's, a policy that led to hard feelings and perhaps contributed to the negative image of Patrick Breen in many subsequent accounts. Nevertheless, when there was no danger to themselves, the Breens often gave food to others.

The Breens saved the four Reed children by taking them into the Breen cabin. One of the Reed daughters, Virginia, prayed every day with the Breens and vowed to become a Catholic if she survived. She did, and kept her promise when she married John Murphy, a son of Martin Murphy, Sr. (*see* Murphys, California).

Several attempts were made to break out, and efforts were made by those who had gone ahead to organize relief parties. But the Mexican War had commenced earlier in the summer and trapped migrants were just about the last thing on anybody's mind in California.

Relief arrived on March 1, the date of Breen's last diary entry. Two of the Breen children had left with an earlier rescue party that took only those best able to travel. Unfortunately, deliverance was not to be theirs. At the place now called Starved Camp, the Breens were finally forced to engage in the practice they had stoutly resisted up to that point: cannibalism. They ate two dead children and an adult woman.

The Breens' ordeal came to a definitive end when a third relief party arrived, which initially was inclined to abandon the family as too far gone to be saved. Instead, a stout Indian named John Stark insisted they be rescued, and he carried many of the smaller Breen children and all their provisions on his back to the safety of Sutter's Fort. All the Breen children remembered him as the true hero of the ordeal.

The banished John Reed was reunited with his wife and children, whom the Breens had saved. The other members of the party did not fare so well, with almost everyone losing someone. George Donner and his wife ended up being eaten by one of the last survivors.

The Breens came through their ordeal remarkably well (a telling refutation of modern theories about children's fragility). Patrick and Margaret were the first English-speakers to settle in San Juan Bautista in San Benito County. Thanks to eldest son John Breen, who brought $12,000 in gold back from the gold rush, the Breens were able to purchase a handsome home and 400 acres. Patrick later served as postmaster and died in 1868. Margaret followed him six years later.

The Breen children all did well. John took over the family estates. James became a state assemblyman and a judge. Edward and Patrick became prosperous ranchers and Simon a noted violinist. Isabella, only a year old at the time of the tragedy, outlived all the other members of the Donner party, dying in 1935.

?? EXHIBITS: The Emigrant Trail Museum displays exhibits of the area's railroad history, natural history, logging and immigrants. There is a plaque near Donner Lake marking the location of the Breen cabin. ?? LOCATION: One mile west of the town of Truckee on Donner Pass Road. ?? HOURS: Park open daily 8–dusk. Museum open daily 10–5 Memorial Day to Labor Day; 10–12 and 1–5 rest of year. ?? ADMISSION: Park admission $5 per car. Museum admission $2 for adults, $1 for children under 12. ?? TELEPHONE: (916) 582-7892.

W O O D S I D E

FILOLI MANSION

William Bourn, who made his fortune from owning the water rights around San Francisco, used some of his money to construct this magnificent house about 25 miles south of San Francisco as a wedding present for his daughter Maud, who was marrying an Irishman. Mr. Bourn also happened to own Muckross Castle in Ireland, and he chose this site for the mansion because the area reminded him of the Lakes of Killarney.

Bourn intended the house, completed in 1916, as a bribe for his new son-in-law, who was a member of the British civil service and had just been named a magistrate in far-off Zanzibar on the eastern coast of Africa. Horrified at the thought of his daughter being taken off to the Dark Continent, Bourn offered Filoli (an acronym taken from the first two letters of Bourn's personal motto, Fight, Love, Live) as an inducement for the family to stay put. Needless to say, the new son-in-law, Arthur Rose Vincent, accepted with alacrity.

Ireland echoes throughout the house. There are scenes from the Lakes of Killarney painted on the walls of the ballroom, and Irish yew trees thrive in the strange climate around the grounds.

The new couple ended up spending much of their time in Ireland rather than California. Maud died in 1929, and in 1931, Vincent gifted Muckross Castle to the people of Ireland as the newly independent country's first national park. Vincent went on to be elected to the Irish Parliament, where he served with distinction for many years.

In 1937, unable to afford the expense of keeping up Filoli, Vincent sold it to Mr. and Mrs. William Roth. In 1975, that family deeded it to the people of California, and it is now open to the public.

If Filoli looks familiar to visitors, it is because it served as the television "home" of the Carrington clan in the longrunning ABC television series "Dynasty". It also made an appearance in the 1979 film *Heaven Can Wait*, starring Warren Beatty.

🍃 **EXHIBITS:** The house contains original furnishings. 🍃 **LOCATION:** Off I-280, via Edgewood Road to Canada Road. 🍃 **HOURS:** Both self-guided and guided tours of the mansion and the 17 acres of gardens are available. Call for times. 🍃 **ADMISSION:** $8; children $4. 🍃 **TELEPHONE:** (415) 364-2880.

YORBA LINDA

RICHARD M. NIXON PRESIDENTIAL LIBRARY AND BIRTHPLACE

Richard Nixon always seemed fated to turn out second-best to John F. Kennedy in almost everything. He lost the 1960 presidential race to him, of course, and Nixon's 1969 inaugural address is without doubt modeled on Kennedy's, yet no one remembers Nixon's speech. Kennedy's raucous 1963 "homecoming" to Ireland was a major event for Ireland and

Irish-Americans alike. Richard Nixon's own pathetic attempt to stage a similar spasm of Gaelic pride, predictably, fell flat.

Nixon's Irish roots are authentic enough. The late president's great-great-great-great grandfather, Thomas Milhous, was from Timahoe, a small village about 20 miles northwest of Dublin. (Nixon named the Irish setter he kept in the White House "King Timahoe.") But when Nixon announced he would visit Ireland October 3–5, 1970, the Irish government could find not a single Milhous relative to greet him. (They were more successful in finding several Ryan relatives related to First Lady Thelma "Pat" Ryan Nixon, who got her nickname because she was born on St. Patrick's Day.)

The problem was complicated because little was known of Nixon's Quaker Irish ancestors. Thomas Milhous's father, John, was said to have been born in 1699 in Carrickfergus, county Antrim (the same home town as Andrew Jackson's parents). The family is supposed to have moved to Timahoe when Thomas was still a small boy. He grew up there, married, started a family, and then left Ireland for Pennsylvania in 1729. John Milhous was said to have been buried in the Quaker cemetery in Timahoe.

By the time the president arrived, however, his dreams of meeting long-lost cousins had been dashed. Not a single relative could be found. Nixon had to be content with being shown the remains of the Quaker graveyard and the foundations of the old Quaker meetinghouse in Timahoe, but little else remained. Several Watergate memoirs recount that the entire trip was a concoction, with virtually no authentic historical value. Also, the "troubles" had just resumed in Northern Ireland the year before, which seemed to overshadow the entire trip.

&. **EXHIBITS:** The museum contains the small house where Nixon was born, as well as original furnishings, plus many exhibits on Nixon's public and private life. &. **LOCATION:** 18001 Yorba Linda Blvd. &. **HOURS:** Monday–Saturday 10–5; Sunday 11–5. &. **ADMISSION:** $4.95. Over 65 $2.95. Ages 8–11, $1. &. **TELEPHONE:** (714) 993-3393.

YOSEMITE

O'SHAUGHNESSY DAM

In an era when battles between environmentalists and developers are a routine occurrence, it's hard to conceive of a time when they were almost unknown. Throughout much of the history of the American West, the population was transient and many prospectors followed a "rape and run" policy of dealing with the land. Early in this century, however, came the first national controversy over a development issue, and an Irishman (several, actually) was right in the middle of it.

Like Los Angeles to the south, San Francisco was wrestling with a water problem early in this century. Although better endowed than its southern rival, San Francisco faced its own "water famine" and consequent limits on its growth. The man who had to solve the problem was, like William Mulholland, (see Los Angeles, California), an Irish immigrant: county Limerick–born Michael Maurice O'Shaughnessy, the city's water engineer from 1912 to 1932.

O'Shaughnessy's parents must have had some means, for, unlike Mulholland, he received a first-class education at Queen's College, Cork and Queen's College, Galway, earning a bachelor's degree with honors in 1884. Almost as soon as he received his degree, young O'Shaughnessy was off to the United States for a career in engineering. He was employed by various railroads and water companies, spending six years in Hawaii at one time building irrigation systems for sugar plantations there.

The idea of damming the Tuolumne River at Hetch-Hetchy in Yosemite was not O'Shaughnessy's, but James Duval Phelan's during his time as San Francisco's mayor. Phelan began the process in 1901, when he applied to the U.S. Interior Department for a permit. The conservation-minded administration of Pres. Theodore Roosevelt denied the application, but Phelan was not to be so easily discouraged.

For 12 years the battle raged. For the first time, a split opened between what would today be called "conservationists" and "environmentalists." The former believed that natural resources should not be wantonly wasted, but could be harnessed for the wise use of all people. The latter wanted to preserve nature as God intended it and for its own sake. John Muir, founder of the Sierra Club, was in the latter category.

Muir made halting the construction of a dam in the Hetch-Hetchy Valley a national crusade. The dam would flood the entire valley, Muir argued, forever obliterating from human eyes a piece of earth thought to rival Yosemite in beauty. Phelan and his supporters argued the lake would be as aesthetically pleasing as the valley.

In the end, Phelan and O'Shaughnessy won, of course, since Pres. Woodrow Wilson was politically beholden to Phelan. Muir died in 1914. Of a broken heart, some said.

With the way now cleared, O'Shaughnessy assembled the massive amounts of men, machines, and money that would labor for 20 years to see the project become reality. The San Francisco aqueduct rivaled Mulholland's in Los Angeles in almost every way. The aqueduct is more than 155 miles long. At one point, the water cascades through a 28-mile-long tunnel, which was then the longest tunnel in the world. All for water.

By the time the dam was completed in 1934, both Phelan and O'Shaughnessy had died, but their work, whatever one thinks of the merits of how it was accomplished, did ensure San Francisco a reliable supply of fresh water for the rest of the 20th century.

&⚫ EXHIBITS: A stone plinth with a plaque marking the "O'Shaughnessy Dam" stands near the summit. &⚫ LOCATION: The O'Shaughnessy Dam is located at the Hetch-Hetchy Reservoir in the northwest part of Yosemite National Park. It is reached from Yosemite Valley via Big Oak Flat Road. (Tire chains strongly recommended in fall, winter, and spring.) A 9-mile paved road from Mather leads to the 312-foot dam. &⚫ HOURS: Yosemite National Park is open daily all year round. Not all park entrances are open all the time, however. Call ahead for detailed information. &⚫ ADMISSION: $5 entry fee. &⚫ TELEPHONE: Recorded information: (209) 372-0200.

COLORADO

MOLLY BROWN HOUSE MUSEUM

Just before midnight on April 14, 1912, the R.M.S. *Titanic*, the world's newest and most elegant steamship, met with disaster on her maiden voyage. Running recklessly at top speed through an ice field, the ship struck an iceberg that ripped an intermittent gash in her starboard side, flooding the ship's forward compartments. In spite of features that her builders said made her "practically unsinkable" (the press later shortened that to "unsinkable"), the ship went down with the loss of nearly 1,600 lives. It became the most famous, but not the most deadly, maritime disaster in history.

Pulling on the oars in one of the *Titanic's* lifeboats was Denver socialite Margaret Tobin "Maggie" Brown. (She was not called "Molly" in her lifetime.) She had been touring Europe in 1912 when she received word her grandson was ill, and she immediately booked passage home on the new steamer.

Shortly after being awakened by the ship's striking of the iceberg, Maggie dressed and went up on deck to find the crew launching lifeboats. Maggie claimed never to have feared for her personal safety and did not take a seat in a lifeboat when it was offered. As she explained later, however, a crew member came up behind her and forcibly dropped her into a boat as it was being lowered into the water.

While her account of that night became more and more fantastic with each telling, what seems fairly certain is that Maggie more or less took charge of the boat from the one timid *Titanic* crewman on board. She was the first to sight the lights of the liner *Carpathia* as it came to the rescue. Once on board the smaller liner, Maggie's knowledge of languages made her a natural for dealing with the many foreign passengers who were rescued from the sunken ship. She compiled a survivors list and saw to it the information was radioed ahead to New York. She organized a fund-raising effort among the wealthier passengers, and more than $10,000 was pledged by the time the *Carpathia* docked.

Maggie became an instant celebrity as she told and retold the tales of her heroism that night. "Typical Brown luck," was her explanation for her survival. "We're unsinkable." That was enough for the press, which took some liberties with her name and instantly dubbed her "the unsinkable Molly Brown."

Margaret Tobin's father, John, was born in Ireland in 1823 and immi-grated to the United States as a boy in the company of an uncle. His first wife, whom he married in Virginia, died only a few years later. John moved west to Hannibal, Missouri, the town that would later be immortalized by Mark Twain. In one of her tall tales, Margaret later claimed her father and Twain had been friends and rivals, but there does not appear to be any support for this story.

Margaret was born in 1867 in Hannibal after her father remarried, this time to another Irish immigrant, Johanna Collins. John Tobin worked at the Hannibal Gas Works and made enough to buy his own home, which has been restored by the Marion County Historical Society.

Separating fact from fiction in Molly's life is difficult, a process that has not been helped along by the 1960s Broadway musical and subsequent movie. Molly claimed later that it was a chance meeting with Mark Twain in Hannibal that encouraged her to try her luck out west. It is possible Molly met the famed author, but biographer Christine Whitacre thinks it more likely that it was her reading of Twain's books that sent her to Leadville (*see* next entry).

Maggie arrived in Leadville in 1886 in the company of her brother Daniel. Their older sister and her husband had come to the mountain mining boomtown three years before. Molly found work in a dry goods store and married James Brown, a young prospector who dreamed of striking it rich. He was one of the few dreamers who actually hit pay dirt, striking gold and becoming a wealthy man in 1893.

The fashion in those days was for the Leadville rich to set up house-keeping in Denver, and the Browns followed the pattern. They built the house at 1340 Pennsylvania Street for the then-incredible sum of $30,000.

Even though Denver was still little more than a crude frontier town, the local establishment shunned the *noveau riche* Browns. The fact Maggie was Irish and Catholic and retained many of her working-class man-nerisms and speech patterns did nothing to improve the family's social position.

She sought consolation in her world travels, where her elegant clothes and fabulous jewels, combined with her wit and down-to-earth manner, were seen as distinctly American. "Without boasting," she once said,

"Molly" Brown's magnificent Queen Anne Revival was built in 1889 for the then-incredible sum of $30,000.

(Synergy Photographics)

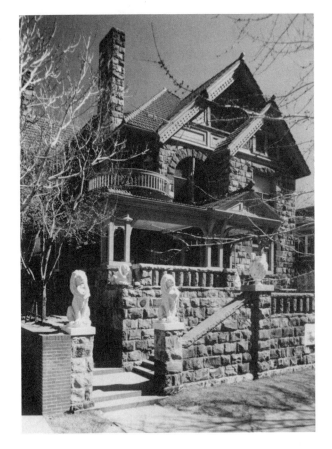

"I can say I know everyone worth knowing from Moscow to the Bosporous."

Maggie's home life was not happy, however. James, or JJ as he was called, suffered a stroke in 1899 and was forced to give up active mining. He and Maggie fought about the upbringing of their children, with Maggie insisting on elite European schools and JJ wanting them closer to home. Maggie got her way on this, as she did on most matters. A major embarrassment was when JJ was sued by a prominent Denver man for alienation of affection, the subject being the plaintiff's 22-year-old wife.

It was the *Titanic,* however, that truly made Maggie Brown into a national figure. She campaigned to end the "women and children" first policy at sea, claiming that it had left numerous widows and children destitute after the disaster. In 1914, she ran unsuccessfully for the U.S. Senate, even though women did not yet have the vote nationally. In the 1920s, she met with Pres. Calvin Coolidge in an unsuccessful effort to get his endorsement of the first Equal Rights Amendment.

Through it all she splashed her opinions on everything throughout the world's newspapers, finding herself on the receiving end of libel suits occasionally. One woman sued Maggie because she claimed the Denver woman had accused her running up and down stairs in only her nightgown.

JJ died in 1922. The family fortune had been dwindling steadily for years, and by the time Maggie died in New York in 1932, there was almost nothing left. The house in Denver fell into disrepair, eventually becoming a rooming house and later a home for wayward girls. It was in danger of demolition in 1970 when a grass roots effort was formed to save it. It was restored as a memorial to this remarkable Irish-American woman who was one of Denver's most famous residents.

🐚 EXHIBITS: The house contains period furnishings and displays on the Brown family. Every St. Patrick's Day, a special "tea" is given in honor of Molly Brown's Irish ancestry. 🐚 LOCATION: 1340 Pennsylvania St. 🐚 HOURS: Monday–Saturday 10–4; Sunday 12–4, June 1 through August 31; Tuesday–Saturday 10–4, Sunday 12–4, September 1 through May 31. 🐚 ADMISSION: $3.50 adults; $2.50 seniors; $1.50 children. 🐚 TELEPHONE: (303) 832-4092.

LEADVILLE

AN IRISH TOWN

In 1876, three Irish-Americans, the Gallagher brothers, showed up in a desolate region of Colorado. With no experience in mining, they nevertheless began to dig and struck silver. They sold out their interest for $225,000, which, although a fabulous sum in those days, was far less than they could have had if they had stayed on.

To see Leadville today is to wonder at how this small town could once have rivaled Denver as the most important town in Colorado. But when the boom was rolling full steam in the late 1870s, Leadville was a thriving center, boasting that it had the finest red-light district in the West. Its solid brick buildings and opera house testify to the prosperity that once reigned here.

The Irish were heavily represented in Leadville, as they were in most mining districts of the West. A delegate from Leadville is recorded as being present at the 1880 national convention of the Ancient Order of Hibernians. A mine called the "Maid of Erin" once operated outside the town.

Today, all of Leadville is one big museum, but there is little that commemorates the presence of the Irish specifically. It is yet another place where the Irish made their mark and blended into the mainstream of American life.

⁄ **EXHIBITS:** The museum contains a diorama of a mining operation in early Leadville, as well as artifacts from the mining era.   ⁄ **LOCATION:** The Leadville Heritage Museum is at 9th Street and Harrison Avenue. ⁄ **HOURS:** Daily 10–6 Memorial Day through October 31; Friday–Sunday 11–4 rest of year.   ⁄ **ADMISSION:** $2.50; $1.50 seniors; $1 children. ⁄ **TELEPHONE:** (719) 486-1878.

IDAHO

O'FARRELL'S CABIN

Idaho's capital city should, by rights, be named "O'Farrell" rather than Boise, since John A. O'Farrell erected the first house and was the first citizen. But things didn't work out that way, and Boise it is. O'Farrell's first house, however, remains standing and is a well-known local landmark.

Idaho was one of the last states to be settled by whites, and there are still a handful of living Idahoans who can remember those first pioneers, many of whom were Irish.

The story of the Irish in the West is largely a story of mining, and John A. O'Farrell was no exception. Born in Ireland February 13, 1833, he was sent to sea at age 13 and traveled the world before he was out of his teens. He was in California during the gold rush in 1850 and, taking advantage of the U.S. government's desire to populate the new state at the far western edge of the continent, took out U.S. citizenship immediately.

O'Farrell had a yen to find gold, and he appears to have found some of it during his time. He was well-off enough in the early 1860s to win the hand of Mary Ann Chapman, the daughter of an established Philadelphia family. In 1863, he moved to the wild, unexplored area of the northern Rockies, east of the Cascades. On a windy, sagebrush plain, he built the first log cabin in the state that, in 1890, would become Idaho. The first settlers were his wife's mother, brother, and other relatives, who arrived soon after the cabin was built in a 14-wagon train.

The cabin was hand-built, using cedar and cottonwood, and although it might not seem much to look at now, it was a veritable palace compared to the adobe shacks local Indians and other settlers were living in at the time. Soon after it was built, other prospectors began arriving in the area,

John O'Farrell's cabin, built in 1863, was Boise's first house, and the site of the first Catholic mass in Idaho.

and the army decided to use the settlement as a frontier post. Boise had begun.

O'Farrell and his wife had seven children, three of whom died in infancy. The family was dedicated to the Catholic church, and it was a source of discontent among them and their fellow Catholic settlers that the church had not seen fit to assign a priest to their area.

Then, one day, according to the story, Mrs. O'Farrell spotted two men riding past the settlement, and she felt confident at least one was a priest. She ran after them, shouting, "Father!" to see if one would turn around. Both did. They were French missionaries on their way to Oregon. The two priests concelebrated the first Catholic mass in Idaho in the O'Farrells cabin.

John O'Farrell made a modest fortune for himself, and the family eventually moved into a comfortable house on Franklin Street. Mary Ann died in 1900, and her husband eight years later. The cabin was preserved by the local chapter of the Daughters of the American Revolution, who moved it to its present site on Fort Street near the main gate of the military reservation grounds in Boise. Derelict for many years, the cabin was restored in 1957 and a granite marker installed outside.

The shutting down of military facilities has thrown the future of the cabin into doubt recently. There has been talk of moving it onto the grounds of the Idaho State Historical Society.

❧ EXHIBITS: There is a stone marker outside detailing the cabin's importance in state history. The cabin itself is not open to the public. ❧ LOCATION: O'Farrell's Cabin is on Fort Street, between Fourth and Fifth streets, in downtown Boise.

MONTANA

HISTORIC ANACONDA

"The Irish did not flock to these places (the mining camps of the West)," writes David Emmons in his excellent study *The Butte Irish* (1989), "but then, neither did anyone else in those years, immigrant or native." Indeed, most Americans, as well as most Irish, stayed on the east coast. Heading out west was for the adventurous, or the desperate. For the Irish who made the journey, it was probably a little of both. Another attraction of the West was that the Irish encountered little prejudice or intolerance in the egalitarian atmosphere of the mining camps.

Enough Irish made the move to build communities in some places. By the turn of the century, Butte was one of the most Irish cities in the entire United States, with no less than 12,000 of the county's 47,000 people claiming to be Irish or first-generation Irish-Americans. In the Anaconda Mine in 1894, there were 1,250 Irish-born miners out of 5,534. Most of these Irish were postfamine immigrants, having come to the United States in the years after the Civil War, and they seem to have come disproportionately from county Cork.

There is no question that the single greatest draw to Butte for the Irish in the 1880s and 1890s was the presence of Marcus Daly (*see* Hamilton, Montana). The Irish-born "Copper King" almost singlehandedly developed Butte as a copper mining center.

Although some have claimed Daly recruited Irish miners specifically to work his mines, that does not appear to have been the case. Daly's Irish origins and reputation for fair dealing and paying above-average wages were all that was needed to bring Irish workers. Daly does appear to have given Irishmen preference in hiring, however. At Anaconda in 1894, for instance, there were only 365 English-born miners at a time when English-born residents of Butte outnumbered the Irish.

Thanks to high wages and a strong sense of ethnic identification, the Irish miners in Montana became powerful advocates of (and sources of support for) the Irish independence movement. They had the time and resources to play the patriot game. Eamon de Valera (*see* Rochester, New York) made two fund-raising visits to Butte before 1920, and membership in such organizations as the Ancient Order of Hibernians and the more secretive Clan na Gael was high.

Eventually, the Anaconda and other mines in the Butte area played out. Many Irish, having made their money in the pits, were all too happy to leave Butte behind for greener pastures elsewhere. Still, enough of them stayed so that 20 percent of Montanans today claim some Irish ancestry, making this isolated state the 10th "most Irish" in the nation.

❧ **EXHIBITS:** A map outlining a walking tour of historic Anaconda is available at the visitor center at 306 E. Park St. ❧ **LOCATION:** Anaconda is about 20 miles from Butte. Take I-90W to Alt. MT Route 10 into Anaconda. ❧ **HOURS:** The visitor center is open Monday–Friday 8–5; Saturday–Sunday 9–5 Memorial Day through Labor Day; Monday–Friday 9–5 rest of the year. ❧ **ADMISSION:** Free ❧ **TELEPHONE:** (406) 563-2400.

HAMILTON

MARCUS DALY MANSION

Butte, Montana, calls itself "the richest hill on earth," and the man who made it so was Marcus Daly, an Irish immigrant.

Born in Ballyjamesduff, county Cavan, in 1841, Daly headed for the United States when he was only 15 years old. For the next 20 years or so, his story differed little from that of the average Irish immigrant, mostly involving poorly paid manual labor. After five years in New York, he headed west, eventually reaching Nevada, where the Comstock Lode silver mines were operating. By all accounts, he was skilled with a pick and shovel and soon worked his way to a supervisory position.

Daly eventually came to the attention of the Walker brothers of Salt Lake City, who owned a mining company. They sent him to Butte in 1876 to investigate the potential of the Alice Silver Mine. Daly recommended they buy it, and threw in $5,000 of his own money toward the purchase. Daly made a great deal of money on the Alice and eventually sold out his interest for $30,000.

Geologists thought the Butte area played out, but Daly thought otherwise and purchased the Anaconda Silver Mine. The silver soon gave out, but Daly sunk a shaft in an area thought to be valueless. When copper was struck instead of gold or silver, even Daly was initially disappointed. But when the exceptional richness of the ore became evident, Daly quietly bought up mineral rights all around the area. Thus was born the fabulous story of Marcus Daly and his Anaconda Copper Company.

Daly's fame grew as quickly as his fortune. Because he paid $3.50 for an eight-hour day—almost double what industrial workers elsewhere could command—thousands of Irish flocked to Butte, and later Anaconda, to work for him. Daly's fortune became one of the largest in 19th-century America. He used his wealth to make dramatic improvements in and around Butte, building and founding power stations, irrigation systems, railroads, lumber mills, and banks.

Daly was a strong Democrat and one of the organizers of the state's Democratic party. He is estimated to have supplied as much as 20 percent of all the money spent by William Jennings Bryan in his unsuccessful 1896 bid for the White House. For over a decade Daly was engaged in the "War of the Copper Kings" with fellow mine owner W. A. Clark for control of the Montana Democratic party. Twice Daly managed to thwart Clark's ambition to become a U.S. senator. Only after Daly's death in 1900 did Clark finally win the seat.

Daly preferred to spend his summers away from Butte, and in 1890 he constructed this 24,213-square-foot Georgian Revival mansion called "Riverside" on 22,000 acres in the heart of Montana's Bitterroot Valley. On its 3 floors are 24 bedrooms, 15 bathrooms, and 7 fireplaces faced with Italian marble. Like many Irishmen, Daly loved the track, and he raised his prize thoroughbred racehorses on the property.

After Daly's death, his widow, Margaret, whom he married in 1872, lived on in the mansion until her own death in 1941. The building was closed from that time until it was reopened to the public in 1987 as a National Historic Landmark.

&. **EXHIBITS:** The house contains many original furnishings and displays on Daly's life and work. A guided tour is conducted hourly. In Butte itself, there is a statue of Daly by Augustus St. Gaudens. It is in the center of North Main Street between Copper and Gagnon streets. &. **LOCATION:** 251 Eastside Hwy., between Hamilton and Corvallis. &. **HOURS:** Tuesday–Sunday 11–4, May through September. By appointment the rest of the year. &. **ADMISSION:** $5 adults; over 62 $4; $2 for children 5–12; $1 grounds only. &. **TELEPHONE:** (406) 363-6004.

HELENA

GENERAL THOMAS FRANCIS MEAGHER
EQUESTRIAN STATUE

Patronage was an important part of organizing the United States for Civil War, particularly on the Northern side. Because there was only a very small cadre of regular army officers (made even smaller by the defection of so many able leaders to the Confederate side), Pres. Lincoln had little choice but to appoint a large number of "political" generals with little or no military experience. A few turned out to be men of ability, but most, unfortunately, were not. "Political general" became a byword in the Union ranks for incompetence.

Thomas Francis Meagher (pronounced MAH-r, though some assimilated Irish-Americans today pronounce it MEE-ger) was a political general, and although he never achieved high command, was well regarded by his fellow Irish-Americans and those who served under him. Born in county Waterford in 1823, Meagher became a fervant Irish nationalist and was one of the leaders of the abortive 1848 uprising (*see* Hampton Park, Virginia). His advocacy of violent methods to end British rule, as opposed to Daniel O'Connell's efforts to win concessions from within the system, earned him the nickname "Meagher of the Sword."

A benevolent British government commuted Meagher's death sentence to banishment to Australia, from which Meagher soon escaped and made his way to New York in 1852. There, he built a successful career as a lawyer, newspaperman, and agitator for Irish independence. He helped raise and organize the Civil War Irish Brigade and later became its best-known commander, leading it in its most famous, albeit disastrous, action at Fredericksburg (*see* Fredericksburg, Virginia and Antietam, Maryland).

Thanks to the influence of patronage in the Union army, however, it was always to the political advantage of Washington politicians to form new regiments rather than rebuild old ones decimated by battle and disease. New regiments meant more high-ranking commissions to be handed out. So, after the carnage at Fredericksburg, when Meagher asked to withdraw the Irish Brigade from front-line service to rest and recruit replacements, permission was denied and he resigned his command.

Meagher served in various minor military posts for the rest of the war, and in the fall of 1865 was appointed territorial secretary of the Montana Territory. Although many Irish-Americans boast he was the first governor, he never held the title. His position actually allowed him only to carry out the duties of a territorial governor for over a year.

Meagher was not merely a functionary, however, for he had ambitions to bring Irish immigrants to the new territory. A movement was developing around this time to lure the Irish away from what many thought to be

*Unveiling of the
Thomas Francis
Meagher statue, in
front of the state
capitol at Helena,
Montana, 1905.*
(Montana Historical Society)

the corrupting influences of urban life in the East and settle them on the Plains. Col. William O'Neill in Nebraska and Father John Ireland of Minnesota both sought to establish colonies on the prairie (*see* O'Neill, Nebraska, and Graceville, Minnesota.) Meagher's ambition was "to be the representative and champion of the Irish race in the wild, great mountains."

Unfortunately for Meagher, he did not live to see large numbers of Irish come west to work for Marcus Daly (*see* previous entry). On July 1, 1867, he fell off a riverboat near Ft. Benton under mysterious circumstances and drowned. His body was never recovered.

He was not forgotten, however. The Irish Montanans, newly prosperous thanks to copper mining, demanded a memorial to their great hero when Montana finally achieved statehood. With Marcus Daly chairing the Thomas Francis Meagher Memorial Association, the equestrian statue of Meagher was unveiled on the grounds of the state capitol in Helena on July 4, 1905.

&· LOCATION: The state capitol is at 6th and Montana streets. The statue stands on the grounds near the west entrance. &· HOURS: The statue can be viewed from dawn to dusk. Guided tours of the capitol are available Monday–Saturday 10–4, Sunday 11–3 from early June through Labor Day. By appointment the rest of the year. The capitol is open daily 8–5. &· ADMISSION: Free &· TELEPHONE: (406) 444-4789.

LITTLE BIGHORN NATIONAL BATTLEFIELD

Two days after Sioux and Cheyenne warriors under the command of Crazy Horse and Gall had wiped out Gen. George Armstrong Custer and 215 troopers of his Seventh Cavalry on June 25, 1876, soldiers of Gen. Alfred Terry's main force cautiously inspected the battlefield. The sight they found sickened them. Bodies of the troopers were stripped naked of their uniforms and possessions and many were mutilated beyond recognition. It was scenes such as this that allegedly caused Irish-American Gen. Phillip Sheridan to make his (in)famous remark, "The only good Indian is a dead Indian."

One body, however, was curiously untouched. It was that of Capt. Myles Keough, the Irish-born commander of Company I, the senior captain in Custer's battalion and one of the most trusted lieutenants of "the boy general." Around his neck was a religious medal, usually described as the *Agnus Dei.* In all likelihood, however, the medal was the *Medaglia di Pro Petri Sede,* awarded Keough by Pope Pius IX for his service with the papal army in the early 1860s. It was a large, impressive award, different from those worn by the other Irish-Catholics in the Seventh Cavalry, and some believe that it caused the superstitious Indians to leave his body alone.

How did this dashing, young (age 36 at his death) Irishman come to meet his fate with America's most romanticized soldier on a bleak prairie hillside 5,000 miles from his birthplace?

Keough's short but tempestuous journey through life began in county Carlow on March 25, 1840. His family were well-off Catholics who passionately detested English rule. (The family, who now spell the name Kehoe, still own and farm the land where the captain was born.) Young Myles seems to have had a wild streak early on, his favorite reading as a boy being the adventure book *Charles O'Malley, The Irish Dragoon.*

Keough received an above-average education at St. Patrick's College and he was good with horses. This latter skill was invaluable in the American Civil War, when the Union armies were particularly short of good horsemen.

*The only body
found untouched
in the aftermath of
Little Bighorn was
that of Capt.
Myles Keough.*

(Courtesy Brian Pohanka)

Initially, Keough sought his fortune in Africa as a mercenary, but he was among the first to respond to the pope's call in 1860 for Catholics to defend the papal states against the forces of Italian unification. The struggle was hopeless and ended quickly, but Keough's reckless courage brought him to the attention of the pope himself, who decorated him.

Now without a war to fight, Keough's eye settled on the United States, where civil war was brewing. Some historians puzzle about why so many Irish joined the Union forces, which were dedicated to freeing the slaves, who would then economically compete with Irish labor. What this analysis overlooks, however, is that the Confederacy was widely seen as pro-British, and the social order in the South looked uncomfortably familiar to Irish eyes. Keough joined the Union army and, because of his prior military experience, was assigned as a staff officer to the Army of the Cumberland in Tennessee.

But Keough did not allow his staff position to keep him out of the action. "Major Keough, Aide-de-Camp, to Major General Stoneman, went forward with a detachment of the 12th Kentucky Volunteer Cavalry . . . surprised and routed the rebels near Salisbury . . . killing 9 and capturing 68 . . . Much credit is due Major Keough . . . ," wrote Gen. George Thomas to General Henry Halleck on April 25, 1865.

Peacetime demobilization temporarily threw Keough out of work, but by the summer of 1866, trouble with the Indians on the Plains created a demand for experienced cavalry officers, and Keough quickly obtained a commission as a captain in the regular army. The Seventh Cavalry was formally activated in September 1866, and Keough was on its original roster.

From the start, the Seventh was an eclectic unit. In addition to Keough, the other officers included a Prussian, a Frenchman, a former member of Congress, a half-breed Indian, a judge, and a grandson of Alexander Hamilton. In the ranks, 40 percent were born overseas, with the Irish forming the largest single contingent and the Germans the next largest. At the time of the Little Bighorn, 128 of the 600 or so men in the Seventh Cavalry were Irish-born, and 31 of them died in the battle. This, of course, did not count the Irish-Americans among the native-born troopers, many of whom sported Irish surnames.

Evan Connell, in his book on Custer and the Seventh Cavalry, *Son of the Morning Star* (1984), says Keough was a drunkard and harsh disciplinarian who was unpopular with his men. There are other accounts, however, which say he was a fair commander who was well respected by his fellow officers and those under him. He was certainly popular with women. All of his photographs convey a dashing sensuality they found well-nigh irresistible.

The destruction of the Seventh Cavalry was part of a long, bitter struggle for control of the northern Great Plains. Gold had been discovered in the Black Hills in 1874, in the middle of an area that had been granted to the Indians by the 1868 Treaty of Ft. Laramie (which had been negotiated by Irish-born "mountain man" Thomas "Broken Hand" Fitzpatrick; *see* Ft. Laramie, Wyoming).

Prospectors flooded into the area, and the Indians left the reservation for the open grasslands of Wyoming and Montana. In 1876, the U.S. government declared the Indians to be in insurrection and dispatched the cavalry to round them up.

The Seventh set out from Ft. Abraham Lincoln near Bismarck, North Dakota, on May 17, 1876, as part of Gen. Alfred Terry's force to trap the Indians. Terry believed there were only 800 Indian warriors in the vicinity. In fact, there were between 4,000 and 6,000.

The Seventh split off from the main force in an effort to catch the Indians in a viselike movement. On the morning of June 25, 1876, Custer spotted some Sioux warriors near his camp and decided to move immediately against the Indians, whom he feared would learn of his position before he had time to make contact with Terry. Custer divided his forces into three battalions and attacked the Indian camp with his 215 men. Vastly outnumbered and outgunned, however (some of the Sioux and Cheyenne carried repeating rifles, whereas the Seventh had only single-shot carbines), Custer and his men were doomed. The "Last Stand" was not a battle in the classic sense, but simply a desperate struggle for survival that lasted perhaps half an hour.

Keough's Company I fought its final battle just to the left of Company F, with which Custer was fighting. According to some Indian veterans, Keough might well have been among the last to fall. Keough's horse, Comanche, was the only Seventh Cavalry survivor.

It was probably Keough's idea to form a regimental band, a notion that Custer, a lover of martial music, thought excellent. The commanding officer personally contributed $50 for the purchase of instruments. Keough probably suggested the old Irish air "Garry Owen" for the regimental march. In her own book, Elizabeth Custer says her husband began whistling the tune at Ft. Riley and she thought Keough had had something to do with it. ("Garry Owen" is a corruption of the Gaelic for "Owen's Garden." Garry Owen is a suburb of Limerick and not far from Keough's birthplace.)

Some of the lyrics, not often heard these days, read like this:

Let Bacchus' sons be not dismayed
But join with me each jovial blade;
Come booze and sing and lend your aid
To help me with the chorus.

CHORUS

Instead of Spa we'll drink down ale.
And pay the reck'ning on the nail;
No man for debt shall go to gaol
From Garry Owen in glory.

At the Battle of Washita River, where Custer surprised the Indians in their winter camp and scored a victory, the signal for attack was when the band struck up "Garry Owen." When the Seventh Cavalry rode out to meet its destiny, the bandsmen were left behind. At Custer's command, they assembled on a knoll outside of camp and struck up the inspirational tune, which they played until the Seventh rode out of sight. Thus, the old Irish marching air was the last tune George Armstrong Custer ever heard played.

🐾 EXHIBITS: There is a visitors' center located at the park entrance with a museum and a bookstore. A film on the battle, "Red Sunday," is shown, and park rangers provide guided tours and information. A plaque on the battlefield tour marks the spot where Myles Keough fell leading Company I in its final battle. 🐾 LOCATION: Sixty-five miles southeast of Billings,

Montana. From Billings, take I-90 to the Little Bighorn Battlefield exit, then drive 1 mile east on U.S. 212 to the park entrance. ❧ HOURS: 8–8 daily Memorial Day through Labor Day; 8–6 from Labor Day through October; 8–4:30 rest of the year. ❧ ADMISSION: $3 per vehicle Memorial Day through Labor Day; U.S. citizens over 62 free. Free to all rest of year. ❧ TELEPHONE: (406) 638-2621.

N E V A D A

CITY NAMED FOR AN IRISHMAN

"What it is about godforsaken patches of the Nevada desert that gives men visions of blooming metropolises is hard to say," says Deke Castleman in his *Nevada Handbook* (1991). That's certainly the case with Laughlin, Nevada, which an Irish-American entrepreneur named Don Laughlin built, in the space of a few short years, from a bankrupt bait shop, in the desert to the third-largest gambling and entertainment mecca in Nevada, after Las Vegas and Reno.

Originally from Michigan, Don Laughlin knew from the 9th grade that he wanted to get into the gaming business, for he made a tidy supplemental living for himself in high school by supplying local bars and restaurants with (legal) pinball and slot machines. At 21, he was off to Las Vegas. After working for awhile as a bartender, he scraped together enough cash to buy a small establishment, which was enough to get him a gaming license. This he sold later for $165,000 and started looking around the place to make his fortune. It was 1969.

He found it in a place called Sandy Point, a spot on the Colorado River where Nevada, California, and Arizona come together. The only establishment for miles around was a bankrupt bait and tackle shop and certainly no one else would have thought it the ideal location for a major entertainment complex. Don Laughlin did, however. He bought six acres of land, including the tackle shop, a ramshackle motel (in which he and his family lived initially), and a six-seat bar.

It didn't stay that way for long. After toying with various names for his new establishment, Laughlin settled on naming it after himself when a local postal worker named O'Reilly suggested he do so because of the Irish "ring" to it.

So it was. And today Laughlin boasts not only Laughlin's own 14-story, 350-room Riverside Hotel and Casino, but a branch of Circus-Circus, Harrah's Hotel, and a Golden Nugget. Laughlin is a booming little city now, attracting 20,000 people on a typical weekend. Apparently, the Irish-American entrepreneurial spirit typified by "the Irish Four" (*see* Flood Mansion, San Francisco, California) and other early prospectors is far from dead.

&⁓ LOCATION: Laughlin is reached via S.R. 163, just off of I-95S from Las Vegas.

R E N O

MACKAY MUSEUM OF MINES AND MACKAY MEMORIAL

In the spring of 1859, a decade after the California gold rush, two Irishmen named Peter O'Reilly and Patrick McLaughlin made their way up Six-Mile Canyon toward Sun Mountain in what is now Nevada. They were prospecting for gold, and they found a small amount, taking out about $12 a day.

Not long after they got started, however, a Canadian blowhard named Harry Comstock came along and insisted the two immigrants were jumping his claim. Instead of telling Comstock to prove his claim or hit the road, as they should have, the two Irishmen took him at his word and cut him in on the action.

The new partners named their mine the Ophir, after the location of the biblical mines of King Solomon. But Comstock talked so loudly and so long about "his" mine that the diggings soon came to be known as Comstock's Lode, or the Comstock Lode.

The readily extractable gold soon played out and the miners found themselves contending with a heavy gray-black mud they had never seen before. Assayed in San Francisco, the mud was found to contain $875 a ton of gold—and $3,000 a ton of silver. The true Comstock Lode had been found.

As Western tradition seems to demand, the men who made the initial discovery earned very little from it. Patrick McLaughlin sold out his claim for a mere $3,500. O'Reilly held out for more, $40,000, but still nowhere near what he could have had had he stuck around. Comstock also sold out for a mere pittance. All three eventually died broke.

But the "silver rush" was now on. As soon as the snow melted in the mountain passes in the spring of 1860, an estimated 10,000 fortune seekers descended on Sun Mountain, the site of present-day Virginia City. For two years, this area was the most raucous boomtown America has ever seen. Violence and lawlessness were the rule, and an estimated 300 brothels flourished.

The boom went bust, however, when all the mines hit solid rock. William Sharon, president of the newly formed Bank of California, however, thought there was more to be had, and he spent huge amounts of money buying up claims thought to be valueless. When mining technology advanced to the point where more ore could be extracted, another boom ensued in 1867. Except for Sharon, only John Mackay was in a position to take advantage of it (see next entry).

After he struck it rich, Mackay generously helped endow the University of Nevada at Reno and its school of mining, which has been named after him.

Improving mining technology kept some mining going on in this area until the onset of World War II. Today, the Reno-Virginia City area thrives, along with the rest of Nevada, on the tourist-attracting vices that were initially ancillary to the mining activity.

❧ EXHIBITS: The Mackay Memorial, a heroic statue of the Silver King, stands just outside the school. The exhibits include displays on most of the minerals that formed the early wealth of Nevada as well as many photographs of early mining boomtowns. There are also rocks and minerals drawn from the Comstock itself, which are displayed inside Mackay's own vault. ❧ LOCATION: On the campus of the University of Nevada at Reno, one of the most attractive in the country. The museum is located in room 112 of the mining school. ❧ HOURS: Monday–Friday, 8–5. ❧ ADMISSION: Free ❧ TELEPHONE: (702) 784-6988.

VIRGINIA CITY

MACKAY MANSION

This 10-room home served first as the headquarters of the Gould and Curry Mine Company and later as the home of John Mackay (pronounced "Mackie"), one of the four Irish "silver kings" of the Comstock lode.

Like so many Irish success stories in the United States, Mackay's began with the unexpected death of his father shortly after the family arrived in New York in 1840, when young John was only 9 years of age. Forced to quit school and go to work, John was apprenticed to a shipbuilder, but his future and his fortune were to be found, not on the open seas, but in the arid deserts of landlocked Nevada.

Mackay followed the gold rush west in 1851. For seven years he drifted around the California mines with indifferent success, but along the way picked up valuable knowledge of mine construction and operation. In 1858, he found himself in the small boomtown of Virginia City as a well-paid (six dollars a day) timberman who worked on the roof shoring of a mine.

Having accumulated experience and a little capital, Mackay struck out on his own. His first effort, the Esmerelda Mine, was a failure, but the Petaluma mill turned a profit. It was around this time, 1864, that he first joined forces with James C. Flood and William O'Brien, two Irish San Francisco bar owners-turned-stock brokers. Four years later, the group was joined by Irishborn James Fair. "The Irish Four" were joined (*see* Flood Mansion, San Francisco, California).

Using his mining expertise, Mackay convinced the others that the old Comstock Lode contained a great deal of low-grade ore that could be profitably mined with the right modern machinery. The partners gained control of the Hale and Norcross Mine in 1865, from which they extracted a very handsome half a million dollars.

A bust intervened in 1870, however, and Mackay and his partners very nearly lost everything. Playing a hunch, Mackay in 1872 quietly purchased the Virginia Consolidated Mine. Ignoring conventional wisdom and sinking a shaft away from the main vein, Mackay and his partners found "the big bonanza." Opened in 1873, the Virginia Consolidated eventually brought forth a staggering $100 million in silver.

There can be little doubt that, of all those thousands upon thousands of penniless men who headed west in the mid-nineteenth century seeking their fortunes in mining, the Irish Four were the most spectacularly successful. Since he had worked in the pits himself, and continued to descend into the shafts on personal inspections long after he became rich, Mackay was probably the most popular with ordinary people.

Mackay lived here for only a relatively brief time, in the early to mid-1870s. His 1867 marriage to Marie Louise Hungerford, a woman of expensive tastes, caused him to spend much of the rest of his life in Europe, mostly Paris and London, where he maintained palatial homes. Like a 19th-century version of Donald and Marla Trump, the activities of the Mackays, especially her spectacular jewelry purchases, were avidly followed in the pages of the world's press.

But it wasn't all spending and parties for Mackay. Indeed, his best work was yet to come. In the 1880s, he set out to do the "impossible" and break Jay Gould's Western Union telegraph monopoly. In 1884, he laid two submarine cables to Europe and had to battle nearly two years in the courts to get their use approved. This bold action won him the admiration and awe of the whole business community, which had taken Gould's monopoly for granted.

Still not satisfied, Mackay next challenged Gould on dry land, founding the Postal Telegraph Cable Company in 1886 to compete with Western Union in the United States. This he did successfully, and Mackay was in the process of planning a trans-Pacific telegraph cable in 1902 when he died in London.

For all his success, the tall, slender, well-built Mackay retained an easy manner. ("The most unassuming American I ever met," said the future King George V.) He was politically unambitious, twice refusing nomination to serve as U.S. senator from Nevada, and his philanthropy was considerable. His money was used to build the School of Mining in Reno (*see* previous entry).

⟐ EXHIBITS: The house contains period furnishings as well as the re-creation of a Chinese laundry once on the site and a woodshed with original implements. ⟐ LOCATION: 120 South D St. ⟐ HOURS: Daily, 9–7, April through November; 11–5 rest of year. ⟐ ADMISSION: $3 adults; children $1; seniors 80 and over free. ⟐ TELEPHONE: (702) 847-0173.

ST. MARY OF THE MOUNTAINS CHURCH

"In Gold We Trust" is supposed to have been mistakenly engraved on some coins of the American West, and it would be no exaggeration to say that it was gold, not God, that preoccupied the thoughts of most of the men who came to these wild, isolated spaces in the mid-19th century.

But God was not a complete stranger in these parts. To be sure, the task of bringing His word to the Wild West was not for the faint of heart. Permanent churches were rare. Such parishioners as could be found often changed from week to week, as men moved in and moved on. Financial support from distant bishops was, at best, irregular, and more often nonexistent. It would take a special breed of holy man to have any success at all in an untamed place like 1860s Virginia City.

In Father Patrick Manogue, the builder of St. Mary of the Mountains, the Catholic church found its man. A one-time miner himself, Manogue could empathize with his flock like few others. He is one of the giants of the all-too-scantily catalogued history of the Roman Catholic church in the American West.

Manogue was from Kilkenny, where he was born in 1831. According to his own account, he and his siblings lost their parents when they were young, and his oldest brother went out to America, sending for the younger members of the family as funds permitted. Seventeen-year-old Patrick immigrated in 1846.

Manogue seems to have early on decided to become a priest, for almost as soon as he arrived he went to a seminary in Chicago to begin his studies. A cholera epidemic, however, swept the city, and some of the young seminarians died and others became very ill. Patrick was among the latter. In the meantime, his brothers had gone out to California for the gold rush, and Patrick thought a spell in the goldfields would help him regain his strength for his eventual return to the seminary.

Manogue was a big, burly, dark-haired man who fit in well in the goldfields. Whereas most miners would work all day and then flop into bed to sleep for the next day's labor, or, if they had some money, head for the saloon and start drinking, Manogue spent part of almost every day reading. He even found time to cultivate a flower bed.

Manogue never seems to have wavered from his vocation during his time in the goldfields. If anything, it grew stronger. His goal was to finish his studies at St. Sulpice's Seminary in Paris, which was known for its demanding curriculum. In the meantime, he became a well-known figure in the goldfields, frequently sought out as a mediator when disputes broke out, as they frequently did.

Manogue wasn't above using some less-than-holy methods when the situation demanded it, however. Anderson reports that when two thugs attempted to seize Manogue's cabin, the big miner seized one by the throat and cuffed him across the face, disarming him simultaneously and sending him flying into the brush. The desperado's partner soon followed.

Manogue spent his four years in Paris at St. Sulpice's, where he was ordained before returning to California to minister among the miners he knew so well. The Comstock Lode had just been opened, and Bishop Joseph Alemany of San Francisco sent his newest priest. Pat Manogue would be the only Catholic priest in all of what is now Nevada.

The Virginia City in which Patrick Manogue found himself was a city in name only. Most of the buildings were little more than shacks, and there was certainly no church. He said his first mass in a tent set up near the livery stables and attracted a surprisingly substantial congregation of Catholics and non-Catholics alike.

Manogue soon made plenty of friends, and one came up with the idea of placing a collection box on every bar in the city (and there were plenty of those). The boxes soon became known as "Manogue's kitty," and that was how he raised the $12,000 he needed to build his first church. The wooden structure, consecrated in 1863, was named by Manogue St. Mary's in the Mountains.

The wooden structure was replaced with a stone one in 1868. But only seven years later, a great fire swept Virginia City, consuming everything in its path, including the church. During the fire, an old Irish woman is said to have run up to John Mackay, who was working furiously to prevent the fire from spreading to the mine shafts, and begged him to save the church. "Damn the church," he is supposed to have replied. "We'll build another one, if we can prevent the fire from going down these shafts."

He was as good as his word. A third St. Mary's in the Mountains rose on the site and was consecrated in 1877. This is the structure still in use today. At the same time, Manogue constructed two schools, St. Joseph's for boys and St. Mary's for girls. They were the first schools of any kind in Nevada. John Mackay was one of St. Mary's most generous benefactors, and he married his wife there, with Father Manogue officiating.

Manogue was appointed an auxiliary bishop in 1881 and bishop of the diocese of Grass Valley (now Sacramento) three years later. He oversaw the construction of the Cathedral of the Blessed Sacrament in Sacramento, which was consecrated in 1889 and is still in use today.

Although he had moved up in the hierarchy, Bishop Manogue didn't lose touch with his former flock in Virginia City, making frequent visits and writing letters. He died in Sacramento in 1895, mourned not only by his own flock, but by many Jews and Protestants that he had befriended over the years, so far from his home in Ireland.

ॐ **EXHIBITS:** St. Mary's in the Mountains is easily the most recognizable site in Virginia City, with its Gothic bell tower dwarfing everything around it. The bell tower is open to the public and offers a million-dollar view of Virginia City and the surrounding mountains. The bell is of solid Comstock Lode silver. ॐ **LOCATION:** Taylor and E streets. ॐ **HOURS:** Daily 9–5. ॐ **ADMISSION:** None, but donations appreciated. ॐ **TELEPHONE:** (702) 847-0797.

NEW MEXICO

ABIQUIU

GHOST RANCH LIVING MUSEUM

Georgia O'Keefe first visited New Mexico in 1917 and began bringing her paints and easel to New Mexico in the early 1930s. She had already found fame and success as an artist in New York, and she was married to Alfred Stieglitz, one of the greatest photographers of the 20th century. But she was seeking a new place to stimulate her creative energies and get over a rough patch in her marriage. She found what she was looking for here at the Ghost Ranch, which had begun as a dude ranch in the late 1920s.

"For Georgia, the experience of being high in the mountains, beneath that sky, among those small, modest, earth formed buildings, was overwhelming," writes Roxana Robinson in *Georgia O'Keefe: A Life* (1991). "Her heart lifted like a bird." The shaded pastel cliffs and deep-red sandstone mesas inspired her to move here permanently in 1949, and she remained until her death in 1986 at age 98.

Georgia's paternal grandparents were Irish immigrants. Her grandfather, Pierce O'Keefe, was a Catholic from county Cork. Unlike so many other famine immigrants, however, O'Keefe's family was well-off, owning a woolen business. Pierce O'Keefe and his wife, Catherine, immigrated by way of Liverpool to New York to escape oppressive British taxation.

Also, unlike many of their compatriots, they did not stop and settle in the great seaport. They continued their journey west, and didn't stop until reaching the small town of Sun Prairie, Wisconsin. Their third son, Francis, had "black Irish" coloring: pale skin, blue eyes, and dark hair. The daughter he would have with his wife, Ida Totto, whose father was an exiled Hungarian patriot, inherited many of these physical traits from her father.

O'Keefe took after her mother in that she refused to be pushed into a "traditional" female role of wife and mother and insisted on going her own way and developing herself as an artist. Very much a stranger in a man's world, she proved to a skeptical art world that a woman could be the equal of any man in her chosen field. Her first public exhibition was in 1916 at Alfred Stieglitz's famed "291" gallery, which was a center of modern art.

Natural forms are the artistic hallmark of O'Keefe's work. Her biographers tell of how she would sit, huddled under a blanket in the cold, waiting for the dawn so she could capture precisely the colors she wanted in her paintings. Mesas glowing red in the sun and bleached cow skulls dot her work.

Although O'Keefe rarely called attention to her Irish roots, she showed in various subtle ways that she had pride in them. At art school, she accepted with alacrity the nickname frequently bestowed on Irish immigrant women, "Patsy." And when she married Stieglitz, she resolutely refused to give up her maiden name, which she thought integral to her success as an artist.

❧ **EXHIBITS:** An intensely private person, Georgia O'Keefe did not want her home opened to the tourist trade, and it remains closed to the public. U.S. Forest Service rangers, however, are happy to point out her house and studio from the ranch's observation tower. ❧ **LOCATION:** The Ghost Ranch is 14 miles northwest of Abiquiu on U.S. 84. ❧ **HOURS:** 9–5:30 April through September; 8–4:30 rest of year. Closed Mondays October–March. ❧ **ADMISSION:** Donations appreciated. ❧ **TELEPHONE:** (505) 685-4312.

LINCOLN

LINCOLN COURTHOUSE MUSEUM

The American West was indeed a wild place. Disputes between neighbors, if they were serious enough, frequently were settled by gunplay, and few questions were asked. Lawmen were few and far between, and even when one was available, it was sometimes difficult to tell what side of the law he was really on.

Two Irishmen were at the center of one such dispute that has gone down in American history as the Lincoln County War of 1878. Laurence G. Murphy was from county Wexford and an ex-soldier. His business partner, James J. Dolan, was a county Galway native. Their enterprises centered around the selling of beef to the army. They had a lot of money and didn't hesitate to use it to buy political influence in the sheriff's and governor's offices. They also were not shy about using more muscular methods when there was no other means to get their way.

The Murphy-Dolan gang's primary antagonist was a cattleman named John Chisum, who had far and away the largest herd in the area (reportedly 100,000 head), which he permitted to roam over free-range land. Rustlers working for the Murphy-Dolan syndicate apparently decided to help themselves to some of Chisum's cattle and were caught.

Murphy sought to hire a Scottish-Canadian lawyer in the area named Alexander McSween to represent the arrested men, which McSween refused to do because he (rightly) believed Murphy to be in cahoots with them. McSween thus found himself almost forced to side with Chisum and another rancher, an Englishman named John Tunstall.

In partnership with McSween and Chisum, Tunstall opened the Lincoln County Bank and General Store, which immediately began undercutting the store owned by Murphy and Dolan. The latter, not at all happy, sought to have Tunstall arrested on trumped up charges, and he was killed by a posse not far from Lincoln.

One man greatly aggrieved by Tunstall's death was an 18-year-old who had worked for him for a time and become almost like a son to Tunstall. In Lincoln County, he was using the name William Bonney, though this was an alias. He had been born (William?) Henry McCarty (or McCarthy, no one seems sure which is right) somewhere around 1860, possibly in New York. His mother, Catherine, was an Irish immigrant who later married a man named William Antrim. That gave the boy one of his early nicknames, Kid Antrim, although he was to become a legend in American history and folklore as Billy the Kid.

No one really knows how Billy got his start in outlawry, though he is reputed to have killed a man while he was still in his early teens (a feat perhaps less shocking today than it was then). When he showed up in Lincoln County around 1878, he already had a reputation. Tunstall, however, took a liking to the youth and needed a man handy with a six-gun. Some historians speculate Tunstall psychologically took the place of the father Billy had never really known.

The Kid certainly was determined to avenge Tunstall's death, and for three bloody weeks in the spring of 1878, Billy and his group of confederates—which included men with names like O'Fiollard and McCloskey—killed five members of the Murphy-Dolan gang. One of their victims was the sheriff, William Brady, another Irish-American, who had led the posse that killed Tunstall.

The Murphy-Dolan syndicate, however, controlled the forces of law in the territory, and the McSween-Chisum faction had little chance. The climactic five-day siege and shootout is supposed to have taken place in the middle of Lincoln at the McSween General Store. (Alexander McSween's widow, however, said it took place at their house.) Regardless, the result

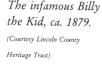

*The infamous Billy
the Kid, ca. 1879.*

(Courtesy Lincoln County

Heritage Trust)

was the death of McSween and the death or wounding of many of Chisum's gunmen.

Billy escaped the flaming building and ran off into the night, wanted on murder and assorted other charges.

Word of the blazing feud now reached Washington and Pres. Rutherford B. Hayes dispatched Gen. Lew Wallace (who was writing his novel *Ben Hur* at the time) to restore law and order in the area. Wallace offered a general amnesty, and Billy met the general alone in a designated house. Two of Billy's sworn enemies, however, were released from jail (probably by Murphy-Dolan sympathizers). Believing he had been double-crossed, Billy went back into hiding, and Wallace placed a $500 price on his head.

For the rest of 1880, Billy and his compatriots rode throughout the area, supporting themselves by stealing cattle and horses. After the outlaws had shot their way out of two ambushes, Pat Garrett, who had just been elected sheriff of Lincoln County, was determined to bring the Kid in, dead or alive. He succeeded in capturing him after a two-day siege near Stinking Springs (now Wilcox Springs), New Mexico.

Billy was imprisoned for most of the winter of 1880–81 and was finally tried for the murder of Sheriff Brady. He was convicted before a Murphy-Dolan judge on April 9, 1881, and four days later was sentenced to hang on May 13 in Lincoln.

Billy wasn't about to die jerking at the end of a rope, however, and on April 28, he saw his chance. Taking advantage of having one of his hands freed from handcuffs to allow him to eat, he felled one guard, took the man's six-shooter, and killed him. The other guard, alerted by the shot, ran to the cell and was also killed. Billy then forced a local blacksmith to cut him free of his chains, mounted a horse, and rode off.

Needless to say, Sheriff Garrett was dismayed at the news and was determined that Billy would never be in a position to escape again. He got word that Billy was hiding at Ft. Sumner, an abandoned army post now being used by a Peter Maxwell as a lodging for his ranch hands. Garrett slipped himself inside the structure and entered Maxwell's bedroom, talking quietly with him. Just then, the door to the hall opened and the unmistakable silhouette of the Kid appeared in the doorway. He was able to ask one question ("Quien es?" or "Who is there?") before being cut down in a hail of shots from Garrett's revolver. At only 21, the Kid's life was over, but his legend had barely begun.

Famous in his own time, Billy was guaranteed immortality by Hollywood. Portrayed by many actors in countless films, Billy has been depicted as everything from a psychotic killer to a misunderstood rebel. Which was the truth?

Physically, he was not the repellant, buck-toothed midget some accounts make him out to be. In fact, as the only documented photograph of Billy shows, he was probably close to 5'8" tall and was not a bad-looking youth. W. N. Burns, in his classic 1926 book *The Saga of Billy the Kid,* in which the author interviewed as many people as could be found who had actually known the famous outlaw, the Kid was described as not lacking in the social graces. It was reported that he rarely swore, had a good sense of humor, often dressed well, and was extremely attractive to women.

That didn't make him a milquetoast by any means, however. Even some who fought beside him said the Kid gave off the aura of a person one crossed at one's peril. He was invariably cool in tight situations, had lightning reflexes, and was a deadly shot. Most of the Kid's victims were ruthless killers themselves, and the lawmen who chased him were frequently little more than bandits with badges. Perhaps these facts account for the sentimental attitude so many Americans seem to have about Billy the Kid.

And, as any fan of Irish ballads such as *"Brennan on the Moor"* and the *"Wild Colonial Boy"* knows, the Irish themselves have a weakness for wild young men who hide from the authorities with the assistance of ordinary people. Although he certainly didn't plan it that way, the story of Billy the Kid thus has a certain Celtic poetry about it.

❧ **EXHIBITS:** Many displays relate to the Lincoln County War and Billy the Kid, as well as the black cavalry regiments that fought Indians in the area. The first weekend in August features a festival that includes a reenactment of Billy's escape from the Lincoln County Jail. The Billy the Kid Museum, located not far from his gravesite in Ft. Sumner, contains memorabilia of his life and legend. ❧ **LOCATION:** The Old Lincoln County Courthouse is located in the middle of Lincoln on U.S. 380. Also, Billy the Kid is buried in Ft. Sumner, which is north and east of Lincoln, under a headstone that proclaims "He died as he lived." Ft. Sumner is at the intersection of U.S. 60 and U.S. 84. ❧ **HOURS:** Tours in Lincoln given daily 9–6, March 1 through November 15. Rest of year schedule varies. The Billy the Kid Museum in Ft. Sumner is open 9–6 May 1 through Sept. 1; 8–5 rest of the year. ❧ **ADMISSION:** $4.50. Under 15 free. Billy the Kid Museum $1. Under 16 free. ❧ **TELEPHONE:** (505) 653-4372; Billy the Kid Museum (505) 355-2573.

O R E G O N

JOHN MCLOUGHLIN HOUSE NATIONAL HISTORIC SITE

Oregonians and others from the Pacific Northwest sometimes joke that the initials "HBC " stand for "Here Before Christ" as well as "Hudson's Bay Company." The HBC certainly is one of the oldest institutions in North America, and John McLoughlin, a Quebec native whose father was born in county Derry, was one of its towering figures.

McLoughlin and his brother were trained as physicians under the tutelage of their Scottish maternal grandfather. Davis became a physician in Paris, but John felt the call of the West and became a partner in the North West Fur Company. When the latter merged with the HBC in 1821, when McLoughlin was 37 years old, he was in charge of the company's important fur trading post at Ft. William on Lake Superior. Three years later, he was given the plum posting of "chief factor" for the Columbia River area, a post he held for 22 years. This was the critical period for the development of what is now the Pacific Northwest.

McLoughlin established Ft. Vancouver in the present city of Vancouver, Washington, as his central trading post for the area. His marching orders from the company were clear: establish a trading system that extracted the maximum amount of furs from the area for the highest possible profit. And, by the way, keep peace among the Indians, prevent Americans from settling the territory, and don't allow farming. This was a tall order, and McLoughlin found it difficult to fulfill.

The tall, white-haired gentleman with his distinctive cane came to rule over the area like a virtual monarch, though a generally benevolent one. McLoughlin ruthlessly suppressed fur competition, but he often extended aid to Americans putting down roots in the area, even helping them with deliveries of food to get through the winter. The company complained to

McLoughlin about this policy. But "the doctor," as he liked to be called, even though he did not practice, replied that simple humanity forbade him from withholding assistance. He also cited the practical concern that niggardly behavior would only inflame anti-British passions in the growing United States.

McLoughlin established what is now Oregon City in 1829 as a company town where he hoped to develop industries that would diversify the local economy away from exclusive dependence on fur trapping. The nearby waterfalls were ideal for powering mills and providing a water route for the shipment of manufactured goods. He placed much of this land in his own name, paying the company $20,000 for the property and constructing this house upon it around 1845–46, roughly the time he was forced to resign from the HBC because of his lenient policies toward American settlements.

The territory passed to American ownership, and McLoughlin took out U.S. citizenship in 1851. That did not prevent Congress from invalidating his claim to ownership of this land, however, and McLoughlin did not receive justice before his death in 1857. In the early 1860s, his heirs settled the claim for a nominal sum.

A strapping six-foot-four with a great main of silver hair, "the doctor" was an imposing presence. As a Roman Catholic in a Protestant territory, however, and because of his long-standing ties to the former British authority, McLoughlin was not chosen for public office. The fact that his wife, Marguerite, was part Indian, also, no doubt, did not help. More than once, apparently, McLoughlin was forced to rebuke a visitor for "your manners sir, before ladies" when they would refuse to remove their hats in her presence.

👈 EXHIBITS: Contains original and period furnishings. 👈 LOCATION: Seventh and Center streets. 👈 HOURS: Tuesday–Saturday 10–4; Sunday 1–4, February through December. 👈 ADMISSION: $2.50; seniors $2; children under 12 $1. 👈 TELEPHONE: (503) 656-5146.

U T A H

GOULDING'S TRADING POST
AND LODGE

 "They say I took pleasure in killing Indians in the movies," a bitter John Ford reflected late in his long life. He went on,

> But while today film people shed tears over the fate of the Indians, write humanitarian pamphlets and make declarations of intention without ever, *ever* putting their hands in their pockets, more humbly I gave them work. . . . More than having received Oscars, what counts for me is having been made a blood brother of various Indian nations. Perhaps it's my Irish atavism, my sense of reality, of the beauty of clans, in contrast to the modern world, the masses, the collective irresponsibility. Who better than an Irishman could understand the Indians, while still being stirred by the tales of the U.S. Cavalry? We were on both sides of the epic.

Indeed, Ford spoke the truth. One reason he kept returning to Monument Valley to make his films was because his Navajo friends needed the work. The Indians employed on his many westerns earned union wages when most Indian extras in other westerns barely commanded 50 cents a day. When a blizzard covered Monument Valley in the 1950s, Ford used his influence in Washington to get army planes to drop food shipments. "To the Navajos," said Harry Goulding, who owned the lodge where the cast and crew stayed, "Mr. Ford is holy, sorta."

Not holy, perhaps, but talented and inspired certainly. More than 20 years after his death, Ford remains the only director to have been awarded no less than five Academy Awards for his work. And although his name conjures up images of Indian raids on wagon trains and strong, silent heros, Ireland was a constant theme of his work as well, and the subject of three of his major films.

He claimed on his passport in later years that his true name was Sean Aloysius O'Feeney, but he appears to have gone through childhood as John Martin Feeney, and he was born in 1894, not the 1895 he claimed. He was one of six children who survived infancy born to Sean and Barbara Feeney. Sean changed his name to John shortly after arriving in the United States from Spiddal, county Galway. He settled in Portland, Maine, where he married his wife, a distant cousin and also an Irish immigrant, and became a ward heeler in Portland's raucous Irish politics (*see* Portland, Maine).

The elder Feeney had high hopes for his son, but young Jack, as he was known, failed the entrance examination for Annapolis and had to be content with the University of Maine. After only the third or fourth day, however, he slugged a fellow student who was taunting him and got sent home. He decided to go join his older brother Frank, who had changed his last name to the more American-sounding Ford and was then making a name for himself in the burgeoning motion picture business in California. It was 1914.

The younger brother adopted Frank's new surname and set to work as "assistant, handyman, everything" at $12 a week. He learned the movie business from the ground up, as an actor, grip, cameraman, and just about everything else. He began making two-reel westerns starring Harry Carey and for a decade labored in obscurity learning his craft. His big break came in 1924 with *The Iron Horse,* an epic about the building of the railroads. It was around this time that he visited Monument Valley for the first time and noted its cinematic possibilities.

In the meantime, Ford kept in touch with Ireland and Irish affairs. His father contributed heavily to the Irish War of Independence and the younger Ford visited Ireland in the troubled year of 1921. On a visit to Spiddal, he learned that a relative was a wanted Irish Republican Army member. Against all advice, he went out into the backcountry and located the young man, bringing him money and whiskey. Word of his escapades got back to the British authorities, however, and Ford was summarily put on a ship and told he would land in jail if he ever showed his face in Ireland again. John Ford gave generously to the IRA for the rest of his life.

In fact, it was an Irish film, not a western, that earned Ford his first Oscar. Ford had become acquainted with the Irish writer Liam O'Flaherty and had read O'Flaherty's novella *The Informer.* Ford shopped the book to every studio in Hollywood without success, until RKO finally loaned him a shabby, broken-down set to make the film.

This dark, brooding film, with its smashing performance by Victor McLaglen as Gypo Nolan, the man who sells out his best friend to the British for 20 pounds, "made" Ford. Critics lauded the symbolism of the dank, mist-filled Irish streets. Ford explained he used the mist to cover up the fact that his budget didn't allow for much of a set.

Ford was now a big-time director who worked with big-time stars. He coaxed out of Henry Fonda two of the best performances of the actor's life in *Young Mr. Lincoln* and *The Grapes of Wrath.* In 1939, he made good his

*Sean Aloysius
O'Feeney (aka
John Ford) earned
his first Oscar not
for a western, but
for an Irish film,
The Novella.*

(Museum of Modern Art)

vow to return to Monument Valley once he had the right script and the right
star. In *Stagecoach* and John Wayne, he had both (*see* Winterset, Iowa).

Ford, with Wayne frequently in tow, would return to Monument
Valley nine more times after *Stagecoach*. Always spectacularly photographed, Monument Valley was every bit as much the star of such films as
Fort Apache, She Wore a Yellow Ribbon, Rio Grande, and *The Searchers* as
the human actors. The Irish-American Wayne, along with Victor Mc-
Laglen, Barry Fitzgerald, and other Ford regulars always managed to
impart an Irish "feel" to a Ford picture, even a western that theoretically
had nothing to do with Ireland.

As his unsuccessful application to Annapolis showed, Ford yearned to
be a man of action, and so it is no surprise that many of his films concern
military men and their lives. He got his chance for real during World War
II, however, when he was commissioned an officer in the naval reserve and
helped make navy films. He was on the scene at the Battle of Midway in
1942 and shot spectacular footage of the actual battle. He was wounded

slightly in the action, but the footage won him another Oscar for best documentary.

After the war, Ford returned to Ireland to make what is probably his best-known film, *The Quiet Man*. In its own way, it is a very sexy film and is evidence of the erotic effect that could be achieved under the old film code that prohibited nudity and explicit language. It is also Ford's most personal film, with John Wayne as Sean Thornton representing everything Ford yearned he could be.

Ford made many more memorable films, including *The Man Who Shot Liberty Valance, The Last Hurrah,* and even tried his hand (successfully) at comedy with *Mr. Roberts.* But his greatest work was now behind him. He died August 31, 1973.

Many critics see Ford's Irish sensibility as a key to the success of his films. His Irish immigrant characters were outsiders in American society, as indeed were many of the members of the audience. His obvious nostalgia for the land of his forebears appealed to many immigrants and children of immigrants, no matter what their country of origin.

One of the best epitaphs for John Ford was given by Orson Welles. When the director of *Citizen Kane* was asked what directors he admired, he answered, "The old masters, by which I mean John Ford, John Ford and John Ford."

&. EXHIBITS: A small museum on the premises has photos and displays on John Ford and the filming of his movies in Monument Valley. There is also a gift shop, and the hotel offers air and ground guided tours of Monument Valley. &. LOCATION: In Monument Valley, 2 miles west of U.S. 163 at Goulding's Junction. &. HOURS: The museum is open 7:30–9 every evening. &. ADMISSION: Free &. TELEPHONE: (801) 727-3231.

SALT LAKE CITY

GOVERNOR'S MANSION (KEARNS MANSION)

Utah was not a major destination for Irish immigrants to the United States or for Irish-Americans, but, as the stories of John Ford and Patrick Connor make clear, individuals did find their way to this isolated state and make their mark. Thomas Kearns was undoubtedly the most successful of all, at least monetarily.

Kearns was born in Ontario of Irish immigrant parents, Thomas and Margaret Maher Kearns, on April 11, 1862. When he was still a child, the family moved to the area of O'Neill, Nebraska (*see* entry), which was one of the few successful Irish "colonies" established on the Great Plains.

The Kearns Mansion, now the Utah State Governor's Mansion, Salt Lake City. (Utah State Historical Society)

Farming the windswept plains of Nebraska, however, was not for him, and he struck out for the mining fields of Deadwood, South Dakota, while still in his early teens. Unsuccessful, he returned home for a time before heading out west again.

Kearns drove a team of horses in Tombstone, Arizona, in the early 1880s, but was in Utah by 1883. He hoped to save enough money to get to Butte, Montana, the destination of so many Irish miners at that time. But instead of going to work for Marcus Daly, the copper king of Montana (*see* Hamilton, Montana), he stayed in Utah, where great wealth was awaiting him.

For seven years he worked the mines, learning the finer points of the business and determining for himself the mineral possibilities of the region. He made many useful contacts among canny miners in the area and he was also fortunate in marriage. Jennie Wilson, also of Irish immigrant stock, provided him with the stability he needed to make his best efforts.

Finally, his big chance came in 1892. He and his associates had taken out leases on several promising areas and they were rewarded when the Silver King Mine came through. Thomas Kearns was a multimillionaire before he was 30 years old.

The rest of his life was spent as the leading Gentile citizen of Utah. Against his desires, he was prevailed upon to serve a single term in the U.S. Senate after Utah was finally admitted to the Union in 1896. He endowed an orphanage and financed many other good works. Like Marcus Daly, Thomas Kearns died young, at only 56, in 1918.

His most visible monument is the great house he constructed on East South Temple Street in Salt Lake City. In the 1930s, the state took it over as the governor's mansion, passing it on to the state historical society in 1957. The latter moved out in 1980 and it once again became the governor's mansion. Unfortunately, a Christmas tree fire in 1993 did considerable damage, and the house is now undergoing several years' worth of restorations, during which it is closed to the public.

❧ EXHIBITS: Not open to the public. ❧ LOCATION: 603 E. South Temple St.

COL. PATRICK EDWARD CONNOR GRAVESITE

Thomas "Broken Hand" Fitzpatrick probably passed through present-day Utah on his travels in the west (*see* Fort Laramie, Wyoming). Of greater importance to Utah history was Edward Creighton, an Irish-American who rode into Salt Lake City in 1860 to help map the route of the transcontinental telegraph from the Missouri River to the West Coast. A year later, he returned to actually lay the telegraph line, one of the most spectacular achievements in the history of the West.

Around the same time, however, Utah was becoming acquainted with an Irish-born man who would be remembered less fondly in the mostly Mormon state. Patrick Edward Connor was born in county Kerry around 1820, immigrated to the United States, and fought in the Florida campaigns against the Seminoles. He was in business in Texas when the Mexican War broke out, rejoined the army, and was wounded at the Battle of Buena Vista.

Connor settled in the area of Stockton, California, where he commanded a militia regiment of volunteers. At the outbreak of the Civil War, he was commissioned a colonel and dispatched to Salt Lake City, where the Mormons, then a polygamist religion considered by most Americans to be a bizarre cult, had established themselves. Although not sympathetic to the Confederacy, the Mormons, because of their polygamist ways, were declared "in rebellion" by the Federal government, which wanted an army unit nearby keeping watch. The War Department also wanted to ensure that lines of communication with the West Coast were kept open from Confederate and Indian raids.

Connor established Camp (now Fort) Douglas, overlooking the city. En route, the men of his command, many of them California goldfield veterans, had not overlooked the possibilities of mining in the area, and it is the opening up of Utah for mining for which Connor's Utah expedition is primarily known. Connor had an ulterior motive besides getting rich, however. He thought that a major gold or silver strike would bring Irish and other miners flocking to the territory and swamp the Mormon population.

To say the least, Connor was not a popular figure among the Mormons, at least during the Civil War. A Catholic himself, he had little use for the new sect and no shyness about telling anyone so. Nevertheless, he also seemed to possess the Irish gift for political maneuver and knew when to be intransigent and when to give a little. E. B. Long's *The Saints and the Union: The Utah Territory During the Civil War*, says that had he not possessed this ability, "Utah could easily have become an armed battleground between the federal authorities and the Mormons, with all the complications and tragedies inherent in such a conflict."

Indeed, as time went on, a certain grudging respect developed between Connor and Mormon leader Brigham Young. When Young and several other Mormon officials were arrested in 1871 for "lascivious co-habitation," Connor is said to have furnished $100,000 bond for their release. Later, Young is reported to have said of Connor, "Men have been here before him; to our faces they were our friends; but when they went away they traduced, vilified and abused us. Not so with Connor. We always knew where to find him. That's why I like him."

Connor seems to have saved his true detestation for the Indians. His "battle" with the Bannock and Shoshoni tribes near Bear River has been described by Bishop Robert J. Dwyer, a not-unsympathetic chronicler, as a "massacre." Though he could show flexibility in his dealings with the Indians as well, Connor's job was to keep the Indians from interfering with the mail routes, and he accomplished that with efficiency bordering on ruthlessness.

Surprisingly, Connor chose to stay in Utah after the war and further develop its mining industries. The completion of the Transcontinental Railroad in 1869 greatly facilitated this effort. He founded several smelting companies and invested in the opening of various mines. He wrote Utah's first mining laws, founded the first newspaper, and also owned the first steamship to regularly navigate the Great Salt Lake. He died in 1891.

ઢ EXHIBITS: The fort's museum contains displays on U.S. and Utah military history from 1858 to the present, including some artifacts relating to Connor and his colorful career in Utah. His gravesite, along with those of his family, is located in the fort cemetery. ઢ LOCATION: Connor was buried on the grounds of Fort Douglas, overlooking Salt Lake City just east of the University of Utah campus on East Wasatch Drive. ઢ HOURS: Tuesday–Saturday 10–12 and 1–4. ઢ ADMISSION: Free ઢ TELEPHONE: (801) 588-5188.

WASHINGTON

BURKE MUSEUM

As a put-upon ethnic group themselves, the Irish-Americans have frequently stood up for the rights of persecuted minorities and other immigrant ethnic groups. Thomas Burke, an attorney who was a son of Irish immigrants and became known as "the man who built Seattle," was in this tradition.

Seattle was still a raw frontier town in 1886. Chinese laborers were present in substantial numbers to build the railroads Seattle needed to survive. Unlike European ethnic groups, the Chinese labored under unique disabilities. They could not take out citizenship papers, and they could not bring women from China for brides. Rootless and easy prey for prostitutes, they thus frequently found themselves in trouble with the law.

Matters came to a head in 1886 when anti-Chinese rioting broke out. Burke, a strong Democrat who had established his law practice in the city 11 years earlier, unhesitatingly and publicly defended the rights of the Chinese to live in the city unmolested. For his trouble, he was pursued by and narrowly escaped becoming the victim of a lynch mob.

Burke was thus a pioneering figure in several ways. A visionar he saw Seattle's future as a western port of trade with the Orient long before almost anyone else. During his long and active life, he made several visits to Japan and China in an effort to encourage businesses from those countries to use Seattle as their port of entry into the United States. As general counsel for the Great Northern Railroad, he was instrumental in convincing railroad magnate J. J. Hill to use Seattle as the western terminus from his railroad from Minneapolis to St. Paul.

Burke's parents, James and Bridget Delia, were famine Irish immigrants who settled in Clinton County in upstate New York. Their son, Thomas, born just before Christmas 1849, received a smattering of education before his mother's death in 1862 caused the family to move to Iowa. The teenaged Burke worked in a store and on a farm and attended school intermittently until 1866 when he moved to Michigan. Attending school and working part-time once again, he graduated from Ypsilanti Academy in 1870 and studied law at the University of Michigan for two years. He continued his studies in a law office in 1872, was admitted to the bar in 1873, and was almost immediately elected city attorney of Marshall, Michigan.

But Burke had his eye on being more than an attorney. He wanted to make money in business as well and thought the West Coast offered better opportunities. In 1875 he headed out to Seattle, where he spent the remaining 50 years of his life helping to build it into the world-class metropolis it has since become.

Like many newly arrived Irish-Americans, Burke had a flair for politics, and the year after he arrived he was elected a judge of the probate court. He was reelected in 1878, and in 1880 and 1882, unsuccessfully sought election as territorial delegate to Congress. He served briefly as chief justice of the territorial supreme court from 1888 to 1889.

Mostly, however, he concerned himself with railroad promotion and litigation, helping establish not only the Great Northern but also the Seattle and Walla Walla Railway and the Seattle, Lakeshore and Eastern Railway to connect with the Union Pacific. All of this, by 1892, gave Seattle the transportation infrastructure it needed to grow.

Politically, Burke had little success. He broke with the Democrats over Bryan's inflationary platform in 1896 and joined the Republican party. He led several diplomatic missions to the Far East for Theodore Roosevelt, and President Taft offered him the ambassadorship to China, but Burke refused in order to run for the Senate instead. Unfortunately for Burke, 1910 was a poor year for the Republicans and he was defeated. He withdrew from general law practice and devoted the rest of his life to various public good works. He died in 1925, recognized as Seattle's foremost private citizen.

❧ EXHIBITS: Unfortunately, there is little relating to Thomas Burke or his remarkable life in the museum that bears his name. Aside from a portrait of Burke and his wife, who endowed it, the Burke Museum is the major natural history museum in the Pacific Northwest and also has many displays on the ethnic groups of the Pacific Rim as well as American Indians. ❧ LOCATION: The facility is on the campus of the University of Washington and is located closest to the 17th Avenue, NE, or western campus entrance. Take I-5 north from downtown, then east on Washington 520 to the university exit. ❧ HOURS: Daily 10–5 and Thursday until 8. ❧ ADMISSION: Adults $3; seniors and students $2; youths 6–18 $1.50; children 5 and under free. ❧ TELEPHONE: (206) 543-5590.

SPOKANE

CROSBY LIBRARY

According to the Guinness Book of World Records, the best-selling single record of all time remains "White Christmas," by Harry Lillis "Bing" Crosby, with nearly 200 million copies sold since its release in 1942. Indeed, Crosby's record company, Decca, used proudly to boast in its advertising, "The voice of Bing Crosby has been heard by more people than the voice of any other human being who ever lived."

The singer-actor was Irish on his mother's side. Catherine Harrigan, Bing's mother, was born above her family's creamery in Stillwater, Minnesota. Her grandparents, Dennis Harrigan and Catherine Driscoll, were "Mirimichi" Irish, immigrants who settled in Mirimichi, New Brunswick, Canada, in the late 1820s and early 1830s. Catherine Harrigan married Harry Lowe Crosby, a bookkeeper, at Tacoma, Washington, in 1894. Harry, a Protestant from an old New England seafaring family, converted to Catholicism to marry Catherine, and they had five sons and two daughters. Bing was the fourth eldest, born in 1903 (not 1904, as the singer claimed in his autobiography).

There are several stories about how Harry got his nickname, but the most credible seems to be that he was an avid reader of a humor feature in the Spokane newspaper called "The Bingville Bugle." A neighbor took to calling him Bingo and his schoolmates took up the name. Soon, the "o" was dropped and he became just plain Bing.

Bing seems to have gotten his musical bent from his father, who could play both guitar and mandolin and was considered to have a fine voice. Around 1910, the elder Crosby brought home a phonograph player and some records, and Sunday nights became music night at the Crosby house. Crosby would get out his guitar and mandolin and the family would sing along to the popular favorites at the time: "In the Good Old Summertime," "In the Shade of the Apple Tree," and Katherine Crosby's all-time favorite, "When Irish Eyes Are Smiling."

At the same time, Kate was a religious, classically domineering Irish mother, and Bing was clearly her favorite. "If it can be said that one can inherit the genetic material of an ancestor who had kissed the Blarney Stone," write Donald Shepherd and Robert F. Slatzer in their biography, *Bing Crosby: The Hollow Man* (1981). "Bing Crosby was so blessed." Kate Crosby, the authors say, ran the house with the "indominitable will . . . of one who had a direct hot line to God." When Bing, after he had become a star, made the mistake of attributing part of his success to luck, his mother swiftly corrected him. "Your luck has been my prayers and the prayers I've asked the Poor Clare nuns to offer up for you."

Bing Crosby has a difference of opinion with "old country" priest, Barry Fitzgerald. (Museum of Modern Art)

While at Gonzaga High School and College in the early 1920s, Bing began fooling around with a set of drums and occasionally a clarinet. He had his mind set on becoming a lawyer, but he found his part-time job in an attorney's office tedious. When a friend suggested he try out as a drummer for a local band called the Musicaladers, Bing agreed and was soon singing vocals as well. After getting rave reviews on a California trip with his then partner Al Rinker, and barely a year after he became a professional musician, Bing Crosby was signed by Paul Whiteman, the great orchestra leader. He was on his way.

Bing's success can only be described as phenomenal. His velvet voice and handsome looks stood him in good stead for the rest of his career. (However, he was almost never photographed directly from the front; his ears stuck out like a car with its doors open.)

Crosby's sedate lifestyle was legendary (incredibly, he never learned to read music), and he was one of the first to appreciate the potential of recording technology, in the service of making his own life easier. According to music critic Gilbert Seldes, Crosby saw no reason why his radio show had to be done "live" at 9 P.M. West Coast time so it could heard at 6 P.M. on the East Coast. He would record the show earlier in the day, and it was played back at 9 P.M. on both coasts. The network chiefs in New York at first hated the idea, but then realized that it brought them a bigger audience on the East Coast, where folks didn't have to interrupt their dinner to hear the program.

Crosby went on to star in more than 70 feature films, his best-known roles being the ones where he played the young "with it" Irish-American priest who, while unquestionably influenced by his background, nevertheless was distinctly *American* in his attitudes. It was an image the many Irish-Americans in the audience could identify with, especially when he played off "old country" priest Barry Fitzgerald in *Going My Way,* for which Bing won an Oscar.

Crosby made fewer films as he got older, and his music fell out of favor in the rock and roll era. But he continued to make his annual Christmas specials (42 in all), his fans remained loyal, and he could still pack concert halls. It was while he was performing in concert in 1977 that he fell off the edge of the stage into an orchestra pit. Although his injuries seemed superficial, he never really fully recovered, and he died of a massive heart attack on October 14, 1977. At the time of his death, he was doing what he loved best: playing golf.

ء **EXHIBITS:** The collections contains letters, photographs, records, and other personal memorabilia of the legendary crooner, including his Academy Award for Best Actor in *Going My Way.* ء **LOCATION:** 502 Boone Ave. at Gonzaga University. ء **HOURS:** September through April hours: Monday–Thursday, 8–midnight; Friday 8–5; Saturday 9–8; Sunday 1–8. Monday–Friday 9-5 rest of year. ء **ADMISSION:** Free ء **TELEPHONE:** (509) 328-4220.

PATSY CLARK'S MANSION

The Pacific Northwest is not a region generally associated with Irish settlements, but Irish place-names can be found throughout Washington State: Burley, Buckley, Carroll, Cunningham and Joyce, to name but a few. And although large numbers of Irish settlers did not come over the Cascade Mountains into the moist, fertile valleys of what is now Washington State, many small groups and individual Irish did.

The story of these Irish is told well by Prof. Timothy Sarbaugh in his article *"Celts With the Midas Touch"* in the excellent book he co-edited with James P. Walsh, *The Irish in the West* (1991). "Some of the region's most prominent and successful pioneer came from Ireland," Sarbaugh writes. "While certainly some filled the traditional occupations of unskilled workers and domestic servants and miners, quite a few achieved financial and civic success with great ease and celerity."

Most of the Spokane Irish did not come to the area directly from Ireland, but were usually migrants from somewhere else, often mining camps elsewhere in the West. Edward Sheehy from Tralee in county Kerry,

Patrick "Patsy" Clark's $1 million legacy to Spokane has 26 rooms and 9 fireplaces.
(Courtesy Eastern Washington State Historical Society, Spokane)

for instance, homesteaded near Spokane after his father had tried mining unsuccessfully in Leadville, Colorado. (The 1862 Homestead Act granted 160 acres to anyone who would agree to live on it for five years, make improvements, and pay a $10 fee.) Sheehy was described in a newspaper article as being "one of the leading figures of the community."

Though never large in numbers, the Spokane Irish were instrumental in helping develop the town from a mere settlement in the late 1860s to the capital of Washington's "Inland Empire" by 1900. The leading personality among the Spokane Irish was Patrick "Patsy" Clark, born in Ireland on St. Patrick's Day in 1850.

Like so many Irish millionaires in the West, Clark made his fortune in mining. He had come to the United States in 1870 and lived with a sister in Pennsylvania for a time. But news of the Comstock Lode in Nevada and other strikes propelled him out west. He tried his luck in California, then Virginia City, and then Utah. But it was when he got to Montana that his luck began changing. There, he hooked with another Irishman, Marcus Daly (*see* Hamilton, Montana), won the latter's confidence, and was named a junior partner. In 1887, he got his lucky break when he helped Daly's Anaconda Copper Company open the Poorman Mine in Coeur d'Alene, Idaho.

The profits he earned from that operation enabled him to buy a mine of his own in British Columbia, which he then sold to Canadian investors at the turn of the century for three-quarters of a million dollars. Clark thus spent the rest of his life repeating the process, opening and developing mines and then selling out, amassing a great fortune for himself in the process.

Clark died suddenly of a heart attack on June 7, 1915, and his death was an occasion for citywide mourning. "Every mining district in the Northwest has at one time or another been his field of operations," opined the Spokane *Spokesman-Review* in its obituary. "Clark was one of the best known mining men in the United States." Alonzo Murphey, a friend, declared, "He was a self-made man, but he was always equal to his enlarged opportunities. . . . Spokane loses an ideal citizen, a man devoted to his family and his Church, and loyal to his friends and to his country."

Clark's most tangible legacy to his adopted city and country is this superb mansion, one of the finest in the Pacific Northwest. Designed by the noted architect Kirkland Cutter, it was built over a two-year period and cost nearly $1 million. The three-story building has 26 rooms and 9 fireplaces. Since Mrs. Clark sold the house in 1926, it has served as a private residence, a rooming house, and an inn. Most recently, it has become Patsy Clark's, one of the area's best-known restaurants. Pres. George Bush and his wife, Barbara, stopped by for dinner during the 1992 presidential campaign.

& EXHIBITS: The house still contains many period furnishings and paintings. Touring is encouraged while waiting to be seated or after dinner. The staff is very helpful. & LOCATION: W. 2208 2nd Ave. & HOURS: 11:30–1:45; 5–9 weekdays; till 10 Fridays and Saturdays; Sundays 10–1:30; 5–9. & ADMISSION: Free & TELEPHONE: (509) 838-8300.

WYOMING

FORT LARAMIE NATIONAL
HISTORIC SITE

"Our ignorance of the route was complete," wrote one member of the first wagon train party headed west. "We knew California lay west, and that was the extent of our knowledge."

Indeed, for Americans used to hopping flights to Los Angeles or San Francisco from the East Coast without a second thought, it is hard to imagine the harshness of the journey in 1841: burning sun in summer, howling winds and snow in winter, and marauding Indians most of the time. Worse, there were certainly no real roads or even trails. The only guides were "mountain men" like Thomas "Broken Hand" Fitzpatrick, an Irish-born scout whose services the first wagon train was fortunate enough to secure. They made it through to California.

Fitzpatrick was born in county Cavan around 1799 and came to the United States as a youth of 17. In 1822, he answered a help wanted ad in a St. Louis newspaper by Gen. William Ashley, who was seeking "enterprising young men" to help him trap beaver on the upper Missouri River. Other men who answered the ad included those would become legends in their own right: Jim Bridger and Jedediah Smith.

The expedition with Ashley was the beginning of a two-decade-long career on the frontier for the young Irishman. Making his living as a trapper and guide, he became a major partner in the Rocky Mountain Fur Company. He also developed a particularly close rapport with the Indians, who trusted him as a fair dealer. They gave him the nickname "Broken Hand" after an accident with a rifle blew off three of his fingers. They also called him "white hair," and the account of how he got his white hair gives some indication of what life was like in the Far West in those days.

Fitzpatrick was guiding a party in 1832 when he was spotted by hostile Indians near the south pass of the Rocky Mountains. Fitzpatrick put the spur to his horse with the Indians close behind. The country was rough, however, and his horse soon couldn't go on. Fitzpatrick took off on foot, eventually finding a small opening in the rocks. He crawled inside and hid the opening with rocks and twigs.

For several agonizing days, Fitzpatrick stayed in his hiding place as the Indians searched the area for him. Although they came close by inches, they never found him. One night, Fitzpatrick was able to slip away unnoticed and start making his way back.

His ordeal was far from over though. Forced to navigate through unfamiliar country, he had to cross the Snake River in a homemade raft, which fell apart in the middle of swift-moving current. He managed to reach the far shore, but he was without his rifle and ammunition.

For five days, he struggled to reach his destination, once forced to take shelter in a tree when pursued by a pack of wolves. Finally, he was found by two scouts sent out to look for him. Although his ordeal had been terrible, his navigation was perfect, and he was only a few miles short of his rendezvous. Nevertheless, the experience had turned his hair snow white, and he looked considerably older than his 33 years.

Eight years later, however, Fitzpatrick secured his place in American history by guiding the first wagon train to California. It almost didn't happen. The 98 emigrants in Westport, Missouri were eager to reach California. They had heard tales of orange groves and olive trees, which was true enough, but also that illnesses were almost unknown among the inhabitants, which was definitely not true.

The group was prepared to set off without a guide when one of their number heard of some Jesuit missionaries who were heading in the same direction accompanied by "an old Rocky Mountaineer." The missionaries were led by the legendary Belgian priest Pierre-Jean DeSmet. The "old" mountaineer, of course, was 42-year-old Broken Hand Fitzpatrick. Fortunately for the wagon train, they decided to bring the missionaries and the mountain man along.

Fitzpatrick guided the group expertly, avoiding all contact with the Indians except for one seriocomic incident whereby one member of the group was stripped of his clothes and belongings by a band of Cheyenne. Fitzpatrick managed to barter for most of the man's possessions back, proving that tact, diplomacy, and knowledge of Indian ways usually trumped shootouts as a problem solver.

It was Fitzpatrick's knowledge of the Indians (he spoke several Indian languages) that led him to believe it was in the interests of all if some kind of accommodation could be reached that would end the violence on the prairie. More and more white settlers were pouring through traditional

Indian hunting grounds on their way to Oregon and California. Along the way, they were slaughtering thousands of buffalo on which the Indians depended for food and clothing and the travelers' horses were consuming all the prairie grass. The Indians were angry and large-scale violence seemed inevitable if something was not done.

As Fitzpatrick saw it, the government had two choices: it could garrison the Plains with huge numbers of soldiers at great expense, or it could effectively buy the Indians off with food and trinkets to compensate them for the losses they were suffering to white wagon trains. He favored the latter course, arguing it would be cheaper and less bloody in the end. Fitzpatrick thought an annual payment worth about $50,000 for 50 years would do the trick.

To modern-day ears, such a bargain might seem patronizing at best and complicity in genocide at worst. It ought to be remembered, however, that for this time and place, Fitzpatrick's proposal was the height of enlightened policy toward Indians.

The result was the Treaty of Ft. Laramie, concluded in September 1851. The Sioux, the Cheyenne, the Crow, the Arapaho, and most other tribes in the area attended (the Comanche stayed away). Under the skillful management of Fitzpatrick, the Indians agreed to the proposed bargain, although Congress later reduced the period for payments from 50 years to 10, which Fitzpatrick considered vastly inadequate.

The treaty, needless to say, did not last, and war broke out repeatedly on the Plains for the next several decades. Fitzpatrick had done what he could, however, and retired to the more sedentary life of an Indian agent, dying in 1854.

One of the best tributes to Fitzpatrick came from the pen of Col. Stephen Watts Kearny, whom Fitzpatrick had guided across the Plains in 1845. "Mr. Thomas Fitzpatrick, who was our guide during the late expedition, an excellent woodsman—one who has been much west of the mountains, and who has as good, if not a better knowledge of the country than any other man in existence."

✿ EXHIBITS: The fort has been restored to its original condition and contains many period artifacts. During summer, guides dress in period costumes and re-create everyday life at the fort during the 19th century. ✿ LOCATION: Three miles southwest of the town of Ft. Laramie in the southeastern corner of the state. ✿ HOURS: Daily 8–7 June 1 through Labor Day; 8–4:30 rest of year. ✿ ADMISSION: $2. ✿ TELEPHONE: (307) 837-2221.

Selected events that are part of or have influenced Irish-American history.

1586   Capt. Richard Lane's diary speaks of one Edward Nugent, an Irishman who killed the Indian chief Pemisapan near present-day Edenton, North Carolina. This makes Nugent the first recorded Irishman to have reached the shores of the present-day United States.

1672   Robert Pollock of county Donegal, great-great-great grandfather of President James K. Polk, arrives in Maryland.

1686   Thomas Dongan, Irish-born royal governor, grants charter to New York colony.

1704   Roman Catholic Church at Bohemian Manor is established on Maryland's Eastern Shore. Charles Carroll of Carrollton, the only Catholic signer of the Declaration of Independence, and John Carroll, the first American Roman Catholic bishop, become students at the school.

1717   The Great Migration of Presbyterian Irish from Ulster to America begins. Between 1717 and the start of the American Revolution, an estimated 200,000 to 300,000 of these "Scotch-Irish" arrive, settling in Pennsylvania, Virginia and especially the Carolinas.

1764   Irish-born Sir William Johnson negotiates an end to Pontiac's War.

1770   Irish immigrant Patrick Carr is one of five people killed in the Boston massacre.

1774–83   American Revolution.

1774   John Sullivan, descendant of a "Wild Geese" refugee, leads seizure of British powder and ammunition at Ft. William and Mary, New Hampshire. This is the first major military action against British forces by American colonists and comes four months before Lexington and Concord.

1775 Don Hugo O'Conor, an Irish-born military officer in the service of Spain, founds the pueblo that would become Tucson, Arizona.

Jeremiah O'Brien leads capture of British schooner *Margaretta* off Machias Bay, Maine. First naval victory of the Revolution.

Colonel William Thompson, a native of county Meath, organizes the 1st Pennsylvania Regiment (also known as 1st Continentals), considered the ancestor unit of the United States Regular Army.

On December 31, Brig. General Richard Montgomery, a native of Dublin, becomes the first United States Army general officer to be killed in action.

1776 Colonel James Moore, descendant of Irish revolutionary hero Rory O'More, defeats a Tory force at Moore's Creek Bridge, North Carolina, one of the first decisive victories of the American rebels over British forces.

George Washington declares the password of the Continental Army for March 17 to be "Saint Patrick."

Three Irish-born men sign the Declaration of Independence: Matthew Thornton of New Hampshire, George Taylor of Pennsylvania, and James Smith of Pennsylvania. Others are of Irish descent, including Charles Carroll of Carrollton, the only Roman Catholic to sign. Charles Thomson, native of Derry, serves as congressional secretary.

Commodore John Barry, a native of Wexford, becomes the first United States naval officer to capture a British warship.

1777 Sharpshooter Timothy Murphy plays a key role in winning the Battle of Saratoga by shooting at long range two high-ranking British officers.

1779 Siege of Savannah. Irish troops in French service participate in unsuccessful effort to eject the British from Savannah, Georgia.

First St. Patrick's Day parade in New York is organized by the Sons of Ireland, a Loyalist regiment in British service.

1780 Colonel Charles Lynch stages a series of summary judicial proceedings against Virginia Loyalists that become known as "lynchings."

1781 Pensacola is captured from the British by a Spanish force spearheaded by the *Regimento de Hibernia*.

1784	Friendly Sons of St. Patrick is organized in New York City.
1789	John Carroll founds Georgetown University.
1790	John Carroll named first Roman Catholic bishop in the United States.
	First U.S. Census records 44,000 Irish-born persons in the United States. Many historians consider this figure too low.
1791	Dublin-born James Hoban wins design competition for "the President's Palace," later known as the White House.
1798	United Irishmen uprising, led by Theobald Wolfe Tone, suppressed with great violence. Denied a "soldier's death" by firing squad, Tone commits suicide rather than face death by hanging.
1803	Uprising led by Robert Emmet fails. Emmet hanged but asks that his epitaph not be written until Ireland is free.
	The Benevolent Hibernian Society of Baltimore is formed by Dr. John Campbell White, an exiled United Irishman.
1804	Thomas Addis Emmet, Robert Emmet's older brother, arrives in the United States to practice law. Named state attorney general in 1812.
1806	Harman Blennerhasset allows his estate on Blennerhasset Island in the Ohio River to be used as an assembly point for Aaron Burr's shady "army." Militia forces burn Blennerhasset's house and he goes into exile.
1808	John Carroll of Baltimore elevated to first Roman Catholic archbishop in the United States.
1810	First Irish newspaper in America, *The Shamrock,* is founded in New York by Thomas O'Connor, refugee from the 1798 uprising.
1814	Irish Emigrant Society formed in New York to assist increasing numbers of Irish immigrants.
	Commodore Thomas Macdonough, grandson of an immigrant from county Kildare, wins the crucial Battle of Plattsburgh on Lake Champlain, helping end the War of 1812 on American terms.
	Andrew Jackson, son of immigrants from Carrickfergus, county Antrim, becomes a national hero by winning the Battle of New Orleans.
1820–29	Records begin to be kept of the ethnic origin of immigrants. Around 50,000 Irish arrive in the United States during this decade.

1825	Erie Canal, dug largely by Irish immigrant labor, opens between Albany and Buffalo, New York.
1828	Andrew Jackson elected President of the United States.
1829	John McLoughlin establishes trading post on the Wilamette River for the Hudson Bay Company.
1830–40	A cholera epidemic in Ireland causes the pace of Irish immigration to the United States to increase. Around 250,000 Irish arrive in these ten years.
1834	Ursuline Convent in Charlestown, Massachusetts is burned to the ground by anti-Irish mob, the first of many acts of nativist "Know-Nothing" violence directed against Irish Catholics.
	Irish empresarios establish settlements in Texas at San Patricio (Saint Patrick) and Refugio.
1836	Ancient Order of Hibernians founded in New York.
	Fall of the Alamo during Texas War of Independence. Twelve Irish-born defenders fall with the rest of the garrison.
1840–49	The Great Hunger more than triples the previous decade's number of Irish immigrants reaching the United States. The new arrivals include the ancestors of Henry Ford and President John F. Kennedy. An estimated 800,000 Irish immigrants settle in the United States.
1844	Anti-Catholic rioting in Philadelphia. An estimated 30 are killed, dozens injured and 3 churches are destroyed.
	James K. Polk, descended from immigrants from county Donegal, elected President of the United States.
1845–49	The Great Famine. One million Irish starve, 1.5 million emigrate, mostly to the United States.
1845	Murphy party becomes first to take wagon train over the Sierra Nevadas to California.
1846–47	Trapped by snow high in the Sierra Nevada Mountains, the Donner Party turns to cannibalism to survive. Irish immigrant Patrick Breen records the ordeal in his diary.
1847	Jaspar O'Farrell begins laying out the streets of present-day San Francisco.
	Choctaw Indian Tribe in Oklahoma takes up a collection to buy food for the victims of the Irish potato famine.
1848	Young Ireland rebellion crushed. Leaders, including Thomas Francis Meagher, Thomas D'Arcy McGee, John Mitchel, and others, transported to Australia; soon after most escape to the United States.

1849	California Gold Rush brings many Irish prospectors to California.

1849   California Gold Rush brings many Irish prospectors to California.

1850–59   Continuing famine in the early part of the decade means continued high Irish immigration to the United States. Over one million immigrants are processed during this decade.

1851   Thomas "Broken Hand" Fitzpatrick negotiates the Treaty of Ft. Laramie, a futile effort to bring peace to the prairie between Indians and white settlers.

1854   John L. O'Sullivan appointed Minister to Portugal, first Irish-American to hold a major diplomatic posting.

1855   "Bloody Monday," August 6, in Louisville, Kentucky. A major anti-Irish riot by the "Know Nothing" Party. At least one priest and several Irish are killed.

1856   James Buchanan, son of an immigrant from county Donegal, elected President of the United States.

    Nativist American Protective Association terrorizes San Francisco Irish. James P. Casey and others lynched.

1858   Nativists burn down a quarantine hospital for diseased immigrants on Staten Island in New York.

    Fenian Brotherhood founded in the United States.

1859   Marine Pvt. Luke Quinn, Irish immigrant, is only fatal military casualty at Harper's Ferry, West Virginia.

    David Broderick, first Irish Catholic U.S. Senator, killed in a duel in San Francisco with state Supreme Court Justice David Terry.

    Peter O'Reilly and Patrick McLaughlin, two Irish prospectors, discover what will become the Comstock Lode. They sell out and the "Irish Four"—James Fair, James Flood, William O'Brien and John Mackay—later become the "silver kings" of Nevada.

1860–69   675,000 Irish arrive in the United States.

1861–65   American Civil War.

1861   Mostly Irish 69th New York Volunteers badly mauled at First Bull Run. Colonel Michael Corcoran, commanding officer, captured.

    Corcoran threatened with execution by Confederates if Union carries out threat to execute captured Confederate blockade runners as pirates. After months-long stand off, Corcoran is spared and exchanged. Forms Corcoran Legion.

1862   Irish Brigade is organized in Union Army and commanded by Brig. General Thomas Francis Meagher. Brigade suffers heavy casualties at Antietam and Fredericksburg.

At Kernstown, Virginia, Irish-born Union Brig. General James Shields becomes only Union general ever to inflict defeat on Confederate General Thomas J. "Stonewall" Jackson.

1863   Irish Brigade saves guns of 5th Maine Battery in Battle of Chancellorsville. Brigade attempts to halt flight of battered Union XIth Corps, but fails.

Irish-born Union Brig. General Michael K. Lawler leads reckless charge at Big Black River, Mississippi, setting stage for capture of Vicksburg.

Battle of Gettysburg. Colonel Patrick O'Rourke, Irish-born commanding officer of 140th New York Regiment, killed in fighting at Little Round Top; Colonel Dennis O'Kane's mostly Irish 69th Pennsylvania repulses Pickett's Charge at High Water Mark; Irish Brigade takes heavy casualties during fighting in Wheatfield.

New York draft riots. Over 100 killed as Irish resist conscription burden they say falls disproportionately on them.

Confederate Irish troops repulse overwhelmingly superior Union force at Sabine Pass, Texas.

1864   Confederates under Irish-born General Joseph Finegan defeat Union invasion force at Olustee, Florida.

Irish-born Confederate General Patrick Cleburne killed in action at Battle of Franklin.

1865   Confederate Irish-American journalist John Mitchel is imprisoned with Jefferson Davis in Ft. Monroe.

1866   Fenians raid Canada in effort to establish Irish republic in North America. Although Fenian forces are victorious at Ridgeway, Ontario, subsequent raids are repulsed.

1867   Canadian Confederation formed in response to Fenian assaults.

Former Irish Brigade commander Thomas Francis Meagher becomes Acting Governor of Montana Territory. Drowns in a fall from a riverboat.

Clan na Gael, the Irish nationalist organization formed out of the failure of the Fenians, organized in New York.

1868   Thomas D'Arcy McGee, leader of 1848 uprising turned Canadian Member of Parliament, becomes only Canadian politician to be assassinated, presumably by Fenians.

1869	Transcontinental Railroad completed, with Irish immigrants providing much of the labor. William Jeffers, son of an immigrant laborer, becomes president of the Union Pacific in 1937.
1870–79	440,400 Irish immigrants arrive in the United States.
1871	The Great Chicago Fire starts in the O'Leary barn.
1872	Daniel O'Connell co-founds San Francisco's Bohemian Club, today one of the pre-eminent organizations of political and business leaders in the world.
1874	"Honest John" Kelly takes control of Tammany Hall after fall of William M. "Boss" Tweed, thus beginning a period of Irish-American control of New York machine politics that lasts for more than half a century.
1875	Archbishop John McCloskey of New York is elevated to the cardinalate, the first American to be so honored.
1876	Lt. Colonel George Armstrong Custer and his entire command slaughtered at Little Big Horn. Capt. Myles Keough and 32 other Irish-born men die with him.
	Marcus Daly strikes copper at Butte, Montana, founding the Anaconda Copper Company.
	John Boyle O'Reilly purchases the *Boston Pilot*.
1877–79	"Molly Maguire" trials in Pennsylvania. Twelve men are executed as alleged leaders of the group that supposedly terrorized the Pennsylvania coal fields. Many claim the organization never existed and blame anti-Irish, anti-union prejudice.
1880–89	660,117 Irish immigrants arrive during this decade.
1880	W.R. Grace, native of county Cork, elected first Irish-Catholic mayor of New York.
1882	Eamon de Valera born in New York City.
1883	John Concannon founds first winery in California.
1886	Hugh O'Brien elected first Irish-Catholic mayor of Boston.
1889	Kate Kennedy wins first "equal pay for equal work" case in ruling by California Supreme Court.
	John L. Sullivan defeats Jake Kilrain to retain his heavyweight championship of the world.
1890–99	430,573 Irish immigrants arrive in the United States.
1892	Ellis Island opened as New York immigration station. Annie Moore, an Irish schoolgirl, is the first immigrant processed.
	Edward Doheny discovers oil in California.
1896	William McKinley, descended from immigrants from county Antrim, elected President of the United States.

1897	American Irish Historical Society founded in New York City.
1900–09	356,000 Irish immigrants arrive during this decade.
1900	United States Navy purchases John Phillip Holland's submarine, the beginnings of the United States submarine service.
1901	President McKinley is assassinated in Buffalo, New York.
1910–19	World War I cuts the number of Irish immigrants by more than half. During this decade, 166,445 arrive.
1912	*Titanic* sinks. Margaret Tobin "Molly" Brown, a passenger aboard the *Titanic,* becomes a hero as the "unsinkable" Molly Brown.
	Woodrow Wilson, descended from immigrants from county Antrim, elected president of the United States.
1913	Belfast-born William Mulholland completes the Los Angeles Aqueduct.
1914–18	World War I. Irish-Americans initially oppose U.S. entry into war on Britain's side, but support the war effort once intervention begins.
1914	Henry Ford declares his "$5 day." Detroit becomes a boomtown almost overnight and the American auto industry comes into its own.
	James Michael Curley wins his first of four terms as mayor of Boston.
1916	Eater Uprising in Dublin. Eamon de Valera saved from firing squad because of his American citizenship.
1919–21	Irish War of Independence. Irish Republican Army vs. British "Black and Tans."
1919	Eamon de Valera makes well-publicized visit to the United States.
1920–29	The end of World War I and the civil war in Ireland causes the number of Irish immigrants to rise again to 206,737.
1920	*Beyond the Horizon* wins Eugene O'Neill the first of four Pulitzer Prizes and begins a revolution in American theater.
	F. Scott Fitzgerald publishes *This Side of Paradise.*
1921	Self-government granted to Catholic-dominated Irish Free State. Partition creates Protestant-dominated Northern Ireland state in Ulster.
1921–22	Irish Civil War between Free Staters and Republicans. The latter are crushed with great bloodshed, making Partition a fact.

1928	Democrat Al Smith, the first Catholic nominated for president by a major political party, is defeated by Herbert Hoover in a campaign that featured vicious anti-Catholic smears.
1930–39	The Great Depression causes the largest fall-off in Irish immigration since before the famine. Only 36,000 immigrants are processed in this decade.
1932	James T. Farrell publishes *Studs Lonigan,* one of the first "realistic" novels of the Irish experience in America.
1936	Eugene O'Neill becomes the second American and first dramatist to win the Nobel Prize for Literature.
1937	Michigan governor Frank Murphy refuses to use the National Guard to eject striking workers from auto plants, resulting in recognition of the United Auto Workers Union.
	Eamon de Valera, prime minister since 1932, proclaims a new constitution, refuses to appoint a new British governor-general and sets Ireland on the road to becoming a republic.
1939–45	World War II. Ireland proclaims her neutrality, a position which leads to tensions between the administration of President Franklin D. Roosevelt and Prime Minister Eamon de Valera.
1940–49	World War II slows down Irish immigration numbers. Just 22,500 Irish are accepted into the United States.
1949	Ireland formally becomes a republic and withdraws from the British Commonwealth of Nations.
1950–59	Irish immigration totals recover, but do not approach those seen in the late 19th and early 20th centuries. During this decade 56,250 Irish immigrants arrive.
1950	"I have in my hand a list. . . ." of known State Department Communists, declares Wisconsin Republican Senator Joseph R. McCarthy in a speech at Wheeling, West Virginia. After nearly five years of "McCarthyism," the senator is censured by his colleagues.
1955	George Meany, president of the American Federation of Labor since 1952, becomes president of the AFL-CIO after merger with the Congress of Industrial Organizations.
1956	Edwin O'Connor publishes *The Last Hurrah.*
1960–69	The 1965 Immigration Act, passed partly at the behest of the Irish government, for the first time seriously restricts Irish immigration to the United States: 44,295 immigrants arrive.
1960	John F. Kennedy, descended from famine immigrants from county Wexford, becomes the first Roman Catholic President of the United States.

1963	Kennedy rapturously received in "homecoming" visit to Ireland.
	Kennedy assassinated in Dallas, Texas on November 22.
1965	Congress passes the 1965 Immigration Act, the effect of which is to sharply limit Irish immigration to the United States.
1968	Robert F. Kennedy, campaigning for president, is assassinated in Los Angeles.
	Richard Milhous Nixon, a descendant of Thomas Milhous of Timahoe, county Kildare, is elected President of the United States.
1969	Inspired by the American civil rights movement, Northern Ireland Catholics begin demanding equal rights. Peaceful marches are attacked by Protestant security forces, the IRA re-emerges and "the Troubles" begin anew. Irish-American leaders express concern, but the Nixon administration takes no action.
1970–79	The full effects of the 1965 act are felt. Just 11,600 Irish immigrants are admitted, the lowest for any decade since records were kept.
1970	In an effort to duplicate President Kennedy's "homecoming" visit seven years earlier, President Nixon visits Ireland. The visit, however, is generally considered a disappointment.
1975	Boston erupts in violence when a federal judge orders black schoolchildren bused to schools in heavily Irish-American South Boston.
1977	Thomas P. "Tip" O'Neill elected Speaker of the House. Serves an unprecedented five consecutive terms.
1980	Ronald Reagan, descendant of Michael O'Regan of Ballyporeen, county Tipperary, is elected President of the United States.
1984	President Reagan makes successful "homecoming" visit to Ireland.
1991	New York mayor David Dinkins is pelted with beer bottles and verbal abuse at the St. Patrick's Day parade because he insists on marching with an Irish homosexual rights group. A court later rules the parade organizers have the right to exclude the group.
1994	Irish Republican Army (IRA) declares a cease fire in its 25–year war with British authorities in Northern Ireland. Under diplomatic pressure from the administration of President Bill Clinton, Britain agrees to begin peace talks.

FURTHER READING

 A selective bibliography of works that were especially helpful in researching this book.

B

Bartlett, Irving H. *John C. Calhoun: A Biography.* New York: W.W. Norton and Co., 1993.

Beatty, Jack. *The Rascal King: The Life and Times of James Michael Curley.* New York: Addison-Wesley, 1993.

Birmingham, Stephen. *Real Lace: America's Irish Rich.* New York: Harper and Row, 1973.

Bredin, A.E.C. *A History of the Irish Soldier.* Belfast, Ireland: Century Books, 1987.

Bultman, Bethany Ewell. *New Orleans.* Oakland, CA: Compass American Guides/Fodor's, 1994.

Burchell, R.A. *The San Francisco Irish: 1848–1880.* Berkeley, CA: University of California Press, 1980.

Butler, Phyllis Filberti. *Old Santa Clara Valley: A Guide to Historic Buildings from Palo Alto to Gilroy.* San Carlos, CA: Wide World/Tetra, 1991.

C

Cahill, Kevin M., ed. *The American Irish Revival: A Decade of* The Recorder, *1974–1983.* Port Washington, NY: Associated Faculty Press, Inc., 1984.

Callahan, Bob, ed. *The Big Book of American Irish Culture.* New York: Viking Penguin, 1987.

Cameron, Gail. *Rose: A Biography of Rose Fitzgerald Kennedy.* New York: G.P. Putnam & Sons, 1971.

Carthy, Margaret. *A Cathedral of Suitable Magnificence: St. Patrick's Cathedral New York.* Wilmington, DE: Michael Glazier, Inc., 1984.

Clark, Dennis. *The Irish in Philadelphia: Ten Generations of Urban Experience.* Philadelphia: Temple University Press, 1973.

Conley, Patrick T. *The Irish in Rhode Island: An Historical Appreciation.* Providence: The Rhode Island Heritage Commission and the Rhode Island Publications Society, 1986.

Connell, Evan S. *Son of the Morning Star: Custer and the Little Bighorn.* San Francisco: North Point Press, 1984.

Conyngham, D.P. *The Irish Brigade.* New York: Fordham University Press, 1994.

Coogan, Tim Pat. *De Valera: Long Fellow, Long Shadow.* London: Hutchinson, 1993.

Cutler, John Henry. *Cardinal Cushing of Boston.* New York: Hawthorn Books, 1970.

D

Davis, Burke. *Sherman's March.* New York: Randon House, 1980.

Davis, Margaret Leslie. *Rivers in the Desert: William Mulholland and the Inventing of Los Angeles.* New York: HarperCollins, 1993.

Dowling, Patrick J. *California: The Irish Dream.* San Francisco: Golden Gate Publishers, Inc., 1989.

Doyle, David Noel and Owen Dudley Edwards, eds., *America and Ireland, 1776–1976: American Identity and the Irish Connection.* Westport, CT: Greenwood Press, 1980.

E

Eastman, John. *Who Lived Where.* New York: Bonanza Books, 1983.

Emmons, David M. *The Butte Irish: Class and Ethnicity in an American Mining Town 1875–1925.* Urbana: University of Illinois Press, 1989.

F

Faust, Patricia, ed. *The Historical Times Illustrated Encyclopedia of the Civil War.* New York: Harper Perennial, 1986.

Fitzgerald, Margaret E. and Joseph A. King. *The Uncounted Irish: In Canada and the United States.* Toronto: P.D. Meany Publishers, 1990.

Flannery, John Brendan. *The Irish Texans.* San Antonio: The Institute of Texas Cultures/University of Texas, 1980.

Foote, Shelby. *The Civil War: A Narrative Vol. 1: Fort Sumter to Perryville.* New York: Random House, 1958.

———. *The Civil War: A Narrative Vol. 2: Fredericksburg to Meridian.* New York: Random House, 1963.

———. *The Civil War: A Narrative Vol. 3: Red River to Appomattox.* New York: Random House, 1974.

Foster, R.F. *Modern Ireland: 1600–1972.* London: Allen Lane/The Penguin Press, 1989.

Furgurson, Ernest B. *Chancellorsville: The Souls of the Brave.* New York: Alfred A. Knopf, 1992.

Furneaux, Rupert. *The Battle of Saratoga.* New York: Stein and Day, 1971.

G

Gallagher, Tag. *John Ford: The Man and His Films.* Berkeley: The University of California Press, 1986.

Garrison, Webb. *A Treasury of Civil War Tales.* Nashville: Rutledge Hill Press, 1988.

Gleeson, Ed. *Rebel Sons of Erin: A Civil War Unit History of the Tenth Tennessee Infantry Regiment (Irish) Confederate States Volunteers.* Indianapolis: Guild Press of Indiana, 1993.

Griffin, William D. *A Portrait of the Irish in America.* New York: Charles Scribner and Sons, 1981.

———. *The Book of Irish Americans.* New York: Times Books, 1990.

H

Heckscher, August. *Woodrow Wilson: A Biography.* New York: Charles Scribner and Sons, 1991.

Henry, William A. III. *The Great One: The Life and Legend of Jackie Gleason.* Garden City, NY: Doubleday, 1992.

Hogarth, Paul. *Walking Tours of Old Philadelphia.* Barre, MA: Barre Publishing/Crown, 1976.

Houghton, Raymond W. *The World of George Berkeley.* Dublin, Ireland: Eason & Son Ltd, 1985.

J

Jones, Virgil Carrington. *Roosevelt's Rough Riders.* Garden City, NY: Doubleday, 1971.

K

Kee, Robert. *Ireland: A History.* Boston: Little, Brown and Co., 1980.

King, Joseph A. *Winter of Entrapment: A New Look at the Donner Party.* Toronto: P.D. Meany Publishers, 1992.

Koppett, Leonard, *The Man in the Dugout: Baseball's Top Managers and How They Got That Way.* New York: Crown Publishers Inc., 1993.

Kurzman, Dan. *Left to Die: The Tragedy of the U.S.S. Juneau.* New York: Pocket Books, 1993.

L

Lavender, David. *Fort Laramie and the Changing Frontier.* Washington, D.C.: National Park Service, 1983.

Leeds, Mark. *Passport's Guide to Ethnic New York.* Lincolnwood, IL: Passport Books, 1991.

Leyburn, James G. *The Scotch-Irish: A Social History.* Chapel Hill, NC: The University of North Carolina Press, 1962.

Lindberg, Richard. *Passport's Guide to Ethnic Chicago.* Lincolnwood, IL: Passport Books, 1993.

Lorant, Stefan. *The Glorious Burden: The American Presidency.* New York: Harper and Row, 1968.

M

Marcus, Sheldon. *Father Coughlin: The Tumultuous Life of the Priest of the Little Flower.* Boston: Little, Brown and Co., 1973.

Mellow, James R. *Invented Lives: F. Scott and Zelda Fitzgerald.* Boston: Houghton Mifflin Co., 1984.

McCaffrey, Lawrence J., et. al. *The Irish in Chicago.* Urbana: University of Illinois Press, 1987.

McCullough, David. *Truman.* New York: Simon and Schuster, 1992.

McShane, Frank. *The Life of John O'Hara.* New York: E.P. Dutton, 1980.

Miller, Kerby and Paul Wagner. *Out of Ireland: The Story of Irish Emigration to America.* Washington, D.C.: Elliott and Clark Publishing, 1994.

Morris, Roy, Jr. *Sheridan: The Life and Wars of General Phil Sheridan.* New York: Crown, 1992.

Mundy, James H. *Hard Times, Hard Men: The Irish in Maine 1830–1860.* Scarborough, Maine: Harp Publications, 1990.

O

O'Laughlin, Michael C. *Irish Settlers on the American Frontier: Gateway West Through Missouri.* Kansas City: Irish Genealogical Foundation, 1984.

Owen, David. *The Year of the Fenians.* Buffalo: Western New York Heritage Institute, 1990.

P

Parmet, Herbert S. *Jack: The Struggles of John F. Kennedy.* New York: The Dial Press, 1980.

Pyron, Darden Asbury. *Southern Daughter: The Life of Margaret Mitchell.* New York: Oxford University Press, 1991.

R

Reedy, George. *From the Ward to the White House: The Irish in American Politics.* New York: Charles Scribner and Sons, 1991.

Regan, Geoffrey. *Great Military Disasters.* New York: M. Evans and Co., 1987.

Revell, Peter. *James Whitcomb Riley.* New York: Twayne Publishers Inc., 1970.

Ridge, John T. *Erin's Sons in America: The Ancient Order of Hibernians.* New

York: Ancient Order of Hibernians 150th Anniversary Committee, 1986.

Robinson, Archie. *George Meany and His Times.* New York: Simon and Schuster, 1981.

S

Sears, Stephen W. *Landscape Turned Red: The Battle of Antietam.* New York: Ticknor and Fields, 1983.

Shannon, William V. *The American Irish: A Political and Social Portrait.* Amherst, MA: University of Massachusetts Press, 1989.

Shepher, Donald and Robert F. Slatzer. *Bing Crosby: The Hollow Man.* New York: St. Martin's Press, 1981.

Slattery, T.P. *The Assassination of D'Arcy McGee.* Toronto: Doubleday, 1968.

Spada, James. *Grace: The Secret Lives of a Princess.* Garden City, NY: Doubleday & Co./A Dolphin Book, 1987.

Sperber, Murray. *Shake Down the Thunder: The Creation of Notre Dame Football.* New York: Henry Holt and Co., 1993.

Stevens, Joseph E. *America's National Battlefield Parks: A Guide.* Norman, OK.: University of Oklahoma Press, 1990.

Sword, Wiley. *Embrace an Angry Wind: The Confederacy's Last Hurrah: Spring Hill, Franklin and Nashville.* New York: HarperCollins, 1992.

T

Tuchman, Barbara W. *The Proud Tower: A Portrait of the World Before the War: 1890–1914.* New York: Macmillan, 1966.

W

Walsh, James P. and Timothy J. O'Keefe. *Legacy of a Native Son: James Duvall Phelan and Villa Montalvo.* Saratoga, CA: Forbes Mill Press, 1993.

Watts, J.F. *The Irish Americans.* New York: Chelsea House, 1988.

Weatherby, W.J. *Jackie Gleason: An Intimate Portrait of the Great One.* New York: Pharos Books, 1992.

Wheeler, Keith. *The Scouts.* Alexandria, Virginia: Time-Life Books, 1978.

Wilkinson, Burke. *Uncommon Clay: The Life and Works of Augustus Saint Gaudens.* San Diego: Harcourt Brace Jovanovich, 1985.

Wood, Ernest. *The Irish Americans.* New York: Mallard Books, 1992.

Wright, Steven J. *The Irish Brigade.* Springfield, PA: Steven J. Wright Publishing, 1992.

NOTES ON SOURCES

 In listing these sources and people, I do not wish to imply they were the exclusive sources of information on the subjects involved. Much of the information was also drawn from the sources listed in the Further Reading section.

ALABAMA: Mary Ann Neeley of the Landmarks Foundation of Montgomery was the source of information on Knox House.

ARKANSAS: I am grateful to Carolyn Cunningham of Helena, Arkansas, for her description of Patrick Cleburne's gravesite.

CALIFORNIA: For much of my information on the Irish of San Francisco, I had the invaluable assistance of Gary Holloway, who conducts the Irish walking tour there. In January 1994, Gary generously gave me two days of his time driving me around the Bay Area and showing me Irish-related sites. ⁊ Sean Prendiville was helpful in providing me with information on the Knights of the Red Branch as well as the photograph of the KRB building reproduced in this volume. ⁊ For information on the Donner Party, I consulted Joseph A. King, author of the excellent *Winter of Entrapment.* ⁊ The staff at the Filoli Mansion in Woodside, California, was very helpful. I also consulted "The Ghost of Muckross Haunts California" in *Irish America* (April 1991).

CANADA: For information on the Battle of Ridgeway, I am indebted to David Owen, who has written the most extensive and serious treatment of the Fenian invasion of Canada, *The Year of the Fenians* (1990). ⁊ For the information on Grosse Isle, I consulted Marianna O'Gallagher's article, "Island of Sorrows," in *Irish America* (April 1991).

FLORIDA: For information on the role of the Hibernian Regiment in the taking of Pensacola, I an grateful to Gayle Shackleford of the Pensacola Historical Society.

GEORGIA: For the information on Flannery O'Connor's family background, I consulted "Root and Branch: O'Connor of Georgia," by Sally Fitzgerald in the *Georgia Historical Quarterly* (Winter 1980). The article, which is also an excellent summation of the story of Catholicism and the Irish in Georgia, was called to my attention by Nancy Davis Bray of Georgia College Dillard Library. ⁊ I am grateful to the brothers William and John Durkin for information on Fr. Thomas Reilly.

IDAHO: I thank the Idaho Historical Society for relaying the history of O'Farrell's cabin.

ILLINOIS: For information on the Vinegar Lead Mine, I thank Mark Furlong, whose ancestors opened the mine. Charles Fanning and Lawrence McCaffrey were also helpful in assembling material.

INDIANA: I am grateful to Susannah Tulloch of the James Whitcomb Riley House in Indianapolis.

IOWA: I received generous assistance from Monsignor Edgar Kurt, director of the Archives of the Archdiocese of Dubuque, Iowa, who sent me the "Parish Profile" of Immaculate Conception. I also received help from Fr. Louis J. Trzil, pastor of Immaculate Conception.

KENTUCKY: I am grateful to Jill Whitten, executive director of the Brennan House Inc., for the information on Thomas Brennan and mid-19th century Louisville. &· Thanks to the staff at Locust Grove for information on the Croghan family.

LOUISIANA: I consulted "The Wild Geese Who Flew South: The Irish in Colonial Louisiana" in *Irish America* (January 1989). Also, Harry Dunleavy's "The Irish in New Orleans" in *Irish America* (May/June 1994). &· Daniel O'Flaherty, the proprietor of O'Flaherty's Irish pub in the French Quarter, went above and beyond the call of duty by driving out to get the exact location of the Celtic Cross in New Basin Canal Park.

MAINE: Thanks to Joanne Williams of the Machias Bay area Chamber of Commerce for the informative package she sent on Jeremiah O'Brien and the *Margaretta;* and to James H. Mundy, who kindly provided me with a copy of his book, *Hard Times, Hard Men: The Irish in Maine* and submitted to several telephone interviews on that subject.

MASSACHUSETTS: The story of the Catalpa rescue has been told many times. I relied on the account in the October 1987 issue of *Irish America.* &· For my information on John Boyle O'Reilly, I consulted the June 1990 issue of *Irish America.* &· For South Boston, I consulted "Southie: A Community in Crisis," by Kate O'Callaghan, in *Irish America* (September 1988).

MICHIGAN: Thanks to the Beaver Island Chamber of Commerce for information on that unique piece of Irish-Americana. &· For information on Frank Murphy, I consulted Marge McCullen's "Murphy's Mark" in *Irish America* (October 1988).

MINNESOTA: For much of the information on Archbishop Ireland and his role in the settlement of the Irish on the frontier, I used Ann Regan's chapter "The Irish" from *They Chose Minnesota: A Survey of the State's Ethnic Groups,* edited by Carlton Zaaley (St. Paul, Minnesota Historical Society Press, 1981). &· For information on the influence his Irish background had on F. Scott Fitzgerald, I consulted Stephan Talty's "F. Scott Fitzgerald: The Irish Scott" in *Irish America* (June 1987). &· For information on Ignatius Donnelly's life and work, I consulted Humphrey Doermann's "All my immense labor for nothing ..." in *American Heritage* (June 1961).

MISSISSIPPI: For information on the Sullivan-Kilrain fight, I consulted John Durant's "Yours Truly, John L. Sullivan" in *American Heritage* (August 1959). &· Information on Gen. Michael Kelly Lawler's attack at Big Black River was generously provided by Terrence J. Winschel, National Park Service historian at Vicksburg National Military Park.

MISSOURI: The Parks and Recreation Department of Kansas City, Missouri, provided information on the statue of James Pendergast. The staff of the Harry S Truman Library in Independence, Missouri, also provided assistance. &· Thanks to Michael

C. O'Laughlin, whose book, *Irish Settlers on the American Frontier* (1984), is an excellent resource on the early Irish settlers of Missouri.

MONTANA: Thanks to Ray O'Hanlon of the *Irish Echo* for supplying me with copies of the stories on Capt. Myles Keough. ❧ Information on Marcus Daly was from Joseph McCarthy's profile of the Copper King in the 1980 volume of *The Recorder*.

NEBRASKA: Some of the information on O'Neill was obtained partially from Kate O'Callaghan's "In the Town of O'Neill" in *Irish America* (February 1986). ❧ The public information office at Boys' Town was the source of most of the information on that institution.

NEW HAMPSHIRE: The staff at the Augustus Saint Gaudens National Historic Site was of great assistance.

NEW JERSEY: For the story of John Philip Holland and the *Fenian Ram*, I consulted "Father of the Modern Submarine" by Courtlanddt Canby and Richard E. Morris in *American Heritage* (February 1961). ❧ For the story of Frank Hague, I consulted Thomas J. Fleming's "I am the Law!" in *American Heritage* (June 1969). ❧ For information on Fr. William McNulty, I am grateful to Vincent Waraske, town historian of Paterson, New Jersey.

NEW MEXICO: For information on Billy the Kid, one of my sources was Dermot P. Duggan's "A Tale from the Old West: Billy the Kid and the Murphy-Dolan Gang" in *Irish America* (October 1991).

NEW YORK: For information on Sir William Johnson, I consulted Francis Russell's profile in *American Heritage* (April 1959). ❧ Information on Timothy Murphy was obtained from the program for the rededication of the Timothy Murphy memorial on July 4, 1976, by the Ancient Order of Hibernians and Ladies Auxiliary. ❧ Jim Devine of the Communications Workers of America Local 1116 was generous enough to provide me with the program for the dedication of the James Connolly Memorial in Troy, New York. ❧ Virginia Bowers, the historian of the city of Albany, New York, provided additional information on the charter granted to Albany by Sir Thomas Dongan. ❧ I relied on C.S. Forester's account of Thomas Macdonough's victory at the Battle of Plattsburgh in "Victory on Lake Champlain" in *American Heritage* (December 1963). ❧ Brian Bennett's "The Ideal of a Soldier and Gentleman" in *Civil War* (March–April 1991), was my primary source material for information on Patrick O'Rourke at Gettysburg. ❧ Barney Kelly of the 69th Veterans' Corps was exceedingly generous in helping me with the history of that unit.

NORTH CAROLINA: For the information on Thomas Kenan's family background, I am grateful to Hortense C. Hasty, assistant curator of the Liberty Hall restoration.

OKLAHOMA: Thanks to the staff at the Choctaw National Museum, which provided the information on Choctaw efforts to assist the Irish during the Great Famine. ❧ Thanks to the Drumwright Chamber of Commerce for information on Shamrock, Oklahoma, and to the staff of the Murray-Lindsay Mansion for information on that site.

OREGON: Thanks to the staff at the McLoughlin House National Historic Site.

PENNSYLVANIA: For the account of the Irish at Gettysburg, I relied on Jack McCormack's "Blue, Gray and Green: The Fighting Irish" in *Civil War* (March-April 1991). ❧ Col. William V. Kennedy, U.S. Army Reserve (retd.), who heads up the Thompson Battalion Memorial Project, conducted extensive original research on the

1st Continental Regiment and was the source for much of the information on that unit. 🙠 Judge John P. Lavelle of the Carbon County Court of Common Pleas generously took time out of his busy schedule to acquaint me with the historical work he had done on the Molly Maguire trials. Judge Lavelle presided over a "retrial" of the Mollies in 1993 and they were found not guilty. 🙠 Clara Pierre's "In the Footsteps of William Penn" in *Irish America* (February 1989) was the source of much information on William Penn's Irish roots. 🙠 Former Navy Secretary John Lehman was very helpful in the research on his cousin, Grace Kelly.

RHODE ISLAND: My thanks to the staff at Whitehall Farm, who showed me around the grounds, and to the staff at Hammersmith Farm.

SOUTH CAROLINA: I consulted Mary Pat Kelly's article "Hibernian Hall" in *Irish America* (March 1991). Thanks also to Carl Pulkenin, the historian of the Hibernian Society. 🙠 *The Defense of Charleston Harbor* (1889) by John Johnson was my source for information on the death of Capt. John C. Mitchel at Ft. Sumter. I also thank Cindy Webb of the Magnolia Cemetery Trust. 🙠 For information on the Irish Volunteers, I consulted "History of the Irish Volunteers Company" by F.M. Salley, a WPA Writer's Project undertaken in 1935–36. It was made available to me by the reference department of the Charleston County Library.

TEXAS: Many thanks to Maxine Reilly and Mildred Rowe of the Refugio County Museum for their help in tracing the Irish of that part of Texas. 🙠 Dennis Hough's article, "The Good, the Bad and the Irish" in *Irish America* (December 1989), is very useful on the Irish in Texas. Also useful was "Remember the Alamo!" by Jay Gaines in *Irish America* (September 1986). 🙠 The Battle of Sabine Pass is well-chronicled in *Blue and Gray* (August-September 1992). 🙠 Thanks go the staff at the Irish Cultural House in Corpus Christi. 🙠 Bob Porter, the director of public relations at The Sixth Floor, helped with information on the Kennedy assassination sites in Dallas. 🙠 Thanks also to the staff at the Greenville Public Library, which maintains the Audie Murphy Room.

UTAH: Helpful was the article "Director John Ford: The Legend Maker" by Sean McGeever in *Irish America* (February 1987). 🙠 For my information on Thomas Kearns, I drew from Bishop Robert J. Dwyer's article, "The Irish in the Building of the Intermountain West" in the *Utah Historical Quarterly* (July 1959). I also used "Thomas Kearns: Builder of Modern Utah" by Newell G. Bringhurst in the book *The Irish in the West*, edited by Timothy J. Sarbaugh and James P. Walsh.

VIRGINIA: The staff at the Ft. Monroe Casemate Museum was helpful in documenting John Mitchel's imprisonment there. Mitchel's life is well-recounted by Raymond Bottom in *The Virginia Magazine of History and Biography* (April 1952). 🙠 "Col. Charles Lynch and the Lynch Law," by Sally Smith Rowbotham, in *Daughters of the American Revolution Magazine* (January 1962) is probably the best explication of Lynch's connection with the coinage of the phrase "lynching." The staff at Avoca was also helpful. 🙠 For the details on the Irish Brigade, I relied on Prof. Lawrence Frederick Kohl's new introduction to D. P. Conyngham's 1867 classic *The Irish Brigade and Its Campaigns* (reprinted by Fordham University Press, 1994). I also consulted Justin F. Gleichauf's article "Mr. Lincoln's Irish Brigade" in *Irish America* (November 1986), and Kevin E. O'Brien's "The Yankees of the hard-fighting Irish Brigade were so brave the Confederates hated having to shoot them" in *America's Civil War* (May 1994). 🙠 For information on Fr. Abram Ryan, I am grateful to my friend Lt. Col. J. Addison Hagan, USMC (Retd.), whose privately published 1973 article, "The True Story of Fr. Abram Joseph Ryan," is an excellent resource. 🙠 For information on the Battle of Cedar Creek, I drew on Caroline Carter's "Family Values at Cedar Creek" in *Civil War* (October 1994) and "At Cedar Creek, the South scored an 'Early' victory, but Sheridan's inspired ride saved the Union's day" in *Military History* (October 1993).

WASHINGTON, D.C.: Information on the nuns of the battlefield was obtained from Jeane Heimberger Candido's "Sisters and Nuns Who Were Nurses During the Civil War" in *Blue and Gray* (October 1993).

WEST VIRGINIA: Thanks to Ray Swick, the historian of the Blennerhassett Historical State Park, Parkersburg, West Virginia, who provided me with information on Harman Blennerhassett and photographs of his restored home.

WISCONSIN: Fr. Jim Kraker of St. Patrick's generously provided me with information about the history of his church in Erin Prairie. Thanks also to Fr. John Holly.

SITE INDEX

Neighborhoods

Parks